An Introduction to
The History
of Sociology

ABRIDGED EDITION

P226 $3.45 (26s net)

Edited by
Harry Elmer Barnes

AN INTRODUCTION
TO THE
HISTORY OF SOCIOLOGY

Abridged Edition

AN INTRODUCTION
TO THE
HISTORY OF SOCIOLOGY

Abridged Edition

Edited by

HARRY ELMER BARNES

Phoenix Books

THE UNIVERSITY OF CHICAGO PRESS
CHICAGO & LONDON

This book is also available in an unabridged clothbound edition from

THE UNIVERSITY OF CHICAGO PRESS

THE UNIVERSITY OF CHICAGO PRESS, CHICAGO & LONDON

The University of Toronto Press, Toronto 5, Canada

To the Memory of

ALBION WOODBURY SMALL

EDITOR'S NOTE

THE original edition of *An Introduction to the History of Sociology*, edited by Harry Elmer Barnes, was published by the University of Chicago Press in 1948. This volume was a collaborative work on the history of sociology covering the growth of sociological thought from its origins to the point of pre–World War II. It contained forty-seven essays and emphasized the period from Comte to Sorokin. Since 1948, six editions have been published, and the book has served as a standard reference in the field.

Because of the continued interest in the book, the University of Chicago Press has prepared this special paperback edition. In consultation with Harry Elmer Barnes, a selection of twenty-one essays have been included. These chapters seek to cover the major figures in sociology and the basic issues in sociological theory of continuing importance and relevance.

TABLE OF CONTENTS

HISTORICAL INTRODUCTION

SOCIOLOGY BEFORE COMTE

CHAPTER I

ANCIENT AND MEDIEVAL SOCIAL PHILOSOPHY

Harry Elmer Barnes

I. SOCIAL THINKING IN THE ANCIENT ORIENT

THE social philosophy of ancient and medieval writers must be gleaned from a large mass of philosophical, theological, economic, political, and legal doctrines, for, as might be expected, there was no strict differentiation between social philosophy, on the one hand, and religious, moral, economic, and political theories, on the other hand. Nor is there to be found in many cases any serious attempt to build up a definite or well-balanced system of social philosophy.

At the same time, the recognition of these facts furnishes no adequate justification for refusing to go back of Comte for the sources of sociological thought. It is hoped that even this brief survey of the pre-Comtian period will substantiate the truth of the statement that, from the time of the Egyptian social prophets onward, thinkers were approaching, and to a certain extent successfully formulating, the chief problems of sociology. Indeed, as Professor A. W. Small pointed out, only the most mediocre writer can be adequately described merely by classifying him as sociologist, historian, economist, or political scientist.[1]* The aim and purpose of the writer constitute the most reliable basis for estimating his contributions to social science. One is, therefore, justified in seeking the origins of sociological thought as far back in the past as a conscious attempt can be discovered on the part of any writer to record or to explain the fundamental problems of social relationships, organization, and development.

In any attempt, however cursory, to trace the development of sociological thought, it is necessary to keep in mind the fundamental truth, so well expressed by Professor Giddings and Professor Small, namely, that the doctrines of any writer lose much of their significance if their relation to the prevailing social environment is not pointed out and

---

* For the greater convenience of the reader, the footnotes in this book are grouped at the end of each chapter.

the purposes of the work clearly indicated. While in this survey the treatment of these important phases of the general topic must, like the summary of doctrines, be extremely condensed, an attempt will be made to indicate the general conditions out of which the sociological thinking of each period developed.

Anything like a systematic discussion of social phenomena began with the Greeks. The writers of oriental antiquity were prevented by the general conditions of their social environment from offering any strikingly original generalizations concerning the origin and nature of social institutions. An agrarian economy, caste, superstition, an inflexible religious system, and sumptuary legislation, begotten of the passion of the antique mind for homogeneity, tended to give social institutions a fixity and sanctity which discouraged any extensive speculation as to their origin, nature, or possible means of improvement. When social institutions were "frozen" by a tyrannical customary code and upheld by an inscrutable Providence, there could be no "science" of society. Consequently, in oriental antiquity most of the thinking upon social problems consisted in formulating justifications of the existence of the given social regime, these mainly centering about the sanctions of a unique revealed religion or the superior wisdom of ancestors.

Fundamental moral and social precepts and ideals of social justice are to be found in the works of the Egyptian scribes; valuable bits of applied and descriptive sociology may be gleaned from the Babylonian records, particularly from the Code of Hammurabi; much of sociological interest may be found in the ancient books of India; the Hebrew legal codes and prophetic teachings are replete with sociological and anthropological interest; and most of the Chinese religious and moral doctrines come from a more remote antiquity than those of the great philosophers of Greece; but the first coherent analysis of social phenomena and processes, so far as extant records furnish the basis for judgment, originated with the Greek philosophers of the post-Socratic period.

The outstanding traits of ancient oriental social thought may safely be characterized somewhat as follows: the social thinking was informal, sporadic, and unorganized rather than systematic or the product of deliberate study. It was highly personal and individual in origin and expression, and not the outgrowth of schools or types of social thought or of conscious social analysis. The individual rather than the group was the center of most social thinking. Social theory was pre-eminently practical and utilitarian, devoted to supplying advice and admonition concerning everyday life. It was decidedly hortatory and emotional in attitude and intent. Such social thinking as related to groups rather than to individuals was concerned mainly with so-called "primary" groups, such as the clan, the neighborhood, and the village. But law and government received some attention. The trend of the social thinking was conservative and traditional, mainly retrospective in outlook. There was no conception of social progress, and such social change as was envisaged was believed to be brought about by supernatural forces, which were held to be the source of all social causation. Professor Joyce O. Hertzler thus summarizes the outstanding contributions of ancient oriental social thinking to our understanding of social processes and problems:

Among a considerable array of specific contributions, those following must be specifically mentioned. We have examined in the preceding chapters much material indicating the development of social consciousness; the recognition of the difficulties arising out of personal contacts in group life; a devotion to thought about man's relationship to man in groups; a discussion of human and social values and philosophies of life; much thought about social control, especially the regulative institutions, such as the state, family, and property; some treatment of certain aspects of social organization; some worry about codes governing almost every aspect of group life; much thought about the importance and nature of man's social duties and obligations, with special reference to moral codes and social proprieties; some thought on the preparation for group life, especially education, its theory and technique, but including other means of inculcating institutional lore; the nature of human nature; occasional thought in the form of deft, though partial, social criticism and prophecy; and some treatment of social differentiation, especially the phenomena of class relations and social inequalities.[2]

II. SOCIAL PHILOSOPHY AMONG THE GREEKS

While it is impossible to account for Greek originality and freedom of thought entirely upon the basis of the surrounding conditions, it is nevertheless true that the characteristic trends in the sociological thinking of the Greeks can be traced back to the social environment.[3]

In the first place, there was rarely any extensive or highly centralized political organization, bringing together in one unified state many different peoples. This allowed the tribal spirit of localism and provincialism to have free play, and this spirit pervaded most of Greek thinking upon social phenomena. With the exception of the Stoics, the contrast between Greek and barbarian stands out clearly in most of the important Greek studies of social institutions. But if the Greek city-state fostered a rather narrow local conceit, it also rendered possible a high degree of like-mindedness on the part of the citizens. This led to that group self-consciousness which lay at the basis of those utopian or idealistic theories of society that appeared in the *Republic* of Plato and the *Politics* of Aristotle.

Again, the freedom and liberty of the Athenian city-state and the absence of a coercive state religion made for that critical philosophy which first appeared on any considerable scale among the Attic Greeks. Despite the pretensions of Athens to commercial empire, Greek civilization was based primarily upon an agricultural economy, which, through its routine and repetition, encouraged a static outlook upon the social process. Consequently, one is not surprised to find Aristotle setting up stability as the most perfect test of the excellence of a state. Despite their intellectual activity, there was little inductive study of social phenomena among the Greeks. Aristotle furnishes the only notable exception to this statement. The Greeks despised the humble and commonplace methods of natural science and preferred the freer and wider ranges of a priori generalizaton. The possibilities of deductive thinking about the social process were, accordingly, exhausted by the Greeks. It was not until natural science had established inductive methods in social science that the *Republic* and the *Laws* of Plato and the *Politics* of Aristotle were surpassed as analyses of social phenomena by the works of Comte, Quételet, Spencer, and Ward.

The period of Greek thought before Plato has left no voluminous textual remains, but, from the sources available, several interesting suggestions and developments may be discovered. Hesiod (eighth century B.C.) outlined the culture ages from the conventional viewpoint of a descent from a "Golden Age" and voiced his protest against existing social and economic conditions. Anaximander (610–546 B.C.) antedated John Fiske by twenty-four centuries in his discussion of the prolongation of human infancy in its relation to human society. Theognis (*ca.* 550 B.C.) clearly expounded the principles of eugenics as applied to the human race. Aeschylus (525–456 B.C.) anticipated Lucretius by more than four centuries in his highly interesting account of the general evolution of civilization. Herodotus (*ca.* 485–425 B.C.), by his acute observations and striking descriptions of the manners, customs, and physical characteristics of foreign peoples, justly earned the title of the first great "descriptive sociologist." The Sophists advanced the conception of a primordial state of nature and a subsequent social, or at least governmental, contract. Hippocrates (ca. 460–380 B.C.), in his work on *Airs, Waters, and Places,* presented the first serious analysis of the influence of physical environment upon human society. He described the effect of climate and topography upon the peoples of Europe and Asia in regard to physical characteristics and political institutions with a sweep and detail not equaled again until the time of ibn-Khaldun and Bodin. He believed that the peoples of warm climates were clever but weak and wicked. Those of cold climates were strong but stupid. The inhabitants of temperate climates, especially the Greeks, combined the good qualities of the others without their weaknesses. They were strong, brave, and wise. Hippocrates' work constituted the point of departure for most treatments of the influence of physical environment on society until the time of Karl Ritter. Finally, Socrates (471–399 B.C.) presented the doctrine of a law of nature, as contrasted with human law, and attempted to reduce ethics to a body of well-reasoned knowledge.

Plato (427–347 B.C.) in his search for an adequate definition of justice, was led into making an analysis of society and of the state. He outlined the organic theory of society and believed that not only the economic but also the ethical basis of society is embodied in the functional division of labor. In this respect his *Republic* contributed what is probably the most satisfactory analysis of the economic foundations of society to be found in the works of any writer of antiquity.[4]

Plato recognized the existence and importance of the social mind, though he wrongly believed it to be merely the sum of the individual minds in the social group. Adopting the premise that man can control his own social relations and that concerted volition is the inevitable result of similar external surroundings, he constructed one of the most nearly complete of the utopian plans for an ideal society of which history bears any record.[5] It is interesting to note that, aside from its communistic aspects, this utopia of Plato provided for the first comprehensive scheme of eugenics in the history of social or biological philosophy. Plato's theory that the élite should govern society stimulated later aristocratic political theory and has been embraced by the Fascist and "managerial" philosophers in our own day.

Especially interesting was Plato's contribution to historical sociology in his *Laws.* With almost the perspective of a nineteenth-century evolutionist, he discerned something of the true nature of social evolution and of the time required for its consummation, and he presented his own theories on the subject, which were exceedingly accurate for one possessed of only his scanty data.[6] Finally, in decided contrast to his predecessors and to many of his successors, Plato tried to comprehend and analyze society as a unity and in its entirety.

Aristotle (384–322 B.C.), the most influential of all Greek writers on social philosophy, both on account of the profundity of his insight into social processes and because of his pontifical relationship to medieval thought, made many advances over Plato in his investigation of the basis of political and social relationships. In the first place, Aristotle's *Politics* introduced to some extent the inductive method of studying social phenomena, while Plato had relied almost entirely upon the far less scientific deductive mode of approach. But probably more important than this was Aristotle's direct and clean-cut assertion that man is by nature a social being.[7] This dictum, had it been heeded by later writers, would have precluded the possibility of such erroneous interpretations of society as that of an original social contract, which was based upon the doctrine of the origin of society in conscious self-interest. As a deduction from this dogma of man's inherent sociability, Aristotle pointed out the necessity of social relations for the complete development of the human personality, and he made plain the abnormality of the non-social being.

Aristotle presented an explanation of social evolution in terms of the social instinct, the expansion of man's social nature, and the widening scope of the desire for, and need of, society.[8] In this respect, he made a considerable advance over Plato, who had adopted the utilitarian and economic interpretation, almost to the exclusion of the instinctive element. Although Aristotle's interpretation of society was more inclusive and well-balanced, it fell far short of the thoroughness of Plato's in its analysis of the economic foundations of society.

In his criticism of Plato's communistic scheme, Aristotle advanced arguments against communism, which, for completeness, were unequaled until contemporary times.[9] But his own project for an ideal commonwealth was not any more satisfactory than that of Plato, for both plans were permeated with the Greek ideals of exclusiveness, provincialism, and localism and with the notion that social stability is the end most to be sought in the institutions of society and that society is prior to the individual in importance.

The subjective basis of organized society Aristotle believed to be embodied in friendship, in the analysis of which he anticipated Professor Giddings' theory of the "consciousness of kind."[10]

Aristotle also gave a more complete statement than did Plato of the analogy between the individual organism and society and of the influence of physical environment upon society. In his theory of the effect of physical surroundings on man and society, Aristotle revived and adapted the theories of Hippocrates, so as to furnish a geographical basis for the alleged superiority of the Greeks. He held that, by their intermediate geographical situation, the Greeks were able to combine the superior mental attainments of southern peoples with the greater bravery of the northerners and, at the same time, to escape the fickleness of the inhabitants of warm regions and the stupidity of the people of the north. The common ancient and medieval doctrine of the general cultural superiority of the inhabitants of the temperate climates was, in all probability, only a statement of observed facts. The detailed explanation, however, was hardly as satisfactory, being based upon the fantastic astrological doctrine of planetary influences on man and the equally grotesque Greek physical philosophy, with its physiological chemistry founded on the theory of the four elements and the four humors.[11]

The distinctive sociological contributions of the Stoic and the Epicurean social philosophies are not difficult to account for on the basis of the conditions of the time. The swallowing-up of the Greek city-states in the imperial system of Alexander and the disorder which followed the disintegration of his empire led naturally, on the one hand, to the cosmopolitan serenity and resignation of the Stoics and, on the other, to the individualistic and materialistic doctrines of the Epicureans, who valued society and the state solely for their aid in securing a superior degree of personal detachment, convenience, and safety.

The Stoics, who represented the school of philosophy which was founded by Zeno (*ca.* 350–*ca.* 260 B.C.) in the latter half of the fourth century B.C. and lasted on until the close of the western Roman Empire, interpreted society in terms of rational thought.[12] They held, with Aristotle, that all men must be social, both for the development of their own personalities and for the proper discharge of their duties toward their fellow-beings. Their conception of society was far broader than that of the other schools of Greek philosophy, to whom the world was either Greek or barbarian. The cosmopolitan Stoic conception of world society and world citizenship did much to develop the idea of the essential brotherhood of mankind, at least the brotherhood of the élite. Especially important in their ethical doctrines was the Stoic emphasis upon the law of nature as the proper guide for moral conduct.

The Epicureans, founded by Epicurus (342–270 B.C.), presented a conception of society diametrically opposed to that held by the Stoics, maintaining that society has its only rational basis in conscious self-interest.[13] This led to the deliberate institution of social relations, in order to escape the evils and inconveniences of a presocial and isolated condition. This theory, it will easily be perceived, was based on a fallacious, intellectualistic conception of society. It opened the way for the later development of the doctrine of the presocial state of nature and the foundation of social relations in a contract based upon the perception of the utility of such an arrangement. With the possible exception of the Sophists and Plato, Epicurus was the first to envisage an original social contract, though it was more after the nature of a governmental, than of a social, contract. As contrasted with the cosmopolitan and idealistic Stoics, the Epicureans were, thus, individualists and evolutionary materialists, though they were by no means advocates of sensuality, as is often asserted.

Polybius (203–121 B.C.), the Greek student of Roman history, is usually overlooked by students of the history of social philosophy, but he is, nevertheless, one of the most important figures in the early development of that subject. His conception of social evolution was, in the main, accurate. He explained the aggregation and association of primitive men as resulting from a sense of weakness and a perception of likeness. Government, he believed, arose in force and was rendered permanent by the reflective action of the social mind, as it gradually perceived more clearly the utility of political relations. This was the argument advanced by Hume, nineteen centuries later, in his assault upon the doctrine of a social contract.[14]

Polybius also made an important contribution in explaining the origin of morality and justice as due to group approval or disapproval of social practices and modes of conduct.[15] In this way he suggested a line of treatment exploited in modern times by writers like Bagehot and Sumner. Polybius also set forth the first clear statement of the theory of reflective sympathy, later developed by Spinoza, Hume, and Adam Smith.[16] Again, he was the first writer on political science who proposed to secure liberty and governmental stability through a system of checks and balances in political organization. Finally, Polybius presented one of the clearest statements of the popular classical conception of the cyclical nature of the historical process—a view taken up by Machiavelli and more recently revived by Le Bon, Gumplowicz, and Spengler.[17]

III. SOCIAL PHILOSOPHY AMONG THE ROMANS

Polybius was the last great Greek social philosopher. The minds of the Romans were of a legal and practical character, little given to constructive speculative philosophy. Their contribution was to adapt Greek social philosophy to Roman conditions and to promote political organization and legal development, not to formulate original theories of the state and society. The Romans, in building up a world empire, came into contact with many different legal codes; and this stimulating "contact of cultures" led to the formulation of theories of the origin and nature of law in general.

While the Romans contributed little to social philosophy in the way of original theories, it is to the Roman followers of the later Greek schools of philosophy that one must look for the most nearly complete statements of such doctrines as have been preserved, for most of the Greek writings of this period have been lost.

The chief Roman representative of the Epicurean school was the great philosophic poet, Lucretius (99–55 B.C.), the most original mind that Rome produced.[18] Acknowledging with pride his obligations to Epicurus, he is entitled, by his sketch of the course of human and social development, to rank as the first great evolutionary sociologist. Combining the current written and oral accounts of the customs of primitive peoples with the previous theories of poets and philosophers, Lucretius produced a theory of social evolution which was infinitely superior, in most aspects, to anything presented by any other writer down to the period of late eighteenth-century social philosophy. The struggle for existence; the survival of the fittest; the mode of life among primitive peoples; the origin of language, fire, industry, religion, domestic relations, and the arts of pleasure; the sequence of the culture ages; and the development of commercial relations are set forth in his great poem,

On the Nature of Things, with a clearness, accuracy, and modernity which preclude the possibility of entire conjecture or of a mere reading into his writings of later ideas which did not occur to him.[19]

But, powerful a thinker as was Lucretius, he had little immediate influence upon posterity, Horace being the only later Roman writer who was deeply affected by Epicurean principles. The Epicurean theories were too rationalistic and dynamic for the Roman mind to approve and were even more repugnant to the Christian writers, owing to their denunciation of *religio* as the chief cause of human misery. So it is to Cicero, a would-be eclectic with strong Stoic leanings, and to Seneca, an avowed Stoic, that one must turn for an exposition of the political and social philosophy generally accepted by the Romans.

Cicero (106–43 B.C.) followed Plato in attempting to describe an ideal commonwealth, but he did not feel the need of constructing a plan for a utopian society, since he thought that the Roman commonwealth possessed all the essential characteristics of the perfect state. He accepted Aristotle's dictum of the natural sociability of man rather than the Epicurean doctrine that society results from a sense of weakness in isolation and a perception of the utility of association. But he did emphasize the advantages of associated life, while denying that they furnish the fundamental explanation of society.[20] He also agreed with Aristotle as to the value of friendship and like-mindedness as a psychological basis of human association. From the Stoics he derived his doctrine of the brotherhood of man, and from Polybius he appropriated the theories regarding the classification and cycles of government and the value of checks and balances. In short, it was his summing-up of the various contemporary theories in a coherent body of social thought that constituted Cicero's main achievement.

Seneca (3 B.C.—A.D. 65) was the next systematic social philosopher after Cicero among the Romans. Seneca's chief contribution to social philosophy was his revival of the ancient Greek conception of the primitive period of society as a "golden age." This was followed by the origin of the conventional institutions of society as a remedy for the evils which crept in and brought the golden age to an end. In the age of "golden innocence" mankind lived without coercive authority, gladly obeying the wise and without any social distinctions based on property or caste. The main reason for the breakdown of this simple primitive arrangement was the origin of private property. People then became dissatisfied with common ownership, and the resulting lust after wealth and authority rendered necessary the institution of political authority to curb these growing evil propensities.[21]

The chief importance of this doctrine is not its enunciation by Seneca but its later adoption by the Christian Fathers. They identified the golden age with the state of man before the "Fall" and thus reinforced the already extremely retrospective character of Christian social philosophy, which rendered impossible any dynamic conception of human progress.

The Stoic doctrines relative to society and politics reached their highest development among the Romans in the writings of Epictetus (about A.D. 90) and the Emperor Marcus Aurelius (A.D. 121-80). In fact, the loss of most of the Greek originals has made these two writers our main sources for the Stoic interpretation of society.

Another philosophic development in the Roman period that had important consequences for the history of sociology was Neo-Platonism, which found its main representative in Plotinus (A.D. 204-70), with its renunciation of the world of sense-perception and its tendencies toward unlimited credulity and bitter hostility to rationalism and skepticism. Neo-Platonism furnished the general intellectual setting adopted by patristic and medieval theology. It militated strongly against any trend toward a rational conception of social processes and institutions. Neo-Platonism, the conception of a former golden age, and the eschatological view of society, which was drawn as much from Persian religions and the pagan mysteries as from Christian texts, all combined to make up the otherworldly and antirational intellectual environment in which Christian theology and social philosophy flourished.[22]

Julius Caesar, in his *Commentaries* on the Gallic wars, and Tacitus, in his description of the early Germans in the *Germania,* presented studies in descriptive sociology and comparative ethnology which were hardly surpassed until the modern studies of primitive-culture areas by trained ethnologists. As is the case with the writings of Herodotus, recent critical historical investigations have tended to confirm, rather than to discredit, the main contentions of both Caesar and Tacitus.

In Roman times the familiar classical theory of the wisdom and physical weakness of southern peoples, the ferocity and stupidity of those of northern climes, and the general superiority of those inhabiting intermediate or temperate areas was carried along by Vitruvius, the chief

Roman authority on architecture; Galen, the leading physician of the Roman period; and Vegetius, an authority on military methods. They interpreted this doctrine to prove the superiority of the Romans, as Hippocrates and Aristotle had exploited it to buttress the notion of Greek ascendency.

Finally, there must be noted the important conception developed by the Roman lawyers regarding the origin and nature of political authority. It is the opinion of recent and reliable authorities that, from the second to the sixth centuries A.D., there was but one legal theory of the origin of political authority, namely, that it had its foundation in the consent of the people. However remote from popular consent might be the method by which the emperor at any time arose to power, the theory remained the same. That this conception had a very great influence upon the later development of the theory of a social, and especially of a governmental, contract and upon the idea of popular sovereignty is beyond doubt. Another important allied Roman legal doctrine was that of the absolute nature of secular authority. It was held that the power of the state transcends that of any other group in society. In later times this was interpreted to mean that the state is superior to the church. Of significance also was the Roman legal theory that our personal rights and civil liberties must be protected by constitutions and laws.

IV. THE SOCIAL PHILOSOPHY OF EARLY AND PATRISTIC CHRISTIANITY

The views of the founders of Christianity in regard to the nature of society were not fundamentally different from that of the Stoics, namely, the brotherhood of man in the spirit of God. The Christians were, however, more universal and democratic in their doctrine, since the Stoics had in reality meant the brotherhood of the wise or of those who could participate through their reason in the divine *logos*. Christianity tended to break down this distinction between the wise and the ignorant and to emphasize the possibility of universal human brotherhood through the medium of faith and belief rather than through the exercise of reason.

The social doctrines of Jesus were embodied in the highly idealistic and plastic exhortations to brotherly love, human service, and the recognition of human brotherhood.[23] They were not reduced, or intended to be reduced, to any rigid scheme of dogma or ritual and were, on that account, all the more valuable and adjustable to changing conditions. It was inevitable, however, that, when the attempt was made to put these lofty ideals into operation on a large scale in secular society and to perfect an ecclesiastical organization, they would, when not entirely forgotten, be compressed within narrow bounds of dogmatic interpretation and ritualistic expression. From such restrictions they have not yet escaped, and, throughout the greater part of the history of Christendom, ecclesiastical organizations have been perverted from a means to an end into an end in themselves.

The first, and perhaps the greatest, figure in this development was Paul. He proclaimed the doctrine of love, the organic nature of society, and the necessity of civil government to repress evil. But, at the same time, he was busy instructing the "brethren" in matters of creed and organization, and he instituted that greatest of Christian rites, the Eucharist.[24] Paul initiated the movement, which was carried on by the Fathers until, by the fifth century A.D., the doctrines of Jesus had been transformed from a few plastic ideals into that rigid, dogmatic, ritualistic, and eschatological system of creed and organization known as "medieval Christianity."

Yet the modern writer must not fail to recognize the very great importance and significance of the Roman Catholic church in medieval life, despite its dogmas and intellectual rigidity. Through its elaborate sacramental system it provided the primitive European mind with an effective instrument for meeting the dangers, mysteries, crises, and perplexities of human existence.

The Christian Fathers, as a source of religious dogma and authority hardly second to the Holy Scriptures, are most important in the history of social philosophy. Although their doctrines cover some six centuries, nevertheless their social ideas possess sufficient coherence to allow the patristic period to be discussed as a unity.

The fundamental doctrines of the Fathers upon the origin, nature, and objectives of society may be summarized under the following propositions:[25] (1) Mankind is by nature social, society thus being a natural product, in agreement with the ideas of Aristotle and the Stoics. (2) Seneca's "golden" state of nature, without coercive government, was identified with the state of man in Eden before the "Fall" of man. (3) Civil government was rendered necessary by that "Fall," as a remedy for the crimes and vices of mankind. (4) While government was thus rendered essential by the "Fall," nevertheless it is a divine institution devised to curb further evil, the political rulers derive their power from God and are the agents of God, and political rebellion is a sin. (5) Whatever practical value social institutions may have in rendering more endurable this earthly life, their service in this respect is only fleeting and, at best, immeasurably less important than preparation for the institutions of the heavenly kingdom. (6) Social reform or progress was thus regarded as relatively unimportant, and it was held that one might better endure serious social inconveniences than jeopardize his salvation by dissipating his energy in attempting to improve earthly conditions. (7) The theory that the poor are a part of the divine order, to promote the spiritual welfare of almsgivers, dominated the ideals and methods of charity and relief until the English Poor Law of 1603.

The eschatological approach to life and society, with its relative disregard of earthly values and institutions, found its highest development in Augustine's *City of God* (written 413–26). Here the doctrine was set forth with great vigor, and the main criterion for measuring the excellence of human institutions was the aid or hindrance which they offered to the attainment of heavenly salvation.

V. MEDIEVAL SOCIAL PHILOSOPHY

The social philosophy of the medieval period grew naturally out of the elements which were fused in the development of medieval civilization. From the Romans there came the conception, most clearly expressed by Seneca, of the conventional or artificial nature of political institutions, as a result of the descent from a primitive golden age and a resulting governmental contract; and the doctrines of the lawyers, upholding the ideas of secular absolutism, popular sovereignty, and popular consent as the basis of imperial power. From Christianity came the notion of the "Fall" of man, which harmonized well with the pagan conception of the descent from a golden age; the doctrine of the divine character of political authority; and the dogma of the autonomy of the spiritual life. The new states of northern Europe contributed the notion that political authority is but the delegated authority of the whole community, thus agreeing with, and giving added emphasis to, the legal theory of the Roman lawyers in regard to popular sovereignty. The basic Christian conception of the brotherhood of man and the organic unity of Christendom, together with the sharp differentiation of classes in the medieval period into ecclesiastics, nobles, burghers, and laborers, tended to revive the Platonic view of the organic unity of society, based upon the functional division of labor. The revival of Aristotle by the Scholastics in the later Middle Ages reintroduced Aristotle's emphasis upon the natural sociability of man and led to the final harmony and synthesis of social philosophy in the medieval period. This maintained that, while society is a natural product, government is equally necessary and natural in order to give stability to society. These are the chief tendencies in medieval social philosophy.[26] Attention may now be turned to the individual presentations of these doctrines and to a consideration of their variation in different periods. There were few advances in social philosophy from the sixth to the ninth century. While the term "Middle Ages," in the old sense, has now been relegated to the field of rhetoric, there can be little doubt of the reality of the term "Dark Ages," when applied to the intellectual life of the period between the beginning of the barbarian "invasions" and the intellectual revival of the ninth century, represented by such men as Agobard of Lyons, Rhabanus Maurus, Hincmar of Reims, and Johannes Scotus Erigena.

So far as there was any interest in the subject of social and political philosophy, the views of the Fathers were adopted without question in the encyclopedic compilations of the time; the chief authority of the period being Isidore of Seville (d. 636), who was a transitional figure between the patristic period and the Dark Ages.

The chief practical political problem was the division of power between state and church. The Fathers had prepared the ground for this struggle by their acceptance of the doctrine of Paul and Peter that government is a divine institution. But the church was also divine, and hence arose the problem of deciding the primacy of two institutions, each with divine and, therefore, infinite powers. The situation was further complicated because the church entered into the feudal system as a great landholder, while the secular rulers aspired to invest churchmen with the symbols of spiritual, as well as secular, authority. The adjustment of the relations between these "two powers"—secular and spiritual—absorbed the writers of this period and later culminated in the extreme theocratic view of the state as presented in the *Polycraticus* of John of Salisbury and in the spirited defense of secular authority by Pierre Dubois and Marsiglio of Padua.[27]

Even the intellectual awakening of the ninth century contributed little new to social and political theory. The writers accepted the common tradition of a primitive state of nature, full of disorder and inconveniences, to remedy which political authority was instituted.[28]

In the eleventh and twelfth centuries, however, there were interesting developments. The revival of Roman law brought with it the theories of popular sovereignty and secular absolutism, and the canon-law doctrine strengthened the patristic conception of a primitive golden age followed by the "Fall," which rendered political organization essential for the preservation of order.

The fiery priest, Manegold of Lautenbach (d. after 1085), in his defense of Gregory VII, clearly enunciated the principle of a governmental compact as the basis of political authority, apparently for the first time in the history of western Europe, though his statement was only a definite formulation of the general theory of the time.[29] Tyranny was defined as the breaking of the original contract by which the ruler was appointed, and it constituted a valid basis for rebellion.

The theocratic doctrine of the state received its fullest exposition in the *Polycraticus* of John of Salisbury (1115–80), an English churchman who had studied under Abélard. The inferiority of the prince to the priest was emphasized at great length, tyranny was defined, and tyrannicide was justified. The ruler or prince was, however, acknowledged to be essential to society, in order to restrain human wickedness.

In addition to these views, John outlined the most detailed analogy between the individual organism and the state that had yet been produced. He suggested that in society we find groups or classes that correspond to the soul, mind, heart, and the other organs in the individual person. The prince is the head of the body politic, the priesthood the soul, the senate the heart, the judges and administrators the sense organs, the soldiers and functionaries the hands, the financial officers the stomach and intestines, and the peasantry the feet.[30]

This notion had been anticipated by Plato and Aristotle. Aquinas elaborated the organic analogy, and it received an even more thorough statement by Marsiglio of Padua and Nicholas of Cusa. It was given special relevance and plausibility by virtue of its compatibility with the medieval system of estates—the ruling princes, the higher clergy, nobility, burghers, peasants, and so on. The functional character of this medieval conception of society has been admirably summarized by Professor J. H. Randall:

The fundamental note in medieval civilization is the complete harmony between the individual and the social. Society is a great hierarchy of ascending orders, in which every man has his God-appointed function and recognized obligations, and at the same time his rights and privileges. Each man is a member of some estate or group, and each estate is an essential organ of the whole, discharging a function at once peculiar to itself and necessary to the full life of Christendom. Only through his participation in this group life can the individual attain his own ends, and conversely, only with the aid of every individual and every group can society afford the appropriate setting for the fullest life of its individual members. All men exist in and for each other, and are bound to each other by an intricate network of mutual obligations.[31]

This functional view of society, in more realistic fashion, has gained popularity in our day with certain liberal economists like R. H. Tawney, and especially with the Guild Socialists.

The mature period of Scholastic political and social philosophy began in the thirteenth century, with the work of Albertus Magnus (1206–1280). It had its origin in the desire to give the Christian viewpoint a systematic philosophical expression, for which purpose the logic and philosophy of Aristotle were admirably adapted. Albertus incorporated the *Politics* of Aristotle in his commentary upon political problems and opened the way for the work of his greater pupil, Thomas Aquinas (1225–74). The latter's *De regimine principum* was one of the most suggestive and systematic of the treatises on social and political philosophy that appeared during medieval times.[32]

As a Scholastic philosopher, Aquinas naturally accepted the dictum of Aristotle regarding the inherent sociability of man. Adopting Aristotle's analysis of political origins, he held that civil society comprehends three ideas: first, that man is by nature social; second, that in society there is a community of purpose and interests, since only through social relations can man realize his own best interests; and, third, that a superior power is necessary to direct society for the common good and to enable the ruler to utilize his greater talents for the benefit of the community. The state had its origin in the natural patriarchal rule of the heads of families. But, in order to create extensive and efficient political organization, it was necessary to delegate this power to a common superior through a governmental compact.

Aquinas proceeded to prove his true Scholastic spirit by blending with this primarily Aristotelian theory the dogma of the church that political authority comes ultimately from God alone, though he may delegate it through the medium of the people. With this goes its corollary that political power is inferior to spiritual power. Departing from Aristotle again, Aquinas denied that the city-state is the ideal political organization and took a step in the direction of Machiavelli by declaring his preference for a province made up of several cities. He also followed John of Salisbury in outlining the organic analogy in the state.

Aquinas' theories regarding the influence of climate upon society and culture embodied the tradition common to classical times, as handed down in the works of Aristotle and Vegetius, with some original comments by himself. It was the usual tradition of the superiority of the peoples of the "middle zones" or temperate climate, now exploited, however, to exalt Christian Europe.

Dante (1265–1321) set forth his political theories in a plan for a universal European monarchy, co-ordinate in authority with the church. This project was designed to put an end to international strife, so that "society might realize its function of unhampered exercise of the intellectual faculties of man in speculation and action."[33] With his co-ordination of state and church, Dante stood in his doctrines midway between John of Salisbury, on the one hand, and the secular absolutism of Pierre Dubois and Marsiglio of Padua, on the other. These last two writers defended the superiority of the state. Dante's book was an epitaph of the political past rather than a prophecy of the future. Protestantism broke up the universal church, while nationalism disrupted both imperial conceptions and the ideals of international order.

In his popular work, *The Banquet,* Dante presented an interesting interpretation of the social process of imitation, thus anticipating Gabriel Tarde. In discussing how fame and notoriety develop, he illustrated the way in which imitation proceeds in a geometric ratio and is refracted by its media.

VI. SOCIAL PHILOSOPHY DURING THE TRANSITION FROM MEDIEVAL TO MODERN TIMES

The marked changes in European society between 1300 and 1600 produced comparable and parallel developments in political theory. Christian supernaturalism, feudalism, imperial ideals, and the struggle between church and state had dominated the medieval period. The growth of monarchies, the increased power of the state, and the origins of representative government brought in new and warmly debated issues after 1300.

Characteristic of the early modern attack on the medieval synthesis was the criticism of the prevailing medieval doctrine of the superiority of the church over the state. Even Dante's notion of the co-ordinate powers and functions of a universal church and empire was viewed with doubt.

The rise of Roman law with the teaching of Irnerius at Bologna (beginning about 1085) revived and encouraged the doctrine of the supremacy of the state over the church and over all other social institutions.[34] The experts in Roman law lined up with kings and emperors in defense of the pretensions of the secular monarchs. Roman law had declared that the power of the state is absolute and can override the opposition of any group within the state. Two of the most notable representatives of Roman legal theory in politics in this age were Pierre Dubois and Marsiglio of Padua.

Pierre Dubois (1255–1321), in his *De recuperatione terre sancte,* defended Philip the Fair in his struggle with Pope Boniface VIII. He warned the Pope not to meddle with temporal affairs, since such interference in the past had cost the Christians the possession of the Holy Land. He outlined a comprehensive program of social reform, in which, among other enlightened suggestions, he advocated a reconstruction of the French government; the reform of law and the expediting of justice; more practical and efficient education—including education for selected classes of women; the confiscation of church property; the revamping of the French army; and international arbitration to settle disputes between nations. He has been hailed by not a few modern scholars as the chief social radical of the Middle Ages. Professor W. I. Brandt and others have, however, thought him interesting primarily as a man who brought together most of the novel political and social ideas of his age without producing much original thought of his own.[35]

Marsiglio of Padua (1270–1342), in his *Defensor pacis,* one of the most important political treatises produced during the late medieval period, attacked the Catholic church with something of the spirit and modernity of the Deists and Voltaire. He offered a powerful criticism of the basic Catholic doctrine of the primacy of Peter. He declared that priests are merely the ministers of salvation, and he denied that they possess the power of forgiving sins or any right to interfere in temporal matters.[36]

In his strictly social and political philosophy Marsiglio was somewhat less original.[37] He accounted for the origin of society on a purely utilitarian basis. Society is essential to mankind, in order that we may carry on those co-operative activities necessary to group existence and human comfort. But unregulated society is likely to degenerate into disorder. Hence civil government is indispensable. Ultimate political authority is merely delegated by the people, in whose hands sovereign power always reposes. Marsiglio was the first notable defender of popular sovereignty and representative government—two of the leading dogmas of modern politics. Marsiglio also emphasized the organic unity and functional character of society by outlining the organic analogy in comprehensive fashion. The six estates or professions were made to correspond to the systems of organs in the individual organism. Further, by his separation of politics from theology, Marsiglio took a step toward Machiavelli's separation of politics from ethics.

Nicholas of Cusa (1401–64), in his *De concordantia catholica,* presented the most elaborate development of the functional analogy between the individual organism and the state that had yet appeared. He also introduced the conception of political pathology and, reviving the Platonic phrase, characterized the ruler as physician-in-chief to the sick state. He must prescribe for its ills according to the best advice of political philosophers, past and present.[38] In the more strictly political aspects of his theories, Nicholas emphasized the notion of popular consent as the basis of politica. authority and outlined an original scheme of representative government.

Aeneas Sylvius (1405–64), in his *De ortu et auctoritate imperii Romani,* advanced the clearest distinction between the social and the governmental contracts that is to be found in the writings of early modern authors. According to his notion, people originally lived in a state of nature. This proved warlike and unsatisfactory, so they agreed to establish orderly social relations through a social contract. Then they found it necessary to institute a government and to set forth the limitations thereupon by means of a governmental contract.[39]

The outstanding political writer of the period conventionally known as the "Renaissance" was Niccolò Machiavelli (1469–1527). He advanced

beyond Plato and Aristotle in separating ethics from politics and proceeded to make one of the most acute analyses of human nature to be
found in the history of early modern social philosophy. A perfect child of
the "conspiral society" that formed his political environment, he frankly
based his analysis of society upon the premise of man's self-interest and
the insatiability of human desire. He further maintained that personal
prestige and material prosperity are amply sufficient to satisfy these desires, in so far as they can be quenched. There was no theology in his
political theory.[40]

In his *Prince* and his *Discourses*—the latter is the less well-known,
but by far the more profound, work—he logically deduced from these
realistic views of human nature the methods that are to be followed by
a successful ruler of a monarchy and of a republic, respectively.

The *Prince* was the keenest sociological study of leadership and political pragmatism that had yet been made. Machiavelli took the position
that the end—success—justifies the means used and that whatever works
well is right. He thus effectively separated political theory from the
ethical elements that had colored it for centuries. In the *Discourses* he
outlined with equal candor the policies that should be followed by the
government of a successful and expanding republic. It was in this work
that he dealt most thoroughly with the problems of social relationships
and political processes. Further, there was a germinal conception of
social dynamics in his criticism of the ideal of social stability and provincialism, as expressed by Plato and Aristotle. He frankly held that a
state must either expand and develop or decay. Finally, Machiavelli
took social philosophy out of the realm of abstract speculation and
made a real start toward putting it on the firm foundation of historical
induction.

Despite these contributions, Machiavelli's analysis of society was not
synthetic or well balanced. His works were more after the fashion of
handbooks of political methods for the use of a self-seeking despot or
an imperialistic republic than systematic social and political theory.
They have, however, enjoyed great popularity and have exerted a very
wide influence upon rulers and practical politics.

The inroads made by the national monarchs upon feudalism and the
growth of the absolutistic national state led to appropriate justifications
of secular absolutism in political writings. This trend was evident in
the writings of Pierre Dubois and Marsiglio of Padua, but it received

a fuller and more resolute statement in the *Six Books concerning the Commonwealth* by the distinguished French publicist, Jean Bodin (1530–96).

Bodin approached nearer to a comprehensive exposition of the social process than any other writer had done since the time of Aristotle. He traced the genesis of society from an original family, which expanded and dispersed but was in time reunited through the operation of the social instinct and a growing perception of the utility of co-operative activity. Society, according to Bodin, is essentially a comprehensive union of lesser constituent groups, organized for the purpose of carrying on trade, worship, and similar activities. But, while society itself had this peaceful origin, the state and sovereign power developed out of force through the conquest of one group by another—an anticipation of social Darwinism.[41]

It is not difficult to discern the similarity between Bodin's conception of the origin of the state and that set forth by Hume and Ferguson and later developed by Gumplowicz and his school. His definition of sovereignty as the "supreme power in a state unrestrained by law" was a starting-point of modern political science. In his doctrine of the single-family origin of society he followed Aristotle and anticipated Blackstone and Maine. His theory of the group basis of civil society gave Althusius the suggestions which he developed to that extreme which is characteristic of the modern writings of Gumplowicz, Gierke, and their many followers. In co-ordinating ethics and politics, Bodin paved the way for Grotius; and his suggestions as to the influence of sympathy in society were in line with the later developments of this doctrine by Spinoza, Hume, Ferguson, Adam Smith, and Sutherland. By assuming a lawless state of primitive freedom, he gave an impetus to that old tradition which received its fullest elaboration a century later in the writings of the social-contract school, with its assumption of an unregulated state of nature.

In his work on historical interpretation, *A Method for Easily Understanding History,* Bodin presented one of the first attempts at a philosophy of history, a line of investigation cultivated earlier by ibn-Khaldun and later exploited by Vico, Voltaire, Turgot, Herder, Condorcet, Hegel, Comte, and Buckle.

Finally, Bodin's analysis of the influence of physical environment upon society and politics was the most comprehensive and systematic that had yet appeared, though not so original as is usually affirmed. He derived his ideas here from tradition and from astrology and the Hippocratic doctrine of the four humors. From these sources he produced the most elaborate discussion up to that time of the effect of climate upon mankind. But it amounted to the same old notion that the people of the south are wise but weak, those of the north fierce but stupid, and those of the middle climates both strong and wise. But, this time, the doctrine was used to vindicate the political and cultural leadership of France rather than of Greece or Italy. In other words, it was, as before, no more than a rationalization of patriotic pride.[42]

It is perhaps typical of the process whereby medieval civilization was disrupted by the intrusion of elements from without, to find that the first writer to possess the modern dynamic ideas of progress and the unity of the social process was the Muslim historian and statesman, ibn-Khaldun (1332–1406). At the outset, in his *Prolegomena to Universal History,* which was the systematic exposition of his theoretical views, he drew a sharp distinction between the popular episodical history and history as he conceived of it—namely, as a science tracing the origin and development of civilization.[43] Man, he maintained, is by nature social, since his wants are so varied and extensive that they can be supplied only through co-operative effort. But the conflict of desires produces quarrels and leads to the necessity for instituting government to insure order and stability. With almost the emphasis of Professor Giddings, he insisted upon the necessity of homogeneity for the existence of a stable state. His analysis of the tribal society of the Arabs was probably unsurpassed as a study of this period of human society until the time of L. H. Morgan. Again, his analysis of the influence of physical environment upon society was more thorough than any other study of this subject until the time of Bodin, if not until that of Montesquieu.

But the most important of the innovations of this interesting writer was his grasp of the unity and continuity of the historical process. In sharp contrast to the static conceptions of the prevailing Christian historiography, he grasped the fundamental conception that the stages of civilization are always in a constant process of change, like the life of the individual. He pointed out clearly the co-operation of psychic and environmental factors in this process of historical development. All in all, Khaldun, rather than Vico, has the best claim to the honor of having founded the philosophy of history, and his view of the factors involved in the historical process was sounder and more modern than that of the Italian of three centuries later.

NOTES

1. A. W. Small, *The Cameralists* (Chicago, 1909), chap. i; and *The Meaning of Social Science* (Chicago, 1910), *passim*.

2. J. O. Hertzler, *The Social Thought of the Ancient Civilizations* (New York, 1936), pp. 340–41. By permission of the McGraw-Hill Book Co.

3. This scanty survey of the social environment of Greek social philosophy may be supplemented by A. E. Zimmern, *The Greek Commonwealth* (Oxford, 1924); G. W. Botsford and E. G. Sihler, *Hellenic Civilization* (New York, 1915), pp. 210–54, 303–48, 423–526, 657–708; and F. S. Marvin, *The Living Past* (Oxford, 1917), chap. iv.

4. *Republic*, in Benjamin Jowett's *Dialogues of Plato*, ii. 369; iv. 433. The best account of Greek political and social thought in English is contained in Ernest Barker, *Greek Political Theory* (2 vols.; New York, 1918).

5. *Republic* iii. 412–17; v. 458–62; see John Wild, *Plato's Theory of Man* (Cambridge, Mass., 1946).

6. *Laws* (Jowett) iii. 676–84.

7. *Politics* (Jowett) i. 2.

8. *Ibid.* i. 1–2.

9. *Ibid.* ii. 2–7.

10. *Nichomachean Ethics,* trans. Peters, viii. 1. 9, 14; ix. 12.

11. Cf. Franklin Thomas, *The Environmental Basis of Society* (New York, 1925), pp. 16 ff.

12. Eduard Zeller, *Stoics, Epicureans, and Sceptics* (New York, 1892), pp. 311–40; G. L. Scherger, *The Evolution of Modern Liberty* (New York, 1904), pp. 18–22; Ludwig Stein, *Die soziale Frage im Lichte der Philosophie* (Stuttgart, 1923), pp. 171 ff.; and the extracts given in C. M. Bakewell, *A Source-Book of Ancient Philosophy* (New York, 1907), pp. 269–89. For a new compilation of the extant writings of Epicurus, Epictetus, Lucretius, and Marcus Aurelius see W. J. Oates, *The Stoic and Epicurean Philosophers* (New York, 1940).

13. The significant passages from Epicurus are preserved in Diogenes Laertius, *Lives and Opinions of Eminent Philosophers* x. 3. 33–35; see also Oates, *op. cit.,* pp. 3–69.

14. Polybius, *History of Rome,* trans. Schuckburgh, vi. 5–6; see also the selections in F. W. Coker, *Readings in Political Philosophy* (New York, 1914), pp. 106–17.

15. *History of Rome* vi. 5–6.

16. *Ibid.*

17. Cf. J. B. Bury, *The Ancient Greek Historians* (New York, 1909), pp. 205 ff., 248.

18. On Lucretius see the commentary of Gustave Masson, *Lucretius, Epicurean and Poet* (2 vols.; New York, 1907–9); and Oates, *op. cit.,* pp. 69–219.

19. Lucretius *De rerum natura,* trans. Munro ("Bohn's Library"), v. 325 ff., 778 ff.

20. *De officiis,* trans. Edmonds ("Bohn's Library"), i. 17, 44; *De republica,* trans. Yonge ("Bohn's Library"), i. 25, 26. For the effect of Cicero's opinion on this point on medieval political theory cf. Otto Gierke, *Political Theories of the Middle Ages,* trans. F. W. Maitland (Cambridge, 1900), n. 306.

21. *Epistularum moralium ad Lucilium,* ed. Haase, xiv. 2; *The Epistles of Lucius Annaeus Seneca,* trans. Morell (2 vols.; London, 1786), ii. 115–36, Letter XC.

22. Cf. Adolf Harnack, *History of Dogma* (7 vols.; London, 1895–1900), I, Appendix, 336 ff.; and T. Whittaker, *The Neo-Platonists* (Cambridge, 1910); for selections from Plotinus see Bakewell, *op. cit.,* pp. 340–93.

23. Shailer Mathews, *The Social Teachings of Jesus* (New York, 1910), pp. 16, 115, 151; and G. B. Stevens, *The Teachings of Jesus* (New York, 1911), pp. 117–18. For opinions and alignment of authorities upon the much-discussed problem of whether the Kingdom of God was an earthly social conception or an eschatological fantasy see Nathaniel Schmidt, *The Prophet of Nazareth* (New York, 1907), pp. 32, 296 ff.; and Stevens, *op. cit.,* pp. 65, 166.

24. A. J. Carlyle, *History of Medieval Political Theory* (5 vols.; Edinburgh, 1903–28), I, 89–90, 97–98; and F. C. Conybeare, *Myth, Magic, and Morals* (Watts, 1909), chaps. i, xiv. For up-to-date interpretations of Paul see F. A. Spencer, *Beyond Damascus* (New York, 1934); and Irwin Edman, *The Mind of Paul* (New York, 1935).

25. Justin Martyr, "First Apology," in *Ante-Nicene Fathers,* Vol. I, chap. xvii; Irenaeus, "Against Heresies," *ibid.,* Vol. I, Book V, chap. xxiv, sec. i; Lactantius, "Divine Institutes," *ibid.,* Vol. VII, Book VI, chap. x; "The Workmanship of God," *ibid.,* Vol. VII, chap. iv.; Tertullian, "Scorpiace," *ibid.,* Vol. III, chap. xiv; "Apology," Vol. III, chap. xxiv; Athanasius, "Against the Heathen," in *Nicene and Post-Nicene Fathers,* Vol. X, Book I, chap. xxviii; Augustine, "On the Good of Marriage," *ibid.,* Vol. III, sec. i; "The City of God," *ibid.,* Vol. II, Book V, chap. xix; Book XIX, chaps. v, xv; Jerome, letter quoted in J. H. Robinson, *Readings in European History* (New York, 1904), I, 86–87; Gregory the Great, "Pastoral Rule," in *Nicene and Post-Nicene Fathers,* Vol. XII, Book I, chap. iii; Isidore of Seville *Etymologies* xv. 2; Carlyle, *op. cit.,* Vol. I, chaps. viii–xv; Gierke, *op. cit.,* nn. 16–18, 137.

26. These diverse sources of medieval political theory are admirably summarized by A. J. Carlyle, "The Sources of Medieval Political Theory," in the *American Historical Review,* October, 1913, pp. 1–12; and more elaborately analyzed in his *History of Medieval Political Theory,* Vol. I, *passim,* and Vol. III, Introd.; see also Ernest Barker, in F. C. Hearnshaw, *The Social and Political Ideas of Some Great Medieval Thinkers* (New York, 1923), chap. i. For political and social thought in medieval and early modern times see Hearnshaw, *op. cit.;* and his *The Social and Political Ideas of Some Great Thinkers of the Renaissance and Reformation* (New York, 1925); C. H. McIlwain, *The Growth of Political Thought in the West* (Macmillan, 1932); Bede Jarrett, *Social Theories of the Middle Ages* (Boston, 1926); W. A. Dunning, *Political Theories, Ancient and Medieval* (New York, 1902); and R. G. Gettell, *History of Political Thought* (New York, 1924).

27. For this period see J. M. Littlejohn, *The Political Theory of the Schoolmen and Grotius* (privately printed, 1895), Part I, pp. 11–48; though somewhat diffuse, this work is the most complete exposition in English of the Scholastic political and social theory.

28. Cf. Carlyle, *History of Medieval Political Theory,* I, 211–12; and Littlejohn, *op. cit.,* pp. 26–33.

29. Carlyle, "The Sources of Medieval Political Theory," *op. cit.,* p. 8; and *History of Medieval Political Theory,* III, 160–69.

30. Carlyle, *History of Medieval Political Theory,* III, 126 f., 136 ff.; Gierke, *op. cit.,* p. 24 and n. 76; Hearnshaw, *The Social and Political Ideas of Some Great Medieval Thinkers,* chap. iii; and Littlejohn, *op. cit.,* pp. 42–47. There is an abridged English edition of the *Polycraticus,* edited by Professor John Dickinson (New York, 1927). It must be borne in mind that these medieval analogies were purely anthropomorphic and not genetically related to the later biological analogies.

What was, perhaps, an even more extreme statement of the ecclesiastical claim for the primacy of the church over the civil power was embodied in the *Summa de potestate ecclesiastica* of Augustinus Triumphus, written in the fourteenth century, during the papal "captivity" at Avignon. However, this had little practical significance, for, as Professor Dunning has well remarked, the papal pretensions increased about in proportion to the decline of the actual powers of the papacy.

31. J. H. Randall, Jr., *The Making of the Modern Mind* (Boston, 1926), pp. 58–59. By permission of the Houghton Mifflin Co.

32. *De regimine principum* i. 1; Littlejohn, *op. cit.*, pp. 69–74, 84–87, 104–8; and Crahay, *La Politique de Saint Thomas d'Aquin* (Brussels, 1896), chaps. i–ii; see also the selections given by Coker, *op. cit.*, pp. 123–35, particularly pp. 129–33.

33. *De monarchia*, ed. and trans. Henry; cf. Littlejohn, *op. cit.*, pp. 219–28; and Hearnshaw, *The Social and Political Ideas of Some Great Medieval Thinkers*, chap. v.

34. P. G. Vinogradoff, *Roman Law in Mediaeval Europe* (New York, 1910).

35. F. M. Powicke, "Pierre Dubois, a Medieval Radical," in *Historical Essays of Owens College*, ed. Tout and Tait (Manchester, 1902), pp. 169–91; Hearnshaw, *The Social and Political Ideas of Some Great Medieval Thinkers*, chap. vi; and W. I. Brandt, "Pierre Dubois, Modern or Medieval?" *American Historical Review*, April, 1930.

36. Cf. selections from the *Defensor pacis*, given in Robinson, *op. cit.*, I, 495–97; and Gierke, *op. cit.*, p. 51 and n. 182.

37. *Defensor pacis* i; see selections in Coker, *op. cit.*, pp. 160–67; Littlejohn, *op. cit.*, p. 230; Hearnshaw, *The Social and Political Ideas of Some Great Medieval Thinkers*, chap. vii; and Gierke, *op. cit.*, pp. 47 f. and nn. 155, 170, 267.

38. Gierke, *op. cit.*, p. 24, n. 79; and Hearnshaw, *The Social and Political Ideas of Some Great Thinkers of the Renaissance and Reformation*, chap. ii.

39. *De ortu* 1–2; Gierke, *op. cit.*, n. 306; and Dunning, *op. cit.*, pp. 282–83.

40. On Machiavelli, see Hearnshaw, *The Social and Political Ideals of Some Great Thinkers of the Renaissance and Reformation*, chap. iv.

41. Jean Bodin, *The Six Books of a Commonweale*, English trans. by Richard Knolles (London, 1606), pp. 47 ff., 262 ff.

42. Thomas, *op. cit.*, pp. 48 ff.

43. Nathaniel Schmidt, *Ibn Khaldun* (New York, 1930).

CHAPTER II

SOCIAL THOUGHT IN EARLY MODERN TIMES

HARRY ELMER BARNES

I. THE COURSE OF SOCIAL PHILOSOPHY DURING THE GENERAL DOMINATION OF THE DOCTRINE OF A SOCIAL CONTRACT

THE great popularity, from 1600 to 1800, of the social-contract theory of the origin of organized society is not difficult to account for in the light of the political and social environment. The late A. J. Carlyle has emphasized the general acceptance of the doctrine of a governmental compact throughout the medieval period, and it has already been pointed out that Aeneas Sylvius apparently made the important distinction between the governmental compact and the more fundamental social contract. Professor Giddings insisted that the social-contract theory grows naturally out of a society in which political relations have been based on parliamentary procedure and sound legal foundations and where there is a considerable degree of homogeneity in the population. The fact that the first definite instances of the enunciation of the social-contract theory may be assigned to churchmen, who had been under the sway of the well-established legal systems of the Catholic church and the Church of England, lends plausibility to this theory. Again, Professor D. G. Ritchie has pointed out the prevalence of many actual contractual associations in the seventeenth century, such as the Mayflower Compact, the Solemn League and Covenant, and the "Associations" of the Commonwealth period. He has also indicated the cogency of the contract doctrine to those writers who were seriously concerned with establishing the basis and justification of political liberty.[1]

Finally, it needs to be noted that the contract theory bore a definite relation to the economic and political conditions of the period. The growth of commerce and capital had made possible the existence of strong national states and had also emphasized the importance of contracts in the sphere of economic activities. The origin and justification of these powerful new political organizations offered an impressive challenge to social and political philosophers, and the doctrine of a social contract was the most important early modern answer to this problem.

It should always be borne in mind that the majority of the exponents of the social-contract theory did not advance this theory as a literal historical account of the origin of the state but set it forth as a logical explanation of its existence. Many eager critics have made undeserved capital out of a misunderstanding of this important aspect of the contract theory, though Hume showed that its logical foundations were as weak as its historical basis.

The increased numbers, power, and ambition of the new middle class produced by the commercial revolution brought them into conflict with the absolute monarchs, who tried to tax and restrict the trade of the merchants in an arbitrary manner. In order to justify bourgeois resistance, the theory of natural rights, the social contract, and the right of revolution were most convenient and appropriate. Such notions had great practical political value in this period.

The work of the English churchman, Richard Hooker (1552–1600), was almost as suggestive as that of Bodin.[2] While his treatise, *The Laws of an Ecclesiastical Polity* (1594–1600), dealt primarily with the defense of the Anglican church, he devoted a portion of the first book to a general discussion of society and government.

Hooker emphasized the fact that government originates in the consent of the governed and must be administered according to law. He thus agreed with the previous doctrines of a governmental compact and popular sovereignty. This doctrine of a contract as the origin of government was, as we have seen, an old one. It had appeared in the writings of the Sophists, of Epicurus, Lucretius, the Roman lawyers, Manegold of Lautenbach, Aquinas, Marsiglio, William of Ockham, Nicholas of Cusa, and the monarchomachs of the sixteenth century, such as Hotman, Languet, Duplessis-Mornay, Knox, and Buchanan. But no previous writer, with the exception of Aeneas Sylvius, had advanced the doctrine of a social contract, namely, the idea that society itself arose out of a deliberate determination of men to escape from the evils of a presocial condition.

Hooker explicitly states this doctrine of social origins through a social contract, and it seems certain that he may be accorded the rather questionable honor of having first expounded the theory in an extended fashion.[3] Hooker did not, however, go so far as Hobbes and claim that men in the state of nature were antisocial. He agreed with Aristotle on this point, but he asserted that sociability had to be supplemented by a covenant which embodies the rules according to which associated life is to be guided and restrained.

Another churchman of this time, the Spanish Jesuit, Francisco Suárez (1548-1617), in his *Tractatus de legibus ac deo legislatore* (1612), expanded the doctrines of Aquinas by devoting especial attention to the function of law as the regulating principle in human association. To Suárez, man was almost a "legal animal," so minutely did he analyze his dependence upon law. It was in this respect that he made his chief advance beyond Aristotle and Aquinas, for he accepted their dictum that man is by nature social.[4] Suárez was also one of the founders of international law and perhaps the first to distinguish clearly between natural law and international law.

Another important element in the work of Suárez was his harmonizing of the doctrine of popular sovereignty with the theory that monarchy is the best type of government. While the supreme power resides in the people, they may alienate it from themselves and confer it upon the ruler by an act of popular will. Once this power is delegated, it is irrevocable, except in the case of tyranny on the part of the monarch. In dealing with tyranny, the delegated leaders of a commonwealth may legitimately depose a monarch, but Suárez denied the right of any individual to slay a tyrant, no matter how base or oppressive the rule of the latter. These political doctrines were contained in his *Defensio fidei catholicae,* a reply to the divine-right doctrine of James I.[5]

Suárez's contemporary and fellow-Jesuit, the Spanish writer, Juan de Mariana (1536-1624), offered an interesting interpretation of the early history of human society in his *De rege et regis institutione* (1605). In the beginning, said he, men had lived like animals, without authority and guided only by instinct. But they were free from the greed and artificial immoralities of civilization. Man, however, had greater wants than other animals; his offspring was less rapid in reaching maturity; and he was less adequately protected from natural dangers and external enemies by his natural endowment. Therefore, to live in safety from hostile attacks, men had to set up group life and submit to the authority of some capable leader who was able to direct the resulting political society for the general welfare.[6]

Mariana's somewhat sentimental picture of the state of nature more closely approached that set forth by Rousseau in his famous second *Discourse* than the views of any other writer of the period. While believing in the natural sociability of man, Mariana clearly implied the existence of a social contract in his theory of civic origins. He also set forth a theory of the influence of the prolongation of infancy upon social life which was directly in line with that elaborated in recent times by John Fiske.

The German jurist, Johannes Althusius (1557–1638), was long regarded as the first Continental writer to elaborate the doctrine of a social contract. His chief expositor, Otto von Gierke, thus interpreted his views. Gierke and Figgis, his English disciple, also regarded Althusius as the founder of political pluralism and of the doctrine of the federal state. There is some basis for such an opinion of Althusius in the first edition of his *Politica methodice digesta;* but Professor Carl J. Friedrich, editor of the latest text of this work, points out that Althusius' mature theory of social and political origins was biological rather than political or legalistic. He held that politics is the science that explains how human beings live together. This process of living together he defined as "symbiosis." The origins of society and the state are not to be sought in any contract but are natural sociobiological phenomena or processes. Society and the state are not the products of conscious deliberation but of a biological drive to close association, in which the community absorbs—"devours"—the individual and the state absorbs the community. He was thus more a forerunner of contemporary totalitarianism than of federalism.[7]

The famous Dutch scholar and statesman, Hugo Grotius (1583–1645), may, for all practical purposes, be regarded as the founder of international law, though Dubois, Gentili, Hooker, and Suárez had earlier made valuable suggestions. He is most noted for his systematic work in this field, which was embodied mainly in the famous *De jure belli et pacis.* In his "Prolegomena" to this work he advanced important doctrines regarding the origin and foundation of social institutions. While he interpreted society, in its most general sense, as being the natural expression of human nature with its "appetite for society," he was convinced, on the other hand, that the state had its origin in a contract. In his work on international law, Grotius endeavored to promote that like-mindedness in regard to the essentials of international policy which Professors Giddings and Tenney have insisted is the indispensable basis of any possible hope for the future peace of mankind. While Grotius' work on international law was an innovation, his confusing and inconsistent theory of sovereignty and his denial of popular sovereignty are considered retrogressive.

The *Patriarcha* of Robert Filmer (d. 1653) was an attack upon the doctrine of the contractual origin of government. While Filmer appealed to reason rather than to authority and made a good case against the contract doctrine, his own substitute, namely, patriarchal authority bestowed upon Adam by God, was even less valid than the contract doctrine. Because he put the case on the grounds of nature rather than of theology, Filmer's notion marks a transition from theological arguments to the use of natural law and utilitarian conceptions in support of the divine right of kings.

Among the chief contributions of the Commonwealth period to social and political philosophy were the individualizing of the conception of a social contract, by assuming that every citizen must be a party to the contract; the appeal to the law of nature to establish the rights of men; and the specific formulation of the doctrine of popular sovereignty and the right of revolution. It was the contribution of John Milton (1608–74) to work these doctrines into a philosophical statement and to promulgate them with sufficient coherence to secure their recognition.[8]

There was one conspicuous democratic development in seventeenth-century England, namely, the rise of the so-called "Levelers" during the period of the Commonwealth. They were made up of real democrats, both within the army and outside, and were led by John Lilburne, who deserves a prominent rank among the leading apostles of democracy.

The Levelers boldly proclaimed the sovereignty of the people and held that Parliament should be the servant rather than the master of the mass of Englishmen. They demanded universal manhood suffrage, excluding only those who were servants or paupers, annual sessions of Parliament, and equal electoral districts. They also espoused a number of other democratic proposals, such as abolition of imprisonment for debt, elimination of monopolies and sinecures, abolition of tithes, and reform of the criminal law. In this program they anticipated some of the policies and demands of the Chartists just two centuries later. The Levelers certainly constitute the most significant democratic development before the days of the Jacksonian Democrats in the United States and the Chartists in England.[9]

Despite the previous developments of the social-contract doctrine, it remained for the English philosopher, Thomas Hobbes (1588–1679), to give that conception its first classic statement. Going far beyond any of the previous writers in the detail and "remorseless logic" with which he analyzed the situation, he assumed the existence of a presocial state of nature, which was "a state of war of all men against all men" and in which the life of man was "poor, nasty, brutish, and short."[10] He flatly denied the dictum of Aristotle that man is by nature social and maintained that all society is for either gain or glory and that any permanent social grouping must originate in the mutual fear which men have toward one another.[11] He was as realistic as Machiavelli in his analysis of human nature and believed with the latter that all human activity springs from man's insatiable desires.[12]

Hobbes held that, to escape the miseries of the turbulent and unregulated state of nature, men agreed to unite into a civil society for their mutual protection. In doing so, they made an inalienable transfer of their individual powers to the general governing agent or sovereign.[13] Hobbes did not, however, hold that either the state of nature or the contract was necessarily true in a literal historic sense. Hobbes's analysis was psychological, and he has been correctly called the "father of social psychology." It was the irrevocable nature of the social contract and the conception of the unlimited sovereign power of the ruler which distinguished the doctrines of Hobbes from those of the majority of the other members of the contract school.

Besides this voluntary contract, Hobbes contended that there might be another type of civic origins based upon force, when a conqueror compelled submission on pain of death.[14] In this latter version Hobbes was in line with the vital principle of the school represented by Gumplowicz. Hobbes's conception of the nature and attributes of sovereignty was an important contribution, but he confused the state and the government and erroneously ascribed sovereign power to the latter.

The German statesman and philosopher, Samuel von Pufendorf (1632–94), attempted a reconciliation of the doctrines of Grotius and Hobbes in his *De jure naturae et gentium*. His ethics were primarily those of Grotius, while his political doctrines were mainly Hobbesian. He held that the social instinct in man can account for the existence of the family and lesser social groups but that a social and a governmental contract were necessary to bring into being the state and government. While Pufendorf began his analysis of the state of nature with the assumption that it was a state of peace, he ended with about the same conclusion as that arrived at by Hobbes.

Pufendorf's conception of the contract was threefold. First, there was a social contract, which embodied the agreement to unite in social life; then a vote was taken to determine the form of government desired; and, finally, the arrangement was ended by a governmental contract between the rulers and the governed, regulating the principles and limits of political administration. Pufendorf thus united more clearly than had Hooker the related concepts of a social and a governmental contract.[15] His conception of sovereignty was as confusing as that of Grotius, for, while defining it as supreme power in the state, he held that it must also be limited to what a sane man would term "just action."

The Jewish philosopher, Baruch Spinoza (1632–77), was, in his political theory, a member of the contract school. He agreed with Hobbes as to the existence of a presocial state of nature which was one of general war and universal enmity.[16] Society, he maintained, had a purely utilitarian basis in the advantages of mutual aid and the division of labor.[17] To render this advantageous association secure, however, it was necessary that its utilitarian basis be supplemented by a contract to give it a legal foundation and to guarantee to each citizen the natural rights which he possessed as an individual prior to the contract. He claimed that the contract was rendered valid only by the superior advantages which it offered and that the sovereign was such only so long as he could maintain his authority. This justification of rebellion Spinoza considered to be the only sure guaranty of just rule and individual liberty.[18] Spinoza was mainly interested in using the contract as a buttress for liberty, while Hobbes had been chiefly concerned in utilizing it to justify royal absolutism.

In his *Ethics* Spinoza gave a clear statement to the theory of reflective sympathy, earlier hinted at by Aristotle and Polybius; later revived and developed by Hutcheson, Hume, Adam Smith, and Alexander Sutherland; and, in our day, occupying a prominent position in Professor Giddings' system of sociology.

The *Patriarcha* of Filmer called forth two better-known works in refutation of its thesis. The first was Algernon Sidney's (1622–83) *Dis-*

courses concerning Government. Sidney criticized Filmer's work in detail, proclaimed that the origin of government is to be found in the consent of the governed, and declared himself for the indefeasible sovereignty of the people. Of all English writers in the seventeenth century, Sidney was, perhaps, the most effective assailant of absolute monarchy and was a martyr to this cause. He favored a mixed government, combining elements of monarchy, aristocracy, and democracy.[19]

The second refutation of the *Patriarcha* constituted the first of John Locke's (1632–1704) *Two Treatises of Government*. But the *Second Treatise* was far more epoch-making in its doctrines, for Locke here set forth his important conception of the social contract and his justification of revolution.

In his views on the state of nature, Locke differed radically from Hobbes, Spinoza, and even Pufendorf, in that he denied that it was by any means a condition of general war and disorder. It was not even a presocial state but was, rather, a prepolitical situation, in which every man had the right to execute the laws of nature.

The very social nature of man, Locke contended, would prevent the state of nature from being one of isolation and unsociability. The most serious deficiency in the state of nature was the lack of an impartial judge who could settle all disputes in an equitable manner and take the power of executing the laws from the hands of each individual.[20] The chief and immediate cause of man's leaving the state of nature was the increase of private property and the desire to use and preserve it in safety.[21] This emphasis upon the security of property might have been expected from the apologist of the bourgeois revolution of 1688. Locke held that the chief purpose of government and law is to protect property.

Locke made the most direct claim of any writer of the contract school for the historicity of the social contract as the means of instituting civil society, and he maintained that it must be assumed to lie at the basis of all the states then in existence.[22]

He differentiated clearly between society, in general, as created by the social contract, and the government, to which society delegates the functions of political control. By so doing he was able to show how government may be dissolved without destroying civil society itself.[23] This dissolution of the government, or revolution, is justifiable whenever the terms or purposes of the social contract are violated by those in power. The majority of the citizens are the only group qualified to judge when the infractions have become sufficient to warrant revolution.[24] Locke thus laid the theoretical foundation for the American and French revolutions, as well as justifying the English revolution of 1688.

The ingenious and romantic Rousseau (1712–78) was the last of the classical contract school.[25] In his earlier writings Rousseau took the position, in opposition to Hobbes, that the condition of man in the state of nature was almost ideal in its rude simplicity and that the state of war was unknown in those idyllic days. Man reached perfection in the age of ancient patriarchs. The development of civilization, while bringing increasing enlightenment, had only contributed to the physical and moral degeneration of the race and to the growth of inequality, corruption, and tyranny.

In his later writings, especially his *Social Contract,* Rousseau abandoned his earlier praise of the natural state of man and took practically the same position as Locke, namely, that, while this condition was not one of war, its uncertainties and inconveniences rendered the institution of civil society imperative. The only way in which civil society could be set up and unified power and general protection secured was through the medium of a social contract. This contract gave rise to the state or civil community and not to the government. Rousseau thus distinguished between the state and government, making sovereign power the prerogative of the state and governmental power purely delegated. His definition of sovereignty as the absolute power of the state, growing out of an expression of the general will, was probably his chief contribution to political philosophy.

Rousseau's notion of popular sovereignty became the doctrinal bulwark of democratic theory. He went on to insist that every governmental issue must be submitted to a popular vote and held that all citizens must obey every measure which has received the approval of a majority of the voters. Rousseau also maintained that voters should register their opinions and elect their candidates in districts based on population and geographical areas. He thus helped to upset the vocational representation of medieval and early modern Europe—representation by estates and interests—and encouraged the trend toward territorial representative units, based on population.

While the importance of Rousseau's conception of popular sovereignty is generally conceded, historians now tend to ascribe less significance to Rousseau's dogmas as direct causal influences in the French

Revolution than was formerly the case. Few men have been further removed from the temperament of the practical revolutionist than Rousseau was.

Finally, Rousseau's important contributions to educational theory in his *Émile* should be mentioned. Here he laid special emphasis upon the value of a spontaneous development of the whole personality rather than upon formal discipline or the mere acquisition of knowledge. He also helped to infuse a democratic tendency into education by declaring it to be the right of every child to have an adequate education, a position even more warmly defended by Helvétius.

Further on, we shall present the criticisms of the social-contract theory by Hume, Ferguson, Burke, and others. Suffice it to say here that among them they completely discredited the doctrine on both psychological and historical grounds.

II. THE RISE OF A THEORY OF PROGRESS

One of the more conspicuous results of the rise of science and the growth of rationalism between 1500 and 1800 was the gradual appearance of an idea of progress. It is a significant fact that more than 99 per cent of man's existence upon the planet was passed through without any consciousness of the actual progress of human culture. Human progress down to the seventeenth century was natural and spontaneous and was in no sense the result of any collective effort to realize a conscious goal of racial and cultural advancement.

The ancient Jews, holding to the doctrine of the "Fall" of man, logically believed that perfection was to be found in the past rather than to be sought in the future. The classical writers shared to some degree a comparable notion, namely, the dogma of a decline from a golden age. Even more popular with the Greeks and Romans was the conception of the cyclical nature of human development. Culture would rise to a certain point and then decline to a level comparable to that which had existed at the beginning. Then the process would start all over again, and the cycle would be repeated. The Christians took over the Jewish notion of the "Fall" of man and combined it with the pagan view of the decline from a golden age. Man could never expect any utopia here on earth. The state of blessedness is to be attained only in the world to come. The Last Judgment and the end of things earthly was, according to the Christian view as stated in the Book of Revelation, to be preceded by unusually horrible and devastating earthly occurrences.

Gradually, however, there arose the conviction that better things might be in store for humanity here on this earth. Back in the thirteenth century Roger Bacon had had a vision of what applied science might do for man. Montaigne had a glimmering of a new idea when he suggested that human learning should be concerned with human happiness here on earth rather than with the salvation of the soul in the life to come. Francis Bacon and Descartes united in decrying the authority of the past. Bacon had contended that the moderns were superior to the ancients and suggested that utopia might be secured through applying science to human problems.

The doctrine of progress, as it is conventionally understood, began, however, with men like Bernard de Fontenelle (1657–1757).[26] In his *Dialogues of the Dead* (1683) Fontenelle hardly went beyond the contention that the ancients were no better than the moderns; but five years later, in his *Digression on the Ancients and the Moderns,* he took a more positive attitude. He held that the ancients and the moderns are essentially alike in a biological sense, there being no progress in this respect. In the fine arts, which are chiefly a spontaneous expression of the human spirit, there seems to be no law of progress. The ancient peoples achieved great things here, but the best modern works in art, poetry, and oratory equal the most perfect ancient examples. On the other hand, in science and industry we find an altogether different story. In these fields development is cumulative. There has been vast progress here since antiquity, and even greater things may be looked for in the future. Moreover, Fontenelle agreed with Francis Bacon that unreasoning admiration for the ancients is a major obstacle to progress. It is doubtful if anybody, even in our own day, has more successfully stated the general principles involved in the problem of what we call "progress" than did Fontenelle.

Charles Perrault (1628–1703) was a contemporary of Fontenelle and expressed very much the same views in his *Parallel of the Ancients and Moderns* (1688–96). But he was so much impressed by what he regarded as the perfection of culture in his own generation that he was not much concerned with future progress—if, indeed, he would have conceded that anything could be better than his own age.

A more dynamic attitude toward future progress was taken by the Abbé de Saint-Pierre (1658–1753). He contended that progress is real and that the achievements of his own age were more notable than those of the era of Plato and Aristotle. He was particularly interested in social progress and believed in the desirability of an academy of political science to guide social advance. He placed great faith in the power of a wise government and was a forerunner of Helvétius and the Utilitarians.

Claude Adrien Helvétius (1715–71) was the foremost of the French social optimists of this period. He believed thoroughly in the possibility of human perfection and thought it could be effectively achieved through universal enlightenment and rational education. He had faith in the equality of men and held that existing inequalities can be eliminated through education.

In the first half of the eighteenth century the Italian, Giovanni Battista Vico (1668–1744), a philosopher of history, worked out a conception of progress in his *La Scienza nuova*. He held that human progress does not take place directly or in a straight line. Rather, it takes the form of a spiral. There may seem to be cycles of development, but they never go back to the original starting-point. Each turn is on a higher level than the preceding.

A little later, in France, a more realistic historical theory of progress was expounded by Anne Robert Jacques Turgot (1729–81), himself an eminent contributor to the philosophy of history. He laid great stress upon the continuity of history and the cumulative nature of progress. He contended that the more complex the civilization, the more rapid is human progress. Hence, cultural advance was very slow in primitive times but has been greatly accelerated in the modern epoch. Even more optimistic was the distinguished writer of the French Revolutionary period, the Marquis de Condorcet, author of *A Sketch of the Intellectual Progress of Mankind*. He not only stated his belief in the reality of progress but presumed to divide the history of civilization into ten periods, each representing a definite stage in the development of human civilization. Nine of these periods had already been passed through, and the French Revolution and modern science were leading us to the brink of the tenth, which would produce an era of happiness and well-being the like of which had never before been known.

There were other men who contributed variously to the notion of progress. The German philosopher, Herder, attempted to work out laws of progress based on the collaboration of nature and God. Immanuel Kant sought to prove the reality of moral progress. The English publicist, William Godwin (1756–1836), believed that perfection might be obtained through the abolition of the state and property and the indoctrination of rationality through private instruction. Henri de Saint-Simon (1760–1825) followed the line of the Abbé de Saint-Pierre in holding that a basic social science must be provided to guide human progress. These notions culminated in the historical philosophy and sociology of Auguste Comte (1798–1857). He worked out a comprehensive panorama of the "laws" governing intellectual progress and formulated an expansive philosophy of history, embodying the division of the past into a large number of periods and subperiods, each characterized by some phase of cultural advance.

III. UTOPIAS, SOCIAL AND REVOLUTIONARY DOCTRINES
AFFECTING THE LOWER CLASSES

The doctrines set forth between 1600 and 1800 justifying revolution that we have discussed above were concerned primarily with the transformation of political institutions and affected mainly the upper-class landowners and the middle-class merchants. But there were many writers between 1500 and 1800 who recognized that political progress means little unless accompanied by comparable social and economic changes. Others saw clearly that no type of social reform is adequate unless it touches the life of the masses of agricultural and industrial workers. They asserted that the doctrine of the equality of man must go deeper than mere beautiful political phrases and must apply to the economic and social status of the various members of society. Some of these proposals for social change took the form of "utopias," or pictures of ideal society, envisaging novel principles not yet adopted in the civilizations of the writers.[27] Locke and other apologists for the rising bourgeois system had contended that the chief purpose of society, government, and law is to protect private property. The radical utopians of this period took the opposite view and held that the ideal society must limit or even, in the opinion of some of these writers, do away with private property altogether.

Programs and movements for social reform date back in their origins almost to the dawn of written history. Oppression of certain classes existed in the first historical societies, and it is not surprising that some of the earliest Egyptian literature reflects the growth of discontent among the subject groups. As Professor E. R. A. Seligman once pointed out, the desire to improve the social environment has been a dynamic impulse encouraging the evolution of economic and social doctrines, though it is quite true that theories which have once been the harbingers of progress may later be utilized as a bulwark of the existing order.

While proposals for the betterment of social conditions have appeared in all ages, they have been most numerous after great social and economic revolutions that have altered the status of existing classes and have brought an unusual amount of misery to those whose condition was most seriously affected by the transition. As Professor Robert Flint expressed it: "It is in their times of sorest depression that nations usually indulge most in dreams of a better future and that their imaginations produce most freely social ideals and utopias."

The growth of wealth and class differentiation in antiquity; the development of Athens into a commercial empire; the growth of the plutocracy in the Roman Republic; the disintegration of Roman society in the fourth and fifth centuries A.D.; the breakdown of feudalism and the origin of the national states; the rise of the *bourgeoisie* following the commercial revolution; and that greatest of all social and economic revolutions, the industrial revolution of the late eighteenth and nineteenth centuries—these are well-known examples of social and economic transformations that brought social upsets and human misery in their train and stimulated the formulation of numerous programs of social reform, written by those who were distressed over the social suffering that ensued. We are here concerned with the transformations, confusion, and misery caused by the breakdown of the medieval system and the origins of modern industry, commerce, and agricultural methods following the close of the Middle Ages.

The first and the most famous of modern utopias was the work of an English scholar and official, Sir Thomas More (1478–1535). More wrote during the Tudor period, when English society, particularly among the lower classes, was feeling the impact of the breakdown of the manorial system and the rise of large-scale sheep-farming. The suppression of the English monasteries by Henry VIII also increased the general misery of the time. In the opening section of his *Utopia* More presents us with a vivid picture of the disorder and suffering of the time.

In order to suggest a remedy for these sorry conditions, More portrayed an ideal society on the fanciful island of Amaurote. Here wealth was to be divided equally, so as to put an end to that avarice and covetousness which More, like Plato, regarded as the root of all human evils. The whole society on the island was to be a well-organized community, based upon co-operative principles. Altruism would prevail, and each person would have in his mind the interests of all others. Everybody was to engage in agriculture and, in addition, to learn some useful trade. The government was to be a combination of aristocracy and the force of public opinion. More did not believe that many laws would be required, since equality and the co-operative principle would automatically bring to an end most of those evil desires and acts which require legislative restraint.

Francis Bacon, as has been noted, advocated the betterment of human society through the application of natural science. His ideal society, described in *The New Atlantis,* was located on an island off the coast of South America. Its central feature was the House of Solomon, where the scientists gathered and worked. They also sent out travelers to visit the rest of the world and to gather in new scientific knowledge. This was to be applied to increasing the happiness and welfare of the population. All superstition was to be rooted out, and social improvements were to be assured through the knowledge acquired by the scientists.

Much more radical were the proposals embodied in *The City of the Sun,* written by an Italian friar, Tommaso Campanella (1568–1639). He maintained that society is based upon the threefold principles of power, love, and intelligence; and he contended that there can be no perfect social system unless this trinity receives due recognition in the organs of social control and political administration. Campanella argued for the complete abolition of all slavery, for the dignity and importance of labor, and for the elimination of the leisure class. Everybody was to work, but he believed that a short day would suffice to produce all the required necessities of life. He favored communism in property. He held that the home and the family are the chief foundation of the property instinct. Hence, property cannot be done away with so long as the individual home is maintained. Community of wives and children he believed to be essential to the elimination of the acquisitive tendency.

The utopia of James Harrington (1611–77), an English publicist, had a much more aristocratic cast. In his *Oceana* he held that society must be organized on psychological principles, so as to make certain the leadership of the intellectually élite. Furthermore, political organization must be so arranged as to secure the predominant influence of the landholding classes, which, he believed, constitute the intellectual aristocracy. He sponsored the equal division of landed property and a wide use of the elective principle in government.

The *Télémaque* of François Fénelon (1651–1715) was a long and fanciful pedagogical novel, which utilized a picture of life in the simple Homeric society in order to inculcate ideals suitable for the education of a modern prince. It endeavored to teach sound principles of government at wide variance with the tyranny and exploitation that then prevailed under the French Bourbons. His ideal government was that of a benevolent monarchy, devoted to peace, economy, social justice, and the development of agriculture. He developed his political doctrines further in his *Tables de Chaulnes*. Among the novel principles that Fénelon suggested was the education of women, to which he devoted an entire book.

The beginning of true social radicalism is to be discerned in *The Code of Nature,* a detailed communistic utopia, written in 1755 by a Frenchman named Morelly, about whose life little is known. He advocated a new social system, based upon the rights of the masses and the laws of nature rather than upon something handed down from above by benevolent autocrats. He took man in a state of nature and primitive society as his standard of comparison. Here, without either property or political force, Morelly pictured man as inherently good. The purpose of government and human institutions should be to preserve this inherent human goodness and social equality. Therefore, he advocated the abolition of private property and the establishment of social equality. His notion of communism was not mere equality of property but actual communal ownership of goods by all members of society. He laid special stress upon the social distribution of the products of industry. He attacked the doctrine of innate ideas and contended that there is no natural idea or instinct of property. Hence there will be no great difficulty in putting an end to the institution of private property. As a form of government, Morelly proposed what he designated as "democracy" but what was really benevolent rule by patriarchs.

Contemporary with Morelly and holding much the same ideas was the Abbé Gabriel Bonnet de Mably (1709–85), especially in his treatise on *Legislation*. He attempted to reconcile the selfish and social tendencies in man by holding that, while self-interest furnishes the basic drive in human activity, true happiness can be found only in social life. Man originally lived in a state of relative perfection but fell from this happy estate into misery because of the rise of private property and the quarrels which this promoted. The underlying cause of human suffering and social evils has been the accumulation and the unequal distribution of wealth. The rise of money helped along this degradation of man and society. Mably held that we cannot suddenly return to perfection by establishing pure communism. We must start by restricting property rights and holdings. We can then work gradually toward communism. The governmental system through which he proposed to achieve this result was about what we should call a "conservative republic."

During the French Revolution a notable movement toward social radicalism was led by François Babeuf (1760–97). He took seriously the "Equality" slogan of the French Revolution and insisted that any equality of real significance must be social and economic, as well as political. These principles he embodied in his *Manifesto of the Equals,* in which he held that, in primitive society, economic and social equality were the rule, and he said that society and government should preserve this equality. To Babeuf they seemed to be defending and perpetuating inequality. He, therefore, advocated communism in property and equality of individual status. He was especially bitter against private property in land. He warmly supported the doctrine of democracy as a form of government. Though Babeuf himself was guillotined, his doctrines cropped up again in the Revolution of 1848 and in the Paris Commune of 1871.

IV. SOCIAL PHILOSOPHY DURING THE PERIOD OF ITS GRADUAL TRANSITION INTO SOCIOLOGY

A. THE CULTURAL BACKGROUND

Around the beginning of the eighteenth century a new era seemed to be dawning in social philosophy. The old a priori speculation and interpretation of society in purely subjective terms was gradually abandoned, though there was a temporary recrudescence in the writings of

Rousseau. Vico presented a theory of progress and a new attitude in studying primitive society. Berkeley and the social reformers reflected the influence of Newtonian natural science. Montesquieu produced the first great objective and descriptive treatise on sociology. Voltaire partially crushed obscurantism. Fontenelle, Turgot, Kant, and Condorcet were the first conspicuous advocates of the doctrines of continuity in history and of the possibility of infinite human progress. Along with Herder and others, they gave an impetus to the philosophy of history. Hume presented the first important psychological interpretation of society, annihilated the social contract, and suggested a naturalistic study of religion as a form of human behavior.

Ferguson and Herder combined the objective and subjective methods of analyzing the social process. Economic influences were studied in detail by the Physiocrats, Adam Smith, and the Classical Economists. The French Revolution emphasized, perhaps to excess, the doctrine of the amenability of social processes to rational and artificial direction. The scientific historical approach to the study of social institutions was manifested in the works of Eichhorn, Savigny, Niebuhr, Ranke, and Guizot. Finally, Saint-Simon classified the sciences and pointed out the need of a synthetic science of society to furnish a reliable guide for reconstructing the social order. The various lines of approach to the interpretation of social processes which were to converge in sociology were, thus, all in process of development during the eighteenth century and the first quarter of the nineteenth. When one reflects upon the situation, it appears neither strange nor miraculous that Comte was able, after 1820, to conceive of, and partially formulate, the laws of a synthetic system of sociology. At best, he only skilfully combined interpretations which were current in his time.

The environmental origins of social philosophy during the period of its transition into sociology are not difficult to discover.[28] The older tendencies, centering about the creation of the national state, furnished the center of orientation for the doctrines of the Mercantilists and the Cameralists, whose influence lasted well into the eighteenth century. The reaction against their excessive emphasis upon the paramount importance of the state and upon the necessity of extensive state activity found expression in the laissez faire doctrines of the Physiocrats and the English Classical Economists.

Natural science, which received its highest expression in Newton, reacted powerfully upon eighteenth-century political and social philosophy. If Galileo and Newton had been able to interpret the physical universe in terms of such simple formulas as the laws of "falling bodies" and "inverse squares," it seemed probable to many social philosophers that equally simple formulas could be found to explain and control social and political phenomena. This idea was a foundation of the prevalent eighteenth-century doctrine that a few "self-evident dictates of pure reason" are adequate to interpret and to adjust social and political relations. It also provided the basic philosophy which buttressed the laissez faire tenets of the Physiocrats and Adam Smith.

The critical spirit of the eighteenth century, which found its ablest representatives in Voltaire, the Encyclopedists, Hume, and Paine, can be traced to a number of sources. Bacon and Descartes, in the previous century, had proclaimed the futility of dependence upon the past. The natural science contributed to a general spirit of skepticism and curiosity. The extensive geographical discoveries and explorations extended the contact of cultures, which is the most potent agency in awakening a criticism of social institutions. The Deists emphasized the necessity of introducing reason into religion, the very possibility of which had been denied by Luther. All these forces and tendencies gave rise to that destructive criticism of old theories and institutions which was necessary to clear the ground for a new synthetic and dynamic study of society.

Montaigne, and Shaftesbury, Pope, and other Deists, attacked the depressing theological view of the inherent depravity and hopeless wickedness of man and made possible a conception of man as a worthy subject for scientific analysis, thus justifying the social sciences.

The critical spirit, the Deistic conception of the reasonable decency of man, and the dynamic type of mind created by the further developments of science, commerce, and industry opened the way to the idea of the future progress of the race, so admirably expressed by Fontenelle, Turgot, Condorcet, and Godwin.

The industrial revolution, the greatest transformation in the history of humanity, broke down the foundations of the previous social system even more completely than the commercial revolution had destroyed the medieval order. Out of the confusion, as an aid in solving the newly created social problems, there came a further development and differentiation of the special social sciences. The necessity of providing a synthetic and systematic science of society, to criticize the validity of the multitude of schemes presented to reconstruct the disintegrating social order, brought into being sociology in its present connotation.

B. GEOGRAPHICAL AND BIOLOGICAL INTERPRETATIONS OF SOCIETY

We have already called attention to the theories offered by Hippocrates, Aristotle, Vegetius, Aquinas, and Bodin relative to the influence of physical factors, especially climate, upon mankind and human society. In the period after 1700 the idea was developed far more completely, and the chief exponent of this interpretation of social and political processes was the French publicist, Charles de Secondat, baron de Montesquieu (1689–1755), author of the famous *The Spirit of Laws* (1748).[29] Montesquieu's notions on the effect of climate on mankind were drawn in part from the English physician and publicist, John Arbuthnot, who, in 1733, wrote an *Essay on the Effects of Air on Human Bodies*. Montesquieu's wide use of examples from the Moslem East was helped along by reading Jean Chardin's *Travels into Persia and the East Indies*.

The purpose of *The Spirit of Laws* was to lay down the fundamental principles of legislation. These Montesquieu found to be: (1) the close adaptation of institutions and legislation to the character of the peoples for whom they are intended, and (2) the harmonious interaction of the various institutions, laws, and other devices for insuring social control which are applied by any group. Such a view led him to investigate the factors which produce the diverse physical and cultural characteristics to be observed among the various peoples of the world. He upheld the notion that the main cause of the diversities among human types and cultures is geographical influences, especially climate. By examining the effects of geographical factors on men, one could understand the traits of the different peoples of the world and thus be in a position to determine the appropriate laws and institutions for each type of man.

Montesquieu frankly abandoned the conventional view that there is some absolutely best state, economic order, religion, form of family, or moral code, and he fully adopted the comparative approach. That institution is "best" which is best adapted to the conditions of the people for whom it is intended. Climate and other geographical factors have created the various types of man, and it is the function of the wise legis-

lator to discover and recognize these types and their traits and to legis-
late accordingly.

To illustrate: Montesquieu maintained that a despotism is best adapted
to peoples dwelling in warm climates, a limited monarchy to those in
temperate climates, and a republic to dwellers in cold areas. Moham-
medanism is eminently suited to those living in the tropics, Catholicism
to those in intermediate climates, and Protestantism to those in colder
zones. Polygamy is particularly practical for the tropics, whereas monogamy is preferable in temperate and cold regions. Drinking should be
tabooed in the warm climates, because no stimulus is needed to produce
vivacity; but heavy drinking may be tolerated in cold areas because of
the need of internal heat, of a stimulation of the senses, and of an
encouragement of playfulness among the "phlegmatic peoples of the
north."

Montesquieu's emphasis on the importance of geographical factors
in shaping social institutions gave an impetus to anthropogeography.
Many writers on history, politics, and economics adopted Montesquieu's
views in whole or in part. Count Buffon held that racial differences are
due chiefly to differences in the geographical habitat of the races. The
German philosopher, Herder, generally agreed with Montesquieu as
to the effects of geographical environment on man, though he laid
rather more stress on organic and psychic forces than did Montesquieu.
He contended that, while Montesquieu's notions regarding climatic influences on man were most suggestive, they must be accepted with careful scrutiny and due discrimination. But he conceded that geographic
factors have much to do with shaping national character. Adam Ferguson
accepted Montesquieu's ideas with some qualification in his *History
of Civil Society*. Montesquieu's notions were critically examined by
Charles Comte in his *Treatise on Legislation*. Much new scientific material on climatic influences was provided by the travels, researches, and
writings of the great German explorer and naturalist, Alexander von
Humboldt, who got away from pure theory and gathered data in the
field in scientific fashion. Such work made possible the publication in
1818 of Karl Ritter's *Die Erdkunde im Verhältnis zur Natur und
zur Geschichte der Menschen,* the first truly scientific work on anthropogeography.

Changes in population levels have naturally aroused the interest of
observers of social conditions. We have already shown that population

problems have been discussed by writers for thousands of years. A scholar in the field of population questions, Charles E. Stangeland, has actually written a good-sized book on the many theories of population growth that were set forth before the time of Malthus, with whom many people believe that the discussion of population problems began. We have no space here for the discussion of historical curiosities in the field of population theory, so we shall limit ourselves to a summary of the notions of Thomas Robert Malthus (1776–1834).[30]

In 1798 appeared the first edition of Malthus' *Essay on Population,* which was destined to have a remarkable influence on economic and social discussions for more than a century. The substance of Malthus' argument was as follows: (1) population tends to increase at a geometric ratio (1, 2, 4, 8, 16, and so on), while the food supply cannot possibly be made to increase at more than an arithmetic ratio (1, 2, 3, 4, and so on); and (2), as a result, population tends always to press upon the underlying means of subsistence.

Malthus saw two kinds of checks to the tendency of population to outrun its food supply—(1) positive: war, pestilence, and starvation; and (2) negative: postponement of marriage to a later age and what he described as "moral restraint." Malthus sincerely believed that a considerable part of the population in the England of his day could hardly escape a life of poverty and misery. He feared that, for the immediate future at least, any increase in the means of subsistence would tend to encourage a more than corresponding increase in the population.

Malthus issued later and more complete editions of his famous work on population. Though he did not alter his basic ideas, as contained in the original edition of his book, later versions did modify certain important details. In the later and more complete statements of his doctrines, Malthus tended to lay less stress upon the alleged precise ratio between the increase of human numbers and the means of subsistence. He was more inclined to emphasize the general tendencies implied in these ratios. He also was willing to admit that many factors, in addition to the pressure of population on the means of subsistence, help to determine the growth of numbers in any given population. Finally, he became rather more optimistic, in that he believed that his proposed negative or preventive checks on population growth were actually beginning to work and were rendering unnecessary the more harsh and drastic conditions involved in the positive checks.

Malthus has been vigorously defended and bitterly criticized in the years which have elapsed since his "law" of population was enunciated. Both his defenders and his critics have usually lacked historical perspective. For conditions as they existed in 1798, Malthus was reasonably sound in his doctrines; but scientific and technological changes in the interval since his day have made Malthusian principles, in large part, an intellectual curiosity in our era.

The two or three "industrial revolutions" have completely altered the situation relating to the food supply. The first industrial revolution gave us the reaper, binder, thresher, and other mechanical methods of carrying on agriculture, the elements of scientific fertilization, and the beginnings of efficient methods of storing and preserving foods. The second industrial revolution carried the process further by providing the tractor, gang-plow, reaping and threshing combine, ultra-scientific soil-testing and fertilization, scientific canning and refrigeration to aid in food preservation, and other comparable advances. So important are these results that Professor O. W. Willcox estimates that we could produce all the food needed in the United States by the scientific cultivation of one-fifth of the land now under cultivation and with the use of only one-fifth of the farm labor now employed. Even more dramatic and portentous for the future is the onset of the third industrial revolution, which offers the prospect of synthetic chemical production of foods in laboratories and factories remote from the farms and with no discernible limit to food production. There are social considerations justifying population limitation, but we can now produce food enough today to support any reasonable or probable population under normal conditions.

Malthus' *Essay* stimulated further interest in population problems. In his *Dissertations on Man* (1806), Dr. Thomas Jarrold denied that economic factors, such as the pressure of population on the means of subsistence, bring about a decline in the birth rate. Like Gini, in our day, he attributed any decline in the birth rate to some occult physiological influence which reduces both fecundity and fertility. In his book on *Current Evils in Ireland* (1828), Michael T. Sadler tried to combine the physiological and economic explanations of birth-rate trends. He held that human hardship and privation tend to increase fecundity, while a state of plenty leads to a decrease. The greater the density of population, all other things being equal, the greater the prosperity and the lower the fecundity. Hence, whenever population becomes dense, the birth rate automatically drops and the population is reduced.

In the eighteenth century there were a number of psychological interpretations of social processes and institutions which were far more realistic and valuable than the dubious hypothesis of a social contract. We shall now present some of the outstanding contributions to this field of social theory.

The work of the brilliant Irish prelate, George Berkeley (1684-1753), was as important for sociology as for philosophy.[31] In his *Sermon on Passive Obedience,* which was largely devoted to a criticism of Locke's theory of revolution, he did not commit himself to the belief in a social contract but held that if such a process be assumed, then its terms must be binding in perpetuity. He assumed the natural sociability of man and the necessity of government to regulate society; from these premises he concluded that obedience to established authority must be regarded as a law of nature.

More important than this bit of reactionary political theory is his generally neglected essay on *The Principles of Moral Attraction,* which is one of the most suggestive essays in the whole history of social philosophy. This was probably the first attempt to interpret social processes in terms of the Newtonian laws of mechanics. Assuming that the social instinct is analogous to the principle of gravitation in the physical world, Berkeley worked out in an ingenious manner the ways in which this socializing force operates to create the various social processes and institutions.

As masses attract each other more strongly when they are closer together in space, so the attraction of different individuals in society for each other increases in proportion to the degree of resemblance which they bear to each other. Again, as the tendency toward sociability and co-operation is the centripetal force in society, so human selfishness and individualistic traits are the centrifugal force, and a stable society can exist only when the former is in excess of the latter. The similarity between these conceptions and certain vital portions of the sociological systems of Herbert Spencer and Professor Giddings is readily apparent.

However, suggestive as Berkeley may have been, there can be little doubt that the contributions of David Hume (1711-76) to social philosophy are the most important that any Englishman advanced before the time of Ferguson and Adam Smith. As Montesquieu had been the herald of descriptive sociology, so Hume came nearer to modern psychological sociology than any other man of this age.[32]

In the first place, he totally destroyed both the historical and the philosophical foundations of the doctrine of a social contract. That Rousseau and others later dared to advance this theory is either a serious reflection upon their intelligence or an indication of their ignorance of Hume's destructive criticism.

Society, according to Hume, has its origin in instinct and not in intelligent self-interest. Man is by nature a social being; the state of nature is only a creation of the imagination in a priori philosophy; and the social-contract theory assumes the impossible condition of knowledge prior to experience—knowledge of the benefits of society before society had ever existed.

As a substitute for this rejected contract doctrine, Hume offered a psychological interpretation of society of the utmost importance. Society originates in the sex instinct, which is the ultimate social fact. This gives rise to the family, which is held together by that sympathy which always springs up among those who are alike and dwell in contiguity. Spontaneous sympathetic bonds are soon supported by custom and habit, which gradually make the group conscious of the advantages of association. This genetic family and community group expands and is at first held together by the influence of sympathy and mutual aid. But human selfishness renders this sympathetic basis of association inadequate, and efficient social control can then be found only in the institution of government. Government originates in force and then develops authority and stability from a growing sense of common interests on the part of the group. The social process thus starts in instinct, develops through feeling and emotion, and, finally, comes under the control of the intellect.

Especially important in Hume's psychological interpretation of society was his emphasis upon sympathy as the chief factor in social assimilation and upon imitation as the basis of "type-conforming" groups. His analysis of imitation as the force which reduces social groups to cultural homogeneity was an attack upon the environmental theories of Montesquieu and was a direct anticipation of Bagehot and Tarde. In addition, Hume was probably the first writer to develop a truly psychological interpretation of religion, which he treated simply as a form of human behavior. Finally, his emphasis upon utility as the criterion by which to estimate the desirability of any institution was the starting-point for the social philosophy and ethics of the English Utilitarians.

A more thorough treatment than Hume's of the social significance of sympathy was contained in Adam Smith's *Theory of Moral Sentiments* (1759).[33] Smith held that no man can be so selfish that he is not interested in the welfare of others. That one weeps over the grief of others is a fact too obvious to take the trouble of proving. Yet, since one cannot experience the feelings of others, this sense of mutual sorrow must arise from one's imagining one's self in the place of the suffering person and as being subject to the same emotions. This changing places with the sufferer, then, Smith asserted to be the only source of fellow-feeling for the sorrow of others.

Not only is this a general reaction; it extends to particular parts of the individual organism. If one is about to be injured or has been injured in a certain part of his body, the observers are immediately afflicted with a sense of shuddering or of pain in a similar part of their own anatomy. Not only pain and sorrow but also pleasurable emotions produce a similar feeling in the mind of the spectator, who puts himself, through the power of imagination, in the place of the person observed. Although "pity" is the term generally used to describe fellow-feeling for a person afflicted with sorrow or pain, Smith consistently employed the term "sympathy," since it may be applied to fellow-feeling for both pleasant and unpleasant emotions. Sight or knowledge of affliction will stir up this fellow-feeling, and in many cases simply the expression of the face which conveys the impression of a certain emotion may set up a comparable one in the spectator.

The social-contract theory represented a form of rationalism in social thought. Rationalism was carried along further in the eighteenth century in the eulogy of pure reason as a dominant social force. The two outstanding exponents of this rationalistic social psychology were the Abbé Sieyès and William Godwin.

An enthusiastic manifesto of rationalistic social theory appeared in the works of Count Joseph Emanuel Sieyès (1748–1836), usually known as the Abbé Sieyès, a French writer of the Revolutionary period and author of *What Is the Third Estate?* When one has worked out in his mind the type of government and society that is desirable, it is possible to set up such a system if adequate popular support can be enlisted for it. In short, institutions do not have to be allowed to change slowly, while old abuses persist. They can be altered to suit the needs of the time and made to produce speedily the results desired by wise men. Such a view justified revolution, if desirable reforms could not be obtained in any other way. This doctrine was a threat to vested monarchical and aristocratic interests, which rested chiefly on tradition, inertia, and the superstition that what is must continue to be.

William Godwin's *Enquiry concerning Political Justice* created considerable excitement when it appeared in 1793. Godwin believed that all human misery is the direct result of the restraining and warping influences of coercive human institutions and that government, at its best, is an evil. He advised the abolition of government, of strict marriage regulations, and of all social groups larger than the parish and declared for the equal distribution of property. Godwin was, on the other hand, emphatic in his praise of the noncoercive and spontaneous forms of society and of co-operative activity. He held that the growing influence of pure reason would be the means by which the ultimate perfection of the human race could be attained. His rosy hopes for the future of mankind were only exceeded by those expressed by Condorcet.

The transition from rationalism to utilitarianism was brought about in the writings of Jeremy Bentham (1748–1842), who first attained prominence through his *Fragment on Government,* published in 1776. This was a relentless attack upon Blackstone's complacent social and political philosophy. While it was in part the rending-asunder of a straw man that Bentham had erected, this work is important in social philosophy for its acute differentiation between natural and political society, its detailed criticism and rejection of the theory of a social contract and natural rights, and its justification of any form of government by the test of its utility. As his slogan for utilitarian ethics and practical reform Bentham adopted the phrase, earlier used by Hutcheson, Beccaria, and Priestley, "the greatest happiness of the greater number"; and his psychology was the simple hedonism or "felicific calculus" which assumes that man is motivated and controlled by the desire to secure pleasurable, and to avoid painful, experiences.[34]

This intellectualistic social psychology of Bentham had an enormous influence on social thought. It was the basis of the so-called "psychological economics," from Stanley Jevons to John Bates Clark, which was not overthrown until the days of Veblen, Wesley Mitchell, and Max Weber. It furnished the foundations of political psychology from Bentham to Bryce, finally punctured by Graham Wallas' *Human Nature in Politics* and Walter Lippmann's *A Preface to Politics*. It deeply influenced the thinking of early sociologists like Spencer and Ward but was ultimately upset by Sumner's *Folkways,* which stressed the importance of custom, habit, and other irrational factors in social behavior.

Bentham produced epoch-making contributions to criminal-law reform, prison reform, the reconstruction of the system of poor relief, the establishment of a public health system, the encouragement of public education, the recommendation of general thrift and savings banks, the reform of local government, colonial self-government, and the like. He is said to have carried in his pockets model constitutions for the leading countries of his time. Constructive legislation in England in the nineteenth century owed far more to Bentham than to any other person.

D. THE HISTORICAL APPROACH TO THE STUDY OF SOCIETY

During this period there were many very interesting advances in the interpretation of social evolution beyond the crudities of the social-contract theory.[35] Some of these have been casually mentioned in connection with the rise of the theory of progress. Perhaps the first of the important historical treatments of human society after the treatise of Bodin was the work of the Italian historian, jurist, and philosopher, Giovanni Battista Vico. His stimulating book, *La Scienza nuova,* is frequently regarded as the starting-point of historical philology, ethnology, and the modern idea of historical progress and is often, but erroneously, described as the first treatise on sociology.

Vico rejected the notion of a social contract and expressed his belief in the natural sociability of man and the necessity of social relationships to produce the well-rounded human personality. He regarded religion as the most vital cohesive principle of society and thus foreshadowed the doctrines of Hegel and Kidd. By making highly original studies in the mental life of primitive man he opened the way for the modern schools of comparative philology, mythology, and religion. He offered a theory of progress which stated that development does not take place in a straight line or through identical recurring cycles but, rather, in a sort of spiral movement, in which every turn is a degree higher and more mature than its predecessor. By discussing the relativity of the excellence of social institutions, as adapted to different external conditions, he led up to Montesquieu's elaborate discussion of this subject.

According to Vico, the essence of historical development consists of the creations and alterations in the collective mind—changes in the character of the "human spirit"—from age to age. Like so many later philosophers of history, he also postulated three major stages of historical development—the divine, the heroic, and the human. The divine period was characterized by the dominion of the feelings and raw emotions in the world of the spirit and by theocracy in the realm of politics. The heroic period displayed the powers of poetic imagination in the collective mentality and gave rise to aristocracy in politics. The third period manifested positive knowledge in the collective mentality and produced political freedom, embodied in constitutional monarchies and republics. As we made plain above, Vico believed that these triadic cycles repeat themselves, but never on the same level. There is a gradual spiral advance in the culture of mankind. Vico's ideas were in harmony with romanticism in many ways, especially his notion of changes in the character of the collective spirit of mankind and his idea of the potency of God in history.

Montesquieu was not only an important contributor to early anthropogeographical ideas but also stimulated the historical study of human society. He emphasized the great variety of forces which promote social evolution, especially geographical and commercial factors. He and his disciples best reflected the reaction of the commercial revolution upon the history of human society. Montesquieu's ideas relative to the social background of history were contained in his *Spirit of Laws,* but his specific contribution to history was his *Causes of the Greatness and Decadence of the Romans* (1734). This proved the profundity of his approach to history, for here he set forth a comprehensive synthesis of the causes of the rise and decline of Roman civilization which anticipated most of the conclusions of historians since his day. He foreshadowed recent specialists in holding that the main reason for the collapse of the Roman Empire was that it grew too large and unwieldy for its rudimentary economy to support.

Montesquieu inspired a number of distinguished historians and historical sociologists. Among the more notable were Arnold Heeren, the able historian of the institutions and commerce of antiquity, and Adam Ferguson, the first real historical sociologist.

Johann Gottfried Herder (1744–1803) is important chiefly as one of the founders of the philosophy of history. His most notable work, *Ideas for the Philosophy of the History of Humanity,* was a composite of many current doctrines. It combined Rousseau's exaggerated enthusiasm for the state of nature and freedom from authority, Voltaire's conception of the reality and permanence of national character, Montesquieu's doctrine of the relation between national character and the physical environment, and the mystical conception, later elaborated by Hegel, of the gradual development of humanity toward a state of freedom. Herder had an evolutionary outlook, and he is credited with being the "father of the historical sense" in Germany: "Every civilization buds, flowers and fades according to natural laws of growth." His special emphasis upon the uniqueness of national character and the organic unity of cultural evolution put him in direct line with the Romanticists and stimulated the trend toward nationalistic sentiment in historical writing.

Immanuel Kant (1724–1804) conceived of history as the record of the unfolding of the plan of nature. This plan is the perfect development of all the latent capacities of man. Kant claimed that the motive power in this process of development is the struggle within the individual and society between the forces of communism and competition. Consequently, this process will move ahead most rapidly in that country which allows the greatest freedom and scope for this struggle and yet provides for individual liberty, protection, and the equitable administration of law.

Such a condition, Kant asserted, cannot be attained until the external relations between societies have been put on a firm, stable, and peaceful basis and the resources of the nations have been set free from war to undertake the great program of progress and enlightenment. The only way to arrive at such a condition of international peace is to establish a universal federation of nations. Looking back over history, Kant thought that he could see in its events evidence of the gradual working-out of this very plan of federation and peace. Kant was an optimist and believed that progress is constantly going on, and he explained the sharp criticisms of conditions in his day as simply manifestations of a more refined moral conscience.

An extremely abstract conception of the philosophy of history appeared in the *Characteristics of the Present Age* by another German philosopher, Johann Gottlieb Fichte (1762–1814). For Fichte, the motive of progress is the quest for human perfection. When there is nothing else left to strive for, we can still strive to create God, a task which we need never fear we shall finish.

Fichte believed that the historical scheme of things, as designed by God, embraces five epochs: (1) the age of innocence, in which reason manifested itself only crudely in the form of blind instinct; (2) the age of authority, demanding the subordination of reason to passive obedience; (3) the age of indifference to truth, thus involving the complete rejection of reason; (4) the age of science, in which truth is revered above all other things and we become conscious of reason; and (5) the age of art, when humanity becomes free and beautifies itself as befitting the image of Absolute Reason.

In his *Addresses to the German Nation* (1807), Fichte held that the hope of the future lay with the German peoples. They are, said Fichte, an *Urfolk,* or unmixed race, possessing "hidden and inexhaustible springs of spiritual life and power." The Romance peoples are a *Mischvolk,* or a product of race mixture. Consequently, they bloomed prematurely in civilization and even in Fichte's day were, so he thought, on the high road to decadence. It is no wonder that Fichte's doctrine was a strong stimulant to the growth of nationalism in Germany.

Most famous of all the Germanic philosophies of history in this period was that of the pontifical dialectician, Georg Wilhelm Friedrich Hegel (1770–1831). Hegel's *Philosophy of History* was a highly subjective work—a record of the unfolding of the self-consciousness of freedom in the human spirit. Like that of Fichte, Hegel's philosophy had a strong nationalistic impulse. It implied that the Germans of the post-Reformation period were invested by God with the mission of bringing the blessings of freedom to mankind.

Though the analysis just given reveals the general pattern of Hegel's theory of history, progress itself comes as the result of conflict and synthesis. A movement or idea—thesis—gets under way. Then its opposite—antithesis—makes it appearance. Out of the clash between the two, there comes an ultimate synthesis, which marks a further step toward truth. The synthesis then becomes another thesis, and the process goes on.

This Hegelian dialectic of progress had much influence on later historical thought, particularly through its partial adoption by Karl Marx and its exploitation by Marx in the service of a materialistic philosophy of history. Hegel stimulated other important work in historical research, especially the magisterial studies of Greek philosophy by Eduard Zeller and the investigation of Christian origins by Ferdinand Christian Baur. While Hegel's historical influence was felt in a double direction—Marxism and nationalism—it is the latter influence which is more prominent today. The celebration in 1931 of the centenary of his death was almost wholly nationalist.

Hegel also revolutionized the development of social thought by repudiating the artificial and intellectualistic notions of the philosophers of the Enlightenment and insisting that social institutions, government, religion, and the like are the natural products of an evolutionary development. The followers of Hegel founded the social sciences and launched the critical study of legal and religious origins.

The contributions of the Scotch philosopher, Adam Ferguson (1723–1816), to the development of historical sociology have not been sufficiently acknowledged.[36] French and German writers, like Comte, Gumplowicz, and Ludwig Stein, have recognized his importance in this field, but English and American students of the subject have until recently minimized or entirely overlooked the genuine worth of his work.

That Ferguson was moving in the right direction may be seen in the fact that he combined the descriptive and historical method of Montesquieu with the psychological and critical procedure of Hume. His treatment was thus both descriptive and analytical. He rejected all a priori methods, as well as the ideas of a state of nature and a social contract. He insisted on studying society as it is, and from such study he found that the primary social fact is the inherent sociability of the human species, arising from instinct and supported by utility.

The dynamic element was emphasized in the work of Ferguson, who ridiculed the ideas of Aristotle and Hobbes that social stability and peace are the chief goal of society. He laid so much stress upon the value of competition and conflict in social development that Ludwig Gumplowicz has claimed him as the first great apostle of the "group-struggle" theory of social development. His *History of Civil Society* was the most valuable and complete study of political and social origins prior to the writings of Auguste Comte and Gumplowicz.

E. THE STUDY OF ECONOMIC FACTORS IN SOCIETY

Important contributions to social thinking came from several different groups of students of the economic factors and processes in social life. The chief trend in German and Austrian economic thought in the middle of the eighteenth century, in so far as it was related to the development of sociological thinking, is to be found in the writings of the Cameralists, of whom Johann Heinrich von Justi (1717–68) and Joseph von Sonnenfels (1733–1817) were the most important.

The Cameralists were a group of technological writers rather than social philosophers. Like the English Mercantilists, they were mainly concerned with providing the national treasury with ample means to maintain its domestic policy and to defend itself against enemies from without. Their chief significance in the development of sociological thought lies in the fact that they furnish an excellent example of a group whose writings were sharply oriented and co-ordinated by the specific purpose which they had in mind. Since the problem of foreign trade in Germanic states was far less important than in England at that date, the German philosophy of extensive state intervention naturally turned toward domestic economic and political problems. This brought up the question of the technique of social improvement by means of public planning, which gave a sociological cast to the whole movement.

An American sociologist, Professor Albion W. Small, has well summarized the sociological significance of the Cameralists.[37] As he points out, cameralism frankly subordinated everything else to control by the state for the purpose of improving national existence. It was an attempt to select and adopt those policies and practices which would help most directly to make the ruler and his people secure at home and to strengthen them against other rulers abroad. It was soon perceived that this program was not merely a matter of material factors but also involved the systematic training and education of the people.

The founders of economic liberalism—the revolt against mercantilism—were the group of French writers in the middle of the eighteenth century known as the "Physiocrats," so named from the work of one of their adherents, Du Pont de Nemours, entitled *Physiocracy, or the Natural Constitution of That Form of Government Most Advantageous to the Human Race* (1767).[38] They derived their basic doctrine from the English Deists and the French *philosophes,* to the effect that social, political, and economic phenomena are governed by the same natural laws that Newton and his associates believed they had proved to rule the physical universe.

The Physiocrats were convinced that the improvement of all human institutions could best be realized by letting them freely adjust themselves to this natural order, a situation which they believed would most certainly be brought about by a regime of unlimited competition. If man refrained from legislation and from any attempt to control economic processes by artificial means, then God and his natural order would have full sway. One reason for human unhappiness and misery, so they said, was the existence of a large number of archaic and restrictive laws which, being statutory and unnatural, were holding back the free dominion of natural law over the affairs of men.

Accordingly, the Physiocrats vigorously advocated the immediate and total abolition of all restrictive legislation and the introduction of an era of laissez faire individualism. They contended that the only desirable functions of the state are the protection of life and property, the enforcement of contracts, the erection of public buildings and other public works, and the promotion of education, so that man might grasp more completely the principles of natural law. Extensive social legislation was regarded as dangerous, since it would surely impede the operation of those beneficent natural principles upon which these advocates placed their chief reliance. The Physiocrats contributed doctrines of less significance in their interpretation of social progress in terms of increasing the net product of agriculture and their scheme of reform in public finance, which centered about the notion of a single tax on land.

The general notions of the Physiocrats concerning individualism and the inactivity of the state received the support of the distinguished French economist and statesman, Turgot, and intrigued the first great systematic writer on political economy, the Scotch philosopher, Adam Smith (1723–90). The chief significance of Adam Smith for the history of economic thought is that he embodied the laissez faire thesis in a notable work, *An Inquiry into the Nature and Causes of the Wealth of Nations* (1776).[39] This received so wide a circulation and attracted so extensive a following for Smith's doctrines that the eminent historian, H. T. Buckle, nearly a century later, regarded this book as the most influential and beneficial one ever written.

Despite his general acceptance of the Physiocratic position as to the proper functions of the state, Smith abandoned to a considerable degree their excessive laudation of agriculture and emphasized the prime value, to a state, of commerce and manufacturing. Especially did he revive the Platonic doctrine of the importance of the division of labor and expert specialization in increasing productivity. His emphasis upon the part played by labor in production paved the way for the later views of Ricardo and the Socialists with respect to the "labor theory of value." His advocacy of free trade, on the ground of the advantages of an international division of labor, was one of the most forceful arguments ever advanced for commercial freedom.

Smith died before the industrial revolution had fully developed even in England, and there is good evidence for believing that he did not even foresee the complete course of this transformation, much less stand out as a conscious apologist of the new capitalist class. But his doctrines were of a sort that fitted in admirably with the popular policy of noninterference with business. The capitalist manufacturers favored this policy, in order that they, if not their employees, might enjoy the alleged "blessings of the perfect freedom of contract." Smith's notions were, therefore, expanded and exploited by the middle class and by sympathetic economists like James Mill, to provide authoritative theoretical foundations for opposition to all social legislation designed to advance the interests of the industrial proletariat.

The most extensive development of the concepts of Adam Smith naturally took place in England, where he had written and where that commercialism which was most congenial to his views was the furthest advanced, but he was honored by reverent disciples in every important European country and in the United States. His most distinguished English disciples, the so-called "Classical Economists," were Thomas Robert Malthus (1766–1834), David Ricardo (1772–1823), James Mill (1733–1836), John Ramsay McCulloch (1789–1864), and Nassau William Senior (1790–1864). The Classical Economists gave systematic expression to the laissez faire dogmas and assumed to found them on "iron laws" of economics. They thus implied that social and economic reforms usually violate both natural laws and economic logic.[40]

F. SOCIOLOGICAL ELEMENTS IN POLITICAL THOUGHT

Of all the writers in the field of political theory in the eighteenth century, one of the most impressive to present-day readers is Montesquieu. He was one of the founders of "rational politics." A member of the French nobility, he was educated for the magistracy, in which he served for many years. Early attracted to the comparative study of human institutions, his first publication was a series of satirical compositions known as *The Persian Letters* (1721).[41] In these he ironically criticized contemporary European society from the standpoint of imaginary travelers. Through the fiction of two Persians traveling in Europe and writing of French society to their friends and relatives back home, he was able to make a witty and spicy attack upon the whole French social system. This clever satire was widely read even in the court circles.

Like Montaigne, to whom we may reasonably compare him in spirit, Montesquieu was fascinated by Plutarch and by the Romans generally. He thought that their history offered a complete historical laboratory for the study of human institutions. In 1734 he published the results of his years of reflection on Roman life under the title *The Greatness and Decadence of the Romans*. Fourteen years later there appeared what is incomparably his greatest work, *The Spirit of Laws*.

Montesquieu differed from most of his contemporary social thinkers in that he did not produce a mechanical solution for social difficulties, nor did he usually bring his findings to the support of any social reform. He developed the "comparative" study of institutions to a very high point. Instead of applying himself to a particular situation, he ranged up and down the known fields of information about social groups, customs, and laws, seeking out the underlying spirit. In addition to feeding his interest through books, he traveled extensively, visiting nearly every country in Europe. Montesquieu distilled his carefully accumulated facts into *The Spirit of Laws*. Very few dogmatic generalizations found their way into this work. Perhaps the distinguishing feature of the book is the number of practical suggestions offered to lawmakers. On the other hand, he made no proposal of drastic reform, and even his admiration for the British constitution, which he misunderstood, did not lead him to advocate its adoption in France.

It was his underlying idea, as we have noted, that laws, customs, and institutions are the product of geographical factors, particularly climatic conditions, and that what might admirably serve one people would be quite unsuitable for another. On this ground he rejected the British system for France, arguing that his country was better served by a more "Gothic" form of government. Yet, despite his own distrust of formulas, his belief that the British government was designedly divided into three departments—the executive, the legislative, and the judicial, operating under a system of checks and balances—had a momentous influence on the makers of the American Constitution.

The fundamental contribution of the political philosopher and orator, Edmund Burke (1729-97), was his eloquent and commanding statement of the corporate unity of society.[42] He ruthlessly criticized the a priori and rationalistic political philosophy of his time and declared that the creation of governments is not a matter of pure reason but of historic growth and long political experience. Burke's view of history, however, was not dynamic; history to him was chiefly an instrument for defending existing institutions and combating social change. While accepting a modified version of the contractual basis of society, he maintained that this contract was universal in scope and binding in perpetuity, and he bitterly assailed the interpretation which justified revolution and led to the French Revolution.

Burke's heated criticism of the French Revolution was effectively answered by Tom Paine (1737-1809) in his *Rights of Man* and his *Dissertation on the First Principles of Government*. According to Paine, man is by nature social, owing to his social instinct and the necessity of co-operative activities. The state of nature was not presocial, but one in which men possessed the natural rights of liberty and equality. This condition had to be abandoned and governmental authority established because of human weaknesses, which made unregulated existence intolerable. Government was created by a contract between the members of society and not between the governed and the governors. Man did not give up his natural rights when government was established but merely added civil rights to them. Paine recognized that social relations, institutions, customs, co-operation, and the like are more important to the individual than government, and he regarded the latter as, at best, artificial and a necessary evil. His criticism of monarchy was an admirable antidote to the doctrines of Bossuet, and he was one of the most ardent advocates of democracy and popular sovereignty in the late eighteenth century. Especially important was his doctrine that the minority must be protected by constitutional checks on absolute majority rule.

The generally reactionary character of the political philosophy of the Romanticist writers on politics and law, such as Burke, Louis de Bonald, Joseph de Maistre, Ludwig von Haller, Herder, Fichte, Friedrich von Schelling, Hegel, and Friedrich Karl von Savigny, has led many to overlook the vital sociological note in these writings. They rejected the ideas of the rationalistic writers of the Enlightenment, who had expounded intellectualistic interpretations of the origin of society and the state as artificial products of conscious choice and deliberation. The Romanticists insisted that social institutions, government, religion, and the like are the natural outgrowth of an organic evolutionary development. This encouraged giving more attention to the social and cultural foundations of all human institutions—a trend of a distinctly sociological nature.

G. NEW CONTRIBUTIONS TO LEGAL THEORY

Much more accurate and illuminating than the application of natural law, with which we are familiar, but of much less practical import for applied jurisprudence and legal processes at the time, was the rise of comparative jurisprudence in the work of Montesquieu and others.[43] It represented, in a rough way, the extension of the conception of the common law to the race as a whole. Just as the common law represented a pooling of the experiences of the various communities in a nation, so law as a whole was a product of the experiences of the many races and nations on the planet. Great interest was taken in comparing the legal codes of diverse peoples, in pointing out their differences and similarities, and in trying to deduce legal principles of broad general application. No other school of law at the time was so civilizing. No man who thoroughly appreciated the great variety of legal concepts and practices among the peoples of the world could well be arrogant concerning the laws of his particular country.

A somewhat more precise application of this approach to law led to the origins of the historical school of jurisprudence. Montesquieu had been concerned with the laws of all peoples. The historical jurists were mainly interested in the evolution of the law within the boundaries of their particular state. Most of them regarded law as an organic outgrowth of the culture of the nation. Of these early historical jurists, perhaps the best known was Burke. Adam Ferguson combined the historical and comparative approaches to law, a procedure that has become increasingly popular from his day to our own. It has served to lessen provincialism and patriotic conceit in jurisprudence.

Rationalism had a decisive but by no means uniform influence upon legal evolution. John Locke tended toward rationalism in philosophy, but he laid special stress upon the law of nature. Many later rationalists departed widely from this precedent. They were prone to stress the deliberate character of sound law and to regard it as the dictates of reason applied to specific social problems. In the opinion of this school, public legislation is the only valid type of law. There was also a tendency to lay stress upon the responsibility of law to insure to every man a right to enjoy life, liberty, and property. It was natural that this group should be in favor of the codification of law, while the historical school was opposed to such a notion. The latter held that an artificial product of reason might be codified but that a living, growing achievement, such as a historical system of law, could not be.

The famous English jurist, William Blackstone (1723–80), ably unified many legal tendencies in his *Commentaries on the Laws of England* (1765–69). He combined Locke's rationalism and Montesquieu's comparative point of view. By giving due attention to both common-law principles and legal evolution, he brought together common-law jurisprudence and the historical approach. In laying stress on the supremacy of parliamentary statutes, he laid the basis for the later analytical jurisprudence of Austin and his successors. His *Commentaries* —the first complete summation and survey of English jurisprudence and legal principles—are notable for their notion that the history of law is a phase of the history of ideas, for their admirable literary quality, and for their comprehensiveness. They had vast influence upon legal thinking in England and America.

In the course of his legal writing, Blackstone made important observations on social and political theory. In discussing the origin of society and government, he refused to accept the doctrine of a state of nature and a subsequent social contract as historic facts. Nevertheless, he claimed that it was man's weakness in isolation that was the primary motive for association and that contractual relations must be implied as the philosophic foundations of society and government. Like Sir Henry Maine, he considered that the original social group was the patriarchal family, and he held that larger societies are but reunited offshoots of the original family that had once dispersed because it had become too large for a single habitation. Blackstone's view of the attributes of sovereignty as supreme, irresistible, absolute, and uncontrolled power in the state greatly resembles the definition of Professor John William Burgess, and it is generally agreed that Burgess' theory stands in a direct line of descent from Blackstone.

It was but a short step from the rationalistic school of law to the Utilitarian—both relied primarily upon human reason; both were interested in reform. Utilitarian jurisprudence was merely a further development and refinement of the rationalistic doctrine. What its chief exponent, Jeremy Bentham, did was to hold that rational jurisprudence must also be a science of social reform, designed in every part to increase the happiness of the largest possible number of men. There was still in it, however, a strong strain of individualism. Bentham believed that every man is the best judge of his own happiness. Hence there should be no restrictions on the acts of anyone except those necessary to secure equal freedom for others. Bentham especially eulogized the importance of freedom of contract. He came closer than others of his day, however, to the notion of law as an adjunct to, or even an instrument of, social engineering.

Friedrich Karl von Savigny (1779–1861) was the true founder of historical jurisprudence. He emphasized the necessity of observing the principle of historical development in the formation of law, maintaining that it evolves unconsciously out of the genius of a people. As a living organic thing, it cannot be codified. In his memorable controversy with Thibaut in 1814, Savigny vigorously opposed the proposal to prepare a code of law for Germany. Like Burke, then, his grasp of history was more apparent than real, and both were equally blind to the practical value of new legislation and a systematic legal code. That a later generation has upheld the judgment of Thibaut is proved by the production of the magnificent German Imperial Code, which was framed between 1874 and 1900.

The most important practical product of legal cogitation during this era was the codification of French law that began in 1793, as a result of revolutionary enthusiasm, and ended in the magnificent *Code Napoléon*. Legal codifications in other European countries followed in the nineteenth century.

One of the worst survivals of barbarism in Europe in the eighteenth century lay in criminal law. Men were still subjected to torture during the process of trial in many countries. Sentences were severe and punishments extremely brutal. The death sentence was often imposed for such a trivial offense as petty theft. Corporal punishment, including branding and mutilation, was still usual. Debtors were commonly imprisoned. Prisons were reserved chiefly for debtors and those accused of crime prior to trial. These prisons were mostly filthy, uncomfortable, and brutally administered.

The barbarous criminal law was attacked by Voltaire and Montesquieu in the middle of the eighteenth century. The latter's *Persian Letters,* especially, satirized the European criminal law of this period. But the most influential reformer in the field of criminal law was the Italian nobleman, Cesare di Beccaria (1738-94). His *Essay on Crimes and Punishments* (1764) was probably the most effective book ever written in the whole history of criminal-law reform. He argued that the prevention of crime is more important than punishment and that capital punishment should be abandoned. Indeed, with the exception of the recent application of psychology and psychiatry to crime, Beccaria suggested most of the essentials of criminological progress that have been achieved in the nearly two centuries since his work was published.

Beccaria's ideas deeply influenced the reform of the criminal codes of the American states after 1776, the new criminal code of Revolutionary France, and the reform of the British criminal code by Bentham, Romilly, Buxton, Mackintosh, and Peel in the first half of the nineteenth century. In 1800 there were about two hundred capital offenses in the British criminal code. By 1861 they had been reduced to three: treason, murder, and piracy. Torture was gradually abolished in European criminal procedure, and fair trials were provided for accused persons. Imprisonment for debt was slowly outlawed. It did not disappear even in the United States, however, until the Jacksonian period, when it was wiped out by the rising tide of democratic enthusiasm.

H. THE RISE OF ANTHROPOLOGY AND ETHNOLOGY

Anthropology, which studies man's physical nature and cultural achievements, came into being during this period.[44] The investigation of man's physical characteristics was forwarded by the anatomical studies of Andreas Vesalius (1514-64) and his successors. Carolus Linnaeus (1707-78), while he still held to the uniqueness of man in possessing a soul, linked mankind to the rest of the animal world in his system of classification, listing man as *Homo sapiens Linnaeus,* of the order of primates, and divided into four species, white, yellow, red, and black.

Johann Friedrich Blumenbach (1752-1840), of Göttingen, founded physical anthropology. He combed the museums for skulls and other physical remains of man and approached physical anthropology and anatomy from the comparative point of view. He amplified and rendered more precise the classification of the human races suggested by Linnaeus. He founded scientific craniology by his concept of the *norma verticalis,* or the shape of the skull as seen from above. Peter Camper (1722–89), a Dutch anatomist and naturalist, advanced the study of craniology by his description of the facial angle and jaw projection.

Even more important was the work of Anders Retzius (1769–1860), of Stockholm, who rendered more scientific Blumenbach's concept of the *norma verticalis.* Retzius devised what is known as the "cephalic index," namely, the ratio of the breadth of the skull to its length as expressed in a percentage. The narrow-skulled type he called "dolichocephalic," and the broad-skulled, "brachycephalic." He adopted from Camper the idea of the facial angle and took over from Friedrich Tiedemann (1781–1861) methods of determining comparative skull capacity. He thus systematized physical anthropology in its earlier stages of development, from which it was carried further by Quatrefages, Broca, Topinard, Virchow, and their successors. A dynamic orientation was given to physical anthropology by the evolutionary biology of Jean Lamarck (1744–1829). From that time onward, anthropology could begin to measure up to the definition of Robert Ranulf Marett as "the whole history of man as fired and pervaded by the idea of evolution."

The expansion of Europe, explorations, and colonization brought Europeans into contact with the most diverse cultures, from the more advanced peoples of the Moslem Near East, India, and China to the most primitive of native peoples. This led to the cultivation of comparative ethnology, religion, and ethics. The prevailing notions of primitive culture were rescued from the mysticism of the "state-of-nature" philosophy and placed upon the substantial basis of concrete descriptions of actual primitive life. To some writers, such as Adam Ferguson, this suggested the idea of the evolution of culture and institutions, though little progress was made here until the days of Sir John Lubbock, Herbert Spencer, and Lewis Henry Morgan.

An extensive literature reflected this growing knowledge of, and interest in, comparative ethnology. We can mention only a few representative examples. The travel literature was well represented by the *Travels into Persia and the East Indies* of Jean Chardin (1643–1715), from which Montesquieu derived most of his ideas of oriental life and customs, polygyny, and despotic forms of governments. Books written by historians of the discoveries and colonization added much to knowledge in comparative ethnology. Such were Oviedo y Valdés' (1478–1557) *Natural History of the Indies;* the *Da Asia* of Joao de Barros (1496–1570), which dealt with Portuguese conquests in Brazil and the East Indies; the works of Bartolomé de Las Casas (1474–1566) on the Indians of the New World; Bernal Díaz del Castillo's (1492–1581) *True History of the Conquest of New Spain;* the *General History of Explorations* by Antoine Prévost d'Exiles (1697–1763); the *General History and Description of New France* by François Xavier de Charlevoix (1682–1761); Richard Hakluyt's *The Principal Navigations, Voyages, and Discoveries of the English Nation* (1588); and William Robertson's *History of America.*

The nearest approach to real comparative ethnology in such writings was embodied in the *Customs of the American Savages Compared with the Customs of Early Times* by Joseph François Lafitau (1681–1746). The general cultural and philosophical impact of overseas contacts on European thought was best expressed in *The Philosophical and Political History of the Settlements and Trade of Europeans in the East and West Indies* by Guillaume Thomas Raynal (1713–96).

When the doctrine of evolution was enunciated in the nineteenth century, the interest in comparative ethnology was given a new and more dynamic turn. What this led to will be described later on, when we discuss such writers as Morgan, Spencer, Sumner, Westermarck, and Briffault.

V. THE INDUSTRIAL REVOLUTION, PLANS FOR SOCIAL REFORM, AND THE RISE OF SOCIOLOGY

The industrial revolution was one of the most sweeping social transformations which had thus far taken place in the history of human society. It tangled and tore the whole web of social life in the Western world and forced extensive readjustments to meet the new conditions of living. The misery and suffering which resulted led to a large number and variety of proposals for social and economic reconstruction. Nothing which had previously taken place had given so tremendous an impulse to the humanitarian movement. These programs of social reform, and the proposals of a social science to guide them, began as the result of the disintegrating influence of the commercial revolution. By the time of

Saint-Simon we have a full reflection of the effects of the industrial revolution.

For the most part, these plans of social reform and reconstruction rested more upon profound sympathy with the unfortunate classes than upon any scientific conception of society and the proper methods of securing social reform. In due time, however, many students of the social problems of the age became convinced that, if social reform was not to be wasteful and misguided, it would have to rest upon a "science of society," which would indicate the nature of, and the limitations upon, social betterment. A. W. Small, in his *Origins of Sociology,* has clearly indicated the interrelationship between these early social-reform movements and the rise of sociology.[45]

The brilliant Abbé Charles Castel de Saint-Pierre seems to have been the first to suggest clearly that man's future lies in his own hands. He embodied his theory of progress in his *Observations on the Continual Progress of Universal Reason* (1737). His predecessors were interested chiefly in showing that there had been some progress since antiquity. The Abbé was more concerned with the idea that man might plan a better future and work directly to achieve this end. In his *Discourse on the Polysynodie* (1718) he anticipated Turgot, Saint-Simon, and Auguste Comte by declaring that we must depend primarily upon social science and an academy of experts to aid us in planning for a happier future. He is also well known for a specific contribution to the betterment of the race, namely, a comprehensive plan for perpetual peace through arbitration, published in three volumes in 1713–17. He regarded war, along with religious superstition and political despotism, as the main obstacles to progress.

The French economist, Turgot, the friend and defender of the Physiocrats, produced an interesting and original interpretation of progress and historical development. In his two discourses, delivered at the Sorbonne in 1750 on the *Advantages to the Human Race from the Establishment of Christianity* and on the *Successive Advances of the Human Mind,* he set forth in clear and unmistakable language the doctrine of continuity in history, the cumulative nature of evolution and progress, and the causal sequence between the different periods of history. He also, doubtless, furnished Comte with the suggestions which grew into the latter's law of the three stages of intellectual progress. While he viewed progress as primarily a matter of intellectual improvement, his conception of continuity in cultural development and of the essential unity of the historic process was a brilliant contribution. Like Saint-Pierre, Turgot believed that we must put informed intelligence to work if progress is to be made more speedy and certain. He definitely implied that scholars could work out a broad science of social progress to guide man in planning for the future.

The Marquis de Condorcet (1743–94) is representative of that group who looked upon the French Revolution as the climax of a long period of preparation for a new era of civilization. Comte pronounced him as much the best student of "social dynamics" in the eighteenth century, as Montesquieu had been of "social statics." His *A Sketch of the Intellectual Progress of Mankind* (1793) was one of the most optimistic and original of the writings of the period. His review of the previous stages of history led him to believe that civilization was rapidly advancing and that the French Revolution might be regarded as the culmination of this process. He developed a theory of historical progress which was far in advance of the earlier doctrines of Vico or Turgot and was expressed mainly in terms of the increase of knowledge and the growth of scientific achievement.

Condorcet's hope for the future of humanity was not less optimistic than his interpretation of the past. He made many remarkably accurate, as well as some extravagant, predictions as to what science would be able to accomplish for the race. He was, thus, one of the first writers to combine the scientific and the utopian theories of society. All in all, his work is most refreshing in contrast to that depressing conception of the descent from a "golden age" which was first expressed by Hesiod and had deeply influenced European thought from that time to the nineteenth century, especially after the classical conception had been reinforced by the Hebrew myth of a primal Paradise, which had come into the current of western European thought with the introduction of Christianity.

Count Henri de Saint-Simon (1760–1825) anticipated the main theoretical positions in the sociological system of Auguste Comte. If one substituted the word "sociology" for the term *science politique,* used by Saint-Simon with practically the same connotation that Comte gave to "sociology," then Saint-Simon may be said to have formulated Comte's chief theses, though even he himself only collected and systematized the doctrines current at the time.

After a critical examination of his works, Franck Allengry enumerates the following as the fundamental doctrines advanced by Saint-Simon: (1) Science must be distinguished from art in all departments of knowledge. (2) The sciences must be classified in the order of their increasing complexity, and a new science—*la science politique*—should be put at the head of the hierarchy. (3) This *science politique* must be based on the solid inductions of history and observation and must be animated by the conception of development and progress. (4) The general law of progress is that formulated by Turgot and Bourdin, namely, the law of the three stages of the psychological evolution of the race: the conjuctural, the "miconjectural," and the positive. (5) All sociological theories of progress must be founded upon this fundamental law. (6) The practical conditions of social life, and not supernatural sanctions, must be made the basis of the new morality, and the happiness of the race must be realized through a transformation of the present social order rather than in heaven. (7) This transformation requires a new industrial organization, a new social and political system, and a union of Europe in a new fraternity, *Le nouveau christianisme.*

One who is familiar with Comte's system need not be told that all that remained was for him to expand and to systematize the outlines laid down by Saint-Simon, and the the best critics agree that such was the primary contribution of Comte to sociology.

In his program of social reform, Saint-Simon proposed to organize society under the control of industrial experts, who were to direct production with a view to bringing plenty to all mankind. The industrial experts, in turn, were to be instructed by a select group of social scientists, who would apply themselves to discovering new truths and to inculcating both the new information and all that was worthy in the old. In this idea, Saint-Simon may be regarded as founder of technocracy and of the "managerial" social philosophy set forth in our day by James Burnham and others.

Auguste Comte (1798–1857) worked over and systematized some of the leading tendencies in social science in the eighteenth and early nineteenth centuries, in order to create a comprehensive system of sociology. His indebtedness to Saint-Simon for many of his leading ideas is obvious. Other influences may be discerned along with those of Saint-Simon. From Hume, Kant, and Gall he derived his chief doctrines as to causation and positivism in method. Comte's peculiar view of history as a combination of the inevitable and the providential may be traced to the opinions of Hume, Herder, and Turgot on historical determinism and to the emphasis of Bossuet, Vico, and De Maistre on the providential element in history. Saint-Pierre, Montesquieu, Turgot, Condorcet, and Saint-Simon had pointed out the need of a broad and fundamental science of society to act as a guide for political theory and practice. Finally, Montesquieu had introduced the modern conception of social law, Condorcet had elaborated the theory of progress, and Saint-Simon had insisted upon the necessity of transforming the social order.

There was, thus, little that was original in the theoretical content of Comte's system of sociology; his main contribution was to integrate and to give a comprehensive and systematic form to some of the most important of the social theories which were current in his time. In some ways, Comte was behind the scientific achievements of his age and failed to absorb some of the most important developments and innovations of the period, which have since entered into the shaping of sociological thought. At the same time, Comte cannot be denied a certain degree of genius, for there have been few minds which have been able to grasp in a more penetrating or comprehensive manner the unity of human society or to appreciate better the vast number of factors which are involved in its organization and development.

This cursory enumeration of the chief tendencies in the study of social phenomena in the eighteenth and nineteenth centuries gives one a basis for testing the validity of the assertion of Professor Small that sociology did not have its origin in isolation from the special social sciences and that the latter had faced and partially solved some of the important problems of sociology. It also throws light on the apparently contrary thesis of Professor Giddings that a new type of approach to the study of social phenomena, which was definitely sociological, began in a systematic way with Auguste Comte and developed directly through the writings of Spencer, Ward, and the sociologists of the present generation.

The reconciliation of these conflicting views of the matter is to be found in their respective opinions of the nature of sociology. If one accepts Professor Small's contention that sociology is the philosophical synthesis of the results of the special social sciences, then his view of the origin of sociology may be regarded as valid. On the other hand, if one agrees with Professor Giddings that sociology is the elemental and basic social science, characterized by the investigation of society in its broadest and most fundamental aspects, then one must concede that the formal differentiation of sociology as a distinct social science began with the systematization of earlier doctrines by Auguste Comte.

If, as Professors Ellwood and Vincent contended, both views are tenable and mutually complementary, then the conflict of opinions is more apparent than real, and one may seek the origin and development of sociology in the last century, both in the works of avowed sociologists and in the increasing tendency of the special social sciences to adopt the broader sociological method of approach to their problems.

On the whole, this last solution of the controversy seems the more accurate and satisfactory. The fundamental fact to be insisted upon is that the essence, if not the name, of sociology was an inevitable result of the necessity of providing an adequate science of society and an equally natural product of a more comprehensive method of analyzing social phenomena. It was not the fortuitous invention of the mind of a single man or the precarious product of a single age.

It so happened that, about the time that the general social, economic, and intellectual setting in western Europe and the advances in positive knowledge and scientific methods first made possible such a thing as a science of society, Auguste Comte, an enthusiastic thinker, with a genius for assimilation and systematization, appeared upon the scene and gave a name and a systematic expression to an already potent and dynamic tendency. That sociology would have come into existence in its present nature and strength, though perhaps under a different name, even if there had been no Auguste Comte, is quite conceivable to one who has read the previous works of Vico, Montesquieu, Turgot, Hume, Ferguson, Adam Smith, Herder, Condorcet, and Saint-Simon or who has investigated the development of social science since 1850.

NOTES

1. "Contributions to the History of the Social Contract Theory," *Political Science Quarterly*, 1891, pp. 665–67.

2. N. Sykes, in F. J. C. Hearnshaw, *The Social and Political Ideas of Some Great Thinkers of the Sixteenth and Seventeenth Centuries* (New York, 1926), pp. 63–89. On sixteenth-century political thought see J. W. Allen, *European Political Thought in the Sixteenth Century* (New York, 1928).

3. Richard Hooker, *The Laws of an Ecclesiastical Polity*, Book I, chap. x; cf. also Allen, *op. cit.*

4. *Tractatus de legibus ac deo legislatore* (1612), Book I, "On Law in General."

5. Cf. J. M. Littlejohn, *The Political Theory of the Schoolmen and Grotius* (privately printed, 1895), pp. 262–96; W. A. Dunning, *A History of Political Theories from Luther to Montesquieu* (New York, 1905), pp. 133–49; and Hearnshaw, *op. cit.*, chap. iv.

6. Juan de Mariana, *De rege et regis institutione* (1605 ed.), chap. i, "Homo natura est animal sociabile." Cf. John Laures, *The Political Economy of Juan de Mariana* (New York, 1928).

7. For the most up-to-date treatment of Althusius see the Introduction to C. J. Friedrich, *Politica methodice digesta of Johannes Althusius* (Cambridge, 1932). On Grotius' contributions to social thought see Albert Salomon, "Hugo Grotius and the Social Sciences," *Political Science Quarterly*, LXII, No. 1 (March, 1947), 62–81.

8. G. P. Gooch, *English Democratic Ideas in the Seventeenth Century* (New York, 1907), pp. 177–83, 241–45, 314–19.

9. T. C. Pease, *The Leveller Movement* (American Historical Association, 1917).

10. Thomas Hobbes, *Philosophical Rudiments concerning Government and Society*, ed. Molesworth, chap. i, secs. 11–12; *Leviathan*, chap. xiii.

11. *Philosophical Rudiments*, chap. i, sec. 2.

12. *Leviathan*, chap. xl.

13. *Ibid.*, chap. xvii.

14. *Ibid.*

15. Samuel von Pufendorf, *The Law of Nature and of Nations*, trans. Basil Kennett and annotated by Barbeyrac (London, 1729), Book I, chap. ii, pp. 102 ff.; Book VII, chap. i, pp. 629 ff.

16. Baruch Spinoza, *A Theological-political Treatise*, trans. Elwes (1887), chap. xvi.

17. *Ibid.*, chaps. v, xvi; *A Political Treatise*, trans. Elwes (1887), chap. ii, sec. 15.

18. *Theological-political Treatise*, chap. xvi. Cf. R. A. Duff, *Spinoza's Political and Ethical Philosophy* (Glasgow, 1903).

19. Algernon Sidney, *Discourses concerning Government* (3d ed.; London, 1751), chap. ii, sec. v, particularly pp. 75 ff.

20. John Locke, *Two Treatises of Government*, ed. Morley (1884), Book II, chap. ii, secs. 6–7; chap. iii, sec. 19; chap. vii, secs. 77, 87.

21. *Ibid.*, chap. ix, secs. 123–24, 127; chap. xi, secs. 135, 138.

22. *Ibid.*, chap. viii, *passim*.

23. *Ibid.*, chap. xix, secs. 211–21.

24. *Ibid.*, chap. xix, sec. 240.

25. G. D. H. Cole (ed.), *Rousseau's Social Contract and Discourses* (New York, 1914).

26. On the theory of progress see J. B. Bury, *The Idea of Progress* (New York, 1932); and F. J. Teggart (ed.), *The Idea of Progress: A Collection of Reading* (Berkeley, Calif., 1925).

27. On the utopian writings of this period see W. B. Guthrie, *Socialism before the French Revolution* (New York, 1907), and Jessica Peixotto, *The French Revolution and Modern French Socialism* (New York, 1901).

28. See H. E. Barnes, *History of Western Civilization* (2 vols.; New York, 1935), Vol. II, Parts I–II.

29. Franklin Thomas, *The Environmental Basis of Society* (New York, 1925), pp. 58 ff.

30. W. S. Thompson, *Population: A Study in Malthusianism* (New York, 1915).

31. Berkeley's *Works*, ed. Frazer (4 vols., 1901), IV, 111–18, 186–90.

32. David Hume, *A Treatise of Human Nature*, ed. Green and Grose (1874), II, 111 ff., 140, 155, 183, 259–73; *Essays, Moral, Political, and Literary*, ed. Green and Grose (1874), Vol. I, Part I, Essay V; Part II, Essay XII. On Hume, Ferguson, and Adam Smith, see Gladys Bryson, *Man and Society: The Scottish Inquiry of the Seventeenth Century* (Princeton, N.J., 1945).

33. Adam Smith's major works, *The Theory of Moral Sentiments* and the *Wealth of Nations*, are available in numerous editions. The notes recovered from his lectures delivered at the University of Glasgow have been edited by Edward Cannan under the title, *Lectures on Justice, Police, Revenue, and Arms* (Oxford, 1896). On Sieyès, Godwin, and rationalistic social thought, see W. A. Dunning, *A History of Political Theories from*

Rousseau to Spencer (New York, 1920), chap. iii, and pp. 362–64; and H. N. Brailsford, *Shelley, Godwin, and Their Circle* (New York, 1915).

34. Wesley C. Mitchell, "Bentham's Felicific Calculus," *Political Science Quarterly,* June, 1918; on Bentham and his followers, see Elie Halévy, *The Growth of Philosophical Radicalism* (New York, 1928).

35. On this section see H. E. Barnes, *A History of Historical Writing* (Norman, Okla., 1937), chaps. vii–viii.

36. W. C. Lehmann, *Adam Ferguson and the Beginnings of Modern Sociology* (New York, 1930).

37. A. W. Small, *The Cameralists* (Chicago, 1909).

38. Henry Higgs, *The Physiocrats* (New York, 1897).

39. A. W. Small, *Adam Smith and Modern Sociology* (Chicago, 1907); and Eli Ginzberg, *The House of Adam Smith* (New York, 1934).

40. Charles Gide and Charles Rist, *History of Economic Doctrines* (New York, 1915), Book I.

41. W. A. Dunning, *A History of Political Theories from Luther to Montesquieu, A History of Political Theories from Rousseau to Spencer;* and C. E. Vaughan, *Studies in a History of Political Philosophy before and after Rousseau* (2 vols.; New York, 1925).

42. Edmund Burke, *Works* (12 vols.; Boston, 1884), Vols. III–IV, esp. III, 358–60. On Burke see J. MacCunn, *The Political Philosophy of Burke* (London, 1913); and A. K. Rogers, "The Social Philosophy of Burke," *American Journal of Sociology,* July 1912.

43. On legal developments in this period see Fritz Berolzheimer, *The World's Legal Philosophies* (New York, 1912), chap. v.

44. A. C. Haddon, *A History of Anthropology* (New York, 1910); and R. H. Lowie, *A History of Ethnological Thought* (New York, 1939).

45. On this section see A. W. Small, *Origins of Sociology* (Chicago, 1924), *passim,* esp. chap. i; and Dunning, *Political Theories from Rousseau to Spencer,* chaps. iii, ix.

PART II

THE ORIGINS OF SOCIOLOGY

CHAPTER III

HERBERT SPENCER AND THE EVOLUTIONARY
DEFENSE OF INDIVIDUALISM

HARRY ELMER BARNES

I. GENERAL NATURE OF SPENCER'S PHILOSOPHICAL
AND SOCIOLOGICAL SYSTEM

A. LIFE AND WORKS

COMTE'S work in the field of sociology was taken up and greatly amplified by the philosopher who, better than anyone else, summed up the main currents of nineteenth-century social thought, Herbert Spencer (1820–1903). This does not mean that Spencer regarded Comte as his scientific precursor. In fact, quite the opposite was the case, for Spencer published his first sociological treatise, *Social Statics,* before he had any detailed knowledge of Comte's ideas, and it seems that in many respects the similarity between the two writers was accidental. On the other hand, it is hard to agree entirely with Spencer in his attempt to prove his complete independence of Comte and his fundamental divergence from the views of the latter.[1] Rather, it would be almost as accurate to accept the verdict of Henri Michel: "It does not follow that the *Principles of Sociology* can actually be regarded as an original book by anyone who has read the *Opuscules* [i.e., the early essays] of Comte. All the leading ideas, and even the method, of Spencer are to be seen in the *Opuscules*. Comte traced the outlines: Spencer only filled them in."[2]

A child of feeble health, Spencer was taught at home and never received any public education. In this aspect of home training he resembled his famous contemporary, John Stuart Mill. His failure to follow a university career doubtless tended to contribute strongly to the refusal of formal academic circles in England to take a lively interest in Spencer's teachings; and his lack of a properly socialized existence in early life certainly had not a little to do with his individualistic tendencies as an adult. Aside from these more strictly personal elements,

Spencer's nonconformist inheritance from his family and his reaction against the radical revolutionary doctrines of his youth are matters which must be taken into consideration when attempting to get an insight into the sources of his philosophic tendencies and an understanding of his intellectual predispositions.[3]

Spencer early acquired a taste for mechanics, and in 1837 he became chief engineer of the London and Birmingham Railroad. He resigned from this position in 1848 to become subeditor of the *Economist;* and during the four years that he served in this capacity he produced (1850) his first important contribution to sociology, *Social Statics*. During the next eight years he developed the basic principles of his system of synthetic philosophy and published them in the *First Principles* in 1863. No one can understand Spencer's philosophy if he has not read this work, any more than one can appreciate Comte's fundamental ideas if one has not read his early essays.

In this volume Spencer disposed of metaphysical theology by relegating it to the realm of the ultimately unknowable; he outlined his theory of universal evolution; and he indicated the main lines of its application to the totality of human knowledge. He did not, as has frequently been asserted, attempt to apply the theories of Darwin to a restatement of science and philosophy. Rather, he applied to this field his own theory of evolution, which had been formulated prior to, and independent of, that of Darwin and was built upon a thoroughly distinct, though compatible, set of fundamental propositions.[4]

B. SPENCER'S PHILOSOPHY OF SOCIETY

This is not the place to attempt to pass final judgment upon the merits of Spencer's system as a whole. It certainly suggested the general line of approach to modern scientific knowledge, which seems, on the whole, essentially correct, namely, the evolutionary viewpoint, however much of Spencer's particular view of evolution may fail to bear the test of later and more specialized inductive and quantitative studies. Again, it is quite safe to say that his system represents one of the most impressive products of a single human mind since the time of Aristotle. Further, there can be little doubt that, for innate mental productivity, Spencer is quite unequaled among modern writers. It requires a remarkable man, for instance, to produce Wundt's treatises on psychology, in which the author seems to have had a good acquaintance with every important work on his special subject. But, though such a work may be infinitely more valuable from a scientific point of view, it requires less genius to produce it than it did for Spencer to create the *Principles of Psychology* from the recesses of his own mind, after having read less formal psychology than the average elementary-school teacher in an American public school.

In short, whatever in Spencer's system may be destroyed by subsequent scientific progress—and it seems that much of it has even now passed into the realm of rhetoric—still he may claim the distinguished honor of having placed nearly all the phases of scientific study upon the road to further progress by making their guiding principle the concept of evolution. The late William Graham Sumner has well stated the significance of Spencer's establishment of the evolutionary principle in social science:

Mr. Spencer addressed himself at the outset of his literary career to topics of sociology. In the pursuit of those topics he found himself forced to seek constantly more fundamental and wider philosophical doctrines. He came at last to the fundamental principles of the evolution philosophy. He then extended, tested, confirmed, and corrected these principles by inductions from other sciences, and so finally turned again to sociology, armed with the scientific method which he had acquired. To win a powerful and correct method is, as we all know, to win more than half the battle. When so much is secure, the question of making the discoveries, solving the problems, eliminating the errors, and testing the results, is only a question of time and of strength to collect and master the data.[5]

The natural and social sciences were thus rescued from the retrospective and obscurantic tendencies with which they had been struggling more or less hopelessly ever since patristic theology had shackled induction and empiricism by reliance upon ecclesiastical authority and justification by faith and by opposition to the discovery of any scientific facts subversive of the tenets of accepted "truth."[6]

As Spencer's whole system of social science was built upon his general laws of evolution, it is essential to understand the fundamental propositions involved in his doctrines on this point. This is incomparably more important in Spencer's sociology than his development of the organic analogy, though most expositors and critics of his sociology have dwelt mainly upon the latter.

Spencer's laws of universal evolution are found in their complete development in the second part of his *First Principles*. In the first place, he finds three fundamental truths or propositions. Of these, the basic one is the law of the persistence of force, which means the existence and persistence of some ultimate cause which transcends knowledge. The two other principles are the indestructibility of matter and the continuity of motion, both being derived from the principle of the persistence of force. There are, in turn, four secondary propositions. The first is the persistence of the relations among forces, or the uniformity of law. The second is the transformation and equivalence of forces, namely, that force is never lost but is merely transformed. The third is the law that everything moves along the line of least resistance or of greatest attraction. The fourth and final law is that of the rhythm or alternation of motion.

To render this system complete, some law must be found which will govern the combination of these different factors in the evolutionary process. This need is supplied by the law that, with the integration of matter, motion is dissipated and, with the differentiation of matter, motion is absorbed. As a result, the process of evolution is characterized by a passage from an incoherent homogeneity to a coherent and co-ordinated heterogeneity. From these foundations, Spencer summarizes his complete law of universal evolution as follows: "Evolution is an integration of matter and a concomitant dissipation of motion during which the matter passes from a relatively indefinite, incoherent homogeneity to a relatively coherent heterogeneity and during which the retained motion undergoes a parallel transformation."

When we add to this basic foundation of his evolutionary system such important corollaries as the instability of the homogeneous, due to the incidence of unlike forces; the spread of differentiating factors in a geometrical ratio; the tendency of differentiated parts to become segregated through a clustering of like units; and the final limit of all the processes of evolution in an ultimate equilibrium, Spencer's system of evolution stands complete in outline. As the reverse of evolution stands dissolution, in which the achievements of evolution are undone through a reversal of the stages in the process.[7]

Spencer briefly applied this evolutionary formula to all phenomena in the remaining portion of his *First Principles,* and the application to social processes therein to be found is the vital portion of Spencer's sociological system. The detailed expansion of this preliminary outline found in the *First Principles* constitutes Spencer's system of "Synthetic Philosophy."

Spencer's formal treatment of sociology, aside from the outline of his system in the *First Principles,* is to be found in the *Study of Sociology* —a sort of prolegomenon to the subject and still an indispensable introduction—and in the three large volumes of the *Principles of Sociology.* While Spencer gave an excellent summary of his whole philosophical system, he failed to present a succinct digest of his sociological theory. Professor Giddings attempted to supply this need and performed the task in a manner satisfactory to Spencer. His lucid and comprehensive summary follows:

Societies are organisms or they are super-organic aggregates.

Between societies and environing bodies, as between other finite aggregates in nature, there is an equilibration of energy. There is an equilibration between society and society, between one social group and another, between one social class and another.

Equilibration between society and society, between societies and their environment, takes the form of a struggle for existence among societies. Conflict becomes an habitual activity of society.

In this struggle for existence fear of the living and of the dead arises. Fear of the living, supplementing conflict, becomes the root of political control. Fear of the dead becomes the root of religious control.

Organized and directed by political and religious control, habitual conflict becomes militarism. Militarism moulds character and conduct and social organization into fitness for habitual warfare.

Militarism combines small social groups into larger ones, these into larger and yet larger ones. It achieves social integration. This process widens the area within which an increasingly large proportion of the population is habitually at peace and industrially employed.

Habitual peace and industry mould character, conduct, and social organization into fitness for peaceful, friendly, sympathetic life.

In the peaceful type of society coercion diminishes, spontaneity and individual initiative increase. Social organization becomes plastic, and individuals moving freely from place to place change their social relations without destroying social cohesion, the elements of which are sympathy and knowledge in place of primitive force.

The change from militarism to industrialism depends upon the extent of the equilibration of energy between any given society and its neighboring societies, between the societies of any given race and those of other races, between society in general and its physical environment. Peaceful industrialism cannot finally be established until the equilibrium of nations and of races is established.

In society, as in other finite aggregates, the extent of the differentiation and the total complexity of all the evolutionary processes depend upon the rate at which integration proceeds. The slower the rate the more complete and satisfactory is the evolution.[8]

Better known than Spencer's interpretation of society in terms of the laws of evolution, though not so vitally connected with his system, is his development of the analogy between society and an organism. This analogy was by no means original with Spencer, as it is to be found in Plato, Aristotle, Paul, and many of the early Christian Fathers. It was common throughout the Middle Ages and had later been considerably elaborated, among others by Comte, Krause, and Ahrens. It was reserved for Spencer, however, to present the first systematic development of the theory.[9]

Spencer enumerates six fundamental similarities between society and an organism. First, both differ from inorganic matter through an augmentation of mass and visible growth during the greater part of their existence. Second, as both increase in size, they increase in complexity of structure. Third, progressive differentiation of structure in both is accompanied by a like differentiation of functions. Fourth, evolution establishes in both society and animal organisms not only differences, but definitely related differences, of such a character as to make both possible. Fifth, the analogy between society and an organism is still more evident when it is recognized that, conversely, every organism is a society. Finally, in both society and the organism the life of the aggregate may be destroyed, but the units will continue to live on for a time.

On the other hand, there are three important differences to be noted between society and the organism. In the first place, whereas in the individual organism the component parts form a concrete whole and the living units are bound together in close contact, in the social organism the component parts form a discrete whole and the living units are free and more or less dispersed. Again, and even more fundamental, whereas in the individual organism there is such a differentiation of functions that some parts become the seat of feeling and thought and others are practically insensitive, in the social organism no such differentiation exists; there is no social mind or sensorium apart from the individuals that make up the society. As a result of this second difference, there is to be observed the third distinction, namely, that, while in the organism the units exist for the good of the whole, in society the whole exists for the good of the members.[10]

Another important phase of Spencer's biological interpretation of society was his famous theory of population trends, first set forth in 1852. He maintained that there is a fundamental antagonism between "individuation" and "genesis." As civilization became more complex, an ever larger portion of the available physiological energy of the race is exhausted in the activities associated with personal development and expression. Hence less energy remains available for reproductive interests and activities. In short, advanced and mature civilizations seem to be unfavorable to high fecundity. This doctrine was an implied criticism of Malthusianism. Adopted by Henry C. Carey in the United States, it was exploited to counteract the pessimism of the social philosophy of Malthus and the Classical Economists.

These two fundamental theories of society—the evolutionary and the organic—comprise the major theoretical contributions of Spencer to sociology. His remaining voluminous works on sociology are primarily descriptive, though in many cases they present a keen analysis of social processes.

Just how Spencer's sociological system will rank in the future, when more refined statistical and ethnological studies permit the general body of sociological theory to assume something like a final form, it is difficult to say. It seems safe to hold that, as a physical interpretation of society, his system will remain, in general outline, the final statement of the subject. The organic analogy will doubtless be accepted as an interesting bit of figurative description but will be discarded as possessing little value as an explanation of social processes. How much will remain of his historical sociology can hardly be estimated at present. Already the researches of the more critical ethnologists, like Professor Ehrenreich in Germany, Professors Durkheim, Hubert, and Mauss in France, Professors Rivers and Marett in England, and Professor Boas and his disciples in America, have challenged in drastic fashion the almost mechanical evolutionary systems of the classical school of anthropology, of which Spencer was one of the most thoroughgoing exponents. One can no longer hold with Professor T. N. Carver that not to have read Spencer's *Principles of Sociology* imposes a handicap greater than would result from the neglect of any other treatise.[11] Still it will probably be accurate to say that, viewed from the standpoint of the historical development of sociology, Spencer's contribution was one of the most far-reaching in its influence that has yet been made. Professor A. W. Small has admirably summarized the significance of Spencer's position, particularly as set forth in the *Principles of Sociology:*

Spencer's scheme is an attempt to give name, and place, and importance to the meaning factors in human association. It is not a system of speculative conceptions.

It is an attempt to represent in language the literal facts of society in the relations in which they actually occur in real life. It is a device by means of which, in proportion as it is adapted to its purpose, we should be able more truly, more comprehensively, and more profoundly to understand, for instance, the life of the people of the United States, than we could without the aid of such description. The fair test is, not to ask whether this scheme leaves nothing in the way of social exposition to be desired, but whether it lays bare more of essential truth about society than is visible without such an interpretation; not whether there is a remainder to be explained, but whether more appears in the confusion of everyday life than is discovered before it is seen in terms of these symbols. Judged by this test the Spencerian scheme is certainly an approach to truth.[12]

II. SPENCER'S LEADING SOCIAL AND POLITICAL THEORIES

A. THE RELATION OF SOCIOLOGY TO POLITICAL SCIENCE AND THE STUDY OF THE STATE

As regards the relation of sociology to political science, Spencer differed from Comte in holding that the special social sciences are distinct, but co-ordinated, branches of sociology and that, as such, they are legitimate bodies of science. However, his differentiation between the scope of sociology and that of the special social sciences was not clearly worked out. His summary of the relation of sociology to political science and of the legitimate treatment of political problems by sociology, as presented in his chapter on "The Scope of Sociology" in the *Study of Sociology,* covered completely the field now generally allotted to political science, though with a distinctly sociological orientation. He says here:

Sociology has next to describe and explain the rise and development of that political organization which in several ways regulates affairs, which combines the actions of individuals for purposes of tribal or national offence or defense; and which restrains them in certain of their dealings with one another, as also in certain of their dealings with themselves. It has to trace the relations of this coordinating and controlling apparatus, to the area occupied, to the amount and distribution of population, and to the means of communication. It has to show the differences of form which this agency presents in different social types, nomadic and settled militant and industrial. It has to describe the changing relations between this regulating structure which is unproductive, and those structures which carry on production. It has also to set forth the connexions between, and the reciprocal influences of, the institutions carrying on civil government, and other governmental institutions simultaneously developing the ecclesiastical and the ceremonial. And then it has to take account of those modifications which persistent political restraints are ever working in the character of the social units, as well as the modifications worked by the reaction of these changed characters on the political organization.[13]

This is an excellent outline of what might constitute a sociological survey, if not a complete sociological theory, of the state. Spencer's full

ilment of this task in the section of his *Principles of Sociology* dealing
with "Political Institutions" and in numerous essays and parts of other
works was doubtless one of the most extensive treatments of political
problems that any sociologist, with the possible exception of Gumplowicz and Ratzenhofer, has attempted.

B. FUNDAMENTAL POLITICAL CONCEPTS AND DEFINITIONS

Spencer seems to have distinguished in a fairly definite manner beween the concepts of society and of state, though he makes no attempt
at a formal treatment of this somewhat academic subject. He unquestionably regards the state as society, politically organized. He conceives
of the state as that conscious organization of co-operative activity in a
society which concerns the group as a whole. "Political organization,"
he says, "is to be understood as that part of social organization which
consciously carries on directive and restraining functions for public
ends."[14]

Thus, Spencer does not make the state coextensive with society or
a further refinement of society but simply regards it as society when
organized as a political unit. Society, as a whole, is supported by two
types of co-operation: spontaneous private co-operation, which is concerned with matters that do not affect the group as a unit except in
indirect ways; and the "consciously devised" co-operation which deals
with the public activities of the group as a totality. It is only the latter
that directly creates and supports the state.

He does not, however, distinguish so clearly between the state and
the government—something that is hard for an Englishman to do, since
in England legal sovereignty and the lawmaking power reside in the
same body. At the same time, it seems reasonably clear that Spencer
would have defined government as the particular form which the political organization may assume at any time or place, in other words, the
correct notion of the government as the mechanism of administration.
Speaking in terms of the organic analogy, the state is the system which
has for its function the regulation of the social organism; the organs
which perform this function are known as the "government." As to
the distinction between the terms "state" and "nation," it seems that
Spencer used the word "nation" as meaning the state in its objective
political and geographic aspects—the conventional use of the term,

though not the connotation given to it by the strict terminology of political science.

Spencer agrees with the usual conception as to what constitutes the fundamental attributes of the state, so far as territory, population, and governmental organization are concerned, but he balks at the notion of an unlimited sovereign authority. To an arch-individualist like Spencer, the conception of an irresistible power in society, against which the individual had no legal right of resistance, was most repugnant. Hobbes, Bentham, and Austin are as scathingly attacked by Spencer as Blackstone was by Bentham: "Analyze his assumption, and the doctrine of Austin proves to have no better basis than that of Hobbes. In the absence of admitted divine descent or appointment, neither single-headed ruler nor many-headed ruler can produce such credentials as the claim to unlimited sovereignty implies."[15]

Natural or, perhaps better, individual rights rather than sovereignty were the cornerstone of Spencer's political theory. But individual rights, as conceived by Spencer, are neither those which are assumed by metaphysical ethics nor those artificial rights conferred by a governmental agent. They are those indispensable rights which must be guaranteed to an individual so that society may exist and function properly. Such a doctrine of natural rights is perfectly valid and is not, as Ernest Barker intimates, entirely incompatible with the doctrine of a social organism. It is chiefly the excessive extent of these natural rights insisted upon by Spencer which may be called in question rather than the theoretical aspects of the problem.

C. THE FOUNDATIONS AND JUSTIFICATION OF POLITICAL AUTHORITY

The question of the origin of the state and the government Spencer treats both analytically and historically. In both senses the immediate basis of political control and that which has made its existence possible through the ages is the "fear of the living," in the same way that the "fear of the dead" is the foundation of religious control.[16] Of course, this fundamental distinction is not perfect, for in some cases political control is furthered by the fear of the dead, as when a chief is believed to be able to control the ghosts of his ancestors; and, likewise, the fear of the existing ecclesiastical hierarchy is an important element in effective religious control. But, in general, this must be admitted to be a valid principle of differentiation.

In an analytical sense the state and the government arise because society cannot function adequately without them. A society is not established by the mere physical contiguity of a mass of individuals. It is constituted only when there is an organized system of co-operation among these units. The state and government not only supply one of the two great types of co-operation, that which controls the group as a whole in relation to public ends, but they also promote the development of private co-operation. They eliminate the conflict among individuals and increase the size of the group in which co-operation may exist. The larger the group, the greater the amount of division of labor and specialization that is possible. In like manner, legal rights and their enforcement find their philosophical justification in the fact that only under political protection can society continue its existence and function properly. Speaking in terms of the organic analogy, the explanation of the state is identical in principle, since in any perfected organism there must be a potent regulating system in order to insure the proper functioning of the sustaining and distributing systems.

The structure of government, similarly, is easily amenable to analysis. There is a natural triune structure, due to the inherent differences in mankind. Whether one examines a primitive tribe or a modern state, the organization for governmental purposes falls into three classes: (1) the *leader;* (2) the small minority of able and distinguished men, i.e., the *consulting body;* (3) the vast mass of inexperienced and mediocre citizens, who simply listen to, and agree with or dissent from, the acts and opinions of the leader and the council, i.e., the *representative body.* Despotism, oligarchy, and democracy simply reflect the undue prominence of one of these three components of government. The great force lying behind political power and the particular structures through which it is manifested is "the feeling of the community." This is based, to a certain degree, upon the reaction of the community to present problems, but it depends to a far greater extent upon the social heritage which is crystallized into custom and tradition. Political organization is simply the public agency for applying this "feeling of the community." This unconscious fear of the dead (the "dead hand"), which is the psychological content of custom, thus aids the fear of the living in maintaining political control. This notion Spencer sums up in the following manner:

We are familiar with the thought of the "dead hand" as controlling the doings of the living in the use made of property; but the effect of the "dead hand" in ordering life at large through the established political system is immeasurably greater. That which, from hour to hour in every country, governed despotically or otherwise, produces the obedience making political action possible, is the accumulated and organized sentiment felt towards inherited institutions made sacred by tradition.[17]

D. THE HISTORICAL EVOLUTION OF SOCIAL AND POLITICAL INSTITUTIONS

Spencer's account of the historical evolution of social and political organization is very elaborate, but his conclusions are open to the same degree of skepticism as is his generalized account of the evolution of institutions. His method was one—that of the classical anthropologists —which is now abandoned by most scholarly and critical ethnologists at the present time. From his voluminous *Descriptive Sociology* he would gather together illustrative material bearing upon the evolution of any particular institution, regardless of the relation of that particular practice to the whole cultural complex of the social groups from which the information was drawn or of the different stages of culture which contributed evidence in support of his thesis. The Shoshonean Indians and the Italian cities at the time of the Renaissance might thus be offered as supporting evidence for a particular process or "stage" in social evolution. The mass of material offered to the reader, its seeming comprehensiveness, as apparently drawn from all parts of the world and from all ages, and the incomparable logical skill with which Spencer marshaled his evidence, all tended for years to make Spencer's historical sociology the *sine qua non* of the subject.[18]

The application of more refined methods in ethnology and the cumulative evidence from intensive original investigation of cultural areas by competent ethnologists have, however, tended to call in question many of Spencer's generalizations. Aside from his faulty methodology, the general assumptions of the classical school of anthropology, of which he was a prominent member, regarding the universality of cultural traits and the orderly progress of institutional evolution have been seriously challenged by later investigations. It is now rather generally conceded by ethnologists that it requires about four specialists competently to investigate any particular cultural area, to say nothing of attempting to survey the whole course of social evolution. An accurate historical sociology can be written only in that distant future when reliable monographs by specialists have summarized what ethnologists and cultural historians have discovered regarding particular areas and special periods. Nevertheless, it is doubtful whether anyone could have reached better logical conclusions by the use of Spencer's methods, and the healthy skepticism which one may entertain regarding his conclusions should not prevent one from having the highest respect for the constructive logic and the brilliant fertility of imagination displayed in Spencer's history of society.

Spencer's main conclusions regarding the evolution of social and political organization may be summarized about as follows: At the outset, society may be assumed to have existed as undifferentiated and unorganized hordes. The beginning of public authority and political organization was the temporary submission of the group to a leader in time of war. The natural prowess of this leader in war was often supplemented by his supposed power to control ghosts and obtain their aid, thus bringing a supernatural sanction to his rule.

In due course of time, with the increasing complexity of society, the more frequent periods of warfare, and the better organization of military activity, this temporary war leader evolved into the chief or king, who held his power for life. In turn, the difficulties and disorder which occurred at the death of a leader and during the period of the choice of a successor tended to establish the principle of hereditary leadership. In this manner stability and permanence of leadership were provided for. Along with this development of the ruler went the parallel evolution of the consultative and representative bodies. At first merely spontaneous bodies meeting in times of necessity, they later evolved into formal senates and assemblies.

The processes of integration and differentiation are exhibited in the development of political organization, as well as in evolution in general. The long period of military activity which characterized the earlier stages of political evolution brought about the consolidation of the petty primitive groups and their respective territory. Because the best-organized groups tended to win in the intergroup struggle, the integration of society and the extension of the range of power of the successful state was a cumulative process. Along with the integration of political authority, both in the scope of its application and in the expansion of the area of control, there went a corresponding increase in differentiation and co-ordination. The differentiation in society, which begins in the family, is extended through the periods of conquest that characterize early political progress, until it has created the classes of wealthy rulers, ordinary freemen, serfs, and slaves. As political power becomes concentrated in a definite ruling class and is increased in scope and applied over a larger territory, it has to be delegated in order to be administered with efficiency. All the vast machinery of modern government, with its ministeries; its local governing agencies; its judicial, revenue, and military systems, is but the further differentiation and co-ordination of the earlier fundamental organs of government, manifested in the simple triune structure of chief, council, and assembly.

The state, at first, centers all its attention upon military organization, conquest, and territorial aggrandizement; but, as time goes on, its concern is turned more and more toward the development of industry. From this moment onward, the process of political evolution becomes a transformation of the military state into the industrial state. This process is still under way. The purely industrial state, however, is not the final goal of social evolution. The ultimate stage to be hoped for is one in which the resources of a developed industrialism may be turned toward the perfection of human character in the higher and more truly socialized aspects of moral conduct, thus bringing into being the ethical state.

Despite his elaborate treatment of the origin and development of the different branches of political organization, Spencer nowhere gives a clear picture of the evolution of the state and sovereign power as a related whole, and this failure doubtless contributed in a large degree to making Spencer unable to grasp and concede the real significance of the state.

E. FORMS OF THE STATE AND THE GOVERNMENT

In his treatment of the forms of the state, Spencer discards for political analysis the conventional classification of states and devotes his attention to a classification based upon the end toward which organized political society functions. Spencer finds that political society has functioned for two specific ends in the course of history—military aggression and industrial development. Comte had suggested such a differentiation, though he had more accurately interpolated a critical and revolutionary period between the primarily military and the primarily industrial eras. These two periods, while sharply differentiated in principle, tend to overlap in a historical sense. The present era, while beginning to be primarily industrial, still contains only too many survivals from the military regime.[19] Nevertheless, close analysis reveals the fact that each of these systems is characterized by a definite set of principles and produces a type of character in its citizens which is almost diametrically opposed to that which is found in the other.

In the militant type of society, unified action is necessary, and all must take their part in this activity. All the energies of the society are devoted to the furthering of military efficiency, since those who cannot fight are busily engaged in providing supplies for the warrior class. The individual is thus completely subordinated to society through the despotic governmental organization which is essential to produce this highly specialized adjustment of society to military activity.

To secure a proper administration of this despotic control over a large area and a considerable population, there must be a thorough regimentation of society, extending from the ruler to the humblest subject. The regulation administered by this despotic and bureaucratic system is both positive and negative. This system of regimentation develops a rigidity in society, owing to the enforced specialization, which makes it difficult for the individual to change his place in society. In fact, the position of the individual in the military era is merely one of status. In order to secure economic independence, so valuable in time of war, the society pursues a vigorous policy of protectionism. Since success in war is the supreme aim of society, bravery and strength are made the chief moral qualities toward which the ambitious individual may aspire. A selfish patriotism that regards the triumph of the particular group or nation as the chief end of social activity is the dominating sentiment in the militant state. The deadening influence of bureaucratic officialdom lessens individual initiative, fosters the belief that universal governmental activity is indispensable, and blinds society to the conception of the evolutionary factors in progress and social evolution.

The industrial type of society is not to be distinguished from the militant solely by the amount of industry which is being carried on, as militant states may be very industrious. Neither can it be completely characterized by having as its chief end the development of industry, for socialistic and communistic states also pretend to aim at this goal. Rather, the industrial type of society is one which combines the goal of industrial development with absolute freedom of individual initiative within the limits of order and equity. In the industrial type of society there is no longer any all-pervading compulsory political activity; the small amount of such discipline that is retained is designed merely to prevent unnecessary interference with individual initiative and freedom. For this type of society a representative, and not a despotic, government is required, and the function of such a government is to administer justice or, in other words, to see that each member of society gets a reward which is directly proportionate to, and resultant upon, his efforts.

The government, instead of being both positively and negatively regulative, as in the militant state, is now only negatively regulative. The position of the individual changes from one of status to one of contract. Individual activity and voluntary co-operation are encouraged. Society in the industrial regime is plastic and easily adaptable to change. Finally, since there is no longer any need of economic self-sufficiency, the rigid protectionist policy must break down, and the economic barriers of nationality tend gradually to be dissolved. A regional form of government, or a federation of governments, may be looked forward to as the goal of political organization. As to the reaction of the industrial era upon the traits of society, patriotism tends to become more refined, society loses its faith in the infallible efficacy of governmental interference, and individuality becomes stronger, more self-assertive, and mutually respectful of rights. Though industrialism is still only very imperfectly realized, it should not be assumed to be the final goal of social evolution. A new era, primarily devoted to the development of man's ethical nature, may be hoped for after the industrial regime has been perfected. The final or ultimate form of social and political organization, then, is the ethical state.

Spencer does not devote any considerable space to the question of the forms of government. His detailed account of the evolution of "political forms" is mainly concerned with an analysis of the development of what are usually known as the "departments" of government. Spencer claims, however, that a close relation exists between these departments of government and the different forms of government, for he revives the old classical doctrine that monarchy is a government characterized by the undue predominance of the single leader; oligarchy a type in which the council is abnormally prominent; and democracy that in which the representative factor has become disproportionately powerful. Though Spencer grants the existence of these three types of government, he really believes that there are only two pure forms—monarchy and representative government, meaning by the latter, democracy.

Between these two extremes, which are based upon the contradictory assumptions that society should obey the will of one individual and that its members should be governed by their own wills, there are a number of different grades of mixed governments. While these mixed forms of government are absurd from the standpoint of logic, they are good enough in practice, as their incongruities agree with those of a society in transition from the rigid military state to the plastic industrial state: "Nevertheless, though these mixed governments, combining as they do two mutually destructive hypotheses, are utterly irrational in principle, they must of necessity exist, so long as they are in harmony with the mixed constitution of the partially adapted man."[20]

Democracy, Spencer defines as "a political organization modelled in accordance with the law of equal freedom."[21] Or, again, he describes it as "a system which, by making the nation at large a deliberative body, and reducing the legislative assembly to an executive, carries self-government to the fullest extent compatible with the existence of a ruling power."[22]

While granting that monarchy and despotism had their historical function, Spencer was wholly in favor of democracy in any society in which the citizens have reached a sufficiently high level of moral and intellectual development to be intrusted with the administration of this type of government. Not every society is fitted for the maintenance of a democratic government. Conduct has to be ruled either by internal or by external restraint; hence, among those people whose moral sense has not been sufficiently developed to furnish an adequate internal restraint, a democracy is out of place and a more coercive type is needed. Not only must there be a high moral sense among the citizens to make democracy practicable, but there must also be a sufficient degree of intelligence and a high enough estimation of the value of freedom to make the citizens alert in detecting infringements upon their liberty and capable in use of the franchise. When such conditions exist, democracy is the ideal type of government. In no case should one put faith in a particular type of government as such. The best is out of place and likely to fail except among a people whose national character fits them by experience for such a form:

Anyone who looks through these facts and facts akin to them for the truth they imply may see that forms of government are valuable only where they are products of national character. No cunningly devised political arrangements will of themselves do anything. No amount of knowledge respecting the uses of such arrangements will suffice. Nothing will suffice but the emotional nature to which such arrangements are adapted—a nature which during social progress has evolved the arrangements.[23]

F. SOVEREIGNTY, LIBERTY, AND THE SOCIOLOGICAL THEORY OF POLITICAL RIGHTS

For the doctrine of legal sovereignty Spencer had little respect. The whole conception was repugnant to his mind. Consequently, he avoided any attempt to trace its origin or to define its attributes. His main concern was to dispute the tenets of the upholders of the doctrine and to establish logical and historical grounds for justifying limitations upon sovereignty.

Spencer was willing to admit that there is such a thing as what Dicey calls "political sovereignty," but he claimed that some higher justification of submission to authority must be discovered. To this quest he devotes the last essay in *Man versus the State,* which he entitles "The Great Political Superstition," meaning by this the doctrine of the sovereignty of the legislature, which had supplanted the outgrown doctrine of the sovereignty of the monarch. In order to find theoretical justification for the submission of the minority to the majority, Spencer formulated the hypothetical question as to just what type of agreement to co-operate the majority of the citizens would enter into with a considerable degree of unanimity. This reminds one of Rousseau's famous problem of establishing political authority and at the same time preserving the liberty of the individual.

Spencer finds, in answer to his query, that practically all would agree to co-operate in defending their territory against external aggression and in protecting their persons and property against internal violence and fraud. To this extent, then, the submission of the minority is valid and legitimate; beyond this point such submission is unjust and illegitimate.

A hypothetical contract thus replaces the old doctrine of an actual contract as the solution of the problem of reconciling liberty and authority. When one remembers that few of the classical writers of the contract school, with the possible exception of Locke, believed in the actual historicity of the social contract, Spencer's solution does not seem to differ greatly in principle from theirs, however different may have been his deductions from that principle.

As to the vital question of the origin of the basic rights of the individual, Spencer claims, in opposition to Bentham and to recent political scientists in general, that they are not historically derived from governmental action but are really antecedent to government. They are those indispensable modes of individual freedom which have been found by ages of experience to be essential to any normal and continuous social life. They existed by sheer social necessity before any legal enactment, and the only role government has played has been to codify and enforce these rights which previously existed in custom and usage.

Such a doctrine of natural or individual rights, however erroneous may be its historical justification, is not logically inconsistent with the doctrine of the social organism. Spencer's theory of natural rights as the product of social experience rather than as derived from a priori rationalization is valid. The most cogent criticism of his theory is that what he assumed to be derived from the experience of the race was quite frequently the outgrowth of his fertile imagination concerning what the experience of the race ought to have been.

G. THE PROPER AND LEGITIMATE SCOPE OF STATE ACTIVITY

With the possible exception of his dogma that sound social reform could not be expected to flow from direct legislative measures, the most famous item in Spencer's political theory was his analysis of the legitimate sphere of state activity. As one eminent sociologist observed, Spencer was so busy throughout his life attempting to formulate a doctrine of what the state should not do that he failed to develop any coherent positive theory of the state. Spencer's well-known vigorous opposition to extensive state activity or positive remedial social legislation seems to have been based upon two main factors: (1) the dogmas of automatic social evolution that were current in the middle and third quarter of the nineteenth century and (2) the traits of his neurotic constitution which made the authority of the state abhorrent to him.

The idea that social development and the proper working of the social process is an automatic and spontaneous affair had been accepted long before the time of Spencer. In its earliest modern form it grew out of the reaction of Newtonian cosmic mechanics upon the social science of the eighteenth century. The English Deists and the French *philosophes* developed the notion that social institutions are governed by the same "natural laws" that Newton had shown to dominate the physical universe. Their assumption was taken up and incorporated in social science by the French Physiocrats and the Classical Economists, the latter employing it as a philosophic defense of the new capitalistic system produced by the industrial revolution. Though this conception was shown to be unsound early in the nineteenth century by Rae, Hodgkin, and Sismondi, it prevailed very generally throughout the century.

With the development of the evolutionary hypothesis, a new "naturalism" was provided. It was believed that the highly organized types of animal life had developed from lower forms in an automatic and independent manner. It was easy to postulate a direct analogy between organic and social evolution and to contend that social evolution is a wholly spontaneous process which artificial human interference could in no way hasten but might fatally obstruct or divert. It was Spencer, more than any other writer, who popularized this view of social development as an argument against state activity—a position which Lester F. Ward, Leonard T. Hobhouse, Ludwig Stein, and Albion W. Small have seriously challenged.

Spencer seems to have derived from some source what the modern dynamic psychologists would designate as an extreme "anti-authority complex." Coupled with what is known regarding his early life, especially his early domination by male relatives, and his confirmed neurotic tendencies, his persistent and ever growing resentment against the extension of governmental activity probably was personally motivated by a subconscious neurotic reaction. It must also be remembered that Spencer came from a dissenting family and was reared in that atmosphere. It seems, on the whole, that his attitude toward government must have had a deep-rooted emotional foundation, since it diverged materially from some of the vital premises of his general philosophy. This inconsistency was constantly causing him trouble and entailed considerable labor in patching up a reconciliation between his political individualism and his sociological principles.

Be this as it may, his attitude in respect to the question of state activity may quite well have been suggested, and it certainly was abundantly nourished, by the political conditions of his lifetime. The revolutionary ideas of the early nineteenth century, with their doctrines of the efficacy of hasty and violent political reform, and the great volume of proposed remedial legislation designed to solve the problems caused by the disorganization of the older social control by the industrial revolution were admirably adapted to awaken sentiments like those entertained by Spencer and to prevent them from becoming dormant.[24]

Spencer published his first essay on this subject, entitled "The Proper Sphere of Government," in 1842, and eight years later there appeared his first substantial treatise, *Social Statics*. The fundamental principle of this work is Spencer's law of equal freedom, which is but a revival of Rousseau's definition of liberty. He contends that each individual is to enjoy as perfect a degree of freedom as is compatible with the equal privilege of other individuals. In this work Spencer states his famous theory of the state as a joint-stock company for the mutual protection of individuals and presents his catalogue of activities from which the state should refrain, with a detailed analysis of his views in support of his position. This list of interdicted or tabooed activities include the following, some of which are rather startling: commercial regulation, state religious establishments, charitable activities tending to interfere with natural selection, state education, state colonization, sanitary measures, regulation and coining of money, postal service, provision of lighthouses, and improvements of harbors. The real duty of the state is to administer justice, which consists theoretically in maintaining the law of equal freedom and practically in protecting the life and property of the citizens from internal robbery and fraud and from external invasion.

In the *Study of Sociology* (1873) Spencer repeats his fundamental notions regarding political laissez faire, especially in the justly famous opening chapter on "Our Need of a Social Science" and in the equally excellent chapter on "The Political Bias." In one passage in his *Study of Sociology*,[25] Spencer anticipates the view of Sumner regarding the "forgotten man" as the one who bears most of the financial burden of state activity and gets the least benefit from this legislation. His political theories, expressed in the *Principles of Sociology*, are mainly historical and analytical and, with the exception of the contrasts between militant and industrial society, deal only incidentally with the question of the legitimate scope of state activity. Between 1850 and 1884, when he published his *Man versus the State*, Spencer contributed a large number of articles on the subject of noninterference. These have been, for the most part, gathered together in the third volume of his *Essays, Scientific,*

Political, and Speculative (1891). Perhaps the most important among them is his "Specialized Administration" (1871), issued in answer to Professor Huxley's attack on Spencerian doctrines in his essay on "Administrative Nihilism" (1870). By the doctrine of "specialized administration" Spencer means the relinquishment by the government of its function of positive regulation of human activities and the perfection of its negatively regulating function. He also published a telling diatribe against socialism under the title "From Freedom to Bondage"; and the second essay in his *Man versus the State*, "The Coming Slavery," is also mainly devoted to a refutation of socialistic propositions.

Finally, in *Man versus the State* and in *Justice*, one may look for Spencer's last word on the subject. In the former he inveighs against the socialistic tendencies of the age and the attempted extension of family ethics into the field of state activity. He attempts a refutation of the contemporary dogma of the sovereignty of Parliament as the representative of the majority. His final doctrine regarding the proper sphere of government, as here stated, is that it should be limited to the provision of safety from physical assault, the freedom and enforcement of contracts, and the protection of the individual from foreign aggression, in other words, to be concerned purely with negative regulations. In the Postscript to the final edition of *Man versus the State*, he admits that he is fully aware that his theory of state activity is far in advance of his age and that it will not be adopted for generations to come, but he justifies his devotion to the cause on the ground that society must have an ideal to guide it toward realization.

Spencer has been roundly criticized by many writers, notably by D. G. Ritchie, for the inconsistency between his doctrine of the social organism and his inference that, with the further evolution of society, the regulating structure of government will gradually disintegrate. That there is a discrepancy here which even Spencer's ingenuity was never quite able to explain away cannot be denied, but the logical completion of the organic doctrine, with its assertion that the function of government must become more and more all-inclusive, is hardly satisfactory. With a type of society in which intellect guides legislation, as was assumed by Comte and later by Ward, progress might be hoped for through an extension of state activity; but, in view of the present general level of intelligence and moral character of the usual run of the governmental officers in modern political systems, many thinkers would rather trust to the efficacy of voluntary organization. It seems that this was essentially Spencer's view.

As to the activity of the state in international matters, it has already been pointed out that Spencer believed that the state should protect its citizens from the aggression of invaders. Spencer was not a believer in the doctrine of passive submission. He did, however, strongly advocate the principle of nonaggression. He believed in the principle of international arbitration and prophesied that, in time, this would be the universal mode of settling international disputes. He looked forward, in the distant future, to a general dissolution of strict national lines and the institution of a universal government or a federation of governments. Spencer followed up his belief in international arbitration by personal activity in promoting a peace society that worked for international conciliation, and he tells in his *Autobiography* of the injury to his health caused by his exertions in this field of effort.

Spencer was also a vigorous critic of the new capitalistic imperialism which developed in England and in the world generally, following the seventies. In one of his latest articles, entitled "Imperialism and Slavery," Spencer criticized British policy in the Boer War as based wholly on the principle of superior force, which he alleged to be the dominating principle of the new imperialism. He further asserted that imperialism inevitably leads to militarism, destroys democracy both at home and abroad, and vastly increases the burdens of taxation. He thus came very near to the position taken by the neoliberals, Hobhouse and Hobson, differing chiefly in not complaining that the expenditures for imperialism reduced desirable appropriations for social legislation at home.

In conclusion, it seems that whatever one may think of Spencer's doctrine of the legitimate field of state activity, no thoughtful person can easily dissent from the assumptions which produced at least half of his opposition to state interference: (1) the present low level of political morality; (2) the general lack of intelligence or, at least, of special competence on the part of the agents of government; (3) the failure of the electorate to exercise any considerable degree of wisdom in the choice of these agents; and (4) the present perversion of the attitude toward government as an end in itself rather than as a means toward an end. He held that these shortcomings all combine to make our governmental machinery miserably incompetent to deal with the complex problems of modern civilization. The improvement of this condition can be effected in but two ways: a decrease in the activity of government or an increase in its efficiency. The latter is held by most contemporary writers to be by all odds preferable, but Spencer considered it so remote a possibility that he chose to put his trust in the former. That he had some valid grounds for his attitude is distressingly apparent.

H. PROGRESS, SOCIAL REFORM, AND STATE ACTIVITY

Spencer's writings on the subject of social reform are about as prolific and spirited as those dealing with the proper field of state activity. In fact, these questions are but different sides of the same problem. As the foundation of his doctrine concerning state activity was equal freedom, natural rights, and negative regulation, so in regard to social reform his central dictum was that results are not proportional to appliances.

Spencer did not deny the need of political reform or the tendency of all governmental structure to become conservative and to resist change. In his *Principles of Sociology* Spencer gives an illuminating discussion of how political organization, like all other social institutions, tends to resist change. It was not the need of reform that he questioned; it was, rather, the efficacy of the methods and principles of reform then proposed.

What Spencer desired to emphasize was that it is futile to expect that any measure directly designed to remedy a certain situation could be successful unless it took into consideration the general cultural complex of which the particular defect was a part and allowed for the interdependence of social forces and institutions. Writers have accused Spencer of dealing with "straight men" and formulating a "political arithmetic," but, in this field of social reform at least, he was sufficiently conscious of the actual conditions which confront the social reformer. His classic statement of this principle is contained in the following paragraph from the *Study of Sociology:*

You see that this wrought-iron plate is not quite flat; it sticks up a little here toward the left—"cockles," as we say. How shall we flatten it? Obviously, you reply, by hitting down on the part that is prominent. Well, here is a hammer and I give the plate a blow as you advise. Harder, you say. Still no effect. Another stroke: well, there is one, and another, and another. The prominence remains you see: the evil is as great as ever—greater, indeed. But this is not all. Look at the warp which the plate has got near the opposite edge. Where it was flat before it is now curved. A pretty bungle we have made of it. Instead of curing the original defect, we have produced a second. Had we asked an artisan practised in "planishing," as it is called, he would have told us that no good was to be done, but only mischief, by hitting down on the projecting part. He would have taught us how to give variously—directed and specially—adjusted blows with a hammer elsewhere: so attacking the evil not by direct but by indirect actions. The required process is less simple than you thought. Even a sheet of metal is not to be successfully dealt with after those common-sense methods in which you have so much confidence. What, then, shall we say about a society? "Do you think I am easier to be played on than a pipe?" asks Hamlet. Is humanity more readily straightened than an iron plate?[26]

Nevertheless, Spencer was not a complete and unqualified advocate of laissez faire. What he was trying to combat was the all too prevalent tendency to repose complete trust in the efficacy of legislation as a cure-all for social ills. As a spirited advocate of the opposite school, he naturally went too far. What he wanted to impress upon society was the necessarily small part which an individual or even a generation can hope to achieve in changing the direction of social evolution. He did not desire to discourage either individual or collective effort toward reform, provided that it recognized the necessary social limitations upon the scope or results of such action. He sums up this position well in the following paragraph:

Thus while admitting that for the fanatic some wild anticipation is needful as a stimulus, and recognizing the usefulness of his delusion as adapted to his particular nature and his particular function, the man of the higher type must be content with greatly moderated expectations, while he perseveres with undiminished efforts. He has to see how comparatively little can be done, and yet find it worth while to do that little: so uniting philanthropic energy with philosophic calm.[27]

Few would today uphold so extreme a policy of laissez faire as Spencer sanctioned or wait so patiently for the impersonal laws of evolution to work out a program of reform as he assumed to be willing to do. Yet we cannot well doubt the wisdom of his advice to beware of the doctrine of the possibility of manufacturing progress by legislation that is not based on the widest possible knowledge of the sociological principles involved. This is the lesson which sociologists are still trying to impress upon well-meaning, but ill-informed, philanthropists.[28]

I. EXTRA-LEGAL ASPECTS OF POLITICAL ORGANIZATION

Spencer offered numerous reflections regarding the extra-legal aspects of political activity and organization. It has already been pointed out that he rightly conceived of public opinion, or "the feeling of the community," as the vital force behind governmental activity which gives it vigor and effectiveness and that he believed that no form of government can succeed unless it is in accord with the public sentiments of the time. His analysis of the overwhelming part which custom and tradition play in formulating public opinion has also been described. As to political parties, Spencer held that their influence is mainly negative. They usually merely becloud the real issues in any political situation by their bias in one direction or the other.

On the general subject of the extra-legal forms of social control, it may be said that Spencer rendered a real service to political and social thought in correlating political organization with general social organization and in showing how hopeless it was for political reformers to attempt any political change or reform without looking at the state in its relation to society and taking into consideration the basic dependence of political activity upon social forces and interests. In this regard he performed the main service which sociologists have to offer to political theory and practice. The significance of this view has been well stated by Professor Small in what he designates as the central notion of the Spencerian philosophy: "The members of society, from the very earliest stages, arrange themselves in somewhat permanent forms; these forms are rearranged in adaptation to varying needs; the forms are related, both as cause and effect, to the individuals who make up the society; they are thus factors that may never be left out of account in attempts to understand real life."[29]

J. SUMMARY OF SPENCER'S SOCIAL AND POLITICAL THEORIES

Spencer's salient social and political doctrines, then, may be summarized as follows: (1) he revived the contract (agreement) doctrine to account philosophically for the justification of political authority; (2) he put forward a strong sociological statement of individualistic political philosophy, in which the state was completely subordinated to the individual and was regarded simply as an agent for securing a greater degree of freedom for the individual than was possible without its "negative interference" with human conduct; (3) he denied the possibility of securing social progress by direct remedial legislation (at least of the type he was familiar with) and asserted that society must wait for the automatic working of the general laws of evolution to bring about permanent progress; (4) he set forth one of the most elaborate expositions ever devised of the organismic theory of society; (5) he developed a philosophy of political evolution based upon the purpose for which organized society functions, finding these purposes to have been, first, military expansion, then industrial development, and, finally, ethical improvement; (6) finally, Spencer made the important contribution of correlating the state with society in the attempt to estimate its position and functions in the wider social process.

In short, Spencer approached public problems from the broad viewpoint of the sociologist, however inconsistent and inadequate at times may have been his application of the principles of his social philosophy to the solution of those problems.

NOTES

1. See Spencer's *Essays, Scientific, Political, and Speculative* (New York, 1891), pp. 118–49, essay entitled "Some Reasons for Dissenting from the Philosophy of M. Comte."

2. Henri Michel, *L'Idée de l'état* (Paris, 1896), p. 462 (author's translation); see also Eugene de Roberty, *Auguste Comte et Herbert Spencer* (Paris, 1904).

3. For a brief statement of the sources of Spencer's doctrines see Ernest Barker, *Political Thought in England from Herbert Spencer to the Present Day* (New York, 1915), pp. 86–90. For his own account of his early years see his *Autobiography* (2 vols.; New York, 1904), I, 48–142. For more bibliographic detail on Spencer, see H. E. Barnes and Howard Becker, *Social Thought from Lore to Science* (2 vols.; Boston, 1938), I, xlix–li.

4. See A. G. Keller, *Societal Evolution* (New York, 1931), pp. 12 ff. *The First Principles* was followed by the *Principles of Biology* (1864–67), the *Principles of Psychology* (1872), the *Study of Sociology* (1873), the *Principles of Sociology* (1876–96), the *Principles of Ethics* (1879–93), and *Man versus the State* (1884). In addition to these systematic works, Spencer published a large number of articles which were collected in numerous volumes of essays. For a complete list of Spencer's works see the article entitled "Spencer" in the eleventh edition of the *Encyclopaedia Britannica;* and in W. H. Hudson, *An Introduction to the Philosophy of Herbert Spencer* (New York, 1894), Appendix, pp. 231–34.

Spencer produced this mass of material under conditions far from conducive to its speedy and efficient execution. He was a chronic neurasthenic during the entire period of the development of his sociological system, and his pecuniary resources were not always sufficient to keep his plan in a normal state of progress. The Preface to the third volume of his *Principles of Sociology*, published in 1896, which completed the work to which he had devoted practically a lifetime, sums up the difficulties of the writer and expresses his satisfaction at his final success.

5. William Graham Sumner, *The Forgotten Man and Other Essays* (New Haven, 1918), p. 401.

6. Four good works dealing with Spencer's philosophical system are: Hudson, *op. cit.;* Josiah Royce, *Herbert Spencer: An Estimate and Review* (New York, 1904); Hector Macpherson, *Spencer and Spencerism* (New York, 1900); and H. Elliott, *Herbert Spencer* (New York, 1916). An authorized and approved digest of his system as a whole is to be found in F. H. Collins, *An Epitome of the Synthetic Philosophy* (New York, 1889). Finally, no one should consider himself thoroughly acquainted with Spencer unless he has read his *Autobiography,* which appeared posthumously in two volumes in 1904, and David Duncan's *Life and Letters of Herbert Spencer* (2 vols.; New York, 1908).

7. For Spencer's summary of his system see his Preface to Collins, *op. cit.*, pp. viii–xi; cf. also Robert Mackintosh, *From Comte to Benjamin Kidd* (London, 1899), chaps. viii–ix.

8. Franklin H. Giddings, *Sociology: A Lecture* (New York, 1908), pp. 29–30.

9. *The Social Organism* (1860); *Specialized Administration* (1871); *Principles of Sociology*, Vol. I, Part I. Citations from the *Principles of Sociology* are from the New York edition of 1896.

10. *Principles of Sociology*, Vol. I, Part II, chaps. ii–ix, particularly chap. ii. More detailed analysis of Spencer's organic theory of society are to be found in F. W. Coker, *Organismic Theories of the State* (New York, 1910), pp. 124–39; and Ezra T. Towne, *Die Auffassung der Gesellschaft als Organismus, ihre Entwickelung und ihre Modifikationen* (Halle, 1903), pp. 41–48.

11. See his review of the work in F. G. Peabody, *A Readers' Guide to Social Ethics and Allied Subjects*, p. 29.

12. A. W. Small, *General Sociology*, p. 130. For estimates of Spencer's importance for sociology see F. H. Giddings, *Principles of Sociology* (New York, 1896), Book I, chap. i, and his adaptations of Spencer's doctrines in all his works; Ward, *Dynamic Sociology*, I, 139–219; Small, *op. cit.*, pp. 109–53; E. A. Ross, *Foundations of Sociology* (New York, 1905), pp. 42–47; and, above all, Leopold von Wiese, *Zur Grundlegung der Gesellschaftslehre: Eine kritische Untersuchung von Herbert Spencer's System der synthetischen Philosophie* (Jena, 1906).

13. *Principles of Sociology*, Vol. I, sec. 210, p. 438; cf. also *Study of Sociology*, chap. i. Among the best analyses of certain phases of Spencer's political theories are D. G. Ritchie, *Principles of State Interference* (London, 1891); Barker, *op. cit.*, chap. iv; and Coker, *op. cit.*, pp. 124–39.

14. *Principles of Sociology*, II, 247.

15. *Man versus the State* (with the abridged and revised *Social Statics* [New York. 1892]), pp. 380–81. As Ritchie points out, part of Spencer's confusion with respect to the problem of sovereignty was due to his tendency to personify the abstract philosophical concept.

16. *Principles of Sociology*, I, 437.

17. *Ibid.*, II, 317.

18. For Spencer's own description of his method see his *Autobiography*, Vol. II, chap. xlvii, esp. pp. 325–27.

19. *Principles of Sociology*, II, 568–605 ff.

20. *Social Statics* (abridged edition with *Man versus the State* [New York, 1892]), pp. 248–49.

21. *Ibid.*, p. 105.

22. *Ibid.*, p. 248.

23. *Study of Sociology* (New York, 1876), p. 275; cf. also *Principles of Sociology*, II, 230–43.

24. For Spencer's own account of the development of his political theories see his *Autobiography*, II, 431–36. This seems to be somewhat of a "rationalization after the fact."

25. *Op. cit.*, pp. 285–86.

26. *Ibid.*, pp. 270–71.

27. *Ibid.*, p. 403.

28. For Spencer's account of his ambitious plan to make a study of the effect of so-called "reform legislation" during the whole period of medieval and modern English history see in *Various Fragments* (New York, 1898), pp. 136–40, an essay entitled "Record of Legislation."

29. *General Sociology*, p. 153.

CHAPTER IV

LEWIS HENRY MORGAN: PIONEER IN THE THEORY OF SOCIAL EVOLUTION

Leslie A. White

I. MORGAN'S LIFE AND WRITINGS

IF IT was Herbert Spencer who was mainly responsible for introducing the concept of evolution into social thought, in general, in the nineteenth century, it was an American ethnologist and sociologist, Lewis Henry Morgan, who applied the notion of evolution to social development and constructed the most impressive system of institutional evolution produced in that century.

"Morgan was undoubtedly the greatest sociologist of the past century," declared the distinguished British ethnologist, Alfred C. Haddon.[1] Judgments may well differ as to who was *the* greatest sociologist of the nineteenth century; but there can be no doubt that Morgan was one of the greatest.

Lewis Henry Morgan was born on a farm near the village of Aurora, New York, on November 21, 1818. He was educated at Cayuga Academy, in Aurora, and at Union College, from which he was graduated in 1840. After studying law at Aurora, he went to Rochester, New York, in 1844 to practice. He married, settled in Rochester, and lived there for the rest of his life. Morgan took an active part in the intellectual life of Rochester of his day and was for many years the guiding spirit in the Pundit Club, which had its first meeting in his home. Many of his contributions to science were first read in manuscript before this club. Morgan was active also in civic matters, serving one term in the Assembly and one term in the Senate of the state of New York. Partly through his legal practice but largely through investments in mining and business enterprises in northern Michigan, Morgan accumulated a considerable fortune, which enabled him eventually to give up his legal practice and to devote himself wholly to his scientific labors.

Morgan's first notable work was the *League of the Ho-de-no-sau-nee or Iroquois* (1851) the "first scientific account of an Indian tribe ever given to the world."[2] In 1868 his classic, *The American Beaver and His Works,* appeared. Two years later, the Smithsonian Institution published his monumental *Systems of Consanguinity and Affinity of the Human Family.* This work may be regarded, in some respects at least, as Morgan's most original and brilliant achievement.[3] But it is his *Ancient Society* (1877) for which Morgan is most widely known. This work, which grew out of his *Systems of Consanguinity,* has been translated into many of the languages of Europe and into Chinese and Japanese and has exerted an influence upon sociological thought that was as profound as it was widespread. Morgan's last work, *Houses and House-Life of the American Aborigines,* appeared in 1881, shortly before his death.

Contrary to a notion that has gained currency in recent decades, Morgan was no mere "armchair philosopher." He did a great deal of field work in a day when investigations in the field were dangerous as well as arduous. In addition to his field work among the Iroquois of New York, Morgan made several long field trips to Kansas and Nebraska territories, to the Rocky Mountains, to Hudson's Bay Territory, and to New Mexico—and made them in a day when hostile tribes still waged war against the whites and when railroads had extended westward hardly as far as the Missouri River.

Although Morgan never taught at a university or held a position with any scientific institution, he nevertheless exerted considerable influence in scientific and educational circles. He was active in the American Association for the Advancement of Science for many years, serving as its president in 1880. He received an honorary LL.D degree from Union College in 1873 and was elected to the National Academy of Sciences in 1875. His death came on December 17, 1881.[4]

II. MORGAN AS SOCIAL EVOLUTIONIST

Morgan was truly a pioneer in social science. He began his work at a time when the Christian cosmogony was accepted without question by virtually everyone. As a young man, Morgan accepted the account of creation in Genesis, just as Darwin had done. But by the time he had come to write *Ancient Society,* Morgan had placed himself squarely against the biblical account of man's origin. Although *Ancient Society* was dedicated to a Presbyterian minister and although God is alluded to in the last paragraph of the book, Morgan specifically repudiated the then current theological explanation of savage cultures, which held that they are the result of degradation after the Fall of Man. This theory, Morgan asserted,

came in as a corollary from the Mosaic cosmogony, and was acquiesced in from a supposed necessity which no longer exists..... The views herein [i.e., in *Ancient Society*] presented contravene, as I am aware, an assumption which has for centuries been generally accepted..... It [the degradation theory] was never a scientific proposition supported by facts. It is refuted.....[5]

Thus Morgan, like Darwin, was obliged to oppose Christian theology in order to establish the views of science. Likewise, both Morgan and Darwin broke with the old and ushered in the new. Morgan did for sociology what Darwin did for biology—introduced and established as a fundamental concept the theory of evolution. And, if anything, Morgan's achievement is even greater than Darwin's, for Morgan was able to show *why* cultures evolve, as well as to describe the ways in which the development came about. Darwin was able to show how evolution occurs as a consequence of organic variations, but he was not able to explain how and why the variations appeared in the first place.

It is in his theory of social, or cultural, evolution, then, that we find Morgan's greatest contribution to sociological thought. To be sure, the idea of social evolution did not originate with Morgan; many writers before him had dealt with this concept in one manner or another. But it is in Morgan that we find, for the first time, a sound, naturalistic theory, one that is adequate to the needs and requirements of modern science. The gist of his theory may be briefly put: Culture advances as the technological means of man's control over his habitat, particularly over his means of subsistence, are enlarged and improved; ".... the great epochs of human progress have been identified, more or less directly, with the enlargement of the sources of subsistence."[6] Man is an animal who "at the outset" lived as a mere beast. But, because of articulate speech with which to communicate ideas from one individual to another and from one generation to the next, man has been able to elevate himself from the brute level and to advance himself from savagery to civilization. Tools and weapons are the principal means by which man increases his control over nature and "enlarges his sources of subsistence." The bow and arrow "must have given a powerful upward influence to ancient society."[7] The discovery of metals, especially iron, and their uses contributed immeasurably to cultural advance.[8] The domestication of animals not only enlarged man's sources of subsistence but "supplemented human muscle with animal power, contributing a new factor of the highest value . . . . the production of iron gave the plow with an iron point, and a better spade and axe. Out of these, and the previous horticulture, came field agriculture; and with it, for the first time, unlimited subsistence,"[9]—i.e., unlimited resources for culture-building. As technology advanced, social institutions changed. The profound change from subsistence upon wild foods to intensive agriculture produced a correspondingly radical change in society: the institutions of tribal society gave way to the institutions of civil society; the clan and tribe were replaced by the political state.

We have here a simple, sound theory of cultural evolution. Man lives by exploiting the resources of nature by technological means. Social institutions are society's ways of organizing itself to wield and use its technology. As the technology advances, social institutions must change also. It is clear, of course, that this theory is applicable to the present as well as to the past. If a social revolution, a change from tribe to state and empire, resulted from the transition from a wild-food technology to intensive agriculture, what social consequences may be expected from the technological revolution of the present power age or the future age of atomic energy?

Although Morgan sets forth this theory of cultural evolution clearly and succinctly in Part I of *Ancient Society,* he does not employ it consistently throughout this work. He speaks of social institutions as developing from a "few primary germs of thought" that were originally "implanted in man's mind." Parts II, III, and IV of *Ancient Society* are concerned with the "growth of the idea of" government, the family, and property, respectively. One frequently gets the impression that the evolution of social institutions (the "growth of primary germs of thought") takes place independently of technological advance, which results from "inventions and discoveries," or, at most, that social evolution and technological evolution run along parallel but independent lines.[10] Morgan does, indeed, speak of "two independent lines of investigation." But it should be noted that he says independent lines of investigation, not independent lines of development. Thus it might appear that Morgan had two theories of social evolution: one in which technology was the determinant; the other in which ideas inherent in man's mind just grew and expressed themselves in social institutions.

We shall not attempt to explain at this time why Morgan expressed his philosophy of evolution as he did. It seems likely that his "primary germs of thought," lodged originally in "man's mind" and subsequently growing from age to age was a concept borrowed from the prevailing psychology of his day.[11] But, apart from a few lapses, as, for example, when he explains the polygamy of the Mormons as "a relic of savagism not yet eradicated from the human brain,"[12] Morgan shows that the growth of social institutions is dependent upon, or even an expression of, technological advances. This interpretation runs through the entire book but is especially evident in Morgan's account of the transition from tribal society to civil society. Morgan's statement of the theory of the technological determination of social evolution is, perhaps, not so explicit, pointed, and emphatic as it might be, and his demonstration of this theory is frequently obscured by his psychology of the "germs of thought." But we must not forget that Morgan was a pioneer; he invented this theory. To demand philosophic purity and perfect refinement of expression of him is, of course, unreasonable; it is enough that he formulated this most basic theory of social science, gave it to us, and showed us how to use it.[13]

III. MORGAN'S THEORY OF THE EVOLUTION OF THE FAMILY

Holding a prominent place in Morgan's theory of cultural evolution is his special theory of the evolution of the family. According to Morgan, the original condition of human society was that of a "horde living in promiscuity." Out of this emerged the Consanguine family, which was the first stage in the evolution of the family. The Consanguine family was "founded upon the intermarriage of brothers and sisters in a group." Next came the Punaluan family, which prohibited marriage between brothers and sisters but constituted "group marriage"— a group of brothers possessed their wives in common, or a group of sisters possessed their husbands in common. In the Syndyasmian family, which came next, we have "the pairing of a male with a female under the form of marriage, but without exclusive cohabitation. It was the germ of the Monogamian Family."[14] The Patriarchal family appeared next and, finally, the Monogamian family, "founded upon marriage between single pairs, with an exclusive cohabitation." Thus Morgan distinguished five stages in the evolution of the family. It will be noted that the course of development assumed by Morgan had a definite direction: from promiscuous and unregulated unions in the original horde through "group marriage," which was progressively reduced by customary restrictions until monogamy was attained.

A vigorous, and sometimes bitter, debate upon the subject of the origin and evolution of the family followed the publication of *Systems of Consanguinity* and *Ancient Society*. It has not become extinguished even yet.[15] But the consensus is that Morgan's theory is untenable. The discovery that monogamy is customary among the most primitive of peoples; the failure to establish Morgan's theory by any method other than Morgan's; and, above all, the modern studies of monkeys and apes, which show fairly conclusively that the family form, as a sociological consequence of physiological processes, is universal among primates (of the Old World at least) have overthrown Morgan's theory once and for all. Morgan formulated his theory of the evolution of the family in his attempt to explain the various systems of kinship terminology which he had discovered. His various family forms were essentially devices to explain systems of kinship nomenclature. It was something like the physicists' creation of "luminiferous ether" to account for the transmission of light from the sun to the planets. Once the Consanguine and other forms of the family had been invented to explain relationship terms, the indisputable fact of the kinship systems made the forms of the family seem plausible. But Morgan did more than reason in a circle; he had the testimony of men who had lived among the Hawaiians which, he believed, established the actual existence of the Punaluan family among the Polynesians.[16] His theory was tested and indorsed by two intelligent and educated men who were intimately acquainted with the aborigines of Australia.[17] Thus he had reason for confidence in his theory.[18] Today we can explain kinship nomenclatures in another way, we know more about primitive peoples, and we know something of the physiology of sex among primates, all of which renders Morgan's theory obsolete. It was a bold and brilliant achievement, like the Ptolemaic system of astronomy or the theory of luminiferous ether. But, like these theories, Morgan's has had to give way to a better one.

IV. KINSHIP AND THE CLASSIFICATORY SYSTEM OF RELATIONSHIPS

In the discovery of systems of kinship we find one of Morgan's most brilliant achievements. Before Morgan's day, a few men here and there had noted that many primitive peoples do not observe the same rules in the designation of kindred that we do. But these differences were merely noted as "strange customs" or dismissed as "heathen practices." It was Morgan who first recognized that the customs of primitive peoples in this respect were indeed systems, governed by definite rules, and not mere savage caprice or vagary; it was he who first formulated, as an objective for science, the problem of kinship nomenclatures; and it was he who laid the foundation upon which our modern studies of kinship systems rest.

Although Morgan failed to see that kinship in human society is primarily and essentially a social phenomenon and only secondarily and incidentally a biological matter,[19] he did discover and appreciate the fact that relationship terms are sociological devices employed in the regulation of social life. A relationship term is the designation of an individual or a class of individuals that is socially significant. Every society of human beings is divided into social classes or groups, which, with reference to any individual in the society, are designated with kinship terms such as "uncle," "sister," "mother-in-law," etc. One's behavior toward one's fellows varies, depending upon the category of relationship in which the person stands. Since the categories are labeled with kinship terms, a close functional relationship obtains between kinship nomenclature and social organization and behavior.[20] These are the views and postulates upon which a modern school of social anthropologists bases much of its work.[21] They were discovered, elucidated, and established by Morgan many decades ago.[22]

v. "SOCIETAS" AND "CIVITAS": THE TRANSITION FROM KINSHIP TO CIVIL SOCIETY

Morgan surveyed the entire span of human history and saw that, with reference to social organization, it is divisible into two great categories: "ancient society" (or "primitive society," as we tend to call it today) and modern, civil society. He called the first type of society *societas,* the second *civitas.*[23] Morgan's distinction of these two great types of human society and his description of each constitute one of his greatest contributions to sociological thought.[24]

Ancient society, the *societas,* was founded upon "persons and upon relationships purely personal." Civil society, the *civitas,* was founded upon territory and upon property. Thus, in primitive society a person's status and role in social life were determined by his personal relationship to other members of the society. And, since in almost all instances all members of a *societas* regard themselves as related to one another, a person's role in primitive society is determined and regulated by ties of *kinship,* as well as by merely personal ties. A *societas* is thus a community of kindred. In a *civitas,* on the other hand, a person's status and role are determined by his place of residence—deme, township, state, etc.—and by his relationship to property. The relationship between persons is thus impersonal. The members of a *societas* are kinsfolk, the members of a *civitas* are citizens. The clan[25] and tribe are the characteristic units of ancient society. The political state is the form characteristic of the *civitas.*

Ancient society is democratic, and all men are free and equal.[26] In civil society there are class distinctions:[27] masters and slaves; lords, vassals, and serfs; kings and subjects; or the rich and the poor.

VI. PROPERTY AND INHERITANCE IN RELATION TO SOCIAL EVOLUTION

Bearing directly upon the differences between these two great types of society is Morgan's treatment of property. This subject is dealt with in various places in *Ancient Society,* but particularly in the fourth and last part of this work, which is devoted to the "Growth of the Idea of Property." This part, although relatively brief—less than a quarter as long as the part devoted to the family and less than one-tenth as long as the part on government—nevertheless contains some of Morgan's most significant contributions to modern sociology and the science of culture.

Peoples with crude and simple cultures have little property, and the problem of inheritance at death is an insignificant one. In many instances the few articles owned by the deceased are either buried with him or destroyed, or they may be divided among his close relatives and friends. But, as culture advances and property accumulates, the problem of inheritance becomes important. The course of social evolution has been profoundly influenced, according to Morgan, by the accumulation of property and by the exigencies of inheritance at death.

The "first great rule of inheritance," according to Morgan, decreed that the effects of a deceased person were to be inherited by the members of his clan, or "gens." "Practically they were appropriated by the nearest of kin; but the principle was general, that the property should remain in the gens of the decedent and be distributed among its members." The second rule limited the heirs to agnates of the deceased, excluding other clansmen, or "gentiles." The third rule restricted heirs to children (unless, of course, there were none), excluding agnates. It was the accumulation of property and the desire of men to bequeath it to their sons that caused a change of descent through females to descent through males, Morgan believed. He points out that the rule prohibiting marriage within the gens among the Greeks was occasionally relaxed in the case of heiresses: marriage within the gens being permitted in such cases in order to keep the property from passing outside the gens. Morgan speaks of the family as a "property-making organization" as William F. Ogburn has, in dealing with the family in Colonial America.[28] Property, "as it increased in variety and amount, exercised a steady and constantly augmenting influence in the direction of monogamy." Thus we note a close relationship between "the growth of the idea of the family" and the "growth of the idea of property." As the family narrowed itself down from the Consanguine family ("group marriage") to monogamy, the body of legitimate heirs of a decedent contracted from the gens as a whole to his own children. And it was property that, to a great extent, determined the course of social or family evolution. As Morgan once put it: "Property became sufficiently powerful in its influence to touch the organic structure of society."[29]

Whatever modification of Morgan's formulations might be necessary or desirable today, his general thesis is as sound and as important as ever: property and the customs of inheritance have exerted a profound influence upon the course of social evolution, affecting directly the form of family, marriage, and divorce and influencing indirectly other aspects of society. An exhaustive sociological study of the influence of property and inheritance upon such things as polygamy, primogeniture, crime, celibacy of a portion of the clergy, divorce, etc., in our own culture for the last fifteen hundred years would be most illuminating.

It is property, its quantity and variety, and its method of tenure and inheritance, Morgan argues, that determine whether a society will have privileged classes or not. Among primitive peoples property is relatively insignificant quantitatively and, apart from "articles purely personal," is owned and consumed in common. This does not mean, of course, that an agricultural tribe had only one big field and no individual fields or gardens, nor does it mean that all food within a tribe was stored in one big warehouse from which it was served in a tribal community mess hall. It means that land and other natural resources were communally *owned,* although individual rights to the use of a plot of ground might exist. There was no private property in land and other natural resources; there was no buying and selling of real estate. Everyone in the tribe had free and unrestricted access to the resources of nature, to the means of life. Herein lay the freedom of primitive society, of the *societas.* Community of effort in production prevailed, as a rule, in situations where it could be carried on effectively. In consumption, the members of a household which in primitive society frequently includes a number of families, were fed from common stores. And between households— who were, of course, groups of kindred—there was often such exchange of goods, especially in times of shortage, that, as many investigators since Morgan have put it, "a whole village (or community) must be without food before a single family can starve." Therein lay the equality of primitive society. Thus, "communism in living," as described by Morgan in *Houses and House-Life,* was the basic principle of society among primitive peoples. The freedom and equality which character-ize primitive society are but social expressions of the customs relating to the tenure, exchange, and consumption of property.

But with advances in culture came changes in customs relating to property and, as further consequences, changes in the organization of society. "Systematical cultivation of the earth tended to identify the family with the soil." The right to cultivate a portion of the land held in common by the tribe passed into ownership in severalty. Commerce grew with the accumulation of wealth through agriculture and manu-facture. With the development of money, everything came to be bought and sold, men as well as land. Private property became established. The constitution of society was transformed as a consequence. Instead of the liberty, equality, and fraternity of the *societas,* there was inequality, class divisions, aristocracy, and slavery. "Property and office were the foundations upon which aristocracy planted itself." The "growth of the idea of property .... introduced human slavery as an instrument in its production; and after the experience of several thousand years, it caused the abolition of slavery upon the discovery that a freeman was a better property-making machine."[30] The transition from democratic gentile society to aristocratic society is seen by Morgan from still another angle:

.... From the increased abundance of subsistence through field agriculture, nations began to develop, numbering many thousands under one government, where before they would be reckoned by a few thousands. The localization of tribes in fixed areas and in fortified cities, with the increase of the numbers of people, intensified the struggle for the possession of the most desirable territories. It tended to advance the art of war, and to increase the rewards of individual prowess. These changes of condition and of the plan of life .... [were] to overthrow gentile and establish political society.[31]

As property has been the great factor in bringing about the transition from primitive society, so has it been the instrument which has formed and shaped the institutions of civil society. "Government and laws are instituted with primary reference to .... the creation, protection, and enjoyment" of property.[32] "It is impossible to overestimate the influence of property in the civilization of mankind,"[33] Morgan declares. The "idea of property," which was so feeble "in the mind of the savage," has grown until it has become the "master passion of civilized man."

Morgan's view of the consequences of this master-passion is set forth in a striking passage:

Since the advent of civilization, the outgrowth of property has been so immense, its forms so diversified, its uses so expanding and its management so intelligent in the interests of its owners, that it has become, on the part of the people, an unmanageable power. The human mind stands bewildered in the presence of its own creation. The time will come, nevertheless, when human intelligence will rise to the mastery over property, and define the relations of the state to the property it protects, as well as the obligations and the limits of the rights of its owners. The interests of society are paramount to individual interests, and the two must be brought into just and harmonious relations. A mere property career is not the final destiny of mankind, if progress is to be the law of the future as it has been of the past. The time which has passed away since civilization began is but a fragment of the past duration of man's existence; and but a fragment of the ages yet to come. The dissolution of society bids fair to become the termination of a career of which property is the end and aim; because such a career contains the elements of self-destruction. Democracy in government, brotherhood in society, equality in rights and privileges, and universal education, foreshadow the next higher plane of society to which experience, intelligence and knowledge are steadily tending. It will be a revival, in a higher form, of the liberty, equality and fraternity of the ancient gentes.[34]

In *Ancient Society,* Morgan has little specifically to say about social classes in modern society, although he declares the question of aristocracy *versus* democracy is one of the "great problems" of modern society, and adds: "As a question between equal rights and unequal rights, between equal laws and unequal laws, between the rights of wealth, of rank and of official position, and the power of justice and intelligence, there can be little doubt of the ultimate result."[35]

But, in his European *Travel Journal,* Morgan discusses the condition of society in Italy, Austria, Germany, France, and England at some length. His comments upon English society are especially interesting. He observes that the aristocracy proper is an obsolete and relatively impotent class. Their place has been taken by "a Plutocracy .... consisting of the great merchants, great manufacturers and great bankers of the Kingdom who are now the governing power, the true ruling aristocracy of the land."[36] He comments upon a meeting of working men in Hyde Park as follows:

These meetings will gradually organise a public sentiment against the existing order of things..... The merchants, capitalists, and middling men keep clear of these meetings because their sympathies are on the other side..... When the time comes, if it ever does, the working men will have to rise upon the merchants and traders as well as the aristocrats and push them out of the way in one body.[37]

VII. AN EVALUATION OF MORGAN'S POSITION IN SOCIOLOGY AND ANTHROPOLOGY[38]

Morgan's eminence and influence were great during his lifetime and for a decade or two thereafter; but he has suffered an eclipse since the turn of the century. The forces of antievolutionism, which fought Darwinism so vigorously, entrenched themselves upon the sociological field after being driven from the field of biology. In America the attack upon Morgan and social evolutionism has been led chiefly by the anthropologist, Franz Boas, and his disciples. One of the latter has gone so far as to declare that the idea of social evolution is "the most inane, sterile, and pernicious theory ever conceived in the history of science."[39] Alexander Goldenweiser has written "critiques" of evolutionism again and again, in which he describes "the downfall of evolutionism." But, if, on the one hand, Morgan has been attacked, on the other hand, he has been ignored. Franz Boas does not even mention Morgan's name in his essay, "The History of Anthropology,"[40] although he discusses the evolutionist school and mentions other evolutionists by name. Radcliffe-Brown does not list Morgan in the bibliography of his long article on "The Social Organization of Australian Tribes,"[41] although it contains 188 references to over a hundred titles by fifty-odd authors, despite the fact that Morgan was the first ethnologist of repute to write on Australian social organization.[42] Indeed, it might fairly be said that it was Morgan, aided by his disciples, Lorimer Fison and A. W. Howitt, whom he taught and guided by correspondence,[43] who founded the science of Australian ethnology. Radcliffe-Brown mentions Morgan in the text of his article only to oppose him.

Morgan has been so grossly misrepresented by some of his critics that it is difficult to believe that they have even read his works. Paul Radin has asserted that "to all Boas' disciples Morgan has since remained anathema and unread."[44] Morgan's biographer, Bernhard J. Stern, has declared that "Morgan nowhere in his books uses the word 'evolution.' "[45] Ralph Linton has made the same charge.[46] The fact is that "evolution" appears on the *very first page* of the Kerr edition of *Ancient Society* and twice in the first four pages of the Holt edition. It is found here and there in subsequent pages of *Ancient Society* and in other books and articles by Morgan. Lowie, Stern, and Linton have pictured Morgan as a man who was never able to free himself from his theological upbringing and accept the philosophy of modern science in general or of Darwinism in particular. Nothing could be further from the truth, as the present writer has demonstrated.[47] Morgan was a staunch champion of science throughout his entire adult life. The high-water mark of misrepresentation was perhaps reached recently by A. R. Radcliffe-Brown, who made the remarkable "discovery" that Morgan was not even a *social* evolutionist but merely a *petit bourgeois* with a simple faith in progress, measured by the provincial standards of his home town, Rochester, New York![48]

Ancient Society came to the attention of Karl Marx, who regarded it as a great work and was much impressed with it. He planned to write a book dealing with Morgan's contributions but was prevented from doing so by his death. The book was eventually written by Frederich Engels, Marx's lifelong friend and co-worker, under the title, *Der Ursprung der Familie, des Privateigenthums und des Staats* (1884).[49] *Ancient Society* became a Marxist classic. This fact has unquestionably had much to do with the change in attitude toward Morgan that has taken place since his day.

No one, of course, would maintain today that Morgan's work was complete, perfect, and final. He had his shortcomings and made mistakes, as many another pioneer in science has. But he was more than a mere pioneer, for he made many contributions of enduring value. His general theory of cultural evolution is perfectly sound today and is as indispensable to sociology as Darwinism is to biology. Culture evolves as the technological means of exploiting the resources of nature are enlarged and improved. Morgan's distinction between primitive society, characterized by communal ownership of the resources of nature and by liberty, equality, and fraternity in social life, and modern civil society, resting upon private ownership of the resources of nature and characterized by aristocracy and plutocracy instead of democracy, is tremendously illuminating. His discovery of kinship systems and their sociological significance laid the basis and showed the way for a modern school of social anthropologists. In some respects modern sociologists and anthropologists have not advanced beyond positions attained by Morgan. Few have gone beyond Morgan in his treatment of the role of property in social evolution and in social life generally. Some have even receded.[50] Few, if any, sociologists or social anthropologists have exploited Morgan's study of house architecture as an expression of social life and organization. Thus, while portions of Morgan's work are obsolete today (his theory of the evolution of the family, for example), much of it is perfectly sound and amazingly "modern." And his thesis of an evolutionary development of culture, repudiated or ignored by so many today, is the most basic concept of social science. Sociologists and social anthropologists would do well not merely to "go back to Morgan" but to return to him, so that they may again go *forward* along the broad highway that he laid out for us long ago.

NOTES

1. *History of Anthropology* (London, 1910), p. 133. Haddon, M.A., Sc.D., F.R.S., was Fellow of Christ's College and University Reader in Ethnology at Cambridge University.

2. J. W. Powell, "Sketch of Lewis H. Morgan," *Popular Science Monthly*, XVIII (1880), 115. As recently as 1922, Alexander Goldenweiser, who had himself done field work among the Iroquois, wrote: "The best general treatise on the Iroquois still remains Lewis H. Morgan's 'The League of the Iroquois,' " (*Early Civilization* [New York, 1922], p. 418)

3. An eminent British anthropologist, the late W. H. R. Rivers, pays this tribute to *Systems of Consanguinity:* "I do not know of any discovery in the whole range of science which can be more certainly put to the credit of one man than that of the classificatory system of relationship by Lewis Morgan. By this I mean, not merely that he was the first to point out clearly the existence of this mode of denoting relationship, but that it was he who collected the vast mass of materials by which the essential characters of the system were demonstrated, and it was he who was the first to recognize the great theoretical importance of his new discovery" (*Kinship and Social Organization* [London, 1914], pp. 4–5; see also p. 93).

4. For biographical accounts of Morgan see, in addition to articles in encyclopedias and dictionaries of biography, (1) the aforementioned sketch by J. W. Powell, written during Morgan's lifetime; (2) Bernhard J. Stern, *Lewis Henry Morgan: Social Evolutionist* (Chicago, 1931), which, however, contains numerous errors and distortions; and (3) Rochester Historical Society ("Publication Fund Series," Vol. II [Rochester, N.Y., 1923]),

which contains a number of sketches of Morgan's life and work, some of them written by men who knew Morgan personally.

5. *Ancient Society* (New York, 1877), pp. 7–8, 506. All page references to *Ancient Society* used in this chapter are taken from the first edition, by Henry Holt & Co., not from the later edition by C. H. Kerr & Co.

6. *Ibid.*, p. 19.

7. *Ibid.*, p. 22.

8. *Ibid.*, pp. 43, 535, 539.

9. *Ibid.*, p. 26.

10. *Ibid.*, p. 4.

11. Adolph Bastian, a contemporary of Morgan, frequently gave expression to this view (see L. Gumplowicz, *The Outlines of Sociology*, English trans. [Philadelphia, 1899], pp. 38–39, 46, 47). Immanuel Kant, too, spoke of the unfolding of "germs implanted by nature" (*The Idea of a Universal History*, trans. Thomas De Quincey [Hanover, 1927], p. 13). Henry Sumner Maine discusses forms of moral restraint "unfolded out of" certain "germs" (*Ancient Law* [3d American ed.; New York, 1888], p. 116).

12. *Ancient Society*, p. 61.

13. See Leslie A. White, "Energy and the Evolution of Culture," *American Anthropologist*, XLV (1943), 335–56, for a modern formulation of Morgan's theory of cultural development.

14. *Ancient Society*, p. 28.

15. See Gerrit S. Miller, Jr., "Some Elements of Sexual Behavior in Primates and Their Possible Influence on the Beginnings of Human Social Development," (*Journal of Mammalogy*, Vol. IX [1928]); B. Malinowski, *Sex and Repression in Savage Society* (New York, 1927); and R. H. Lowie, *The Family as a Social Unit* ("Papers of the Michigan Academy of Arts and Sciences," Vol. XVIII [1932]), pp. 53–69.

16. Morgan, *Ancient Society*, p. 427.

17. See Lorimer Fison and A. W. Howitt, *Kamilaroi and Kurnai* (Sydney, 1880).

18. Cf. Leslie A. White (ed.), *Pioneers in American Anthropology* (2 vols.; Albuquerque, N.M., 1940), which depicts the support and encouragement which Morgan received from an able and erudite scholar who was to become one of America's most distinguished anthropologists and documentary historians, Adolph F. Bandelier.

19. Many social anthropologists, even today, think of kinship as something biological, as is indicated by their use of such terms as "fictitious kinship" to designate the sociological phenomenon of kinship.

20. In 1909 A. L. Kroeber challenged this thesis in "Classificatory Systems of Relationship," *Journal of the Royal Anthropological Institute*, Vol. XXXIX. Kroeber's position has received some support from other students; but, after more than a half-century of testing, the sociological interpretation of kinship terms still stands (see R. H. Lowie, "Relationship Terms," *Encyclopaedia Britannica* [14th ed.]).

21. Social anthropologists do not always acknowledge their indebtedness to Morgan, however. A. R. Radcliffe-Brown, one of the foremost students of kinship in recent years, occasionally refers to Morgan to criticize or oppose him (see, e.g., "The Social Organization of Australian Tribes," *Oceania*, I (1931), 426; "Kinship Terminologies in California," *American Anthropologist*, XXXVII [1935], 530–35, in which recognition of Morgan's contributions is conspicuously lacking; and "The Study of Kinship Systems," *Journal of the Royal Anthropological Institute*, LXXI [1941], 1–18). In only one instance, so far as I am aware has he taken cognizance of Morgan's part in founding the science of kinship ("Some Problems of Bantu Sociology," *Bantu Studies* [Johannesburg, 1922], I, 40).

22. "To Morgan we owe a discovery and analysis of classificatory kinship terminologies, with all that they mean, and that is really a vast aspect of primitive sociology" (B. Malinowski, in his Introd. to H. Ian Hogbin, *Law and Order in Polynesia* [London, 1934], p. xlv).

23. R. H. Lowie (*Primitive Society* [New York, 1920], p. 391, and *History of Ethnological Theory* [New York, 1937], p. 50) and Stern (*op. cit.*, p. 138) have pointed

out that Maine formulated a like distinction sixteen years before Morgan; and they give one the impression ("a distinction adopted by Morgan . . . . [Lowie, *History of Ethnological Theory*, p. 50]) that Morgan merely developed Maine's idea. It is true that, in 1861, Maine distinguished between blood tie and local contiguity as bases of political organization (*op. cit.*, pp. 124–26). Morgan, however, emphasized the property basis of civil society as well as territorial boundaries, whereas Maine did not. Morgan's use and development of this idea are distinctly his own.

24. "Indeed we may agree with Morgan that the passage from lower forms of civilization to higher forms such as our own was essentially a passage from society based on kinship to the state based on political organization" (Radcliffe-Brown, "Some Problems of Bantu Sociology," pp. 40–41).

25. Morgan used the word "gens," of Greek derivation, instead of the Gaelic "clan." We employ the latter term, as it is more widely used and understood.

26. This is not wholly and absolutely true. There are minor and insignificant exceptions to this, as to many another generalization in science. But, by and large, it holds.

27. In primitive society we find distinctions which rest upon such things as the exclusive right of one group in a tribe to certain titles or crests. But this does not constitute a *class* division as the term is here used. By "class division" we mean that one group in society is supported by the labor of another group.

28. "The Family and Its Functions," *Recent Social Trends* (New York, 1933).

29. *Ancient Society*, p. 389.

30. *Ibid.*, p. 505.

31. *Ibid.*, p. 540.

32. *Ibid.*, p. 505. "Government, institutions and laws are simply contrivances for the creation and protection of property," observes Morgan (Leslie A. White [ed.], *Extracts from the European Travel Journal of Lewis H. Morgan* ["Rochester Historical Society Publications," Vol. XVI (Rochester, N.Y., 1937)], p. 269).

33. *Ancient Society*, p. 505.

34. *Ibid.*, p. 552. This noble passage has inspired and impressed many. The distinguished German sociologist, Ferdinand Tönnies, quoted it more than once (see "The Problems of Social Structure," *Proceedings of the Congress of Arts and Sciences at St. Louis, 1904* [Boston and New York, 1906], V, 839).

35. *Ancient Society* p. 551.

36. *Extracts from the European Travel Journal*, pp. 263–64.

37. *Ibid.*, p. 376.

38. See also Lowie's appraisal of Morgan, "Lewis H. Morgan in Historical Perspective," in R. H. Lowie (ed.), *Essays in Anthropology* (Berkeley, 1936); and *History of Ethnological Theory*, chap. vi.

39. Berthold Laufer in his review of Lowie's *Culture and Ethnology* (*American Anthropologist*, XX [1918], 90).

40. *Science*, XX (1904), 513–24.

41. *Oceania*, Vol. I, Nos. 1–4 (1930–31).

42. Morgan wrote the following on Australia: "Australian Kinship, from Original Memoranda of Rev. Lorimer Fison," *Proceedings of the American Academy of Arts and Sciences*, Vol. VIII (1872); "Organization of Society upon the Basis of Sex," *Ancient Society*, Part II, chap. i; and Introd. to Fison and Howitt, *op. cit.*

43. They dedicated their book, *Kamilaroi and Kurnai*, to Morgan.

44. "The Mind of Primitive Man," *New Republic*, XCVIII (1939), 303.

45. *Op. cit.*, p 23.

46. In an essay entitled "Error in Anthropology" (in Joseph Jastrow [ed.], *The Story of Human Error* [New York, 1936], p. 313, which was, perhaps, not the most fortunate place in which to make such a claim).

47. "Morgan's Attitude Toward Religion and Science," *American Anthropologist*, XLVI (1944), 218–30. Lowie's contribution to this conception of Morgan, which was not cited in the essay just mentioned, is to be found in *History of Ethnological Theory*, p. 54.

48. "On Social Structure," *Journal of the Royal Anthropological Institute,* LXX (1940), 11.

49. English translation by E. Untermann (Chicago, 1902); also an English translation, containing Engels' prefaces to the 1st and 4th eds. (New York, 1942).

50. Professor R. H. Lowie has, in his chapter on "Property" (chap. ix), in *Primitive Society,* made a heroic effort to obscure the distinction which Morgan drew between the communal tenure of property (or natural resources) in primitive society and the institution of private property in modern society. This chapter in Lowie's book was singled out for special praise by Edward Sapir in his review of *Primitive Society* (*Freeman,* Vol. I, June 30, 1920).

CHAPTER V

LESTER FRANK WARD: THE RECONSTRUCTION OF SOCIETY BY SOCIAL SCIENCE

HARRY ELMER BARNES

I. GENERAL CHARACTERISTICS OF WARD'S SOCIOLOGICAL SYSTEM

AMONG American writers it can be said that Lester F. Ward (1841–1913) produced the most impressive and comprehensive system of sociology and was also the earliest systematic American sociologist. His *Dynamic Sociology,* which many critics consider his *magnum opus,* appeared in 1883, about midway between the publication of the first and last volumes of Spencer's *Principles of Sociology*. In addition to many articles in periodicals, Ward's sociological system was embodied in six considerable volumes.[1]

Whatever may be the estimate of the future regarding the place of Ward in the history of sociology, it is certain that no other sociologist approached the subject equipped with a body of scientific knowledge which equaled that possessed by Ward. Herbert Spencer's *Synthetic Philosophy* may display more acute reasoning powers and a greater talent for the logical marshaling of evidence, but his scientific knowledge was not at all comparable to that possessed by Ward.

Ward's formal scientific career was that of government expert in paleobotany, to which he made contributions only second in importance to his work in sociology.[2] Ward's predilection for introducing his botanical terminology into his sociology often gives the latter as strange, technical, and repellent a tone as is to be found in the writings of the extreme "Organicists." Some of his scientific terms, however, such as "sympodical development," "synergy," "creative synthesis," "gynaecocracy," and "social telesis," are rather ingenious and have been fairly widely absorbed into conventional sociological thought and expression. A complete exposition of Ward's sociological system is manifestly impossible within the scope of the present work. Attention will be confined to his cardinal contributions.

As to the subject matter of sociology, Ward says: "My thesis is that the subject matter of sociology is human achievement. It is not what men are but what they do. It is not the structure but the function."[3] Since nearly all the earlier sociologists had been chiefly concerned with an analysis of social structure, Ward's point of approach was novel and epoch-making. The divisions of sociology are two—pure and applied. Pure sociology is theoretical and seeks to establish the principles of the science. Applied sociology is practical and points out the possible applications of pure sociology to social betterment. It "deals with artificial means of accelerating spontaneous processes of nature."[4]

Ward divides the body of his sociological system, accordingly, into "genesis" and "telesis." The former treats of the origin and spontaneous development of social structures and functions and the latter deals with the conscious improvement of society. In the department of social genesis, Ward's most important contributions may be summarized under the following headings: sympodial development, creative synthesis, synergy, the law of parsimony, the functions and biological origin of mind, social statics and dynamics, and the classification of the social forces.

The natural or genetic development of society is "sympodial." By this, Ward means that type of development found in certain plants in which the trunk, after developing to a certain extent, gives off a branch or sympode, which, from that point onward, virtually becomes the trunk, until it is, in turn, displaced by another sympode. The doctrine of "creative synthesis," which Ward adopted from the German psychologist, Wilhelm Wundt, he explains as denoting that "each combination is something more than the mere sum of its component factors."[5] Every synthesis of nature is, like the chemical compound, a new creation. This is probably the most useful of the contributions of Ward's pure science to his sociology. "Synergy," a word derived in part from botany and in part from Hegelian dialectic, is defined as "the systematic and organic working together of the antithetical forces of nature."[6] This is one of the basic conceptions underlying the theory of the spontaneous development of society. Finally, the "law of parsimony," which is the basic law of social mechanics, is described as the tendency of natural forces to work along the line of least resistance or greatest attraction.[7] The identity of this with Spencer's principle of motion along the line of least resistance is obvious.

With his characteristic daring and confidence, Ward describes the origin of life and the biological basis of mind. Life originated through the process of "zoism," which was a creative synthesis taking the form of the recompounding of the highest known chemical properties.[8] The mind is also a creative product of "zoism." It originated in the fact of "awareness," and its irreducible element is the capacity of detecting and differentiating painful and pleasurable stimuli coming from the environment.[9] Feeling and desire, which had an earlier origin than the intellect, are the dynamic and impelling forces of mind; intellect, which is a later and higher product, is the directive faculty.[10]

Ward considered his distinction between social statics and social dynamics and his discussion of the nature of each of these to be one of his most important theoretical contributions. Social statics deals with social equilibration and the establishment of a social order—the building-up of social structures.[11] The development of the social order is a "struggle for structure" rather than a struggle for existence. The best structures survive. In the growth of social structures social synergy is the most important principle. It is the force which creates all structures and explains all organization. Through this principle of synergy there is brought about the collaboration of the antithetical forces of nature in the following sequence of processes: collision, conflict, antagonism, opposition, antithesis, competition, interaction, compromise, collaboration, co-operation, and organization.

Synergy, in the development of the social order, takes place mainly through the process that Ward calls "social karyokinesis." This is the social analogue of fertilization in the biological field and is manifested in the contact, amalgamation, and assimilation of different social groups. All the stages enumerated in the above sequence are exemplified in this process, which ends in the production of a homogeneous nation. Ward here follows the theory of Ratzenhofer and Gumplowicz regarding the "struggle of races and social groups" as the main factor in state-building.

Social dynamics deals with social progress or the changes in the structure of society.[12] In social dynamics there are three fundamental principles—difference of potential, innovation, and conation. The difference of potential is manifested in the crossings of cultures which take place through social assimilation and amalgamation. Progress comes from a fusion of unlike elements. Innovation, which is the social analogue of the sport or mutation in the organic world, is the product of psychic exuberance. Conation, or social effort, is that application of social energy from which achievement results. This achievement takes the form of the satisfaction of desire, the preservation of life, and the modification of the environment.

Ward classifies the social forces as ontogenetic or preservative, phylo-genetic or reproductive, and sociogenetic or spiritual.[13] It is in connec-tion with his discussion of the phylogenetic forces that Ward develops his famous theory of "gynaecocracy," according to which he holds that the female sex was the original sex in nature and was the most important until it was subordinated by the social restraints imposed upon it after man discovered his relation to the child.[14]

In his exposition of the principle of social telesis, Ward lays down the fundamental proposition that energy must be controlled if evolution is to result. There are two possible methods of control: the unconscious control of nature manifested in *genesis* and the conscious direction by mind involved in *telesis*.[15] The conscious method of control by mind is manifestly superior to the unconscious control of nature. Nature is wasteful in providing an immense mass of raw materials and leaving them to be improved very slowly through natural selection. The tendency of mind is to economize through foresight and the adjustment of means to ends. This control of the dynamic forces of nature and society through the adjustment of means to ends is what Ward designates as "telesis."

In this process of conscious or telic control of the social forces, the development of the state was the most important step ever taken by man or society.[16] Nevertheless, though the state is the chief agent through which the conscious control of the social process is and will be carried on, society cannot perfect this conscious control through any agency until there is developed an adequate and sufficiently diffused knowledge of the nature and the operation of the social forces. Therefore, the pro-vision of a system of education which will make possible the universal diffusion of this essential knowledge is the indispensable prerequisite to the complete development of collective or social telesis.[17]

In conclusion, one may safely say that Ward's outstanding contribu-tions to sociology were his grasp of the relation between cosmic and social evolution and his doctrine of the superiority of the conscious to the unconscious control of the social process. In neither of these respects has he been surpassed by any other sociologist.[18] Of these two cardinal contributions the latter is by far the more important, for the obvious reason that the former is at best but picturesque and eloquent guesswork and must always be so until the range of human knowledge is greatly extended. The latter, however, is perhaps the most important single contribution of sociology to human thought, and Ward's significance rests mainly upon the fact that his presentation of this conception has been the most effective that sociology has so far produced. Professor F. H. Giddings has summed up this aspect of Ward's system with characteristic clarity:

> Throughout all Ward's work there runs one dominating and organizing thought. Human Society, as we who live now know it, is not the passive product of unconscious forces. It lies within the domain of cosmic law, but so does the mind of man: and this mind of man has knowingly, artfully, adapted and readapted its social environment, and with reflective intelligence has begun to shape it into an instrument wherewith to fulfill man's will. With forecasting wisdom man will perfect it, until it shall be at once adequate and adaptable to all its uses. This he will do not by creative impulse evolving in a void, but constructive intelligence shaping the substantial stuff of verified scientific knowledge. Wherefore, scientific knowledge must be made the possession of mankind. Education must not merely train the mind. It must also equip and store with knowledge.
>
> This great thought Dr. Ward apprehended, expressed, explained, illuminated, drove home to the mind of all who read his pages, as no other writer, ancient or modern, has never done. It is his enduring and cogent contribution to sociology.[19]

II. SPECIFIC CONTRIBUTIONS TO SOCIAL AND POLITICAL THEORY

A. THE RELATION OF SOCIOLOGY TO POLITICAL SCIENCE

The conception which Ward holds of the relation of sociology to political science is apparent from his view of the general relation between sociology and the special social sciences. The special social sciences furnish the data which the more comprehensive social science—sociology—co-ordinates and uses as the basis of its generalizations. But sociology is more than the mere sum of the special social sciences. It is the true creative synthesis and, like a chemical compound, is a new product and of a higher order than the constituent units. Political science, as a special social science, furnishes the data for the generalizations which sociology offers upon political problems. Ward's famous and authoritative statement of the nature of sociology and its relation to the special social sciences is worth quoting:

> It is not quite enough to say that it is a synthesis of them [the special social sciences] all. It is the new compound which their synthesis creates. It is not any of them and it is not all of them. It is that science which they spontaneously generate. It is a genetic product, the last term in the genesis of science. The special social sciences are the units of aggregation that organically combine to create

sociology, but they lose their individuality as completely as do chemical units, and the resultant product is wholly unlike them and is of a higher order. All this is true of any of the complex sciences, but sociology, standing at the head of the entire series, is enriched by all the truths of nature and embraces all truth. It is the *scientia scientiarum*.[19a]

B. GENERAL DEFINITIONS AND CONCEPTS

Ward's distinctions, if they may be called such, between the terms "society," "state," "government," and "nation" are very vague and unsatisfactory. He certainly did little to clarify the terminology of political science. He does not employ any of the above terms in a consistent or uniform manner, nor does he in any place define any of them in an exact sense.

"Society" is used as the generic term for associated life and also to describe advanced forms of human associations. That he did not regard the distinction between the terms "state," "government," and "nation" as fundamental is apparent from the following passage: "If anyone objects to the use of the word government, there is no reason why the word nation or state may not be substituted. The name is not essential."

However careless Ward may have been in his use of terms to describe the fundamental political organization of society, he was not in the least equivocal in regard to its importance.[20] He invariably insists that the state or the government is the most important social institution. He repeatedly emphasized the value of the organic analogy which represents the state as the brain of the social organism. The following paragraph, which is almost Hegelian in spirit, best summarized Ward's conception of the state:

We thus see that the state, though genetic in its origin, is telic in its method; that it has but one purpose, function, or mission, that of securing the welfare of society; that its mode of operation is that of preventing the anti-social action of individuals: that in doing this it increases the freedom of human action so long as it is not anti-social; that the state is therefore essentially moral and ethical; that its own acts must necessarily be ethical; that being a natural product it must in a large sense be representative; that in point of fact it is always as good as society will permit it to be; that while thus far in the history of society the state has rarely performed acts that tend to advance mankind, it has always been the condition to all achievement, making possible all the social, industrial, artistic, literary, and scientific activities that go on within the state and under its protection. There is no other institution with which the state may be compared, and yet, in view of all this, it is the most important of all human institutions.[21]

Ward did not enter into any formal discussion of the problem of sovereignty. He defines liberty as "the power to act in obedience to desire."[22] The love of liberty has thus been instinctive and universal in mankind. In theory, government is the necessary foe of liberty. In fact, however, government, by checking license, has prevented man from losing more liberty than it has taken away. The restraint of absolute liberty by government has made possible the development of man's intellectual powers, so that ultimately he may be restored to the possession of his complete original liberty, but not a liberty which is based upon ignorance. The liberty of the future will be one that is founded upon an intelligent comprehension of man's relations to society and will not require crude artificial restraints to prevent its enjoyment from threatening the disintegration of society.

Ward relates his interpretation of political parties very definitely to his theory of social mechanics. The fundamental principle underlying his sociological interpretation of the struggles between different political parties is that of "social synergy." Party antagonism, in reality, brings about a co-operation between seemingly antithetical forces and secures their working together toward an end of which they are unconscious:

The vigorous interaction of the two forces, which looks so much like antagonism, strife, and struggle, transforms force into energy and energy into power, and builds political and social structures. And after they are constructed, the same influences transform them, and it is this that constitutes social progress. Political institutions —the laws of every country—are the product of this political synergy, the crystallized action of legislative bodies created by political parties.[23]

In the same way, therefore, that the struggle between races and groups creates society and the state, the struggle between political parties within the state transforms the state and produces political progress. Moral, rather than technical, questions are best adapted for political issues. The progressive and liberal parties, which are characterized by the advocacy of an extension of governmental activity, are the real friends of individualism and liberty. The "coming slavery," to use Spencer's term, has already arrived, says Ward, in the form of the plutocratic, laissez faire control of society and political organization by the conservative capitalistic parties. The progressive parties, which stand for collective action, are the force which is attempting to secure emancipation from this slavery and exploitation.

C. THE ORIGIN OF SOCIETY AND THE STATE, AND THE STAGES OF POLITICAL EVOLUTION

While Professor Small remarked with accuracy that Ward modified his sociological thought but little between the publication of his *Dynamic*

Sociology and his death, this is decidedly not the case with his theory of the origin of the state.

The theory which he advanced in the *Dynamic Sociology* was quaint and curious, being virtually a combination of Hobbes's view of a pre-social state of nature with Rousseau's conception of the origin of the state through an artifice of the most powerful individuals.[24] In the first place, Ward here envisages four broad stages of social development. The first was the solitary or "autarchic" stage, in which man lived in solitude and as far from a social state as was in keeping with the possibility of propagating and rearing his kind. The earliest condition of man was thus presocial, if not antisocial. The second stage in social evolution was the "anarchic," or that of the "constrained aggregate." Social groups had expanded through natural or genetic increase, but, being without government, they lived in a "state of utmost liberty and utmost license." The third stage he designates as the "national" or "politarchic" stage, which was distinguished by the origin of a crude form of government. The wars which took place between these first national groups led to the formation of larger political societies and will ultimately lead to the development of the fourth or final stage in social evolution. This ultimate stage, which he designates as the "cosmopolitan" or "pantarchic," will come when social integration has produced the world state.

In his specific account of the origin of the state in the *Dynamic Sociology,* Ward starts with the utterly untenable theory of the antisocial nature of primitive man. He denies the validity of the Aristotelian tradition regarding the sociability of man. Since the passions of primitive man were intense and the means of satisfying them limited, the condition of life must have been one of conflict, and orderly society could not have been possible until the development of political control and protection. The origin of society and government must have been coeval. But mankind did not find its way out of this state of primitive anarchy through the social contract. The people as a whole never sought government; government always created itself. Government was initiated by a few especially ambitious individuals who were possessed of superior sagacity and who desired social power and position. They disguised their real intentions by claiming to intervene to protect the weak and oppressed: "The plan must have consisted in speciously claiming as the real object the protection of the injured and the punishment of the injuring. This, as the sagacity of the founders of government foresaw, would secure them adherents and confirm their authority."[25] Owing to this insidious and oppressive origin of political authority, man has ever since that time been trying to escape from the burdens which government has imposed. But the many evils that have accompanied the development of government are not the result of the application of the principle of political control; they are a consequence of the perversions of sound and wise government by mankind.

During the interval between the appearance of his *Dynamic Sociology* and the publication of the *Pure Sociology,* Ward became acquainted with the now generally accepted theory of Ferguson, Spencer, Bagehot, Gumplowicz, and Ratzenhofer, to the effect that the state, as it is defined by political science, originated through the processes of group conflict, amalgamation, and assimilation. This doctrine Ward accepted with great enthusiasm. He says of it: "It furnishes the first scientific, or in the least satisfactory, theory that has been advanced as to the origin and true constitution of the state, so that, after grasping this principle in its entirety, all the old notions about the state become rubbish, and any work on the nature of the state that does not recognize and start from this standpoint is superficial and practically worthless."[26]

D. THE FORMS OF GOVERNMENT

As a general classification of the forms of government, Ward proposes the terms "autocracies," "aristocracies," and "democracies." Within the general classification of democracy, Ward distinguishes three distinct variations: "physiocracy," "plutocracy," and "sociocracy." Physiocracy is that type of government which developed in western Europe as a result of the teaching of the Physiocrats and Adam Smith and of such individualistic writers as Wilhelm von Humboldt and Spencer. It is that sort of laissez faire government that is based upon honest but wrongheaded individualistic political philosophy.

Plutocracy is that perversion of physiocracy that resulted when, in the early nineteenth century, the corrupt and selfish vested interests of capitalism exploited the individualistic political philosophy for the purpose of maintaining themselves in their position of ascendancy.. The exponents of this theory make a wide use of the individualistic appeal for governmental inactivity and utilize the deep-seated prejudice of the masses against government, so that they may be allowed to continue their exploitation of society. This perversion of individualism, which originated a century ago, is still the current form of contemporary political theory and organization.

Sociocracy is the next logical stage in political evolution. It is, in reality, the ideal democracy from which the current partisanship, ignorance, hypocrisy, and stupidity have been eliminated. In short, it is administration of the government by society for the public interest, and not the present exploitation of society for the benefit of a particular party or group of interests. Sociocracy does not lay stress primarily upon the external form of government but "goes to the substance, and denotes that, in whatever manner organized, it is the duty of society to act consciously and intelligently, as becomes an enlightened age, in the direction of guarding its own interests and working out its own destiny."[27] Under a sociocratic form of government "society would inquire in a business way without fear, favor, or bias, into everything that concerned its welfare, and if it found obstacles it would remove them, and if it found opportunities it would improve them. In a word, society would do under the same circumstances just what an intelligent individual would do. It would further in all possible ways its own interests."[28]

E. THE FUNCTIONS OF THE STATE

In his theories regarding the function and sphere of state activity, Ward was the most vigorous and consistent opponent of Spencerian and Sumnerian laissez faire individualism among the strictly sociological writers of his time.[29] In fact, Ward's treatment of this subject is the most satisfactory and important division of his social and political theories. While no writer has been more scathing in his condemnation of the defects and evils in contemporary political systems, Ward always distinguished carefully between the institution of government and its perversions. For the latter he had unlimited contempt, but he never lost his faith in the efficacy of the government as an agent of social reform, if it could be put on a scientific basis and purged of its corruption and stupidity.

Ward enumerates four chief functions of government: the restraint, protection, accommodation, and amelioration of society.[30] The first of these has never been a legitimate function; the second will be necessary so long as men do not refrain from injuring their fellows; the third is, and always will be, an indispensable function of government; while the fourth, which is the most important of all, has been scarcely put into action at all.

The restraint of the citizens by the government is not conducted in the interests of the community but is designed to allow the ruling classes to proceed with their exploitation. How long it will be before society divests the government of this function will depend upon the rapidity of the growth of social intelligence and enlightenment. By the "protective" function of government Ward means the "police" function, which is concerned with the prevention of fraud and violence. This cannot be dispensed with until the fraudulent and violent elements in society are eliminated by the general advance of enlightenment and intelligence. The function of accommodation, however, is never likely to be outgrown:

Man is neither ubiquitous, omniscient, nor omnipotent; hence he needs agents to transact business in localities where he cannot be; to acquire skill and dexterity in subjects with which everyone cannot afford time to acquaint himself; and to perform duties by means of organization which individuals, acting independently, would not possess the strength to perform. In short, society needs and must always have an organized agency to represent it.[31]

In carrying on its restraining, protecting, and accommodating functions, government has not directly promoted progress. But, while possessing no directly progressive element, it has been the indispensable prerequisite of all progress. Government can directly improve the condition of society in a conscious or telic manner if the legislators will only become social scientists. There can be no scientific government, no important development of the ameliorative function of government, until legislators have gained a knowledge of the nature and means of controlling the social forces, in the same way that the natural scientist discovers the physical laws of nature and applies this knowledge in controlling natural laws and adapting them to the service of technology.[32]

Ward's whole defense of government as the most effective instrument of society in promoting progress rests primarily upon his abovementioned distinction between honest and intelligent government and its past and present perversions. As to origins, the extant governments almost universally arose in exploitation. They were established by, and have been conducted in the interest of, those who desired to govern and exploit. A rationally constituted government should be instituted by, and conducted for the benefit of, those desiring to be governed. Again, whereas in our actual governments the people look up to the government as their master and the government regards the citizens in the light of subjects, in a rational political system the officers of government would be viewed as public servants and would be compelled, upon pain of removal, to perform their stipulated duties. In a model government the social distance which separates the governing and the governed would be eliminated. The people would recognize that they are the source of political authority and that the government is merely their agent. Governments are at present analogous to large stock companies conducted in the interest of the officers and not for the profit of the stockholders. Progress toward the perfection of government must first come "in the direction of acquainting every member of society with the special nature of the institution, and awakening him to a more vivid conception of his personal interest in its management."

In his essay on "False Notions of Government,"[33] Ward points out the unfortunate results which have come about as a result of the failure to distinguish between the true principles and the actual practices of government. The deep-seated popular distrust of government was very beneficial in the earlier periods of despotism, but the recent democratization of government has removed the need for this suspicious and wrongheaded attitude toward political control and direction, and its persistence is detrimental. It keeps good men from entering public life; it perverts the notion of the true purpose of government; it intensifies party strife by emphasizing the aspect of spoil; it makes government worse by encouraging the politician to live up to his unsavory reputation; and, finally, it deprives government of much of its usefulness by weakening its protective function.

These "false notions of government" must be removed. The people must be made to grasp the correct conception of government and take the proper steps to remove its abuses and use it for their own ends. Accordingly, Ward severely criticizes as obstructionists those "Misarchists," of whom the most conspicuous examples among sociologists have been Herbert Spencer, W. G. Sumner, and Jacques Novicow, for their strenuous attempts to perpetuate this "pernicious view of government." The exploitation of society by organized wealth requires the intervention of government at present, just as the exploitation by individuals, tyrants, nobles, and lawless characters created a need for the origin of the protective function of government.

The basic principles of Ward's sociology are nowhere better displayed than in his doctrines regarding the solution of social problems and maladjustment through the agency of governmental activity—in other words, his treatment of government as the chief instrument in collective or social telesis.

That the government must be the seat of control of the social process is evident from the fact that it alone can be viewed as the social analogue of the brain in the individual organism. The present stupidity of the personnel and activities of governments is the basis of the familiar argument that government can never give evidence of any creditable degree of intelligence. When the general level of social intelligence is raised, there is every reason to believe that the knowledge of those in control of the government will be proportionately improved.[34]

In his *Psychic Factors of Civilization*,[35] Ward summarizes what he regards as the indispensable prerequisites for the successful operation of social or collective telesis through the instrumentality of government. The legislators must either be social scientists or work in co-operation with sociologists. The prevalent confusing legislative methods must be eliminated. This can best be brought about by an extension of the use of the committee system and by conferring upon the executive the power to participate in legislation. Finally, there must be a greater use of statistics as the data upon which all scientific lawmaking must be based.[36]

Like Comte, to whom he was much indebted for many of his political theories and much of his political terminology, Ward placed his chief reliance on sociology as the source of the information which is essential for any extensive development of scientific government. Ward's legislators, like the priests of the Positivist regime, were to be trained sociologists. Hence the diffusion of a knowledge of fundamental sociological principles must precede the scientific development and application of governmental activity in behalf of social reform. The legislators must be thoroughly acquainted with the nature of, and the method of controlling, the social forces. In current jargon, Ward was an ardent supporter of government through a "brain trust" and the great sociological forerunner of the "social-planning" program. Unfortunately, however, says Ward, sociological knowledge itself is as yet in a very imperfect and undeveloped stage. In 1903, according to Ward, it was in practically the same stage of development that physics and chemistry were in during the fifteenth century. This indispensable sociological knowledge must be imparted by an improved system of education.

Ward takes as his point of departure in discussing the social function of education the thesis that the social forces can be directed into safe and useful channels only if their nature and the means of their control are understood. Education should thus be valued in proportion "as it gives to its possessor correct views of life, of his relations to society, and to nature." The educational system which embraces this useful type of information should be carried on by the state and should be universal. The whole sociological problem and significance of education he sums up in the following characteristic paragraph:

It is the question whether the social system shall always be left to nature, always be genetic and spontaneous, and be allowed to drift listlessly on, intrusted to the by no means always progressive influences which have developed it and brought it to its present condition, or whether it shall be regarded as a proper subject of art, treated as other natural products have been treated by human intelligence, and made as much superior to nature, in this only proper sense of the word, as other artificial productions are superior to natural ones.[37]

When this revised and universal system of education is put into effect, government, which will be sociocratic in form, can be conducted on truly scientific principles, and it will then be in a position to promote progress by the indirect or telic method of "social invention" and "attractive legislation." True social invention "consists in making such adjustments as will induce men to act in the manner most advantageous to society." These adjustments must take the form of "attractive legislation," which will replace the wrongheaded and repressive legislation of the present day.

This principle of "attractive legislation" Ward explains in the following manner: The "desire, passions, and propensities of men" are the great impelling forces of society. They have vast potentialities for both good and evil. Repressive legislation, which constitutes the vast majority of modern laws, simply curbs this energy without deriving any benefit from it. Attractive legislation would not aim to check or restrain this vital energy of society but, instead, would divert it from harmful forms of expression and would direct it into constructive channels. In terms of the new dynamic psychology, it would provide a rational method of *sublimating* social energy.

The scientific statesmanship of the future must attempt to guide and utilize social forces and energy in the same manner that the applied scientists of today control and utilize the physical energy of nature. Ward's best summary of the fundamental characteristics of the political regime based upon the principles of attractive legislation and collective telesis is contained in the following paragraphs, which are, at the same time, a fairly adequate summary of his whole social philosophy:

As a scientific investigator, the legislator would then set for himself the task of devising means to render harmless those forces now seen to be working evil results, and to render useful those now running to waste. Not only would the present prohibitive legislation, which seeks to accomplish its ends by direct, or brute method, be rapidly supplanted by attractive legislation accomplishing its purposes by the indirect, or intellectual, method, and thus fulfilling the protective functions of government at a saving of enormous loss through the friction of opposition, but the accommodative function would now be in condition to advance toward the position of a truly ameliorative one.

Society, possessed for the first time of a completely integrated consciousness, could at last proceed to map out a field of independent operation for the systematic realization of its own interests, in the same manner that an intelligent and keen-witted individual pursues his life-purposes. Not only would protection and accommodation be secured without loss of liberty and at the least possible cost to society, but directly progressive measures would be adopted looking to the organization of human happiness.

Fully realizing the character and mode of operation of the truly progressive agencies of society, government would not simply foster and protect these, but would increase and intensify them and their influence. No longer doubting that progress, upon the whole, must be in proportion to the degree and universality of intelligence, no effort or expense would be spared to impart to every citizen an equal and adequate amount of useful knowledge.[88]

Ward's prophetic vein was not entirely exhausted by this eloquent picture of the scientific legislation of the future. He even dared to predict that, in the still more remote future, with the perfection of the intellect and the completeness of knowledge, the state and government may disappear. This seems to be a denial, however, of Ward's statement mentioned above, to the effect that society would never outgrow the need for the accommodating function of government.

III. SUMMARY APPRAISAL OF WARD'S SOCIAL THOUGHT

In summarizing Lester F. Ward's contributions to social thought, it is fair to say: (1) that Ward made the most impressive effort by a sociologist to link up the concepts of natural and social science; (2) that he was the first notable sociologist of post-Darwinian days to emphasize the difference between biological and social evolution and to contend that the latter can be brought under social and mental control; (3) that he clearly distinguished between the genetic method of organic evolution and the telic processes of social development; (4) that he forecast the growing trend toward state interference and governmental planning and urged that these be guided by realistic social education; (5) that he was, thus, the father of the "social-studies" movement, in so far as this is related to public advancement and social progress; (6) that he anticipated by several generations the current social emphasis in education; and (7) that he stressed the fact that the data and laws of social science are chiefly useful in promoting social betterment and finding a short cut to utopia, which can otherwise be reached only by the slow and wasteful methods of naturalistic evolution.[39]

NOTES

1. *Dynamic Sociology* (2 vols.; New York, 1883); *The Psychic Factors of Civilization* (Boston, 1893); *The Outlines of Sociology* (New York, 1898); *Pure Sociology* (New York, 1903); *Applied Sociology* (Boston, 1904). His *Pure Sociology* appeared in a reduced and clarified form in J. Q. Dealey and L. F. Ward, *Textbook of Sociology* (New York, 1905). Ward's minor works and notices of his major contributions are brought together in his "mental autobiography," *Glimpses of the Cosmos* (8 vols.; New York, 1913).

Of these works, *Dynamic Sociology* is the best extended exposition of his whole social philosophy, a briefer and clearer presentation of which is to be found in the second part of his *Outlines of Sociology*. *Pure Sociology* is the authoritative exposition of his sociological system, which, again, is more clearly presented in Dealey and Ward's *Textbook of Sociology*. His social psychology is best brought together in *Psychic Factors of Civilization*, while his *Applied Sociology* is the classic exposition of his conception of social telesis.

His *Pure Sociology* is reviewed by H. H. Bawden in *American Journal of Sociology*, IX, (1903–4), 408–15; is criticized in detail by A. W. Small, *American Journal of Sociology*, IX (1903–4), 404–7, 567–75, 703–7; and is critically analyzed by J. M. Gillette in *American Journal of Sociology*, XX (1914–15), 31–67.

Estimations of Ward's significance for sociology by eminent sociologists appear in *American Journal of Sociology*, X (1904–5), 643–53; XIX (1913–14), 61–78; XXI (1915–16), 748–58, 824.

The most complete treatment of Ward as man, scientist, and sociologist is the enthusiastic book by Samuel Chugerman, *Lester F. Ward: The American Aristotle* (New York, 1939). There is a well-selected anthology of Ward's sociological writings in Clement Wood, *The Substance of the Sociology of Lester F. Ward* (New York, 1930). For biographical details see E. P. Cape, *Lester F. Ward: A Personal Sketch* (New York, 1930).

2. His academic career was limited to lectures at several university summer-school sessions and six years (1906–12) as professor of sociology at Brown University. For the formative experiences in Ward's life see B. J. Stern, *Young Ward's Diary* (New York, 1935).

3. *Pure Sociology*, p. 15.

4. *Ibid.*, pp. 3, 431.

5. *Ibid.*, p. 79.

6. *Ibid.*, p. 171.

7. *Ibid.*, p. 161.

8. *Ibid.*, pp. 115–19.

9. *Ibid.*, pp. 119–35.

10. *Ibid.*, pp. 97, 99 ff., 124 ff., 142, 467 ff.

11. *Ibid.*, p. 175 ff.

12. *Ibid.*, pp. 221 ff.

13. *Ibid.*, p. 261.

14. *Ibid.*, pp. 296 ff., 336–41, 345.

15. *Ibid.*, pp. 463 ff.

16. *Ibid.*, p. 551.

17. *Ibid.*, pp. 573–75; *Dynamic Sociology*, Vol. II, chap. xiv; *Applied Sociology, passim.* With this outline of Ward's sociology based upon his *Pure Sociology* compare his own summary in the Preface of his *Dynamic Sociology.*

18. Cf. A. W. Small, *American Journal of Sociology*, XXI (1915–16), 752; F. H. Giddings, *American Journal of Sociology*, XIX (1913–14), 67–68.

19. Giddings, *loc. cit.* It is hardly necessary to point out that this is essentially a contradiction of Spencer's thesis and that it constitutes the chief difference between the social philosophy of the two men who were to sociology what Niebuhr and Ranke were to history and Turgot and Adam Smith to economics.

19a. *Pure Sociology*, p. 91.

20. *Psychic Factors of Civilization*, p. 297. Cf. *Pure Sociology*, p. 188, where, in opposition to the conventional view, he argues that the institution of government by society required and produced the state.

21. *Pure Sociology*, p. 555.

22. *Dynamic Sociology*, II, 233.

23. Ward, "The Sociology of Political Parties," *American Journal of Sociology*, XIV (January, 1908), 440–41.

24. As expressed in Rousseau's famous *Second Discourse*. For Ward's own frank admission of the archaic and erroneous nature of his earliest theory of the state see his "Sociology and the State," *American Journal of Sociology*, XVI (March, 1910), 679–80.

25. *Dynamic Sociology*, II, 224. This tendency of the few to dominate in political control has been scientifically analyzed by F. H. Giddings, who designates it as the principle of "protocracy" (see his *Responsible State* [Boston, 1918], pp. 19 ff.).

26. Ward, *American Journal of Sociology*, VII (1901–2), 762; cf. also *ibid.*, XV (1909–10), 679–80; *Pure Sociology*, pp. 204 ff. As Ward agrees entirely with Gumplowicz and Ratzenhofer upon the subject of the origin of the state, it will not be necessary to repeat his version of their doctrine. In addition to the reference to *Pure Sociology*, Ward's interpretation of the Gumplowicz-Ratzenhofer theory of the origin of the state is best summarized in *American Journal of Sociology*, X (1904–5), 643–53; and *Publications of the American Economic Association* (3d ser., 1904), V, No. 2, 187 ff. The criticisms which can be directed against this group-struggle origin of the state are best formulated by J. Novicow in his *La Critique de Darwinisme social* (Paris, 1910); and E. C. Hayes, *An Introduction to the Study of Sociology* (Philadelphia, 1915), pp. 538 ff.

27. *The Psychic Factors of Civilization*, p. 311, introductory note.

28. *Ibid.*, p. 327.

29. See, in particular, his "Professor Sumner's Social Classes," in *Glimpses of the Cosmos*, III, 301–5; and "The Political Ethics of Herbert Spencer," *ibid.*, V, 38–66.

30. *Dynamic Sociology*, II, 212, 217, 231.

31. *Ibid.*, pp. 241–42.

32. *Ibid.*, pp. 245–50; *Pure Sociology*, pp. 568–69; *Outlines of Sociology*, pp. 187–89; *Psychic Factors of Civilization*, pp. 309–12. Ward, then, essentially adopted the doctrine of Plato and Comte that perfect government could come only when society and government were controlled and directed by sociologists.

33. *Dynamic Sociology*, II, 243.

34. *Outlines of Sociology*, pp. 187–89, 268–76; *Pure Sociology*, p. 565; and *Psychic Factors of Civilization*, p. 297.

35. Pp. 309–12.

36. Cf. Ward's article on "The Way to Scientific Law-making" (1877), reprinted in *Glimpses of the Cosmos*, II, 168–71. This is one of the earliest and clearest statements of the value of statistics in scientific legislation and antedated by five years Jevons' classic exposition of this subject in his *The State in Relation to Labor* (London, 1882); cf. also Graham Wallas, *Human Nature in Politics* (Boston, 1909), pp. 121 ff., 132 ff.

37. *Dynamic Sociology*, II, 632–33; cf. also *Applied Sociology, passim.* Ward's best brief statement of the sociological significance of education is to be found in his address, "Education and Progress," in *Glimpses of the Cosmos*, VI, 333–40. See also E. P. Kimball, *Sociology and Education* (New York, 1932).

38. *Dynamic Sociology*, II, 249–50.

39. For further authoritative material on Ward's significance in social science see J. Q. Dealey, "Lester Frank Ward," in H. W. Odum (ed.), *American Masters of Social Science* (New York, 1927), chap. iii.

CHAPTER VI

THE SOCIOLOGICAL SYSTEM OF FERDINAND TÖNNIES: "COMMUNITY" AND "SOCIETY"*

RUDOLF HEBERLE

I. MAIN FACTS CONCERNING TÖNNIES' LIFE AND ACADEMIC CAREER

FERDINAND TÖNNIES was born in 1855 on a farm in Eiderstedt on the west coast of Schleswig-Holstein. Originally Dutch settlers, his paternal ancestors had been farmers in those parts for over two hundred years. The Tönnies were one of the leading families in this Frisian region, where serfdom had never developed and where many elements of the ancient Germanic rural community had been preserved. His mother came from a rural family in the east of Holstein, which had given to the country many Lutheran pastors and professional men of distinction.

In 1864 the family moved to the small town of Husum. Here the young Tönnies formed a friendship with the much older poet, Theodor Storm, which became one of the important influences in his life.[1] He was graduated from the Gymnasium in 1872, and, not yet seventeen years of age, he began to study classical philology and philosophy at the University of Jena and later at Leipzig, Bonn, Berlin, and Tübingen, where he received the degree of Doctor of Philosophy in 1877. From then on, Tönnies, following his genuine intellectual interest, devoted himself to social philosophy and the social sciences. The influence of the philological training is, however, quite conspicuous even in his later writings.

Among those who, during these student years, left the most lasting imprint on Tönnies' mind were his countryman, Friedrich Paulsen, noted philosopher; Adolph Wagner, the economist; and Wilhelm

* Revised and supplemented reprint from *American Sociological Review*, Vol. II, No. 1 (February, 1937). This article was originally written in German. For the translation, the author is indebted to Mrs. Frank D. Graham, of Princeton. He assumes, however, full responsibility for the present form of the essay.

Wundt, the sociopsychologist.[2] Wagner, with his idea of an increasing regulation of social life by the state, influenced Tönnies' thinking in the direction of state socialism. Wundt's theorem of *Zweckwille* and *Triebwille* obviously left its mark on his thought.

As early as 1877, Tönnies had become interested in Thomas Hobbes, the most outspoken advocate of state omnipotence.[3] His Hobbes studies led him to comprehensive reading in the fields of political philosophy and natural law, as well as in the more recent social sciences. He acquired a thorough knowledge of the German, English, and—to a lesser extent— the French literature. In these years of private studies his main object became the understanding of the true meaning both of the rational school of natural law and of the opposing historical and romantic theories. To him it appeared that "all irrational and less rational forms of thought .... were never simply unreasonable but that they had their peculiar meaning which finally was a derivation from human will."[4] The social theories became to him sociological data in themselves, expressions of social volition and reflections of actual social conditions. It became clear to him that ideas like communism and socialism were to be regarded not as mere phantasms, as thought-out utopias, but as forms of actual social life. The existence of primitive communism had, he believed, been proved by recent ethnological studies, and Tönnies began to conceive of the history of mankind as a movement from original simple communism through various stages of individualism and finally to state and international socialism.[5] These ideas were presented in 1887 in his now famous book, *Gemeinschaft und Gesellschaft*.

Six years earlier Tönnies had become a lecturer (*Privatdozent*) at the University of Kiel, with which he remained affiliated until his dismissal by the National Socialists in 1933. Although Tönnies' connection with the University of Kiel lasted through more than half a century, he always remained in a sense an outsider. Only for eight years, six of which were war years, when the universities were almost deserted, did Tönnies hold the rank of a full professor. While this limited his influence on the younger generation, it gave him leisure for work and liberty to travel, which he did extensively and with great pleasure.[6]

Though conservative in temperament, Tönnies took part in virtually all the more important progressive movements of his time. His special sympathy belonged to the two branches of the organized labor movement—the consumers' co-operatives and the labor unions. In them he saw the beginnings from which a better society might develop.

Tönnies was one of the founders of the German Sociological Society and was its president for many years; he also was an honorary member of the American Sociological Society. His professional contacts and personal friendships with the prominent men and women of his time were numerous and covered a wide range of scholars, writers, artists, and statesmen. While his life lacks any dramatic aspects, it was, never-theless, a rich, intensive life in close contact with the historical processes of the period.

Tönnies died in 1936, over eighty years old, one of the last scholars in our time who could be said to possess a truly universal erudition in the humanities and the cultural and social sciences.

II. TÖNNIES' CHIEF WRITINGS

The works of Ferdinand Tönnies cover so many topics and such wide fields of sociology, social philosophy, economics, and politics that, at first glance, it seems almost impossible in a short essay to do justice to the lifework of a man who, at his death, had surpassed the biblical age by a decade. The task, however, is made lighter by the fact that the focus of Tönnies' scheme of thought lies in the concepts which first appeared in *Gemeinschaft und Gesellschaft*. On this theory Tönnies' international reputation rests. In vigor of thought and beauty of style, *Gemeinschaft und Gesellschaft* has hardly been surpassed by any of the numerous later writings of the author. Here, already, the social-psychological foundations and the fundamental sociological categories of Tönnies' scheme are well and truly laid.

In a large part of his later work Tönnies has "applied" the funda-mental concepts of *Gemeinschaft und Gesellschaft*[7] to special phenomena of social life, as, e.g., morals and folkways[8] or public opinion.[9] The broader public knows Tönnies merely as the author of *Gemeinschaft und Gesellschaft,* but it would be unjust to identify his scientific life-work with the theorem of that book and its application, for, on the one hand, his sociological system was fully developed only in later years and, on the other, his achievements in the social sciences reach far beyond the narrower field of theoretical sociology.

Tönnies' sociological system as a whole was for many years known only to his personal students. It has, indeed, never been published in adequate form but only in some short essays and in the *Einführung in die Soziologie,* a book of his maturer years which did not attain to the classic form of the *Gemeinschaft und Gesellschaft.* The *Einführung,* nevertheless, is quite indispensable to the understanding of Tönnies' theory and, because of its easy style, will be found to be very useful in the teaching of sociology.

Tönnies' interest in sociological problems was stirred by his studies of Thomas Hobbes's philosophy of law and theory of the state and, as we shall see, his own sociology cannot be rightly understood or fully appreciated unless these early studies are kept in mind. In his book on Hobbes and in numerous later papers on problems more or less closely related to Hobbes's philosophy, Tönnies has made valuable contributions to the theory of the modern state and to the philosophy of law. These deserve recognition quite apart from Tönnies' purely sociological writings.

The third and least-known phase of Tönnies' work is that of the empirical investigations to which a considerable part of his lifework was devoted. Among these studies the following may be mentioned here: the surveys of the socioeconomic situation of longshoremen and seamen in Hamburg and other ports, which Tönnies was asked to undertake after a big strike in Hamburg;[10] a study of the relationship between certain moral phenomena and socioeconomic conditions in Schleswig-Holstein;[11] a series of papers on criminality in Schleswig-Holstein,[12] based upon material collected in the chief prisons of the province; a study on suicide [13] in Schleswig-Holstein; a paper on cyclical changes in marriage rates and in the proportion of male to female births in relation to certain economic data,[14] unhappily published during the first year of World War I. This was one of the first German contributions to the empirical study of business cycles. For these investigations he had developed a method of correlation of his own invention.[15]

III. LEADING PHASES OF TÖNNIES' SOCIOLOGICAL THEORY

A. SOCIOLOGICAL THEORY AND RESEARCH; THE THREE SPHERES OF SOCIOLOGY

It was detrimental to the appreciation of Tönnies in America that these studies attracted scarcely any attention there and that, at the time when *Gemeinschaft und Gesellschaft* gained a broader public in Germany, there was among American sociologists little interest in what they held to be "armchair sociology." And yet Tönnies, believing firmly in the possibility of "exact" methods in the social sciences, never thought of sociological theory as being an end in itself or as independent of research. Tönnies distinguishes three disciplines of sociology,[16] distinct in their epistemological aspects and in the methods essential to each:

1. Pure or theoretical (*reine, theoretische*) sociology
2. Applied (*angewandte*) sociology
3. Empirical (*empirische*) sociology or sociography

This division relates to sociology in the narrower sense. Besides this, Tönnies asserted the validity of a wider concept of sociology, which had come to general recognition outside of Germany and which included social biology, demography, and social psychology.

Tönnies' idea of "pure" sociology corresponds approximately to "general sociology"[17] in the meaning which has now become rather generally accepted. It is a logical system of concepts of "normal" or ideal types (in the meaning of Max Weber) of *soziale Wesenheiten* ("social entities") in a static condition. Such a system of concepts is a necessary means to the description and understanding of empirical social phenomena.[18]

The "application" of these "pure" concepts to the analysis and explanation of concrete historical societies (*Kulturen*) and to historical processes of social evolution is the field of *angewandte Soziologie*.[19] Here the original meaning of sociology as a scientific philosophy of history, as conceived by Lorenz Stein and A. Comte, is restored. Tönnies planned a comprehensive treatise on the evolution of modern society, which he intended to be the complement to *Gemeinschaft und Gesellschaft*. He published some papers on the subject of *Progress and Evolution in Society*[20] and, a half year before his death, the first volume of the larger work was published under the title *Geist der Neuzeit*. The difference beween *reine* and *angewandte* sociology is not only that between a static and a dynamic theory of society but also, and primarily, that between a constructive and a deductive approach. In *angewandte* sociology empirical data are to be systematized and interpreted according to the principle of evolution from "Gemeinschaft" toward "Gesellschaft."[21]

The sociographic study of present social conditions and processes, or *empirische Soziologie,* can proceed by inductive or empirical methods,[22] since in this field almost any data required are available or can be made available. But, of course, even in these empirical studies the concepts of pure sociology will be used in order to select and organize the "facts."[23] This concept of *Soziographie* corresponds approximately to the more recent type of American social surveys and ecological studies as a scientific representation of sociologically relevant facts in concrete communities or groups. This threefold system of sociology, in the special sense, can be said to combine in an organic unity the main approaches to the subject of society which have led to the development of different and apparently irreconcilable schools of sociological thought.[24]

B. GEMEINSCHAFT AND GESELLSCHAFT

The core of Tönnies' system lies in the doctrine of human relationships or social entities (*soziale Wesenheiten*). This doctrine is based on the distinction between the two "fundamental concepts" *Gemeinschaft* and *Gesellschaft.* The historical importance of this theorem for the social sciences lies in the synthesis of the rational and the Romantic conceptions of society. The two concepts of social life which, since the days of Aristotle, have been the principal subject of discussion among social philosophers are held to be one-sided pictures of the reality of social life. The essential contribution is not the mere construction of two antithetic concepts (we shall see that they are not at all meant to be strictly antithetical) but the clear conceptual differentiation of two fundamental patterns, representing opposite potentialities of concrete social formations, and, furthermore, the recognition that the difference between the two schools of social philosophy is due to the fact that their proponents have each taken only one of the two spheres into their conception of the whole of social reality.

It is true that we find the inception of this recognition with Hobbes in the distinction between natural and political commonwealths. But the clear formulation in the concepts of *Gemeinschaft* and *Gesellschaft* was possible only after the Romantic theory of state and society had prepared the way; the knowledge of the social life of primitive peoples, which, during the nineteenth century, was attained through cultural anthropology, comparative philology, and the studies of comparative law, was also a prerequisite.

It is impossible within the limits of this chapter to trace in detail the influence on Tönnies of German natural-rights philosophers and thinkers of the Romantic school and, above all, of English and American scholars (e.g., Morgan, *Ancient Society*). In *Gemeinschaft und Gesellschaft* Tönnies has especially acknowledged the decisive stimulus which he received from Sir Henry Maine's antithesis of status and contract.[25]

The distinction between *Gemeinschaft* and *Gesellschaft* as fundamental concepts of social groups recalls the distinction between organic and mechanical social entities (even Tönnies occasionally employs these pictures, but only as analogies) or between those relationships which have grown naturally out of sympathetic sentiments and those which have been set up consciously and for a definite purpose.

The essential points in Tönnies' theory, however, are as follows:

1. All social relationships are to be regarded as creations of the human will. They exist as social facts only through the will of individuals to associate.

2. This will and, along with it, the inner relationship of the associated individuals with one another can be of very varied character: a group or relationship can be willed either because it is desired to attain through it a definite end (with complete indifference toward, or even antipathy against, partners, e.g., a business co-operation), or because, from sympathy with the partners, it is felt that the relationship is valuable in itself (e.g., friendship). Tönnies designates the two types of will as *Wesenwille* and *Kürwille*. *Kürwille*[26] means the rational will which distinguishes between end and means (the concept corresponds fairly exactly to Max Weber's concept of the *zweckrationale* behavior). *Wesenwille* means any process of willing which springs from the temper and character of an individual, whether it has its origin in inclination, in habit, or in conviction.[27]

3. The *Wesenwille*, therefore, is by no means necessarily irrational. On the contrary, one can distinguish rather between degrees of rationality of the *Wesenwille* and of the "communities" which derive therefrom. The scale runs from those in which the instinctive sympathy of biologically related individuals determines the individual will to those which are based solely on a relationship arising out of common adherence to certain values (e.g., blood-relationship, neighborliness, friendship; family, community, guild). The wholly mental forms (stages) of *Gemeinschaft*[28] come nearest to the *gesellschaftlichen* relationships, which are always purely mental.[29]

The two categories of *Gemeinschaft* and *Gesellschaft* stand in a complicated relationship to each other which is not always understood by critics. The objection has been raised[30] that these concepts represent, on the one hand, antithetical conceptional categories and, on the other hand, stages of historical development and that they also are mere classificatory concepts. The last of these is certainly not Tönnies' meaning. Though he sometimes designates the family or the village as a *Gemeinschaft* and the city or the state as a *Gesellschaft,* this is only as a paradigm. To him *Gemeinschaft* and *Gesellschaft* are pure concepts of ideal types which do not exist as such in the empirical world. They cannot, therefore, be applied as classificatory concepts. Rather, they are to be regarded as traits, which, in empirical social entities, are found in varying proportions. If one should, for example, define the family as a *Gemeinschaft,* the road to sociological understanding would thereby be barred; it is the peculiar task of the sociologist to find out to what extent a family in a concrete situation (e.g., a wage-earner's family in a great city) corresponds more to the type of *Gesellschaft* than does a family in another situation (e.g., on a farm).[31] If one takes the concepts in this sense, it will be possible to apply them to historical phenomena without doing violence to the logic of the system.

A peculiar difficulty lies in the fact that the two categories are not strictly antithetical, inasmuch as a purely *gesellschaftliche* empirical condition of social life is, for Tönnies, inconceivable; for, since man in his behavior is never motivated alone by intellect and reason but, whatever the stage of social development, by inclinations and emotions, that is to say, fundamentally by *Wesenwillen* and only partially by *Kürwillen,* all empirical "associations" must have a *Gemeinschafts,* or "community," basis.[32]

c. THEORETICAL (PURE) SOCIOLOGY; SOCIAL GROUPS

The social entities are classified as (1) social relations (*Verhältnisse*); (2) social collectives (*Samtschaften*); and (3) social corporations (*Körperschaften*). These social entities are to be conceptually distinguished from natural and psychic relations. Natural relation by common blood does not, per se, constitute a social relation. A social relation springs from a psychic relation "in the measure in which the latter is felt not only as such but is also willed to exist and persist"—and in so far as certain common and mutual rights and duties of the participants are derived from it (e.g., courtship developing into marriage).

A social relation, thus, is thought of as something "valid"—not only by the participants but, if it is not a secret relation, by other persons. These, however, can refuse to recognize the validity, e.g., if parents refuse to recognize the engagement of their daughter. A complex of social relations between more than two persons is called a "social circle" (*sozialer Kreis*), e.g., a circle of friends. This is the link between social relation and social collective (*Samtschaft*).

Under collective, or *Samtschaft,* we are to understand a group of individuals who, because of common natural or psychic traits, are regarded as units (race or language groups); social *Samtschaften* are such natural or psychic groups, in so far as they are recognized by the associated individuals themselves as units, to which their assent is given and which they will to persist. A people would be the best example of a *Samtschaft* resting on natural and psychic common characteristics; the political party may be considered as an example of a purely psychic or mental *Samtschaft*.

"Corporations"—social bodies or social unions—are to be distinguished from the two former categories inasmuch as they possess an organization, that is, that definite persons can perform definite functions, which are regarded by the members of the corporation, and even by outsiders, as the acts of the corporation. The corporation is thought of as a person, which possesses a rational will to which it can give validity through its organs or functionaries. Thus the idea of social entity comes to full expression in the concept of the corporation.

A corporation may be based on a social *Samtschaft,* as the church rests in the community of believers, or it may originate from a social *Samtschaft,* as the party machine from the mass of those who feel that they are bound together by similar political ends.

All three categories of *soziale Wesenheiten* can be willed predominantly by *Wesenwillen* or by *Kürwillen* and therefore predominantly correspond to the type of *Gemeinschaft* or *Gesellschaft,* as the case may be.

While, as a rule, in social philosophy a "superindividual" character is attributed only to corporations, in which case the concept of the juristic person is usually employed, it is an essential feature of Tönnies' theory that even the "social relation" is conceived as a creature of the will of the partners, which exists in their consciousness as something objective toward which the partners recognize that they have definite obligations, and from which they acquire certain rights. Thus, one may say "My friendship to X binds me to do or refrain from doing this or that." When social relations are legally sanctioned as, for instance, in marriage or the relation of employer and employee, the identity, in principle, of their mode of existence with the corporations becomes obvious

And with that we define the point at which the objects of sociology and social psychology diverge. Sociology deals with types of social relationship, not with the typical psychic attitudes of the persons related.

The state, as the most important corporation, has been the object of philosophical and sociological speculations and theories ever since antiquity. Tönnies considers the so-called *Allgemeine Staatslehre* as a part of sociology,[33] so far as it deals with the *Sein* and not with the *Sollen,* i.e., with really existing states and not with ideals of the state. Several of his most important writings are concerned with problems of the theory of the state, and, during the first World War, Tönnies wrote an excellent comparative study of the English and the German state.[34]

D. SOCIAL NORMS AND VALUES

It is the criterion of the social life of human beings, as distinguished from the mere living-together in groups, such as occurs also among animals, that it is subject to a normative order; for this reason the theory of social norms and social values—from which these norms derive their meaning—is the necessary complement to the theory of social entities. Tönnies was always particularly interested in the theory of social norms, and therefore we find it more systematically developed in his work than is the theory of social values.[35]

In this paper only the elementary features of Tönnies' theory of norms can be presented. Social norms are defined as all commandments and inhibitions, of general validity to individuals linked together in a social entity, which regulate the conduct of those individuals toward one another and toward outsiders. These regulations gain validity by the agreement (consent)—expressed or tacit—of the individuals; they may be norms autonomous or heteronomous; and they may be followed from conviction of their rightness or merely in order to avoid the detrimental consequences of disobedience.

Tönnies distinguishes (1) three classes of norms: order, law, and morality, and (2) the following kinds of social will, by which the norms (as objects of will) are created:[36] (*a*) *gemeinschaftliche* forms of social will: (i) unanimity, or concord, as the general trait of all common willing, which, based upon relations formerly described as of "community" type, appears to be natural and necessary per se, (ii) custom, based upon habits in common, (iii) religion, based upon faith in supernatural commanding powers; (*b*) *gesellschaftliche* forms of social will:

(i) convention, (ii) legislation, (iii) public opinion (based upon common interests).

"Order" is the most general complex of norms, primarily based upon either concord or convention. It might be said that it comprises those norms which are valid through the normative power of facts.

Law is the complex of norms, which, according to their idea, are to be interpreted and enforced by judicial decision. Law is created either by custom or by formal and intentional "legislation."

Morality is the complex of those norms the interpretation and application of which are thought of as the function of an imaginary judge (God or conscience). The norms of morality are sanctioned more or less either by religion or by public opinion.

All these distinctions, however, are of purely conceptual character; in reality, transitions exist between the various types of norms, and each category contains elements of the others. The systems of norms of the various social entities are composed of norms of order, law, and morality.[37]

Tönnies' concept of custom is defined in a manner slightly different from the usual concept: for him custom is not the original unity (or common origin) of all norms, out of which law and morality develop at a higher level of culture. And, again, custom is not a definite body of norms. It is the will of a social entity rooted in common habits, by which definite norms attain content and validity.

The distinction between customary law and law by legislation is not identical with the distinction between codified law and unwritten law, for even customary law is liable to become codified and sanctioned by legislation. But, in order to regulate constantly arising new conditions, the modern state has to establish laws which are sanctioned by no "sacred" customs but only by their being generally reasonable or by their serving certain interests, as, for example, most rules of modern transportation and traffic law.

Thus the systematic theory of law, in so far as law is factually effective and can, therefore, be studied by empirical methods, forms an essential part of pure sociology. But for Tönnies even those ideas of the origins of law and of laws valid under all conditions of human society which form the theory of "natural law" become essential subjects of sociological theory because of their great importance in political respects. Tönnies has added to the well-known rationalistic theory of natural law—of which he considers Hobbes to be the classic philosopher—the principles of a modern "community-law of nature."

By resuming Aristotle's idea of man as a being by nature destined to live in communities, the concept of a legal order based upon natural altruism and not on conflicting interests restrained by reason could be constructed. In every social relationship based upon mutual sympathy and upon the feeling of duty arising from it, there would lie hidden the bud of a system of law, which could be called "natural law of community."[38] This system of law would, in every one of its institutions, express the principles of solidarity within the community and of the immediate interdependence of rights and duties. It would especially presuppose common property in land and in other means of production of primary importance, and even common use of these.[39] This type of law, being motivated only by the common good of the people, would not permit of any disparity between law and morality. These ideas and their explication, especially with regard to the legal status of wage-earners as given in the *Einführung*,[40] have attained a high degree of actuality in spite of their perversion by the National Socialist regime; they might also be interesting to American social reformers, since they furnish arguments against an individualistic philosophy of law, which is likely to bar the way to social reform. Law, in so far as it results from legislation by democratic procedure, is, according to Tönnies, an emanation of public opinion.

E. TÖNNIES' THEORY OF PUBLIC OPINION

The phenomenon of public opinion was especially attractive to Tönnies, who, after more than a decade of theoretical and historical studies, published in 1922 a comprehensive work on this subject. The *Kritik der öffentlichen Meinung*[41] contains in the first book the theory of Public Opinion; in the second book, empirical "applications" and observations on the characteristics, contents, and functions of public opinion; the third book deals with public opinion on social problems and public opinion concerning the first World War. The present discussion has to be restricted to the theoretical part. Tönnies himself summarizes his theoretical contributions as follows:

1. *The* Public Opinion of a country or nation, or the Public Opinion in the strict sense, is distinguished conceptually as an expression of group will from the popular notion of public opinion as a conglomeration of various diverse and contradictory views.

2. The Public Opinion as the politically valid opinion is distinguished conceptually from local or apolitical public opinions.

3. This Public Opinion can be of a more or less fixed, fluid, or gaseous condition
of aggregation, depending on the issues involved.

4. In conformity with Giddings' distinction between popular beliefs and "genuine public opinion," Tönnies distinguishes both public opinion and *the*
Public Opinion from popular sentiment and feelings—Public Opinion is,
by contrast, a product of critical, i.e., intellectual, thinking.[42]

These distinctions are, of course, intended only for strictly conceptual,
critical, and dialectic thinking.

All social phenomena, according to Tönnies, can be properly understood only by an inquiry into the notions which people themselves have
of them. Language offers a first clue. Tönnies, therefore, in an instruc-
tive etymological discussion, traces the relation of individual and collective opinion to the basic forms of will and to belief and knowledge.
He shows that, while opinions are dependent on sentiments and interests are conditioned by the situations in which individuals and groups
are living, the holding of an opinion presupposes a mental decision and
determination.

Since like conditions and like interests tend to result in like opinions,[43]
there will be in a complex society many such public opinions, representing the essentially unanimous thought of various social collectives. In
this sense, *a* public opinion is found in small towns, as well as in occu-
pational or other groups.[44] This "unarticulated" public opinion is to
be conceptually distinguished from *the* Public Opinion of an entire
nation. This latter concept refers to the collective will, not merely a
point of view, of the political body or community. *The* Public Opinion,
in this specific sense, deserves its name in a threefold sense: first, with
regard to its subject, which is the politically conscious public of a nation;
second, in so far as it is opinion publicly expressed; third, in so far as
it refers to public affairs.[45] The popular notion of public opinion is
vague, not distinguishing sharply between the clamor of many and
often disharmonious voices of public opinions and the collective will
of a people which is thought to be as unified as the will of a person.[46]
It is in this articulate or specific sense that *the* Public Opinion, as a
political power, is often contrasted to the power of governments and
parliaments, to which it is thought to be superordinated.[47]

Empirically, in modern society, this Public Opinion tends to be actually the opinion and political will of the propertied, urban, and edu-

cated upper classes. It is, however, presented to the less wealthy, the rural, and the uneducated classes with the claim of authority, as the correct opinion which every respectable citizen and loyal patriot is expected to share. As a means of social control, Public Opinion takes in modern society the place which was occupied by religion in medieval communities, although its claims are based on intellectual, i.e., critical, scientific thought, unlike religion, which is based on faith and belief in the inconceivable, the miraculous.

Not only this intellectual basis but also the fact that Public Opinion can be "made" to suit the aims of groups in control of the means of expression and communication of ideas make it essentially a phenomenon of rational group will. Doubt or deviation from Public Opinion is, however, considered and treated very much like religious heresy.

It should be noted that Tönnies' treatment of Public Opinion differs in two respects from that of many other authors on the subject. His conceptual distinction of *the* Public Opinion from *a* public opinion and public opinions in general enables him to point out the essentially rationalistic or intellectual nature of *the* Public Opinion, while others have been more impressed with the emotional aspects of public opinion. For the same reason, Tönnies emphasizes the tendency of Public Opinion to assume the characteristic of a doctrine, while the popular notion is rather that of the wavering, chameleon-like nature of public opinion.

The link between pure and applied sociology is furnished by the theory of *soziale Bezugsgebilde,* i.e., of those systems of activities of economic, political, and spiritual or moral character "in which social will finds its fields of action."[48] This part of Tönnies' sociological system may be said to be the least developed. Here a general sociology of religion or of art and similar theories would find their place within the system.

F. APPLIED OR SPECIAL SOCIOLOGY—TÖNNIES AND MARX

Tönnies shows that, in the course of social evolution, *kürwillige* attitudes and *gesellschaftliche* social entities and norms arise pre-eminently from trade, from the modern state, and from science. As to the question which of the three spheres of economics, politics, and culture, into which we are accustomed—under the necessity of analytical abstraction —to divide the unity of social life, should be given the leading role in social evolution or, rather, the highest degree of variability, Tönnies commits himself to the economic interpretation of history or, as he preferred to say, to a realistic interpretation of social evolution.[49] In this regard, Tönnies stood perhaps less under the influence of Karl Marx than in accord with seventeenth- and eighteenth-century social theory in England and France. In Germany this tradition had been interrupted by the philosophic school of idealism and, being restored by Karl Marx, was adopted as a slogan in political conflict, thereby losing credit with the great public. While Marx attributes to technological conditions an important role among the "forces of production," thereby relying largely upon an extra-economic factor for the explanation of social evolution, Tönnies conceives capitalism as an outgrowth of trade, in particular of large-scale and foreign trade, which is not limited to the simple exchange of goods for money and of money for goods but whose function consists in the profitable use of money as "capital." The infiltration of this kind of trade into the realms of industrial and agricultural production, in the shape of the plantation economy, home industry, the sweatshop, and the factory, tends to burst all the old traditional "community" conditions of economic life.[50]

And yet Tönnies, being vitally interested in questions of theological and philosophical doctrine, has certainly not underestimated the importance of ideas in social life. For him, the economic (realistic) interpretation of history was a useful device of analysis but not the last word in wisdom. However, he held the opinion that only those ideas which, regardless of their "rightness," had actual validity and significance in society because they express the real or assumed interests of influential social groups could, in fact, exert their sway on social life. Therefore, he expected social reforms to result not from propagation of ethical social doctrines but from appeal to the well-understood group interests of the parties involved in social conflicts. For the same reason Tönnies disapproved of the opinion, chiefly shared by political reactionaries, that the faults of the modern social system were due to the heretical doctrines of individualistic social philosophy. He considered these theories rather as attempts at an understanding and justification of the modern social order. That Thomas Hobbes should have recognized the radically new principle of the modern state as opposed to all earlier "communal" forms of political bodies and should have undertaken to make it conceivable by the doctrine of a social covenant, Tönnies appreciated as the sociologically significant feature of Hobbes's theory of the state and of the rationalistic doctrine of social contract in general; for the modern omnipotent centralistic state, independent as it was in principle of any ethnic basis, could, in fact, be understood only by a rationalistic construction, and the principle of sovereignty could be justified only by some such fictional devices of thought. The modern state is, in this regard, distinct from both the antique *polis* (representing, in principle, a "community") and from the feudalistic and *ständischen* medieval realms. Tönnies conceives the state as a revolutionary force, which tends to weaken and even to destroy most of the older community elements of the social order and which establishes a new "associational" order in its place.

G. POLITICAL ATTITUDE AND PERSONAL EXPERIENCE

Tönnies has been blamed for the bias which his theory implied. He has been called a pessimist and even a romantic. Against such criticism —brought, at first, by his elderly friend, Harald Höffding, the famous Danish philosopher, and only recently by L. von Wiese—Tönnies would defend himself by explaining that his intention was simply to describe the irreversible course of social evolution which he occasionally compared to the life-cycle of human beings. Nobody could say whether youth or old age was "better," and there was no sense in putting the question in this fashion. And yet it could not be denied that youth, in certain respects, was preferable to age and that, in other respects, old age had its own advantages. Thus Tönnies' verdict on the development of scientific thinking and its victory over theology and metaphysics— a victory he welcomed—was absolutely positive. He had been a supporter of the movement for the establishment of "ethical culture," independent of religion in its narrower sense. He considered the modern state, although he labeled it an "associational" group, all but an evil; on the other hand, he believed the solution of many social problems arising from the evolution of modern capitalism to be possible through a combination, in some way, of the efforts of co-operative and trade-union movements with those of state socialism.[51] Tönnies was, however, a man of firm judgment and, on many things, he held rather fixed opinions. Thus it cannot be denied that antipathy toward many features of capitalism and industrial society crops out quite obviously in his writings. But, if he had written on feudal society, he would not have failed to condemn in no less cogent fashion certain features of precapitalistic society. There was, however, no reason for such criticism in *Gemein-schaft und Gesellschaft,* since this book was intended as a critique of the present and not of the past.

The strong and far-reaching influence[52] of this chief book of Tönnies was due not only to the fact that in it was attained a synthesis of the strivings of social philosophy and political theory since more than three centuries, but also to the enthusiasm of a vigorous thinker whose theories sprang not from mere intellectual interest but from intensive experience. Tönnies had himself gone through the process of assimilation from a social background predominated by "community" values and norms to a social milieu of essentially "associational" type, when, as a young man, he had left a countryside of farms and small towns for the world of big cities. He had, morever, in those political changes and social conflicts which occurred during his childhood and youth, observed with vigilant eyes the full unfolding of the modern state and of the capitalistic middle-class (*bürgerliche*) society in Germany. In his native Eiderstedt he had observed the influence of the capitalistic commercial spirit on the life and character of a society of cattle-grazing farmers. But he had also seen how Eiderstedt, on the incorporation of the duchies of Schleswig and Holstein into Prussia, had lost considerable remnants of self-government preserved under the Danish regime and had been converted from a semi-medieval political community into a mere administrative district within a modern state. During his early manhood there occurred the first big strikes of labor and the attacks of Bismarck on the Socialist labor movement. When Tönnies took sides with the laborers, he was motivated not merely by his sociological theory. Having an extraordinary facility in making contacts with plain people and gaining their confidence, he had, quite early, acquired a comprehensive knowledge of the conditions of life of the working-class people and of "what was on the worker's mind." He was, however, concerned not only about the well-being of the laboring class but also about the future of the whole nation. Like his friend and teacher, Adolf Wagner, and the other so-called *Kathedersozialisten,* he was convinced that social peace could be guaranteed for the future only by radical social reforms.[53] A peaceful condition of group life appeared to him so obviously to be the end and meaning of any social order, that, even in pure sociology, he would admit as its essential subject only the peaceful relations between men.[54] He therefore condemned any kind of social revolution, since he believed that a sudden and doctrinaire recasting of existing institutions would not lead to better conditions but, rather, would give rise to new and unforeseen social evils.[55] On the other hand, he held his own science justified and necessary, just because of the existing conflicts and tensions in modern society. Tönnies wrote in 1926:

It is the recent gigantic change in the fundamental conditions of social life, a change that, for the last hundred years, has been increasingly endangering the very existence of society—it is the Social Problem which proves unquestionably the necessity for and the importance of the new science of sociology. In it the cultural sciences find the same systematic completion that Biology intends to give the descriptive natural sciences. Necessity decides. The Labor Movement has been, from its beginning to the present day, an important stimulant for the thinking about the relations and antagonisms of the social classes.....

Sociology, he said, was the science of the statesman—if not of the statesman of today, then inevitably of the statesman of the day after tomorrow. In the Preface to the *Einführung* we read, however, that the future of nations would be shaped by politicians and diplomats only within comparatively narrow limits. The essential factor was, rather, the general conditions of life, the well-being or the ill-feeling which would influence the willing and not-willing of the broad masses of a nation; these, however, were the working people, together with the intellectually farsighted, experienced, and thinking elements, so far as the latter are earnestly and persistently devoted to the improvement of the conditions of the people. It was generally known how wide and deep were the divergencies of opinions in this regard and that there were but few people who were willing and also able to think and to strive, not for the benefit of a certain class or rank but for the future life and welfare of their nation and (just for the sake of their nation) of all humanity. Sociology would be best justified if it helped to increase the number of these friends of the people and of humanity at large and if it contributed to a strengthening and deepening of their knowledge.

The following are the main sociological writings of Tönnies, together with a selected list of leading commentaries thereon:

I. WORKS OF TÖNNIES

Gemeinschaft und Gesellschaft (1887), 8th ed. Leipzig, 1935.
Fundamental Concepts of Sociology: Gemeinschaft und Gesellschaft. Translated and supplemented by CHARLES P. LOOMIS. New York, 1940.
Thomas Hobbes, Leben und Lehre (1896). 3d ed. Stuttgart, 1925.

Die Entwicklung der sozialen Frage (1907). 4th ed. Berlin, 1926.

"Das Wesen der Soziologie" (Vortrag in der Gehe-Stiftung), *Neue Zeit- und Streit-fragen,* Vol. IV (1907).

"Entwicklung der Soziologie in Deutschland im 19. Jahrhundert," *Entwicklung der deutschen Volkswirtschaftslehre im 19. Jahrhundert: Festgabe für Gustav Schmoller.* Leipzig, 1908.

Die Sitte. Frankfurt am Main, 1909.

Der englische Staat und der deutsche Staat. Berlin, 1917.

Marx Leben und Lehre. Berlin, 1921.

Kritik der öffentlichen Meinung. Berlin, 1922.

"Zweck und Mittel im sozialen Leben," *Hauptprobleme der Soziologie: Erinner-ungsgabe für Max Weber.* München and Leipzig, 1923.

"Die Einteilung der Soziologie." *Zeitschrift für die gesamte Staatswissenschaft,* Vol. LXXIX (1925); also published in *Atti del 5. congresso internazionale di filosofia.* Naples, 1925.

Fortschritt und soziale Entwicklung: Geschichtsphilosophische Ansichten. Karls-ruhe, 1926.

"The Concept of Law and Human Progress." Translated by KARL J. ARNDT and C. L. FOLSE in *Social Forces,* Vol. XIX, No. 1 (1940).

Soziologische Studien und Kritiken, Vols. I (Jena, 1925); II (Jena, 1926); III (Jena, 1929).

Einführung in die Soziologie. Stuttgart, 1931.

Inledning till Sociologien. Translated by E. BOSSE. Oslo, 1932.

"Eigentum," "Moderne Familie," "Gemeinschaft und Gesellschaft," "Stände und Klassen," articles in *Handwörterbuch der Soziologie.* Stuttgart, 1931.

Geist der Neuzeit. Leipzig, 1935.

"Mein Verhältnis zur Soziologie," in R. THURNWALD (ed.), *Soziologie von heute: Ein Symposion der Zeitschrift für Völkerpsychologie und Soziologie.* Leipzig, 1932.

"Philosophical Terminology," *Mind: Quarterly Review of Psychology and Philos-ophy,* Vols. VIII (new ser., 1899) and IX (1900).

"The Problems of Social Structure," *Congress of Arts and Science: Universal Ex-position.* St. Louis, 1904.

II. CRITICISMS AND EXPOSITIONS

STOLTENBERG, H. L. *Ein Führer durch F. Tönnies "Gemeinschaft und Gesellschaft."*

ROSENBAUM, EDUARD. "Ferdinand Tönnies' Work," *Schmoller's Jahrbuch für Gesetzgebung,* XXXVIII (1914), 14.

WIRTH, LOUIS. "The Sociology of Ferdinand Tönnies," *American Journal of Sociology,* Vol. XXXII (1926).

LEEMAN'S V. *Ferdinand Tönnies en de duitsche sociologie.* Brugge, 1932. *F. Tönnies et la sociologie contemporaine en Allemagne.* Paris, 1933.

HEBERLE, R. "Ferdinand Tönnies," *Internationales Handwörterbuch des Gewerk-schaftswesens.* Berlin, 1932.

JAHN, GEORG. *Ferdinand Tönnies.* Leipzig, 1935.

FREYER, HANS. "Ferdinand Tönnies und die deutsche Soziologie," *Weltwirtschaft-liches Archiv,* Vol. XLIV (1936).

SALOMON, ALBERT. "In Memoriam Ferdinand Tönnies (1855–1936)," *Social Research*, Vol. III (1936).

For the most comprehensive bibliography see: *Brencke, Else*, "Verzeichnis der Schriften von Ferdinand Tönnies aus den Jahren 1875 bis 1935," *Reine und angewandte Soziologie: Eine Festgabe für Ferdinand Tönnes zu seinem achtzigsten Geburtstage*. Leipzig, 1936.

JURKAT, ERNST. "Die Soziologie von Ferdinand Tönnies," *Geistige Arbeit*, November, 1936.

Kölner Vierteljahrshefte für Soziologie, Vol. V, Heft 1/2 (1925). Contains several articles dedicated to Tönnies on account of his seventieth birthday.

ERNST JURKAT (ed.). *Reine und angewandte Soziologie: Eine Festgabe für Ferdinand Tönnies zu seinem 80. Geburtstage*. Leipzig, 1936.

PARSONS, TALCOTT. *The Structure of Social Action*. 1937.

ZIMMERMAN, CARLE C. *The Changing Community*. New York, 1938.

NOTES

1. Heinrich Meyer, "Theodor Storm und Ferdinand Tönnies," *Monatshefte für deutschen Unterricht*, Vol. XXXII (Madison, Wis., December, 1940). This publication of the correspondence between Storm and Tönnies in the years 1872–88 contains valuable biographical information.

2. See H. E. Barnes and Becker, *Social Thought from Lore to Science* (Boston, 1938), II, 881.

3. "Mein Verhältnis zur Soziologie," in R. Thurnwald (ed.), *Soziologie von heute: Ein Symposion der Zeitschrift für Völkerpsychologie und Soziologie* (Leipzig, 1932), p. 103.

4. *Ibid*. (Translation by R. Heberle.)

5. *Ibid.*, p. 104.

6. In 1904 Tönnies visited his intimate friend, Professor Kuno Francke, head of the German Department at Harvard, and read a paper at the Congress of Arts and Sciences held in connection with the Exposition at St. Louis. Following that time he developed an intense interest and comprehensive knowledge of American life and affairs.

7. *Gemeinschaft* can be translated by "community," *Gesellschaft* by "society," or in some cases more adequately by "association." In order to avoid any misunderstandings and to emphasize that these terms designate the specific concepts of Tönnies, the German words have been retained throughout this paper.

8. *Die Sitte* (Frankfurt, 1909).

9. *Kritik der öffentlichen Meinung* (Berlin, 1922).

10. "Hafenarbeiter und Seeleute in Hamburg vor dem Strike [sic] 1896–97," *Archiv für Sozialwissenschaft und Sozialpolitik*, Vol. X (1897); "Der Hamburger Strike von 1896–97," *ibid.*; and "Die Ostseehäfen Flensburg, Kiel, Lübeck," in "Die Lage der in der Seeschifffahrt beschäftigten Arbeiter," *Schriften des Vereins für Sozialpolitik*, Vol. CIV (1903).

11. "Studie zur schleswig-holsteinischen Agrarstatistik," *Archiv für Sozialwissenschaft und Sozialpolitik*, Vol. XXX (1910).

12. "Verbrechertum in Schleswig-Holstein," *ibid.*, Vols. LII (1924) and LVIII (1927); "Die schwere Kriminalität von Männern in Schleswig-Holstein in den Jahren 1899–1914 in Verbindung mit Dr. E. Jurkat," *Zeitschrift für Völkerpsychologie und Soziologie*, Vol. V (1929); "Ortsherkunft von Verbrechern in Schleswig-Holstein," *Deutsches statistisches Zentralblatt*, Vol. XXI (1929); *Uneheliche und verwaiste Verbrecher* ("Kriminal statistische Abhandlungen," Heft 14 [Leipzig, 1930]).

13. "Der Selbstmord in Schleswig-Holstein: Eine statistisch-soziologische Studie," *Veröffentlichungen der schl. holst. Universitäts-Gesellschaft* (Breslau, 1927); "Der Selbstmord in Schleswig-Holstein," *Nordelbingen,* Vol. VIII (1930).

14. "Die Gesetzmässigkeit in der Bewegung der Bevölkerung," *Archiv für Sozialwissenschaft und Sozialpolitik,* Vol. XXXIX, No. 1 (1914), and No. 3 (1915).

15. "Eine neue Methode der Vergleiche statistischer Reihen," *Schmoller's Jahrbuch,* Vol. XXX (1909); see also H. Striefler, "Zur Methode der Rangkorrelation nach Tönnies," *Deutsches statistisches Zentralblatt,* Vol. XXIII, No. 5 (1931).

16. Ferdinand Tönnies, "Die Einteilung der Soziologie," *Zeitschrift für die gesamte Staatswissenschaft,* Vol. LXXIX (1925).

17. With Tönnies the term *generelle Soziologie,* however, has a different meaning: it comprises all disciplines pertaining to human society, whereas *spezielle Soziologie,* or sociology in the proper sense, is confined to the study of "social entities" and excludes, for instance, social psychology and social biology.

18. In "Wege und Ziele der Soziologie," the presidential address at the first conference of the German Sociological Society, Tönnies said that sociology was fundamentally a philosophical science: "....As such Sociology is mainly concerned with concepts.....It has to formulate these concepts, i.e., make them ready for use, ...so as to hang upon them like on nails or to seize as with clamps, the facts of experience. In this realm, it is not so much its task to perceive facts but to construct the handiest, the most useful implements for their perception: a task of supreme importance, which is, frequently to their own disadvantage, not much appreciated by the mere empiricist" (*Soziologische Studien und Kritiken,* II [Jena, 1926], 131).

19. "As long as Pure Sociology is not established as a fairly solid system of concepts and theories, Applied Sociology should only be regarded as an attempt to apply certain concepts and theories which are, perhaps provisionally only, accepted for the interpretation of historical developments. Applied Sociology will always be in touch with what has gained a certain amount of importance under the name of Philosophy of History.....A task which is closer to Applied Sociology insofar as it wishes to be more scientific than Philosophy of History, is the study of separate periods of culture, of cultures themselves, in their development and decline.....With the aid of sociological terminology and theory, Applied Sociology could follow the course of the European....development in its fundamental phases up to the present hour. Thus it will end up with the inquiry into present day social life, a research that should be as thorough as possible. However, a third part of Special Sociology makes this research its task; a part which by its method is to be distinguished both from Pure as from Applied Sociology. Its method is....the empirical, i.e., the inductive method. Therefore, we call it Empirical Sociology or Sociography" (*Einführung in die Soziologie* [Stuttgart, 1931], pp. 317, 319–21). (Author's translation.)

20. *Fortschritt und soziale Entwicklung: Geschichtsphilosophische Ansichten* (Karlsruhe, 1926).

21. Cf. the quotation in n. 19.

22. Statistics will be employed as much as possible. Tönnies liked to explain his idea of *Soziographie* by comparison with the older type of German *Statistik,* of which he considered *Soziographie* to be an improved renovation.

23. See R. Heberle, "Soziographie," *Handwörterbuch der Soziologie* (Stuttgart, 1931) Here Tönnies' concept of *Soziographie* is criticized, and the subject is more strictly defined.

24. Tönnies shows especially the possibility of combining "formal" sociology with historical sociology.

25. Tönnies gives a short enumeration of the sources of his theory in "Mein Verhältnis zur Soziologie," in Thurnwald (ed.), *op. cit.*

26. *Küren* means "to choose."

27. It is obvious that the idea of *Wesenwille* is derived from Schopenhauer's *bewusstloser Wille.*

28. For the concept of *Gemeinschaft* see Tönnies. *Studien und Kritiken,* II. 271.

29. Thus the concept of *Wesenwille* corresponds approximately to Max Weber's types of emotional-affectual, traditional, and *wertrationales* behavior.

30. Cf. Theodor Geiger, *Die Gestalten der Gesellung* (Karlsruhe, 1922), pp. iii, 22.

31. An individual *gemeinschaftliche* relation (e.g., a love-match) can change into a *gesellschaftliche* relation (if the marriage is preserved only for reasons of respectability).

32. Certainly, Tönnies does not distinguish between the categorical relation of the members of a group to the whole and their personal relation to one another. For example, a joint stock company as a social form remains also a *Gesellschaft,* if the stockholders or, at all events, the active elements among them are personal friends or even connected by kinship. This distinction has been elaborated by Max Graf Solms, *Gestalt und Gerüst der Menschenwelt* (Karlsruhe, 1929).

33. The differentiation between sociology and political science does not go so far in Germany as it does in the United States.

34. *Der englische und der deutsche Staat* (Berlin, 1917).

35. This theory has been elaborated very ably by E. Jurkat, *Das soziologische Wertproblem* (dissertation, Kiel, 1930).

36. "Einteilung der Soziologie," *Studien und Kritiken,* II, 438.

37. *Ibid.,* pp. 438 ff.

38. *Einführung in die Soziologie,* p. 218.

39. *Ibid.,* p. 220.

40. Pp. 217 ff.

41. Also, "Macht und Wert der öffentlichen Meinung," *Dioskuren: Jahrbuch für Geisteswissenschaften,* ed. Walter Strich, II (1923), 72–99.

42. *Kritik,* pp. vi–vii.

43. *Ibid.,* p. 27.

44. *Ibid.,* p. 130.

45. *Ibid.,* p. 131; "Macht und Wert," p. 82.

46. "Macht und Wert," p. 83.

47. *Ibid.,* p. 73.

48. "Einteilung," p. 441; *Einführung,* Book V.

49. *Einführung,* pp. 270 ff.

50. The explanation in detail of these ideas was reserved for the above-mentioned treatise on the evolution of modern society.

51. "Vorrede zu *Gemeinschaft und Gesellschaft*" (3d ed., 1919); reprinted in *Studien und Kritiken,* I, 58 ff.

52. This influence cannot be discussed here. It reaches far beyond Germany; more or less obvious symptoms of Tönnies' influence are to be traced in Austria and southeastern Europe, in Scandinavia, and even in Japan and China. It may only be mentioned that Sombart and Max Weber both accepted the concepts of *Gemeinschaft* and *Gesellschaft.* Spengler's *Untergang des Abendlandes* is supposed to have been influenced largely by Tönnies' ideas, although Tönnies is never quoted. In the United States, Tönnies' ideas have been recognized recently by an increasing number of sociologists, of whom only a few can be mentioned here: H. Becker, E. F. Eubank, R. M. MacIver, T. Parsons, Carle C. Zimmerman, and Charles P. Loomis, the translator of *Gemeinschaft und Gesellschaft.*

53. Cf. *Die Entwicklung der sozialen Frage bis zum Weltkrieg* (Berlin, 1926).

54. Compare the criticism by Wiese and the reply by Tönnies in *Soziologie von heute.*

55. *Einführung,* p. ix.

CHAPTER VII

EDWARD ALEXANDER WESTERMARCK AND THE APPLICATION OF ETHNOGRAPHIC METHODS TO MARRIAGE AND MORALS

C. Wright Mills

I. THE LIFE AND WORKS OF WESTERMARCK

IT DEPENDS on the definition into which the tally is made, but, not counting hillbillies, peasants, and folk-societies, there are something under one hundred major cultural types of nonliterate people on the globe today. Since the eighteenth century they have been "data" for social thinkers. Exhausting work, good minds, and a lot of money have been spent in exploiting them. Many of their languages have been learned. Detailed graphs have been constructed of their family and social organization. They have been lived among. Thin, mensurative instruments have been pushed around their heads. Their very existence, as well as the details of their lives and minds, have been the object of many theories. They have been much explained, and they have been used in various and imaginative explanations of the development of mankind.

If we conceive of the history of intellectual doctrine as a series of learned conversations, we may designate Westermarck as one given to monologues. Twice he monopolized the round table—on two topics: (1) the origin and history of kinship structures and rules and (2) the character and history of moral ideas.[1] He also spoke on ethics,[2] but the philosophers could not believe it, and the ethnologists, although respectful, were not interested in "philosophy."

Most of his traveling was to the British Museum and in shuttling between London and Finland, but he left the round table occasionally and went to Morocco and came back with three collections which had only a small audience.[3] A triangle with points in London, Finland, and Morocco encompasses the major movements of Westermarck's life. He was close to academic contexts by antecedents and location. Born in Helsingfors, in 1862, he breathed out a sickly childhood, being barred

from the romp and game of associates of his own age. As an under-
graduate he took a strong dislike to German metaphysics, was attracted
greatly to English empiricism, and became an agnostic. He remained
an agnostic, being quietly but firmly hostile to religion all his life.

He must have conceived of the marriage study around 1887; in that
year he came to the British Museum for library materials. Fourteen
years later the book appeared. In the meantime, as a professor of moral
philosophy he taught at Helsingfors, escaping these duties in 1893
and 1897 for periods of work in London. He met and was associated
with such men as Shand, Tylor, Marett, Branford, and the Maecenas,
J. Martin White, who was instrumental in securing for him a university
lectureship in sociology at the University of London in 1907. At the
same time he held the chair of moral philosophy at Helsingfors and
spent his summers in field work in Morocco. Intermittently, he was
active in Finnish politics. But his life was filled mostly with scholarship up to the last days. He died on September 3, 1939.[4]

II. THE ORIGINS, EVOLUTIONS, AND FORMS OF MARRIAGE

The "conversation" into which Westermarck plumped his monu-
mentally sized tomes on marriage and the family had been going on
for some time. Since many of the logically possible positions concerning
the origin and early forms of marriage had already been taken, it is to
be expected that Westermarck had antecedents. There were those who
were upholding and those who were contraverting theories similar to
those with which Westermarck's name was to be connected. Sir Henry
Maine (*Ancient Law* [1861]) had held the primordial cell of social
development to be the patriarchal family and had voiced other views
similar to those that Westermarck was to enunciate. However, Maine
had not supported his notion with primitive materials; his sources were
largely Roman. Bachofen (*Das Mutterrecht* [1861]), using Greek data
primarily, had challenged the notion of the patriarchate as the first form
of the family. Tylor, in his review of *The History of Human Marriage,*
made it clear that Westermarck was not the first to reject primitive
promiscuity; Tylor himself had never sponsored it.[5]

The primary objective of those who have studied family organizations and marriage rules among primitive peoples has been the reconstruction of the sequence of forms which are antecedent to those now
existent. Taking existent types as the end-product, other forms have

been scaled according to their degrees of difference and similarity to them; various features of contemporary culture have been treated as survivals from, putatively, earlier stages that no longer exist; also the mating behavior of anthropoids have been used analogously.

Perhaps the prevailing views on the topic were those of the classical evolutionists, represented by such men as Post, McLennan, Lubbock, and Morgan. Using the comparative method and positing certain stages to have been universally followed, the evolutionists set forth the following scheme:

In the beginning was promiscuity. "Society" was without form; chaos prevailed and unregulated sex intercourse. Then groups of women, related or not, were looked upon as wives of groups of men, related or not. But the clans came forth: tribes were divided into these hereditary social units, and these were composed of blood relatives and also of some who were not so related. Thus social organization became more clearly formed. At first, and dominantly, this form was maternal in principle: the children belonged to the clan of their mothers. Later the gens developed: the children belonged to the gentes of their fathers. Finally, after all this had passed, the monogamous family (and the village) became the basic units of organization.

It was against this view that Westermarck formulated what impressed many as a definitive and adequate counterstatement. He did not think mankind had to go through so much to reach monogamy. Man was originally monogamous. Rejecting primitive promiscuity in the first well-rounded attack on that notion, Westermarck asserted that a paternalistic family was the earliest, and universal, social unit. It was present in the most primitive tribes, in those having no clan structure; and it persisted among all those which had acquired such structures of kinship. Westermarck attempted to refute the precedence of matrilineal over patrilineal descent. He set forth alternative explanations for observed social forms which had been explained by the evolutionists as survivals of group marriages and promiscuity.

His evidence was gathered, as seems to have been a custom of the day, illustratively; it was of two kinds—ethnographic and from the anthropoids, which he indicated as being given to pair arrangements of some permanence. In both cases his evidence has been strongly imputed to have been selected for the theory. He profusely illustrated the alleged fact that hunters and fishers, whom the classical evolutionists considered "most primitive" economically, were, in the main, monogamous. He set forth many detailed cases around which argument over the question could swirl.

Besides these two modes of proof there was another: Westermarck grounded the idea of a universal and original monogamous patriarchate in the realm of Darwinian biology and in what passed (and "still passes") for a psychology. He supported the Darwinian view of the family, bottomed on male possessiveness and jealousy, with monopoly by force later becoming enshrined in custom. He argued from supposedly universal "psychological causes" to social forms. He accepted "mere instincts" as playing a "very important part in the origin of social institutions."[6] This mode of proof supported and was supported by the evidence from the anthropoids. I shall comment later upon the psychological inadequacy of Westermarck's thinking.

How do present-day American ethnologists stand on the question of the origin and sequence of marriage forms? In so far as they permit themselves an opinion on such a large question, they are, as a group, closer to Westermarck than to the Morgan type of evolutionist. But their reasons are not his. Such men as Boas, Kroeber, Lowie, and Malinowski hold that the biosocial unit of the monogamous family seems to be a very fundamental and prevailing one in existent preliterate societies. However, properly speaking, we know of no such institution as *the* primitive family"; there are many and diverse types of organization among primitive peoples, some quite similar to "modern" forms, some not. At the "lowest levels" of society, family life is quite varied. There seems to be no thoroughly acceptable evidence that a "stage" of promiscuity ever existed. The father, the mother, the child, and their net of relationships are primary. By various types of extension their interrelationships have grown into such (often complex) groupings as the clan and into such arrangements as group marriage. The latter occurs but rarely and then as an outgrowth of previous conditions of individual marriage. The family and village groupings are near-universal units of social organization; they extend "from the beginning"; they persist through all the other forms.

But, in the main, modern ethnologists have not answered the sort of questions and topics which formed the theme of the evolutionists' and Westermarck's work on marriage and family structures. They have dropped the questions. They have given up the search for origins.

They no longer seek all over the world, albeit via libraries, for "the fundamentally primitive" condition. It is a methodological refusal to ask a question whose answer presumably would rest upon evidence that is not available. And, more important, the quest for origins is a significant and compulsive problem only within a framework which assumes the fundamental conception of evolutionism: a universal uniformity of development through stages. The legitimacy and the significance of the origin hunt died with the evolutionists.

From present elements found in nonliterate cultures, modern ethnologists do not *readily* infer into a constructed past, certainly not into a "stage" arbitrarily postulated as previously existent. Such an element is studied functionally in a context that is seen; it is not interpreted as evidence for an affiliated context supposed to have been there but which is now forever vanished.

III. ON METHOD AND COMPILATION

In a growing science it is often over questions of method that arguments hover; and it is through this sphere that individuals really shape deeply and lastingly the contour of their science. If you spread out the histories of various sciences, you see that compilations of fact are not important unless they are logically connected with sharp theory and incisive method. Theory, fact, and method are the inseparable rungs of the ladder to scientific fame. Methodology is what others can take away from an individual's work and use themselves. You will learn very little, save industry, from Westermarck as methodologist.

The model of thought which informed the classical evolutionists was not the paradigm drawn from physics of Descartes; nor was it the scheme of Hegel. It was Spencer's, and back of Spencer lay the geology and biology of the early nineteenth century, and alongside of him sat Darwin. Among others, Comte had used a comparative method. Spencer used it more generously, and it was from Spencer that the classical evolutionists derived their way of thinking. Like them, Westermarck used the comparative method, but with this scheme and method he dug out of the British Museum, and presented to the round table, an alternative sequence of the forms of marriages and families and of kinship structures in general.

Unlike the classical evolutionists, Westermarck rejected *in toto* the small interpretative trick with which any kind of rabbit can be made to appear from anybody's sleeve of abstractions: the theory of survivals. He thought it was based on speculation, that it took unfair advantage of empirical materials. And in this he has been vindicated.

But the concrete way of work utilized by Westermarck was the famous little-slips-of-paper-piled-topically-and-write-it-up-method.[7] It was the encyclopedic and comparative method. The data so collected suffer in general in that they are not oriented so as to be crucial empirical evidence in the solution of carefully defined problems. In ethnological work this method has been rejected for a more specialized reason: it dislocates particular phases and bits of a "total culture" and tears societal features from their contexts.[8] Given the present ethnographic norms for the determination of whole facts, the result is plain and simple inaccuracy.[9] Also, since the cultural world is a big place with a lot in it, such grab-bag methods are bound to result in ethnographic inadequacy, for even encyclopedias are selective. A severe appraisal of Westermarck's method, sources, and work has been written by R. Lowie. After commenting on the profusion of documents used in an amazingly uncritical way, he states: "Not only are there inconsistencies .... but bad, good, and indifferent sources are cited indiscriminately .... even good sources are abused..... Westermarck neither appraises his evidence discriminatively nor becomes absorbed in his cultural phenomena; and while his views on early family life largely coincide with current doctrines, we are not able to discover any signal advancement of ethnology due to his writings."[10] Yet, in so far as ethnography in its quest for facts and more facts around the turn of this century implemented a concretizing of social science, Westermarck's Darwinian ethnography helped. He did live with the Moors for nine years.

For many ethnologists, however, Lowie has carved an epitaph that cannot easily be rubbed off the tomes of Westermarck with their six to twelve footnotes per page.[11]

IV. THE NATURAL HISTORY OF SOCIAL INSTITUTIONS

But other thinkers with other interests sat at the round table of intellectual history. Some of them listened to Westermarck's monologue and took away certain influences and certain models of thought. By some sociologists, Westermarck is remembered as among the first to shift the focus from old-fashioned history to the "natural history of social institutions." If a sociological standpoint occurs when historical studies become studies of the regular growth of institutions, then Wester-marck's *History of Human Marriage* is one of the earliest wholesale sociological studies. The book may be viewed as a large-scale natural history of a social institution. In this connection Westermarck writes:

> Like the phenomena of physical and psychical life those of social life should be classified into certain groups and each group investigated with regard to its origin and development. Only when treated in this way can history lay claim to the rank of a science in the highest sense of the term, as forming an important part of Sociology, the youngest of the principal branches of learning. Descriptive his-toriography has no higher object than that of offering materials to this science.[12]

The sociological interest in historical and ethnological materials was greatly augmented by Darwinian doctrine, and Westermarck's work is dominated by the Darwinism of *The Descent of Man*. The direct translation of Darwinian principles into social interpretation imagina-tively ran itself to a brief end in such men as Gumplowicz. The other line of development was the classical evolutionist and, following in partial reaction to it, the historical and institutional evolutionism of such men as Westermarck.

England was one of the several places where idiographic facts got caught up in a level of abstraction. In England, history and ethnography were used as stuffing for natural histories. In so far as English thinkers have imprinted patterns upon American sociology, it is by means of this notion of the natural history of social institutions. And Westermarck was a big man among them.

His view of sociology is indicated clearly in the above quotation. He had no systematic view of the scope of the discipline; it was synthetic, a collection of studies dealing with all aspects of social life. His own interest was in the comparative study of social institutions, which he thought of as sets of social relations regulated and sanctioned by "society." In American publications he is also classed as a forerunner of folk, or, more usually, of "cultural," sociology. In this connection, W. I. Thomas, in his influential course on social origins, told his classes that *The Origin and Development of Moral Ideas* was an important book to pur-chase, but, he added, "because of the wealth of material rather than for theory."[13]

Ward and Giddings and their generation knew Westermarck at firsthand, and he seems to have influenced Cooley in his formulation of the importance of primary groups, although how much or in what way, we do not know. Cooley writes: "The best comparative studies of the family, such as those of Westermarck or Howard, show us . . . . a universal institution . . . . . as more alike the world over than . . . . an earlier school had led us to suppose."[14] Cooley also cites him as rendering evidence for Cooley's cherished primary ideal of "the universality of kindness and the kindly ideal."[15] Yet it cannot be denied that Westermarck has not been, and is not now, of any focal importance in the actual work of American sociologists.

V. THE PSYCHOLOGICAL MODE OF EXPLANATION AND
BIOLOGICAL METAPHYSICS

Closely tied in with the comparative method but also standing weakly by itself, there is in the recorded thinking of Westermarck an instinctivist psychology. This psychology is linked to a model of causal explanation, and both are determined by the Darwinian notion of survival value. Westermarck used "cause" interchangeably with "origin." By these terms he meant the *biological* condition which determined a phenomenon or which lent to it a biological survival value. Thus the cause and origin of marriage lie in the need of prolonged parental care and protection. Mammals, including human beings, with such instinctive proclivities are favored by processes of natural selection. Upon such instincts (in 1936 Westermarck called them "primeval habits," and "feelings"[16]) rests the origin and persistence through various kinship vicissitudes of the family grouping. The basic explanatory apparatus upon which rests the application of causal analysis is, for Westermarck, the Darwinian theory of natural selection. This theory is used in accounting for the "psychological" tendencies and structures of men. Such tendencies and structures are the causes and lead to the motives underlying social groups and relationships. Hence, "in the last analysis," the *real* hub of the wheel of social life is found to be biological conditions. This was the metaphysical bent which underlay the psychology of the day.

It is because the "instincts and sentiments" underneath it are deep in the universal organic makeup of man as animal[17] that the family existed "from the beginning" and will probably continue to exist in times not yet here. Any reconstruction or explanation of social institutions must be based on "the fundamental causes" which Westermarck took to be biological and psychological in nature. "I put particular stress," he says, "upon the psychological causes . . . . and more especially I believe that the mere instincts have played a very important part in the origin of social institutions and rules."[18]

Thus, although Westermarck treated his ethnographic data in terms of the concept of social institution, he relied for their ultimate explanation upon psychobiological theory. Robertson Smith[19] criticized his *History of Human Marriage* on two related grounds: It is not "natural" history, for an institution is "controlled by public opinion and regulated by law." Second, to treat the study as a *natural* history of pairing involves the assumption that "the laws of society are at bottom mere formulated instincts, and this assumption really underlies all our author's theories. His fundamental position compels him .... to hold that every institution connection with marriage that has universal validity, or forms an integral part of the main line of development is rooted in instinct, and that institutions which are not based on instinct are necessarily exceptional and unimportant for scientific history."

Such a writer as Sir Edward B. Tylor considered that Westermarck had executed a valuable attempt to work out the biological and cultural sides of anthropology into a connected scheme.[20] But today, when one of the major emphases in ethnology is sociological psychology, it is not necessary to detail the reasons why Westermarck's formulation and assumptions are outmoded and otiose. The Durkheim school and also Rivers[21] criticized him for "explaining" social phenomena on a "psychological" basis, told him to watch it, but he shook them off.

VI. THE SOCIOLOGY OF MORALS AND THE THEORY OF ETHICS

Perhaps the ground tone of all Westermarck's writing is a persistent interest in moral codes and in ethical theories. The initial problem which led to the three volumes on marriage was that of sexual modesty. Later this concern expanded to include all relations between the sexes.

This drive toward a sociology of morals is one component of Westermarck's work which I believe could, but probably will not, influence the direction of American sociological interests. A sociology of morals, worthy of the name, cannot be said to exist among American social thinkers. Their intellectual tradition harbors certain hard phrases, distinctions, and many logical knots, which hang by the neck any attempt really to analyze moral phenomena. The theoretically inadequate work of Sumner is still for most the last word. An adequate social psychology of moral rules and judgments has not yet been written.

But if a sociology of morals were to be developed, Westermarck[22] would be written of as *one type* of its "forerunners." His voluminous synthesis of ethnographic material[23] was one of the pioneering books that placed the *historical* and *grossly empirical* aspect of ethics on a much more secure foundation. He documents moral variability; he presents data on the evolution of ethical behavior; his collection of facts shows a "connection" of custom with morals.[24] He shows morals as an early religious function.[25] One comes from his books with an absorbed realization of the *factual*[26] relativity of moral ideas. In his books the divine-origin view of morals is bathed in a lethal bath of facts. His name must be placed on the list of those who helped hammer out a naturalistic view of morals, even though *its* theoretical basis was mistaken. There is in Westermarck much timber that was growing in his time and that must be cleared from his work by a sociology of morals. Perhaps the utilization of his large body of anthropological materials in reconstructing the evolution of morals is vitiated by an uncontrolled comparative method. But the generic weakness in his thought on morals, as in his thought on kinship, lies in its psychological foundations.

His data show custom to be related to morals. It may be said that Westermarck misstates the point of these data: although he recognizes a certain objectivity and distinterestedness[27] as a characteristic of custom, he is so dominated by a subjective psychology that he is able to write: "Custom is a moral rule only on account of the indignation called forth by its transgression . . . . it is nothing but a generalization of emotional tendencies."[28]

The ultimate basis of moral judgments is individual and emotional. Moral concepts are generalizations of emotions that are within us. In certain cases specific emotions underpin certain moral concepts. Moral disapproval is a form of resentment, and moral approval is a form of retributive kindly emotion.[29] These two are distinctly *moral emotions*. Psychologically, Westermarck is not a bad bedfellow for McDougall, and certainly he would not fail to welcome Adam Smith if he had brought his "sentiments" with him.[30] Moral judgments spring from the individual's "own moral consciousness; they are judgments of other's conduct from one's own point of view and in accordance with one's own feelings and opinions about right and wrong." Although relative, they are not arbitrary, for we approve and disapprove "because we cannot do otherwise; our moral consciousness belongs to our mental constitution which we cannot change as we please."[31]

Yet, factually, "there is no absolute standard in morality."[32] Hence Westermarck must posit innate emotional differences to account for the ethnographic fact of a variety of moral judgments. He falls back upon the notion of an innate "emotional constitution."[33] The basic moral factor in evolution springs not from social relations but from individual sentiments of praise and blame. Westermarck evolutionized the Adam Smith of the "Moral Sentiments."

He speaks of "the evolution of the moral consciousness" which to "a large extent consists in its development from the unreflecting to the reflecting, from the unenlightened to the enlightened."[34]

Although, as I have indicated, the excessively psychological and subjective interpretation given by Westermarck to his data makes it necessary to give us the explanatory structure of his thought, the gross data are still valuable for certain purposes and there are also scattered inklings which a sociology of morals would wish to consider carefully and possibly to develop.

VII. THE MORAL

The younger generation of American ethnologists and sociologists do not know Westermarck at firsthand. It is possible to receive gracefully the Ph.D. degree in ethnology, and certainly in sociology, without ever opening any one of his books. In diluted fashion his effort lives in passages in histories of social thought and in the chapters of symposiums.[35] But he is not a direct determinant of the working day of American social scientists.

Searching the pages of contemporary texts, monographs, and symposiums you will find few references to Westermarck. You do find scattered bits of information ("In Java, among the ...."), with his name footnoted, or references to, or paragraph summaries of, his theories of incest and ornament and the monogamic family.

Why is this? Why did this man have his best time in other times and then drop from the running in the operative, the pivotal, footnotes of fresh writing? Many general and perhaps some social reasons could be given, but I think there are two more or less specific ones.[36]

One reason is that between Westermarck and us there stands a modern sociological psychology which comprises a new view of the role of biological elements in social systems and which excludes the psychological as explanatory, making physiological science a strict counterpart and a parallel endeavor to work within a sociological perspective. With varying degrees of adequacy, ethnologists are grasping and using this view; it forms one of the more fruitful trends of interest in modern American ethnology. The past is written and used in terms of the present, and Westermarck does not contribute to this trend.

The other reason is the changed status of "fact" within the accepted models of inquiry. Westermarck got hold of a lot of "facts," but he used them either in a kind of planless empiricism or like a philosopher illustrating his feelings in the grand manner. His facts do not now appear to be crucial. They are not caught up in a firm mesh of theory, which they prove or disprove. The comparative method and the evolutionist theory, within which his facts make sense, have been overthrown for new models of inquiry and new and perhaps more modest theory. That is the history of the changing content of science. And so his books bore us a little because their masses of fact seem irrelevant to our theoretic directions. Encyclopedic compilation prevails over analytic theory, and he is heavy with obsolete problems. The undisturbed dust on his volumes is an object lesson in method and in the ways of setting up problems.

These things might have been forgiven if he had possessed the synoptic mind that can squeeze from masses of data the analytically characterizing sentence. But Westermarck did not write such sentences. Maybe he made some of the men at the intellectual round table get up and thenceforth look to their facts. But he does not give us anything to look to them through; he sat at some other round table with other chairmen.

NOTES

1. *The History of Human Marriage* (London, 1901). The major propositions of these three volumes are to be found in a one-volume edition, *A Short History of Marriage* (New York, 1926); and in *The Origin and Development of Moral Ideas* (2 vols.; London, 1906). He also considered *The Future of Marriage in Western Civilization* (New York, 1936).

2. *Ethical Relativity* (New York, 1932).

3. *Marriage Ceremonies in Morocco* (London, 1914); *Ritual and Belief in Morocco* (2 vols.; London, 1926); *Wit and Wisdom in Morocco: A Study of Native Proverbs* (London, 1930); see also "The Belief in Spirits in Morocco," *Acta academiae Aboensis, Humaniora,* I (Helsingfors, 1920), 1–167.

4. The best life-history in brief compass is to be found in M. Ginsberg's "The Life and Work of Edward Westermarck," *Sociological Review* (Eng.), January–April, 1940; see

also, for self-told account, Westermarck's *Memories of My Life* (New York, 1929), trans. A. Barnewl.

5. *Academy*, XL (October 3, 1891), 288 ff.

6. *History of Human Marriage*, p. 5.

7. See Westermarck, *Memories of My Life*.

8. It is interesting to note the way in which museum arrangements reflect ethnological theory and vice versa. Westermarck's books are arranged like the museums set up by Pitt-Rivers. Both reflect evolutionist theory. The present method of arrangement is "regional," and the corresponding theory incorporates such notions as "cultural area" and the necessity for contextual work.

9. There is a remarkable criticism of Westermarck written in 1900 by Karl Pearson (*Grammar of Science*). After criticizing the "obscurity attaching to the use of the words force and cause" (p. 132), he adds that "to find sequences of facts .... we must follow the changes of one tribe or people at a time. We cannot trace the successive stages of social life except by minute investigation of facts relating to one social unit" (p. 359).

10. *The History of Ethnological Theory* (New York, 1937), p. 98–99.

11. Before leaving Westermarck as ethnologist, however, it must be recorded that the common idea of him as merely an armchair librarian is mistaken. Those who hold such a view are sentenced to thirty days with the very flat idiographic descriptions in *Ritual and Belief in Morocco* and the ethnographic pages of "The Belief in Spirits in Morocco." These works show that Westermarck knew what a campstool felt like; they do not harbour any conclusions, and they have not entered into the stream of American social science. Although the bulk of *Wit and Wisdom in Morocco* consists of a mere compilation of proverbs (with full Arabic texts), there is a 63-page Introductory Essay (embodying the Frazer lecture of 1928), which contains a neat set of characterizing criteria for *proverbs*, an empiric taxonomic scheme, and notes on their societal function. It should also be mentioned that two of Westermarck's more specific theories still run through writers on these topics (see the *Encyclopaedia of the Social Sciences*, articles by Reo Fortune on "Incest" [VII, 621] and by Ruth Bunzel on "Ornament" [XI, 496]).

12. *The History of Human Marriage*, p. 1.

13. *Source Book for Social Origins* (Boston, 1909), p. 911 and 869.

14. *Social Organization* (New York, 1909), p. 24.

15. *Ibid.*, p. 40.

16. *The Future of Marriage in Western Civilization*, pp. 5, 264.

17. Hence, given the biologistic premises, the relevance of the mating habits of the cognate species of anthropoid.

18. *The History of Human Marriage*, p. 5.

19. *Nature*, XLIV, 270 (cited by Park and Burgess, *An Introduction to the Science of Sociology*, pp. 16–17).

20. Tylor, *op. cit.*, pp. 288 f.

21. See the critical reviews in *Revue philosophique*, 1907, pp. 409 ff.; *L'Année sociologique*, X, 283 ff., XI, 274 ff.; W. H. R. Rivers, "Survival in Sociology," *Sociological Review*, VI, 304 ff., and "Sociology and Psychology," *ibid.*, IX, 3 ff.

22. Along with Hobhouse, *Morals in Evolution* (London, 1906); Sumner, *Folkways* (Boston, 1906); and Spencer, *The Data of Ethics* (New York, 1879).

23. *The Origin and Development of Moral Ideas* (2 vols.; London, 1906).

24. But see below.

25. *Op. cit.*, II, 745.

26. But, as we shall see, in his interpretation of moral phenomena and in his ethics it is clear that moral ideas are relative to "the emotions they express" and not to social factors, e.g., custom (see *Ethical Relativity*, p. 289).

27. See, e.g., *Origin and Development of Moral Ideas*, I, 120–21; cf. also A. Smith's notion of the "impartial spectator" and "sympathetic resentment."

28. *Ibid.*, I, 121.

29. *Ethical Relativity*, p. 89.

30. *Ibid.*, see p. 71 for laudatory references to *The Theory of Moral Sentiments*.

31. *Ethical Relativity*, pp. 58–59.

32. *Ibid.*, p. 59.

33. *Moral Ideas*, I, 11: "The emotional constitution of man [which underlies moral phenomena] does not present the same uniformity as the human intellect." The very engaging manner in which Westermarck uses his very pliable psychology to account for what he considers to be another fact should be noted: "The general uniformity of human nature accounts for the great similarities which characterize the moral ideas of mankind. ....But at the same time these ideas also represent racial differences" (*ibid.*, II, 742). Although "different external conditions" and "different measures of knowledge" [*Ethical Relativity*, p. 187] may also be reasons for these variations, "the most common differences of moral estimates have undoubtedly a psychical origin [ultimately 'emotional']" (*Moral Ideas*, II, 742).

34. *Moral Ideas*, I, 10.

35. See H. E. Barnes and Howard Becker, *Social Thought from Lore to Science* (Boston, 1938), and *Contemporary Social Theory* (New York, 1940).

36. I am here concerned *only* with immanent reasons, not those, if any, to be found by a sociological analysis of his work in its various societal contexts. See V. F. Calverton's ideological imputations, "The Compulsive Basis of Social Thought," *American Journal of Sociology*, March, 1931; also Westermarck's reply (*ibid.*, March, 1936).

CHAPTER VIII

THE SOCIOLOGICAL THEORIES OF FRANKLIN HENRY GIDDINGS: CONSCIOUSNESS OF KIND, PLURALISTIC BEHAVIOR, AND STATISTICAL METHOD

CLARENCE H. NORTHCOTT

I. DISCURSIVE AND EVOLUTIONARY CHARACTER OF GIDDINGS' WRITINGS

IN ATTEMPTING to give an outline of the sociological theories of Professor Franklin Henry Giddings,[1] one is beset by the difficulty of finding them in any complete and final form. His writings are scattered over a period of more than thirty years.[2] Each book is, to a certain extent, complementary to all others in the series, so that a study of them in chronological order gives a realistic impression of the open mind and analytic power of the author, without affording anything that even he would claim to be a completed system of sociological theory. The absence of revision and co-ordination also bewilders the student as to what part, if any, Giddings accepted or rejected at the end of his life and what he would have modified. Moreover, personal contact with him in the lecture-room does not help one greatly. His custom of applying his analytical mind to any pressing question of immediate import, whether suggested by the publication of a new book, the exposition of a new theory, or the application of some political policy, and his habit of injecting the results of his analysis as new wine into old bottles shatter the outline and symmetry of any tentative system. Nevertheless, the fundamental theories on which his sociological system is built are so clearly stated that an attempt may reasonably be made to synthesize them.

While Giddings was a man of great mental originality, his sociological system and ideas were also based on a wide reading of his sociological predecessors and contemporaries. From Auguste Comte he derived the idea of the need for a basic or fundamental social science. As Giddings once forcefully expressed this conviction: "To teach ethnology, the philosophy of history, political economy, and the theory of the state, to men who have not learned the first principles of sociology, is like teaching astronomy or thermodynamics to men who have not learned the Newtonian laws of motion." From Comte's *Positive Polity* he drew his outline of the main stages in the history of civilization. He also fully adopted Comte's repudiation of theological and metaphysical thinking about society and upheld the contention that sociology must always be an empirical science, worthy of our scientific age. From Darwin and Herbert Spencer he learned that scientific social thinking, in turn, must be evolutionary thought, and he held tenaciously throughout his life to a stalwart evolutionary naturalism. Giddings' earlier sociological system was essentially an adaptation and elaboration of Spencer's system, as stated in the latter part of *First Principles*. From Lester F. Ward he took over the notion that a main purpose of sociology is to furnish scientific guidance for civic reform and social betterment. His conception of the "consciousness of kind" was derived mainly from Adam Smith's notion of reflective sympathy. He leaned heavily on Tarde for some of his social psychology, and his views of social constraint were affected by the conceptions of Darwin, Durkheim, and Sumner. His psychology of social values was in part derived from a reading of the economic theories of the Austrian school and John Bates Clark. Finally, Giddings' ideas of scientific method and social statistics were taken over mainly from John Stuart Mill, Stanley Jevons, Leon Walras, and Karl Pearson.

II. THE ORIGIN AND EVOLUTION OF HUMAN SOCIETY

To Giddings there are four general problems for the sociologist to study: (1) the origin and evolution of society; (2) social constraint and the conformation of behavior and character to type as the immediate and general function of society; (3) the effect of social constraint upon selection; and (4) the final consequence of social constraint, conceived of as an amount or rate of progress. The greater bulk of his own thought has been devoted to the first problem, though he has given many significant sidelights in his later works upon all the others.

Society, which in his later writings he distinguishes from all swarms, herds, and packs of animals, he regards as a product of association, which he is at pains to differentiate from gregariousness. All these phenomena —namely, gregariousness and the herd, association and society—are products, as he contends, of a collective or pluralistic mode of the struggle for existence. Pluralistic behavior is the behavior of a "plural," that is, many creatures (animals or human beings) in one place at one time, played upon by the same set of circumstances and acting and reacting upon one another. Behavior is affected by the material environment, which supplies "an infinitely differentiated group of stimuli."[3] These play upon beings who have held together from birth or have assembled under the stress of the struggle for existence. The multiplication of off-spring not only aids the collective life but insures a mutuality of needs and capacities for either attainment or resistance. A given habitat will include a number of groups of this kind, whose points of resemblance will measure the degree of their similarity.

Their most important similarities will be found in their behavior. The primary activity of the living organism is to adapt the environment to itself in order to satisfy its primary needs of safety and food. In the human being these adaptations are the basis of appreciation, that is, a change in consciousness describable as the attaching of more interest or value to one thing than to another. Appreciation arises out of those reactions, which are, first, instinctive, then habitual, and later on are rationalized. When, at length, man finds the limits which restrict the adaptation of the environment to himself, he begins the reverse process of the adjustment of himself to the environment. His interest is attached to the behavior of his fellows, who, by reason of their biological relationship and the pressure of a common environment, are at the same time interested in his behavior. His reactions and those of his fellows tend to be alike, and there arises a perception of the likeness of external stimuli to self-stimuli. This is co-ordinated with the adjustment of one organism to the like behavior of similar organisms, a process furthered by imitation and reflective sympathy. This interstimulation produces dramatic behavior: "In the presence of fellow-beings action becomes acting."[4] When language arises, such behavior is conversationalized: it is talked about, and differences and similarities among objects, activities, behavior, and persons are felt and perceived. Out of this arises a consciousness of kind, compounded of "organic sympathy, the perception of resemblance, conscious or reflective sympathy, affection, and the desire for recognition."[5] There is a distinct stimulus in "kind," a direct reaction to it, and presently a discriminating awareness of it. Natural selection works upon this; and, since competition and the struggle for survival lead to co-operation and preferential association, there is produced that collective behavior with which social organization begins. So it comes about that talk and the consciousness of kind convert gregariousness into association and the herd or pack into society.

Among the most elementary similarities of behavior are habits of toleration. Individuals living in a group necessarily come to tolerate one another. Conflict is natural in a group, since, by reason of original differences of nature and habit, the imitation involved in consciousness of kind is never perfect, and because of the drive toward domination and conquest: "Antagonism, however, is self-limiting; it necessarily terminates in the equilibrium of toleration."[6] Individual members of the group prove to be too evenly matched to make fighting worth while. Thus primal natural rights, in the sense of the immunities and liberties of toleration, come to be enjoyed long before they get conscious recognition. Soon, under the pressure of a common danger or a common opportunity, these similarities of behavior develop unconsciously into spontaneous collective action. This effect is produced under the stimulus of communication, imitation, suggestion, and, later, leadership and subordination. The group which acts collectively represents an assembling and economizing of effort. The assembled effort of the group becomes co-operation, that is, conscious practical agreement for the better realization of common purposes.

The organizing force or influence whereby this type of social organization is launched is to be found in an analysis of the degrees of reaction. Some individuals react more promptly, some more effectively, some more persistently. The first type of reaction is mainly one of sensation and emotion, which practically all share. Some, fewer in number, will examine, inquire, think, and discuss, while the remainder, forming the minority, will initiate action. In so doing they create new situations to which others must adapt themselves. The protocracy, or the nucleus of the ruling minority, seek the co-operation of the group which has given them power and authority, and the latter must either co-operate or oppose. But the protocracy is in a position to see opportunities of wealth and power before others and to dispense patronage on a definite understanding of loyalty and allegiance. Where the protocracy does not actually rule, it dominates by virtue of ability, integrity, or beneficent purpose. Thus, "in terms of like or of unlike, of prompt or of slow, of persistent or of intermittent response, all the phenomena of natural grouping and of collective behavior can be stated and interpreted."[7]

Social organization began with the few exercising rule or domination; later, collective choices or decisions were made, and concerted volition came into existence. The concert of wills, of which this consists, is of various degrees of completeness, according to the proportion of individuals who are instinctive, sympathetic, dogmatic, or deliberate. Many fewer persons share in approving a collective deliberative decision than in one requiring an instinctive or sympathetic attitude. From this arises a law of concerted volition, that "in a normal population, the percentage number of individuals participating in a collective decision diminishes as the intellectual quality of the decision rises."[8] With increasing necessity for collective action, social organization tends to develop internal complexity and to assume a hierarchical form.

From one point of view these grades represent the divisions which the collective struggle and the reactions of the majority and minority upon one another create. Through conquest, the assertion of privilege and authority, and the use of the *commendatio,* there are produced within the social organization groups that may be privileged and closed, selectively open, or indiscriminately open:

> Eligibility to membership in a privileged and closed group is governed by consideration of source. Descent from members of the group in a former generation is one of the oldest and best-known requirements. Membership in an antecedent group or category may be the requirement. Eligibility to membership in a selectively open group is determined by the functioning value of members individually for the functioning of the group collectively. In the indiscriminately open group there are no eligibility tests.[9]
>
> In the historical evolution of social organization, intragroup conflict develops between closed and open groups.[10]

The group based on ethnic unity or kinship is replaced by one based on civil unity. The alien is admitted to the privileges of the folk and to the obligations of tax-paying and military service. This mutuality of obligation and opportunity is the basis of civilization, which may, therefore be defined as "modally and characteristically a substitution of the open for the closed group in politics, religion, trade, and education."[11]

Through the organization of relations within the open group and the establishment of co-operation, the protocracy acquires political power or sovereignty. This can never be an unconditional power to compel obedience but is finite and conditional, dependent on the balance and composition of forces. In social evolution, sovereignty has assumed four distinct modes. The personal sovereign, the strong personality, commands obedience but cannot compel it. The class—aristocracy, capitalists, or labor—can inspire obedience, if mentally and morally superior, or exact it through the control of wealth. In mass sovereignty the majority has the power to compel a large measure of obedience for a time through numbers or the potentialities of superior force. Finally, an organized, enlightened, and deliberative community may evoke obedience through a rational appeal to intelligence and moral sense.[12]

When the supreme will of society is organized for requiring and directing obedience, government comes into existence and, like sovereignty, is determined by the prevailing conditions of the social mind and the degree of circumstantial pressure. In times of chaos and insecurity the forceful personality crushes his competitors and, with the active co-operation of the community born of their dislike of anarchy, sets up an absolute government. Where there is much spontaneous co-operation and more like-mindedness than difference and antagonism, with a fair resistance to arbitrary power, government takes the form of limited minority rule. Where revolutionary conditions exist, whether political or industrial, absolute majority rule tends to be found as a product of the revolt. Finally, in a community that is, on the whole, homogeneous and composed of individuals approximately equal in ability and condition, limited majority rule is the form of government.[13] In the latter form, constitutional limitations are stated to insure the rightful balance between the coercion through which government as a form of social control operates and the liberty associated with that full development of personality that is the purpose of social organization.[14]

But liberty, says Professor Giddings, is not guaranteed by a written constitution; it is determined by the composition of sovereignty, which is the real constitution. The bond by which the most democratic form of sovereignty is held together is the agreement to abide by the decision of the majority. The conditions implied in this form of organization of majority rule are twofold: (1) the majority may not and does not override certain rights agreed on by the majority and most of the minority, and thereby guaranteed to all the minority. These rights must be set forth in a constitution, which is necessary for minorities and for democracies generally. The defense and the safeguard of liberty, however, does not lie in this constitution but in the maintenance of this condition and the establishment of a second. (2) Minorities must have freedom of speech, of the press, of meeting, and of orderly and peaceful agitation, to the end that they may be able to turn their minority into a majority. The repression of minorities throws society back onto lower planes of organization, where patriotism and various forms of lordships are the chief characteristics.[15]

III. THE NATURE OF SOCIAL ORGANIZATION

With this as an inadequate presentation of the account that Giddings has given of the processes involved in the genesis and evolution of human society, let us now attempt to summarize his analysis of social organization. In a community there are two forms of organization: one called the "social composition," combining those who dwell together in one specified place; the other, a constituent society, combining those who are desirous of carrying on special forms of activity or of maintaining particular interests. Each group in the social composition may be called a "component society." The earlier tribal forms of component societies were brought together by genetic aggregation, while the later civil component societies are the product, in addition, of congregation. Tribal societies insist on kinship as the bond of association; civil societies have broken that bond of ethnic unity. The path of development toward a civil organization of society, where kinship is of less value, has lain in the transition from the loosely knit, even segregative, matronymic group, generally the more primitive, to the more compact and powerful patronymic group, in the establishment of a barbaric and pastoral feudalism and in the effect of migration and settlement in producing a varied demotic composition in which the bond of kinship is no longer adequate. With the establishment of male descent and ancestor worship, clan headships and tribal chieftainships tended to become hereditary in certain families. Barbaric feudalism arose as the chief became wealthy in cattle and land, which he received as rewards from his tribe. It became his duty to protect the borders of his land, and for this purpose he used the broken and ruined men, the landless and the refugees from other clans, and bound them to him as feudal dependents in a bond of uncritical and unquestioning obedience. The development of this form of organization and a synchronous development of agriculture led to civil society, based on neighborhood, mutual interest, and co-operation.

In civil society, constituent societies wherein membership is not an incident of birth became possible. Constituent societies grow out of, and are differentiated from, component societies through a specialization of function; they are voluntarily formed purposive associations.

Their chief characteristics are co-ordination, mutual aid, and division of labor.[16] The chief of these purposive organizations in civil society is the state, through which the social mind operates to achieve the co-ordination and domination of the whole community and its lesser purposive associations. Its functions are coextensive with human interests, for its primary purpose is to perfect social integration. In so doing, it is carried into economic activities and cultural functions. Yet equally vital to social organization are the various private and voluntary associations which arise, duplicating in many cases the functions of the state: "The state, so far from being the only political organization, could not exist in a free or republican form, were there not voluntary and private political associations."[17] It follows, therefore, since the compulsory state and the voluntary association are both vital and essential, that "whatever belittles the state or destroys belief in its power to perform any kind of social service, whatever impairs the popular habit of achieving ends by private initiative and voluntary organization, endangers society and prevents the full realization of its ends."[18]

IV. SOCIAL CONTROL AND SOCIAL CONSTRAINT

Turning, now, to the second problem which Giddings enunciates as facing the sociologist, that of social constraint, we find him defining his point of view thus:

We make the initial assumption that the institutions of human society and all the events of history, including the migrations of men from place to place, the great enthusiasms, the intellectual awakenings, the wars and the revolutions, may be regarded as responses to varying stimuli, and that they are governed by certain laws of combination or by certain facts of resemblance or of difference among the minds responding.[19]

That is, social constraint and the conformity of behavior and character to type are functions of the operation of the social mind. This social mind is no abstraction, nor, on the other hand, is it a mere summation of individual minds. It is an integration of them, born of their interaction: "The social mind is the phenomenon of many individual minds in interaction, so playing upon one another that they simultaneously feel the same sensation or emotion, arrive at one judgment and perhaps act in concert."[20] It is to be explained in terms of response to stimulation, of consciousness of kind, and of concerted volition.[21] From like response spring the phenomena of agreement and co-operation; from differences of response in kind, degree, and completeness come the innumerable phenomena of unlike interest, antagonism, conflict, rivalry, and competition.[22] The process of interstimulation is carried on by suggestion, impression, example, and imitation, with conflict as a co-efficient, and with forms of expansive association, such as travel, commerce, diplomacy, and war, as further determinants. With the accumulation, through the advance of socialization, of innumerable conditions, events, relations, acts, ideas, beliefs, plans, and ideals, there are created large classes of secondary stimuli which, in modern social life, play a greater role in the formation of the social mind than do the primary stimuli: "The very arrangements under which we live, the groupings of human beings, their ideas and purposes, their aims, their ideals, their laws and institutions are ever-present, ever-potent causes of continuing collective action."[23] These secondary stimuli are divisible into four classes: the ideomotor, directly inciting the motor system; the ideo-emotional, awakening chiefly emotional reactions; the dogmatic-emotional, appealing to emotion and belief; and the critically intellec-tual, appealing to the higher intellectual processes. Corresponding to these stimuli are classifications of like-mindedness, according to whether the individuals are swayed by feeling, emotion, belief, or reason, respec-tively. A correlation can be established between these psychic traits and the extent of the forms of like-mindedness. This correlation is expressed in the law: "More individuals agree in feeling than agree in belief. More agree in belief than concur in reasoned opinion. Sympathetic like-mindedness is more extensive than dogmatic like-mindedness, and dog-matic like-mindedness more extensive than deliberate like-mindedness."

This movement of the social mind may also be viewed from the stand-point of the modes of activity of the individual, the types of character that shape it, and the motives and ideals that are indorsed. The modes of activity of the individual are fourfold. There is, first, *appreciation,* the seizing of the facts of experience and their organization into knowledge, preference, and values. Next comes *utilization,* the turning to use of the objects of the external world. Then the conscious individual adapts him-self to his situation, to the opportunities and activities possible to him, which constitute the process of *characterization.* Finally, conscious indi-viduals adapt themselves to one another in the process of *socialization.*[24] Parallel with the complex of psychic states involved in appreciation are the motor, emotional, and intellectual types spoken of above. Parallel, in the same way, with the four degrees in which utilization is carried out are four types of disposition—the aggressive, the instigative, the domineering, and the creative. Thus, also, four types of character come into existence in the process of characterization—the forceful, the convivial, the austere, and the rationally conscientious. The former emphasizes the qualities of courage and power; the convivial is of the pleasure-loving type; the austere is the product of reaction against the excesses of convivial indulgence; while the last is a product of the reaction against and progress beyond the austere type.[25]

Correlated with the phenomena of the social mind and the form and degree of social constraint is the type of human rational society. Of this there are eight subdivisions: (1) A homogeneous community of blood relatives, among whom the chief social bond is sympathy—the *sympathetic* type. (2) The *congenial* type, made up of like spirits drawn together by similarity of nature and agreement in ideas. Illustrations of this type are found in the Mayflower band, the Latter-Day Saints, partisan political colonies, and communistic brotherhoods. (3) The *approbational* type, a community of miscellaneous and sometimes lawless elements drawn together by economic opportunity, where a general approbation of qualities and conduct is practically the only social bond. (4) The *despotic* type, where the social bonds are despotic power and a fear-inspired obedience. (5) The *authoritative* type, where the arbitrary power has identified itself with tradition and religion, and reverence for authority is the social bond. (6) The *conspirital* type, where intrigue and conspiracy are the social bonds. (7) The *contractual* type, such as the league of the Iroquois and the confederation of American commonwealths in 1778, where the social bond is a covenant or contract. (8) The *idealistic* social type, where a population collectively responds to certain great ideals, where the social bonds are comprehension of mind, confidence, fidelity, and an altruistic spirit of social service.[26]

The genetic standpoint from which Giddings approached sociology prompted him to lay slight stress upon the modes and forms of social control. He gives little space to the tribe in primitive society, the state and municipality in civil society, or the instruments of social control therein adopted. Only brief sketches are devoted to the influence of custom, law, the church, parental authority, and various voluntary associations.

Social control is compared with that of natural selection: it is control of variations from type. In the organic struggle for existence "there is

an environmental constraint compelling conformity of organic structure and of life to certain adapted or adaptable types, from which variation is possible only within somewhat definite limits."[27] In group life
"human beings, instinctively, by habit, and rationally, manifest a dominant antipathy to those variations from type which attract attention."[28]
Among savages and barbarians such persons are killed or abandoned.
In civilized societies they are suspected or avoided, guarded or restrained.
In savage and barbarian communities a considerable degree of uniformity of conduct is obtained: "by the conscious coöperation of elders
in directing the rearing of children by young parents, by organized initiation ceremonies, by clan and tribal councils, each new generation is
remorselessly trained in those beliefs, habits and loyalties which the
group regards as vital to its existence." While in civilized communities,
such "restraints, inculcations and obedience-compelling devices" are so
greatly interlaced as to be difficult to distinguish, they are found, when
stripped of all adventitious features, to be means to the same end, to
"determine, limit, and control variation from type, now extending its
range, now narrowing it and compelling a closer conformity."[29]

The method of constraint may be summed up in the one word "discipline." The methods are described in greater detail in the following
sentence: "By praise and blame, by avoidance and rebuke, by indulgence
and license, by penance and fine, by suspension and expulsion, by
corporal punishment and maiming, by imprisonment and execution,
men are forced to desist, to obey, to help; their conduct is educated into
habits; their efforts are stimulated or goaded to acceptable degrees of
intensity and persistence; their characters are moulded to approved
types."[30] These particular methods are employed in the "conviction that
such conformity to kind or type or standard is essential to security and
to coöperative efficiency."[31]

Social constraint is affected by environmental pressure and by the
composition and the degree of homogeneity of the population. The
character of the environment "determines the composition of a population as more or less heterogeneous, more or less compound," while "the
composition of the population determines the character, the complexity
and the range of its reactions to stimulation,"[32] including its mental
characteristics, its potentialities of co-operation, its capacity for progress,
its ideals, and the degree of its democratic organization. Environments
are either poorly or richly endowed, and each is either accessible or iso-

lated. The poor and isolated environment is filled with a sparse, relatively simple, and homogeneous population, where the struggle for existence causes a large proportion of the people to fall into the "middle age frequencies." A poor country, easy of egress, contains an equally homogeneous population, but one which, under the attraction of more favorable lands, suffers from the emigration of its more virile members. A rich land, but relatively isolated, like several of the South Sea island groups, carries a dense population in which every inequality of energy or ability counts. From this more favored land, under the pressure of the food supply, vigorous elements go forth to conquer new homes. Or, where a stronger race can do so, distant populations come to invade and exploit these rich natural resources. The bountiful and accessible environments furnished, for instance, by the great river valleys of the world form the seats of composite and varied populations, welded into an amalgam by conquest, immigration, and intermarriage.

The composition of the population limits the vigor and adaptiveness of its reactions to stimulation. A vigorous reaction is characteristic of adolescence and maturity; adaptation is difficult to the old. The ethnic composition of a population determines whether its total reaction to stimulation will be relatively simple or complex. A homogeneous population may be expected to show a reaction uncomplicated by conflicts between differing groups. A heterogeneous population will react to a greater number of stimuli; it will have a wider circle of interests. In the more heterogeneous populations, stimulation must be stronger before like behavior will result.

Social pressure generates countless forms of co-operation that can most appropriately be called "folkways." When these folkways have been affected by emotion, belief, reflection, and conscious inculcation and are to some extent socially enforced, they become "mores." Usage, custom, fashion, manners, ceremonies, ritual, morals—all these indefinable and flexible forms of social pressure operate upon the individual chiefly through penalties of disapprobation and ostracism.[33] More important mores, such as religion and justice, which apply social pressure through "boycotting, outlawry, and other social dooms, including death,"[34] are called "themistes."

On the third problem, the effect of social constraint upon selection, Giddings recognizes that association, though involving scarcely anything beyond involuntary social control, gives advantage in survival. It assists in perpetuating the race, in diminishing the expenditure and waste of energy, and in favoring the growth of intelligence. He holds a view differing in a measure from that of Fiske in regard to the relation of prolonged infancy to social development. He contends that association stimulated conceptual thought, which, in turn, reacted upon mental activity until it became man's dominant interest. A slower development of the individual and a longer infancy resulted.[35] Association favors survival by providing greater power of defense for the group, by affording a longer and more certain food supply, and by making maturity and reproduction of the race more certain. It makes variation more fruitful and gives survival-value to such social characteristics as toleration, sympathy, and compassion.

By emphasis upon the value of toleration, social constraint modifies selection. In the conflict which preceded the establishment of toleration "the very strong kill off the weak. Then the very strong in turn are overborne by the numerical superiority of the individuals of average power. The majority then left is composed of those that are too nearly equal in strength for one to hope to vanquish another, and they are obliged to live on terms of toleration that make possible the reassertion and renewed activity of the socializing motives."[36] Along with these objective conditions go subjective consequences, the chief of which is an idea of toleration, finding expression in rules of custom, formulating "those enjoyments and immunities that are habitually allowed."[37]

Society is a selective agent, for social selection converts survival of the fit into survival of the better. This is both an individual and a social matter: "Social conditions determine for each individual what elements of his personality shall be played upon by the influences that strengthen or weaken; what suggestions shall consciously or unconsciously give direction to his thoughts, quality to his feeling and so, at length, determination to his will."[38] The aim of society is to carry on the process of individuation without endangering race survival. The function of social control is "to increase the practical effectiveness of society as an instrumentality for the protection and improvement of life."[39] The social discipline in which it consists secures the extermination or restraint of the antisocial and the selection for survival and encouragement of the sympathetic, the intelligent, and the self-controlled. But social pressure, being mainly repressive and destructive, has distinct limits of utility. It curtails variation, limits differentiation, checks spontaneity, restricts individuality, and tends toward rigidity of social organization. There must, therefore, be a balance between the restraint that it imposes upon the antisocial and the freedom that it gives to the elements adapted to a social life. If it offers opportunity for the development of individuation without endangering race survival, it has turned the selective struggle of evolution into progress. For "race maintenance and evolution with diminishing cost of individual life, with increasing freedom, power and happiness of the individual person—is progress."[40]

V. CO-OPERATION, SOCIAL DISCIPLINE, AND SOCIAL INSTITUTIONS

The fourth problem, the final consequences of social constraint, conceived of as an amount or rate of progress, has much more attention given to it. Social constraint, which is, to Giddings, a form of concerted volition, co-operation, and discipline, is a chief factor in the organization of society. Organized society, in contrast to any of those imaginary states where every man's hand was against his neighbor, has become a mutually beneficial association for attaining security, opportunity, enjoyments, or improvements: "Society is a means to a definite end—namely, the survival and improvement of men through a continuing selection of intelligence and sympathy."[41] The development of community life meant more than the establishment of social order; it meant greater security, a social and economic surplus, more definite rights for the individuals, and the definition of those rights in codes of law interpreted and applied by specialized talents and institutions. Administrative agencies came to shape activities of society and were, in turn, reacted upon by the collective organization. Civil society gave opportunities and problems to intelligence and, in application and reaction to the economic, cultural, and political environment, produced a civilization that stands for the vast complex wealth of an intelligent humanity.

After this general statement we turn to an analysis of the policies whereby this co-operation was effected. Such policies are formed "through deliberation upon the composition, the character, and the circumstances of the community."[42] They are of two types, internal and external. The former have for their object the achievement of certain relations of unity, liberty, and equality within the group; the latter aim to achieve policies of subjugation, exploitation, and assistance between one group and another. Policies of unity aim to perfect the cohesion, the homogeneity, and the solidarity to the group through control of amalgamation and assimilation, of language and religion, of law and conduct. Policies of liberty are reactions against the restraints of excessive unification. They depend for their origin upon diversity of social composition, incomplete assimilation, and freedom of communication: "No scheme of unification ever quite destroys the restless individualism of the rational mind." Hence, when unifying policies have produced administrative order, and in part set the mind free for, and in part instigated it to, public agitation, destructive criticism, and even overt rebellion, an ideal of liberty arises, becoming actualized in the establishment and protection of individual liberty by forms of constitutional law. Policies of equality are reactions against the abuse of liberty and a limitation of it, so as to procure equality of liberty and opportunity. These policies include political and legal equality, the abolition of state-created privileges in economic activities, equality of educational opportunities, and socially remedial measures.

Policies of subjugation result in the integration of small ethnic groups into larger tribal systems and in the consolidation of small civil states into great political systems. Race struggles and class conflicts have also been, to a great extent, expressions of consciously formulated policies of subjugation. In policies of exploitation the economic motive has become ascendant. In most advanced modern civilizations both these policies tend to be superseded, in part, by policies of assistance, where "the powerful and prosperous classes of the relatively strong people extend educational advantages, relief of acute distress, and, to some extent, economic opportunity to the wage-earning classes, to inferior races and to dependent peoples."[43] It is of interest here to trace the connection that Giddings establishes between surplus energy and the policies of assistance.[44] Certain organisms develop surplus energy, which enables them to survive under the circumstances that cripple other organisms and to transmit to posterity a rich legacy of ability or to give their own generation much socially beneficial help. In the social sphere America, which has developed this surplus energy, has been able to extend assistance to Europe and the Orient:

Of all the modes of socially distributed surplus energy, the most important are sympathy and its allied elements in the consciousness of kind. Given this force, the transformations of the weak by the strong necessarily become to some extent an uplifting instead of an exploitation. Given the equilibration of energy through uplifting, there is a necessary growth of equality and an increasing possibility of successful democracy of the liberal type.[45]

In the development of these policies the internal and external varieties come to be combined in highly complex schemes. Thus internal policies of unification become combined with external policies of subjugation to produce militarism. Prior to attack, unity and cohesion are demanded in the attacking state, and to a great extent the organization of society becomes coercive. After the conquest and the establishment of a heterogeneous people, policies of unification again come into play, to secure uniformity in language, religion, and conduct, through criminal law, sumptuary administration, and isolation. Successful militarism prepares the way for exploitation and stimulates it; but in the long run militarism works out its own destruction. With the downfall of militarism, much administrative energy hitherto devoted to political integration, much economic activity hitherto diverted, and much intellectual energy hitherto suppressed are freed, and the result is a growth of liberalism. Diversity of peoples, laws, manners, and customs in the heterogeneous nation has a stimulating effect. Physical and mental plasticity results. The investigating, critical, and philosophical spirit arises. The nation becomes liberal and progressive and has to face the problem of pursuing policies that will maintain unity and stability and yet guarantee liberty and equality. To solve this problem it must perfect legal and rational methods of government and procedure.

The political ideas which come to guide this latter form of social development are transformed and converted into highly complex social values. Subjectively considered, these are judgments of the "utility, or goodness, or dignity, or importance, of any object, act or relation."[46] Socially considered, they are "the social estimates of things that are socially important."[47] First among these social values comes the type of conscious life characteristic of the society; next comes social cohesion; third, the distinctive possessions and properties of the community, such as territory, sacred places, national heroes, ceremonies, laws, worship, and amusements. Last in order of evolution are the "values attaching to certain abstract conditions that are favorable to social integrity and development, and to certain modes of effort that are intended to extend or to perfect the social type. The conditions are liberty, equality, and fraternity."[48] Social value, in the singular, means "regard or esteem for any social habit, relation, or institution which makes men cherish and defend it."[49]

What is the relation of this form of social valuation to progress? To this Giddings makes two answers, which differ only in their point of view: (1) "The rational improvement of society proceeds through a criticism of social values."[50] Society must accurately estimate the utility of every institution or custom and the cost and sacrifice involved not only in defending the old but also in renovating it and making possible developments along new lines. By this criticism the foundations of a rational social choice will be secured. (2) Social conduct is the resultant of a certain combination of social values, determined by rational choice. Group the social values in a certain way, and a certain form of social conduct will follow in obedience to the unchanging relations embodied in the laws of social choice. Progress then is dependent on (a) the formulation of the laws of rational social choice and (b) the combination of social values.

The laws of social choice may be formulated under two heads: (1) the law of preferences among ends to be achieved and (2) the law of the relation between interests and social choices.[51] These two laws, first sketched in the *Principles,* receive fuller statement in *Descriptive and Historical Sociology*.[52] The first one in full runs:

In all social choice, the most influential ideals are those of the forceful man, the powerful community, of virtue in the primitive sense of the word; second in influence are ideals of the convivial man, the prosperous and pleasure-loving community, the utilitarian or hedonistic virtues; third in influence are ideals of the austere man, the righteous or just community, the Stoic or Puritan virtues of self-restraint; fourth in influence are the ideals of the rationally conscientious man, of the liberal and enlightened community, of the virtues of reasonableness, broad-mindedness and charity [but, if mental and moral evolution are to continue], the higher ideals [must] become increasingly influential.

The second law is formulated in terms of interests, that is, of "the elements, modes and means of good." Varied experiences and manifold interests lead any distinct section of society to "choose, select or decide, strictly in accordance with the mental characteristics that these different experiences have developed."[53] The law runs:

A population that has only a few interests, which, however, are harmoniously combined, is conservative in its choices. A population that has varied interests, which are as yet inharmoniously combined, is radical in its choices. Only the population that has many, varied and harmoniously combined interests is consistently progressive in its choices.[54]

Functionally, therefore, progress depends upon the establishment, step by step, of the higher ideals named in the first law and the creation of the many, varied, and harmoniously combined interests named in the second. To that end certain "public utilities" must be realized. First in functional importance, though often last in genetic order, stands security of life, of territory, and of institutions. This security includes both international peace and domestic peace and order: "To secure and to maintain these, as far as possible, is the supreme function of the political system."[55] Next in functional order comes equity, "a certain compromise and reconciliation of the differing interests and claims of the individuals, the racial elements and the classes, making up the social population." To adjust these differing interests and claims requires some restriction of the liberty of the strong to curtail the liberty of the weak. The only practical method for conserving and extending liberty has been by establishing certain objective modes of equality. Only an approximation to such equality will insure progress in liberty, prosperity, and enlightenment. Springing out of this principle of utility comes public control of the economic system, in the interest of a greater equality of economic opportunity, and a tendency toward complete equality of cultural advantages.[56] To these public utilities, as the functional content of social progress, must be added a formal test of efficiency. The organization must benefit the organized and must be regarded by the members as beneficial.

Considering progress as an end to be attained, these public utilities fall into place as means to an ultimate end, which is "life in its higher developments, especially its moral and intellectual developments.... a social nature, or personality, adapted to social coöperation and enjoyment. This social personality .... is the ultimate end of social organization."[57] The development of the social personality is measured both positively and negatively. Positively it consists in the increase of vitality, sound mentality, morality, and sociality. Negatively it connotes a decrease in the number of the defective, the abnormal, the immoral, and the degraded. Practically it includes a eugenic program, based along its positive side on a "pure and sane family life, which disciplines the welcome and untainted child in the robust virtue of self-control, and in an unswerving allegiance to duty,"[58] and, on the negative side, on a ruthless suppression of the feeble-minded and other dysgenetic stocks.

VI. THE QUANTITATIVE METHOD IN SOCIOLOGY

In handling the descriptive and historical material of sociology, Giddings took a position in which, as a sociologist, he stood almost alone at the time. His evolutionary standpoint enabled him to pass naturally and logically to a statistical treatment of the objective subject matter of sociology. Collective behavior is typical and modal: "To the extent that safety and prosperity depend upon group cohesion and coöperation, they are seen to depend upon such conformity to type as may suffice to insure the cohesion and to fulfil the coöperation."[59] "Sociology is the science of the origin, the process, the extent and the results of type control of variation from itself, within a group of more or less freely associating individuals."[60] "Society is a type, controlling variation from itself for its own survival and further evolution."[61] Therefore it preeminently calls for precise or quantitative study by the statistical method;[62] for the phenomena of type can always be expressed in the statistical terms of "frequency" and "mode." When the full significance of the many statistical reports available today is realized, greater progress will be made in statistical sociology. There may also be needed some development of statistical terminology and methodology, for frequencies of sort, which predominate in our large collections of data in census and other reports, are not held to be so amenable to the present statistical methods as frequencies of size. Rates of births and deaths, of marriage and divorce, are numerical and measurable, being items of number and size. But numbers of illiterates, of foreign- and native-born, of adherents of religious denominations, of delinquents and dependents, and so on are frequencies of sort.

Some of the feasible points of attack have been suggested by Professor Giddings. From an analysis of the statutory enactments of legislative bodies, it is possible to obtain index numbers to measure social pressure.[63] The work of state and municipal commissions could be tested statistically, as also could the struggle for mastery between integral society and the corporations. More important are such problems as the measure of social constraint, the extent of human variation, and the range of socialization and individuation. The first of these affords an instance of the value of a knowledge of normality and of the meaning and significance of variation.

The extent of social mutation, in which the ameliorative effects of social organization are reflected, is obviously a matter for statistical investigation.[64] While measures of such variations and especially of the preferences and characterizations which are called for in many sociological inquiries have not yet been adequately established, the purpose and method of sociology must be to discover "ratios, modalities, coefficients of variation and correlations."[65]

The question, how much restraint, how much liberty, how much conformity to type, how much variation from it, are conducive to the general welfare, is the supremely important question in all issues of public policy. The right answer to it turns upon the determination of the previous question, namely, what is normal social constraint in a given community, at a given stage of its evolution, and what at a given moment is the actual range of fluctuation? .... To obtain, then, determinations of normal social constraint for modern communities, including municipalities, commonwealths and nations, and to perfect the methods of measuring fluctuations must, I think, be regarded as the chief object of sociological effort in the immediate future. That that effort will be successful is, I am convinced, a fairly safe prediction.[66]

To sum up, Giddings approaches the social process from the standpoint of a psychologist who is also a statistician and a scientist. In one single sentence he defines the subject matter of the science and determines its method: "Pluralistic behavior is the subject matter of the psychology of society, otherwise called Sociology, a science statistical in method, which attempts, first, to factorize pluralistic behavior, and, second, to explain its genesis, integration, differentiation and functioning by accounting for them in terms of the variables, (1) stimulation, and (2) the resemblance (more or less) to one another of reacting mechanisms."[67] Around these two variables his whole sociological theory revolves.[68]

NOTES

1. Franklin Henry Giddings (1855–1931) was probably the ablest sociologist that the United States has ever produced, and among sociologists abroad perhaps only Durkheim, Hobhouse, and Max Weber would rank with him. He was less impressively erudite than Lester F. Ward, but he had a more penetrating mentality and greater capacity for theoretical formulation and analysis.

Giddings was born in Sherman, Connecticut, in 1855. His father was an orthodox and puritanical Congregationalist minister, and Giddings' strong reaction in mature life against orthodoxy and puritanism can probably be traced mainly to his early surroundings. He received an engineering training at Union College but entered journalism in Springfield, Massachusetts, where he remained for ten years on the *Springfield Republican* and the *Springfield Union*. He succeeded Woodrow Wilson as professor of politics at Bryn Mawr College in 1888 and accepted the newly created chair of sociology at Columbia University in 1894. Here he taught as professor of sociology and the history of civilization until shortly before his death in 1931.

Giddings possessed a most impressive personality and a remarkable gift for both the oral and the written exposition of his thoughts. Had he entered public life he would have been a distinguished political orator. He impressed his students with his personal vigor and gusto, but the more serious and alert among them were disconcerted by the often careless and informal conduct of his classes. No other American sociologist could lecture with the power, conciseness, and organization that Giddings could exhibit when he wished to do so, but he rarely conducted a course systematically, and, at times, a course of lectures might bear little apparent relation to the subject matter announced. This was especially true after 1914. In a certain sense, Giddings was an intellectual "war casualty." He was veritably obsessed with anti-Germanism, which, after 1918, turned into anti-Bolshevism, and for years his lectures were more often diatribes against his pet hates than calm sociological analysis. But, however little they might contribute to sociological clarification, they were always interesting and stimulating.

While of a kindly and sympathetic disposition, Giddings was a markedly dominating personality and very dogmatic in his views. He insisted upon doctrinal loyalty, not to say worship, from his departmental colleagues. For this reason he surrounded himself with satellites rather than equals or professional rivals. In this way he stood at the opposite extreme from the other leading academic sociologist of his day, Dean Albion W. Small, of the University of Chicago, and was prevented thereby from building up anything like the impressive department of sociology which Small created at Chicago. (This biographical material is supplied by the editor and Dr. Northcott has no responsibility for the opinions expressed.)

2. Among Giddings' more important books are the following: *Principles of Sociology* (New York, 1896), far and away his most important work and probably the most important single volume yet to be published in the sociological field; *Elements of Sociology* (New York, 1898), the best brief statement of Giddings' early sociological ideas; *Democracy and Empire* (New York, 1900), the best synthesis of Giddings' views on public questions and a defense of American imperialism; *Inductive Sociology* (New York, 1901), a syllabus of principles and problems, with suggestions for further research; *Descriptive and Historical Sociology* (New York, 1904), a further summary and development of sociological principles, with illustrative readings; *The Responsible State* (Boston, 1918), the application of sociological principles to political science, colored by Giddings' wartime psychology and anti-Germanism; *Studies in the Theory of Human Society* (New York, 1922), the most important restatement of his theoretical sociology since the publication of the *Principle of Sociology; The Scientific Study of Human Society* (Durham, N.C., 1924), the most extended of Giddings' arguments for the inductive and statistical method in sociology; *The Mighty Medicine* (New York, 1930), an application of sociological principles to education and religion; and a posthumous volume, *Civilization and Society* (New York, 1932), summarizing his theories and principles.

For good surveys of Giddings' life and contributions to sociology see J. L. Gillin, in H. W. Odum, *American Masters of Social Science* (New York, 1927), chap. vii; and F. H. Hankins, "Franklin Henry Giddings, 1855–1931: Some Aspects of His Sociological Theory," *American Journal of Sociology*, November, 1931, pp. 349–67. Gillin is strongest on the personal side and Hankins on the theoretical.

3. Cf. *Sociology* (New York, 1911), p. 32.

4. *Theory of Human Society*, p. 259.

5. *Descrptive and Historical Sociology*, p. 289; cf. also the treatment in the *Theory of Human Society, passim.*

6. *Principles of Sociology*, p. 114.

7. *Sociology*, p. 32; cf. also *Theory of Human Society*, pp. 267–68.

8. *Ibid.*, p. 261.

9. *Theory of Human Society*, p. 274.

10. Quoted from unpublished lectures; cf. also *Theory of Human Society*, p. 87.

11. Quoted from unpublished lectures; cf. also *Theory of Human Society*, p. 87.

12. *Descriptive and Historical Sociology*, p. 359; *The Responsible State*, chap. iii.

13. Cf. *Descriptive and Historical Sociology*, p. 373.

14. *Principles of Sociology*, p. 421.

15. Cf. *The Responsible State*, pp. 75–78.

16. *Theory of Human Society*, pp. 269–72.

17. *Inductive Sociology*, p. 217.

18. *Descriptive and Historical Sociology*, p. 515.

19. "Theory of Social Causation," *Publications of the American Economic Association*, 1903, p. 144.

20. *Principles of Sociology*, p. 134; cf. also *Theory of Human Society*, p. 266.

21. *Inductive Sociology*, p. 68.

22. *Descriptive and Historical Sociology*, p. 128.

23. *Ibid.*, p. 176.

24. *Ibid.*, p. 127.

25. *Democracy and Empire*, pp. 317–20.

26. *Descriptive and Historical Sociology*, pp. 11–13.

27. *Theory of Human Society*, chap. xii; cf. also p. 202.

28. *Ibid.*, p. 203.

29. *Ibid.*, p. 204.

30. *Ibid.*, p. 206.

31. *Ibid.*

32. *Ibid.*, p. 147; cf. chap. viii.

33. *Ibid.;* cf. also pp. 192–94, 264.

34. *Ibid.*, p. 264.

35. *Principles of Sociology*, p. 229.

36. *Descriptive and Historical Sociology*, p. 315.

37. *Principles of Sociology*, p. 142.

38. *Ibid.*, p. 380.

39. *Sociology*, p. 34.

40. *Ibid.*, p. 36; cf. also *Theory of Human Society*, pp. 118–19.

41. *Theory of Human Society*, p. 246; cf. also chap. xiv.

42. *Descriptive and Historical Sociology*, pp. 395 ff.; cf. also *Theory of Human Society*. pp. 278–81.

43. *Descriptive and Historical Sociology*, p. 415.

44. *Theory of Human Society*, p. 280.

45. *Descriptive and Historical Sociology*, p. 416.

46. *Ibid.*, p. 393.

47. *Principles of Sociology*, p. 147.

48. *Ibid.*, p. 149.

49. *Democracy and Empire*, p. 59; cf. also *Theory of Human Society*, p. 173.

50. *Democracy and Empire*, p. 59.

51. *Principles of Sociology*, pp. 409–11.

52. P. 351.

53. *Inductive Sociology*, p. 181.

54. *Ibid.*

55. *Descriptive and Historical Sociology*, p. 526.

56. *Ibid.*, pp. 526–28.

57. *Ibid.*, p. 523.

58. *Principles of Sociology*, p. 352.

59. *Political Science Quarterly*, XXIV, 575; see also *Theory of Human Society*, pp. 202, 206–8, 282, 286.

60. *Political Science Quarterly*, XXIV, 578.

61. *Ibid.*, p. 580; cf. also *Theory of Human Society*, pp. 202, 206.

62. For a full discussion see his *Scientific Study of Human Society*.

63. *Quarterly Publications of the American Statistical Association*, March, 1908.

64. *Ibid.*, p. 286.

65. *Ibid.*, p. 300.

66. *Theory of Human Society*, p. 208.

67. *Ibid.*, p. 252.

68. *The Scientific Study of Human Society*, several chapters of which appeared in the *Journal of Social Forces*, 1923–24; and an article, "Stimulation Ranges and Reaction Areas," *Psychological Review*, November, 1924.

PART III

THE EMERGENCE OF

SYSTEMATIC SOCIOLOGY

CHAPTER IX

THE SOCIOLOGISM OF ÉMILE DURKHEIM AND HIS SCHOOL

ÉMILE BENOIT-SMULLYAN

I. DURKHEIM'S PREDECESSORS

SOCIOLOGISM, as we use the term here, is a synthesis of a positivistic methodology[1] with a particular set of substantive theories, for which we have invented the name "agelecism" (from $\dot{\alpha}\gamma\acute{\epsilon}\lambda\eta$, meaning "group").[2] By "agelecism" we mean the general sociological doctrine which maintains the reality *sui generis* or the causal priority of the social group *qua* group. Agelecism in its modern form was introduced into the stream of French social thought by De Bonald and De Maistre, who maintained that the social group precedes and constitutes the individual, that it is the source of culture and all the higher values, and that social states and changes are not produced by, and cannot be directly affected or modified by, the desires and volitions of individuals.

Positivism, the doctrine that the social sciences should adopt the methods or schemas of the physical sciences, was first given self-conscious development by Saint-Simon, who sketched a program for a "social physics" or "social physiology" which would search for the "necessary" laws of social development. He laid the basis for a sociologistic theory of morals by treating morals as relative to group structure and pointing out the analogy between an applied science of morals and medicine or hygiene. This synthesis of agelecism and positivism was further elaborated and systematized by Comte. By reviving Bonald's criticism of introspective psychology and by omitting psychology from his classification of the sciences, he introduced an important antipsychologistic bias into the methodology of sociologism. His strongly anti-individualistic program of social control, his theory of social consensus, his conception of society as a "Great Being," and his emphasis on the family as the true social unit all contributed elements to the development of a comprehensive theory of agelecism. De Roberty, who, although a Russian, has figured prominently in the evolution of French sociologistic thought, contributed the biosocial hypothesis which viewed psychology as a concrete and dependent science derived from biology and sociology and explained culture and the higher faculties of the human mind as the product of human interaction and the group situation. The latter doctrine was later echoed and elaborated by Izoulet and Draghicesco. Finally, the biologistic theorist, Espinas, working under the inspiration of Comtean positivism, proclaimed that the individual was only a society of, cells and, conversely, that society might legitimately be considered a kind of superindividual possessing a collective consciousness.

The essential dependence of Durkheim on this particular stream of thought would be difficult to deny.[3] Durkheim disagrees with Comte's law of the three stages and with his conception of humanity as composing a single society; and he disagrees with Espinas's biologistic assumptions. But he is profoundly in sympathy with the particular combination of methodological positivism and agelecism which constitutes the essence of the sociologistic tradition as here defined. Durkheim's achievement may be summed up under three heads: first, his brilliant synthesis of positivism and agelecism into a single theoretical structure; second, his investigation and analysis of a number of empirical problems in terms of this theoretical scheme; third, the founding and editing of the *Année sociologique* and, in connection with it, the guidance of an enthusiastic group of collaborators and disciples in a wide but unified program of empirical research.

The purpose of the present chapter is to present a brief exposition and analysis of the Durkheimian sociology conceived as a single integrated system of thought. We shall not, except incidentally, concern ourselves with the historical problem of the succession of Durkheim's ideas and their process of development. Nor will there be any attempt to present a detailed or adequate criticism, although the notes will contain brief criticisms on a few major points.[4] It goes without saying that only the most salient features of the Durkheimian sociology can be treated at all within the confines of a single chapter.

II. METHODOLOGY IN DURKHEIM'S SOCIOLOGY

Some students of Durkheim have maintained that Durkheim's whole sociological system rests at bottom on a few methodological intuitions.[5] There can be no doubt at least that methodological preconceptions played a very important role in shaping the Durkheimian sociology. Our first task, accordingly, is to analyze the essential elements in the Durkheim methodology and to trace their derivation from the positivistic faith with which Durkheim was inspired.[6] Durkheim's continuity with the main Positivist tradition is immediately evidenced in his stand on the relation between sociology and philosophy. He begins by rejecting the assumption that sociology needs to rest on any philosophic presuppositions whatever. Sociology is to be completely independent of philosophy; yet this independence is not reciprocal, for an adequate philosophy will, of necessity, incorporate important elements contributed by sociology, especially an understanding of the basic processes of association. This is clearly in line with the essential element in the positivistic philosophy, namely, the rejection of the main philosophic traditions as unscientific, together with the attempt to erect a new philosophy by generalizing scientific conclusions or by utilizing scientific methods to tackle such theoretical questions as still appear to be meaningful. Like Comte, Durkheim expects the renovation of philosophy to be based particularly on the results of the new science of society.[7] His blueprints for methodological reform in this new science we now propose to examine.

According to his own statement, Durkheim's most basic methodological postulate is that we should "treat social facts as things."[8] The intended meaning of this formula has never been clear, because Durkheim used the term "thing" in four different and not closely related senses, viz., (1) an entity possessing certain definite characteristics which are independent of human observation; (2) an entity which can be known only a posteriori (as opposed, for example, to a mathematical relation); (3) an entity, the existence of which is independent of human volition; (4) an entity which can be known only through "external" observation (as, for example, the sensory observation of the behavior or physiological states of others, in psychology) and not by introspection.

The meaning of the prescription that we ought to treat social facts as things varies with the sense of the word "thing," taken as intended. In the first sense of the word, the prescription means little more than that the sociologist has a real subject matter. In the second sense it means that social facts can be known only through *some type* of experience, and not by an a priori insight. These two contentions would be admitted by virtually all sociologists. In the third and fourth meanings the prescription becomes more controversial. In the third sense it seems to require the assumption of determinism in interhuman relations.[9] In the fourth sense it limits us to external observation of social facts and forbids the use of introspective evidence even if it is selected and checked with scientific caution.

The classical sociological systems of Comte and Spencer, as well as virtually the whole body of jurisprudence, economics, and the theory of morals, are all vitiated, Durkheim feels, by an excessive dependence upon deductive reasoning and by a normative or evaluative approach. Both these errors spring from the same source: a failure to treat social facts as things; for, if social facts are things, then they must be empirically observed at every stage and not merely deduced from certain initial asumptions; and, moreover, we must strive merely to know them and adapt ourselves to them. Valuation is irrelevant. To insure scientific objectivity, the sociologist must begin not with concepts but with sensory data. These will supply the elements of his definitions.[10] The sociologist must find some "objective" set of sensory data, the variations of which will measure the variations in the internal life of society, just as the oscillations of the thermometer provide an objective index to replace the subjective sensory data of temperature. There are three such orders of facts which Durkheim accepts as possessing this objectivity and, at the same time, as being collective rather than individual. They are legal codes, social statistics, and religious dogmas.[11]

Durkheim's basic rules of sociological explanation are, first, that the social fact should always be viewed as mechanically determined and, second, that it should be explained in terms of another social fact, never by a fact of a lower order (e.g., a biological or psychological cause). In his discussion of this topic[12] Durkheim attacks two opponents simultaneously: psychologism and individualism—as well as that particular mixture of the two which constitutes utilitarianism. The common procedure of explaining a social fact in terms of its utility or in terms of the satisfaction it yields to individuals is, Durkheim maintains, entirely fallacious, since our needs do not of themselves create conditions which satisfy those needs; and only an explanation in terms of efficient causation is scientifically acceptable. Furthermore, if we supposed the cause of the social fact to lie within the individual, we should be unable to explain the constraint which the social fact, by definition, exerts over the individual. Hence "the determining cause of a social fact must be sought for among the antecedent social facts..... The function of a social fact must always be sought in its relationship to some social end."[13]

There still remains the question as to which particular order of social facts is to provide the ultimate explanatory principle. Durkheim reasons that, since social facts arise out of the act of association, they must vary in accordance with the forms of this association, "that is to say, according to the manner in which the constituent parts of the society are grouped." Thus "the ultimate origin of all social processes of any importance must be sought in the constitution of the internal social milieu."[14]

This internal social milieu, to which Durkheim elsewhere refers as the social "substratum"[15] is comprised of such morphological elements as: the number of people in the group, the degree of their proximity, the evenness with which they are diffused over a given area, the number and dispositions of the paths of communication and transport, etc. It is, therefore, essentially a matter of the spatial distribution of physical entities (even persons are here considered in their physical aspect). The asserted ultimacy of this factor has caused Durkheim to be taxed, by several writers, with sociological materialism.[16] This criticism Durkheim attempts to avoid by maintaining that it is not simply the number of people in a given area (the "material density") which is important, but the number of people who have established effective *moral* relations ("dynamic density"). However, by introducing this nonmaterialistic element into the concept, Durkheim sacrifices much of its operational value, since the degree of its applicability can no longer be determined by wholly external observations.[17]

An interesting phase of Durkheim's positivism is his program for an applied sociology to formulate rules for social guidance.[18] This science not only would advise us as to the best way in which to achieve social objectives but also would select the ends which a given society ought to pursue, and would do so entirely on the basis of scientific observation of empirical data. This can be accomplished, Durkheim claims, by finding an objective criterion of social health and social pathology. Once in possession of such a criterion, social science can apply the general laws of sociology to the preservation of social health, just as the science of medicine applies the laws of physiology to the preservation of the health of the individual organism.[19]

Durkheim is quick to dismiss the criterion of utility, as requiring an appeal to the subjective states of individuals and, hence, as lacking in scientific objectivity. Instead, he defines health in terms of "normality" and adopts *generality* as the criterion of "normality." The socially healthful is that which is normal; and as "the normal type is identical with the average type .... every deviation from this standard is a pathological phenomenon."[20] In the application of this criterion Durkheim is led to paradoxical conclusions. Since crime is prevalent in all or most societies, it must be considered normal and as an element in social health. On the other hand, certain phenomena which have been common in all the societies of Western civilization for the last century, such as a rising suicide rate, a weakening in the moral condemnation of suicide, and certain types of economic maladjustments, are all classified by Durkheim as pathological.[21] Critics have pointed out also that this criterion of normality leads to an ultra-conservative morality of sheer social conformism, since every deviation from what is general in a society is classified as pathological.[22] An implicit concession to this criticism is perhaps apparent in Durkheim's admission that, in periods of great social change (like the present), phenomena which are general may have only an "appearance of normality"; and some phenomena which are exceptional may be normal because they are closely bound up with the conditions of social existence.[23]

III. DURKHEIM'S SUBSTANTIVE THEORIES

A. THE SOCIAL FACT

Durkheim places great emphasis on his definition of the social fact in terms of constraint and exteriority. Unfortunately, the precise meaning of these criteria has never been clear. From his fundamental methodological postulate that we must treat social facts as things, Durkheim infers that the social fact must possess two important characteristics of a thing: it must be *exterior* to (in the sense of not identical with) the idea in the mind of the scientist, and it must impose a certain constraint on the scientist (in the sense of possessing independent characters not influenced by the scientist's volition, to which the scientific theory must conform, or which it must express, if it is to be true). By shifting the center of reference from the *scientist* who *studies* social facts to the acting *individual* who *lives* in an environment of social facts, Durkheim is able to endow the criteria of exteriority and constraint with a new and purely substantive set of meanings. To the acting individual the social fact is exterior in the sense that it is experienced as an independent reality which neither he nor any other individual created and which literally forms a part of his objective environment. In the same way the social fact possesses the characteristic of constraint in that it does not conform to the volitions of individuals but, on the contrary, imposes itself upon individuals, regulating their behavior and even their volitions.

The substantive doctrine of the exteriority of the social fact is thus identical with what we have called "agelic realism." It asserts that society is a reality *sui generis,* above and apart from the individuals. The evidence adduced by Durkheim in defense of this doctrine is of four main types. The first is the alleged heterogeneity of individual and collective states of mind. Thus it is asserted that in a time of national danger the intensity of the collective feeling of patriotism is much greater than that of any individual feeling and society's willingness to sacrifice individuals is greater than the willingness of individuals to sacrifice themselves. Similarly, the individual's hesitant and vague condemnation of dishonesty is said to stand in marked contrast to the "unreserved, explicit, and categorical disgrace with which society strikes at theft in all its forms."[24] A second type of argument, which in one form or another is to be found in practically all Durkheim's writings, stresses the difference in individual attitudes and behavior which results from the group situation. When in a crowd the individual thinks, feels, and acts in a different fashion. It follows, thinks Durkheim, that a new reality must be created by the association of individuals and that this reality reacts upon the sentiments and behavior of the individuals and changes them. A third type of evidence is supplied by the uniformities of social statistics. Many types of social facts, like crimes, marriages, and suicides, show a surprising degree of numerical consistency from year to year, either remaining virtually unchanged or maintaining a uniform rate of change. Such uniformity, Durkheim argues, could not derive from the personal motives or characteristics of individuals, which are so variable as to comprise what is practically a random distribution. Nor can they be satisfactorily explained, Durkheim attempts to prove, by physical, biological, or psychological uniformities. The only remaining explanation is to be found in the influence of certain real social currents which form a (hitherto undetected) part of the individual's environment.[25] A fourth line of argument is based on analogy and on the philosophical theory of emergence.[26] Just as the phenomenon of life is not to be explained by the physicochemical properties of the molecules which form the cell, but by a particular association of molecules, and just as the phenomenon of consciousness resides not in the physiological nature of the cell but in a particular mode of molecular association, so we must assume that society is not reducible to the properties of individual minds but that it constitutes a reality *sui generis* which emerges out of the collocation and interaction of individual minds.

The other characteristic of the social fact, the "constraint" which it exercises over the individual, may be viewed as a simple corollary of its externality. Since the social fact is both real and external, it forms part of the individual's environment and, like the physical and biological parts of his environment, exerts upon him a certain constraint; for the hallmark of an independent reality is the resistance it opposes to our volitions and the counterpressure it exerts on our behavior. Moreover, the fact of social constraint enters into the direct experience of the individual. Legal and moral rules (which are the most typical orders of social facts) cannot be flouted by the individual without his experiencing the tangible evidences of social disapprobation. But if constraint is such an essential element in legal and moral rules, it cannot be wholly absent in other types of social facts.[27]

B. THE DIVISION OF LABOR

The principal problems treated by Durkheim in his book on the division of labor, *De la division du travail social,* concern the nature and the cause of social evolution.[28] Durkheim agreed with Spencer and the Utilitarians that one important aspect of the change from primitive to civilized modes of social existence was to be found in the increase in the amount of division of labor, or specialization. But he felt that the Utilitarians in their description of social evolution unduly emphasized the economic changes and misunderstood or neglected the far more important moral and legal changes. As Durkheim sees it, the fundamental difference between primitive and civilized societies is in the type of morals or social solidarity,[29] which is, in turn, reflected in the type of legal codes.

In primitive society, where division of labor is rudimentary, individuals are relatively homogeneous and bound together by a "mechanical" solidarity characterized by blind acquiescence to the dictates of public opinion and tradition. The legal system is designed primarily to

punish those who violate the collective will and offend collective sentiments and to restore by this punishment a moral equilibrium. In such
a society, moral and legal responsibility is collective, social status tends
to be hereditarily fixed, and a relatively small part of social life is ordered
by the contractual principle. In civilized societies, where division of labor
is well developed, individuals have diverse personalities, experiences, and
functions, and they are bound together by an "organic" solidarity rooted
in their need for each other's services. The primary purpose of the legal
system is to restore to the individual that which has been wrongfully
taken away from him. In this sort of society individualism is the dominant morality, but individualism in a very special sense. Individualism,
as a conscious moral attitude appropriate for our type of society, is
not a claim for the unlimited right of the individual to pursue his immediate desires; it is, rather, an obligation laid upon him to individualize
himself by intensive specialization in order to make his distinctive contribution to social welfare. It is a stern injunction to avoid the delights
of dilettantism and to further the division of labor.[30] Durkheim is intensely concerned to demonstrate that a purely egoistic and hedonistic
individualism could never produce social solidarity or serve as a basis
for social cohesion. He is at pains to point out that peaceful and beneficial contractual relations can exist only in the framework of a legal
and moral order which limits the types of contracts that are valid, gives
the definitive interpretation as to the obligations arising out of the contracts, and enforces their performance.[31]

Still more sharply does Durkheim disagree with the Utilitarians as
to the *causes* of social evolution. They had assumed that the division of
labor and the resulting gains in economic productivity and material
civilization derived, quite simply, from the desires of individuals for
greater wealth and higher planes of living. Durkheim makes this a test
case in his war against the explanation of social facts in terms of the
motives of individuals and the tendencies of human nature. The general
line of the argument is as follows.[32] Human beings have only a limited
and moderate capacity to enjoy economic goods, and therefore they
would long ago have stopped increasing their wealth if happiness had
been the motive for increased production. Happiness is connected with
social health, which is imperiled by excesses of every sort, including a
superabundance of material luxuries. Great social changes which dis-
rupt settled habits create much suffering, and it could not be a desire

for happiness which would lead a whole generation to make such sacrifices in order to produce luxuries which it did not consciously desire and from which only succeeding generations would profit. Finally, there is no evidence that material progress and civilization make men any happier. In fact, the apparent contentment in primitive society and the relative infrequency of suicides and neuroses reveal a far higher degree of average happiness than that in contemporary civilizations. Therefore, it is not the desire for happiness which created civilization.[33]

Having disposed of the psychologistic and individualistic explanations of the division of labor, Durkheim now turns to his own morphological explanation, which accords very well with the requirements set forth in the *Règles de la méthode sociologique*. Division of labor is due to changes in social structure arising out of an increase in material and moral density. The increase in population intensifies competition and thus forces individuals to specialize, in order to survive. Thus Durkheim, rather reluctantly, comes to rest his entire explanation upon the factor of an assumed natural increase in population. This is obviously a biologistic rather than a sociologistic type of explanation and comes closer to an outright materialism than anything in Durkheim's later work.[34]

C. SUICIDE

Durkheim's intensive study of suicide[35] is more than an interesting statistical analysis of an important empirical topic. As usual, Durkheim is vitally concerned to show how the empirical data support a theoretical doctrine, in this case the exteriority and constraining power of a given order of social facts.

He begins by refusing to define suicide as an intentional act of self-destruction, because intentions are not externally observable and are too variable to define a single order of phenomena. He then proceeds to an ingenious statistical refutation of theories which explain suicide in terms of various climatic, geographic, biological, or psychological factors. As an alternative he proposes a conception of suicide as a social fact, explicable in terms of social causes. The social, superindividual nature of suicide is supported by the observation that the rate of suicide (or its rate of change) in a given society is remarkably constant from year to year. Durkheim argues that such constancy woud be inexplicable if the suicide rate depended on the highly variable and practically random traits of individual personality and volition. He infers that suicide must emanate from a single type of causal factor which preserves a uniform strength from year to year. Since climatic, geographic, biological, and psychological factors have been excluded by his statistical demonstrations, he concludes that only in the social realm can a comprehensive explanatory factor be found.

The social factors influencing the rate of suicide are revealed by the correlation of suicide rates with group affiliations and with important collective processes. Thus Durkheim uncovers evidence to prove that free thinkers have the highest suicide rates and Protestants the next highest; that Catholics have low rates, and Jews the lowest of all. The essential difference here, according to Durkheim, is not in the religious beliefs themselves but in the degree of integration of the religious group. Protestantism involves a higher degree of religious individualism than Catholicism, and the religious group is less integrated by uniformities of belief, while Judaism, because of its heritage of persecution, strongly binds its members together to face a hostile environment. Durkheim infers that one important type of suicide ("egoistic") is caused by an insufficient participation by the individual in the life of a group. The individual in himself is of little value; it is only what he derives from participation in a social group that can give his private existence purpose and significance. Hence the individual who remains aloof from strongly integrated social groups, who pursues his own personal ends exclusively, is more liable than others to be overcome with ennui and to find no reason for continuing his existence.

Another important type of suicide described by Durkheim is *"suicide anomique,"* or "normless" suicide. He observes that bachelors have much higher suicide rates than married men and that the general suicide rate decreases in time of war and increases in times both of sharp economic depression and of exceptional prosperity.[36] Durkheim supposes that the individual's desires are in themselves boundless and insatiable and that mental health and contentment require that fixed limits be placed by society on the individual's expectation of personal gratification. During a period of exceptional prosperity, customary standards of living are easily surpassed, and no new norms or appropriate living standards are established. But unlimited expectations must sooner or later engender disappointments, which may easily prove fatal to the individual lacking a strong moral constitution. Similarly, the bachelor, who is less restricted in his sexual life than the married man, is easily disenchanted and disgusted with life. The degree of integration of the society is important, because upon it rests the capacity of the society to discipline the individual. Thus in wartime, when there is normally a strong unification of the society in response to an external threat, it imposes a firmer discipline on the individual and thereby preserves him against suicide. A serious depression, on the other hand, involves social disorganization, and the suffering which this disorganization produces in the social mind is reflected in the minds of individuals, a greater number of whom commit suicide.[37]

The conclusion to which Durkheim comes is that there exist "suicidal currents" produced by the varying states of social organization, which act mechanically upon individuals and force a certain number of them to commit suicide. These suicidal currents are just as real and just as much external to the individual as are the physical and biological forces which produce death by disease. The suicidal current, like the biological epidemic, has a predetermined number of victims, selected from those who can offer the least resistance. There is an individual factor in suicide, just as there is in disease; but it determines who in particular will succumb and not the number of deaths.[38] The individual may appear to himself and to others to be committing suicide from personal motives, but in reality he is being impelled to commit the act by impersonal forces, of which (unless he is a sociologist!) he is presumably unaware. Perhaps nowhere in the literature of sociologism has the doctrine of agelic fatalism been given a more dramatic application![39]

D. AGELIC TRANSCENDENTALISM

Around 1898, Durkheim entered on a new and distinct phase of his work. It is characterized, in the first place, by a more idealistic conception of the social group, with more emphasis on "collective representations" and less on the internal social milieu; and, in the second place, by adventurous speculation concerning the social origin of morals, values, religion, and knowledge. The social group is successively endowed by Durkheim with the characteristics of hyperspirituality, personality, creativity, and transcendence. The inception of this phase is marked by the publication of Durkheim's paper on individual and collective representations.[40]

The chief conclusion of this paper is that there exist collective mental states which are no more reducible to the mental states of individuals than the mental states of individuals are reducible to the physiological states of independent brain cells. The association of individuals gives rise to an emergent reality—society—which is relatively independent of the properties of the constituent individuals. Collective representations are undoubtedly influenced in their formation by the conditions of the material substratum; but, once formed, they are partially autonomous realities, which combine according to their own natural affinities and which are not closely determined by the character of the milieu in which they originated.[41] This conception of social facts as constituting an independent reality is very far from materialism, says Durkheim. If the individual mind is a spiritual reality, social facts must be granted the attribute of "hyperspirituality."

E. AGELIC PERSONALISM AND THE THEORY OF MORALS

The second major step in the development of a transcendental theory of the social group was taken by Durkheim in connection with the development of a sociologistic theory of morals.[42] To begin with, he holds that the moral fact presents a peculiar duality. The moral rule inspires us with respect and with a feeling of obligation which is quite independent of its content; but, on the other hand, we must assume that this content is good and desirable (even if it does not at the moment correspond with our personal desires).[43]

Now if we seek for the origin of the moral rule, we perceive immediately that it cannot emanate from the individual, since no act has ever been called "moral" which had as its exclusive end the conservation or self-development of the individual. If the agent in himself cannot be a source of moral obligation, neither can *other* individuals, for they are not essentially different from the agent. But disinterestedness and devotion are essential characters of the moral act, and these sentiments are meaningless or impossible unless we subordinate ourselves to another conscious being (preferably of higher moral value than ourselves). If, however, all human beings are excluded, there are only two further alternatives: there is God, and there is society. At bottom these two alternatives are the same, for God is only society "transfigured and conceived symbolically."[44] Thus, if the moral life is to have any meaning, we must assume that society itself is a true moral person, formed by a synthesis of individuals and qualitatively distinct from all the individuals taken distributively.

This solution accounts for the dual character of the moral fact. It is obligatory because it is the command of society, and society so infinitely surpasses the individual, both materially and morally, that its commands carry sufficient authority to produce unquestioning obedience. But, on the other hand, it seems good and desirable, because society is the source of all the higher values of civilization and the creator of that element in the individual which raises him above the animal level. Without society, language would not exist; and without language, the higher mental processes would be impossible. Without science, which is a social product, man would be helpless before the blind forces of nature. So it is to society that the individual owes his real liberty. "We cannot wish to leave society without wishing to cease to be men."[45]

Durkheim ends by drawing certain important relativistic conclusions. Moral rules are always the product of particular social factors, and every moral system is closely dependent upon the social structure of the society in which it exists. There is no single moral system which would be moral for every society, and diversity of morals among different societies is not to be explained by ignorance or perversity. Each society has the moral system it needs, and any other morality would be injurious to it. The social scientist may sometimes help society by showing what moral judgments are truly consistent with the actual state of social organization, but this is as far as anyone can go. "To wish for a different moral system from the one which is implied in the nature of society is to deny society, and consequently to deny oneself."[46]

F. AGELIC CREATIONISM AND THE THEORY OF VALUES

The final stage in the completion of a doctrine of agelic transcendentalism was reached in 1911 with the elaboration of a general theory of value, which portrayed the social group as the transcendental creator of *all,* not merely of all moral, values.[47] As his point of departure, Durkheim calls attention to the apparent objectivity of value-judgments. Assertions that Beethoven's music has aesthetic value, that honest behavior has moral value, that a diamond has economic value, are not intended as mere expressions of personal preference but as characterizations of an external reality.

They cannot, therefore, be supposed to refer to the personal likes and dislikes of myself or any other *individual,* or even of a majority of individuals. Since value-judgments do not refer to any individual's preference, they must express the hierarchy of preferences which society has established—and the fact that it is society which has established and imposed them gives them their objectivity.

The basic problem, however, concerns the source of the whole realm of values. How is it possible that man, who lives in a world of merely factual existence, should conceive and refer to an ideal world of values? How can we pass from what is to what ought to be?

According to Durkheim, the only natural forces which could suffice to account for the emergence of an ideal realm of values are those which are liberated by the association of individuals in the social group. When individuals come together and have vigorous mental interaction, "there emerges from their synthesis a psychic life of a new sort."[48] It is in such periods of effervescence and collective enthusiasm, when gatherings and assemblages are more frequent and the exchange of ideas more intense, that the great ideals of civilization have been formed. Examples are offered by the student movement in Paris in the twelfth and thirteenth centuries, the Reformation, the Renaissance, the French Revolution, and the socialist upheavals in the nineteenth century. In such periods the individual lives a higher life, almost completely devoid of egoistic and vulgar considerations. Then, for a time, the ideal seems to coalesce with the real, and it almost seems as if the Kingdom of Heaven were about to be achieved on earth. However, this illusion cannot last, because the exaltation is too exhausting to be maintained indefinitely. "Once the critical moment has passed, the social network relaxes, the intellectual intercourse slows down, and the individuals fall back to their ordinary level."[49] What is left behind is only a memory, a group of *ideas,* which would soon evaporate if they were not revivified from time to time by celebrations, public ceremonies, sermons, artistic and dramatic performances, and other forms of group concentration and social integration.

Society must be conceived as a mind composed of collective ideas, but these ideas are not simply cognitive representations. They are strongly imbued with sentiment and have important motor elements, i.e., they are stimulants to action. They are the expression of forces which are both natural and ideal at the same time. This is possible because society has a dual character: it comes out of nature, but it synthesizes natural forces to produce a result which is richer, more complex, and more powerful than these forces. "It is nature which has risen to the highest point in its development and which concentrates all its energies in order, in some fashion, to transcend itself."[50]

It must be noted that Durkheim has arrived here at a definitely ambivalent conception of society. On the one hand, it is a transcendental reality, which can plausibly be considered the source of all the transcendent elements in human experience; and, on the other hand, it is still a natural phenomenon (a number of individuals in spatial proximity). An increase in the proximity of the members of the group provides a "naturalistic" explanation for the creation of the transcendental elements in experience, and a decrease in proximity provides an equally naturalistic explanation for the nontranscendent, secular, *alltäglich* element in experience. With the further assumption that the life of the group goes through a natural and necessary rhythm of concentration and dispersion, the doctrine of agelic fatalism becomes practically omnipotent as an explanatory hypothesis.[51]

G. THE THEORY OF RELIGION

As is generally known, the fundamental idea of Durkheim's *Les Formes élémentaires de la vie religieuse*[52] is that religion is entirely a "social thing." This involves two distinct theses: first, that religious ideas and practices refer to or symbolize the social group and, second, that association is the generating source, or efficient cause, of the religious experience. As usual, Durkheim begins with the careful framing of an *ad hoc* definition of the object of investigation.[53]

The next step is the elimination of the chief individualistic and psychologistic theories of religion, especially the animistic theories of Sir Edward B. Tylor and Spencer and the naturistic theory of Müller. The chief objections brought against these theories are that they are unable to account for more than a part of the whole body of religious phenomena; that they fail to explain the radical heterogeneity between the sacred and the secular, which is the essential characteristic of religion; and, finally, that they "explain religion away" by interpreting it as an illusion without any basis in the real world.

Durkheim proceeds next to an examination of the totemic practices of the Aruntas in Australia. The assumption is that this society is about the most primitive society in existence and that its religious practices will therefore exhibit in its simplest form the original nature of religion.[54] The fundamental characteristic of totemism is that the clan takes the name of, claims descent from, and exercises certain ritual restraints toward, some object in the environment, usually an animal or plant. According to Durkheim's analysis, the most fundamental belief implicit in totemism is the belief in a mysterious and sacred force or principle which animates the totem, provides a physical sanction for violation of the totemic taboo, and inculcates moral responsibilities. Now the strong emotions of awe and reverence for the totem can hardly have been derived from the physical properties of the totem itself, since this latter is usually some harmless and insignificant animal or plant. The totem must therefore be considered as a symbol. It symbolizes, first, the sacred totemic principle or god and, second, the clan itself, with which the totem is closely identified. Durkheim infers from this that the totemic divinity and the clan are really the same thing and, more generally, that God is only a symbolic expression of society.[55]

The next problem concerns the origin of the religious experience; and Durkheim's explanation runs as follows:[56] The life of the Arunta is divided into two phases. In the first, or secular, phase the clan is scattered in small groups of individuals pursuing their private economic objectives and living a life which is "uniform, languishing, and dull." In the second, or religious, phase the clan gathers together, and "the very fact of the concentration acts as an exceptionally powerful stimulant." A sort of electricity or collective euphoria is generated, which soon lifts the individuals to miraculous states of exaltation. The effervescence is so intense that delirious behavior and altogether exceptional actions (like violations of the most well-established taboos) are common. It is in these periods of intense agelic concentration and violent interaction that religious sentiments and ideas are born, and it is the sharp contrast between these periods and the dull and languishing periods of group dispersion which explains the radical heterogeneity between the sacred and the profane.

These general conclusions are reinforced by certain considerations concerning the similarity of our attitudes toward society and toward God.[57] Society, it is asserted, is quite capable of inspiring the sensation of divinity in the minds of its members because of its power over them. The individual's feeling of perpetual dependence is alike in each case. Society, like God, possesses moral authority and can inspire disinterested devotion and self-sacrifice. It is also capable of endowing the individual with exceptional powers and is the source of all that is highest and

best in human personality. Therefore, the religious man, who feels a
dependence upon some external moral power, is not the victim of a
hallucination. There is such a power: society. Of course, he may be
mistaken in supposing that the religious forces emanate from some
particular object (like a totem), but this is simply a mistake in the
"letter of the symbol." Behind this symbol there is a reality which does
have the ascribed properties.[58]

H. THE THEORY OF KNOWLEDGE

In recent years one major development in sociology has been the
elaboration of a "sociology of knowledge," an explanation of knowledge itself as a product of social conditions. In this field Durkheim
must rank as one of the most important pioneers. Going beyond the
generalities of his predecessors (to the effect that thought depends upon
language, and language upon society), he tries to show in detail how
both the forms of classification and the basic categories of cognition
have been produced by society.

The problem of classification is treated in a monograph on primitive
forms of classification (written in collaboration with M. Mauss).[59] The
present concept of a "class," we are told, does not go back beyond
Aristotle; and our contemporary forms of classification (in terms of
class and subclass, species and genus, etc.) are not innate but based
upon "a hierarchical order for which neither the sensory world nor our
own minds offer us a model."[60] If we observe the classifications of
primitive peoples, however, we discover that these classifications closely
reflect the social organization of the tribe. The first "classes" were classes
of men, and the classification of physical objects was simply an extension of previously established social classifications, since all the animals
and objects in the environment were classified as belonging to this or
that clan, phratry, or other kinship group. The hierarchy of type and
subtype in logical classification reflects the hierarchical character of
earlier forms of social structure. The imagery in which, even today,
logical relations are expressed, reveals their social origin: things which
are alike "belong to the same family"; an entity "possesses" certain
characteristics; and one concept is "dependent upon or subordinate to"
another.

Primitive classification is not primarily conceptual but is based largely
on emotion and social sensibility. Scientific classification emerges when

social sentiment becomes less important and when individual observation and speculation have more freedom. But the very framework of classification—the mental habits by which we organize facts in groups (themselves hierarchically related)—bears the indelible mark of a social genesis.[61]

The last and most daring of Durkheim's speculative flights is a sociologistic explanation of the categories of thought and the forms of intuition.[62] As usual, he begins with a criticism of existing theories. Empiricism, he holds, cannot account for the universality and necessity of the categories (i.e., why it is that the individual cannot "think away" or alter essentially his conceptions of space, time, substance, cause, etc.). The aprioristic point of view does not explain where these ideas originate and how it is that we can arrive at knowledge of objective relationships transcending our personal sensory experience. A theological explanation is not "experimental" and cannot account for the variation of the categories in different societies.

Durkheim's own explanation is that the categories are collective representations. As such, they are imposed upon the individual and create in him the impression of being universal and necessary. The uniformity of the categories within a given society is easily explained by the fact that agreement about such fundamental modes of thought as the categories is absolutely essential for social co-operation and thus for the very existence of society. In the interest of self-preservation, the society must impose a minimum of logical conformity. Our obligation to think in terms of space, time, cause and effect, etc., is "a special form of moral necessity which is to the intellect what moral obligation is to the will."[63]

But the categories are not only imposed by society; they reflect its most general characters, and they are in this sense a social creation. The sense of time was derived from the rhythms of group life; "the territory occupied by the society furnished the material for the category of space"; and the power of the social group gave rise to the idea of an efficient force, upon which the category of causality depends.[64] From his own limited temporal and spatial intuitions the individual could never derive the idea of space or time in general. It was necessary, first, to have the concept of totality, and only society, "which includes all things," could give rise to the concept of totality.[65] With the world "inside of society," however, the space occupied by society becomes identified with space in general. Similarly, social rhythms, based on the concentration and dispersion of the social group, supply the generalized notion of time. The divisions of time into days, weeks, months, and years corresponds to the periodic recurrence of social functions; the calendar both expresses the rhythm of social life and assures its regularity.

The dependence of our conception of space on the regions occupied by the society is shown by the following:

> There are societies in Australia and North America where space is conceived in the form of an immense circle, because the camp has a circular form; and this spatial circle is divided up exactly like the tribal circle, and is in its image. There are as many regions distinguished as there are clans in the tribe, and it is the place occupied by the clans inside the encampment which has determined the orientation of these regions. Each region is defined by the totem of the clan to which it is assigned.[66]

Durkheim even hopes that evidence may yet be found to show conclusively that the principle of contradiction itself is a function of a given social system. He thinks that it has already been shown that the extent to which this principle has influenced human minds has varied historically from one society to another.[67]

I. DURKHEIM'S ETHICAL AND POLITICAL ORIENTATION

In the history of thought, agelecism has usually been accompanied by anti-individualism in ethics and conservatism in politics. This combination of elements is well exemplified in many phases of Durkheim's work. His sociology is primarily concerned with the problem of social control and is negatively disposed toward individual deviation from accepted social norms. Both the reality and the value of individual invention are systematically denied. It is a sociology of a static and monistic type, with no adequate explanation for social change.[68] Moreover, it displays a remarkable lack of interest in those structures and processes of group life which are connected with internal division and conflict. There is little concern with social classes, with the clash of interest groups, or with processes of revolution and war.[69]

It is not surprising, therefore, that Durkheim's diagnosis of our social ills and his therapeutic program of social reform should have assumed a pronounced anti-individualistic character. The prevalence of suicide, nervous disorders, and other pathological symptoms were due, he thought, to the fact that the individual was no longer sufficiently restrained by a social group. With the decline in the influence of the neighborhood, the religious group, and the extended kin group and with the increase in the size of the state and its impersonality and distance from the individual, there was no group left which could successfully impose a wholesome moral discipline on the individual. To remedy this deficiency, Durkheim proposed the creation of a type of corporatism which would endow the trade-union or professional association with sufficient authority to enter actively into the regulation and direction of the personal lives of its members.[70] This program bears some resemblances (the importance of which should not, however, be exaggerated) to the corporatism established by Fascist regimes.[71]

Yet, if we would do justice to Durkheim's thought, we must admit a complexity which baffles any simple interpretative pattern. Scattered throughout his work, but especially in the *Division of Labor* and in the *Suicide,* are numerous passages of praise for individualism. In his politics, moreover, he was regarded as a liberal. Certain biographical facts are of considerable relevance here. Durkheim was born in 1857 and came to intellectual maturity in a period when France was exerting enormous efforts to recover from the effects of the Franco-Prussian War. The unification and reintegration of the French nation was considered by most intellectuals of the period to be of the utmost urgency. An intense sentiment of nationalism provided the emotional background for Durkheim's belief in the transcendental reality of the social group (which, ordinarily, he implicitly identifies with the nation) and for his unvarying emphasis on the problems of social control. But the intellectuals were hopelessly divided in their opinions as to the proper *basis* of that social reintegration, the necessity of which they uniformly conceded. On the one hand, the conservatives urged a reversion to Catholicism, royalism, and traditionalism. On the other hand, the intellectuals who most staunchly supported the Third Republic hoped for a secular basis of integration, resulting from the growth and diffusion of scientific information. Durkheim's position was naturally with the latter group. As a social scientist of the positivistic persuasion, he could not fail to support the position that science could provide a new and quite adequate basis of social organization. As a scientific rationalist, he was necessarily distrustful of those *mystiques* which the traditionalists were offering as a substitute. Two other factors inclined him in the direction of liberal individualism: his own struggle against race prejudice, and the strong influence upon him of Renouvier's moral personalism.

What is truly distinctive, however, about Durkheim's individualism is that it is supported by entirely agelic arguments. The individual is sacred, it is claimed, because he bears within himself that culture which has been created by the group; and in doing violence to him we should be indirectly attacking the group. Moreover, the ideals of individualism and liberalism need no metaphysical justification: their rightness *for us* is guaranteed by the fact that they are implicit in our whole contemporary social organization (based on division of labor and specialization). We cannot restore this or that institution characteristic of an earlier civilization, because individualism and liberalism offer the only *possible* basis for integration in a society of our type.[72]

The adequacy of this relativistic and pragmatic defense of individualism is highly questionable. It is not based on any appreciation of the intrinsic value and creative potentialities of the individual in himself but upon the assumed inevitability of individualism at a given stage in the fixed evolutionary pattern of social change. In Durkheim's system, it appears as a paradoxical rationalization of an ideal which he found useful and which he wished to defend but which was, at bottom, incompatible with his fundamental sociological beliefs. The reversion, in recent years, of several civilized nations to a more barbaric principle of law and social organization dramatically illustrates the unsoundness of the doctrine of linear evolution. It may be true that individualism and liberalism are necessarily bound up with our present type of society, but Durkheim, who died too soon to see a Fascist revolution, apparently never realized that a society may actually change over—and quite rapidly—from a more to a less individualistic and liberal type. His relativistic defense of liberal individualism gives us no basis for deciding which of the two *types* is preferable.

IV. THE DURKHEIM SCHOOL IN FRENCH SOCIOLOGY

Durkheim's enormous influence in French sociology arose not only from his research and publications but very largely from his teaching and from his exceptional ability to guide and co-ordinate the research of others. In his position as editor of that remarkable sociological journal, *L'Année sociologique* (1896–1913) he gathered around him most of the best sociologists in France, as well as a considerable number of specialists in other fields (ethnology, law, economics, statistics, history, comparative languages, etc.), who were interested in the sociological aspects of their special fields. The work of this group has been described by Mauss in the following words:

> The *Année* was not only a publication. . . . . Around it was formed . . . . a "group" in the full sense of the word. Under the authority of Durkheim at the outbreak of the war, it was a sort of society fully developed both on the intellectual and on the spiritual side. A great number of investigations and ideas were being elaborated. . . . . We practised a true division of labor.[73]

The history of the Durkheim school bears eloquent testimony to the destructiveness of modern war. In 1914 the group was shattered by the necessary suspension of all scholarly activity and by the loss of almost all the promising young men upon whose expected contributions the pre-eminence of the school and of French sociology largely depended.[74]

After the war and Durkheim's death (possibly hastened by the loss of his son), Marcel Mauss, a relative and intimate disciple of Durkheim, bent all his efforts toward the maintenance of the tradition. He edited several of the posthumously published works of Durkheim and of the younger members of the school; and in 1923 he made a valiant, but financially unsuccessful, attempt to revive *L'Année sociologique* (published only during 1923 and the first part of 1924). In 1934, under a new board of editors and with a more flexible organization, it was launched again under the name *Annales sociologiques*. With the approach of another war, the work was again discontinued.[75]

The most orthodox of the followers of Durkheim have been Marcel Mauss, Georges Davy, and Paul Fauconnet. On the theoretical side they have done little more than to expound, rephrase, and defend against various critics the fundamental views of the master. Mauss has been much interested in methodological problems, such as the organization of the special divisions within sociology[76] and the relation of sociology to psychology. He has not hesitated to tell psychologists that sociology is, for the most part, entirely independent of psychology and that, even in the field of collective representations, sociology contributes more to psychology than it derives therefrom.[77] His chief contribution, however, probably lies in his numerous ethnological monographs, which often succeed in illuminating important social processes.[78] Of these, the monograph on the Eskimos is probably the most celebrated. It tries to prove that the intensity of Eskimo social and religious life is directly correlated with the degree of concentration of the social group. The fundamental pattern of this monograph was later used by Durkheim in his studies on value and on religion.

Georges Davy, for many years Dean of the Faculty of Letters at Dijon, has loyally and eloquently defended the Durkheimian position.[79] As a contributor to the great co-operative *Traité* of Georges Dumas, he has given forceful and unqualified expression to the sociologistic point of view in psychology. In the chapter devoted to "Sociology" he defends quite unequivocally the theses of agelic realism and agelic creationism.[80] In a statement on "the moral and the social sentiments," he reaffirms Durkheim's stand that moral obligation is first experienced as an external social constraint which is only gradually interiorized, and that the moral and the social sentiments can therefore never be entirely separated from each other. Each is the product of social organization; consequently, they cannot be explained adequately in terms of biological or psychological forces.[81]

Davy's chief empirical investigation, *La Foi jurée* (1922) is an important contribution to juristic sociology, offering, as it does, a completely sociologistic theory of contract. The attempt is to show that the institution of the legal contract grew originally out of familial relations and obligations and has only gradually assumed an individualistic character. In his study of the origins of Egyptian civilization (in which he collaborated with the eminent Egyptologist, A. Moret), Davy finds evidence to support Durkheim's position on the primacy of the totemic over either the familial or the political group, as well as to corroborate the Durkheimian explanation of the incest taboo.[82] However, he does concede the existence in religion of nonsocial elements.[83]

Paul Fauconnet, who took over Durkheim's chair of pedagogy and sociology at the Sorbonne in 1921, had collaborated with him earlier on a methodological article concerning the relation of sociology to the other social sciences;[84] and he later collaborated with Mauss in an article, "Sociologie," for the *Grande Encyclopédie,* which is perhaps the most authoritative brief statement of the fundamental position of the Durkheim school. His empirical investigations have been concerned mainly with the subject of responsibility.[85] Starting with Durkheim's conception of crime as an act which offends strong and well-defined states of the collective conscience, and of punishment as the result of the need for a restoration of emotional equilibrium, he tries to show that the function of "responsibility" is simply to provide a focus for the application of punishment. In former times children, the insane, and even physical objects have been held responsible and have been punished; and only by a gradual process of social evolution has there emerged the modern conception of responsibility as limited to the free and rational agent.

Maurice Halbwachs, for many years professor at the University of Strasbourg, but more recently at the Sorbonne, has been one of the most eminent and productive of the Durkheim group. He ranks, moreover, as the most able statistician among contemporary French sociologists. His first major work attempted a sociologistic explanation of social classes and standards of living[86] and filled an important lacuna in the Durkheimian sociology. He maintains that social classes are based on differences in the intensity of social existence. In our society the proletarian is desocialized by the mental isolation in which he works and by his low income. This lack of sociality is reflected in the disproportionately small share of his income spent on rent.

An important contribution to the sociology of knowledge is contained in Halbwachs' brilliant, but daring, monograph on "the collective framework of memory."[87] Beginning with the assertions that we never remember in our dreams and that it is in our dreams that we are furthest from the influence of society, he infers that personal memory depends on the objective structure of memories common to the social group. This is further evidenced by the fact that, in order to localize our memories, we customarily relate them to important episodes in group life—episodes such as births, marriages, deaths, holidays, festivals, etc. The rhythm of group life, as expressed in the calendar, provides an objective framework, in the absence of which the individual would be unable to remember. Furthermore, families, social classes, and other social groups all have their own memories, which serve as an indispensable principle of integration and coherence.

Halbwachs' treatment of suicide[88] brings up to date Durkheim's work on this topic and introduces some very significant concessions and modifications. While insisting that "the sentiment of a definitive and irremediable solitude is the unique cause of suicide"[89] and that this sentiment is always at least partially a social product, he admits that the individual motive (even if socially generated) plays a necessary part in the causation of suicide, which therefore always involves a psychological, as well as a social, element. He thinks that the increasing rate of suicide characteristic of the last century is now leveling off and that this rate was caused chiefly by a rapid urbanization, which exposed the individual to more shocks and rebuffs and to frequent feelings of maladaptation.[90]

Célestin Bouglé, from 1927 until his death a director of the Ecole Normale Supérieure, was a balanced and eclectic thinker who actively collaborated in the work of the Durkheim school but who remained highly critical of many of the assumptions upon which it was based. On various occasions he explicitly rejected the doctrine of the independence and externality of the *conscience sociale,* the sociologistic theory of knowledge, the identification of the pathological with the abnormal, the sociologistic derivation of values, and the methodological exclusion of motivation and other psychological data from sociology.[91] His own interests were very largely centered around the problems of equality and democracy. In an early study he clearly formulated a conception of social equality as the provision of equal opportunities for self-development by the elimination of nongenetic hereditary advantages.[92] He tried to show that equality in this sense was a natural and inevitable product of the intensification of such morphological processes as population growth, mobility, centralization, urbanization, and social complication. However, although he succeeded (in his interesting treatment of the caste system) in *describing* the social structure of India in primarily morphological terms, he did not deny that this structure is very largely sustained by ideological forces (particularly the Hindu beliefs in reincarnation and in the peculiar holiness of the Brahmin caste).[93] A defense of the democratic ideals from the attacks of the social biologists is the subject matter of another important monograph.[94] It is urged that the biological processes of differentiation and natural selection cannot be transposed to the social plane except metaphorically; that on the social level it is not the differentiation of hereditary castes but the diversification of individuals in accordance with their different capacities and interests that is to be desired; and that the inheritance of property and privilege falsifies the whole conception of natural selection in the social world, since it no longer follows that the biologically fit survive.[95]

Two eminent French sociologists who are not members of the Durkheim school deserve mention because of their peculiar relation to it. The first, Gaston Richard, was an associate of Durkheim at Bordeaux and played a not inconspicuous role in the early history of *L'Année soci-*

ologique. However, he found himself unable to accept most of the chief sociologistic doctrines and was genuinely shocked by the Durkheimian theory of religion; so that he became, by stages, one of the most explicit and relentless critics of the school.[96] Quite a different case is presented by René Maunier, the genial and eclectic professor of colonial sociology at the University of Paris; he has continued to co-operate with the school,[97] although his own theoretical position combines elements from both Durkheim and Tarde and is far from sociologistic orthodoxy. The social fact is defined as one which is repeated and common in a given society (which accords with Tarde's definition in terms of imitation) but which is also "traditional" and "obligatory for the individual" (which thus conforms to Durkheim's definition as well).[98] Maunier is a sober empiricist, who shares with the Durkheimians a great interest in the morphological type of explanation but who has not found the theory of collective representations a useful hypothesis.[99]

It is necessary, before concluding, to give brief mention to the many specialists in related fields who have been directly influenced by, or who have been more or less associated with, the Durkheim school. Lucien Lévy-Bruhl, the philosopher of neo-Comtian positivism, was never a member of the Durkheim school and has been subjected to criticism by its members on certain points; but between his work and that of the school there is an important parallelism, if not an actual convergence. In *La Morale et la science des mœurs,* he takes the position, closely resembling Durkheim's, that an empirical science of morals can and should be constructed and that this science, by an objective study of existing moral attitudes and practices, will provide a scientific basis for social guidance.[100] Moreover, in his numerous and well-known studies on the thought-processes of primitive peoples, he has tried to show that their mentalities are "pre-logical" and essentially different from our own, because they are dominated by "collective representations."[101] The precise role of morphological factors in the creation of these alleged differences has not been sufficiently examined to satisfy M. Mauss and other orthodox Durkheimians, who, moreover, have preferred to stress the evolutionary continuity between primitive and civilized thought forms rather than their heterogeneity. On the whole, however, these researches of Lévy-Bruhl have been taken as additional corroboration of Durkheim's contention that the fundamental forms of thought are not uniform and universal but are variable because they are socially conditioned.

Charles Blondel, the eminent psychologist of the University of Strasbourg, was much interested in the collective elements in mental life and showed clearly the influence of the sociologistic point of view. According to his analysis, the chief cause of insanity is a desocialization and progressive isolation of the individual mind.[102] Volition reduces to little more than individual obedience to collective imperatives. Both will and reason are gifts which we derive from society ready-made and which for most men involve no more than the application of accepted ideas and rules (collective representations) to their daily experience.[103] In his *Introduction à la psychologie collective,* Blondel comes to the conclusion that, although psychic facts exist only in the individual mind, they are, in large part, of a collective character; that only collective psychology (which studies the collective element in the individual mind) can explain the higher mental functions (intellectual, affective, and volitional); and that a sound psychology of the individual must be based upon the conclusions of psychophysiology and collective psychology.[104]

Two other French psychologists who have shown an active sympathy for the sociologistic point of view are Georges Dumas and Henri Wallon. Dumas, in his monumental treatises, *Traité de psychologie* and *Nouveau traité de psychologie,* has invited Georges Davy to express the Durkheimian position and has himself asserted that collective patterns largely determine the emotional life of the individual, even when the individual is in a state of isolation.[105] Wallon has given us an analysis of child mentality, which is markedly similar in certain respects to Lévy-Bruhl's study of pre-logical thinking in primitive societies.[106]

Among the historians, the one who comes closest to sharing the Durkheimian point of view is the eminent Sinologist, Marcel Granet; he takes a definitely sociologistic approach to the study of Chinese civilization.[107] In particular, his treatment of the influence of group structure on the basic modes of thought in China constitutes the most impressive attempt thus far made at a detailed substantiation of the sociologistic theory of knowledge.[108] Henri Berr, another outstanding French historian, has sponsored a type of synthetic history which lays considerable, but not exclusive, emphasis upon social factors.[109]

François Simiand, one of France's leading economists, was from the beginning an active participant in the work of the Durkheim school. He was an able critic of the orthodox conceptions of economics; his own approach resembled somewhat that of the American Institutionalists.[110] Beginning with the assumption that economic phenomena are primarily an expression of collective judgments of social value, he did several exhaustive statistical studies of wages and prices.[111] Among the jurists who have been influenced by sociologistic theory, the most outstanding have been Léon Duguit, Emmanuel Lévy, and Paul Huvelin. Duguit's "positive" theory of law probably owes something to Durkheim's positivistic methodology and certainly owes much to his doctrine of organic solidarity, which, in Duguit's hands, becomes the objective basis of modern law.[112] Emmanuel Lévy was one of the original collaborators of the *L'Année sociologique,* and he consistently maintained the position that law rests on beliefs which emanate from the *conscience collective.* Paul Huvelin, the jurist and legal historian, was one of Durkheim's first pupils. He emphasized the role of magic in the origin of private law and the influence of social structure on the evolution of commercial law.[113]

Finally, the science of comparative linguistics in France has shown the influence of Durkheim to a remarkable degree. To all appearances, no other order of social phenomena depends less on individual creation or better illustrates the imposition of collective patterns of behavior on the individual. From the beginning, *L'Année sociologique* had the active co-operation of the great and highly revered philologist, Antoine Meillet, who contributed to it a now classic monograph on the influence of social groups in bringing about changes in the meanings of words.[114] In his monumental *Histoire de la langue française* and in his systematic discussion of the relation of thought to language, [115] Ferdinand Brunot has frequent recourse to a sociological (though not always a clearly sociologistic) point of view. But the philologist who shows the influence of Durkheim most clearly is Jacques Vendryes, who has been intensely concerned to prove that linguistic innovations by individuals are only apparent and that all linguistic changes are, at bottom, of social origin.[116]

NOTES

1. We wish to distinguish carefully between *substantive* theories, which attempt to tell the truth about the actual object of scientific investigation in a general field, and *methodological* doctrines, which analyze and evaluate the cognitive processes by which the object is studied.

2. The adjectival form of the term "agelecism" is "agelic." "Agelic realism" asserts that the group is a real entity outside of, and apart from, its members. "Agelic personalism" asserts that the group is, or must be considered, a mind, soul, person, or moral agent. "Agelic transcendentalism" asserts that the social group is a hyperspiritual, ideal, or supernatural entity. "Agelic creationism" maintains that values, culture, and all the higher elements of human personality are of collective origin and that the individual is therefore, in a radical sense, a group product. "Agelic fatalism" asserts that the individual is power-less to influence the course of social change, since the group is bound by necessary laws emanating from its own structure which determine its evolution.

3. Durkheim freely acknowledged his indebtedness to Comte and Espinas (cf. S. Deploige, *Le Conflit de la morale et de la sociologie* [2d ed.; Paris, 1912], pp. 393–413). And Durkheim's disciples and close associates consider him "le véritable héritier d'Auguste Comte sur le terrain de la recherche scientifique" (C. Bouglé, *Bilan de la sociologie française contemporaine* [Paris, 1935], p. 2). See also G. Davy, *Sociologues d'hier et d'aujourd'hui* (Paris 1931), p. 2. For a comprehensive Durkheim bibliography and a survey of the sources of Durkheim's sociological thought see Harry Alpert, *Émile Durkheim and His Sociology* (New York, 1939).

4. The reader interested in a more detailed analysis and criticism of Durkheim's system is referred to the author's unpublished doctoral dissertation, "The Development of French Sociologism and Its Critics in France" (Widener Library, Harvard University) (also avail-able on microfilm from the Library of the University of Wisconsin).

5. Roger Lacombe, Daniel Essertier, Célestin Bouglé, among others. This is probably an overstatement, since important elements of agelecism are to be found in the tradition from which Durkheim springs, and these are apparent in his earliest work. However, the term "methodological" is used by Lacombe *et al.* in a broader sense than that in which we use it.

6. Durkheim rejected the appellation of "Positivist" as applied to himself, probably because he took it as denoting an unreserved adherent of the system of Comte.

7. Durkheim's attempt to "renovate the problems of philosophy" and his preoccupation with problems of morals, values, religion, and epistomology in his later work have been mistakenly criticized by Gaston Richard (in *La Sociologie générale* [Paris, 1912], pp. 364–65) and others, as involving the abandonment of his early positivistic program and his announced separation of science and philosophy. This criticism rests on a mistaken conception of the *kind* of separation between science and philosophy which positivism envisages. In fact, Durkheim made it quite clear in his earlier period that sociology, when developed, would have important philosophical *implications*, though it would never have any necessary philosophical *presuppositions* (cf. *Les Règles de la méthode sociologique* [3d ed.; Paris, 1904], pp. 172–75). (Hereafter cited as *"Règles."*)

8. *Règles*, Preface to 2d ed., p. x.

9. In his Latin thesis on Montesquieu, Durkheim made it quite clear that treating social facts as things required the abandonment of the assumption of free will in favor of a uni-versal determinism. Montesquieu is praised for abandoning occasionally the older concep-tion "that social facts depend entirely on the will of man and that consequently they are not true things" (Durkheim, *Montesquieu: sa part dans la fondation des sciences politiques et de la science des sociétés, Quid secundatus politicae scientiae institundae contulerit* [Bordeaux, 1892]; translated into French by F. Alengry in the *Revue d'histoire politique et constitutionnelle*, I, No. 3 [July–September, 1937], 410).

10. *Règles*, p. 54.

11. It is interesting to note that Durkheim's three empirical studies rely almost entirely upon these types of data: *De la division du travail social* (Paris, 1893), mainly upon law codes; *Le suicide* (Paris, 1897), upon social statistics; and *Les Formes élémentaires de la vie religieuse* (Paris, 1912), upon religious dogmas, myths, and rites.

12. *Règles*, chap. v.

13. *Ibid.*, p. 135.

14. *Ibid.*, p. 138.

15. "Morphologie sociale," Introduction, *Année sociologique*, II (1899), 520.

16. By P. Barth, R. Worms, G. Richard, and R. Lacombe, among others.

17. Durkheim is inclined to hedge on the causal ultimacy of even this attenuated morphological factor, stating that *no* factor is truly ultimate for science and that morphological facts are themselves influenced by other types of social changes (*Règles*, p. 142).

18. Durkheim was bitterly opposed to the introduction of practical considerations and problems into sociology itself, but, on the other hand, he expected sociology to have important practical *applications*. In fact, he states, "we would not consider our scientific labors worth an hour's trouble if they were to have only a speculative interest" (*Division du travail*).

19. *Règles*, pp. 61 ff. This recourse to the analogy of the science of medicine is characteristic of the sociologistic tradition and is found in Saint-Simon, Comte, Roberty, and Espinas. Durkheim, however, is the first one to give serious consideration to the difficulties involved in this conception.

20. *Ibid.*, p. 70.

21. Halbwachs, a follower and close student of Durkheim, maintains that, on the basis of his own criterion, Durkheim should have judged the rising suicide rate to be normal. It seems apparent that the ascription of normality or abnormality is not an entirely objective and mechanical procedure but that it rests upon certain concealed and relatively subjective standards of value.

22. Among the able critics of Durkheim's theory of social pathology may be mentioned G. Tarde, R. Lacombe, G. Belot, C. Bouglé, G. Richard, G. Cantécor, and A. Fouillée.

23. *Règles*, p. 76. This seems to make survival or utility the ultimate criterion.

24. *Le Suicide: étude de sociologie* (new ed.; Paris, 1930), p. 357.

25. *Ibid.*, pp. 346 ff.

26. It is most fully expounded in Durkheim's "Représentations individuelles et représentations collectives," *Revue de métaphysique et de morale*, Vol. VI, (May, 1898). Reprinted in Durkheim's *Sociologie et philosophie* (Paris, 1924), chap. i, pp. 1–48.

27. One of the chief difficulties in understanding Durkheim arises out of the great (and probably unwarranted) extension given to the meaning of the term "constraint." The writer has distinguished *seven* distinct senses in which this term is used by Durkheim, as illustrated by the following cases, all of which are offered by Durkheim as examples of social constraint: (1) A law compels an individual's obedience by penal sanctions. (2) A moral rule is observed by an individual through fear of public opinion. (3) An ideal or value which an individual may have imbibed from his culture influences him to act in a certain way. (4) An inhabitant of France is forced to speak French if he wishes to be understood; similarly, a merchant must pay prevailing rates of interest and wages if he is to continue in business. (5) The paths of transportation and communication influence the course of migrations and the diffusion of culture. (6) The individual in a crowd is led to act in ways in which he would not act when alone. (7) Education or inculcation produces an acceptance of the truth of certain doctrines.

In the writer's opinion, only the first and second cases are true examples of collective constraint. In general, Durkheim fails to note the important distinctions between: (1) *collective constraint*, where the *group* deliberately represses certain types of actions which individuals would like to commit; (2) *cultural determination*, where ideas, values, and action patterns passed on by education and imitation influence what people believe and the way they *want* to act; (3) *physical determination*, where the topography or the material culture influences the unfolding of various social processes; and (4) *psychological compulsion*, where the crowd situation provides certain unusual psychological stimuli, which produce strong emotional reactions and aberrant behavior.

28. Durkheim, *De la division du travail social: étude sur l'organization des sociétés supérieures* (Paris, 1893).

29. As we shall see, individual morality and social solidarity are so closely connected in Durkheim's mind as to form virtually a single entity.

30. *Division du travail*, pp. 450–52.

31. *Ibid.*, pp. 230 ff.

32. *Ibid.*, pp. 256 ff.

33. *Ibid.*, pp. 269 ff. This has often been pointed out as an amazing non sequitur. G. Belot remarked that one might as well say of a bankrupt merchant that he could not have been motivated by the hope of profits. Moreover, the whole argument rests on premises which are inadmissible by Durkheim's own methodological criteria. His discussion about man's capacity for happiness or about the different degrees of happiness enjoyed by primitive and civilized peoples unfortunately relies upon arbitrary and subjective psychological intuitions which Durkheim elsewhere condemns as *prénotions*. Moreover, the conception of human nature as essentially static, and easily satisfied in its desires, appears just as unrealistic as the diametrically opposite, but equally one-sided, conception of human nature which Durkheim elaborates in *Le Suicide* (cf. below, p. 509).

34. Since Durkheim's day, there has been much anthropological evidence to show that in primitive society an increase of population is an exceptional rather than a normal phenomenon and that the size of the population is itself determined by numerous social and cultural factors (see Carr-Saunders, *Population Problem* [Oxford, 1922]). It should, moreover, have been apparent to Durkheim that an increase of population, where it did occur, might have been met by emigration or war and that, where division of labor was selected as a preferable alternative, individual motivation and consideration of personal or collective welfare must have been influential in bringing about a decision. Hence the causation could not have been completely "mechanical."

35. Durkheim, *Le Suicide* (Paris, 1897).

36. The observed increase in suicides during periods of exceptional prosperity has not been corroborated by further investigation.

37. A third type of suicide ("altruistic suicide") is explained by Durkheim as resulting from an excess of social integration. Unfortunately, the nature of this type of suicide is far from clear. Durkheim so defines it as to include apparently the willing sacrifice of life for the benefit of another (as by a soldier to save his comrades or by a mother for her child). Yet, as Halbwachs subsequently pointed out, these are not considered by society to be suicides; and this is therefore not a good sociologistic definition. Moreover, it is curious to note that Durkheim himself forgets about "altruistic suicide" in important parts of his study. Thus he uses the ordinary statistics of suicide in estimating the total number of suicides, entirely overlooking the fact that most of his "altruistic suicides" are not commonly considered to be suicides and do not enter into the official suicide statistics. This error is particularly glaring when he asserts that the total number of suicides decreases during a war. If cases of deliberate self-sacrifice were included, the rate might be vastly increased. He also seems to have forgotten "altruistic suicide" in his blanket condemnation of suicide as a moral evil.

38. *Le Suicide* pp. 366 ff.

39. Two of the chief lines of criticism which we feel might well be brought against the Durkheimian theory of suicide are: (1) Durkheim hypostatizes a statistical average. The uniformity of the suicide rate might arise from the uniform strength from year to year of a great number of suicide-producing factors. (2) Where factors of group composition, social integration, etc., are influential, they probably act on the suicide rate by influencing the motives of individuals; and these form an indispensable link in the causal chain. Society's influence on the suicide rate is not so much a matter of collective compulsion as of cultural determination. Thus, e.g., the suicide of individuals who have lost their money in a depression is to be explained largely by the fact that they have acquired from their culture certain value-judgments stressing the unconditional desirability of maintaining their socio economic status.

40. Durkheim, "Représentations individuelles et représentations collectives," *Sociologie et philosophie* (Paris, 1924), chap. i, pp. 1–48.

41. This constitutes a major breaking-away from the position adopted in the *Règles*—that the sociologist should explain all social changes in terms of changes in the internal social milieu.

42. This theory was first presented by Durkheim in 1906 at two meetings of the Société Française de Philosophie, held on February 11 and March 22. The paper and subsequent discussion are reported in the *Bulletin de la Société Française de Philosophie*, VI (Paris, 1906), 113 ff.

43. *Ibid.*, pp. 121 ff. Durkheim also notes that the same duality is to be found in the notion of sacredness, which is both forbidden and inspiring. He maintains that there is a very close relation, both logically and historically, between religion and morality.

44. "Now in the world of experience, I know of only one subject which possesses a moral reality which is richer and more complex than our own: it is the collectivity. No, I am mistaken; there is another being who could play the same role: namely, the divinity. Between God and society we must make our choice. I will not here examine the reasons which could militate in favor of one or the other solution. Both solutions are, moreover, perfectly compatible. I will add that from my point of view this choice is a matter of indifference, for I do not see in the divinity anything more than society transfigured and conceived symbolically" (*ibid.*, p. 129). Note how clearly this anticipates the fundamental idea of Durkheim's study of religion.

45. *Ibid.*, p. 132.

46. *Ibid.*, p. 116. The *chief* defects in Durkheim's theory of morals, as they appear to the writer, may be summarily stated as follows: (1) Other individuals may legitimately be the object of moral behavior and may properly inspire moral devotion. It is not that they are *better* than we are but that they are *other* than we; and this quality of "otherness" makes possible an element of devotion which no narrowly egoistic objective can inspire. Besides, it is by no means certain that the individual's desire to improve or develop himself is completely lacking in moral content. It is therefore not necessary to postulate that society is a person. (2) The social group conserves culture, but it has not yet been shown that it *creates* culture. Our devotion to culture and to civilization does not necessarily require us to be loyal to the particular group with which we happen to be associated. If that group betrays or inhibits culture, we may be justified in abandoning it or in trying to bring about a radical reorganization. In short, our devotion to the social group is conditional upon *its* loyalty to the fundamental values transmitted by culture. (3) The extreme relativism of Durkheim's theory makes it impossible to criticize an existing moral system "from the outside," in terms of wider and more general standards. If every society has the moral system it needs, there is no basis for fundamental moral criticism and no possibility of moral progress. Mere conservation is not for society, as it is not for the individual, a completely adequate moral objective. The individual may willingly sacrifice his personal existence for a moral end, and a society is similarly dedicated to ends beyond its own mere existence.

47. Durkheim, "Jugements de valeur et jugements de réalité: communication faite au Congrès international de philosophie de Boulogne, 6 avril, 1911," published in *Revue de métaphysique et de morale*, July 3, 1911, pp. 436–53; reprinted in *Sociologie et philosophie*, chap. iv, pp. 117 ff. Our references will be to this reprint.

48. *Ibid.*, p. 133.

49. *Ibid.*, p. 135.

50. *Ibid.*, pp. 141–42.

51. Such universal explanations are obviously of small scientific value. In further criticism the writer would maintain that *mental* interaction is only slightly dependent upon physical contiguity and that it is *mental* interaction which is important in the development of new ideals or values. Durkheim has presented very little evidence that the increase in physical

proximity (as in crowds) plays an important part in the *creation* of ideals. It is probably much more important in creating emotional attitudes favorable for their rapid diffusion.

52. Paris, 1912. References are to the excellent English translation by J. W. Swain, *The Elementary Forms of the Religious Life* (London, 1915).

53. "A religion is a unified system of beliefs and practices relative to sacred things, that is to say, things set apart and forbidden—beliefs and practices which unite into one single moral community called a Church, all those who adhere to them" (*ibid.*, p. 47). The *ad hoc* nature of this definition is implicitly admitted by Durkheim when he writes: "The second element which thus finds a place in our definition is no less essential than the first; for by showing that the idea of religion is inseparable from that of the Church, it makes it clear that religion should be an eminently collective thing" (*ibid.*).

54. This evolutionary approach to the problem of social origins exposes Durkheim to many serious criticisms. For example, some authorities have claimed that other peoples (as, e.g., the African pygmies, who are alleged to be monotheistic) are more primitive than the Aruntas. Moreover, Sir James Frazer, who first revealed to Durkheim the religious nature of totemism, later changed his mind and decided that totemism is not really a religion at all. Perhaps the most serious objections, however, concern the validity of the whole evolutionary approach in sociology. Do primitive peoples represent an earlier phase of our own evolution, or are they end-products of a long and largely independent line of evolution? Can primitiveness be equated with simplicity? Will the essential characteristics of religion be more clearly revealed in a primitive society, where religion is closely bound up with many other phases of social life (kinship groups, tribal patriotism, technological procedures, etc.) or in a highly civilized society, in which all the institutions have been to a much higher degree differentiated and purged of extrinsic elements?

55. ". . . . If it is at once the symbol of the god and of society, is not that because the god and the society are only one? How could the emblem of the group have been able to become the figure of this quasi-divinity, if the group and the divinity were two distinct realities? The god of the clan, the totemic principle, can therefore be nothing else than the clan itself, personified and represented to the imagination under the visible form of the animal or vegetable which serves as totem" (*ibid.*, p. 206).

56. *Ibid.*, pp. 214–16.

57. *Ibid.*, pp. 206 ff.

58. Three of the many possible criticisms of the Durkheimian theory of religion may be briefly indicated here: (1) The group always remains a purely secular and existential reality. It is difficult to see how it could give rise to the ideal and the sacred merely by an increase of density. Crowd excitement is not necessarily of a religious character; and the intense states of excitement aroused in an Australian *corrobori* or in a revival meeting may be very largely nonreligious in origin and nature. We must also remember that many of the most intense and authentic religious experiences occur in solitude. (2) Our attitudes toward God and toward society are not nearly so similar as Durkheim tries to make out, especially if we distinguish between the social group and the culture—which is, in large part, borrowed from other groups. And such similarity, if established, would by no means prove that God and the society are the same entity. (3) Since Durkheim's theory of religion deeply shocks the sentiments of religious people (cf. G. Richard, "L'Athéisme dogmatique en sociologie religieuse," *Revue d'histoire et de philosophie religieuse*, 1923), it seems likely that his theory, no less than the theories he criticizes, portrays religion as resting on an illusion. The religious believer does not consciously worship society, and to say that the entity he worships is only a symbol of society is to accuse him of a gross error if he does not *understand* its symbolic character. If its symbolic character *were* understood, few religionists would continue to worship, because they would not recognize in the empirical reality—society—an adequate substitute for God, unless they had, like Durkheim, begun by deifying society.

59. Durkheim and Mauss, "De quelques formes primitives de classification," *Année sociologique*, VI (1901–2), 1–72.

60. *Ibid.*, p. 6.

61. Perhaps the chief criticism of this theory of classification is implicitly contained in a footnote in which Durkheim admits: "It is probable that from the beginning man has always more or less clearly classified his sources of food" (*ibid.*, p. 66). But if primitive man could always classify his foodstuffs (and, in general, the technological elements in the situation), then the logical powers of classification were already his, anterior to and independent of the classificatory powers derived from the structure of the group. If nature or the structure of his own mind could create a classification in one field, why could it not also create classifications in other fields; and what could prevent classificatory habits exercised in one field from being extended gradually to others? Durkheim's assumption that contemporary scientific classification has its source in the emotional, mythological classifications based on collective representations seems very arbitrary, since our contemporary scientific classification seems logically and "temperamentally" much closer to the utilitarian technological classifications by means of which primitive man was able to exercise some slight degree of prediction and control over the material conditions of his existence. From another point of view, we may also ask whether, if individuals did not already possess at least a general power of classification, they could recognize human beings as constituting a class distinct from the animals or could arrive at such notions as a clan, phratry, or family.

62. This subject is treated in the Introduction and in the Conclusion of *The Elementary Forms of the Religious Life* (see esp. pp. 10 ff. and 440 ff.).

63. *Ibid.*, p. 18.

64. *Ibid.*, p. 440.

65. Here Durkheim lapses into language which brings him very close to an absolute idealism, with society as the Absolute. "Since the universe does not exist except insofar as it is thought of, and since it is not completely thought of except by society, it becomes a part of society's interior life, while this is the totality, outside of which nothing exists" (*ibid.*, pp. 441–42). One puzzling aspect of the situation is that, while the Absolute Idealists believe in only *one* Absolute, Durkheim, as a sociological relativist, insists that there are *many* societies and that they are radically heterogeneous. The simultaneous existence of several societies *each* of which contains the whole universe reminds one of a congress of philosophical solipsists!

66. *Ibid.*, pp. 11–12.

67. There are many points of view from which Durkheim's theory of knowledge can be (and has been) criticized. From the point of view of empiricism, the following objections will appear pertinent: Extension, duration, etc., are real properties of the physical world, not something created by the social mind. It is absurd to say that society imposes categories of space and time on individuals in order that they may meet at a given place and time and otherwise co-operate; for, if the world were not already spatial and temporal, there could not be any problem of "meeting." The rhythm of group life is superimposed upon, and measured by, astronomical time (days, months, seasons, etc.), and the spatial formations which a social group assumes is simply a particular distribution of its members and their possessions over the earth's surface, which possesses fixed spatial properties independent of any society. In the example given, it is not the *society* which is circular, but the camp site; and *its* circularity could be perceived by the individual if the site were uninhabited. The primary function of the categories is to enable us to adapt ourselves to the physical world; and, if they simply reflected the organization of a particular society, they would not so well fit the physical world or enable members of *different* societies to co-operate. The apriorist would urge the following type of objection: If the individual mind did not naturally receive its experience in a spatial and temporal order, society could not possibly impose such an order on the individual minds. The *meaning* of time would be quite incommunicable to one who initially lacked all sense of time. To perceive the rhythm of social processes or the pattern of a camp site, we must first be able to experience temporality and spatiality. Society may influence the conventional methods of dividing or

describing space and time, but it could not give us the fundamental forms of intuition. The same may be said for such categories as cause, substance, etc.

68. The only serious attempt to find an explanation of social changes occurs in the book on the division of labor, and this attempt is generally conceded to have been unsuccessful (see above, p. 508 and nn. 33 and 34).

69. Durkheim's interest in socialism appears to have been chiefly in the history of its ideology. He indicates that, while he has considerable sympathy for its ideal of justice as a principle whereby excessive individual demands may be regulated (he calls this principle "communism" as distinct from socialism), he is opposed to that type of socialism which is interested chiefly in raising the standard of living and which favors collectivism as a more efficient type of economic organization for the creation and distribution of wealth (*Le Socialisme, sa définition, ses débuts, la doctrine Saint-Simonienne*, ed. M. Mauss [Paris, 1928]).

70. This program is presented in an Introduction to the second edition of *De la division du travail social*, written in 1902. Further treatment of the problems of social pathology is to be found in the *Règles*, in the *Suicide*, in *L'Education morale* (Paris, 1925), and in the articles "La Morale," *Revue philosophique*, LXXXIX (1920), 81–97), and "Morale professionnelle," *Revue de métaphysique et de morale*, XLIV (1937), 527–44, 711–38). The last three titles were published, after Durkheim's death, by Marcel Mauss.

71. Under fascism the professional associations are not really autonomous and are simply an additional instrument for bringing the ubiquitous power of the state to bear on the individual. Durkheim's scheme, in contrast to totalitarianism, involves no increase in state power but proposes a decentralization of authority by means of an increase in the powers of vocational associations.

72. It was this type of argument which he adopted against the traditionalists at the time of the Dreyfus trials ("Individualisme et les intellectuels," *Revue Bleu*, X (1898), 7–13).

73. Marcel Mauss, "In Memoriam," *Année sociologique* (new. ser.), Vol. I.

74. Among those lost may be mentioned: Robert Herz, Maxim David, Antoine Bianconi, Jean Raynier, R. Gelly, and André Durkheim, son of Émile Durkheim.

75. By 1939 a new generation of scholars had grown up and entered the group. In general, they adopted a less doctrinaire line and were moving in the direction of the abandonment or modification of agelecism. Among them were included such promising younger men as Raymond Aron, Robert Marjolin, and Raymond Polin.

76. "Divisions et proportions des divisions de la sociologie," *Année sociologique*, Vol. II (new ser.; 1924–25). "Fragment d'un plan de sociologie générale descriptive," *Annales sociologiques*, ser. A, Fasc. 1, 1934.

77. "Rapports réals et pratiques de la psychologie et de la sociologie," *Journal de psychologie*, Vol. XXI (December 15, 1924); see also "L'Expression obligatoire des sentiments," *ibid.*, 1921.

78. Such, e.g., are his studies on the seasonal variations in Eskimo religious life (*Année sociologique*, Vol. IX, in collaboration with H. Beuchat); on primitive forms of classification (*ibid.*, Vol. II, in collaboration with Durkheim); on the nature and function of sacrifice (*ibid.*, Vol. II, in collaboration with H. Hubert); on the general theory of magic (*ibid.*, Vol. III, in collaboration with H. Hubert); and on the gift as an archaic form of exchange (*ibid.*, [new ser.], Vol. I). Note also the following studies in the *Revue de l'histoire des religions*: (1896–97) "La Religion et les origines du droit pénal"; (1901) "Leçon d'ouverture du cours d'histoire des religions, etc."; see also "L'Arte et le mythe, d'après Wundt," *Revue philosophique*, 1909; "L'Origine de la notion de mana," *Anthropologie*, 1914; and "L'Ethnographie en France et à l'étranger," *Revue de Paris*, 1913.

79. *Durkheim: Introduction et morceaux choisis* (Paris, 1911); "Emile Durkheim: l'homme et l'œuvre," *Revue de métaphysique et de morale*, 1919, 1920; and *Sociologues d'hier et d'aujourd'hui*.

80. G. Davy, "La Sociologie," in G. Dumas, *Traité de psychologie*, Vol. II (Paris, 1924).

81. In G. Dumas, *Nouveau traité de psychologie,* Vol. VI (Paris, 1939).

82. Davy and Moret, *Des clans aux empires* (Paris, 1924). Davy has made other contributions in juristic and educational sociology.

83. *Le Droit, l'idéalisme et l'expérience* (Paris, 1922); *Eléménts de sociologie appliquée à la morale et à l'éducation,* Vol. I: *Sociologie politique* (1924).

84. "Sociologie et sciences sociales," *Revue philosophique,* 1903.

85. *La Responsibilité* (Paris, 1920).

86. *La Classe ouvrière et les niveaux de vie: recherches sur le hiérarchie des besoins dans les sociétés industrielles contemporaines* (Paris, 1913).

87. *Les Cadres sociaux de la mémoire* (Paris, 1925).

88. *Les Causes du suicide* (Paris, 1930).

89. *Ibid.,* p. 425.

90. Other important publications of Halbwachs are: "La Doctrine d'Émile Durkheim," *Revue philosophique,* 1918; *Le Calcul des probabilités à la portée de tous* (in collaboration with M. Frechet) (Paris, 1923); and "Matière et société," *Revue philosophique,* July–August, 1920, pp. 120–22; also, "La Nuptialité en France, pendant et depuis la guerre," *Année sociologique,* ser. E, Fasc. 1, 1935.

91. Cf. particularly *Les Sciences sociales en Allemagne, les methodes actuelles* (Paris, 1896), pp. 147 ff.

92. *Les Idées égalitaires* (Paris, 1899).

93. *Essais sur le régime des castes* (Paris, 1908).

94. *La Démocratie devant la science: études critiques sur l'hérédité, le concurrence et la différenciation* (Paris, 1903): 3d ed. with a Preface on "La Sociologie monarchiste" (1923). Some of this material was first presented in two brilliant articles devoted to a criticism of the biologistic sociology: "La Sociologie biologique," *Revue philosophique,* 1900; and "Le Procès de la sociologie biologique," *ibid.,* 1901.

95. Bouglé has also made numerous contributions in the fields of sociological pedagogy and the history of social thought. Under the former heading we may list the following books: *Qu'est-ce que la sociologie?* (Paris, 1907) (an excellent introductory statement); *Guide de l'étudiant en sociologie* (in collaboration with Déat) (Paris, 1921); *Eléments de sociologie* (a source book, edited in collaboration with J. Raffault (Paris, 1926); Bouglé's work on the history of social thought has dealt mainly with socialists and social reformers: *Chez les prophètes socialistes* (Paris, 1918); *La Sociologie de Proudhon* (Paris, 1911); *La Doctrine de Saint-Simon* (in collaboration with Élie Halévy) (Paris, 1924); *L'Oeuvre d'Henri de Saint-Simon* (selected passages) (Paris, 1925); *Proudhon* (Paris, 1929). He has also proved himself a keen and well-balanced commentator on the development of academic sociology (cf. *Les Sciences sociales en Allemagne, les méthodes actuelles* (Paris, 1896); "Un Sociologue individualiste: G. Tarde," *Revue de Paris,* 1905; "Individualisme et sociologie," *Revue bleu,* November, 1905; "La Sociologie et le droit comparé," *Revue de l'enseignement français hors de France,* 1926; "Sociologie et psychologie," *ibid.,* 1927. Especially notable is his useful outline of modern French sociology, *Le Bilan de la sociologie française contemporaine.* We must also make mention of an interesting series of lectures entitled *Leçons sur l'évolution des valeurs* (Paris, 1922), which was translated into English by Helen S. Sellars in 1926 as *The Evolution of Values,* which takes only a moderately agelic point of view with respect to the nature and origin of social values. Bouglé has also written numerous articles and pamphlets on problems of politics and social policy.

96. G. Richard, *La Sociologie générale* (Paris, 1912); "Nouvelles tendences sociologiques en France," *Revue internationale de sociologie,* XXXVI, 648 ff.; "A. Comte et E. Durkheim," *ibid.,* XL, 603 ff.; "La Pathologie sociale d'Émile Durkheim, *ibid.,* XXXVIII, 119 ff.; "Le Conflit de la morale et de la sociologie," *Revue philosophique,* 1911; "L'Athéisme dogmatique en sociologie religieuse," *Revue d'histoire et de philosophie religieuse,* 1923.

97. He has been a collaborator both on *L'Année sociologique,* to which he contributed a monograph on the rituals of exchange in North Africa (Vol. II [new ser., 1924]), and

on *L'Annales sociologiques*, in which he published an important memoire on "Interest Groups and the Idea of Contract in North Africa" (ser. C, Fasc. 2, 1937).

98. Cf. René Maunier, *Introduction à la sociologie* (Paris, 1929), pp. 15 ff.

99. Other important publications of Maunier are: *L'Economie politique et sociologie* (Paris, 1910); *L'Origine et la fonction économique des villes* (Paris, 1910); *La Construction de la maison en Kabylie* (Paris, 1926); and *Essais sur les groupements sociaux* (Paris, 1929).

100. Paris, 1903, and many later editions. Albert Bayet has pushed this view even further in: *La Morale scientifique* (Paris, 1905); and *La Science des faits moraux* (Paris, 1925). In *Le Suicide et la morale* (Paris, 1922), he has carried out his methodological program by a voluminous and painstaking investigation of the history of moral judgments and attitudes bearing on a specific act.

101. Lévy-Bruhl, *Les Fonctions mentales dans les sociétés primitives* (1923); *La Mentalité primitive* (1925); *L'Ame primitive* (1927); *Le Surnaturel et la nature dans la mentalité primitive* (1931); *La Mythologie primitive* (1935); and *L'Expérience mystique et les symboles chez les primitifs* (1938). These are all issued by Alcan in Paris; and the first four have been felicitously translated into English by Lilian A. Clare under the following titles: *How Natives Think* (New York, 1927); *Primitive Mentality* (New York, 1923); *The "Soul" of the Primitive* (New York, 1928); and *Primitives and the Supernatural* (New York, 1935).

102. *La Conscience morbide: essai de psychopathologie générale* (Paris, 1913).

103. Blondel, "Les Volitions," in G. Dumas, *Traité de psychologie* (Paris, 1924), II, 333–425.

104. Blondel, *Introduction à la psychologie collective* (Paris, 1928). However, Blondel has criticized Durkheim's theories of knowledge and of religion (*ibid.*, pp. 96 ff.); and in a more recent work (*Le Suicide* [Strasbourg, 1933]) he presents a formidable criticism of the sociologistic explanation of suicide, emphasizing for his own part the psychophysiological, and particularly the psychopathic, elements in this phenomenon.

105. G. Dumas, "L'Expression des émotions," in his *Traité de psychologie*, I, 641. However, he has seriously criticized an exclusively sociologistic explanation of the mental life (*ibid.*, II, 1150–53).

106. *L'Enfant turbulent* (Paris, 1925); also "La Mentalité primitive et celle de l'enfant," *Revue philosophique*, 1928.

107. Cf. Granet, *Fêtes et danses anciennes de la Chine* (Paris, 1919); *La Polygynie sororale et le sororat dans la Chine féodale* (Paris, 1920); *La Religion des Chinois* (Paris, 1922); *Danses et légendes de la Chine ancienne*, Travaux de *l'Année sociologique* (2 vols.; Paris, 1926); *La Civilisation chinoise*, "La Vie publique et la vie privée," "L'Evolution de l'humanité" (Paris, 1929).

108. *La Pensée chinoise* (Paris 1934). Cf. the author's critical review in the *American Sociological Review*, I, 487–92.

109. Henri Berr, *La Synthèse en histoire* (Paris, 1911). Berr is also the founder and editor of *La Synthèse historique*, and of the series, Bibliothèque de synthèse historique."

110. Cf. *La Méthode positive en science économique* (Paris, 1912); *Statistique et expérience: remarques de méthode* (Paris, 1922); "Méthode historique et science sociale," *Revue de synthèse historique*, 1903; and "La causalité en histoire," *Bullétin de la Société française de philosophie*, 1907.

111. *Salaire des ouvriers des mines de charbon en France* (Paris, 1907); and *La Formation et les fluctuations des prix du charbon en France pendant vingt-cinq ans, 1887–1912* (Paris, 1925). Simiand has had an important influence on Halbwachs.

112. Cf., among other works, *Traité de droit constitutionnel* (1911); *Le Droit social, le droit individuel et la transformation de l'état* (Paris, 1911); *Les Transformation générales du droit privé* (1912); and *Les Transformations du droit public* (1913).

113. "Magie et droit individuel," *Année sociologique,* Vol. X (1907); and *Histoire du droit commercial* (Paris, 1904).

114. Meillet, "Comment les mots changent de sens," *Année sociologique,* Vol. IX 1905–6). A similar sociologistic emphasis is found in his *Les Langues dans l'Europe nouvelle* (Paris, 1918); in *Linguistique historique et linguistique générale* (Paris, 1921); and in many articles.

115. *La Pensée et la langue* (Paris, 1922).

116. "Le Caractère social du langage," *Journal de psychologie* (1921); and "Le Progrès du langage, *Bulletin de la Société française de philosophie,* 1922. Also, *Le Langage: introduction linguistique à l'histoire* ("Bibliothèque de synthèse historique" [1922]).

CHAPTER X

MAX WEBER'S SOCIOLOGICAL ANALYSIS OF CAPITALISM AND MODERN INSTITUTIONS

Talcott Parsons

I. WEBER'S LIFE AND ACADEMIC CAREER

MAX WEBER was born in Berlin in 1864.[1] His father was a rather prominent man in the politics of the day, being for many years a member of the Reichstag and a leader in the affairs of the National Liberal party. When Max was a young man he met many of the leading political personalities of the time in his own home. At the university Max studied law under the influence of the historical school, which was dominant in the German universities at that time. Among his more important teachers were Theodor Mommsen and Adolf Goldschmidt.

From his earliest period he was marked off as a particularly able student, and he embarked, apparently without question, on the path leading to an academic career. In due course he was made *Privatdozent* in jurisprudence at the University of Berlin and could have been expected to become a professor of law. His career was, however, dramatically changed by his being called, in 1893, to a professorship of economics at the University of Freiburg. This was followed within a few years by a call to one of the most prominent chairs of economics in Germany—Heidelberg—the previous incumbent of which was the well-known historical economist, Karl Knies.

Weber's shift from jurisprudence to economics was not altogether illogical. His legal interests had, from the first, been historically directed, and in this connection he had become increasingly interested in the relations between law and the economic organization and conditions of the societies he studied. His doctor's dissertation on trading companies in the Middle Ages already showed this trend, and he tended to shift more and more from legal history with an economic slant into economic history.

His career in its earlier stages was undoubtedly one of the most brilliant of his day in the German academic world, with advancement to high position and great reputation at an unusually early age. It was, however, in 1900, suddenly interrupted by a severe illness, reported as a "nervous breakdown," which kept him entirely out of work for about four years. His breakdown was so protracted that it enforced his resignation from his professorship; and, since he was never in good health after his resumption of work, he lived for many years in Heidelberg as a private scholar without official position. Only toward the end of his life, in 1918, did he resume teaching. The summer semester of 1918 he spent as a visiting professor at the University of Vienna and from there soon went to a regular professorship in economics at Munich, as successor to Lujo Brentano. There, in only the second semester of his teaching, he died suddenly of pneumonia in 1920, at the age of only fifty-six.

During these intervening years Weber was active not only as a scholar and in the promotion of scholarly enterprises but in politics as well. He was always passionately interested in political affairs and followed them extraordinarily closely. In 1905 he learned to read Russian in an incredibly short time, in order to be able to read the newspapers in connection with the abortive Russian Revolution of that year. He was personally acquainted with many important political figures and gave a good deal of advice behind the scenes. He was one of the first prominent men in Germany to turn against the regime of Kaiser Wilhelm II. During the war he wrote a notable memorandum in opposition to the unrestricted submarine warfare, predicting that it would inevitably bring the United States into the war against Germany. Toward the end of the war he wrote many articles for the *Frankfurter Zeitung,* and, with the revolution, it seemed as though he might emerge as an important political leader. He served as a member of the commission which presented the famous memorandum on German war guilt to the Peace Conference at Versailles and was also a member of the commission which drew up the first draft of the Weimar Constitution. He failed, however, through a political mischance, of election to the Constitutional Assembly, and his death came soon after.

In the academic world, apart from his own scholarly work, Weber was notable for his part in two important enterprises. It was he, more than any other single person, who was the dominant influence in the

Archiv für Sozialwissenschaft und Sozialpolitik and who made it the most notable social-science periodical in Germany. He was also the moving spirit in developing the plan for the great collaborative work, the *Grundriss der Sozialökonomik,* which was to be as near a complete study of the society of the Western world as German scholarship could produce. His own *Wirtschaft und Gesellschaft* was ultimately published as part of this series.

II. THE NATURE OF WEBER'S SOCIOLOGICAL WRITINGS

Though a many-sided individual and to all who knew him apparently a notably impressive personality, Weber's greatest significance undoubtedly lies in his scholarly achievements. In this respect there is an important reorientation which became evident on his partial recovery from the long illness that divided his career into two parts. Almost at the same time, in 1904 and 1905, he embarked on two different series of studies, both of which resulted in some of the most notable developments in modern social science. The first was a series of critical essays on the methodology of social science, which were directed, in the first instance, against the doctrines then current in the historical schools, especially of economics. These essays were not brought together and published during his lifetime but have been collected since his death in the volume entitled *Gesammelte Aufsätze zur Wissenschaftslehre.* The second development was initiated by his now famous essay, *The Protestant Ethic and the Spirit of Capitalism.* This was not the completion of a program but the beginning. It was followed by the series of comparative studies in the sociology of religion,[2] a number of which were published in subsequent years, but was left unfinished at his death.

Not immediately, but within a few years, Weber embarked on a third related, yet distinct, program of work. He apparently more and more felt the need for the systematic conceptual formulation and collection of material, which, organized under a systematic conceptual scheme, was to be brought to bear on the problem of understanding the position of modern Western society in his time. The work he had done along these lines was, so far as it had been completed, published in *Wirtschaft und Gesellschaft,* only a small part of which had been prepared for publication before his death.

Weber's sudden death occurred at just the time that he was beginning to reap systematically the harvest of a lifetime of research and thought.

It is questionable whether he ever intended to publish a systematic work on methodology; but in the fields of the sociology of religion and of the analysis of Western society, he had just begun to bring his material together and publish it in systematic form. Only one volume[3] of the studies of the sociology of religion was prepared for publication by his own hand. Two other volumes[4] were in sufficiently good condition to be published, but the series was very far from being complete. None of *Wirtschaft und Gesellschaft* had been completed beyond the first section, and the editors were left without even an authoritative table of contents to guide their arrangement of the material. He apparently worked on a number of different things simultaneously, and many of the chapters break off suddenly in manuscript. From internal evidence it is also clear that he intended to write on other subjects on which he did not leave even fragments of manuscript.

III. WEBER'S APPROACH TO SOCIAL SCIENCE AND ITS METHODOLOGY

Weber's approach to social science and the change that it underwent during his lifetime should be understood in terms of the particular intellectual situation in Germany. Germany was the home of idealistic philosophy and of the related attempt to draw a particularly sharp methodological distinction between the natural sciences and the disciplines dealing with human action. It had become almost a dogma in Germany that the latter could not be treated in natural-science terms. It was variously thought of as the sphere of free will, of the development of *Geist,* of the unfolding of cultures, and of the intimate understanding of subjective feelings and ideas, but, above all, it came to be held that it was only in the natural sciences that the use of generalized theoretical categories was admissible. As over against this, explanation in the social field was thought to be essentially historical, to consist in the tracing of genetic sequences of motivation and cultural influence.

It was at this point that Weber's critique of the historical schools began. His essential thesis was that it is only by the use of generalized theoretical categories, implicitly or explicitly, that it is logically possible to demonstrate the existence of causal relationships. This view necessitated a radical reconstruction of the logical structure of the social sciences, since it had become essential to pay attention to questions of systematic generalized theory. It was in undertaking this reconstruction that Weber developed his celebrated doctrine of the ideal type. In a word, to Weber, theory in the field of human action consists in systems of ideal types. In developing this, Weber did not pretend to put forward anything new but merely to formulate more precisely than others what social scientists actually did and what logical canons they were subject to when they claimed to prove causal relationships.

As distinguished from concepts current in the natural sciences, the ideal type had, in Weber's view, three primary characteristics. In the first place, it was formulated in terms of subjective categories—that is, in his own phrase, "of the intended meaning" of an action to the actor. This category—in German referred to as *Verstehen*—had played an important part in the discussion of the distinction between the natural and the social sciences. Weber took it over, but he used it quite differently from such other writers as Dilthey and Simmel.

Second, however, the ideal type did not formulate the actual concrete meaning of an action but an extreme limiting case, in which certain elements were stated in their logically pure form and others intentionally neglected. This gave the ideal type a particular character of abstraction in a special direction. Although he did not hold to it consistently in practice, in some of his most important general statements Weber contended that the ideal type should formulate the rational elements of a pattern of action, leaving those not fitting the rational norm to be treated residually as the sources of deviation from the rational pattern of action. This calls attention to an aspect of the peculiar kind of abstraction involved, which Weber himself did not stress. In fact, what is formulated in most of his ideal types is a description not of concrete action but of the normative patterns which may be considered binding on the actors.[5] There are serious difficulties involved in Weber's treatment of the problems of rationality which cannot be gone into in this chapter.[6]

Thirdly, Weber insisted that the formulation of generalized ideal types could not be treated as the goal of social science. Such types were to be formulated only as instruments for the analysis of concrete historical problems. This view was, in part, based on the conviction that anything like a stable and permanent system of theory was impossible in the social field, since the problems investigated, and hence the concepts useful for their solution, were inevitably relative to the particular values involved in the situation and to the scientific interests of the observer. This he formulated in his well-known concept of *Wertbeziehung*.

While Weber's basic insight on this point is undoubtedly correct, it seems to be clear that his position cannot be upheld as he himself formulated it. On the one hand, he neglected elements in the determination of scientific interests and problems other than their relation to the values of the observer. On the other hand, it can be shown that the difference between the natural and the social sciences in this respect is not so great as he thought it to be. Indeed, this doctrine constitutes the principal barrier to the completion of a very far-reaching methodological unification of all the empirical sciences which Weber's own work, starting from the background of the German doctrines, went far to prepare. It should be noted, in this connection, that Weber's critique of both groups of sciences showed, with a clarity remarkable for the time, that their pretensions to a full grasp of concrete reality were entirely unfounded. One of the principal obstacles to a methodological unification has been this naïve empiricist realism on both sides, for which Weber's critique is one of the best available correctives. But, once this empiricism is abandoned, the harmfulness of systematic theory to the legitimate interests of social science largely disappears.

IV. THE SOCIOLOGY OF RELIGION AS AN INSTRUMENT
OF SOCIAL METHODOLOGY

Weber's importance in social science does not, however, rest primarily on his methodological writings as such. Indeed, unlike many German scholars, he did not carry on methodological investigation for its own sake but rather as a means of clarifying the problems encountered in his empirical research. This program of research centers on a very comprehensive attempt to understand some of the most important aspects of the social and economic order of the modern Western world. Undoubtedly, the studies in legal, economic, and social history made before his illness contributed in important ways, but his maturer general conclusions first began to take shape in connection with the study for which he is best known—*The Protestant Ethic and the Spirit of Capitalism*.

Though this study was an essay in historical research, its importance does not by any means lie entirely in its contribution to our understanding of the forces which account for the development of "modern capitalism." At least equally important is Weber's conception of what elements in the modern social structure were particularly distinctive and of central importance to society as a whole. Most economic historians had paid primary attention to the development of a system of profit-making activity, along with the process by which mechanisms facilitating its functioning, such as credit and banking institutions, markets, and the like, had developed. Weber's primary interest was neither in acquisitive activity, as such, nor in the development of such mechanisms, but in the emergence of a distinctive set of institutional patterns, in so far as these regulated the market activities of business itself—not merely their sanctioning of the goal of profit, which was important, but their subjection of such activity to a certain kind of discipline—and its pursuit in terms of a specifically patterned type of institutional role and social organization. Business activity was regarded as a "calling," as a job in which, in an impersonal and specialized function, an individual proved his competence and his primary qualities of character. Weber thought it particularly significant that such roles were organized to a very high degree into complex bureaucratic structures, with individuals subjected not only to the informal ethical discipline of institutional patterns but also to a rigorous system of formally organized hierarchical authority.

Undoubtedly, in the earlier stages of the vast program of research which Weber devoted to these problems, he laid undue stress on the central importance of acquisitive activity for modern society and neglected the central position of such groups as the professions. The most important results of his analysis are, however, applicable to a considerably broader field than that of business life. Similarly, perhaps under the influence of the special conditions in Germany, he also laid undue stress on the significance of large-scale bureaucratic organization, although the phenomena he was talking about are undoubtedly of great prominence throughout the area of highly developed industrialism.

In formulating the problem of historical origins Weber was undoubtedly influenced by the Marxian point of view. For the fully developed system he accepted the Marxian position that the acquisitive activities of the individual businessman were adequately motivated by the pressures of the situation in which he was placed. He felt, however, that this interpretation could not be applied to the process of development of the system and that it was necessary to find patterns of orientation in terms of which this kind of activity was comprehensible—in terms of its own direct value and not merely as a means of survival on various levels of established conditions. Such an orientation he found in the basic ethical attitudes associated with what he calls the "ascetic" branches of Protestantism—namely, Calvinism and the Protestant sects like the Baptists, Quakers, and Methodists, which, though differing in theology, had very similar ethical orientations.

Weber admitted, quite readily, that these religious movements, far from positively sanctioning materialism and acquisitive greed, were fundamentally otherworldly and suspicious of the temptations of the flesh. But it was precisely this otherworldly ascetic orientation which made the specific pattern of activity in a "calling" meaningful. It provided adequate motivation for devoting one's life to a specialized and impersonal task, with the attendant sacrifice of many otherwise legitimate interests and of the sanctity of traditional ways of life. The positive sanction of acquisitiveness was, at least partly, a consequence of partial secularization, whereby prosperity in the affairs of this world came to be interpreted as a sign of grace. Since, however, acquisitive activity was only one of many different acceptable callings, this fact is not the central basis of Weber's thesis but essentially a secondary phenomenon.

Weber most explicitly repudiated any idea that he was developing a monistic religious interpretation of even one great development in history. On the contrary, he always insisted that many mutually independent conditions were necessary in order to make the development of modern capitalism. He did, however, equally definitely maintain that the Protestant ethic was a necessary condition and that, without it, the development would have been radically different. Weber did not, however, stop with this essay. He made it rather the starting-point of a much more extended program of investigation, partly to verify the interpretation of the importance of Protestantism in this particular historical connection, partly to clarify his analysis and place his empirical material in a more adequate perspective.

The course that he took in pursuing these aims is of the greatest significance, particularly in Germany, where the influence of the historical schools was predominant. Even with this background the normal thing, in the face of any uncertainty, would have been to engage in more and more detailed research into the specific historical antecedents of Western culture. Weber was undoubtedly an unusually competent social and economic historian in the relevant fields and could easily have devoted the rest of his scholarly life to completing a great historical study. Instead of this, he turned to radically different sources, embarking on a large-scale program of comparative studies of the relation between religious ethics and social and economic organization in all the great world religions.

Underlying this choice was a profound methodological insight. His problem was not elucidation of the specific facts of historical sequence but, rather, the definite isolation of the most important variable elements and the demonstration of their causal significance by studying their operation under variant conditions. The comparative method, as Weber used it, is the direct methodological equivalent of experimentation in the laboratory sciences. Only by studying cases which are similar in some respects but different in others would it be possible to arrive at a judgment of the causal influence of any factor. It was a consequence of his criticism of the logic underlying the historical school of economics that he saw that his problem could not be solved by further elaboration of a single historical process. Though he did not say so directly, he must have realized that the same fundamental criticism is applicable to the Marxian analysis of history. In order to achieve determinate results, it is essential to focus attention on a small number of factors.

To Weber the problem was that of the order of influence which can be attributed to what he called a "religious ethic." It was this which he treated as a variable factor. The broad conclusion to which he came was that a critical significance could be attributed to the variations in this factor in the process of the *differentiation* of the institutional structures of the great civilizations from each other. The ranges of variations in which he was interested were precisely those defined by the dominant characteristics of "modern capitalism," as they have been outlined above. He was particularly interested in the conditions favoring a rational orientation, as opposed to traditionalism, a prominent position for functionally specific roles, and, finally, elements of universalism not merely in personal ethics but in the institutionalized definitions of situations.

Weber isolated the influence of the religious ethic by a rough but, for his broadest purposes, adequate method. What he attempted to do was to judge whether, at the time preceding the emergence of the religious movement in question, the general character of the social structure, apart from religion, was more or less "favorable" to the development of the institutional patterns characteristic of the modern Western world. In the two cases most fully worked out—namely, China and India—his conclusion was that at comparable stages, that is, comparable to Europe on the eve of the Reformation, the situation was, in all the relevant respects at least, as favorable as it was in western Europe.

The problems involved in this judgment are too detailed and technical to review here. The religious movements—namely, Confucianism, Hinduism, and Protestantism—however, which came to dominate in these three cultural areas were radically different from one another. If these differences had any influence, it could not have been in the direction of assimilating the three societies to a common institutional pattern. Moreover, in broad terms, in each of the three cases the institutional structure which emerged was of a kind which would have been expected, had the basic attitudes toward social life inherent in each of the three great religious movements exerted a decisive influence.

The case of India is, perhaps, the most obvious because the contrast of attitude with our own is sharpest. Not only were the basic goals of religion in India, as in all such cases, transcendental, but the situation was defined in such a way that these goals could be meaningfully pursued only by turning one's back on everyday social interests and responsibilities, by engaging in mystical contemplation or otherworldly asceticism. The pursuit of salvation in this radical sense was, to be sure, not traditional; but in the nature of the case it was a goal accessible only to a small minority. For the great majority, Hinduism resulted in the most radical sanction of the existing traditional order and ways of doing things that has ever been developed anywhere. In the caste system the only form of virtuous behavior consisted in the conscientious performance of the traditional obligations, especially the ritual obligations, of the station in life in which one was born. Only by such faithfulness to tradition was there any prospect of improvement of one's fundamental religious status by being reborn in a higher caste position.

Though the Indian case is the more obvious, that of China is even more telling, because on a certain level there seems to be a striking resemblance between the typical Chinese and Western attitudes. At least in the Confucian tradition the Chinese have been notable for their shrewd practical worldliness. They have been contemptuous of metaphysical speculation, of mysticism, of transcendentalism. Far from being averse to acquisitiveness, they have been a people who have notably valued the good things of this life with money conspicuously placed among them. What, then, is the difference? It is precisely, as Weber succinctly puts it, "that, while Calvinism was a doctrine of rational *mastery over* the world, Confucianism was a doctrine of rational *adaptation to* the world."

The notable feature of the Chinese social structure is not only its complete failure to root out traditionalism but a sanctification of tradition, second only to that of India. The attitude that the classics, which were the subject of education of every scholar, could never be improved upon is to be contrasted with the inherently dynamic character of Western science. In addition, in China there is a notable absence of any sanction for impersonal specialized functions. The educated man is never the technical specialist but rather the well-rounded cultivated gentleman. Finally, there is also a notable absence of universalism in Confucian ethics. Loyalty to one's own kinship group and one's own particular friends and associates supersedes all generalized obligations as to honesty, truth, and so on.

It is important, in this connection, that, though Weber never came to formulate the results of his comparative studies in any single systematic statement, there is discernible in the later development of the studies and in relevant parts of *Wirtschaft und Gesellschaft* a certain shift of perspective. The problem of accounting for adequate motivation of acquisitive activity, even in the special forms described above, becomes considerably less important, and a broader contrast between the institutional structures of the modern Western world and of China and India becomes more prominent. It is not the existence of a business economy but of patterns which underlie not only business but many other equally important features of our world, such as science and learning, the professions, and governmental administration.

At the same time, there is a certain shift in the perspective on Protestantism itself. In the earlier essay Weber was particularly concerned with the contrast between "ascetic" Protestantism and Catholicism. Comparison with the religions of China and India considerably reduces the significance of this contrast. From the latter point of view the Calvinistic pattern is to be regarded as the most complete realization of possibilities in one particular direction. Catholicism, from this point of view, considerably mitigates the rigor of the Calvinist doctrine; but, by contrast with Confucianism and Hinduism, all branches of Christianity are seen to have much in common.

So far only the "religious ethic" has been mentioned as an object of Weber's analysis. It is this aspect of a great religious tradition which impinges most closely on concrete social activities in the secular sphere. Weber, however, went much further to analyze the structure of a religious tradition itself and to explain the deeper motives underlying the particular attitudes central to the religious ethic in question.

The essential feature of this analysis is a theory of the relation in his own terms between ideas and religious interests.[7] As he repeatedly said, it is not ideas but religious interests which motivate action. The function of ideas is, to borrow W. I. Thomas' term, to "define the situation." At least on the level in which Weber was concerned with the problem, the interest in salvation can be regarded as a constant, in particular as sharing common features between India and the Western world. But pursuing such an interest as salvation is a matter of action, a matter of doing something about an intolerable situation. Unlike the solution of technological problems, the question of *what* to do cannot be answered by merely observing empirical facts. What it will make sense to do will depend upon the cognitive interpretation of the meaning of salvation and the possible paths to its attainment. On the basis of Brahman philosophy, salvation in a radical sense could only mean "escape from the wheel of Karma"; but this goal could not possibly be attained by excelling others in worldly accomplishments of any sort. It could be accomplished only by complete dissociation from all worldly interests and immersion in communication with the Absolute. It furnished, as Weber says, no motive for any positive interest in secular goals.

In Christianity, on the other hand, from the very beginning, salvation has meant fundamentally an act of grace on the part of a transcendental deity; and the deity has often attached specific conditions to the granting of grace. In some branches, good works—that is, the fulfilment of positive ethical norms in secular activity—have been a direct means to the attainment of salvation. In strict Calvinism this was not so. The state of grace was predetermined, which might seem to favor a fatalistic attitude, but at least two factors have operated in the opposite direction. The very doctrine of predestination emphasized more sharply than any other version of Christian thought the complete dependence of man on the will of God, and, since it was His will that man should work in the building of His kingdom, any person with sufficient faith to accept pre-destination would be bound to take seriously his religious duties to fulfil God's commandments. Beyond that, however, for the serious Protestant the doctrine of predestination left him in a state of extreme emotional tension relative to his state of grace. Though he could not by his own action earn salvation, he could prove to himself that he was worthy of it and hence, in all probability, was one of the elect, for "a good tree cannot bear evil fruit." And there was no question about it—God's will was that man should build a Christian society in this world as well as in the next.

The difference between Weber's analysis of motivation on this level and his agreement with Marx as to the automatic enforcement of discipline in a developed capitalistic society is, in one sense, not so great as it appears at first sight. To be sure, the devout Calvinist is not explained mainly in terms of external sanctions, but two things may be said. In so far as his interest in religious salvation is a genuinely powerful emotional force, external sanctions become unnecessary. There is probably far more of this disinterested attachment to secular activity than most utilitarian thinkers have understood. The addition of external sanctions is not primarily the result of the fact that, to Marx, the interests are acquisitive rather than religious but of the fact that the definitions of the situation have become institutionalized. Comparative study, to which Weber made a great contribution, has shown conclusively that particular goals, when they have become institutionalized, universally become attached to a widespread variety of different interests—that is, of deeper-lying elements of motivation. Indeed, almost any goal, provided it is integrated with a meaningful definition of the situation and institutionalized, can become a focus not only of economic interests but of a very wide variety of interests. Indeed, one of the most important consequences of Weber's work is to suggest that what we talk about as "economic" interest is not an ultimate category of motivation but is, rather, a consequence of the institutionalization of whatever patterns may be dominant in any given social system.

V. THE CHARACTER OF WEBER'S GENERALIZED SYSTEM
OF SOCIAL THEORY

It has also been pointed out that Weber did not believe in the possibility or desirability of attempting to formulate a permanent generalized system of social theory. At the same time, there is, especially in his later work, much which constitutes systematic theoretical construction, though he was probably himself unaware of the full theoretical significance of what he was doing.

So far as Weber could be said to have formulated a generalized system of theory, it is most completely stated in the early part of *Wirtschaft und Gesellschaft*.[8] On the explicit level this took the form of a classification of ideal types of social action and relationships. Weber started off by distinguishing four basic types of action. The first two are characterized by certain modes of rationality. In the case of one, *Zweckrationalität,* action is conceived as rationally oriented to the maximum attainment of a plurality of ends which are weighed against one another, and in the choice of means not merely technical efficiency but also cost is considered. In the second case, that of *Wertrationalität,* a given clearly formulated value is put into practice by the most effective available means, regardless of cost or bearing on other values. The other two constitute residual categories in different directions. In the one case, that of traditional action, the departure from rationality consists in the absence of calculation in terms of efficiency or effectiveness and in the adherence to established patterns without further question. The fourth type, affectual action, consists in any mode of orientation which is neither rational nor traditional but motivated in terms of feeling, emotion, sentiment, and so on. There is no point in attempting to specify the meaning of these terms, since the category is, for Weber, residual and its content is not specifically clarified.

Weber employs these concepts throughout his work in a variety of different ways. Systematically, however, the next step is to attempt to work out their various possible permutations and combinations in the structure of more and more complex systems of social relationships. Though Weber does proceed to systematize his types on the relationship level, he nowhere attempts to follow out the logic of this procedure systematically. What he does is, rather, to select among the many logical possibilities a relatively small number which he finds to be of particularly great significance. In certain directions, however, the classifications trail off into endless subdivisions in such a way that it becomes quite arbitrary as to where the process is halted.

Since the mere logical possibility of combinations is not adequate to determine the direction that his systemization takes, we must look for other principles of selection. These it would seem are to be found in two principal directions, which are roughly, though by no means fully, integrated with each other. On the more abstract level, Weber seems to have developed, largely implicitly, a scheme of the generalized structure of systems of social action.[9] The basic categories of this scheme are not types of action but are structural elements which underlie any classification on the type level.

The starting-point for this scheme is clearly the rational means-ends analysis. When this is followed through to a certain point, it becomes necessary to differentiate ultimate goals or ends from those elements of the means-ends system which are primarily significant as means to other ends. The role of ultimate values as the direct goals of chains of action is completely clear in Weber's work. Furthermore, in complex systems the intermediate factors of the means-ends chains are not undifferentiated but involve a series of analytical distinctions which come out clearly in his work. The most important of these is that between the technological and the economic aspects, on the one hand, and between economic allocation and the employment of authority and coercion, on the other.

This direct analysis of means-ends systems, however, is far from exhausting this aspect of Weber's systematic thinking. Action is not oriented merely toward specific goals but also in social systems to an order which defines, within certain limits, the conditions under which goals may be pursued. The systems of order which are of greatest significance in social life Weber found to be characterized by one peculiarly important feature: they are treated as "legitimate." Though conformity with them is generally enforced by various forms of the mechanism of reward and punishment, they are also supported by common moral sentiments, so that conformity is widely treated as a moral obligation and is exacted on the part of those in authority as a morally legitimized right. The element of legitimacy underlying forms of order Weber connects closely with the basic values which enter into means-ends systems. Both of these are derived from the basic ethical orientations of the members of social groups.

These ethical orientations are not isolated phenomena. They always stand in close relation to those aspects of cognitive and affective orientation which we generally call "religious." The typical attitude of respect for moral authority and moral obligation which is the distinguishing feature of legitimacy is closely related to the respect for "sacred," or, in Weber's term, "charismatic," persons and things. For an order to be legitimized and ultimate values to be justified, they must, as a matter of empirical generalization, be closely integrated with man's orientation toward the problems of meaning and the world of sacred entities and symbols. Just as, in Durkheim's work, moral authority in the secular sphere is integrated with sacredness in the religious, so in Weber's is legitimacy bound up with patterns of charismatic prestige and authority. In the concepts of the means-ends system, of ultimate values, legitimacy, charisma, and systems of religious ideas is contained a systematic outline of the generalized structure of systems of action. It is from these that the structural relationships of Weber's more concrete ideal types are derived, so that they constitute a structurally integrated system rather than a mere elaborate spinning-out of logical possibilities.

There is, however, a second aspect of Weber's theoretical systematization. In addition to the comparative studies in the sociology of religion, which have been reviewed above, and closely connected with them, Weber carried out for many years a program of study in comparative institutional structures primarily in the fields of economic and political organization. This interest grew out of his early studies in comparative law and in economic and social history and was extended and refined as his systematic thinking developed. It is this material which forms the main substantive content of his greatest systematic work, *Wirtschaft und Gesellschaft,* unfinished though it remained to his death.

In this context he pursued the same fundamental interests in the forms of, and deviations from, rationality in social affairs which had been basic to his studies in the sociology of religion. Hence he was particularly preoccupied with the status and institutional peculiarities of rationalized patterns, particularly in three most important fields; the system of market exchange and money accounting, the rationalized formal-legal procedure and administration, and the structure of bureaucratic administrative organization with legal control.

In all three of these fields he attributed great importance to patterns of what he called "formal rationality," which in each case came into inevitable conflict with considerations of "substantive rationality." In the case of money and capital accounting, the formal perfection in a free-exchange economy inevitably results in deviations from substantive standards of the satisfactory provisions for the economic wants of a population, as well as in deviations from standards of distributive justice and the like. In the legal sphere formal rational procedure results in conflict with the moral sentiments of substantive justice; and in the sphere of the exercise of authority in administrative procedure strict adherence to formal bureaucratic patterns results in corresponding strains in relation to important interests and sentiments.

Thus in all three spheres a high level of formal rationality is particularly unstable and can be maintained only by overcoming formidable resistance. These three types of formal rationality Weber considered the most distinctive institutional features of modern Western society. He attempted to throw light on the conditions necessary for their development and maintenance in terms of a comparative analysis which showed the most important patterns by which, in each case, they could become transformed by imperceptible degrees into radically different institutional patterns.

In the economic sphere Weber tended to contrast the pattern of free-market economy with a maximization of the use of money and of accounting in money terms with situations in which the orientation of economic activity was, on the one hand, forced to calculate in terms of qualitative comparisons of heterogeneous goods and services and, on the other hand, to take account of considerations not of direct economic significance and not expressible in terms of a numerical unit. He did not in this field develop a specific type classification but devoted much effort to showing the precariousness of the modern market system and the fact that deviation from it tended in the direction of the traditional stabilizing of economic relations through their entanglement in structures of primarily noneconomic significance, such as relations of loyalty between superiors and subordinates in an organization, political, religious, or otherwise. Though his judgment may have been faulty in detail, Weber presented important evidence that the shift to a large-scale planned economy would probably give powerful impetus to the tendency to traditional stereotyping of the economic system.

A second field of analysis is that of property relations. There Weber showed that the modern market economy and many other features of modern society rest on a particular combination in the structure of property rights which he characterized as the full appropriation of the nonhuman factors in production by owners and the complete lack of appropriation of human factors by owners—that is, full private property of natural resources and goods and complete absence of property rights in human beings or their services.

This particular combination is unique and subject to deviant tendencies in very important respects. There are tendencies, on the one hand, to place limitations on full property rights of owners and, on the other, to limit the freedom of the human agents in production. In particular, Weber maintained that, while the tendency of workers to appropriate rights in their jobs and in the means of production and the tendency of employers to appropriate property rights in the services of the workers were formally antithetical, there is a fundamental tendency for them both to lead into the same general consequences—restrictions on the formal rationality of the economy and tying both worker and the material means of production to a traditionally stereotyped system of relationships. Though any such formula is subject to numerous qualifications, one may say that for Weber the basic alternative to our system of free property and free labor was a feudal type of organization of economic life in which the freedom of the worker was traded for a combination of security and dependency; and the employer, though receiving a kind of right over his workers which is now prohibited, would be restricted in the freedom of disposal both of his workers through discharge and of material property. In terms of Weber's more general scheme on both these levels, the alternative to formal rationality in economic life as a stable routine economy is traditionalism.

In the field of the institutionalization of authority, Weber's analysis runs somewhat parallel. There, however, he distinguishes three basic types: rational-legal, traditional, and charismatic. In the case of rational-legal authority, authority is exercised by virtue of incumbency of office under a system of generalized rules. The sources of legitimacy do not lie in the personal prestige of the individual but in the authority of the rules under which he holds office. By the same token, its scope is limited to that which is specifically authorized by the terms of the system of rules. There is a fundamental separation between the individual's sphere of official authority and that outside it, in which he is a private individual. In a complex system such authority tends to be organized hierarchically, with a system of higher and lower authorities, each specifically limited by the terms defining the official role. This type is closely integrated with the property system and the monetary economy, in that there is a rigid distinction between property over which the individual has control in his official capacity—that Weber calls the "means of administration"—and the private income and possessions of the individual. Similarly, the ideal form of remuneration is fixed money salary in such a way that the organization has no control of the specific channels of expenditure.

In the case of traditional authority, authority is not exercised by virtue of an office but of a traditionally sanctioned status. This status is defined in terms of a traditional order which both legitimizes the assumption of authority and, in certain respects, defines its scope. But outside the provisions of the traditional order there is a sphere of arbitrary will in which the individual exercises authority by virtue of his personal prestige and status. There is no clear separation of the sphere of office and the capacity of the incumbent as an individual. Nor does there tend to be a clear segregation between means of administration and personal property. Provision both for expenses of the function and for personal expenditure are met from benefices—that is, handing over to the individual property rights in sources of income over which the organization has command. Just as rational-legal authority is closely correlated with the formal rationality of economic life, so is traditional authority unfavorable to it and correlated to a traditionalized economic order, with a limitation both on full private property in goods and on personal freedom, at least for the more dependent elements of the population.

The third category is that of charismatic authority. This Weber defines as not a form of stable routine organization at all but as a pattern taken by movements of change as such. The charismatic leader claims legitimacy for his demands upon other people by virtue of a personal authority which is in specific conflict with any established order; this is neither an office nor a traditional legitimized status but is, in some respects, in overt conflict with either or both. In contrast to the other two, the charismatic leader claims obedience as a matter of personal devotion to him and his cause. There is, again, no clear separation between his sphere of office and that of private life, or between official property and private resources.

Charismatic authority is not, like the others, linked to a specific form of economic organization, because Weber treats economic organization as a phenomenon of settled routine. The effect of a charismatic movement is to upset whatever settled economic conditions exist; but, like any other social movement, it is bound to economic conditions, and this forms one of many fundamental reasons why the charismatic phase is inherently temporary. There are two typical forms of charismatic provision with means—gifts and booty, that is, resources acquired by coercive methods, whether by force or not. But, once the position of authority becomes established, these must be transformed into regular sources of income which take the form of acquiring segregated property or of granting benefices in the traditional form. According to circumstances, the authority structure of the charismatic movement may change in either a traditional or a rational-legal direction.

This scheme of comparative institutional analysis is by no means complete in Weber's work but nonetheless forms a set of tools of analysis which fits into his generalized analysis of social action and has also been built up in the direct treatment of empirical problems of very wide scope. In a sense in which it has rarely been attempted or even partially achieved, Weber undertook to diagnose certain of the basic institutional features of the social situation of the modern Western world in terms of a comparative perspective of exceedingly broad scope. His emphasis throughout was on the uniqueness and the relative instability of the most important institutional features of our society. It is a diagnosis which, in many respects, has been verified by events since his death and is one of the most impressive demonstrations of the power of careful logical discrimination, combined with extensive and accurate empirical knowledge, in understanding social phenomena on a grand scale.

BIBLIOGRAPHY

A. WORKS OF WEBER

Essays on Sociology. Translated and edited by H. H. GERTH and C. WRIGHT MILLS. New York, 1946.

General Economic History. Translated by F. H. KNIGHT. London: George Allen & Unwin, Ltd., 1927.

Gesammelte Aufsätze zur Religionssoziologie. 3 vols. Tübingen: J. C. B. Mohr (P. Siebeck), 1920–21.

Gesammelte Aufsätze zur Sozial- und Wirtschaftsgeschichte. Tübingen: J. C. B. Mohr (P. Siebeck), 1924.

Gesammelte Aufsätze zur Soziologie und Sozialpolitik. Tübingen: J. C. B. Mohr (P. Siebeck), 1924.

Gesammelte Aufsätze zur Wissenschaftslehre. Tübingen: J. C. B. Mohr (P. Siebeck), 1922.

Gesammelte politische Schriften. Munich: Drei Masken Verlag, 1921.

Grundriss der Sozialökonomik, Part III: *Wirtschaft und Gesellschaft*. 2 vols. Tübingen: J. C. B. Mohr (P. Siebeck), 1925.

The Protestant Ethic and the Spirit of Capitalism. Translated by TALCOTT PARSONS.
London: George Allen & Unwin, Ltd., 1930.
The Theory of Social and Economic Organization. Translated by TALCOTT PARSONS.
London: Hodge & Co., Ltd. New York, 1947.
Wirtschaftsgeschichte. Edited by S. HELLMAN and M. PALYI. Munich: Duncker
& Humblot, 1923.

B. SECONDARY SOURCES

ABEL, THEODORE F. *Systematic Sociology in Germany.* ("Studies in History, Eco-
nomics, and Public Law," edited by the FACULTY OF POLITICAL SCIENCE OF
COLUMBIA UNIVERSITY, No. 310 [New York: Columbia University Press, 1929].)
BARKER, ERNEST. *Church, State, and Study.* London: Methuen & Co., Ltd., 1930.
BENNION, L. L. *Max Weber's Methodology.* Dissertation, University of Strasbourg.
Paris: Les Presses modernes, 1933.
FREYER, HANS. *Soziologie als Wirklichkeitswissenschaft.* Leipzig: B. G. Teubner,
1930.
HALBWACHS, MAURICE. "Max Weber, un homme, une œuvre," *Annales d'histoire
économique et sociale,* I (January, 1929), 81–88.
——— "Les Origines puritaines du capitalisme moderne," *Revue d'histoire et
philosophie réligieuses,* V (1925), 132–34.
JASPERS, KARL. *Max Weber: Deutsches Wesen im politischen Denken, im Forschen
und Philosophieren.* Oldenburg: G. Stalling, 1932.
MERTON, R. K. *Science and Society in Seventeenth Century England.* ("Osiris:
History of Science Monographs," Vol. IV, edited by GEORGE SARTON [Cam-
bridge, Mass.].)
MISES, L. VON. "Soziologie und Geschichte," *Archiv für Sozialwissenschaft und
Sozialpolitik,* LXI (1929), 465–512 (on Weber, pp. 470–97).
PARSONS, TALCOTT. "H. M. Robertson on Max Weber and His School," *Journal of
Political Economy,* XLIII (1935), 688–96.
ROBERTSON, HECTOR M. *Aspects of the Rise of Economic Individualism: A Criticism
of Max Weber and His School.* Cambridge, England: At the University Press
(John Wilson & Son, Inc.), 1933.
SALOMON, ALBERT. "Max Weber's Methodology," *Social Research,* XI (1934)
147–68.
———. "Max Weber's Political Ideas," *ibid.,* II (1935), 368–84.
———. "Max Weber's Sociology," *ibid.,* pp. 60–73.
SCHELTING, ALEXANDER VON. "Die logische Theorie der historischen Kulturwis-
senschaften von Max Weber und im besonderen sein Begriff des Idealtypus,"
Archiv für Sozialwissenschaft und Sozialpolitik.
———. *Max Weber's Wissenschaftslehre.* Tübingen: J. C. B. Mohr (P. Siebeck)
1934.
SCHÜTZ, ALFRED. *Der sinnhafte Aufbau der sozialen Welt.* Vienna: Julius Springer
1932.
SPANN, OTTMAR. *Tote und lebendige Wissenschaft.* 2d ed. Jena: Gustav Fischer
1925.
TAWNEY, RICHARD H. *Religion and the Rise of Capitalism.* New York: Harcourt
Brace & Co., 1926. 2d ed., 1929.
TROELTSCH, ERNST. "Max Weber," in his *Deutscher Geist und Westeuropa*
Tübingen: J. C. B. Mohr (P. Siebeck), 1925.

TROELTSCH, ERNST. *The Social Teaching of the Christian Churches.* Translated by OLIVE WYON. 2 vols. New York: Macmillan Co., 1931.

WEBER, MARIANNE. *Max Weber: Ein Lebensbild.* Tübingen: J. C. B. Mohr (P. Siebeck), 1926.

NOTES

1. On Weber's life see the excellent biography by his widow, Marianne Weber, *Max Weber: Ein Lebensbild.* This also contains a complete bibliography of his writings.

2. *Gesammelte Aufsätze zur Religionssoziologie* (3 vols.; Tübingen, 1920–21).

3. Containing a revision of the essay on the Protestant Ethic, some introductory and interstitial material, and the study of Confucianism and Taoism.

4. Containing, respectively, the studies of Hinduism and Buddhism and Ancient Judaism.

5. Weber himself was always careful to point out that this did not imply that a given norm was considered binding by the observer. He left room for an important range of cultural relativity, which was yet consistent with the view that action was best understood in terms of orientation to normative patterns, whatever their particular content happened to be in a given case.

6. See the Introduction to the author's translation of Part I of *Wirtschaft und Gesellschaft.*

7. Cf. the author's article, "The Role of Ideas in Social Action," *American Sociological Review,* October, 1938.

8. Soon to appear in English translation under the title "The Theory of Social and Economic Organization," translated by A. M. Henderson and Talcott Parsons, and to be published by Hodge & Co., Ltd., London, and Oxford University Press, New York.

9. In the author's *Structure of Social Action* (New York: McGraw-Hill Book Co., 1937), chap. xvii.

PART IV

EUROPEAN AND BRITISH THEORISTS

CHAPTER XI

THE SOCIOLOGY OF GEORG SIMMEL: THE
FORMS OF SOCIAL INTERACTION

RUDOLF HEBERLE

I. SIMMEL'S LIFE AND CHIEF WRITINGS

GEORG SIMMEL (1858–1918) belongs to the generation of European scholars who, at the end of the nineteenth century, broke
with the "classical tradition" in sociology and originated a renaissance
of sociological theory and research. Born in Berlin of Jewish parentage,
he became a lecturer in philosophy (*Privatdozent*) at the age of twenty-
seven at the University of Berlin, in which position he remained until
1914, when he was called to Strassburg as a professor of philosophy.
He taught there under the adverse conditions of wartime until he died
in the fall of 1918.

Simmel was primarily a philosopher, whose interests were not at all
confined to the problems of society; in fact, his sociological essays form
only part of his lifework. He had a strong interest in history, in the fine
arts, and in literature. Perhaps the most adequate characterization of
his work as a whole would be to say that it represents a philosophy of
contemporary culture.[1] It is in this context that his sociological work
has to be appraised—as *one* among several approaches. Simmel rose soon
to international reputation as a sociologist; several of his studies were
published almost simultaneously in German, English, and French. This
accessibility of his sociological work is partly responsible for the fact
that he was probably better known in his time in the United States than
most of the other leading German sociologists of his generation.

II. SIMMEL'S CONCEPTION OF THE SCOPE AND
METHOD OF SOCIOLOGY

To represent within the framework of a single chapter the sociological
work of Georg Simmel involves some difficulty which arises from the
peculiarity of his work. Simmel himself admits that he did not develop

a system. His sociological work consists of a series of essays on subjects not systematically related but selected because of their importance for the study of forms of social interaction. This was the aspect of social life which Simmel considered to be the specifically sociological problem. His essays, therefore, represent a highly personal choice of subjects, and, moreover, their content is the highly personal work of a brilliant, analytical mind. Their attractiveness and their value is largely conditioned by the form of presentation; the mere skeleton of basic ideas and concepts would be a very dry and unimaginative affair if deprived of the brilliancy of illustration, the striking analogies and differentiations, and the often surprising indication of structural similarities between apparently very disparate phenomena. Even in Spykman's able condensation of Simmel's essays, much of their intellectual and aesthetic qualities is lost. Therefore, no attempt will be made here to present in a comprehensive summary the contents of Simmel's writings. For this purpose the reader may be referred to Spykman's book and to the numerous papers by Simmel which are available in English translations. Instead, this chapter deals, rather, with the methodological principles of Simmel's sociological work. Only by way of illustration will some of the main theorems be discussed. This procedure is, in fact, congenial to Simmel's own style of work.

Simmel is generally considered to be the founder of the so-called "formal school" in sociology. This is certainly an adequate designation of his main contribution to the development of sociology. How far this was an original idea is problematic.[2] The essence of Simmel's position is that sociology, in the strict sense, or "pure" sociology, in distinction from the other social sciences which deal with special fields of human social life, has, as its specific object of cognition, the forms of social interaction that occur in all those spheres of social life and really constitute the essence of society.

Such phenomena as superordination and subordination, the specialization of functions, the phenomena of conflict and competition, the formation of parties, and the like can be studied as such, irrespective, in principle, of the fields (economic, political, religious, etc.) which form the "content" of the action of those groups in which they occur; for— and this is the empirical justification for this concept of form—the same pattern of interaction occurs in connection with quite different aims or purposes, while, on the other hand, the same aims or purposes can be realized through quite different forms of social interaction. This circumstance permits the isolation by abstraction of the various forms of interaction of the different kinds of combinations of men as such, for the purpose of analytic and comparative inquiry.[3] In these "forms" of association and dissociation we have the phenomenon of society as such, in pure essence, separated theoretically from all its particular contents.

When Simmel first presented his ideas, he found that sociology was widely conceived of as a comprehensive study of all social facts and that, since everything in human life has a social relevance, sociology would be "the science of everything human"—except for those subjects reserved for the sciences of external nature.[4] This position would, according to Simmel, mean merely a dumping of all existing sciences dealing with social phenomena "into one great pot," or it would reduce sociology to a mere method of investigation, a directive principle which can be applied in the most varied and diverse fields of science, without itself constituting a science.[5]

This concept of sociology lacks a definite object of cognition (*Erkenntnisobjekt*). In a similar way psychology has been considered as a solution of the problems of all the sciences; and yet psychology, as a science, is concerned solely "with the functions of the mind as such" and is separated from "the special sciences which from particular points of view investigate the particular contents of perceptive knowledge."[6] "Just as psychology as a science does not deal with everything conditioned by consciousness, so sociology does not necessarily include everything that belongs in a society or that is conditioned by its existence."[7] New sciences, Simmel points out, arise if the inquisitive mind is focused on certain aspects of the chaos of existence which can be isolated by a process of abstraction. Thus mathematics deals with the formal and numerical aspects of physical bodies, while chemistry and physics deal with the qualitative aspects of substances of those bodies. Since economics, politics, law, and the "cultural sciences" deal with the contents or the substance of society, sociology, it appears, would deal with the social as such, that is, with society in its essence. Hence the conception of the isolability of the "forms" of social interaction furnishes the basis for the abstraction of a new object of cognition. Pure sociology thus becomes a sort of geometry of social interaction.[8]

Before entering on a further discussion of this position, some of Simmel's arguments in its defense have to be presented. One objection to the very notion of a science of society is that society is an abstraction, that only the individuals are real. Simmel, however, points out that the concept of the "individual" is also an abstraction. "Society" or human groups appear just as real, if one looks at human existence from a perspective[9] where the single individual disappears. What is really decisive is the cognitive intention (*Erkenntnisabsicht*) : "the special ends of cognition determine whether immediately manifest or experienced reality shall be inquired into with regard to a personal or a collective object."[10]

> Any science selects from the totality of immediately experienced phenomena one series or one aspect under guidance of a certain concept; sociology thus is justified in dissecting the individual "Existenzen" and bringing them together again according to its own concept by thus asking: according to what "laws" do human beings move, in so far as they form, by interaction, groups, and in so far as they are determined by this existence in groups?[11]

Although the primary motivation for this construction of the object of cognition of pure sociology is epistemological, Simmel is, of course, aware that a living science could develop only around significant problems. He considers, however, the systematic study of the pure forms of society as of fundamental importance. In a critical comment on historical materialism he suggests that the "real substance of the historical process" might be found in the change of sociological forms, as such, with the economic system being merely one of several "superstructures" conditioned by the basic interrelations of human beings.[12]

While Simmel limits the field of sociology proper in this way, he does not want to see sociology restricted to the organized and "permanent" interrelations only. Besides the state, the family, the guilds and classes, and other "permanent" associations, there exists an indefinite variety of seemingly less important forms of relations and types of interaction which "by filling in the spaces between those, so to speak, official formations bring really into existence the society that we know."[13]

Simmel's new concept of pure sociology is also directed against the identification, quite common at his time, of sociology with philosophy of history. In contrast to the latter, which always involves metaphysical, aesthetic, or religious interpretations of history, sociology "restricts itself entirely to the realm of phenomena and their immediate psychological explanation."[14] On the other hand, he thought that sociology, by separating out the phenomena of socialization, might lead to the discovery of "historical laws" within one special field, whereas the nonspecialized historical studies had failed to reveal such laws for the historical processes as a whole.[15] Two other concepts of sociology have to be distinguished from this concept of pure sociology:

1. In so far as economic, political, or other cultural phenomena and historical processes can be studied as phenomena of group life, as results of interaction between individuals, that is, under application of the sociological *method,* such studies might be labeled "sociology," though in a vague and inaccurate sense. However, by way of abstraction, a complex of problems can be lifted from such studies which Simmel considers as sociological in a rather specific sense. These problems are all related to the elaboration of those *general* characteristics of the realities of life which result from the fact that life occurs within the framework of social groups. The attempt to discern a general, socially conditioned "law" of historical evolution, such as Tönnies', Durkheim's or Comte's, would belong here. And so would the inquiry into the conditions of the power and value of groups and of collective action, as contrasted to power and value of individuals and their action. Simmel refers to these problems as "general sociology."[16]

2. Any empirical science is framed by two philosophical disciplines: its epistemology and its metaphysics. Sociology, in so far as it deals with fundamental categories of social life, serves as an epistemological foundation for the special social sciences.[17] On the other hand, there are other questions which go beyond the scope of these necessarily fragmentary special sciences. All those questions of the signficance and meaning of economic, political, etc., phenomena and processes and the final question of whether the meaning and purpose of human existence are embodied in the individual or in the association—these are questions of interpretation, which cannot be solved by empirical studies. Nor is the discussion of such questions independent of personal value-judgments. Simmel suggests that this discipline be called "philosophical sociology."[18] His main work, however, is devoted to pure sociology."

When Simmel in his *Grundfragen* wanted to exemplify his idea of pure sociology, he included a paper originally read at the first congress of the German Sociological Society in 1910, entitled "The Sociology of Social Entertainment."[19] It may, therefore, be summarized here for the same purpose, namely, that of conveying an idea of Simmel's approach and procedure and the kind of insights at which he arrives.

"Social gatherings" or sociables—or *Geselligkeit*—are a manifestation of the social urge as such. Since such social gatherings, in their true form, are not motivated by any special concrete purpose, as are all other types of associations, they represent, in a playful way, the essence of all social life. Their relation to the concreteness of society resembles the relation existing between a work of art and reality.

The relations of the individuals in social gatherings are regulated by a peculiarly ambiguous principle of a quasi-ethical nature: on the one hand, everything referring to, or reminiscent of, the roles played by the participants in their working-day life (e.g., their rank and occupation) has to be ignored; on the other hand, the most intimate and personal qualities of the individuals are also barred from entering into the relations. Every participant will use restraint in expression of his personality and of his impulses and will avoid engaging in too personal and intimate psychic relations. The participants come together "merely as human beings," and yet they refrain from letting the whole of their personality enter into the interaction process. This polarity of the behavior pattern is the essence of "tact." Furthermore, social gatherings are the artistic stylization or play-form of real society: sociable "games" and other forms of entertainment imitate societal processes of competition, conflict, and co-operation. "Flirting" is the play-form of erotics, and "conversation" becomes an end in itself, whereas, in "real society," talking serves the purpose of conveying certain "contents"—here, in social gatherings, one talks for entertainment; and, while the conversation is the better, the more interesting and significant its subject, the subject matter does not constitute its purpose. It can, therefore, be changed quickly and will never be taken seriously. Finally, social entertainment also symbolizes the ethical forces of society. The integration of the individual into the social whole, on the one side, and the enrichment of the individual by the pleasure, prestige, and other compensations received, which is the very essence of the ethical function of society, on the other side, are also found in *Geselligkeit*—in abstract form, free from all concrete ends or purposes.

However, "all *Geselligkeit* is merely a *symbol* of life, as it is reflected in the flow of an easygoing happiness-bestowing game or play, and yet it is a symbol of *life;* the picture of life is modified only as far as the distance requires, just like the most subjective and phantastic art, that renounces all copying of reality, is still nourished by a profound and

faithful relation to reality—otherwise, its effect will be empty and in-
sincere. Thus, if conviviality severs all ties connecting it with the realities of life, it changes from a play to a vain playing with meaningless
forms."[20] This phenomenon of decadence can be observed in the autumn
of the *ancien régime* and similar periods.

Social entertainment is, in its true form, a stylization of society; it is a
game in which one behaves "as if" everybody was everybody else's equal
and friendly companion. This is no more a deception than art and play,
with their deviations from reality, can be considered lies. Only when
such gatherings become mere means for the promotion of aims of other
than a mere sociable quality or for the concealment of such purposes
does the element of lie and deception enter and the true meaning of
the forms of polite sociability become corrupted. Simmel concludes:

These forms of entertainment would not mean relief and pleasant relaxation
from the ever-present burdens of life for so many serious people, if they were merely
devices of escape, merely a momentary avoidance of life's seriousness. This may
often be actually the case, but the liberation and relief which are enjoyed precisely
by the more serious personalities is due to the fact that the being together and the
interaction through which life in all its gravity is realized can here be enjoyed in
the form of an artful play—in sublimation and dilution.....[21]

III. THE LEADING CONTRIBUTIONS OF SIMMEL TO SOCIOLOGICAL THEORY

A. THE NATURE OF SOCIETY

Society is, for Simmel, essentially psychic interaction between human
beings[22] both as individuals and as group members. Society is really
not a substance but a process, a happening (*Geschehen*), or "something
functional," something that human beings do and experience. One
should perhaps, avoid the term "society" and, instead, use the term
"association" to denote the true nature of social reality.[23] However, not
all psychic interaction constitutes a process of association, e.g., not the
mere exchange of glances between two individuals who pass each other
on the street.[24] Such are "border phenomena," which, by repetition and
intensification, may assume the character of social processes. The criterion
seems to be that in association processes the individuals become "linked
together" by "mutual influence and determination." One will, therefore, have to assume that between a mere being together and a perfect
association there is a continuous range of more or less intensive mutual
influencing. Even the large, interindividual groups (organizations),
with which the idea of society is usually identified, are to Simmel

"nothing but solidifications of direct interactions between individuals."[25] However, social relations, in the perfect sense, are not only psychic but *moral* relations.

This involves the following two main principles: (1) In the case of any kind of interaction in which one party loses all human significance for the other, any relationship in which one party considers the other merely as a means for an end which is not related to this other party, or where an attitude of complete indifference of the one party to the other is existent, such relations are not *social* relations at all, in the strict sense of the term. No association exists in such cases, just as it does not exist between the carpenter and his bench. (2) "Society can be regarded as a system of relations of morally, legally, conventionally, and in many other ways, entitled and obliged beings,"[26] or association involves reciprocity of rights and duties.

This principle is of consequence in the analysis of relations of power, domination, and authority. To speak of "compulsion" in social relations is usually incorrect, since such interaction involves in most cases a measure of voluntary decision and action on the part of the "compelled" individuals.

In the *Philosophy of Money*, Simmel points out[27] that even the modern state can seldom really compel citizens, it can merely induce them into certain actions because of fear of punishment. Only in matters of taxation can the state use direct compulsion, in so far as monetary wealth can be seized by force. Simmel elaborated this idea again in "Superordination and Subordination" and pointed out that this is one reason why despotic regimes tend to favor the substitution of money taxes for contributions in kind or in services. Consequently, any kind of domination is possible only in so far as and as long as a minimum of consent is existent among the dominated—even if such consent merely takes the form of avoidance of the greater evil of disobedience.[28]

It should also be noted that this concept of social interaction excluded the man-object relations, as such, from the realm of sociology; they constitute objects of sociology only in so far as they involve relations between persons.

The same functionalistic approach, which dissolves all social phenomena into complexes of relationships, is apparent in the treatment of social types likes "the stranger,"[29] or "the poor."[30]

From Simmel's point of view, processes that seem to cause dissocia-tion are as important in the life of groups as are the associating processes. There are no completely harmonious groups; and, if such a group could be found, it would not show any life.[31] A certain amount of conflict is, for example, an organic element in marriage relations. The attitude of opposition is often the only means by which antagonistic individuals can tolerate being together in the same association.[32] Of course, conflict relations cannot, by themselves, result in social forms but only in con-nection with associating forces—both together constitute the concrete living unity of a group.[33] However, the function and effect of conflict vary with the structure of the relationship, and it requires a casuistic[34] analysis to understand these variations. Opposition, competition, jealousy, envy—all such conflict phenomena vary with the basis and degree of likeness and integration in the groups.[35]

There exists a definite correlation between the structure of any social group and the amount of antagonisms permissible among its mem-bers.[36] Here, as in many cases, Simmel shows the ambiguous nature of social constellations: "The same centripetal structure of the group makes it either more resistant against dangers arising from antagonism among its members or weakens its ability to resist—depending upon the addi-tional conditions." Among the large groups, those that are highly organ-ized will stand a greater degree of friction and partition than the more mechanical conglomerations.[37] However, in so far as conflicts, in socie-ties of the less elaborately organized type, can more easily be localized, the group as a whole will be less sensitive. On the whole, the larger group will have more reserves of uniting energies. The modern state, for example, can tolerate the strife of political parties and can even utilize these antagonisms for its very equilibrium and development, while the Greek city-states were destroyed, torn to pieces by the internal party struggles.[38]

The same principle can be observed in the effect of intergroup conflict on the solidarity of the conflicting groups; it may compel factions to unite, or it may lead to a complete seccession of minorities already dis-contented with the course of action pursued by the majority. Simmel seems to have been deeply impressed by this ambiguity of social situa-tions, which is one reason why accurate prediction of social events is so difficult. He refers to it on many occasions.

278   AN INTRODUCTION TO THE HISTORY OF SOCIOLOGY

B. THE STRUCTURE OF SOCIETY AND THE PROBLEMS OF SOCIAL INTERACTION

In spite of Simmel's functional concept of society, the notion of "form" is largely identical with what may be more properly called "structure." His excellent study of the determination of the character groups by the number of members[39] shows this very clearly. Among the structural problems discussed by Simmel, that of superordination and subordination deserves special consideration because of the basic importance of the phenomenon.[40]

Three main types of domination and authority are distinguished: (1) domination by a single person, (2) domination by a group of several persons, and (3) subordination to an impersonal objective principle. The value of the treatment lies, however, not in this classification but in the execution of a minute analysis of specific situations under each of these main types.

Simmel assumes that an inverse relation exists between the extent to which each individual enters into the group with his personality and the extent to which a single ruler can dominate the group modified by the size and homogeneity of the group.[41] While an absolutely rigid authoritarian rule is intolerable in a family group in which every member participates with almost his entire personality, it becomes possible and tolerable in a very large group into which every individual enters only with a small "quantum" of his "personality."[42]

Rule by a body of several persons, while it can be as "absolute" and as "hard" as monocracy, is likely to be more objective and impersonal.[43]

One of the main cases of subordination to an objective principle is the so-called "rule of law"; the others are those forms of authority which are derived from the position of the ruling person in a kinship or household group (patriarchate, matriarchate, patrimonial rule, etc.).

Simmel assumes that the development of subordination proceeds from personal rule to impersonal authority: as in the intellectual field the trend is from subordination under society (i.e., the authority of prevailing opinion) to subordination under objective (scientific) truth. Thus in the political field the ruler himself is finally subordinated to the objective principle of a social order by which his own will is bound.

This evolutionary trend can be traced in the family, in the state, and also in the economic system. In the relations between employer and employees the same evolution occurs to the extent that both parties become subordinated to the objective principle of contract, especially if the contract is based on a collective agreement between an employers' association and a labor union.[44]

Simmel, although he is aware of the possible advantages for the subordinated individuals of the personal elements in authority, thinks that, in general, depersonalization of authority relations makes subordination more tolerable and less humiliating. In connection with this idea he offers some observations on the alternation of superordination and subordination by limitation of terms of office and other devices, which should be interesting to the student of democratic institutions.[45]

Simmel then discusses the selection of the best-fitted individuals for positions of authority. He points out that a perfect correspondence of personal qualifications and social position is, in principle, impossible because of the always existing surplus of qualified individuals.[46] The development of a bureaucracy with elaborate specialization of positions and the detailing of functions of authority to experts tend to minimize the required personality standards for most positions of authority. On the other hand, the highest offices in the modern states would require extraordinary personal qualifications if the officeholder were chosen strictly on account of his relative personal ability, as compared with those of other minor functionaries. The difficulty arising from the scarcity of such highly qualified individuals is often mitigated by the adaptability of men to new and larger tasks; in other cases the device of conveying an objective dignity of office, which is not based on personal qualification, is resorted to.

Since the questions "What contributes to the integration or disintegration of groups?" and "What keeps groups together over a long period of time?" may be considered as the central theme in all society, Simmel's discussion of the *self-preservation of groups*[47] may be regarded as a testing ground of his contributions to theoretical sociology. Simmel refers here to those groupings which ordinarily last much longer than the life-span of their individual members and therefore assume, from the point of view of the individual, a relative permanence of existence.

The first problem which arises is that of the continued identity of the group, in spite of change in its membership composition.[48] The continuity of the group as an identical unit is effected, in the first place, by the persistence of the locality or territory in which it exists, in so far as in many—though not in all—groups the sentiments and intellectual contents are definitely related to a certain special unit, to the domestic "soil" or the "fatherland."[49]

In this connection Simmel presents a most important principle, that "the sociological characters of relationships otherwise perfectly alike, will be significantly differentiated on account of the notions of their different duration that are effective in them."[50]

The second condition of group persistence is the physiological connection of the generations and the web of kinship relations in general. The connection of the generations is of such great importance for the preservation of the larger groups, because the replacement of one generation by the next does not occur all at once, but step by step, so that at any moment those who have already belonged to the group for some time will always be in the overwhelming majority. This permits the conservation and transmission of the objective culture which has been developed and is characteristic of the group.

The same process of gradual replacement of membership occurs in other organized groups, even where no biological relation exists between the generations, e.g., in the Roman Catholic clergy. The gradualness of the change in membership composition serves to preserve the identity of the group, even where, after a long period, the entire culture of the group has changed.

Sometimes a group, originally not based on kinship, will resort to closing its ranks against persons not related to the present members in order to preserve its existence, e.g., the guilds in their late stages or the Russian clergy, who, by contrast to the Roman Catholic clergy, developed into an inbred caste.

Simmel points out that the transmission of the objective spirit of a group through "ordination" and co-optation is superior to the system of heredity of social positions.[51] Gradualness and slowness in the turnover of membership is, thus, a condition of the immortality of groups.[52] Therefore, it is necessary to provide special precautions in such groups whose existence is essentially dependent on the life of a single leading or ruling individual.[53] The main device used in such cases is the objectification of the ruler's position, that is, the development of the idea that the individual ruler is merely the personification of a supra-personal spirit or principle attached to the "office," together with the hereditariness of the ruler's position.[54]

Most essential, however, for the continuity of any group is organization. All associations exist "originally" in immediate interaction between individuals, in their roles as group members through organization; the functions which affect the unity of the group are transferred to officials or functionaries; the direct interaction between members is replaced by interaction between members and these organs. The interrelation of individuals, which, in nonorganized groups, is purely functional, acquires through organization a separate objective existence. Originally merely interaction, the group is now represented by a particular structure.[55]

In addition, there are the well-known technical reasons which make an organized group more resistant to dangers from without or within than an unorganized group.[56] On the whole, this discussion may be taken as a strong plea in favor of the rational forms of association. Nevertheless, Simmel makes the interesting remark that a group which in a crisis can fall back on the unorganized interaction of the rank and file of its members has a better chance to survive than a group that cannot dispose of the functions of specialized organs or offices.[57]

This leads to the further observation that, in some cases, a variability of structure is desirable for the preservation of the group,[58] as evidenced by the history of the Jews.[59] This, however, presupposes a high degree of homogeneity. In groups consisting of heterogeneous elements in latent or open conflict, greater stability of structure and conservatism with respect to changes in institutions and regulations are advisable, for in such situations any change is likely to arouse opposition in some quarters.

It is, therefore, understandable that ruling groups which are on the defensive avoid progressive changes;[60] if they agree to reforms, they do so not because they want the change but because they want, by minor concessions, to preserve their own essential traits—a policy especially noticeable in decaying aristocracies.[61]

Conservatism is, however, also characteristic of groups that are determined in their structure not by a dominating minority but by the broadest social stratum. This is most conspicuously the case in agrarian societies composed of freeholders. The farmer wants security more than change. Where, however, the urban middle class determines the structure, there will be change, for the continuity of such society depends on the chances for individuals to rise to higher social positions. Thus the form or structure of societies is determined by the nature of the social interests.[62] Again, the ambiguity of social situations is apparent—stability and elasticity can both contribute to the chances of group preservation, depending on several other variables, both of structural and of substantial nature.

While the main discussion is kept within the framework of structure analysis, the psychic factors involved are dealt with in a long note on loyalty and gratitude.[63] The structural phenomenon of group persistence after disappearance of the original purposes or motivations is one of the essential principles of sociology. Loyalty is that psychic disposition which produces this phenomenon. It is obvious that "without this phenomenon of loyalty society could not in the actually observed way exist over any length of time."[64]

Gratitude is another essential psychic factor, since all social interaction rests on the scheme of gift-receiving and equivalent giving. The latter can be obtained by compulsion in only certain cases.[65] Gratitude, therefore, is an indispensable complementary element in the maintenance of social interaction.

Every individual belongs as a social being to a variety of social circles which are partly overlapping[66] and, from a different point of view, can be thought of as concentrically arranged. The narrower the circle, the less the individuality for the individual; the circle itself, however, will be something individual, sharply distinct from other circles. If the circle within which one acts expands, the margin for individuality development increases, but the circle itself, as a social whole, will show less individuality.[67]

Simmel explains that this theorem is not meant as a sociological law but merely as an attempt to summarize by a "phenomenological formula," without any reference to causality, the uniform effects of what may be very heterogeneous "causes" in each case.[68] If he offers a psychological explanation, he does so merely as a "heuristic principle."[69]

It seems as though the individual was dominated by a dual urge: to differentiate himself from the social circle to which he belongs and at the same time to differentiate himself as a member of this circle from those who do not belong to it. The more the urge for differentiation from the fellow group members is satisfied, the less will the group itself be differentiated.[70]

Certain kinds of groups assume under this aspect an intermediate position. It seems that the most unreserved emotional attachment is directed only to the most narrow and to the largest circles,[71] not to the intermediate ones. One is willing to sacrifice one's self for one's country and for one's family, but not for the township in which one lives.[72] While this is primarily a static principle, it lends itself obviously to application with regard to social evolution.

C. THE SOCIAL IMPLICATIONS OF A MONEY ECONOMY

Although Simmel's *Soziologie* is chiefly concerned with logicosystematical inquiry into structure elements of society in general, it also contains rather definite ideas on the main social changes in contemporary Western society. Moreover, the *Philosophy of Money* represents in the second, synthetic part, in a more organized form, his ideas on this matter.[73] Simmel accepts here the basic notions of historical materialism or, as he suggests it should be called, "historical sensualism." His position is, however, that this theory has to be modified, in so far as the concrete economic forms are, in their turn, conditioned by profounder evaluations and by psychological, as well as metaphysical, "currents," which, again, are conditioned by profounder economic factors and so on.[74] The main changes resulting from money as an all-pervading institution in modern society can be summarized as follows:

1. An increase of freedom of the partners in any kind of social relations: landlord and peasant, employer and employee. When contractual social relations become possible on a basis of compensation in money rather than in services and kind, they can become depersonalized, in the sense that every moral consideration or interaction process extraneous to the specific kind of relation tends to be eliminated.[75] This gives a freer choice of action to all persons concerned, especially so far as the choice of partners is concerned and also with regard to the place of residence of each partner. There can be no doubt that the general tendency is to make man, on the one side, dependent on the services of more and more people, but, on the other hand, to make him more and more independent of the serving personalities as such.[76]

2. The ensuing separation of objects possessed from the person of the owner permits combinations of ownership between otherwise unrelated individuals. The institution of money makes it possible for the individual to associate himself with others for a common purpose,

merely by contributing money, without getting involved and bound with his entire personality—as was characteristic of the medieval corporation.[77]

3. This depersonalization of social relations makes possible associations for limited purposes of individuals not personally attached to one another: the purely purposive voluntary association.

Consequently, the entire *style of life* is changed under the impact of money as one of the main economic institutions. The trend toward rationalistic attitudes is increased through the development, alleviated by money use, of the habit of calculation—a habit that is spreading into all spheres of life. Even time assumes a money value in Western society with the full unfolding of money economy[78]—an idea which, later on, was elaborated by Oswald Spengler. The trend of social change is thus toward greater rationalization and depersonalization of all human relations, that is, toward a form of society in which the individuals, highly specialized in their social functions (divisions of labor), as personally free atoms tend to be related merely by purposive relations in which, again, the kind of interrelation effected by combinations of monetary wealth or by monetary compensation of services tend to become prevalent.

IV. CRITICISM AND EVALUATION

It is clear from these examples that Simmel actually intended more than a mere systematization of social forms. He made it clear enough that the conceptual distinction between "form" and "content" of society was "really nothing but an analogy," that both are "in reality inseparable elements of any social existence and process."[79] In his sociological papers he refers repeatedly to the "meaning" of social "forms." The two questions—"What do the individuals mean by behaving in a certain way?" and "What is the objective meaning of the described action patterns in their lives?"—are constantly suggested, if not expressly put, to the reader.

As already pointed out, the search for the objective meaning leads beyond sociology, in the strict sense, into metaphysical interpretation. The inquiry into the subjective meaning requires the application of psychological knowledge and methods; yet, in its final intention, it does not aim at the regularities (laws) of psychic processes in the individual but at the causal understanding of the social interaction patterns by which individuals are united into groups.

The objects of sociology are psychic processes which can be conceived by psychological categories. These are indispensable for the description of the facts, but they do not enter into the sociological intention which aims at the association process as such—like the intention of a drama, which, although it can be understood only psychologically, is not directed at psychological insights but at those syntheses which the psychic processes form under the points of view of the tragic or of style or symbols of life.[80]

The problems of social psychology are, according to Simmel, merely special problems of individual psychology. Therefore, these arguments also apply to the objection that Simmel's sociology is not clearly distinguished from social psychology.

The nonpsychological character of Simmel's pure sociology can be exemplified by the principle of correlation between individuality and the expansion of the social circle.[81] The principle, as such, does not contain any psychological theorem; it merely states an observable relationship between two elements of group structure.

Here, however, one weakness of Simmel's approach is revealed. Some of the phenomena could be made intelligible, even as evidence of structural principles, only by careful inquiry into psychic attitudes and processes. Simmel, instead, merely applies a rather general psychological hypothesis as "heuristic principle." The result is often mere conjecture rather than a real insight and secure knowledge. Furthermore, one can scarcely escape the impression that Simmel views society as an interplay of structural factors, in which the human beings appear as passive objects rather than as live and willing actors. Frequently, he refers to the inherent regularities of form principles as if these were the real moving forces in social life. Nowhere do we find a systematic analysis of the will-currents, the antagonisms and harmonies of interest and will which determine the course of individual and collective action and on which the very existence of associations depends.

However, the precise determination of the nature of social forms and the skilful application of the idea in Simmel's essays have opened a new angle of perception—a new outlook on social phenomena—which proves very fruitful in the analysis of concrete social situations—if applied with the necessary discretion. Simmel's procedure of staking off a field of investigation by abstracting a certain aspect (the "form" of social inter-action) from the chaos of experienced reality, is not unique, not peculiar to sociology; rather, it is the principle on which *all* specialization of the actual sciences has developed.[82] Simmel applied this principle to a field (sociology) in which, hitherto, the notion had prevailed that its specific object of cognition was not a new abstraction but, rather, a synthesis of the insights into social life gained by the existing specialized social sciences.

Among the critical objections to this idea of pure sociology, those offered by Hans Freyer deserve special attention because they raise a question of fundamental importance. Freyer points out that the con-ception of pure sociology as a sort of geometry of social phenomena may prove fatal, since it leads sociological thought off on a wrong track; phenomena that ought to be conceived as historical processes, imbedded in the context of the more or less unique situation in the flow of time, become fixed as static structures. Simmel, according to Freyer's criticism, tried to establish sociology as a *Logos-Wissenschaft,* which Freyer be-lieves to be foreign to the very nature of its subject. Freyer, however, emphasizes the fact that, in spite of this fundamental error, Simmel's essays contain "excellent sociology," because, with a fine scientific tact, Simmel applied his approach only to such subjects as lend themselves to this kind of treatment, since they are, indeed, "timeless."[83]

The "formal," or, as one might better say, the "structural" or morpho-logical approach, applied even to the apparently most fluid social unions or groupings, is so widely different from the layman's point of view that it becomes immensely stimulating and challenging. The student who is habitually inclined to think in compartments or fixed "contentional" categories is suddenly forced to draw comparisons between phenom-ena that seem to be distant in time or space and unrelated in quality, focusing his attention on the strictly social, that is, interactional, as-pects. This, in itself, would be valuable in a propaedeutical sense. In addition, this approach is carried out with a meticulous casuistry in analysis. Never is Simmel content with general notions of social types; always he insists on defining the specific situations in which the phe-nomenon arises; always he forms, from general concepts, specific type concepts of well-defined "cases" of the general phenomenon studied.[84] In this respect, he is perhaps surpassed among his contemporaries only by Max Weber. Among the generation of his followers, Max Graf zu

Solms and Leopold von Wiese have carried on this work of classification of forms of social interaction.[85]

While this method would finally result in a fruitless play of the mind —and, in fact, this danger zone is often touched in Simmel's essays— Simmel succeeds in making it a meaningful endeavor. This is accomplished by the introduction, into the "form" analysis, of psychological interpretations, often of a very subtle character. Spykman[86] points out that Simmel agreed that pure sociology alone cannot convey a full understanding of society, that it needs supplementing by psychological and "factual" inquiries. As an illustration we may note his observation that conflicts between individuals intimately related by kinship or other close personal ties tend to be more bitter than those between comparatively strange and loosely related individuals. This is in itself a rather common-sense observation. The real value of Simmel's analysis lies in the fine distinctions between various typical constellations and in the sociopsychological explanations or interpretations.[87] The same manifestations of conflict may be due to a wide variation of motivations and may, therefore, be of quite different meaning for the life of the social groups in which they occur. Furthermore, violent conflicts, such as occur in intimate relations (e.g., in marriage), just because of a profound community of values among the partners, without endangering the relation as such, would definitely destroy any relation of less intimate character. Incidentally, these subtle differentiations of configurations (or "forms") and motivations in social relations suggest the necessity of careful theoretical preparation and utmost caution in any quantitative inquiry into social attitudes and processes.

Simmel's interpretation of the trends of social change in contemporary Western society can hardly be said to be original. It is essentially a synthesis of the ideas developed previously by Marx, Tönnies, Durkheim, and others.

On the whole, his sociological interpretations, although extremely intelligent and subtle, do not betray a great deal of firsthand experience and contact with the great social movements and important societal events of his time. This may partly explain the lack of new original insights into the great social questions of the period.[88]

It seems that Simmel's interest in sociology originated not from an immediate concern with the social problems of contemporary society but rather from a philosophic endeavor to clarify its position in a system of sciences. Obviously, Simmel's occupation with problems of ethics and morals (*Moralphilosophie*) also led him into a discussion of norms and values in their relation to social life.

These reservations have to be made in order to arrive at a fair appreciation of Simmel's work. Its real and lasting value lies not so much in the new knowledge of society it conveys as in the contribution to the classification of the purpose and procedure of sociology.

Even his most severe critics acknowledge the significance of Simmel's idea of sociology as a systematic analysis of social forms. "The influence of Simmel's concepts of 'social form' is present in contemporary sociology, even where the idea of Pure Sociology in Simmel's sense is rejected."[89] It is Simmel's method and procedure of analysis rather than the content of his findings which constitute his unique and lasting contribution to the advancement of sociology. Thus we are confronted with the paradox that the philosopher who started out to redefine the subject matter of sociology gained his place among sociologists rather because of his methodological ideas.

The following selected bibliography will indicate the main sociological and philosophical writings of Simmel and the chief commentaries on his work.

I. BOOKS AND ARTICLES BY GEORG SIMMEL

Soziologie: Untersuchungen über die Formen der Vergesellschaftung. Leipzig, 1908.

Grundfragen der Soziologie. Leipzig, 1917.

Die Probleme der Geschichtsphilosophie. Leipzig, 1892.

Einleitung in die Moralwissenschaft. 2 vols. Berlin, 1892–93.

"Moral Deficiencies as Determining Intellectual Functions," *International Journal of Ethics,* III (1893), 490–507.

"The Problems of Sociology," *Annals of the American Academy of Political and Social Science,* VI (1895), 412–23.

"Das Problem der Soziologie," *Jahrbücher für Gesetzgebung, Verwaltung und Volkswirtschaft,* XVII (1894), 1301–7.

"Le Problème de la sociologie," *Revue de métaphysique et de morale,* II (1894), 497–504.

"Superordination and Subordination as Subject-Matter for Sociology" (trans. Albion W. Small), *American Journal of Sociology,* II (1896–97), 167–89, 392–415.

"The Persistence of the Social Group (trans. Albion W. Small), *ibid.,* III (1897–99), 662–98, 829–36; IV (1897–99), 35–50.

"A Chapter in the Philosophy of Value" (trans. Albion W. Small), *ibid.,* V (1898–99), 577–603.

Philosophie des Geldes. Leipzig, 1900.

"Tendencies in German Life and Thought since 1870" (trans. W. D. Briggs), *International Quarterly,* V (1902), 93–111, 166–84.

"The Number of Members as Determining the Sociological Form of the Group" (trans. Albion W. Small), *American Journal of Sociology*, VIII (1902–3), 1–46, 158–96.

"Grossstädte und Geistesleben," in *Die Grossstadt: Vorträge und Aufsätze zur Städteausstellung* (Dresden, 1903), pp. 185–206.

"The Sociology of Conflict," *American Journal of Psychology*, IX (1903–4), 490–525, 672–89, 798–811.

"A Contribution to the Sociology of Religion" (trans. Albion W. Small), *American Journal of Sociology*, XI (1905), 359–76.

Philosophie der Mode. "Moderne Zeitfragen," No. 11. Berlin, 1905.

Die Religion. "Die Gesellschaft, Sammlung sozialpsychologischer Monographien," ed. M. BUBER, No. 2. Frankfurt, 1906.

"The Sociology of Secrecy and of the Secret Society" (trans. Albion W. Small), *American Journal of Sociology*, XI (1905), 441–98.

"The Problem of Sociology" (trans. Albion W. Small), *ibid.*, XV (1909), 289–320.

"How Is Society Possible?" (trans. Albion W. Small), *ibid.*, XVI (1910), 372–91.

"Soziologie der Geselligkeit," in *Schriften der Deutschen Gesellschaft für Soziologie: Verhandlungen des ersten deutschen Soziologen-Tages, 1910* (Tübingen, 1911), pp. 1–16.

Philosophische Kultur: Gesammelte Essais. "Philosophisch-soziologische Bücherei," Vol. XXVII. Leipzig, 1911.

II. CRITICISM AND INTERPRETATION

SPYKMAN, NICHOLAS J. *The Social Theory of Georg Simmel.* Chicago, 1925.

VIERKANDT, A. "Simmel," *Encyclopedia of the Social Sciences.*

FREYER, H. *Soziologie als Wirklichkeitswissenschaft* (Leipzig and Berlin, 1930), pp. 46–57.

BARNES, H. E., and BECKER, H. *Social Thought from Lore to Science* (Boston, 1938), II, 889–91.

WIESE, L. VON, and BECKER, H. *Systematic Sociology.* New York, 1932.

MACIVER, R. M. "Sociology," *Encyclopedia of the Social Sciences.*

ROSENTHAL, ERICH, and OBERLAENDER, KURT. "Books, papers, and essays by Georg Simmel," *American Journal of Sociology*, LI, No. 3 (November, 1945), 238–47.

NOTES

1. Nicholas J. Spykman, *The Social Theory of Georg Simmel* (Chicago, 1925), p. xxvi.

2. P. A. Sorokin, *Contemporary Sociological Theories* (New York, 1928), pp. 497–98. Sorokin thinks that the idea is very old, dating from the Roman jurisconsults.

3. G. Simmel, "The Problem of Sociology," *Annals of the American Academy of Political and Social Science*, VI (1895), 54–55, 63; *Soziologie: Untersuchungen über die Formen der Vergesellschaftung* (Leipzig, 1908), pp. 6–7; and *Grundfragen der Soziologie* (Leipzig, 1917), pp. 28–29.

4. "The Problem of Sociology," *American Journal of Sociology*, XV (1909), 290; see also "The Problem of Sociology," *Annals*, pp. 52–53.

5. "The Problem of Sociology," *American Journal of Sociology*, p. 291.

6. "The Problem of Sociology," *Annals*, p. 53.

7. *Ibid.*, p. 54.

8. *Soziologie*, pp. 9–11; *Grundfragen*, p. 28.

9. *Grundfragen*, p. 11.

10. *Ibid.*, p. 12.

11. *Ibid.*, p. 15. Translations of all quotations from works not published in English are by the author.

12. *Ibid.*, pp. 20–21.

13. *Ibid.*, pp. 12–13, 14.

14. "The Problem of Sociology," *Annals*, p. 59.

15. *Ibid.*, p. 60.

16. *Grundfragen*, pp. 25–28 and chap. ii, which gives an example.

17. *Ibid.*, p. 32.

18. *Ibid.*, pp. 32–33 and chap. iv.

19. "Die Soziologie der Geselligkeit," in *Schriften der Deutschen Gesellschaft für Soziologie: Verhandlungen des ersten deutschen Soziologen-Tages, 1910* (Tübingen, 1911), 1–16; also *Grundfragen*, chap. iii, pp. 50–71. This paper has not been translated into English, nor has it been abstracted by Spykman. The term *Geselligkeit* in this connection designates the kind of more or less formal conviviality characteristic of the middle and upper classes. The title of Simmel's essay might be freely translated as "Sociology of the Drawing-Room."

20. "Die Soziologie der Geselligkeit," p. 14.

21. *Ibid.*, p. 16.

22. *Grundfragen*, p. 12.

23. *Ibid.*, pp. 14–15.

24. *Ibid.*, p. 12.

25. *Ibid.*, p. 14.

26. *Soziologie*, p. 345.

27. *Philosophie des Geldes* (Leipzig, 1900), p. 417.

28. *Soziologie*, p. 102.

29. "Exkurs über den Fremden," *ibid.*, chap. ix, pp. 509–12.

30. "Der Arme," *ibid.*, chap. vii.

31. *Ibid.*, p. 187; also the "Sociology of Conflict," *American Journal of Sociology*, IX (1903–4).

32. *Soziologie*, p. 189.

33. *Ibid.*, p. 191.

34. The term is used here in its original meaning, free of all pejorative connotations, to designate a procedure of analyzing general concepts of social phenomena (like "competition") by stating very specifically the various "cases" which result from a change of variables.

35. *Soziologie*, p. 205. Simmel's discussion, for example, of jealousy in its morphological and sociopsychological aspects is a masterpiece of analysis. The same may be said of the discussion of competition, its forms, limitations, and effects (*ibid.*, p. 213). One observation deserves quotation because it shows the brilliancy of Simmel's formulations: "Jealousy tends to destroy the very relationship for the preservation of which the jealous individual is striving."

36. *Ibid.*, p. 219.

37. Note the influence of Durkheim.

38. *Soziologie*, p. 220. The entire discussion shows the strength but also the weaknesses of the "form" approach. Clearly, Simmel neglects to mention the decisive fact that party antagonism is destructive to the extent that it involves the fundamental values of the group. The existence of the group is not endangered so long as the strife of parties keeps within the sphere of means or minor ends and does not involve the basic ideas on which the group life rests.

39. *Ibid.*, chap. ii; also "The Persistence of the Social Group," *American Journal of Sociology*, III (1897–99), 662–98, 829–36.

40. *Soziologie,* chap. iii; see also "Superordination and Subordination as Subject-Matter for Sociology," *American Journal of Sociology,* II (1896–97), 167–89, 392–415.

41. *Soziologie,* pp. 115–17.

42. Obviously, this principle holds only for a basically liberal regime, in which private and public matters are separable. It has been disproved by the recent phenomenon of totalitarianism. The principle does not consider the possibility of despotic rule over a heterogeneous mass of subjects with the aid of an organized political machine or gang, although Simmel's discussion of the various forms of hierarchic organization in monocracies (*Soziologie,* p. 120) contains some valuable contributions (the function of patronage, of the idea of service, etc.) to a sociology of authoritarian rule.

43. *Ibid.,* p. 131.

44. Simmel, of course, could not foresee that this "law" would be modified through the emergence of quasi-charismatic leadership regimes. The sociological explanation lies in the fact that subordination to an objective principle presupposes consensus of the group members on at least the fundamental issues of social life. It also requires a certain stability of objective social conditions. Where the latter change quickly, frictions arise, and emergency powers will be given to the authority-bearer who represents the objective principle, and if, in addition, the basis of consensus becomes too narrow, a transition to personal leadership may take place.

45. *Soziologie,* p. 174. He also mentions the device (later utilized in the Fascist countries) to appropriate authority in some functions to individuals otherwise subordinated, thus letting the individual alternate in the roles of superordinated and subordinated.

46. *Ibid.,* p. 183.

47. *Ibid.,* chap. viii; and "The Persistence of the Social Group."

48. *Soziologie,* p. 377.

49. *Ibid.,* p. 378; see also "Der Raum und die räumlichen Ordnungen der Gruppe," *ibid.,* chap. ix.

50. *Ibid.,* p. 378; cf. also the excellent discussion on pp. 500–502.

51. *Ibid.,* p. 383.

52. The ways in which entrance to, and exit from, an association are regulated are therefore important for the chance of longevity of the group. Simmel, with mathematical precision, distinguishes four principal possible combinations: (1) entrance and exit equally easy: as in most voluntary organizations; (2) entrance difficult, dependent on conditions—resignation difficult: secret associations, criminal gangs, etc.; (3) entrance easy—resignation difficult: most proselyting associations; (4) entrance difficult—exit easy: aristocratic associations (*ibid.,* p. 401).

53. *Ibid.,* p. 385.

54. *Ibid.,* p. 389, and the "Exkurs über das Erbamt," pp. 391–96.

55. *Ibid.,* p. 409.

56. *Ibid.,* pp. 410–30.

57. *Ibid.,* p. 433.

58. *Ibid.*

59. *Ibid.,* p. 449.

60. *Ibid.*

61. *Ibid.,* p. 450.

62. *Ibid.,* p. 451.

63. *Ibid.,* pp. 439 f.

64. *Ibid.,* p. 439.

65. *Ibid.,* p. 443.

66. Simmel develops in chaps. vi and x of his *Soziologie* the theorem that the chances of personality development increase with the number of circles to which the individual belongs and also with the degree to which the social circle expands.

67. *Ibid.,* pp. 531–33. In one of his illustrations Simmel refers to the structural differences between northern and southern states in the United States. In the South, where

settlement was carried on by highly individualistic adventurers, one finds political life centering in the more abstract, colorless structure of the states, while the more socially regulated settlers in the North tended to more narrow municipalities, which, however, showed strong individual characteristics and enjoyed privileges of autonomy.

68. *Ibid.*, p. 532.

69. *Ibid.*, p. 533.

70. *Ibid.*

71. *Ibid.*, p. 539.

72. The weakness of this theorem is obvious. It is derived mainly from experiences in the age of liberalism and does not take account of the factors of power and compulsion that can be used by the larger social circle to restrict the chances for individuality development.

73. In accordance with Simmel's ideas on the relation between philosophy and the special sciences, the first part of this work deals with problems preceding the actual economic theory of money, that is to say, with the conditions which make a monetary system possible (for a fuller account see Spykman, *op. cit.*, pp. 219 ff.).

7⁴. *Philosophie des Geldes*, p. viii.

75. The ideal partner for money transactions (*Geldgeschäfte*), in which, as the saying goes, *Gemütlichkeit* ceases to exist, is the completely indifferent personality, biased neither for nor against us (*ibid.*, p. 211). On the other hand, for this very reason, one should not engage in money transactions with one's friends or foes.

76. *Ibid.*, p. 293; see also *ibid.*, p. 338, on spatial separation of the owner from his property.

77. *Ibid.*, pp. 351–52.

78. *Ibid.*, p. 546.

79. *Soziologie*, pp. 4, 5; also p. 10.

80. *Ibid.*, pp. 17–19; cf. also the "Exkurs über Sozialpsychologie," *ibid.*, pp. 421–25.

81. Compare with pp. 254 ff., 262, above, where this has already been discussed.

82. Teaching disciplines which are formed for practical purposes may combine several such "sciences," e.g., geography. The field taught in the departments of sociology is, of course, composed of bits from a great many sciences, more or less well integrated by relation to the subject proper of sociology: the types of groups and social processes. Where "theory" is in disrepute, syncretism and a lack of interior, epistemological, and methodological order will be the consequence. Where Simmel's concept of "formal" sociology is adhered to with pedantry, the teaching will very likely lack substance and relevance to the significant problems of contemporary society.

83. Hans Freyer, *Soziologie als Wirklichkeitswissenschaft* (Leipzig and Berlin, 1930) pp. 46 ff., and 56–57. The same may be said of the work of Simmel's followers, especially L. von Wiese, who has attempted to develop systems (or parts of systems) of formal sociology. As long as they deal with phenomena of *universal* significance, especially with simple processes and relations, the approach proves satisfactory. Where, however, complex structures of a historically determined nature like the modern state are subjected to the same treatment, the approach has to be modified, or the resulting insights are of little significance.

84. Compare Simmel's own statement (*Soziologie*, p. 10): "Even an approximate dissolution of societal forms into simple elements [as in geometry] cannot be hoped for in the near future. Consequently, sociological forms if they are to be to some degree definite can be valid only for a relatively small range of phenomena. If one says, for instance, that super- and subordination is a form found in almost any human society, little will be won with such general statement. What is necessary is the consideration of the various ways of super-and subordination, of the special forms of their realization. These will lose in universality of validity the more concretely they are defined."

85. Max Graf zu Solms, *Bau und Gliederung der Menschengruppen*, I. Teil (Karlsruhe, 1929); and *Führerbestellung: Bau und Gliederung der Menschengruppen*, II. Teil (Leipzig, 1932); also L. von Wiese and H. Becker, *Systematic Sociology* (New York, 1932).

86. *Op. Cit.*, p. 74.

87. Simmel, *Soziologie,* pp. 205–10.

88. It seems symptomatic that Simmel's illustrations referring to the labor problem are almost exclusively taken not from German conditions but from the British Labor Movement or from the sphere of the domestic-servant problem, where Simmel had, of course, firsthand experiences. It is, furthermore, symptomatic that the rich sources of socioeconomic surveys, dissertations, and semiofficial inquiries which had resulted from the influence of the historical school in economics in Germany have scarcely been utilized by Simmel, while he gives ample references to ancient and medieval history. The question of the sources of Simmel's knowledge of the social world can, of course, merely be stated, not answered, in the framework of this chapter.

89. Freyer, *op. cit.*, p. 47. The influence of Simmel's ideas on American sociology cannot be traced within the limits of this chapter.

CHAPTER XII

THE SYSTEMATIC SOCIOLOGY OF LEOPOLD VON WIESE: THE ORIGIN AND STRUCTURE OF INTERHUMAN RELATIONS

J. Milton Yinger

I. THE INTELLECTUAL BACKGROUND AND MAIN SOCIOLOGICAL WRITINGS OF VON WIESE[1]

LEOPOLD VON WIESE was born in Silesia in 1876, the son of a Prussian cavalry captain. At eight years of age he was sent to an academy for cadets; but, chafing under the severe discipline there, he was always in trouble. At about eighteen he ran away. Though he secured a job with a German exporting house in Bombay, his restlessness continued. He fell in love with a Ceylonese girl—an affair which found literary expression in a novel, *Nava*.

Returning to Germany, Wiese resumed his education, pursuing graduate work in economics. He lined up, in the economic controversies of the time, with the psychological school. In 1905 he joined the faculty of the Cologne School of Commerce and Finance but was not altogether happy there. He was married and divorced several times. In 1918 the Cologne School of Commerce was made a university—one of several municipal schools that were expanded at the time, partly to counteract the rigidities of the old universities. In this more important academic setting, Wiese became the editor of a sociological journal, the *Kölner Vierteljahrshefte für Soziologie,* which carried a great many important articles and published most of the empirical data gathered by Wiese and his students. Later he developed a research institute for social science, which occupied a large share of his attention. *The Kölner Vierteljahrshefte* was last published in 1934, and the institute was closed in 1935. Wiese's position during the period of National Socialism was one of decreasing influence and security. Most of his classes were taken over by men in favor with the party. Since the end of the war, however, he has come back into prominence as president of the newly organized Deutsche Gesellschaft für Soziologie.

Wiese's own statements, as well as basic similarities to the work of several other writers, make it fairly easy to determine the chief sources of influence of his thought. Most important is the influence of Simmel, who, in maintaining that the isolation of the form of social relations is the peculiarly sociological problem, furnished the general pattern for Wiese's system. In emphasizing the dynamic, sociation aspects, however, Wiese approached the problem from a somewhat different point of view. More than most German sociologists, Wiese was influenced by American writers, particularly Ross, whose work directed his attention not only to the systematic arrangement of societal processes but also to many concrete problems. Park and Burgess, who were also influenced by Simmel and were concerned with problems of systematic sociology, should also be mentioned, as well as Thomas and Znaniecki. Waxweiler, a Belgian sociologist and director of an outstanding research institute, emphasized the importance of the processes of interhuman adjustment, through language, as the source of social life. His *Esquisse d'une sociologie* (1906) helped to focus Wiese's attention on the sociation frame of reference.

The trend of Wiese's thought is evident even in his early essay on Spencer,[2] which contrasts Spencer's cosmic scheme with Simmel's detailed studies, much to the advantage of the latter. Although Wiese is often considered to be too unconcerned with factual material, the error of such an interpretation is seen even in this early essay. Emphasizing the need for a natural-science approach to the study of society, Wiese is consistently empirical in his method.

The work on which his fame as a sociologist rests, however, and with which this paper is largely concerned is his *Allgemeine Soziologie.* Part I, the *Beziehungslehre,* appeared in 1924; Part II, the *Gebildelehre,* in 1929.[3] A recent English translation of three papers by Wiese, entitled *Sociology,*[4] furnishes a succinct and relatively complete statement of Wiese's point of view and system. His short essay, *Soziologie: Geschichte und Hauptprobleme,*[5] is also of value in showing his approach to the problems of sociology and his analysis of its history.

II. ESSENTIAL ELEMENTS IN VON WIESE'S SOCIOLOGICAL SYSTEM

Two elements are of greatest importance to Wiese's conception of the nature of sociology, the first of which is his emphasis on sociology as a science. Wiese is in the tradition of scholars who insist that sociology

can begin to make contributions to the understanding of social relationships only when it has profited by the example of the natural sciences,
broken away from speculative social philosophy, freed itself from the
reform efforts, and eliminated value judgments. Unlike most social
scientists in Germany, he was strongly influenced by the Western
natural-science tradition.[6]

Secondly, Wiese's whole work is orientated toward the idea that sociology is a special social science, with a clearly defined and delimited
area of investigation which differentiates it from the other social sciences.
It does not seek to draw together the results of the other social sciences
in order to get a total view of "concrete reality" but makes an abstraction
of its own, from an entirely unique point of view, in order to contribute
to the understanding of social life. The peculiarly sociological abstraction is the isolation of the processes of sociation, of approach and with-
drawal, which characterize all social behavior. Moreover, sociology is
interested not in the purposes served by social relations, which are the
concern of the other social sciences, but only in the direction (approach
and avoidance) and the rhythm of sociation. "Rhythm of sociation"
refers to sequences and repetitions of social relations which establish observable patterns. Sociology, then, in brief, is the study of interhuman
relations as such; its special problem is the analysis of the direction and
patterning of sociation of all human behavior which has as its object
other human beings.

The greater part of Wiese's work is devoted to the systematizing of
the processes of sociation and their recurrent patterns. Part I of his
Allgemeine Soziologie, the *Beziehungslehre,* concerns itself with the
theory of interhuman relations, which Wiese divides into association,
dissociation, and mixed processes. Each of the two main processes—
association and dissociation—is analyzed into many subprocesses, which
are situated along a continuum, according to the degree of association
or dissociation which they represent.[7] The first tentative stages of association are included under "advance," a process in which "there always
remains some feeling of hesitation," of reserve; the participants look
upon the association as a kind of "doubtful experiment." Wiese gives
adoring, enticing, consulting, thanking, and the like as examples of
advance.

Indicative of a greater degree of association is the process of "adjustment," which implies the modification of differences among the persons

involved. This adjustment may be one-sided or mutual; the former usually signifies a condition of dependence on the part of the individual who does the adjusting; the latter is the result of reciprocal influence, generally in the pair-relation, which continues the tendencies initiated in the compromise: "Actions which in compromise are unrelated and transitory become incorporated in an on-going, continuous configuration in adjustment."[8] Wiese gives instilling knowledge, agreeing, imitating, and coming to terms as examples of adjustment.

Adjustment "....does not wipe out feelings of difference...., although they are usually somewhat less intense..... When once the stage of accordance is reached, however, mutual participation in emotions, memories and habitual attitudes ensues....."[9] Behavior of the participating individuals becomes more and more similar. Deferring to another's judgment, forming a friendship, and mediating are examples of accordance.

Most complete of the processes of association is that of "amalgamation," which, however, in the human sphere never represents complete coalescence. This process is seldom descriptive of association in mobile and anonymous groupings, such as the modern city, which preclude intense attachment to any one plurality pattern, but is more often found in isolated social structures. Amalgamation finds expression in the formation of pairs and other small groups and in the association of a large number of persons for co-operative purposes.

This analysis of the processes of association is not intended, of course, to correspond to empirical reality. One cannot easily classify concrete interhuman relationships in one category or another; they are set up as analytic devices. Three factors lead to association on all the different levels, although their influence becomes continually greater as one moves from advance to amalgamation: emotionally toned urges and sympathetic impulses; "interests which, although emotionally toned in some degree, usually are consciously recognized as conducive to the enhancement of self";[10] and objective factors in the situation which make association almost inevitable. Wiese thus summarizes the processes which flow from these influences: "By advance, we understand the preparatory steps to coming together; by adjustment, association through simultaneous and mutual recognition of differences; by accordance, the attempts to overcome differences; and by amalgamation, the establishment of some association which is conceived as a new state or condition."[11]

Dissociation, the other main process of interhuman relations, is also influenced by the three factors of emotionally toned urges, interests, and objective factors. Wiese insists that in the treatment of the processes of dissociation, value judgments must be checked even more rigorously than usual, for associative tendencies are likely to be regarded as worthy of diligent cultivation, while dissociation is to be avoided. The sociologist, says Wiese, can make no such distinction.

Dissociation as well as association can be expressed in terms of social distance: " .... any social process is a sequence of occurrences through which the distance prevailing between human beings .... is increased or decreased."[12] The three main processes of dissociation—competition, contravention, and conflict—signify increasing social distance. They also imply a "gradual increase of definitely antagonistic activity."

Competition, the least dissociative of the three processes, " .... may be defined as the general social process comprising the dissociative tendencies inseparably connected with efforts on the part of persons or plurality patterns to attain an identical objective."[13] The objects in view are drawn from every field of human activity. The sociological study of competition, however, refers not to the goals but to competition "as an interhuman relation *per se*." It involves not only dissociative elements but many tendencies toward association—sufferance, compromise, advance, or even adjustment—which limit the degree of dissociation.[14] There is also a tendency, however, for competition to pass over into contravention and conflict, where dissociative influences are stronger. The two main varieties of competition are rivalry and striving; the former contains a larger subjective element or reference to the competitor, while the latter arises from a consciousness of scarcity of desired objects.

Contravention[15] is a process of dissociation which contains, on the one hand, more antagonistic elements than competition but includes, on the other hand, more uncertainty over the nature and extent of the antagonism than conflict. Contravention may be fostered by the emotional factors of exasperation, dislike, and resentment and by antagonistic interests, convictions, and temperaments which preclude agreement. These factors operate in contravention between the sexes and between generations and in majority-minority disputes, in all of which there is a strong clash of interests but also many associative traits which inhibit the appearance of overt conflict.

Conflict is the most extreme process of dissociation. It includes, however, a large variation in intensity of antagonism, ranging from that bordering on contravention to open combat. The latter is the most distinct form of dissociation, but by no means is it always reached in conflict processes. It involves, furthermore, an approximate equivalence in the strength of the contending parties. Conflict does not necessarily result in continuing dissociation; it may, in fact, result in well-marked association. "The more equivocal and latent dissociative processes, particularly contravention that never comes to the surface, may be greater barriers to future amalgamation than the most violent forms of open combat."[16] Attacking, persecuting, blaming, lynching, and abhorring are examples of conflict; and dueling, carrying on a feud, and ejecting a rival are examples of its combat phase.

Wiese's first discussion of these main processes of association and dissociation centered about "common-human" relations, that is, relations which are not specifically channelized by a more or less permanent pattern of behavior which delimits or circumscribes them. Other processes, "circumscribed action patterns," may also be analyzed into associative and dissociative, still with the dynamic point of view as the central concept. The only difference in this approach to the problem is the addition of the influence of plurality patterns,[17] which constitute the background of circumscribed processes and tend to condition the direction and intensity of the sociation. "Common-human relations" and "circumscribed action patterns" are, of course, only heuristic terms, not descriptions of empirical reality. All concrete interhuman processes contain both common-human and circumscribed elements, but the proportion varies greatly.

Turning, then, to the analysis of sociation, as it is circumscribed by more or less permanent patterns of behavior, we have the following statement by Wiese:

All circumscribed processes fall in one of two categories, differentiation or integration.... : disparities and uniformities develop; the growth of plurality patterns brings with it stratification .... individuation perpetually takes place; concomitantly, the associative network within plurality patterns becomes increasingly ingrained in the neuropsychic structures of its members, so that the associative bonds which unite them come to be regarded as more or less necessary, desirable, and justifiable, a consequence which renders the term "socialization" applicable..... Accompanying all these processes is the social ascent and descent of various members of the plurality patterns involved; the ensuing domination and submission are inseparable from group life.[18]

We have space here only to outline the processes of differentiation and integration which Wiese discusses with a wealth of detail. Among the differentiating processes are: the genesis of disparities; domination and submission; gradation, stratification, and selection; individuation, separation, and estrangement. These processes of differentiation follow certain channels which are marked out by the patterns of human relations; they are the circumscribed varieties of dissociation.

On the other hand are the integrating processes, the complements to differentiation. Both are always at work, although they do not balance each other. Uniformation; ordination, superordination, and subordination; and socialization are the main processes of integration. Wiese did not attempt to rank the circumscribed relations, as he had the common-human processes, according to the degree of sociation which they represent.

Using the same dichotomy from the point of view of the impact of differentiation and integration on the continuance of existing plurality patterns, one may speak of "constructive" and "destructive" processes. These are not wholly distinct from integration and differentiation. Constructive processes, for instance, " .... are simply regarded as those special types of integration that produce new plurality patterns from old. Of course, all integrating processes are in some measure adapted to this end, and we merely select those which experience shows to be particularly adapted to the construction of new plurality patterns....."[19]

The main destructive processes are: exploitation, favoritism, formalism (ossification), radicalization (attack on old patterns without qualification), commercialism (undue subjection to economic criteria), and perversion (substitution of goals). The principal constructive processes are: institutionalization (the ordering of social relations), professionalization, and liberation (abolishing hindering restrictions).

The study of social processes and distances is central in Wiese's systematic sociology. In the *Gebildelehre,* however, he has extended the analysis of sociation to include the systematization of plurality patterns —the relatively continuous social structures which channelize inter-human relations. In harmony with his conception of sociology, Wiese confines his interest in plurality patterns to the investigation of the ways in which they influence association and dissociation. The bases of classification of social structures are (1) relative duration and (2) degrees of abstractness. By means of these criteria the author distinguishes three types of plurality patterns: crowds, groups, and abstract collectivities, which are consecutively less influenced by the behavior and characteristics of the "concrete human being," are consecutively more durable, more highly organized, and more abstract. "Crowds are very much like the empirical individual in his characteristics .... *groups* .... possess an *organization* which prescribes the activity of the individual .... *abstract collectivities* are considered to be supra-personal, and thus removed as far as possible from the empiric individual man."[20] That is, there is a progressive decrease in common-human behavior patterns and a progressive increase in circumscribed behavior patterns as one moves from crowds to abstract collectivities.

The two chief varieties of the crowd are the concrete (visible and temporary) and the abstract (amorphous and of indefinite duration). The former is a type of social grouping which lies between a leaderless aggregation, on the one hand, and the group, on the other. The latter is the transition between the concrete crowd and the abstract collectivity; it corresponds quite closely to what has become known in the United States as the "public." The term "crowd" is used to designate both concrete and abstract groupings because there is a close empirical connection between them: "there would be no concrete crowd if the abstract were not already present, and the abstract is perpetually rebuilt and renewed by the concrete."[21] The group is defined as " .... those interhuman plurality patterns .... which are of such relatively long duration and relative solidarity that the persons therein affiliated come to be regarded as a relatively homogeneous unit."[22] Duration and solidarity clearly distinguish the group from the crowd. In his classification of groups, Wiese uses size as the main criterion and discusses sociation influences in the pair, the triad, and larger groups. The abstract collectivity is distinguished from the crowd and the group by the lack of "affiliative homogeneity of definite, empirical human beings." That is, more attention is given to the organizational structure and less to the particular members.[23] The main types of abstract collectivities are the state and the church.

The analysis of these social structures—the crowd, the group, and the abstract collectivity—reveals the *patterns* of sociation; it defines the interhuman relations that tend to be continued or repeated, and it is therefore a valuable source of knowledge of the processes of sociation, which continues to be the main concern of Wiese's systematic sociology.[24]

III. CRITICAL APPRAISAL OF VON WIESE'S SOCIOLOGY

Wiese's systematization of sociology has received wide attention. Its scientific usefulness therefore needs careful appraisal. It is not necessary to discuss it on any other grounds than those of its scientific validity and utility, for they are the criteria which it is intended to satisfy.

The question that first arises concerns the validity of *any* attempt to systematize a science, to pay specific reference to the conceptual apparatus. Such activity is held by some to be idle armchair philosophizing which entirely contradicts the scientific pretensions under which it is pursued. One who holds such a position will immediately discount Wiese's system. The result of such a position, however, is not to eliminate the process of concept-building but to hide it, allowing implicit and unwarranted concepts to condition the data. The chief value of Wiese's work is precisely that he has contributed to the methodological "self-consciousness" of sociology, its scientific sophistication, by means of which its concept-building becomes explicit and planned with direct reference to its data. This is the central value of his emphasis on sociology as an abstracting science and as a special discipline.

Having said this, however, in regard to the general value of the development of a systematic frame of reference, one must investigate the usefulness of Wiese's specific systematization. The basic concept of sociation is doubtless a useful descriptive device; but for the most part —and here the critics of the system-builders have legitimate cause for complaint—it has preceded too many of the sociological problems with which it is concerned and has not, therefore, developed methodological tools for research. One must consider, in this connection, the concrete studies which have grown out of Wiese's systematization in order to see whether or not the conceptual apparatus which it furnishes has proved to be a valuable scientific tool. Granting that the analysis and prediction of the types and degrees of sociation are valid social scientific problems (whether or not it "is sociology" is unimportant), may one, by using the sociation frame of reference developed by Wiese, go into an agricultural village or ghetto or city and heighten his ability to say: "Given these conditions, these people will associate or dissociate thus—here competition, there accommodation, there conflict"? A scientific study does not simply record instances of a predetermined classification of processes; it seeks to discover relationships.

Many of the studies by both Wiese and his students[25] indicate that the orientation from which they have worked has proved valuable. It is a conceptual "pair of glasses" that sharpened their vision in studying the family, the village, and the ghetto. No startling new relationships have been discovered, to be sure—few theoretical developments force a sharp new orientation—but the sociation concept has been a clear way of analyzing, for instance, many aspects of the community-society dichotomy which has been important in the work of many writers. Its usefulness as a perspective is probably greatest when it refers to direct interhuman relations and least when applied to abstract crowds and abstract collectivities, such as the state.

Usefulness as a tool for certain sociological problems, however, is a long way from an all-embracing sociological system. It is a futile argument, in fact, from the scientific point of view, to try to decide whether or not Wiese's work is an accurate and complete sociological system. The only question is: Is it a useful conceptual tool for analyzing the data to which it refers? In so far as orderly description is of value in this regard, Wiese's system is only to be praised; but, because it is not oriented toward prediction, it has not generally achieved a more rigorous scientific level.

The felt need for *inclosing* a science in some particular systematization is a manifestation of lack of awareness of the function of that systematization in the scientific process. The history of science is the story of old problems attacked with new weapons, of new insights from fresh orientations. A systematization, by focusing attention, may prove to be a source of these new insights. To concentrate on the system itself, however, as Wiese too often does, is to shut off this source.[26] He himself finds it impossible to keep within the sociation frame of reference in his own concrete studies of interhuman relations. This is as it should be—a system is a tool, not a boundary. There is a good deal of truth in Abel's remark, made in a slightly different connection, that the controversy over Wiese's limitation of sociology " .... resolves itself .... into a mere struggle for a name and thus is without foundation."[27]

A further criticism of Wiese can be made in regard to his oft repeated dictum: No value judgments in science. He does not keep sharply enough in mind the distinction between values as biasing factors in research and values as data for the sociologist, although he accepts Max Weber's definition of sociology as one of the "understanding" sciences, which, in their search for predictive power, attempt to understand not only objectively observable behavior but subjectively intended meaning. This "meaning" is not something mysterious; scientists are not even concerned with its "reality"; but it proves to be a useful concept for the analysis of human behavior.[28] Although Wiese accepts this definition, he never uses it. His system is behavioristically (in a narrow sense) inclined. By insisting so strongly that sociology is a science, upon which there is now almost unanimity of opinion among professional sociologists, he is led to avoid, more than is necessary, the dangers that inhere in the idealistic tradition. Because he sees a need for following the work of the natural sciences, he is unable to develop a strictly sociological method devised for the analysis of "meaning."

Furthermore, there is a danger in the absolute denial to value judgments of a place in science. Value judgments make the positive contribution of sensitizing one to certain data and problems; they may be a source of insights. The danger is not so much the holding of a position as the failure to recognize the bias and thus to make allowance for it. If perspectives distort, it is not enough to deny them. Therefore, if the continued emphasis on elimination of value judgments from science tends only to prevent their explicit recognition, it hinders the scientific process. If, however, it stresses the dangers of biasing factors, it is a useful and necessary emphasis.

In sum, Wiese's work, in so far as it attempts to demonstrate what sociology "really is," has failed to established its point, as, indeed, any such effort must fail when tested by scientific criteria; for, to repeat, such a delimitation is not a surveying activity but a tool-building process. Wiese has failed to pay sufficient heed to concrete methodological tools in relation to specific problems. On the other hand, in the elaboration of his system he has, of course, collected a wealth of valuable detail and made valid empirical insights, the value of which is independent of the system itself. Moreover, when properly qualified, his emphasis on the need for explicit theoretical orientation is essential to the scientific quest; and his insistence upon the special nature of scientific sociology —irrespective of whether or not one accepts his definition of that specialty[29]—is fundamental to a nonempiricist, abstracting science.

NOTES

1. The writer wishes to express his thanks to Professor Howard Becker for making available his excellent library of books and documents on Wiese.

2. *Zur Grundlegung der Gesellschaftslehre: Eine kritische Untersuchung von Herbert Spencers System der synthetischen Philosophie* (Jena, 1906).

3. All references to *Allgemeine Soziologie* given below are to the American adaptation by Professor Becker, *Systematic Sociology* (New York, 1932) (cited hereafter as "Wiese-Becker"). It should be noted, however, that this volume is not simply a translation but a thoroughgoing adaptation of Wiese's work in terms of American material. Though there have been no basic shifts, there are different points of emphasis and several additions. In studying Wiese's work from *Systematic Sociology*, therefore, one must take account of these differences.

4. Edited and annotated by Franz H. Mueller (New York, 1941).

5. This appears in English both in Wiese-Becker, *op. cit.*, Part IV, which is a free translation and adaptation, and as a separate volume, *Sociology: Its History and Main Problems* (Hanover, 1928).

6. Some German writers—Sombart, for instance—spoke with great disdain of Wiese's *westlich* ideas.

7. As Abel and Becker have pointed out, this is not a genuine quantification of sociological data, because the essential requirement of quantification—a scale—is lacking. It is only a ranking procedure (cf. Theodore Abel, *Systematic Sociology in Germany* [New York, 1929], pp. 102–7; and Wiese-Becker, *op. cit.*, p. 59).

8. Wiese-Becker, *op. cit.*, p. 198.

9. *Ibid.*, p. 206.

10. *Ibid.*, p. 230.

11. *Sociology*, p. 60.

12. Wiese-Becker, *op. cit.* p. 243.

13. *Ibid.*, p. 248.

14. In the second edition of *Allgemeine Soziologie*, in fact, the author discusses competition as a mixed, not a dissociative, process.

15. Wiese uses the more general term "opposition," which Becker, however, has changed to "contravention" in order to avoid the confusion which surrounds the former term in English (cf. Wiese-Becker, *op. cit.*, pp. 260–61).

16. *Ibid.*, p. 272.

17. This, again, is a free translation of the German term *Gebilde* ("structure"), in an attempt to catch the meaning more exactly.

18. Wiese-Becker, *op. cit.*, pp. 284–85.

19. *Ibid.*, p. 369.

20. Wiese, *Sociology*, p. 72.

21. Wiese-Becker, *op. cit.*, p. 457.

22. *Ibid.*, p. 489.

23. It should be noted here that Wiese explicitly rejects any notion of "social realism." Though the focus of attention may be on the pattern of abstract collectivities, not on the members, that pattern does not constitute a substantive reality: ".... Social structures do not exist in space..... If we attribute to them any reality it cannot be the reality of the perceivable but reality in the sense of an active force affecting and influencing life" (Wiese, *Sociology*, p. 39). This quotation also reveals the connection, according to Wiese, between social process and social structure: the latter is but a static picture of the former.

24. The second edition of *Allgemeine Soziologie*, which appeared in 1933, has several minor changes which should be mentioned, since we have drawn on the English adaptation of the first edition. The author gives a greater place to mixed processes of sociation, among which he includes competition; he elaborates his discussion of social distance; and he develops the application of his system to economic and biosociology. In his chapter on

306 AN INTRODUCTION TO THE HISTORY OF SOCIOLOGY

biosociology he denies the Nazi race doctrine and stresses the mixed racial character of the German people.

25. Cf. various chapters in *Allgemeine Soziologie,* those on the dyad and the triad, for example, and numerous studies by Wiese published in the *Kölner Vierteljahrshefte;* cf. also such studies as Willy Gierlichs, "Zwischenmenschliche Probleme der Ghettos," *Kölner Vierteljahrshefte,* X, 3; and Willy Latten, "Die niederrheinische Kleinstadt," *Kölner Vierteljahrshefte,* XIII, 3.

26. It is difficult to estimate how much the emphasis in Germany on the autonomy of sociology was due to the struggle for academic recognition against intrenched disciplines. It was probably an important influence, fostering an overemphasis on academic boundaries and elaborate system-building—from which Wiese's work suffers. In the polemical situation sociologists were at pains to prove that their science encroached on no other domains and hence paid too much attention to boundaries.

27. Abel, *op. cit.,* p. 10. That is not to imply, of course, that, because this unacceptable element is present in Wiese's work, the whole of it is to be dismissed lightly.

28. Note that not all sociologists who hold the discipline to be an understanding science would agree with this statement: some are concerned with "real meaning."

29. As Abel says: "The primary object of v. Wiese's sociological writings so far has been the establishing and justification of sociology as an independent science. His achievement on this point is not invalidated by the criticism which we advanced against his proposals according to which the various tasks of sociology are to be carried out" (*op. cit.,* p. 114).

CHAPTER XIII

THE SOCIOLOGY OF RELIGION
OF ERNST TROELTSCH

J. MILTON YINGER

I. TROELTSCH'S TRAINING, INTERESTS, AND WRITINGS

ERNST TROELTSCH was born in Augsburg in 1865, the son of a physician and ardent scientist, who hoped his son would study medicine. With that in view, he introduced him at an early age to the natural sciences; but Troeltsch's preferences moved toward history, philosophy, and religion. As a student of philosophy he came under the direction of Gustav Class, who introduced him to the Kantian tradition, to Hegel, Fichte, and Schleiermacher. Troeltsch was also influenced by Lotze and by the work of his teachers, Harnack, Ritschl, and Lagarde.

He began his teaching career as a lecturer in Göttingen in 1891; after a year he moved to Bonn as professor of theology, 1892–94; and then to Heidelberg, where he taught for twenty-one years. In 1915 he became professor of philosophy at Berlin. He concerned himself there not only with teaching but with politics, was elected to the Prussian Diet in 1919, and served as parliamentary undersecretary to the Prussian minister of education. He died in 1923.[1]

Troeltsch's chief writings, extending over many years, have been published together in his *Gesammelte Schriften*,[2] Volumes I and III of which particularly have established him as a scholar of the first rank. Volume I, translated into English as *The Social Teaching of the Christian Churches*,[3] first appeared in German in 1912. It represents the fruits of many years of research and, it might be added, of invaluable association at Heidelberg with Max Weber, who was at least partially responsible for the shift of Troeltsch's main interest from theology to the philosophy and sociology of religion.

Volume III of the collected works, *Der Historismus und seine Probleme*, was first published in 1922. There is general agreement with

Mannheim's statement that this book "....belongs among the foremost contributions to the history of German philosophical ideas."[4] In it one finds the finest expression of Troeltsch's philosophy of history which, although it lies outside the subject of this paper, may be characterized briefly. It was strongly influenced by Dilthey. Troeltsch held that one cannot understand the life of the "human spirit" by the methods of natural science, for science is unable to reveal the unique and individual character of any event. The historian's understanding of a situation is different from the naturalist's precisely because he attempts to discover the individuality, the "quality" of a particular event, not to develop general laws of human behavior.[5]

Among Troeltsch's important writings one should also mention *Zur religiösen Lage, Religionsphilosophie und Ethik* (1913), *Aufsätze zur Geistesgeschichte und Religionssoziologie* (1925), which compromise Volumes II and IV of his collected works; and *Die Bedeutung des Protestantismus für die Entstehung der modernen Welt* (1906).[6]

II. THE SOCIOLOGICAL STUDY OF RELIGIONS AND THEIR EVOLUTION

As a sociologist of religion, Troeltsch continually posed this problem: To what extent are the various elements of a society conditioned by religious beliefs and organizations and to what extent are they entirely independent of such an influence; and, on the other hand, how far are religious beliefs an outgrowth of purely nonreligious factors, and how much do they have their own independent inner dialectic? In his search for an answer to this extremely difficult and tenuous problem, Troeltsch has brought together an amazing amount of historical detail, which allows him to see a situation in all its complexity. Unlike Weber, who also had at his command an enormous amount of empirical material but who, by means of "mental experiments," attempted to control certain interacting factors in order to focus on some specifically defined problem, Troeltsch, for the most part, sought to trace the whole range of interacting factors in order to discover the precise place of religious groups in the total setting.

In his masterful *The Social Teaching of the Christian Churches,* Troeltsch sets himself the task, as Mannheim says, "....of solving the problem of how far the origin, growth and modifications of Christianity as well as the arrest of that growth in modern times were sociologically determined."[7] But he also sought to discover the reciprocal influence of the churches on the other aspects of social organization. Thus, for example, after tracing the importance of many influences in shaping the medieval church, he says that we must now inquire "....to what extent the Christian ideal determined the social development of the Middle Ages after it had itself been effectively and even decisively influenced in its development of a social philosophy by the actual conditions of the life of the day."[8]

The primitive Christian movement was, Troeltsch declared, a purely religious upsurge, conditioned, to be sure, by the social crises of the time but focused not on the demand for reform and justice in this world but on equality before God. This does not mean, however, that the secular order was not affected by its appearance, for the Christian ethic has a dual impact: It contains not only this thoroughgoing religious asceticism, emphasizing the universalism of love, but also an ethical-prophetic strain, with a radical individualism. Although the former element is dominant, the latter is never eliminated and continues as a latent challenge to the existing order which comes to the fore in times of crisis. During the period of a unified church civilization, both elements were included in the church organization, the radical force being drained off, for the most part, into the monasteries. With the breakup of this unity, however, two distinct types of religious groups emerged: the churches (the successors to the religious world unity) and the sects (which contain the explosive elements). Troeltsch uses this distinction, the methodological importance of which was first suggested to him by Weber, to great advantage in analyzing the place of religious groups in the historical process. The analysis of religious organizations into sociological types is, in fact, crucial to an understanding of their various roles and in Troeltsch's work, even more than in Weber's, is of the utmost importance.[9]

As ideal types,[10] the church and the sect are thus described by Troeltsch: The church is built upon development and compromise; it accepts the secular order but claims universal dominion over it; it is mobile and adaptive. The church is the great educator; "it dominates the world and is therefore dominated by the world." The sect, on the other hand, is usually associated only with the lower classes; it stresses radicalism and literal obedience of the Synoptic Gospels; it has voluntary membership, is small, lacks continuity. The sect rejects compromise with the world and the church's conception of relative natural law.

It is lay religion, free from worldly authority, able therefore, on the one hand, to forget the world in asceticism or, on the other, to fight it in radicalism.[11]

The Social Teaching traces the history of the churches and sects up to the eighteenth century, when, as Troeltsch says, the church civilization was finally replaced by a secular order. The sociological analysis of religious groups is extended to the modern scene in *Protestantism and Progress,* which, although published earlier than the longer work, is a complement to it and attacks the same fundamental problems. In this essay Troeltsch attempts to analyze the complex interacting factors at work in contemporary civilization, to discover ".... how much the Modern Spirit actually owes to Protestantism." The author concludes that ".... Protestantism cannot be supposed to have directly paved the way for the modern world. On the contrary, it appears at first, in spite of all its great new ideas, as a revival and reinforcement of the ideal of authoritatively imposed Church-civilisation, of a complete reaction to medieval thinking, which sweeps away such beginnings of a free and secular civilisation as had already been toilsomely established."[12]

The impact of Protestantism on the modern world was ".... mainly in indirect and unconsciously produced effects, nay, even in accidental side-influences, or again in influences produced against its will....."[13] The indirect influence which has received most attention concerns the importance of Protestantism for the modern economic system. In his study Troeltsch was led inevitably to the problem which Weber had highlighted in *The Protestant Ethic and the Spirit of Capitalism.* There is no question, says Troeltsch, of Protestantism having created capitalism. Can one discover, however, in its economic ethic (especially in Calvinism) the kind of rigorous, this-worldly asceticism which indirectly (and generally against the will of its adherents) encourages the severely rational economic action which typifies modern capitalism? Troeltsch accepts, with some modifications, Weber's thesis that Calvinism was an important influence[14] in the early stages of capitalism:

Weber has, in my opinion, completely proved his case; though perhaps it ought to be more strongly emphasized that the special character of Reformed asceticism was partly determined by the special conditions of the commercial situation in the Western countries, and more especially by the exclusion of Dissent from political life, with its opportunities and responsibilities, just as, on the other hand, the traditional Lutheran view became emphasized during the economic decline of Germany.[15]

This emphasis is a sharper criticism against Weber's thesis than Troeltsch seemed to realize, for Weber's point was precisely that, *in the beginning,* religious movements have importance for economic systems. Even Marx could agree that religious doctrines, after they have been selectively modified, reinforce the system which modified them. In another place, when Troeltsch says, "I would rate still higher the difference which *Weber* emphasizes between Calvin and Calvinism ....,"[16] he again underestimates the importance of his criticism of Weber, who did not stress the difference between Calvin and Calvinism nearly enough. These statements by Troeltsch require drastic modifications of Weber's thesis—and the present writer considers them to be necessary modifications—but Troeltsch was not fully enough aware of the sharpness of his criticism.

Having denied any direct and initiating power to Protestantism in creating capitalism and secularism, Troeltsch does not, however, consider it to be uninfluential in the contemporary world. He says:

.... We must not allow ourselves to be deceived by all the hostility to the churches and to Christianity, by all the naturalistic or aesthetic pantheism, which prevail at the present day. The present-day world does not live by logical consistency, any more than any other; spiritual forces can exercise a dominant influence even where they are avowedly opposed. Were it not for the religious Personalism which we have had ingrained into us by prophetism and Christianity, individual autonomy, the belief in progress , the all-embracing community of mental outlook, the indestructibility and strength of our confidence in life and of our impulse to work, would be impossible.[17]

The chief influence of Protestantism, however, the unique and immediate influence, is to be found, says Troeltsch, in the purely religious domain which is its central concern.[18] This point is in harmony with his insistence that religion has its own inner dialetic, an intrinsic element which cannot be reduced to other sociological factors.

III. APPRAISAL OF TROELTSCH'S SOCIOLOGICAL STUDY OF RELIGION

Troeltsch's importance for the development of a sociology of religion derives from his great ability to take into account so many of the interacting factors in a complex situation, an ability which enables him to escape a one-sided interpretation of any social movement. He had at his command a vast amount of historical detail, both through his own research and through a thorough acquaintance with the work of others in the field. His religious preconceptions were never denied, but, be-

312

cause he was explicitly aware of them, they did not condition his historical and sociological writings. Troeltsch's work, in fact, is an outstanding example of the possibility of scholarly research stimulated, rather than obscured, by judgments of value, provided only that one is thoroughly self-conscious in regard to those judgments.

The chief value of Troeltsch's work to the student of the sociology of religion, however, is that of a mine, not of a tool. His own work is a model of undogmatic and scholarly research and an invaluable source of information on the whole field of interaction of the Christian churches. But the questions he poses are more often historical than sociological. He asks himself: How must one describe the complete interaction which took place here? The sociological question—What does this situation reveal in regard to general laws of interaction between religious teachings and other life conditions?—is not his central concern. His elaboration of the church-sect dichotomy is a notable exception to this statement, for this has proved to be an important analytic tool for predicting the behavior of religious groups.[19] For the most part, however, Troeltsch is not concerned, as is Weber, with the development of a scientific methodology for the investigation of stated hypotheses. The importance of his work rests, rather, upon the exhaustive treatment that he has made of the complex history of Christianity—a complete and penetrating "intellectual history" which interprets the development of the church in terms of its total cultural setting.

NOTES

1. Cf. Albert Dietrich, "Ernst Troeltsch," *Deutsches biographisches Jahrbuch,* Vol. V: *Das Jahr 1923* (Berlin, 1930), 349–68.

2. Tübingen, 1912–25.

3. Translated by Olive Wyon (New York, 1931).

4. *The Encyclopaedia of the Social Sciences,* XV, 106. (It should be noted that this article seems to refer to Troeltsch's brief essays, *Der Historismus und seine Überwindung,* translated into English, by several authors, as *Christianity: Its History and Application* (London, 1923). This is probably an error, inasmuch as the more important work, *Der Historismus und seine Probleme,* is not mentioned). Dietrich says of this volume: ".... in the great definitive work of his life .... 'Historismus und seine Probleme' .... he has thrown a final and great illumination on German idealism and romanticism, from the point of view of the philosophy of history, of intellectual development and the dialectic, above all the work of Hegel" (*op. cit.,* pp. 357–58).

5. On Troeltsch's philosophy of history cf. Eugene Lyman, "Ernst Troeltsch's Philosophy of History," *Philosophical Review,* XLI (September, 1932), 443–65; H. E. Barnes and Howard Becker, *Social Thought from Lore to Science* (Boston, 1938), I, 767–68; and F. A. Christie, "Spiritual Values in the Work of Ernst Troeltsch," in *Methods in Social Science,* ed. Stuart A. Rice (Chicago, 1931), p. 416.

6. Translated into English by W. Montgomery under the title *Protestantism and Progress* (New York, 1912).

7. *Op. cit.*, p. 106.

8. Troeltsch, *The Social Teaching of the Christian Churches*, pp. 323–24.

9. Howard Becker has expanded the dichotomy of church sect into a fourfold classification—ecclesia, sect, denomination, cult—which is a valuable addition to the usefulness of the type concept as applied to religious groups (cf. Leopold von Wiese, *Systematic Sociology*, adapted and amplified by Howard Becker [New York, 1932], pp. 624–42). J. M. Yinger has also developed a more detailed classification in *Religion in the Struggle for Power* (Durham, 1946).

10. It is perhaps no longer necessary to say that an "ideal type" is not a "desirable type" but a conceptual tool, ideal only in the sense of not corresponding to empirical reality.

11. Cf. *The Social Teaching*, pp. 331–49.

12. *Protestantism and Progress*, pp. 85–86; on this point, cf. also Barnes and Becker, *op. cit.*, pp. 319–30.

13. *Protestantism and Progress*, p. 87.

14. Owing to frequent misunderstandings, one should perhaps stress the point that Weber, as well as Troeltsch, was thoroughly aware of the other very important influences in the development of capitalism. His only point was that Calvinism must also, along with economic and political factors, be given a place. It must be added, however, that he was careless, at some points, in his discussion of the interacting factors.

15. *Protestantism and Progress*, p. 138.

16. *The Social Teaching*, p. 894 n.

17. *Protestantism and Progress*, pp. 38–39.

18. Cf. also on this point A. C. McGiffert, *Protestant Thought before Kant* (New York, 1911).

19. Cf. H. Richard Niebuhr, *The Social Sources of Denominationalism* (New York, 1929), which, in addition to being an important work in its own right, has also made excellent use of Troeltsch's material and method. Cf. also Yinger, *op. cit.*

CHAPTER XIV

THE SOCIAL AND ECONOMIC PHILOSOPHY OF WERNER SOMBART: THE SOCIOLOGY OF CAPITALISM

F. X. Sutton

I. SOMBART'S LIFE AND WRITINGS

WERNER SOMBART was born on January 19, 1863, at Erms-
leben-am-Harz, a small town near Madgeburg. His ancestors
were of French and Dutch origin, largely Calvinists. Anton Ludwig
Sombart, his father, was a liberal, self-made landowner, who took an
active part in the social and political affairs of his day, becoming a
member of the Prussian Diet in 1861 and a member of the Reichstag
in 1867. After 1875 he moved to Berlin, in order to devote the whole
of his time to his political activities. The young Sombart was thus early
transported from his rural life on his father's estates to the intellectual
and cultural surroundings of the capital. Here he pursued his education until graduation from the University of Berlin in 1885, when his
health induced him to seek the warmer climate of Italy. Two years
were spent in Pisa preparing his dissertation, *Die Römische Campagna*
(1888), a study of Italian agricultural conditions which reflected his
father's intense concern with agricultural problems. Returning to Germany, he took his degree at the University of Berlin (1888), where he
remained until his first academic appointment at Breslau in 1890.

During this early period of his life, Sombart was subjected to the
impact of the social problems of late nineteenth-century Germany. While
he never took the active part in politics that his father did, he did not
hold aloof from the controversial issues of his day. His socialist sympathies early became known and acquired for him a considerable reputation. A series of lectures on socialism, given in 1896 at Zurich, were
published in the same year under the title *Sozialismus und soziale
Bewegung,* a work which went through many editions and was translated into more than twenty languages. This work established him as

314

a sympathizer with the socialist movement and apparently satisfied all but extreme Marxists; indeed, he was regarded by many as a coming socialist leader. It seems very probable that this sympathy retarded his academic advancement; it was not until 1906 that he left the "exile" of Breslau to accept a post at the newly created Handelshochschule in Berlin. Only in 1917 was he finally called to the University of Berlin to fill the chair in economics vacated by Adolf Wagner.

After his dissertation was completed, Sombart turned his attention from agricultural problems to the wider problems of modern capitalism, which became his lifework. The first edition of his magnum opus, *Der moderne Kapitalismus,* was published in 1902 and was subjected to severe criticism, which stimulated him to a thoroughgoing revision of the work. A series of studies appeared during the next decade, which were in a sense preparatory, special studies for this revision. Important among these were *Die Juden und das Wirtschaftsleben* (1911), *Luxus und Kapitalismus* (1912), *Krieg und Kapitalismus* (1912), and *Der Bourgeois* (1913). Gathering together the fruits of these studies and a vast amount of other material, he published the second edition of *Der moderne Kapitalismus,* the first two sections appearing in 1916–17, the concluding section somewhat later, in 1927.[1]

Paralleling this lifelong preoccupation with the problems of modern capitalism was a continued interest in the problems of socialism. Through successive editions the treatise on socialism grew from the little booklet of 1896 to the pair of large volumes in the ninth edition of 1918. After World War I, Sombart underwent a definite change, revealed in the tenth edition of this work, which appeared under the new title *Der proletarische Sozialismus* (1924). The change of title was symbolic of a complete change of attitude, from one of sympathy with the movement to strong antipathy and bitter denunciation. From an admittedly "convinced Marxist" he had come to a bitter retraction of the beliefs for which he had given enormous effort and delayed his academic advancement. In 1934, with the publication of *Deutscher Sozialismus* (translated into English by K. F. Geiser, under the title *A New Social Philosophy*) the transition became complete in a pledge of allegiance to the new regime in Germany. Further evidence of Sombart's new trends under the Third Reich are to be found in the work *Vom Menschen* (1938), which is subtitled *Versuch einer geistwissenschaftlichen Anthropologie.* This work, an "anthropology" in a sense unfamiliar to American readers, is representative of considerable German literature which attempted to analyze the essential nature of man; it is a treatise more philosophic than scientific and certainly not free from Sombart's particular Weltanschauung.

One more important work remains to be mentioned. In various scattered articles and remarks in his works on capitalism, Sombart set forth his views on methodology; but it was not until his scientific work was essentially complete that he wrote extensively on the subject in his *Die drei nationalökonomien* (1929). This involved and difficult book has been the subject of much controversy because its frequent obscurity and the general diffuseness of Sombart's style in this work invite varied interpretations.

In all his work Sombart reveals a great erudition, and his writings speak of the energy necessary to its acquisition. He frequently expressed dislike for the heavy and unbending seriousness of German scholarly writing and offers in his own works a flowing and vigorous style which has been universally commended. Until his death on May 19, 1941, his prolific pen continued to add more items to a bibliography already of imposing length.[2]

II. SOMBART'S METHODOLOGY AND LEADING CONCEPTS

To those immersed in the traditions of Anglo-American thought the understanding of Sombart's work presents very considerable difficulties. While insisting that his work on modern capitalism is not merely historical but theoretical as well, he adopts a negative attitude toward the great bulk of classical economic theory and hence presumably utilizes some theoretical system of a different nature. To elucidate this theoretical background of his work it will be necessary to examine his views on the nature and methodology of economic research in some detail.

For Sombart the field of economic research is that range of concrete human activity which arises from the fact of environmental resistance to the satisfaction of human needs; as he is fond of saying, it is concerned with the fact that man must obtain the means of his subsistence by the sweat of his brow. The basic methods by which this range of phenomena may be studied are conceived to be three, namely, (1) the evaluative and metaphysical, (2) the natural scientific, and (3) the *geistwissenschaftlich.*

The first of these methods, exemplified by Aristotle, the Scholastics, Adam Mueller, Spann, and a host of others, is concerned less with detached analysis than with the formulation of doctrines as to how human economic activity should proceed. When this program is carried through to its ultimate implications, it inevitably leads into metaphysical or religious systems. The relativity and individuality of such systems make them objectionable, if we are seeking widely acceptable systems of valid knowledge about this or other ranges of empirical fact. Hence we must turn to the nonevaluative methods of study wherein this objectionable regression into metaphysics or theology may be avoided. Concerning the possibility of such a study of social phenomena independent of one's value-judgments, Sombart has written frequently, arguing stoutly in the affirmative.[3]

The other two methods of economic research, which Sombart calls the *ordnend* and the *verstehend,* correspond to his conception of a fundamental distinction between two classes of sciences, the natural sciences and the *Geistwissenschaften.*[4] This distinction, popularized by Rickert and Dilthey, is widely accepted in German social science.[5] It is conceived to involve distinctions of a logical, as well as of a substantive, order. For Sombart this takes the form of characterizing the method of the natural sciences as an "external" ordering of phenomena, ultimately to the end of forming laws of nature *(Naturgesetze),* which he apparently conceives as empirical generalizations. This method *(ordnend),* proper to the natural sciences and supposedly most typically found in their supreme representative, physics, may be applied to the data of the social sciences but is much less productive than a method proper to these data.[6] This, the so-called *verstehend* method, is described as a "grasping of meanings" *(Sinnerfassen).* The scientific study of phenomena by this method consists in relating them to a system of known relationships in such a way that they make sense in terms of this system.[7] It particularly demands the use of subjective categories. The contrast between the type of knowledge which we possess of the formation of wild geese flying and the orderly movement of a military parade is emphasized. The latter case is *verstehbar,* in that the subjects of the scientist's observation are in some sense like himself and may be assigned motives for acting as they do, these motives finding their place in a meaningful complex in the soldier's subjective experience.

In the former case no such ready penetration of the meaning of the formation seems possible.

While admitting the importance of such analysis for the interpretation of human action, it may be seriously contended that, logically, there are no grounds for concluding that the process of *Verstehen* (as Sombart formulates it) is foreign to the natural sciences. Such a conclusion, obviously most damaging to Sombart's position, is supported by the fact that the elaboration of complexes of meanings (*Sinnzusammenhängen*) is one of the most important products of the process of *Verstehen;* inasmuch as no place is left for the development of such systems by other means, we must conclude that mathematics falls under the rubric of the *Geistwissenschaften*. This Sombart explicitly admits.[8] Physics, utilizing mathematical systems, then seems paradoxically close to the *Geistwissenschaften*. In particular, it is difficult to see how Sombart can conceive classical mechanics to be a part of the natural sciences as he understands them, since it certainly does not consist of a body of empirical generalizations. The distinction thus seems to be clearly untenable.

This apparent misconception of the nature of the natural sciences would not entail serious consequences for the development of social science were it not coupled with an empiricist interpretation of the system of meanings to be developed by the *verstehend* method. It has been characteristic of much German economic thought that the abstractness of the great bulk of economic theory has not been recognized. Interpreting the "laws" of economic theory as purporting to be determinant of concrete action, this tradition has rejected them both on the ground of empirical inadequacies and on the philosophic ground of the supposed rigorous subjection of human action to general laws. This methodological difficulty has been described by Professor Talcott Parsons as "idealistic empiricism."[9] It has the expected consequences in Sombart's work.

He begins by emphasizing the organic character of any system of meanings, hence the essential uniqueness of any complex system. This does not mean that a *verstehend* economics must be devoid of "laws" but that these can only be internal to a given system or purely formal characteristic of such systems in general. The so-called "laws of orthodox theoretical economics" have a heuristic value as aids to the process of *Verstehen* but are accorded the status of fictions. Clearly, from the empiricist standpoint, this view of the fictional character of these laws is inevitable. They are not admitted to the respectable status of scientific laws, whatever their heuristic worth. Moreover, they are applicable only within a given system of meanings.[10] Thus he is led to the curious position that classical economics is applicable in this sense only to the capitalistic system, not because of restricted empirical adequacy but because of logical necessity. This fictional status is assigned to rational schema in general, wherein the implications of completely rational action on the part of given actors are traced out; they are a scaffolding and no part of the final building. This does not, of course, exclude rationality as an important distinguishing characteristic of economic systems.

The contrast between the types of knowledge of human action that one can obtain, admitting the accessibility of the subjective aspect and the "externality" of knowledge concerning nonhuman objects, leads Sombart to the conception that this former type of knowledge is ultimate—is knowledge of the essence of things. "Behind the phenomena that we 'understand' there is nothing."[11] This dubious epistemological proposition leads to the position that the fundamental conceptions used in the formulation of a *verstehend* social theory are not arbitrary in any sense but are determined through the character of the phenomena in hand. It is not through mere convenience or adequacy for explanation that the fundamental concepts are chosen; they are forced upon the scientist by their very ultimateness. Sombart has noted in several places[12] the precarious position of the *Geistwissenschaften* between the natural sciences, on the one hand, and metaphysics, on the other; the tendency of the whole system to depart from the canons of general scientific methodology into metaphysics should be evident from this view of the role of general theoretical concepts. While certain basic metaphysical assumptions are necessary to any scientific research, it may be said that in Sombart's formulation of the *verstehend* method there is an objectionable intrusion of unnecessary metaphysics.

The implications of such a general position for an attack on the problems presented by modern capitalism should be reasonably clear. Insofar as it represents self-conscious use of theory, it will not be an application of general theoretical systems, such as, for example, one makes of the classical mechanics in studying the solar system. Sombart is emphatic that his treatment of capitalism is both theoretical and historical,[13] but enough has been said to show that the "theory" involved does not, in his conception at least, transcend the particular economic system which is under consideration. It involves essentially a tracing-out of the possibilities, probabilities, and "necessities" in a given economic system.[14] Always theory is to be subordinated in importance to the understanding of the particular historical individual under consideration. Sombart's interest is not in developing a general analytical social theory; for him only so much theory should be developed as is of apparent use in the study of particular economic systems.

From his earliest days, Sombart rejected the sharp separation of theory and empirical research represented in the famous *Methodenstreit* between Schmoller and Menger. While a student at Berlin, he divided his attention between Wagner and Schmoller, the local representatives of the controversy, and continued throughout his later life to proclaim the necessity of a union of theory and empirical study. What he brought forth from his union we may observe in his study of modern capitalism.

III. THE NATURE AND EVOLUTION OF CAPITALISM

Capitalism, for Sombart, is a unique historical phenomenon, a particular economic system. While it characterizes a particular period in the development of Western civilization, it is not merely the totality of "economic life" during this period. Nor is it conceived as a particular step in the process of economic or, more generally, social evolution. Unlike Weber, Sombart does not regard capitalism as of more general occurrence than is the case in the modern Western world; the emphasis is on the individuality and peculiarity of the system.

The study of this unique historical phenomenon has been Sombart's lifework and is represented most fully in the large volumes of *Der moderne Kapitalismus.* This work falls roughly into three parts. The first is concerned with setting the background for the emergence of modern capitalism in depicting two contrasting economic systems, the self-sufficient (*Eigenwirtschaft*) and the handicraft systems; the second treats the early stages of the capitalistic system; and the third, capitalism in full bloom.

Essential to any economic system are three elements: (1) a system of economic value-attitudes (*Wirtschaftsgesinnung*), i.e., a set of basic goals and rules of economic conduct; (2) an economic order given in some objective organization of economically significant activity; and (3) a technique. Each economic system is characterized by a particular form and combination of these elements. The key differences between the possible forms of the *Wirtschaftsgesinnung* are those between the principle of satisfaction of relatively fixed needs (*Bedarfsdeckungsprinzip*) and the principle of unlimited acquisition (*Erwerbsprinzip*), on the one hand, and that between traditionalism and rationalism, on the other.[15] The former elements in these pairs characterize the pre-capitalistic forms of economic activity. In these systems, economic activity is directly tied to obtaining the means for satisfying stable, traditional needs. In this aspect of the system, there is no significant distinction between the self-sustaining economy and the handicraft economy. Such distinctions as exist must be sought in the organization of economic life. The self-sustaining economy, characterized by the villages and manors of the Middle Ages, was gradually supplanted in the thirteenth and fourteenth centuries by the development of exchange in many branches of economic life. This development, stimulated by the increase in the supply of money and the growth of cities, resulted in the appearance of a new system—the handicraft economy. It was a distinct economic system but remained characterized by traditionalism and production for the satisfaction of existing needs. Like the earlier self-sustaining economy, its technology remains traditional, empirical, and largely bound to organic natural resources. In the late Middle Ages, according to Sombart, this was the dominant economic system, and it continued in control until the emergence of the capitalistic system. The similarity of these two systems is evident, and it is difficult to see why Sombart distinguished between them, apparently on the same level as he distinguished them from the capitalistic system. Perhaps his curious predilection for classification in triads is responsible.[16]

Against the earlier systems, the capitalistic system stands in sharp contrast. It is characterized as a system based on exchange, in which normally two different groups are involved: (1) the possessors of the means of production, who, at the same time, control the economic unit, and (2) the propertyless workers. These groups are bound together through the market. The economic spirit is that of unlimited acquisition (*Erwerbsprinzip*), and rationality is dominant economically and technologically.[17] This system first made its appearance in Italy in the thirteenth century and remained in faint beginnings for over two centuries. In the sixteenth and seventeenth centuries it definitely emerged in the form of early capitalism and passed into full-blown capitalism near the end of the latter century.

It is quickly apparent what is to become the central element for Sombart in characterizing this system. A new economic spirit had arisen, which was to create and characterize capitalism. In this new spirit there are two main elements, the spirit of enterprise and the bourgeois spirit. The former of these, the dynamic element, is the same restless Faustian spirit which has created the modern state, modern science, and technology. It is a spirit of unlimited worldly striving. Interwoven with this is the calculating bourgeois spirit, which provides the element of rationality.[18]

These contrasting economic systems which Sombart sets up do not correspond to clear-cut historical periods. In any given period characteristics of all three systems may be, and, indeed, are, present.[19] The empirical systems, thus dissected out, may exist simultaneously, differing in relative importance through successive stages of historical development. That period during which some part at least of economic activity is in recognizable conformity with a given system is called an "economic epoch." In any given period, there may or may not be effective dominance of any one system; thus in the period of early capitalism the capitalistic system had not arisen to sufficient prominence to give a characteristic stamp to the period, as it did later in the age of high capitalism. While Sombart's systems divide the historical development of Western economic life into radically distinct units, this does not imply a sharp division of concrete historical periods. Actually, between the periods of dominance of the various systems there is a shading-off of one into the other.

To the emergence of the capitalistic system, which for Sombart is the product of the capitalistic spirit,[20] certain conditions were necessary. Outstanding among these were the development of the modern state, certain technological advances, and the discovery of increased supplies of precious metals. The coincidence of these elements made possible the accumulation of wealth in cities, with a subsequent transformation of the demand for goods. The age of early capitalism thus ushered in bears many characteristics of the new capitalistic system but also involves a considerable heritage from the previous system. The new spirit of enterprise, directed toward profit alone, slowly makes its appearance. The beginnings of modern double-entry bookkeeping make possible an accurate accounting of profits and losses and encourage the separation of the funds of business enterprise from private funds. New forms of business association develop, which increase the depersonalization of economic activity. Technology moves from its traditional ways but remains empirical, i.e., based on rules discovered through experience and deprived of the rational understanding that science was later to supply. The formation of demand still rests with the ultimate consumers, but harbingers of the formative influence of capitalistic enterprise appear.

Conditions hampering the full development of capitalism are still, however, in evidence.[21] The drive to unlimited acquisition was not yet fully evident, and the tendency to abandon business enterprise to become inactive landowners dissipated the forces aiming toward high capitalism. In addition, there were political and religious restrictions, technical inadequacies, and the fortuitous adversities of war and pestilence. Indeed, the exhaustion of the wood supply threatened the whole development.[22] It was not until the latter half of the eighteenth century that conditions necessary to the full unfolding of capitalism were in evidence; after 1760 the age of high capitalism had begun.

In the age of high capitalism, which Sombart delimits by the first application of a coking process in 1760 and the outbreak of World War II in 1939, the capitalistic system was realized in a very notable degree and took its place as the clearly dominant economic system. The objectification of acquisition through the depersonalization of business enterprise gave the system its mechanical compulsive character, which Marx, before Sombart, had stressed. The growth of credit structures released the energies of impecunious enterprising spirits like Solvay, Rathenau, and Ford. Rationality, already gained on an empirical level in technology, was immensely furthered by the wedding of science and technology; this same rational spirit pervades the whole system. In short, the conditions which had fettered the capitalistic spirit fell away, and it attained to full expression, patterning economic life in its own image.

This brief sketch gives only the barest account of a vast canvas on which Sombart has lavished enormous energy and erudition. It is, of course, impossible here to criticize the work in detail, but certain aspects of it may be noted in their importance for the problems of general sociology and the particular problem of modern capitalism.

We have seen that the spirit of capitalism stands at the center of Sombart's scheme; he states quite simply that it has created capitalism. The status of this spirit, for all its central importance, is not completely clear. In one aspect, it seems clearly related to the *Wirtschaftsgesinnung* and thus may be interpreted as a complex of value-elements.[23] The realization of the spirit of capitalism may then be interpreted as the effective patterning of action in terms of these value-elements. On the other hand, this realization comes to be closely identified with the realization of an "idea" of capitalism, much in the Hegelian fashion.

If we accept this latter conception in its most innocuous form, i.e., regard it as the emergence of a definite pattern in modern economic life, the reason for its close association with the realization of the spirit of capitalism in the former sense is not far to seek. For Sombart the driving forces in the development of any economic system and of capitalism in particular must be found in the value-attitudes of some group of actors in the system. This group of prime movers may change radically in the course of development of a system, as it did during the movement of capitalism from the early to the mature stages, but in some form it is always present. To the effective formation of economic activity in accordance with a particular spirit, certain situational conditions are necessary. We have had occasion to note some of these conditions. However crucial they may be, they remain necessary and not sufficient conditions. Sombart criticizes Marx on just this score. While he admits and, indeed, strongly emphasizes the compulsive power of the capitalistic system, it is so only after the capitalistic spirit has been sufficiently realized to permit the system to run under its own power. Technological development, increase in population, and the like are not in themselves capable of providing a dynamic element in the capitalistic system, any more than is the "reproductive tendency of capital," of which Marx made so much.

The emphasis for Sombart is thus on the value-elements in action rather than on the situational conditions—a placing of emphasis quite opposed to that common in the positivistic tradition. Since it has produced capitalism, Sombart concluded that this spirit must have preceded the development of the system. Whence, then, this all-important spirit of capitalism? Sombart can be said to give no satisfactory answer to this problem. In *Der Bourgeois* he argued that Weber's famous association of the spirit of capitalism with the Protestant ethic was unacceptable, but he offered nothing substantial in its place. We are left with a description of its embodiment in certain groups, but otherwise it hovers unexplained as a mysteriously potent force behind the development of capitalism.

Whatever the uncertainty of the provenance of this capitalistic spirit, its prominent position in Sombart's account of capitalism serves to emphasize the peculiarity of the system in a way which has been unfortunately neglected in much discussion of capitalism. In making the action of the capitalistic entrepreneur an expression of a unique spirit, he avoids the plaguing tendency to see acquisitiveness in our economic system as instinctively determined. Sombart inherited from Marx the insight that, whatever may be the ultimate aims of the capitalistic entrepreneur, he must make a profit as a necessary prerequisite to the attainment of these aims. The unlimited character of acquisitiveness in a capitalistic system, wherein the goal is not merely the attainment of an income appropriate to a given status but rather its maximization, is derived from two sources. One is the result of rationalization of business enterprise in money terms. The wide and indeterminate applicability of money profits as a means to further ends makes them particularly prone to take the character of unlimited desirability. Moreover, the dynamic spirit of enterprise, which is one major part of Sombart's capitalistic spirit, is expressed in a competitive preoccupation with business enterprise as a source of power and enhanced status through "success." In short, Sombart's position leads him to a recognition of what may be called the "institutionalization of self-interest" in the modern capitalistic system. His description of the progressive emancipation of capitalistic economic activity from considerations other than the maximization of profit is thoroughgoing and fascinating.[24] In particular, one sees clearly the progressive autonomy of modern capitalistic enterprise from involvement in any particularistic consideration of individuals.[25]

It may now be seriously questioned whether Sombart's emphasis on the peculiarity of the modern capitalistic system is justified. This splitting of the course of development of Western society into distinct units, each characterized by its own special spirit, has been a source of much criticism of Sombart's work. It seems unquestionable that this criticism is justified, inasmuch as he has gone too far in reacting from the Marxian conception of progressive development through necessarily related stages.

This can be seen most clearly in the treatment of technology. As noted above, the technologies of Sombart's systems possess special character-istics. The traditionalism of the precapitalistic era gives way to empirical rationality in the age of early capitalism and, finally, to scientific ra-tionality in the age of high capitalism. Certainly, Sombart makes out a good case for the accuracy of these designations as empirical descrip-tions, but it seems much more satisfactory to regard the process roughly as one continuous development than as the expression of at least two distinct spirits.

Certain other features of Sombart's general scheme may possibly be traceable to polemical overcompensations. It has already been noted that his first two systems are not very clearly differentiated, notably in the all-important spirit. On the other hand, the periods of early capitalism and high capitalism are distinct in very important characteristics, notably in the role of the state and the character of technology; the spirit, while capitalistic in both cases, is described as "bound" in the one case and "free" in the other.[26] Sombart's strong reaction against those who would find the beginnings of capitalism in eighteenth-century English inven-tions and his consequent desire to exhibit typically capitalistic character-istics in previous periods may account for this delineation of the system. In any case there seems to be good reason for distinguishing two systems since the Middle Ages, rather than one.[27]

Sombart's ethical attitude toward the subject of his life's work is negative and pessimistic. For all of Marx's revolutionary antipathy to capitalism, Marx saw in it a necessary and proximate stage on the way to a better society. What for Marx should be honored as a mother, bearing a savior in her womb, becomes for Sombart a sterile monster, from which nothing can be expected. Man must seek salvation through other means than capitalism.

This antipathy has been fairly constant through Sombart's intellectual development, and hence it is not accurate to say, as sometimes has been done, that after World War I he transferred the source of all evils from capitalism to socialism and, in particular, Marxism. Nonetheless, after the first World War he abandoned a long-held sympathy for social-ism and heaped much responsibility for the miseries of the world onto it. Essentially, it was a reaction similar to that against capitalism.[28] He found in the materialism of socialism the same inadequacies as he had found in the dehumanizing mechanical monster of capitalism. A transition took place, now grown familiar among intellectuals of our time, in which he became definitely religious and insistent on spiritual values. Coupled with this was a growing nationalism, which had begun with his patriotic wartime writings and maintained its strength during Germany's travail of the twenties. Against this background it is evident that his pledge of allegiance to the Third Reich in the *Deutscher Sozialismus* was not merely an accommodation to a new state of affairs. His renunciation of Marxian socialism contained therein is scarcely more complete than it is in the much earlier *Proletarische Sozialismus,* written under the Republic, a work in which he endeavored to show that none of the socialist leaders were true Germans. In *Deutscher Sozialismus,* "the eternal German spirit" replaces the spirit of capitalism as the dominant element in Sombart's thinking. The book is unquestionably a sincere presentation of the beliefs of Sombart, the man and the patriot. As such, we cannot here quarrel with him, except when he intimates that his discussion is within the bounds of science; such vagaries are difficult to accept from one who argued so stoutly for the *Wertfreiheit* of science.[29]

Fortunately, this dissatisfaction with capitalism and its social products did not keep Sombart from giving an objective account of its development. *Der moderne Kapitalismus* is a highly individual work, and, though its accuracy in detail has been attacked by historians, it stands as the most vivid and comprehensive picture of the growth of capitalism which we possess. In concentrating attention on capitalism, it does not do full justice to other equally distinctive features of the organization of economic activity in our society, notably those centering around the professions.[30] The tendency is thus to give capitalism too exclusive importance in characterizing modern Western economic life. Proper adjustment of perspective in this respect is one of the promising tasks for social scientists of our time.

IV. SOMBART AND GENERAL SOCIAL THEORY

In summary, we may briefly consider the significance of Sombart's work for social theory. His own conclusions as to the possibility and utility of general social theory we have seen to be negative. In general, his own work supports his contention for the type of theory he uses. The individuality of his system offers little encouragement to those convinced of the fruitfulness of comparative institutional studies. It may be that the organic complexity of a system like capitalism is so great that its emergent properties make it, in a high degree, incommensurable with other systems of possible use in comparative work. That this is not entirely the case may be argued from the patent fruitfulness of Weber's comparative studies in support of his thesis that the Protestant ethic was a necessary condition to the emergence of capitalism. Sombart's treatment of capitalism seems, further, to involve a personal element, akin to an artistic production, which makes it difficult for subsequent workers to add more than criticism or commentary. This is consonant with Sombart's conception of the nature of the *Geistwissenschaften*. In these sciences it is not possible for a generation of scholars to stand on the shoulders of their predecessors, as it is in the natural sciences. Understanding social systems for Sombart is not a matter of successive approximations to the goal of complete understanding but an irregular process, dependent on the appearance of individual genius. Whatever may be said for such a point of view on other grounds, it is unattractive to those preoccupied with the task of building a body of general theory in the social sciences. To these latter, whatever his own theory in the matter, Sombart's work offers much that is suggestive for this ambitious building. In this respect, we may apply to him his own remark on Taine: He was better than his theory.[31]

NOTES

1. A translation of *Der moderne Kapitalismus* by K. F. Geiser has been promised. A condensed form of this work has been published in English by F. L. Nussbaum, under the title *A History of the Economic Institutions of Europe* (New York, 1933). *Die Juden und das Wirtschaftsleben* and *Der Bourgeois* have been translated by M. Epstein under the respective titles *The Jews and Modern Capitalism* (London, 1913), and *The Quintessence of Capitalism* (London, 1915). The later work, *Deutscher Sozialismus,* has been translated by K. F. Geiser under the title *A New Social Philosophy* (Princeton, N.J., 1937).

2. Biographical material and a bibliography may be found in M. J. Plotnik, *Werner Sombart and His Type of Economics* (New York, 1937).

3. See *Die drei Nationalökonomien* (Munich, 1930), pp. 288–91. His position in these matters is similar to Weber's, with whom he participated in historic discussions of the problem. For Weber's position see Talcott Parsons, *Structure of Social Action* (New York, 1937), pp. 591–601.

4. *Die drei Nationalökonomien, passim.*

5. For a brief summary of this position as presented by Rickert and Dilthey see the article of Alexander Goldenweiser in H. E. Barnes, H. Becker, and F. B. Becker, *Contemporary Social Theory* (New York, 1940), pp. 93–109.

6. In particular, *Die drei Nationalökonomien,* pp. 125–37.

7. In no place does Sombart give a clear statement of his position (see *ibid.,* chap. xiii. "Das Verstehen").

8. *Ibid.,* pp. 174–75.

9. Parsons, *op. cit.*, pp. 476–77. My debt to Professor Parsons in all these matters is profound (see also the paper in Barnes, Becker, and Becker, *op. cit.*, pp. 620–27).

10. *Die drei Nationalökonomien*, p. 301.

11. *Ibid.*, p. 196.

12. See, e.g., *Vom Menschen*, p. xxi.

13. *Der moderne Kapitalismus*, I, xi-xii. All references are to the 2d ed.

14. *Die drein Nationalökonomien*, pp. 299–300.

15. *Der moderne Kapitalismus*, I, 13 ff.

16. This tendency is especially marked in *Die drei Nationalökonomien*, which is literally a hierarchy of triads and strongly suggests artificial organization.

17. *Der moderne Kapitalismus* I. 319.

18. *Ibid.*, pp. 327 ff.

19. See, e.g., *ibid.*, III, 951 ff., where he traces the persistence of the self-sustaining and handicraft economies into the heyday of capitalism.

20. *Ibid.*, I, 329.

21. *Ibid.*, II, 1111 ff.

22. *Ibid.*, pp. 1137 ff.

23. For this aspect see especially *Der Bourgeois*, pp. 441 ff.

24. Especially *Der moderne Kapitalismus*, II, 99–173.

25. These matters are discussed in T. Parsons, "Capitalism in Recent German Literature," *Journal of Political Economy* (1928), XXXVI, 641–61.

26. *Der Bourgeois*, p. 461.

27. Parsons, "Capitalism," pp. 656–58.

28. See R. Michels, *Bedeutende Männer* (Leipzig, 1927), pp. 140 ff.

29. For a highly critical appraisal of *Deutscher Sozialismus*, see Paul K. Crosser, "Werner Sombart's Philosophy of National-Socialism," *Journal of Social Philosophy*, April, 1941, pp. 263 ff.

30. See Talcott Parsons, "Professions and Social Structure," *Social Forces*, XVII (1939), 457–67.

31. *Vom Menschen*, p. 98.

CHAPTER XV

LEONARD TRELAWNEY HOBHOUSE: EVOLUTIONARY PHILOSOPHY IN THE SERVICE OF DEMOCRACY AND SOCIAL REFORM

HARRY ELMER BARNES

I. GENERAL NATURE OF HOBHOUSE'S WORKS AND OF HIS SYSTEM OF THOUGHT

A. HOBHOUSE AND SPENCER

IT MIGHT seem unusual that England, the country of Herbert Spencer, should, in the five decades following the publication of the first volumes of his *Principles of Sociology,* have produced but one scholar whose writings are of a sufficiently high order to mark him as the worthy successor of England's great philosopher and sociologist.[1] This writer was Professor Leonard Trelawney Hobhouse (1864–1929).[2]

Like Spencer, Hobhouse developed his sociological system as a part of a general philosophy of evolution. There is a still closer similarity between the two systems, in that Spencer conceived of the evolutionary process as one of progressive differentiation and better adjustment, and Hobhouse viewed it as a growth in correlation and harmony, and both looked upon society as an organic unity. But here the resemblance ceases. Spencer held that the course of evolution moves on automatically, regardless of the interference of man. He believed that the latter could, at best, have only an indifferent effect and was extremely likely to hinder the process. Hobhouse claimed, on the contrary, that, however much the evolutionary process may depend upon automatically working factors, such as the struggle for existence, social evolution has come to rest more and more upon conscious control by the human mind. From our period onward, progress will depend primarily upon the conscious direction of the social process by the social mind. Again, while Spencer's conception of the organic nature of society rested upon a wide use of the biological analogy, Hobhouse eschewed the use of technical biological

330

terms and only implied the essential unity and interdependence of social life.

While both were avowed Liberals in English politics, Spencer's liberalism was of the "mid-Victorian" individualistic brand of Cobden and Bright, while Hobhouse was a supporter of that newer liberalism of Asquith and Lloyd George which abandoned most of the laissez faire tenets of the earlier period. It was the growth of this modern phase of liberalism which compelled Spencer in his later years to find himself more inclined to favor the policies of the Conservative party.[3]

One thus finds in Hobhouse the interesting combination of a writer who approaches the problems of society from the standpoint of a philosopher of evolution of a most thorough and recent type, of a sociologist unsurpassed in any country for breadth and profundity of learning, and of a liberal democrat in politics. From a writer who thus combined some of the best elements of sociological thought, one can look for a fair sample of what the sociologists have to contribute to a theory of society and the state.

B. THE FOUNDATION OF HOBHOUSE'S SOCIAL PHILOSOPHY

Attention may now be turned to a brief summary of the main propositions in Hobhouse's general philosophical system which he consistently carried over into his explanation of social phenomena.

In the first place, Hobhouse lays down the premise that any valid body of thought must rest upon the methods and discoveries of the most recent scientific endeavor. Its truth must be ascertained by testing it out through a study of experience, carried on according to scientific principles. Since evolution is the basis of all modern science, it may rationally be assumed to be the cornerstone of any modern system of social thought. As a philosopher, Hobhouse may, therefore, be classed as an evolutionist and an empiricist. He sums up his position on these points as follows: "In the meantime, I was convinced that a philosophy that was to possess more than a speculative interest must rest on a synthesis of experience as interpreted by science, and that to such a synthesis the general conception of evolution offered a key."[4]

The contradictions in the evolutionary theory as applied to human progress, which were so strikingly pointed out by Huxley, were due to the attempts of extreme exponents of evolution and pseudo-Darwinian writers to reduce all mental and social processes to one common level of interpretation and to ignore or deny any real differences of kind between biological and social processes. The real solution of the difficulty lies in an impartial and dispassionate study of mental and social evolution to see what has really been its course.[5]

The process of evolution may have been mainly automatic in the development of the animal kingdom prior to man, and even among primitive men. But there is an increasingly conscious control of the mind over material factors, and, at a certain stage in the development of humanity, the whole process becomes predominantly dependent for its future course upon rational control by the collective mind of society. Hence human progress cannot be assumed to be either inevitable or automatic. The struggle for existence and natural selection predominated in evolution until the gradual development of the human mind was able to produce sufficient mental advantages and compensations to overcome physical handicaps.

Until these mental advantages were sufficient to compensate for weaker physical powers, a stronger and more brutal civilization was likely to wipe out a more cultivated one. Such danger was averted only when mental evolution had reached such a stage that it could control all the vital conditions of human life: "Now it seemed to me that it is precisely on this line that modern civilization has made its chief advance, that through science it is beginning to control the physical conditions of life, and that on the side of ethics and religion it is forming those ideas of the unity of the race, and of the subordination of law, morals, and social constitutions generally to the need of human development which are the conditions of the control that is required."[6]

The similarity of this thesis to Lester F. Ward's main contribution to sociology is obvious, but Hobhouse's originality is vindicated by his divergence from Ward on many points and by the numerous scholarly volumes in which he develops this doctrine in detail. Morever, Hobhouse's far greater command of the data of social and cultural evolution allowed him to speak with greater exactness and authority than did Ward.

Evolution, thus, according to Hobhouse, may be viewed as the stages in the development of consciousness and self-consciousness and the resultant control of mind over the conditions of life.[7] Hobhouse admits the broad similarity of this doctrine to that of Hegel and holds that he accepts the element of truth advanced by Hegel, while rejecting his metaphysical vagaries and his contention that reality is entirely spiritual.[8] His system may, then, be regarded as an attempt to harmonize the valuable parts of the systems of Spencer and Hegel, in other words, to effect a scientific reconciliation of evolutionary materialism and metaphysical idealism. Spencer's attempt to explain reality by a purely mechanical and materialistic system and Hegel's insistence upon spiritual reality are rejected, while Spencer's conception of evolution as a synthesis is combined with Hegel's doctrine of the development of consciousness and purpose as the vital factor in human progress.

If the growth of conscious control over the conditions of life is the essential element in the evolutionary process, then some method must be provided for measuring the growth of consciousness, if the investigation is to have any scientific interest or validity. This standard of measurement Hobhouse finds in the principle of correlation: "I came to take the correlation which is effected in consciousness between different portions of our experience or between different acts and purposes as the basis of classification..... It is by correlation that the mind introduces order and establishes control."[9] The principle of correlation is particularly useful, since it will serve for measuring the elementary mental states of lower organisms, as well as the higher mental processes of man, the evolution of social structures, and the progress of civilization. There is a broad correlation between the growth of mental range and control and the development of human culture, which, in turn, provides an evolutionary basis for a sound sociological ethics.

As a result both of a detailed inductive study of the evolutionary process, taking the growth of consciousness as measured by correlation as the central theme, and of a philosophical analysis of the conception of evolution, thus considered, Hobhouse was led to accept the view of evolution as a purposive process: "It is submitted as a sound working hypothesis that the evolutionary process can best be understood as the effect of a purpose slowly working itself out under the limiting conditions which it brings successively under control."[10]

While at first opposed to the teleological view of the evolutionary process, Hobhouse was compelled by his detailed empirical studies to accept this conclusion. This purposive element, thus revealed, may be summarized as "a development of organic harmony through the extension of control by mind operating under mechanical conditions which it comes by degrees to master.....[11] In the higher organisms the work of establishing new correlations, and therefore in particular the work of adapting the organism to a higher synthesis, is the function of the mind, and in particular of that union of mind-functions which constitutes consciousness. The *growth of harmony* becomes, if not from the first, identical with the growth of mind."[12]

This vital principle of harmony, which reveals the universal purpose, he defines briefly as "mutual support between two or more elements of a whole."[13] A *harmonious system* is, then, one in which the parts work in coherence and co-operation. Progress may be regarded as the evolution of harmony, demonstrated by the increased co-ordination and correlation between the parts of the whole. As Morris Ginsberg puts it, Hobhouse conceived of development as "consisting in the extension of harmony through a series of syntheses, effected by the liberation of elements originally in conflict and the building up of structures of varying degrees of plasticity, scale and coherence."

In the development of this harmoniously organized system, which is the essence of the evolutionary process, reason comes to play a dominating part. Hobhouse thus takes a stand against the anti-intellectualistic attitude of some present-day psychological sociology. He says:

Reason is a principle of harmony pervading experience and working it into an organic whole. So understood, reason is supreme in the mind simply as that which embraces every element of experience, interconnects every feeling and thought, takes account impartially of every suggestion and every impulse, and weaves of them all a tissue which is never ossified but always plastic and recipient. It is the conscious expression of that impulse to harmony which dominates the entire evolution of mind, and the rationality of the process is the best guaranty of its ultimate success.[14]

While Hobhouse lays stress upon mental development as the most vital aspect of the evolutionary process, he disclaims any support of a spiritualistic monism. He simply maintains that the mental element becomes increasingly prominent as evolution proceeds: "There is a spiritual element integral to the structure and movement of reality, and evolution is the process by which this principle makes itself master of the residual conditions which at first dominate its life and thwart its efforts."[15] To put it concisely, mind provides the principle of orderly growth within reality.

Professor Hobhouse first developed this system of thought in four large and scholarly works which consumed twenty-six years in preparation. They form successive stages in the development of his system.

The foundations and presuppositions requisite for the construction of a valid system of thought were laid down in *The Theory of Knowledge,* published in 1896. The evolution of animal consciousness and the transition to human mentality were set forth in *Mind in Evolution,* published in 1901. The evolution of human and social consciousness is analyzed at length in *Morals in Evolution,* first published in 1906.[16] Finally, the results of the empirical studies carried on in *Mind in Evolution* and *Morals in Evolution* were reconciled with the philosophical implications of the process of evolution in *Development and Purpose,* published in 1913. In that work the process of evolution is set forth as a purposive development expressing itself in the working-out of a harmonious and rational system of mental processes and social relationship.

While the writer could by no means assume to pass competent technical judgment on any of these works, with the exception of *Morals in Evolution,* the almost unanimous praise of their high quality by a large number of specialists whose reviews have been consulted, as well as their comprehensive scope, would seem to accord Hobhouse the supreme place as a constructive philosopher among modern sociologists. Of course, his rank at present as a systematic sociologist would be much lower. Morris Ginsberg pays Hobhouse the following tribute in his article on Hobhouse in the *Encyclopaedia of the Social Sciences:*

> The range of Hobhouse's work was encyclopaedic. He was one of the pioneers of comparative psychology; he developed a technique for the handling of the vast and chaotic data of anthropology; he laid the foundations of a scientific sociology; in ethics and social philosophy he gave a penetrating and fruitful restatement of rationalism; and he attempted a synthesis of his scientific and philosophical studies on a scale which must win for him a high place among the systematic thinkers of the world.

Hobhouse re-wrote, condensed, and clarified his social philosophy in four brief books, *The Metaphysical Theory of the State* (1918), *The Rational Good* (1921), *Elements of Social Justice* (1921), and *Social Development: Its Nature and Conditions* (1924).

The Metaphysical Theory of the State was primarily a war product and represented Hobhouse's revulsion against the notion of political omnipotence and *Realpolitik* in the political writings of Hegel and the German idealistic philosophers. It is comparable to John Dewey's book on *German Philosophy and Politics.* It is valuable as a corrective but is the least calm and philosophical of Hobhouse's writings.

The Rational Good is an expansion of the basic theme in Hobhouse's writings, to the effect that the true social good consists in the triumph of harmony, co-ordination, and adjustment in society. This principle of harmony is the key to Hobhouse's system of social ethics. The *Elements of Social Justice* repeats this notion and works out Hobhouse's theory of social ethics in such practical fields as rights and duties, liberty and freedom, justice, property, the redistribution of wealth, and the realization of democracy. *Social Development* is the final statement of Hobhouse's conception of the principle of correlation as the measure of mental and social development. It is combined in this book with the notion of harmony and adjustment, as emphasized by a reasonable interpretation of the organic theory of society. This volume is the condensed synthesis of Hobhouse's social philosophy, combining his basic doctrines of evolution with his interpretation of social ethics. He ends on the theme of how far social science may formulate social laws to guide the quest for social justice and the common weal.

While these books cannot be ignored by the student of Hobhouse's social thought, they do not supersede the fuller and richer treatment of most of these topics in his earlier writings.

In any survey of Hobhouse's writings one must include one of his latest products, written just before his death, his magisterial article on "Christianity" in the *Encyclopaedia of the Social Sciences*. This is one of the ablest sympathetic interpretations of Christianity from the rationalistic point of view ever written. Hobhouse found the essence of Christianity to conform to his view of harmony and adjustment as the basis of social ethics. He concludes that the essence of the social teachings of Christianity "must be absorbed into anything that can call itself a rational reorganization of society."

C. THE GENERAL NATURE OF HOBHOUSE'S SOCIAL PHILOSOPHY

Hobhouse consistently carried over his general evolutionary doctrines into his sociological system as a means of interpreting social processes. His sociological doctrines are summarized in his suggestive little work on *Social Evolution and Political Theory*, which may be said to stand in much the same relation to Spencer's *Study of Sociology* that Hobhouse's volumes on the philosophy of evolution do to the *Synthetic Philosophy*. The *Social Evolution and Political Theory* epitomizes the sociological generalizations developed in Hobhouse's works dealing with his evolutionary system, as well as those put forth in two other works on political theory—*Democracy and Reaction* and *Liberalism*.

In the first place, as to the general field or scope of sociology, Hobhouse holds that it may be regarded chiefly as the science of human progress. He says:

> To form by a philosophic analysis a just conception of human progress, to trace this progress in its manifold complexity in the course of history, to test its reality by careful classification and searching comparisons, to ascertain its conditions, and if possible to forecast the future—this is the comprehensive problem towards which all sociological science converges and on the solution of which reasoned sociological effort must finally depend.[17]

The basic element in the social process, as well as the central subject of social evolution, is the interplay of human motives and the interaction of individuals: "The interplay of human motives and the interaction of human beings is the *fundamental fact of social life,* and the influence which it exercises upon the individuals who take part in it constitutes the fundamental fact of social evolution."[18]

Social progress, which is the prime object of sociological study, is not identical with social evolution. The latter term is the more comprehensive and may include retrogression as well as advance: "By evolution I mean any sort of growth; by social progress, the growth of social life in respect of those qualities to which human beings attach or can rationally attach value."[19] Nor is social progress primarily dependent upon biological factors. It is a cultural item and is chiefly a result of psychological and social forces:

> That is to say, there is progress just where the factor of social tradition comes into play and just so far as its influence extends. If the tradition is broken, the race begins again where it stood before the tradition was formed. We may infer that while the race has been relatively stagnant, society has rapidly developed, and we must conclude that, whether for good or for evil, social changes are mainly determined, not by alterations of racial type, but by modifications of traditions due to the interactions of social causes. Progress is not racial, but social.[20]

> So far as the eugenic principle advocates the substitution of rational for natural selection, it is, in the abstract, upon firm ground. Where it can be clearly established that a stock is tainted with a hereditary blemish so great as to outweigh its merits, it is desirable that the stock should not be perpetuated. . . . . On the other hand, the use of eugenic arguments against legislation designed to replace the struggle for existence by ordered social coöperation is at bottom a misapplication of the principle. It rests on the survival of the older ideas of natural selection under a new form, in a new terminology.[21]

Social progress, in the last analysis, Hobhouse regards as an increase in the harmonious adjustment of man to society, of the different types of social organization to each other, and of society as a whole to its environment: "Social progress may be regarded as the development of the principle of union, order, cooperation, harmony, among human beings."[22] The ideal society, toward which social progress should lead, is one in which this harmony is realized: "The ideal society is conceived as a whole which lives and flourishes by the harmonious growth of its parts, each of which in developing on its own lines and in accordance with its own nature tends on the whole to further the development of others."[23]

This growth of harmonious adjustment in society, which is the essence of social progress, is not solely the result of automatically working factors; it can be completely achieved only by the conscious action of will and intelligence: "But in all its meaning harmony, as already hinted, is something which does not come of itself, but is achieved in greater or less degree by effort, that is to say, by intelligence and will."[24] The growth of rational social control over the conditions of life may thus be taken as the test of social progress: "We may therefore take the growth of social mind and its control over the conditions of life as the measure of progress."[25]

The most significant fact in the modern stage of civilization is that it has now reached the point where the social mind has obtained control over the external conditions of life: "The distinguishing characteristics of our time are that civilization for the first time has the upper hand, that the physical conditions of life have come and are rapidly coming more and more within human control, and that at least the foundations have been laid of a social order which would render possible a permanent and unbroken development."[26]

D. THE NATURE OF HOBHOUSE'S POLITICAL WRITINGS

Professor Hobhouse's political writings, the chief conclusions of which are summed up in *Social Evolution and Political Theory,* are in the main contained in three works—*Democracy and Reaction* (1905), *Liberalism* (1912), and *The Metaphysical Theory of the State* (1918). The first two are devoted to an exposition of the principles of English liberalism and, to a less degree, of the general sociological foundations of democracy. *Democracy and Reaction,* which is the most vigorously phrased of the three works, deals mainly with an elucidation of those liberal and sociological principles which are opposed to nationalistic imperialism and to the doctrine that progress comes from a physical struggle for existence. It is one of the keenest indictments of imperialism and national egoism and was written to combat the imperialistic Unionists, led by Joseph Chamberlain, the party which Hobhouse believed was attempting to deprive England of all the social gains she had made during the last half of the nineteenth century. The *Liberalism* is less polemic in character and is unrivaled by any other work as a brief historical and analytical exposition of the growth of, and changes in, British Liberal policy.[27]

Hobhouse's political doctrines clearly reflect the conditions under which they were written. They are a reaction against: (1) the dominant anti-intellectualism, based upon the mistaken interpretation of biological factors of evolution, which led to a fatalistic trust in natural selection; (2) the imperialistic program, which he demonstrates to be an offshoot of this theory; (3) all one-sided and hasty attempts at social reform, so common in contemporary society; and (4) metaphysical adulation of an absolute state.

II. SPECIFIC CONTRIBUTIONS TO SOCIAL AND POLITICAL THEORY

A. GENERAL CONCEPTS AND DEFINITIONS

In discussing the question of the relation of sociology to political science, Hobhouse holds that the latter is one of the specialisms which grow out of the basic method of general sociology, namely, that specialism which studies the state as a political organization within society. The older discipline of political philosophy, which was in vogue from Aristotle to Bentham, was wider than either. It included what is now known as "sociology," in a rough way, as well as political science and moral philosophy.[28]

Hobhouse apparently looks upon sociology as neither the basic and elemental science of society, as maintained by Professor Giddings, nor the synthetic social science, as held by Professor Small. Rather, he regards it as a broad method of approach to social problems—a view very similar to that held by Professor Durkheim. Not that he holds it to be simply a method but rather that its scope is determined primarily by its method. He says on this point:

Properly considered general sociology is neither a separate science complete in itself before specialism begins, nor is it a mere synthesis of the social sciences consisting in a mechanical juxtaposition of their results. It is rather a vitalizing principle that runs through all social investigation, nourishing and nourished by it in turn, stimulating inquiry, correcting results, exhibiting the life of the whole in the parts, and returning from a study of the parts to a fuller comprehension of the whole.[29]

His conception of the subject matter of sociology as consisting chiefly of a study of social progress in its broadest aspects has already been pointed out above.

Professor Hobhouse's view of the nature of the state is particularly sane and up-to-date, and his distinction of the state from society, government, and the nation is clear. Society, he holds to be a plural number of interacting individuals held together by mutual interest—a product of physical and psychological forces resulting from the "interaction of individuals under the conditions imposed by their physical environment."[30] Society is, thus, the broadest and most comprehensive type of human grouping.

The state is that form of human association which is distinguished by the possession and use of coercive power. Of course, other forms of association have and exercise coercive power, but the members can escape from the coercion of a voluntary form of association by leaving it. In the case of the state, however, the citizen cannot escape from this power unless he leaves the territory under the jurisdiction of the state, and even this avenue of escape is not always open: "The state is one form of association among others, distinguished by its use of coercive power, by its supremacy, and by its claim to control all who dwell within its geographical limits."[31] The state is, however, only one of the associations, among many, which are striving for the maintenance and improvement of group life, and it has no claim to be viewed in the Hegelian spirit of adulation as an ineffable and mystic entity:

The State is an association of human beings—with the exception of the great world churches the greatest of all associations. It has no mystic sanctity or authority rendering it superior to morality or emancipating it from the laws by which transgression brings its own retribution in the lowering of character. It is an association which has its own special constitution and circumstances, and in the concrete its duties and rights, like the duties and rights of every other association and every individual, must be judged in relation to this constitution and to these circumstances.[32]

In his *Metaphysical Theory of the State,* Hobhouse makes a devastating attack upon the Hegelian theory of the state, as set forth by Hegel himself and by such English disciples as Bosanquet. He contrasts in the following manner the Hegelian theory of the state and the modern democratic conception of the state:

Herein lies the issue between these two views of the state. In the democratic or humanitarian view it is a means. In the metaphysical view it is an end. In the democratic view it is the servant of humanity in the double sense that it is to be judged by what it does for the lives of its members and by the part that it plays in the society of humankind. In the metaphysical view it is itself the sole guardian of moral worth. In the democratic view the sovereign state is already doomed, destined to subordination in a community of the world. In the metaphysical view it is the supreme achievement of human organization.[33]

Hobhouse calls attention to the fact that, while the Hegelian theory of the state has long been familiar to students of political philosophy, its practical significance has scarcely been recognized, and it has been passed over as the creation of a detached metaphysician:

In older days we passed by the Hegelian exaltation of the state as the rhapsodical utterances of a metaphysical dreamer. It was a mistake. The whole conception is deeply interwoven with the most sinister developments in the history of Europe. It is fashionable to conceive German militarism as a product of the reaction against a beautiful sentimental idealism that reigned in the pre-Bismarckian era. Nothing could be more false. The political reaction began with Hegel, whose school has from the first to last provided by far the most serious opposition to the democratic and humanitarian conceptions emanating from eighteenth century France, sixteenth century Holland, and seventeenth century England. It was the Hegelian conception of the state which was designed to turn the edge of the principle of freedom by identifying freedom with law; of equality, by substituting the conception of discipline; of personality itself, by merging the individual in the state; of humanity, by creating the state as the supreme and final form of human association.[34]

Hobhouse believes that the Hegelian view of the state is not only a generally dangerous and pernicious doctrine but that it also specifically encouraged that view of international relations which produced the first World War.

As to the relation between the state and the government, Hobhouse agrees with the general consensus in modern political science and sociology, namely, that the government is the agent to which the state delegates the practical function of political control: "Government is conceived not as itself the source of unquestioned authority, but as a function which certain individuals are delegated to perform as servants, 'ministers' of the public as a whole."[35]

Hobhouse distinguishes in an equally clear manner between the state and the nation. Logically speaking, the concept of a nation is quite different from either the state or a race. Nationality is primarily a psychic and cultural matter—a sentiment of unity which is apparently a direct heritage or an expansion of the older sentiment of unity based upon the kinship which existed in tribal society:

> Nationality, indeed, is not properly a matter of race. Most of the bodies of people which feel themselves to be nations are of highly complex racial origin. Yet the sentiment of nationality is confessedly analogous to that of kinship: it is a natural unity stronger in the fact than in the logical analysis, a composite effect of language, tradition, religion, and manners which make a certain people feel themselves at one with each other and apart from the rest of the world. Pride and self-respect are closely bound up with it, and to destroy a nationality is in a degree to wound the pride and lower the manhood of those who adhere to it.[36]

Yet, however different the state and nation may be as logical concepts, their practical relation is most intimate and important. If a state happens to embrace a unified nation, the difficulties of political administration are much less than is the case when political sovereignty is extended over a heterogeneous assemblage of different nations:

> Analyze it away as we may, it [nationality] remains a great force, and those states which are rooted in national unity have in them a great living power which will carry them through much adversity. But few states are fortunate enough to be one in nationality, and the problem of dealing with the minority nation is the hardest that statesmen have to solve.....[37]
>
> Analyze the difference as you will, and explain it as you may, the State which is also a nation will have a different life from the State which is a fortuitous concourse of atoms, or the mechanical aggregation of a series of conquests. To ignore the difference is to leave a huge sunken rock unmarked on the chart of political prophecy.[38]

To the generally agreed-upon attributes of the state—territory, population, and sovereign power—Hobhouse would, as has been pointed out, add that the state should be looked upon as primarily a product of social conditions and as the public form of association for advancing the collective interests of mankind. Like most sociologists, Hobhouse regards the state as originating out of the matrix of society and not as prior to other forms of association.

B. THE HISTORICAL EVOLUTION OF SOCIAL AND POLITICAL INSTITUTIONS

Professor Hobhouse's survey of the origin and historic development of the state is one of the best summaries of that subject to be found in any language. In any account of the origin of the state which purports to conform to historic accuracy, one must start with the assumption of mankind as already socially organized. The doctrine that the political bond was the first which held men together in groups finds no support in either history or psychology. The cohesive principle which formed the foundation of human association was mutual interest and sympathy, corresponding in a broad way to the schedule of vital human interests suggested by Professor Small, combined with Professor Giddings' theory of the "consciousness of kind."

This social bond is resolvable into many components, such as sympathy, interest in one's fellows, altruism, and combination for mutual defense against enemies and for the advantages of industrial co-operation. In addition to this general basis of human association, one may find in each period of social evolution some dominating social bond. While not so fundamental as that of mutual interest, it is more direct and apparent and serves to "give character to the society as a whole." The history of social organization has revealed three such characteristic social bonds—kinship, authority, and citizenship.[39]

The principle of kinship is the dominant social bond in primitive society. The crudest type of social organization among primitive peoples is that of the endogamous horde, but its form is rather exceptional among existing human societies. The most characteristic primitive group is the exogamous clan based on blood relationship, real and fictitious. The clan is, roughly speaking, an enlarged family, living in a group and held together by ties of descent through either male or female ancestors. If the descent is traced through the male, the clan is paternal; if traced through the female, maternal.

Hobhouse wisely refrains from committing himself to the view that the horde, the maternal clan, and the paternal clan represent an invariable serial sequence in the history of institutions, thus avoiding the chief pitfall of those historical sociologists who base their generalizations upon the work of the early evolutionary ethnologists and sociologists.

The larger groups of primitive society were normally the local community, usually composed of a number of contiguous exogamous clans, and the larger tribal union, which included several of these local communities.

In describing the form and degree of government found in this kinship stage of society, Hobhouse makes use of the statistical data gathered in his *Material Culture and Social Institutions of the Simpler Peoples,* written with Ginsberg and Wheeler. He finds that those groups that possess no effective government, aside from the household, constitute about one-half of the lower hunters, one-tenth of the agricultural and pastoral peoples, and are practically absent among the higher agricultural grades. Those which have a recognized governmental organization make up from one-quarter to one-third of the hunting peoples, about one-half of the agricultural and pastoral peoples, and over three-fourths of the higher agricultural peoples, often developing an embryonic kingdom in the latter type. These kinship associations "have much vital force, compactness, and endurance, but they are narrow and in proportion to their strength tend to be hard, self-contained, and mutually hostile. They are, moreover, adapted only to rude economic conditions and a rudimentary condition of the arts of life. Hence, they yield with advancing civilization to the rule of force, by which, in the guise of kingly authority far larger aggregations of men can be held together and a more regular order can be maintained."[40]

The very limitations of the kinship principle thus naturally led to that type of political organization which is first based upon force but is later transmuted into the principle of *authority*. This transition usually comes when a strongly organized paternal clan, for one reason or another, starts on a career of conquest. In this transitional process, personal liberty has usually been forfeited by both conquerors and conquered. The conquerors, in order to preserve the coherence and discipline essential to success, were compelled to confer almost unlimited authority upon the chief, while the conquered peoples, though sometimes slaughtered, were usually reduced to a condition of slavery or serfdom. The conquest usually increased the power of the victorious chief, who became converted into a king, with a religious sanction for his superiority.

There thus came into existence a political society, based upon despotism and reinforced by religion. This new type of political order could not long be based upon force alone, but had to develop a theoretical justification for its existence: "The simple but comprehensive code of despotism merely lays down that one man is divinely appointed to determine what is best for all others, and therewith transmutes arbitrary power into righteous authority and slavish subjection into loyal service."[41] Hobhouse sums up the characteristics and contributions of this type of political order as follows:

To sum up the results which the despotic principle—whether we regard it as authority resting ultimately upon force or as force transmuted into authority—has given us:

1st. as to the form of Society, we have—

(a) *The Absolute Monarchy*, where the king is divine and lord without restraint of the persons or properties of his subjects. This form has most vitality in relatively small and barbaric communities.

(b) *The Feudal Monarchy*, suited to wider areas where power is delegated, and the governing class form a hierarchy.

(c) *The Empire*, founded by the aggregation of kingdoms, overstepping national boundaries and exihibiting very varying degrees of unity and local freedom.

2nd. as to the nature of Government, the conception of a moral duty to the governed develops in proportion to the degree of unity achieved, but throughout law is conceived as based upon authority and the social system upon the subordination of class to class. For this order a religious sanction is found, generally in the special association of the ruler with the deity, often also in the semi-divine character of the ruling race, or caste, or finally, in the belief in their conquering and civilizing mission.

If, finally, we may endeavor to sum up in a sentence the function of this principle in human evolution, we may say that it belongs to the epochs of expansion in culture and improvement in the arts of life. It is one method by which large communities can be formed with greater facilities for self-government and for the maintenance of internal order than the primitive clan or village community can enjoy.[42]

The third type of political order is that which is based upon the bond of *citizenship* and which seeks to secure the recognition of personal rights and the advancement of the common good. The two fundamental features of any state based upon citizenship are "the responsible individual fully seized of civic rights and obligations, and the responsible government expressing the will of the whole society in law and administration."[43] In this third type of political order the relations between the governed and the governing, as compared with conditions in the previous stage of authority and force, are reversed. Government is no longer the source of final or sovereign authority, but merely the delegated agent of the people as whole. Law is no longer the ordinance of a despot, but the will of the people expressed through their elected agents: "The subjects of a government have now become citizens of a state, and the citizen has rights which are no less important than his duties. These rights hold good against the government just as they hold against other individuals, for it is a prime characteristic of the state based upon citizenship that it establishes the reign of law, and subjects its officers to this impersonal sovereign."[44]

This type of political organization, based upon citizenship, first came into being among the Greeks of Athens, where civic idealism probably reached the highest level in all history. At the same time there were inherent weaknesses in the Greek system that rendered its perpetuation impossible. The so-called "democratic" Athenian state included a large slave class, and the lack of unified action in the administration of government, together with petty jealousies among the separate city-states, prevented the formation of that large-scale political federation which was essential to self-preservation.

The Roman system degenerated into a political order based upon authority rather than citizenship. The Roman system of republican city-state government could not adapt its administrative mechanism to territorial expansion with speed or success; and, by the time that the idea of federation had made headway, the Roman republic had passed away.

The medieval city-states escaped the blight of slavery, which had been a curse to the Greeks and Romans, but their internal dissensions and their spirit of local isolation and exclusiveness were, if anything, more extreme than among the Greeks.

Because of these earlier failures, the experiment of founding a political system on the principle of citizenship had to be tried over again in the rise and development of democracy and the national state. In this last experiment there have been two stages—the period of absolutism, bringing political concentration and territorial aggression comparable to that during the earlier domination of the authoritative principle, and the period of the democratic reaction against absolutism. As a result of this latter struggle, which has occupied the greater part of modern history,

government has come to recognize that its position is only justified by its function in serving public order and the general happiness. .... The principle of personality has won the successive recognition of one right after another—the right to the protection of the tribunals or immunity from arbitrary punishment, freedom in religious matters, first freedom of conscience, afterwards freedom of expression and public worship, the right to discuss and criticize the acts of government, the right of meeting and association, ultimately the political right to secure these liberties by an indirect share in the government of the country—all the rights which, when taken together, make the modern state what it is.[45]

Hobhouse recognizes that the evolution of the modern state, based on the principle of nationality, has been an important progressive step in the history of human liberty, but he is also alive to the menace of nationalistic aggression:

Nationality is a Janus. It looks both ways—towards freedom and towards aggression. The struggles of subject nationalities with oppressors and conquerors have filled a great chapter in the history of freedom. Yet nationalities that have become free have often gone on to enslave others. . . . . Hence the rise of nationality, essential in its first stages to political liberty, is also a permanent menace to peace and order.[46]

Yet the emancipation of suppressed nations is the indispensable preliminary prerequisite of a permanent and enduring internationalism: "In proportion as political unity can be brought into accord with national sentiment the chances of international union are improved."[47]

The national territorial state is not likely, however, to be the final stage in political development, on account of one inherent weakness. The military ambition, which is based upon nationalism, is incompatible with the development of internal liberty and social harmony within the state itself. The growth of imperialism, with its double code of political ethics—one for home government and another for dependencies—has already seriously threatened the existence of liberal and democratic institutions.

Hobhouse maintains, as Kant and others had a century before, that the political prospects of the future depend upon the development of a spirit of internationalism, which will put an end to national aggression, with its wasting of the national resources and its encouragement of political despotism, and will allow a nation peacefully to devote itself to the settlement of its internal problems and the realization of social justice:

The future of the State is bound up with Internationalism. If the rivalries and jealousies of the civilized nations can be so far overcome as to admit of combined action in the cause of peace, there is every reason to expect that within each nation the rule of right will be maintained and developed. If, on the contrary, wars are to give way only to periods of armed peace, each country alike must gradually relapse into the rule of a dictatorship. The country state, therefore, can hardly be the final word of politics, but if progress continues it must consist in the quickening into active life of those germs of internationalism which the best statesmen of the nineteenth century helped to bring into a precarious existence.[48]

Federalism, as a principle, has suggested a method of reconciling the ideas of empire and democracy, while international arbitration is an equally effective agent for settling international disputes, if its aid were only more frequently and universally invoked.

In concluding the discussion of political evolution, Hobhouse makes it clear that he does not imply that these three broad stages in the development of the state have always followed one another in a uniform sequence in all cases. He simply holds that they are the dominant features of political evolution: "It follows that we cannot say that any of these forms succeeds another in serial form as we ascend the scale of culture. The history of society unfortunately is not so simple. All that we can say with certainty is that the three principles can be distinguished and the forms of social union arising out of them predominate at successive stages in the order named."[49]

Hobhouse's masterly excursion into historical and comparative jurisprudence cannot be analyzed in this discussion, but it might be mentioned in passing that nothing to equal it exists in any language within the same number of pages. He summarizes the main conclusions in the following paragraphs:

Briefly to resume the main phases in the evolution of public justice, we find that at the outset the community interferes mainly on what we may call supernatural grounds only with actions which are regarded as endangering its existence. Otherwise justice, as we know it, in the sense of an impartial upholding of rights and an impartial punishment of wrong-doing, is unknown. In the place of that we have at the outset purely private and personal retaliation. This develops into systematized blood-feuds of consolidated families and clans. At this stage, responsibility is collective, redress is collective, intention is ignored, and there is no question of assessing punishment according to the merit of the individual. When retaliation is mitigated by the introduction of money payments no change in ethical principle occurs. It is only as social order evolves an independent organ for the adjustment of disputes and the prevention of crime that the ethical idea becomes separated from the husk, and step by step the individual is separated from his family, and his intentions are taken into account, his formal rectitude or want of rectitude is thrown into the background by the essential justice of the case, appeals to magical practices are abandoned, and the law sets before itself the aim of discovering the facts and maintaining right or punishing wrong accordingly. ·

The rise of public justice proper necessitates the gradual abandonment of the whole conception of the trial as a struggle between two parties, and substitutes the idea of ascertaining the actual truth in order that justice may be done. That is at first carried out by supernatural means, viz., by the Ordeal and the Oath. These in turn give way to a true judicial inquiry by evidence and rational proof. The transition occurred in England mainly during the thirteenth century, the turning-point being marked by the prohibition of the ordeal by Innocent III in 1215. The early stages of public justice administered by the recently developed central power led to excessive barbarity in discovery and punishment of crime. It took some more centuries to prove to the world that efficacy in these relations could be reconciled with humanity and a rational consideration of the best means of getting at the truth. By so long and round-about a process is a result, so simple and obvious to our minds, obtained.[50]

With respect to the various forms of government, Professor Hobhouse had little to say about any type except democracy. His discussion of the nature, value, and limitations of democracy is extensive and illuminating.

First, as to the meaning of democracy, Hobhouse correctly points out that the term may be used in two different senses. It may mean the direct participation of the mass of the people in the affairs of government. Democracy in this sense—as a form of government—is, however, no longer practicable. The affairs of government have become so complex and multifarious that the citizens have neither the training nor the time to handle the business of government. Even in America, the land which has most cherished this conception of democracy, it has been recognized that it is a forlorn ideal, and a specialized and trained civil service has developed.

The other conception of democracy is that which is based on the idea of ultimate popular sovereignty—the idea of a democratic state as contrasted with democratic government, though Hobhouse does not make this vital distinction explicit. The successful operation of democracy, even in this second sense, is difficult, though not impossible. This is due to the complexity and remoteness of most political issues and agencies which cannot attract a high degree of interest on the part of the average voter. The problem is increased by that confusion of issues which is partially the result of deliberate obfuscation and evasion by party organizations and leads the voter to despair of intelligent action. Hobhouse agrees with Graham Wallas that one of the most essential steps which need to be taken to clarify issues and awaken a sense of interest and responsibility on the part of the mass of the voters in the affairs of government is to revive the vitality of local self-government.

That which may be reasonably expected of the mass of the citizens under a regime of popular sovereignty is that they will give their assent to those measures which will promote the common welfare. They cannot be expected to make independent investigations into the merits of every public question, but a successful democracy presupposes that there will be able leaders to enlighten the people and that the people, on their part, will be sufficiently interested to give heed to this advice of the leaders. Democracy need not be assumed to give a more efficient government than monarchy or bureaucracy, but it may be justly claimed that, by interesting and informing the people, democracy can develop the individual personality to a greater extent than any other type of government. If the people cannot be induced to study public questions, then the time is not yet ripe for democracy. Hobhouse sums up the advantages of democracy in the following paragraph:

Self-government, with all its defects, implies a recognition of the duties of government and the rights of the people; it postulates a measure of personal freedom and of equal consideration for all classes. It is the natural instrument of a growing sense of social solidarity, and the appropriate organ of a stirring national life. In a word, it is the political expression of the idea of Right on which the modern State rests, and if there be any other mode of government which would maintain that idea equally well, it has yet to be produced.[51]

If democracy is as important as this, it is worth while to examine some of the difficulties which it faces and to suggest some of the improvements needed to make its operation more effective in the future.

Hobhouse devotes the majority of his work on *Democracy and Reaction* to a substantiation of the thesis that nationalistic imperialism, with the resulting despotic government of inferior races, is incompatible with the existence or success of democratic self-government at home. It is impossible to develop an arrogant and overbearing bureaucracy to deal with foreign administration without suffering from a reaction of the same principle upon domestic affairs. On the other hand, there is no necessary conflict between democracy and an extension of imperial federation, which permits local self-government within the larger units. But, on the whole, internationalism rather than imperialism is the ally of democracy.

There is, again, the serious handicap, already pointed out, of the "dilution" of responsibility and of the complexity and confusion of issues in a modern democracy: "All that the ordinary voter feels about a given act of government, then, is that it is an act of men to whose return to power he contributed one vote out of some two million or more it may be three or four years ago, when probably quite other questions were under discussion, and whom he will not be able to dislodge until perhaps two or three years more have passed, by which time again other questions have come up."[52] One remedy that he suggests for this difficulty—an increase of the vitality of local self-government—has already been pointed out.

Another of the difficulties of democracy is to provide adequate leaders. No form of government is more dependent upon able statesmen for its success than democracy, yet it must be admitted that democracy is not well adapted to produce such men. A certain amount of brazenness is required of any man who puts himself forward as a public leader in a democracy, and this is a quality which few great men possess, while it is a quality which the politician possesses in an egregious degree. Therefore, while democracy is particularly in need of men who can guide public opinion with wisdom and discretion, this form of government makes it especially easy for quite the opposite type of person to assume the function of political guidance:

Finally, every form of government must be held responsible for the type of man whom it tends to bring to the front, and he who would weigh the merits and defects of democracy must take into account the character of the democratic leader. He must measure the power of brazen self-assertion and unblushing advertisement to bring a man to the front in a society like ours; he must allow that the capacity of gaining power depends more on the effective use of the rapier or the bludgeon in debate than on any proof of capacity to serve the country, while the art of maintaining power resolves itself into the art of so keeping up appearances as always to maintain the show of success for the moment, trusting to the levity of the public and the shortness of political memories to let the real final reckoning go by without close inquiry. A popular leader is not wont to take long views. He seldom looks farther than the next General Election. It would sometimes seem that he looks no farther than the next Parliamentary division, and as long as he keeps his majority, recks little of the effect his words may produce—it may be, on the future of a historic party; it may be on the broad interests of the nation; it may be in deepening the wretchedness of some persecuted people in a distant land. If sufficiently endowed with sophistical skill and debating readiness, a democratic ruler may become a very irresponsible being.[53]

Then, on the psychological side, democracy has to make assumptions which render its position precarious in proportion as they are not verified by experience. Democracy, of all forms of government, assumes the existence of a common or public will. Without such an organization of the will of the community, the democratic system must fall flat or degenerate into mere forms to which the real substance of democracy is foreign. Since it is well-nigh impossible for the mass of the people to study in detail the issues at stake, arrive at a common opinion, and manifest a united interest in public matters, it is particularly necessary that they be instructed by the press, "but the bulk of the press will lay before the public nothing that will not be popular. Its business is to tickle its master's vanity, to tell him solemnly that his duty lies there whither his prejudices already lead him, and to cover up and hide away all things done in his name which might be hurtful to his self-esteem. The few who persist in telling the truth share the traditional fate of the honest counsellor at the hands of the mob of courtiers."[54]

Finally, there are the problems of majority rule, including the protection of the minority and the avoidance of precipitate legislation. This problem has usually been looked upon from the standpoint of preventing radical legislation, and the aristocratic and conservative second house has been hit upon as a device to prevent undue haste in progressive measures. Hobhouse quite rightly points out that there is another side to be considered. At present, the restraints are all placed upon progressive tendencies and none on reactionary movements. There is nothing to frustrate extreme measures proposed by a conservative majority, while a liberal majority has to face the aristocratic upper chamber, the bench, and the conservative tendencies in society, in general, which are now usually upheld by minorities. Hobhouse, of course, wrote these passages several years before the Parliament Act of 1911 had shorn the House of Lords of its veto power.

A way to make the protection of the minority operate impartially, Hobhouse suggests in his proposal for an impartial second chamber, without the power to overthrow the government but with the right to refer appropriate measures to the vote of the people. He thus advocates a limited use of the referendum but stipulates that financial measures and others affecting only certain interests or localities should be eliminated from this sort of procedure.

Hobhouse points out how the English experience has disproved at least one common charge against democracy, namely, that it plays into the hands of the rabble. No sooner had the people finally been enfranchised in England in 1867 and 1884 than they put the Conservative party back into power and kept it there most of the time for two decades: "The first act of the new British democracy was to install the Conservatives in power, and to maintain them with but partial exceptions for nearly twenty years. Never were the fears or hopes of either side more signally disappointed."[55]

Hobhouse considers the question as to whether an efficient bureaucracy or a partially bungling democracy should be preferred. He believes that, with all its faults, the latter promises more for the future of mankind. Bureaucracy provides an excellent means for efficient administration but is very poorly adapted for determining policy on a large scale. It is "the means to an end rather than the means for determining an end." Again, a bureaucracy tends to become mechanical in its action and makes no provision for the development of the individual personality: "When administrative efficiency is made the supreme end, personal liberty, and religious and national divergencies become secondary and subordinate matters. There is not much consideration for the weaker brother, nor much patience with the offender. The grinding of the machine wears away these graces of humanity."[56]

Hobhouse makes it clear how, in the last analysis, the future of democracy is involved in the general progress of civilization and in the development of a socialized theory of politics. No people is fully enjoying political liberty when its industrial conditions are such as sap the vitality of the people or when its international affairs are in such a condition that armed preparedness is necessary: "We may fairly conclude that the ideas of democratic government, personal liberty, the supremacy of law as against arbitrary rule, national rights, the wrongfulness of aggression, racial and class equality are in principle and in practice closely interwoven."[57]

D. SOVEREIGNTY, LIBERTY, AND NATURAL RIGHTS

Hobhouse's use of the term "sovereignty" is hardly clear or consistent. It seems that in most cases he uses it to mean the lawmaking and enforcing power, though at times he appears to mean by it the ultimate power behind the constitution, which in democratic countries resides in the mass of the people. While this is essentially Dicey's distinction between legal and political sovereignty, Hobhouse does not explain explicitly which use he has in mind at different times.

In his *Morals in Evolution* he states that the distinguishing characteristic of the state based upon citizenship is the fact that law is now the embodiment of popular will and that government is subjected to the sovereignty of law. Again he asserts that the federal system in the United States is characterized by the division of sovereignty between the states and the nation. Of course, it is a cardinal quality of sovereignty, in the generally accepted sense, that it cannot be divided; but here Professor Hobhouse seems to refer to governmental power. Then, in his work on *Liberalism*,[58] he contends that "the old doctrine of absolute sovereignty is dead. The greater states of the day exhibit a complex system of government within government, authority limited by authority." Here, again, he must mean by "sovereignty" governmental power, for in no important modern state is actual sovereign power divided and distributed.

In his *Democracy and Reaction,* in discussing the possibility of an international state or of an enforcement of international agreements, he argues that law may be enforced without any sovereign power behind it if the customary precedent for the enforcement of law is strong enough. But he refers in many places to the conception of ultimate popular sovereignty as the indirect control of the government by the people—the ultimate power of the electorate to determine questions of law and political policy. In spite of these seeming inconsistencies, however, it need not be assumed that he does not have clear and definite conceptions about the nature of sovereignty, since nothing more than casual references to the term occur in his works and nowhere does he attempt a formal definition and interpretation of the concept.

Hobhouse's discussion of liberty and its reconciliation with authority is particularly clear and satisfactory. Liberty he defines in its most general sense as "the condition of mental and moral expansion, and of all forms of associated as well as personal life that rest for their value on spontaneous feeling and the sincere response of the intellect and of the will."[59] Practically, however, liberty means the freedom of individual conduct along those lines of activity which do not interfere with the similar privileges of all other normal members of society. Hence liberty, by definition, implies the presence of restraints, and, as a matter of fact, the task of realizing liberty in a society resolves itself into the problem of successfully organizing a system of restraints within the group. The old tradition of the antithesis between liberty and authority therefore vanishes—the former cannot exist as a universally realized ideal without the existence of the latter: "The function of State coercion is to override individual coercion, and, of course, coercion exercised by any association of individuals within the State. It is by this means that it maintains liberty of expression, security of person and property, genuine freedom of contract, the rights of public meeting and association, and finally its own power to carry out common objects undefeated by the recalcitrance of individual members."[60]

Hobhouse resolves liberty into its various aspects—civil, fiscal, personal, social, economic, domestic, local, racial, national, international, and political. By pointing out the degree and quality of freedom which each implies, as well as the corresponding restraints which are required, he gives a high degree of concreteness to a discussion which is otherwise wont to run into metaphysical generalities.

The question of liberty and the restraints which it involves, both upon individuals and upon society as a whole, naturally leads to the question of what justification there is for restraints. This justification is usually found in the so-called rights of individuals, and Hobhouse devoted his attention to an analysis of just what these "rights" actually mean and imply from a sociological viewpoint. A right, in its most general sense, he finds to be an expectation which will appeal to an impartial person as being adapted to the promotion of the general welfare of the community. There can be no right of the individual which conflicts with the common good of the community or is independent of society. Hence, there can be no "natural rights" in the older metaphysical and juristic sense, according to which man was assumed to possess rights antecedent to, and independent of, society and government. Yet if one conceives of the harmonious functioning of an evolving society as something natural, then one may readily discern natural rights in a sociological sense. Such natural rights would be those indispensable liberties and immunities which society would guarantee to the individual in order to secure proper adjustment between the welfare of society as a whole and the good of its constituent members:

> The rights of man are those expectations which the common good justify him in entertaining, and we may even admit that there are natural rights of man if we conceive the common good as resting upon certain elementary conditions affecting the life of society, which hold good whether people recognize them or not. Natural rights, in that case, are those expectations which it would be well for a society to guarantee to its members, whether it does or does not actually guarantee them. If this view is accorded, the more developed the conception of the common good the more completely will a society guarantee the natural rights of its individual members.[61]

Therefore, a right is virtually only a condition of social welfare, and there must be many such rights; it is the "problem of social philosophy to define in principle, and of statesmanship to adjust in practice the bearing of these several conditions."[62]

Liberty is, thus, a social conception which involves such a degree of restraint upon individual and group conduct as will insure the maximum freedom for society and for its component members. This restraint is, in turn, justified by the rights of individuals, which are the essential conditions of public welfare. Both liberty and rights are, thus, social in origin and justification, and liberty is reconciled with authority by a demonstration that it is really dependent upon authority for its origin, existence, and maintenance.

E. THE PROPER SCOPE OF STATE ACTIVITY

In handling crucial problems in every theory of the state—the function and sphere of political action and the reconciliation of authority and liberty—Hobhouse's treatment is among the best to be found in sociological literature. In the first place, he lays down the general rule that it is useless to try to define the sphere of legitimate state activity in specific terms, and at the same time hope to make that definition valid for every society. The scope of state activity is dependent upon the fundamental social conditions existing in any society. If the society is highly homogeneous, the state may successfully develop a considerable degree of activity and interference, while a similar program would cause a revolution in a society made up of many different nationalities with diversified customs and ideals. To give the problem a mathematical statement, the scope of state activity is a function of the composition, progress, and organization of the society under consideration: "The legitimate functions of the state must depend upon the whole circumstances of the society which is under consideration. The kind of compulsion that is necessary, the degree of success with which compulsion can be applied, and the reflex consequences of its employment upon the general life of society will depend essentially upon the composition of the community and the relation of the government to its subjects."[63]

But this does not mean that it is impossible to define in general terms the proper scope of state activity which will apply to any society. It may be stated, as a general principle, that the proper sphere of state activity lies in carrying out those lines of activity in which uniformity and concerted activity on the part of the society is necessary:

This function of state activity may now be defined in general terms as that of securing the best conditions for the common life, (a) so far as these are best obtained by the use of public resources and governmental machinery, (b) so far as such conditions are only obtainable by the use of compulsion; that is to say, where action is frustrated if not universal, and again where in the absence of regulation one man can directly or indirectly constrain another, infringe his rights, obstruct his rational choice, or take advantage of his weakness or ignorance.[64]

The state is an association for dealing with men in mass and with highly generalized matters and hence cannot possess that plasticity in administration which is essential in handling the higher aspects of social life or those questions in which variations of opinion and action are desirable. Its function is primarily to deal with the fundamental commonplace foundations of social welfare, which will allow the superstructure of voluntary effort and activity to function in safety and harmony:

> The life of the state is crystallized into the form of definite institutions, its ordinances have to be incorporated in laws and rules of universal application, and it must deal with men in masses and with problems in accordance with what is general and not with what is particular. Hence it is with difficulty adapted to the individuality of life; it is a clumsy instrument, as it were, for handling human variation. It is inadequate, to adapt Bacon's phrase, to the subtlety of human nature. Its sphere is the normal, the prosaic, the commonplace; its business is to solidify the sub-structure of society rather than to pursue its adornment. It can handle the matters upon which ordinary people agree rather than those upon which there is a variety of opinion.[65]

This conception is, indeed, far removed from Hegel's conception of the state as "perfected rationality," but it is probably far closer to the truth.

Hobhouse thus established in general terms the sphere of legitimate state activity as that which is primarily concerned with producing a coercively secured uniformity where necessary; with promoting the conditions which make possible an organic and harmonious development of society and of the individual; and, finally, with handling commonplace and routine affairs. He then turns to analyze more in detail some of the specific activities which the state might undertake within this general sphere of justifiable activity.

First, as to the desirable attitude of the state toward private property, he tries to steer a middle course between the antiquated metaphysical and legalistic theory of an inherent natural right of property and the socialistic view, which so far emphasizes the social basis of property that it ignores the psychological importance of the element of personal possession. The foundations of property are essentially social, for, without protection through the organized force of the community, the property of the individual would be very insecure and, without the co-operative industry of society, the production of wealth would be very small indeed:

> In spite of all criticism many people still seem to speak of the rights of property as though they were conferred by Nature or by Providence upon certain fortunate individuals, and as though these individuals had an unlimited right to command

the State, as their servant, to secure them by the free use of the machinery of law in the undisturbed enjoyment of their possessions. They forget that without the organized force of society their rights are not worth a week's purchase.[66]

On the other hand, one must not ignore the value of individual property rights in stimulating effort. Without this personal initiative, society would function as inefficiently as it would if the social basis of economic life were left insecure: "To maintain and stimulate this personal effort is a necessity of good economic organization, and without asking here whether any particular conception of Socialism would or would not meet this need we may lay down with confidence that no form of Socialism which should ignore it could possibly enjoy enduring success."[67]

The proper solution of the problem of property lies in allowing to individual effort a reward which will insure its efficient functioning and putting the remaining wealth at the disposal of society for the furthering of the collective welfare:

The central point of Liberal economics, then, is the equation of equal service and reward. This is the principle that every function of social value requires such remuneration as serves to stimulate and maintain its effective performance; that every one who performs such a function has the right, in the strict ethical sense of that term, to such remuneration and to no more; that the residue of existing wealth should be at the disposal of the community for social purposes.[68]

The method which Hobhouse recommends for dealing with the large fortunes of today, which represent a control of property and of politics quite out of proportion to the services of the individual possessor of wealth, is a progressive scheme for taxing inherited wealth, socially created forms of individual wealth, and excessively large incomes: "The true function of taxation is to secure to society the element in wealth that is of social origin, or, more broadly, all that does not owe its origin to the efforts of living individuals."[69]

Had Hobhouse lived to the present day, he would have seen his ominous predictions as to the disastrous effects of imperialism and war and his proposals as to drastic taxation of the very rich borne out with dramatic and drastic thoroughness. The second World War transformed the British Empire from a creditor to a debtor state and shattered its prosperity and solvency. The burdens thus entailed brought about a tax schedule so crushing that, in the fiscal year ending March 31, 1947, less than fifty persons out of a total population of about fifty millions retained an income of over \$24,000 after payment of taxes.

Society must try, as far as possible, to discriminate between earned and unearned incomes. It should levy a very considerable tax upon the unearned type and a sufficiently high one upon the earned incomes so as to prevent their rising unduly above what the receiver of the income contributes to society. Hobhouse admits that it would be hard to determine just what amount a great genius contributes to society, but he contends that this is never a practical question, "for the man of genius is forced by his own cravings to give and the only reward he asks from society is to be let alone and have some quiet and fresh air."[70]

This social appropriation of unearned incomes raises the question of what is to be done with the revenue thus obtained. This by no means so difficult a problem as it is to provide a method whereby society will be able to get a just reward for its share in the creation of wealth. The opportunities for fruitful expenditure in the realms of public education and sanitation have by no means been exhausted. Then there is the ever present question of improving the lot of the poor. Hobhouse points out the fallacy in the argument against the taxation of the rich for this purpose, which is expressed in the phrase of "robbing Peter to pay Paul." He shows how this charge is groundless, since, in the first place, to allow a person to absorb more wealth than he creates is to allow him to rob society and, in the second place, the fulfilment of the requirement of an organic and harmonious social life requires that no one be allowed to suffer from the lack of adequate physical comforts. He believes, further, that the proper method of handling the question of poverty is to aim at socialized prevention rather than the mere relief of individual destitution. Old age pensions and social insurance are steps in the right direction.

The discussion of the sphere of the state in regard to poverty naturally leads to an analysis of what the general attitude of the state should be in regard to labor. The basis of the legitimate interference of the state in problems of labor is twofold. In the first place, it is the duty of the state to control industrial contracts which are made under conditions in which one party is at a distinct advantage. It is perfectly obvious that the individual laborer is at a disadvantage in bargaining with his employer. Out of the recognition of this duty has grown the legislation that resulted, first, in the regulation of laboring conditions among women and children and then, gradually, an extension of the supervision of the state over the condition of adult male laborers. The second justification

of state interference with labor is to be found in the duty of the state
to provide for the normal functioning of the life of the mass of its citizens:

> If we grant, in accordance with the idea with which we have been working all
> along, that it is demanded of all sane adult men and women that they should live
> as civilized beings, as industrious workers, as good parents, as orderly and efficient
> citizens, it is, on the other side, the function of the economic organization of society
> to secure them the material means of living such a life, and the immediate duty of
> society is to mark the points at which such means fail and to make good the
> deficiency. Thus the conditions of social efficiency mark the minimum of industrial
> remuneration, and if they are not secured without the deliberate action of the State
> they must be secured by means of the deliberate action of the State.[71]

Furthermore, there is the problem of how far the state may rightfully
interfere in family affairs, and in matters of religion and education. The
state is justified in interfering in the affairs of the family in preventing
it from interfering with the liberty of individuals and on "the basis of
the rights of the child, of his protection against parental neglect, of the
equality of opportunity which he may claim as a future citizen and of
his training to fill his place as a grownup person in the social system."[72]
In the matters of religion, the state should refrain from any attempt to
prescribe a specific form of worship, but at the same time it should prevent such religious practices as contravene the welfare of society: "It is
open to a man to preach the principles of Torquemada or the religion
of Mahomet. It is not open to men to practice such of their precepts as
would violate the rights of others or cause a breach of the peace."[73] With
respect to education, the whole theory of the harmonious adjustment
of the individual to society and of the organic functioning of society,
which is the basis of Hobhouse's social theories, demands that the individual shall be fitted for an active participation in social life. Hence the
state cannot neglect the duty of providing adequate education for its
future citizens without being guilty of the gravest inconsistency.

Hobhouse agrees with the position taken a century earlier by Kant,
to the effect that the improvement and perfection of the internal arrangements of a political society are inseparably bound up with the provision
of external security. Throughout his *Democracy and Reaction* and in
his books written during the first World War, Hobhouse shows with
great clarity the fundamental antithesis between socialized democracy
at home and militarism and imperialism in foreign policy: "The supporter of the League of Nations finds in the requirement for internal

reform nothing but a pious platitude as long as security against external disturbance is not guaranteed."[74]

F. IS SOCIAL PROGRESS TO BE ACHIEVED BY CONSCIOUS EFFORT?

In his discussion of political and social reform Hobhouse emphasizes two of his fundamental theses—the idea of progress as an ever more successful achievement of social harmony and the doctrine that Western society has now reached the stage where it can achieve further development by the deliberate action of the social mind. In the first place, the old Spencerian and pseudo-Darwinian conception of "continuous, automatic, inevitable progress" must be given up, since social evolution is more or less distinct from biological evolution and its elements are quite different in their operation from the biological factors in organic evolution. Though, in the earlier stages of human development, consciously and deliberately planned legislation to achieve social progress was uncommon, if not unknown, society has now come to the point where it can, if it will, control the direction and degree of its own development. Here Hobhouse gives his assent to Ward's major thesis: "The turning-point in the evolution of thought, as I conceive it, is reached when the conception of the development of humanity enters into explicit consciousness as the directing principle of human endeavor, and, in proportion as the phrase is adequately understood, is seen to include within it the sum of human purpose in all its manifold variety..... Progress has consisted in the realization of the conditions of full social co-operation and in the extension of the rational control of life."[75]

Not only should progressive measures be brought under the deliberative control of the social mind; they must also be synthetic in outlook and designed to promote the harmonious development of society, for this is the essence of progress. This is where the danger enters from narrow-minded agitation for social reform that takes into account only one need for, or one method of, improvement. No plan for social reform can be permanently successful unless it recognizes the necessity for the harmonious and organic development of all society. What is needed to make this synthetic view possible is a comprehensive and well-balanced science of society.

G. THE SOCIOLOGY OF INTERNATIONAL RELATIONS

In treating international relations, Hobhouse was one of the most uncompromising critics of modern nationalism and imperialism. He stood firmly as a foe of manifest destiny, of the idea of the necessity of war to promote social progress, and of the notion that foreign affairs are a field where the ethics of personal relations do not apply. This was, of course, in keeping with the Liberal tradition established by Cobden and perpetuated by Gladstone. In a splendid paragraph he exposes the basic hypocrisy of the imperialistic apology for territorial aggression at the expense of a weaker people:

Of course in every case of aggression some excellent reason has been forthcoming. We were invariably on the defensive. We had no intention of going to war. Having gone to war we had no intention of occupying the country. Having occupied the country provisionally, we were still determined not to annex it. Having annexed it, we were convinced that the whole process was inevitable from the first to the last. On each several occasion we acted purely on the defensive, and on each several occasion we ended by occupying the land of our aggressive neighbors. Such is the fiction still solemnly maintained. The naked fact is that we are maintaining a distinct policy of aggressive warfare on a large scale and with great persistence, and the only result of attempting constantly to blink that fact is to have introduced an atmosphere of self-sophistication or in one syllable, of cant, into our politics which is perhaps more corrupting than the unblushing denial of right.[76]

Of course, each imperialistic country suffers at home for its crushing of the rights of others. As has been pointed out above, Hobhouse holds that imperialism and democracy are mutually exclusive and that the pursuing of an imperialistic program abroad reacts at home in destroying the reform program of a democratic regime. Along with the unfortunate general reaction of imperialism upon democracy, it diverts the attention of the people from the need for improvement at home and causes the revenues of the state to flow into costly armaments rather than into channels for the improvement of domestic social conditions.

As a remedy for the problem of imperialism, Hobhouse suggests an extension of the accepted code of individual ethics to the conduct of one nation with another. He believes that each nation should devote itself to the improvement of its internal conditions and leave other nations free to do the same. If there is ever any excuse for the voluntary interference of one nation with another, it must be on purely humanitarian grounds. He recognizes "that the nation which would endeavour to follow a lofty standard of duty and honour would, in the present state of international morality, be in the position of a man who should carry Christian principles into effect upon the Stock Exchange, or of a Quaker who should adhere to the strict tenets of his religion in the company of highwaymen."[77] Nevertheless, he feels that if each nation stopped short at insisting on the maintenance of its own rights, it would find its neighbors much more willing to co-operate in this respect. Finally, he believes that, in spite of the absence of an international sovereign to enforce the enactments of international law, the force of custom and the fear of ostracism would be entirely adequate to secure the enforcement of international law if the nations would co-operate heartily and sincerely in submitting their difficulties to arbitration.[78]

As might have been expected of an alert and thoughtful student of human relations, Professor Hobhouse was deeply interested in the fundamental sociological problems involved in the first World War, its causes, and probable results. These he briefly analyzes in his little book entitled *The World in Conflict*. He finds that, at just the time when the old European alliances and concerts were disintegrating from moral dry rot and were leaving Europe without any international guaranty against aggressive militarism, a very dangerous philosophy of force and *Realpolitik* was being developed out of a perversion of the biological formula of the survival of the fittest:

The biological theory of evolution which was the crowning glory of nineteenth century science could be interpreted as a justification of force and self-assertion. It then became a theory of revolt against law and morals, and more particularly against the morals of Christianity..... The idea of violence was in the air, then, in the years before the war; and it was not merely the violence that comes naturally from despair of all legal remedy. There was a deliberate theory of force. Men were being taught not to look too far ahead, not to wait till they could see where they were going, not to follow deliberately a reasoned policy, but rather to throw themselves on instinct, to strike a blow which would smash something and make an echo in the world even if they did not quite know what they were breaking or what would follow.[79]

This doctrine, which was fairly general in the Western world before 1914, was intensified and exaggerated in Germany through the addition of certain associated obsessions of recent origin: "Hegel's divine State, Treitschke's power, Nietzsche's contempt of restraint are fused together in the faith which animates the governing classes of Germany, political, military and academic—fused in the medium of some misty conception of the progress of mankind through competition and the fated superiority of the German race."[80]

In the latter part of this work and in the concluding chapter of his *Questions of War and Peace*, Hobhouse deals with the question of the necessary reconstruction of international relations which should follow the war if there was to be any hope that the world would be henceforth free from such calamities as the cataclysm of 1914–18.

Hobhouse sees two alternatives facing the states of the world—a continuance of militarism, preparedness, more wars, and the cumulative self-destruction of Western civilization, on the one hand, and the provision of "some orderly mode of governing the intercourse of nations," on the other.[81] The old cosmopolitanism, based on humanitarianism and free trade, died with Cobden. There is no longer any hope of reviving cosmopolitanism; only an internationalism based upon the recognition of both the independence and the interdependence of national states can serve as an adequate foundation for the international relations of the future. Hobhouse regards as insufficient guaranties of future peace such proposed solutions as the Hague Tribunal and arbitration agreements, union against an aggressive state which violates international law, and the economic boycott of offenders against the law of nations. "I am forced, therefore," he says, "to the conclusion that we must either go further or not attempt to move at all, and I should agree with my friend, Mr. Hobson, that there is no formal guarantee of a permanent peace except in the formation of an international state."[82] Hobhouse believes that the most practicable method of erecting a world state consists in developing a federation out of the Entente Alliance of 1914–18, then uniting this with a federation of neutrals, and finally taking in Germany, when it becomes certain that the pacific elements dominate that country. The following paragraph briefly summarizes his plan: "I would look forward, then, to the conversion of the existing Alliance into a permanent League or Federation, with a regular constitution and definite functions, which should include some measure of control over the production of munitions of war. But from the outset I would contemplate the extension of the League by the free entry of new members..... This would at once transform it from an ordinary alliance into something approaching a world-federation."[83]

There is little doubt that the events and outcome of the peace conference at Paris in 1919 disillusioned Mr. Hobhouse, as it did so many other hopeful liberals, on the matter of the adaptability of the Entente Alliance to furnishing the foundation of a just and durable league of nations.[84] No one can doubt, however, that the moral collapse of the peace conference and the events since that time have substantiated, rather than discredited, Hobhouse's thesis that some kind of world organization had to be provided if peace was to endure longer than was necessary for the European nations to recover from the losses sustained in the first world conflict.

H. EXTRA-LEGAL FORMS OF SOCIAL CONTROL

Of Hobhouse's detailed discussions of the origin and growth of those extra-legal forms of social control exerted by society over the individual, available space forbids more than a casual mention. In substance, he demonstrates how great a part of human conduct is the result of the more or less unconscious coercive power of social customs and traditions, which are often more tyrannical in their domination than the coercion of the codified law but are less odious to the individual because he accepts them as a matter of course or quite unconsciously bends to their sway:

> The greater part of each man's personal experience is made up out of his inter-action with others in the multifarious relations of life, and these relations, from the earliest known phases of human society, are controlled by customs which arise out of the needs of social life and are maintained by the social tradition. Through this tradition society exerts a continuous control over the individual, of which avowed and obvious coercion is the least important element. The vital fact is that from infancy upwards the social *milieu* into which he is born interpenetrates his thought and will, and turns his individuality into a creation of the time and place of his life.[85]

In conclusion, Hobhouse points out at length how the political and social theory of a period is a reflection of the social and intellectual conditions at the time that it is produced. He traces this in detail in regard to the development of the political creed of the English Liberals.[86]

I. CONCLUSION

To sum up very briefly the nature of his writings and the contributions of Professor Hobhouse to social and political theory, it might be said that his method of presentation is characteristically English. Like most English social scientists, he steers clear of abstract metaphysical questions in his strictly social theories and is eminently practical, concrete, and matter-of-fact in his analyses.

His insistence upon the necessity of harmonious social development as the proper goal of social evolution and upon the desirability of applying the best constructive thought to this problem, thus making it an artificially directed movement, cannot be too highly commended.

Again, his candid analysis of democracy, in which he makes plain its many defects and yet demonstrates with equal clarity that no adequate alternative for it has yet been discovered, is one which is likely to startle the complacent apologists of democracy but is equally designed to give courage to those who are seeking to eliminate its defects and to save its virtues for the benefit of humanity. Moreover, he clearly outlines what so many writers have ignored, namely, the very intimate relation and interdependence between social, economic, and political democracy.

He is also one of those clear-headed thinkers who understand that the modern state is not an isolated unit but is dependent for its internal prosperity and progress upon security against external aggression and upon freedom from the paralyzing expense of providing extensive armament for potential wars and imperialism. He therefore lent the weight of this authority as a student of social science to the support of those who are working to secure a stable and pacific international order.

NOTES

1. For Professor Small's explanation see *American Journal of Sociology*, XVIII (1912–13), 206–7. The best analysis of the social philosophy of Hobhouse is Hugh Carter, *The Social Theories of L. T. Hobhouse* (Chapel Hill, N.C., 1927).

2. Martin White Professor of Sociology in the University of London (1907–29) and first editor of the *Sociological Review*. Of course, this statement refers to sociologists in the strictest sense of the term and thus excludes the many brilliant English ethnologists, social psychologists, political scientists, moralists, eugenists, and metaphysical students of social phenomena.

3. Hobhouse's little volume, *Liberalism* (New York, 1911), is probably the best analysis of this fundamental transition in British liberalism.

4. *Development and Purpose* (New York, 1913), Introd. p. xviii. On Hobhouse's general philosophical approach to social issues and problems see Carter, *op. cit.*, chaps. i, iv, vii.

5. *Development and Purpose*, p. xix; *Social Evolution and Political Theory* (New York, 1913), chaps. i–ii.

6. *Development and Purpose*, Introd., pp. xx–xxii; cf. *Social Evolution and Political Theory*, chaps. ii, iv, vii; *Democracy and Reaction* (London, 1904), chap. iv; *Morals in Evolution* (New York, 1915), p. 637; see also *Social Development: Its Nature and Conditions* (New York, 1924), chaps. iv–x.

7. *Development and Purpose*, Introd., pp. xix–xxiii, and 364.

8. *Ibid.*, pp. xxvii, 154–55. Hobhouse's qualified acceptance of Hegel's evolutionary formula does not by any means imply that he accepts the Hegelian theory of the state. This he repudiates and severely criticizes (see *The Metaphysical Theory of the State* [New York, 1918], pp. 6, 23–24, 137).

9. *Development and Purpose*, Introd., p. xxiii; see also *Social Development*, pp. 301 ff.

10. *Development and Purpose*, p. xxvi.

11. *Ibid.*, p. 372.

12. *Ibid.*, p. 364.

13. *Ibid.*, p. 284.

14. *Ibid.*, p. xxix; cf. also *Democracy and Reaction*, chap. iii.

15. *Development and Purpose*, Introd. p. xxvii.

16. Third and revised edition (1915). Reviewed by Norman Wilde in the *Journal of Philosophy, Psychology, and Scientific Methods*, 1907; pp. 183–86, and by James Seth in *International Journal of Ethics*, 1907–8, pp. 375–81. This work is one of the most notable single contributions to the study of the mental and cultural evolution of humanity. This estimate is made in full knowledge of the bulky volumes of Frazer's *Golden Bough* and Westermarck's *Origin and Development of the Moral Ideas*. The former is no longer taken seriously in its theoretical aspects by any scientific student of ethnology, and the latter, while infinitely better, partakes of many of the faults of classical anthropology and manifests a far less subtle insight into the nature of human cultural evolution than Hobhouse's volumes (see Carter, *op. cit.*, chap. iii).

17. Editorial Introd. to the *Sociological Review*, I, ii.

18. *Social Evolution and Political Theory*, p. 33.

19. *Ibid.*, p. 8.

20. *Ibid.*, p. 39.

21. *Ibid.*, pp. 75–76; cf. also *Democracy and Reaction*, chap. iv.

22. *Social Evolution and Political Theory*, p. 127, cf. also p. 185. For a more complete treatment of harmony as the essence of social well-being see *Elements of Social Justice* (London, 1921), chap. i; and *The Rational Good* (London, 1921), chaps. iv–vi.

23. *Liberalism*, p. 136; cf. also *Social Evolution and Political Theory*, pp. 87, 92–93, 204–5; and *Social Development*, chap. iii.

24. *Social Evolution and Political Theory*, p. 93; cf. also pp. 162 ff.

25. *Ibid.*, p. 101.

26. *Ibid.*, p. 163. Contrast this view with that expressed by Graham Wallas, *The Great Society* (New York, 1914), p. 323, where he maintains that the distinctive characteristic of the present state of society is that, for the first time, society has allowed the conditions of its collective life to get beyond its control.

27. Mention might also be made of Hobhouse's remaining works, *The Labor Movement* (3d ed.; London, 1912), an analysis of the labor movement in England and its economic limitations and justification; *The Material Culture and Social Institutions of the Simpler Peoples* (London, 1915), a pioneer treatise in the extension of statistical methods to the study of comparative ethnology; *The World in Conflict* (London, 1915), a brief but penetrating analysis of the sociological causes and implications of the world war; and *Questions of War and Peace* (London, 1916), a profound dialogue on the causes, progress, and issues of the war, with a final chapter on the future of international relations. For a good account of the career and literary activity of Hobhouse see J. A. Hobson and Morris Ginsberg, *L. T. Hobhouse: His Life and Works* (London, 1931). On Hobhouse as a metaphysician and philosopher see J. A. Nicholson, *Some Aspects of the Philosophy of L. T. Hobhouse* (Urbana, Ill., 1928). The best summaries of Hobhouse's social philosophy are J. S. Burgess, "Certain Concepts and Contributions in the Social Science and Social Philosophy of L. T. Hobhouse," *Chinese Social and Political Science Review*, XIII (1929), 119–43; and Carter, *op. cit.* (see pp. 133 ff. of the latter for a bibliography of Hobhouse's writings and of comments on Hobhouse's contributions to philosophy and social science).

28. "Editorial Article" in the *Sociological Review*, I (1908), 4–9.

29. *Ibid.*, p. 8.

30. *Social Evolution and Political Theory*, pp. 29–30, 127–28; see also *Social Development*, chap. ii.

31. *Liberalism*, p. 133.

32. *Democracy and Reaction*, p. 207.

33. P. 137.

34. *Ibid.*, pp. 23–24. Hobhouse calls attention to Mr. Clarke's famous article in the *Contemporary Review* for January, 1899, pointing out the relation between the Hegelian philosophy and the Bismarckian policy.

35. *Morals in Evolution* (3d ed., 1915), p. 60; cf. also *Democracy and Reaction*, p. 221.

36. *Social Evolution and Political Theory*, p. 146; cf. also *Democracy and Reaction*, pp. 158 ff.

37. *Social Evolution and Political Theory*, p. 146.

38. *Democracy and Reaction*, p. 160.

39. *Ibid.*, p. 128; *Morals in Evolution* (3d ed., 1915), pp. 42–43; cf. also *Social Development*, chap. xi. For Hobhouse's handling of the problems of social evolution through a discreet use of the comparative method see Carter, *op. cit.*, chap. iii.

40. *Social Evolution and Political Theory*, p. 147.

41. *Morals in Evolution*, pp. 57–58.

42. *Ibid.*, pp. 59–60; cf. also *Social Evolution and Political Theory*, pp. 138–39.

43. *Morals in Evolution*, p. 63; cf. also *Social Evolution and Political Theory*, p. 140.

44. *Morals in Evolution*, p. 60.

45. *Ibid.*, p. 67; cf. *Liberalism*, chaps. ii–iii.

46. *The World in Conflict*, p. 63.

47. *Ibid.*, p. 86.

48. *Morals in Evolution*, p. 68.

49. *Ibid.*, p. 69; cf. also *Social Evolution and Political Theory*, p. 148.

50. *Morals in Evolution*, pp. 130–31.

51. *Democracy and Reaction*, pp. 186–87; for Hobhouse's final estimate of democracy see *Elements of Social Justice*, chap. xi.

52. *Democracy and Reaction*, pp. 182–83.

53. *Ibid.*, pp. 184–85.

54. *Liberalism*, pp. 183–84.

55. *Democracy and Reaction*, p. 50.

56. *Ibid.*, pp. 119–24.

57. *Ibid.*, p. 166; cf. also *Liberalism*, *pp.* 248–51.

58. P. 238.

59. *Social Evolution and Political Theory*, p. 200; cf. also *Elements of Social Justice*, chaps. iii–iv.

60. *Liberalism*, pp. 146–47.

61. *Social Evolution and Political Theory*, p. 198; cf. also *Elements of Social Justice*, chap. ii.

62. *Social Evolution and Political Theory*, pp. 198–99; cf. also *Liberalism*, p. 127, and *Democracy and Reaction*, pp. 131–37.

63. *Social Evolution and Political Theory*, p. 188.

64. *Ibid.*, pp. 200–201; for Hobhouse's detailed analysis of social and political justice see *Elements of Social Justice*, *chaps.* v–vi.

65. *Social Evolution and Political Theory*, pp. 186–87. This is practically identical with Durkheim's view.

66. *Liberalism*, p. 189; on Hobhouse's notions of property see, further, *Elements of Social Justice*, chaps. viii–ix; and Charles Gore (ed.), *Property: Its Rights and Duties* (New York, 1922), chap. i.

67. *Liberalism*, p. 191.

68. *Ibid.*, p. 209; cf. also *Elements of Social Justice*, chap. ix. Probably Professor Hobhouse would agree that this generalization is a good summary statement of the problem rather than its practical solution.

69. *Liberalism*, p. 202.

70. *Ibid.*, pp. 195–202.

71. *Ibid.*, pp. 204–5; cf. also pp. 163–64, 185–86.

72. *Ibid.*, pp. 39–40.

73. *Ibid.*, pp. 29–31; cf. also *Social Evolution and Political Theory*, pp. 181–82.

74. *Metaphysical Theory of the State*, p. 106; cf. also *Democracy and Reaction*, pp. 49 ff.

75. *Social Evolution and Political Theory*, pp. 155–56; cf. also *Development and Purpose*, pp. 281 ff.

76. *Democracy and Reaction*, pp. 28–29; for an excellent treatment of Hobhouse's application of sociological principles to world affairs see Carter, *op. cit.*, chap. v.

77. *Democracy and Reaction*, pp. 204–5.

78. These arguments are summarized in *Democracy and Reaction*, chap. viii. In the 1915 edition of his *Morals in Evolution*, Hobhouse mentions in a footnote that his statement that the future of democracy and social progress was bound up with the progress of internationalism was written before the outbreak of the first World War.

79. *The World in Conflict*, pp. 38, 50.

80. *Ibid.*, p. 56.

81. *Questions of War and Peace*, pp. 183–86.

82. *Ibid.*, pp. 192–99.

83. *The World in Conflict*, p. 94.

84. See J. M. Keynes, *Economic Consequences of the Peace* (New York, 1920), for the most trenchant analysis of the manner in which the old diplomacy and international policies dominated the Paris conference.

85. *Social Evolution and Political Theory*, p. 94; cf. also *Morals in Evolution*, Part II.

86. Cf. *Liberalism*, *passim*, particularly chap. iii; and *Democracy and Reaction*, chaps. i–ii, ix.

CHAPTER XVI

PATRICK GEDDES, VICTOR BRANFORD, AND APPLIED SOCIOLOGY IN ENGLAND: THE SOCIAL SURVEY, REGIONALISM, AND URBAN PLANNING

Lewis Mumford

I. INTRODUCTORY REMARKS

NOTWITHSTANDING the fact that Patrick Geddes (1854–1932) and Victor Branford (1864–1930) devoted a good part of their lifetimes to the advancement of sociology, their contributions are scarcely known. What accounts for that fact? Three things: the originality of their thought, the completeness of their presentation, and their use of schemata and diagrams and other forms of graphic notation that are still relatively unfamiliar in sociology—particularly among the more literary and philosophical schools.

In one sense it is still too early to judge their life-work or render an adequate account of it. Sir Patrick Geddes, who was the older man and the more profoundly creative mind, left behind him an enormous mass of unpublished material: lectures, unfinished books, and diurnal notes —great heaps of them—some of which have been sorted and put in order at the Outlook Tower in Edinburgh, to be published when sufficient aid is forthcoming. These notes and papers are comparable to the notebooks that Leonardo da Vinci left behind: indeed, Geddes possibly bears the same relation to the biotechnical period which he anticipated that Leonardo now plainly bears to the mechanical and scientific developments whose growth after the seventeenth century was finally to outstrip Leonardo's boldest dreams. At all events, the notes outweigh Geddes' published work in bulk and probably in importance. In the meanwhile, however, it may be useful to sum up Geddes' life work and make a preliminary appraisal of his contributions both to sociology proper and to social philosophy.

II. THE PERSONALITY AND WORK OF PATRICK GEDDES

Patrick Geddes was born in Perth, Scotland, in 1854. After showing an adolescent interest in chemistry and physics, which never came back with any force until he wrote his biography of the Indian biophysicist, Jaghadis Chandra Bose, Geddes became a student of biology. In the seventies he studied under Huxley at South Kensington, where he occasionally met Darwin; and after that he studied under Lacaze-Duthiers in Paris and Haeckel in Jena. His early connections with France never weakened. France, as with so many Scotch thinkers, even before Hume and Adam Smith, was his second home. Le Play, Demolins, Reclus, Durkheim, to say nothing of the French town-planners, historians, and philosophers (Bergson especially), all made contributions to his thought. At the end of his life he founded a students' hostel, which he called the Collège des Ecossais, on the outskirts of Montpellier, the birthplace of that other great sociologist, Auguste Comte, whose essential contributions to historical sociology he sought, among other things, to continue.

Thanks to Huxley and Haeckel, Geddes received an early initiation into ecology; and he passed beyond Huxley's neat morphological studies, with their emphasis upon the dead and the mechanical, to a biology concerned with living organisms reacting upon one another and upon their various environments. The central motif of biology for Geddes was precisely this functioning of the organism in its environment. This led to an early appreciation of Frédéric Le Play, whose formula, *lieu, travail, et famille,* was—Geddes perceived—the equivalent of "environment, function, and organism," as used by the biologist. So, while Geddes rejected the easy metaphorical comparisons of society with an organism, which Spencer and later sociologists pushed to absurdity, he regarded social life in man as continuous with the life of other organisms, and the realities of *organism, function, environment* were translated, in a slightly broader conception than Le Play's, as *folk, work, place.*

Returning to Edinburgh after his studies, Geddes took up a university career by becoming a lecturer in zoölogy at the School of Medicine. Throughout his life his interest in the biological sciences was a deep and central one: indeed, the chair of professor of botany at Dundee, which he held for many years, he did not relinquish until the end of the first World War. One of Geddes' earliest books, on the *Evolution of Sex,* written with his pupil, J. Arthur Thomson, became a pioneer classic on the subject; and the two men published a number of books, *Sex, Evolution,* and *Biology,* in the "Home University Series." In all these collaborations, Geddes' contributions are easily identified by reason of his compact style, with an irregular rhythm and various characteristic elisions and manufactured words—prose, in other words, with a touch of Meredith and Carlyle in it, and at times something of their epigrammatic concentration, as in his description of "good form" as "shamming dead," or in his characterization of specialized knowledge as "knowing more and more about less and less." As for his neologisms, he was as prolific here as was Jeremy Bentham, whose utilitarian limitations Geddes so heartily despised: "paleotechnic," "neotechnic," "geotechnic," "eutopian," "eupsychic," "bio-psychosis," "dis-specialism," "verbalistic empaperment," "biotechnic," were but a few of them.

While Geddes himself was pre-eminently a botanist, if one can pick out a single subject among the many of which he made himself master, he regarded the mathematical and physical sciences as basic to further work in biology or sociology. In the eighties the concept of energy was making its way into the physical sciences, and Geddes was quick to perceive its importance and to trace out its implications in society itself. His earliest contributions to sociology were, in fact, two papers, one on "The Classification of Statistics" and the other on the "Principles of Economics." In these papers he applied the doctrines of energetics to the tabulations of the census-taker and to the formal concepts of official political science. These papers antedated Ostwald's *Energetische Grundlagen der Kulturwissenschaften* by almost a generation, and they anticipated the views and methods of Frederick Soddy by an even longer period.

Meanwhile, Geddes' interest as a naturalist in the society about him was deepening. From his vantage point—a top-floor flat in a renovated tenement in the old town of Edinburgh, later in a new co-operative apartment house just below the Castle esplanade—he became conscious of the social world about him. The historic mile from the Holyrood to the Castle is a veritable mine of social and cultural history; and Geddes became more and more aware of the city itself as the special environment created by man for the transmission of his social heritage.

By the middle of the nineteenth century the city had all but dropped out of consciousness as a subject of thought. Here and there, in Paris and Vienna, a little of the traditional baroque planning was still being done in a grandiose way. But the new factory towns were mere agglomerations of mean hovels, cut through by railway yards and chopped up by dirty factories, disorderly storage yards and slag heaps, and smoky factory districts. The new city had become a by-product of the factory in its most antisocial phase: it exhibited neither technical competence nor social co-operation. And the city had dropped out of political thought. Legally, it was looked upon as a mere creature of the state; and in the new sociologies the city was nonexistent. The individual, the class, and the state were, in general, the only realities recognized.

Geddes was perhaps the first modern sociologist to appreciate the role of the city in the development and continuation of the social heritage. Fustel de Coulanges had in effect demonstrated this in his treatise on *La Cité antique;* but Geddes generalized that approach and carried it further. At the Outlook Tower, which he founded in 1892 as a civic and regional museum and as a sociological laboratory, he carried on a systematic study of the city, beginning with that which was immediately around him. While Geddes' survey of Edinburgh was contemporary with Booth's massive survey of London, Geddes' superior equipment in history and sociology enabled him to give the survey a more useful form. It was he who formulated the procedure—survey before action—as the basis for civic and social planning, and it was from the Outlook Tower that this idea was brought back to America in the nineties, partly through Charles Zueblin, of Chicago, to form the basis of the survey movement.

Through summer meetings that were held at the Outlook Tower, Geddes began in the nineties the assimilation of the best thought on the Continent, repeating in his day what another Scotchman, Carlyle, had done sixty or more years before. Élisée Reclus, the world geographer, and Peter Kropotkin, the brilliant author of *Mutual Aid* and *Fields, Factories, and Workshops* were among the lecturers at the summer school, and Geddes started to weave another thread into his sociology—that of geography. The concept of the human region, as developed by the French human geographers, became an essential part of his thought. Here the two poles of nature, nature as given and nature as modified by human action—to use G. P. Marsh's phrase—are brought together. Geddes, by the way, greatly valued G. P. Marsh's pioneering work on human geography and geotechnics; and he kept his memory alive while Marsh's own countrymen permitted his work to slide into oblivion. A pupil of Geddes', Herbertson, became the exponent of the new regional geography in Great Britain; and out of this came the Oxford School of Geography.

During the 1900's, Geddes began to spend a good part of his time in London. With his pupil and colleague, Victor Branford, he busied himself in 1903 with the foundation of the Sociological Society; and in the years immediately after—as again toward the end of both men's lives—Geddes was an active contributor to the *Sociological Review,* as well as a frequent lecturer at the society. From this London sojourn dates a series of important university extension lectures, whose syllabuses, even today, are vivid and stimulating. Among these are a course on "Country and Town," another on "Contemporary Social Evolution," a third on "Cities," and a fourth on the "Evolution of Occupations: Introduction to the Sociology of Labour."

This career as a professing sociologist was at first abortive: the Martin White professorship at the University of London, originally intended for Geddes, went, by some unhappy accident connected with Geddes' original lecture, to the philosophic liberal, Leonard T. Hobhouse. But in 1920, Geddes was called to a professorship in civics and sociology at the University of Bombay, a post which he held for four years. By this time, unfortunately, Geddes' encyclopedic range of learning and his extensive systematization had taken on such huge proportions that he could scarcely handle them. He cried aloud for a collaborator capable of living with the same intensity, working with the same terrific energy, and writing on the same heroic scale as he himself lived and worked and thought. The collaborator did not appear: those who had the mind had not the strength and stamina, and those who had the necessary capacity for sacrifice and self-annihilation alas! did not have sufficient mind. And while Branford remained closer to Geddes in sociology than any other disciple, it remains true that Branford's best works were those he wrote by himself.

Meanwhile, Geddes had brought to scientific sociology an intellectual equipment and a practical experience that few sociologists could boast. As a biologist, he remained an active student, if not an experimenter, to the end of his days; and he was, incidentally, coplanner with his son-in-law, Frank Mears, of one of the best of the new naturalistic zoos after the pioneer but overrated example of Hamburg—that at Edinburgh. As an educator and civic administrator, Geddes had cleaned up some of the filthiest slums of Edinburgh, had instituted the gardening of leftover open spaces, had built a series of university student halls, and had planned and developed the Outlook Tower. From 1914 to 1924 he surveyed and planned fifty cities in India and Palestine. Among other things, he selected the site for the University of Jerusalem and, with Mears, did the early planning of its buildings. His two-volume *Report on Indore* includes a magnificent critique of the modern university: it is in every way a classic. In short, Geddes knew "cities, climates, councils, governments" as no one since Aristotle had known them. Although a prodigious reader and scholar, no one relied less upon books than he did, unless they had been personally verified by observation and experience.

So much for what went into Geddes' sociology. Let me now try to outline its main points of approach and the particular orientation of his social philosophy. But, before I can do this, I must say a word about Branford, who was Geddes' collaborator in a whole series of undertakings, beginning with the Sociological Society itself and going on to the series of books on the "Making of the Future."

III. THE PERSONALITY AND CONTRIBUTIONS OF VICTOR BRANFORD

Victor Branford was Geddes' junior, and, like Geddes, he began as a student of biology. But family circumstances cut him off from his natural career as teacher, and he became a certified accountant and financier. In the latter capacity his work brought him to South America, where he had interests in a Paraguayan railroad, and to the United States, where Geddes had preceded him and had, in Chicago, discovered Veblen.

Victor Branford was a remarkable man and a pregnant thinker; but, because he was out of the fashion of his time, he was scarcely known in America, and in England, where he led an active, indefatigable life, he was hardly better appreciated, although he had a wide circle of acquaintances and moved freely among financiers and scholars.

Victor Branford was a unique combination of the man of affairs and the speculative thinker, a type England has so often produced from the time of Sir Walter Raleigh and Sir Francis Bacon. By profession he belonged to the abstemious guild of certified accountants, the medical diagnosticians, as he used to say, of business; by interest and attainment, he was a sociologist, a historian, and a philosopher; and in his character were mingled a wordly shrewdness, an ability to appraise all the mischief and madness of his fellows, with a wild devotion to losing causes and remote ideals.

Victor Branford's first book of importance was his *Interpretations and Forecasts,* which was published by Mitchell Kennerley in America on the eve of the first World War; and the book that sums up his observations and his philosophy of art and science and religion and life is *Science and Sanctity*—a treatise whose audacious title is in itself a volume. By indefatigable effort he founded the Sociological Society in London, and by continuous preaching and practice he did his utmost to carry on the substantial tradition of Auguste Comte and Frédéric Le Play, endeavoring to make sociology a true observational science, dealing not with abstractions, such as the "herd instinct" or the "common will," but with the actual processes and functions of definite regional societies. This method has been independently developed and fruitfully used by the American school of anthropologists in dealing with primitive peoples; but because of their original bias, the anthropologists have until recently been reluctant to take over more complex societies, particularly contemporary ones; and in their isolation of the concept of culture, they originally too complacently ignored the data of geography and psychology.

Unlike the American sociologists, who have at last adopted the notion of the survey as an instrument of exact thought in sociology, Victor Branford did not confine the survey to the purely spatial society of the present, without reference to its complex historical filiation, its heritage of mores, customs, laws, ideas, and ideals. Outdoor observation was for him an essential of both life and thought; a sociology of the chair was little better than so much stuffed upholstery for the mind; and Branford invented many ingenious ways of seeing the country, one of them, as I remember, from the top of a moving van—a useful expedient in the days before the double-decker bus began to ply the English roads.

Walking with Branford through Westminster or Oxford or the New Forest was one of the liveliest pleasures in the world; every stone came to life, and the very advertisements on the hoardings became pregnant commentaries upon our venal and life-starved civilization. His conversation had something that his books lacked: a certain spice of worldly observation that might have become cynicism in a less generous soul or have led to despair in a less hopeful one. He would gleefully point out some sinister exhibition of the social process, as in the combination of a bank with a meeting hall in the Methodist center in Westminster, or the juxtaposition of the bust of Cecil Rhodes with the new examination buildings in Oxford, which sorted out the brains of an imperial bureaucracy.

Acquainted with the statistical predictions of that remarkable prophet of modern warfare, Jean Bloch, and himself a keen observer in the financial centers of Europe, Branford was perhaps less surprised by the outbreak of the European War than were any of his contemporaries. As early as 1911, in collaboration with Geddes, he circulated a memorandum among his intellectual associates, pointing out that, unless there was a decisive reversal in policy, the nations of Europe would be at each other's throats by 1915. He proposed, therefore, to issue a series of books which would analyze the economic and spiritual causes of the approaching conflict—the lack of vital economy, the competition of rival megalopolies, the debauchery of all ideal values in a slavish financial and bureaucratic and military regime—and would, before the actual conflict broke out, lay down a positive program of reconstruction which might either help avert the disaster or salvage the ruins.

This proposal sounded so fantastic even to watchful, sober minds in 1911 that Branford and Geddes were forced to drop it; but they had the sad triumph of seeing their prophecy come true; and toward the end of the war, in the midst of the intellectual helterskelter, Branford began to publish—with the advice and help of his colleague Geddes—a series of books called "The Making of the Future," in which he and his contributors sought to embody a more adequate conception of life, economics, and polity. It is interesting to note, by the way, that in the original memorandum, Thorstein Veblen figured as one of the possible contributors.

Neither these books nor Branford's series of postwar pamphlets, called "Papers for the Present," received the attention they deserved; although, if I am not mistaken, his pamphlet, *The Drift to Revolution,* has a fairly wide circulation. In that pamphlet Branford analyzed the historic aims and programs of the "party of order" and the "party of revolution." He showed how one tended to beget the other—hence an oscillation of ferocious dictatorships and a deadlock in the fulfilment of all that was positive in their programs. He suggested a composition of forces, not a compromise, which would achieve nothing that either party sought, but a disinterested effort to get beyond the regime of power into one which would depend more completely upon the verified knowledge of science and that nonpartisan good will which is latent in all the arts and professions. This he called the "party of the Third Alternative," differing from the other two in that its emphasis was not upon abstract shibboleths but upon definite, concrete, realizable aims: reforestation, better houses, more adequately designed towns, co-operative agriculture, socialized credit, regenerated schools. The radical New Towns policy of Britain today, which has both Tory and Labour sponsorship, is an admirable example of Branford's "Third Alternative"—and a confirmation of his political realism.

An expert in finance, he proposed to substitute insurance, plus a definite charge for actual service, for the haphazard and often extortionate incidence of interest. He had no doubt that finance and industry could bring forth disinterested minds, quite as much as medicine and science could—indeed, he was one of them; and, though he had much in common with Thorstein Veblen, whose genius he was one of the first in Europe to recognize and hail, he was far from placing his hopes for a more vital and better-integrated society in the ministrations of some single class, such as the engineers. He knew that social counterpoint was a more complex matter, and his ideal figure for a fine society was that of a symphony orchestra.

The deeper that Branford's feet sank into the muddy slough of finance, the more passionately he longed for social deliverance. So that there is, in Branford's writings, a recurrent note of almost apocalyptic yearning for a grand conversion which would alter all the dominant values of imperialist society, even as Christianity had transformed those of Rome. In consequence the orderly pattern of Branford's thought is sometimes broken by an unexpected emotional eruption, not always justified by the immediate context or the general train of his argument. This defect, which makes some of his writing seem obscure and wilful, is, however, associated with a real quality. Both he and Geddes looked upon thought as an organic process. Instead of ejecting feeling and sentiment, they sought to integrate them in rational thinking, so that the subjective element, eliminated by the Cartesian methods inherited from seventeenth-century science and thereafter discarded as "unreal," should not come back again in a perverse and morbid form. Hence the paradoxical title of perhaps the best of Branford's books, *Science and Sanctity,* is a clue to his whole philosophy. The synthesis of facts and values, of the sciences and the arts, of the practical and the poetic, was his leading interest as a philosopher. Geddes went further than Branford in expressing this synthesis systematically by means of his brilliant diagrams; but Branford was the more active in translating these ideas into literary form.

In 1903, as we have noted, Branford and Geddes were the leading figures in the group that founded the Sociological Society in London, with Spencer's papal blessing and with Galton as the first president and a host of distinguished names in social science and politics on the Council. During the first five years of its existence the society had a healthy growth and showed a stir of intellectual activity. After this the absence for long periods, first of Branford, then of Geddes, and the hiatus of the war interfered with its development. At the end of the war, Branford, by assuming the financial responsibilities for its life and supplying it with a house in Westminster (Le Play House), attempted to resuscitate it and put it on its feet.

Unfortunately, personal rivalries and doctrinal divisions had broken up the original consensus. Neither Branford nor Geddes suffered fools, particularly academic fools, very gladly, nor were they sparing in their criticism of the verbalistic, fragmentary, and unscientific work that often passed for sociology or the social sciences in the established schools. They sought to create a coherent framework that would make possible a co-ordinated attack on the whole sociological front. But those who needed their rigorous discipline most were least ready to receive it. Sociology remained, for most of their opponents, another name for social philosophy; and there were as many schools of this as there were philosophers.

What influence the Sociological Society and the *Sociological Review* exercised was a personal influence. It had brilliant contributors, like Christopher Dawson, the Catholic historian; and, besides Geddes' and Branford's work, it published some notable regional surveys, done under the guidance of Alexander Farquharson; but the core of the review was the contributions of Branford and Geddes. One real victory, however, both Geddes and Branford had, even in their own lifetimes. The method of civic and regional survey, first developed by Geddes at Edinburgh, took on in the schools and exercised a positive influence on the teaching of history, civics, geography, and nature study in the elementary and secondary schools of Great Britain. The incomparable city-development reports of Sir Patrick Abercrombie and his school have their source in Geddes' teaching and example. The land-utilization survey of England was another direct outcome of his work. In the universities, Fleure at Aberystwith and Marett at Oxford, like J. L. Myres, remained natural allies, though not disciples. Other one-time students, like Marcel Hardy and C. C. Fagg, have carried the Geddesian doctrines into geography.

Branford's main contribution, perhaps, was as an expositor and continuator of the Geddesian outlook and vision of life. But the two men, in association with Branford's partner, John Ross, were pioneers in still another department. Following up Ernest Solvay's effort to arrive at a system of social accountancy to replace the pecuniary accountancy of capitalism, they did a series of studies on the nature of modern finance. Branford, out of his vast experience and sharp insight, wrote a number of papers upon banking and credit which were published in the afore-mentioned series of postwar pamphlets issued from Le Play House, called "Papers for the Present."

As sociologist, Branford's mature point of view is perhaps best expressed in the two articles on sociology which he wrote, respectively, for the recent edition of *Chambers' Encyclopaedia* and for the fourteenth edition of the *Encyclopaedia Britannica.*

For Branford the tradition of modern sociology has a double origin. On one side, it begins with Vico's conception of the philosophy of history as expressed in the *New Science* and runs through Herder and Condorcet, until finally it is systematized and set in order by Comte. On the other side, it begins with Montesquieu and the Physiocrats and the cultivators of the special social sciences, and in turn it is synthesized by Le Play in his threefold study of work, place, and people. From this point of view the adequate systematization of sociology in its temporal and spatial aspects would put an end to that abortive series of "systems of sociology" which have succeeded each other since the middle of the nineteenth century. Branford states his point of view succinctly in the *Britannica* article as follows:

From the foregoing psychological approaches collectively there is growing up a doctrine of society, its structure, functions, origins, and purposes which, in popular estimation, probably outranges any sociological presentation yet made. Similarly, the anthropologists are in course of creating a sociology of their own. Ignoring the vast and profound labors of Comte in establishing and elaborating the concept of the Social Inheritance as the essential subject-matter of sociology, those anthropologists who emphasize and work out the idea of cultural diffusion are in danger of substituting a biased particularism for the synthetic generality which a genuine sociology demands. And the same criticism could be levelled against the more generalizing exponents in each of the many specialized sub-sciences found within the social field. Since these specialisms began under the influence of the evolutionary spirit to orient themselves in a sociological direction .... they have collectively accumulated a body of more or less verified knowledge which today must be held to constitute the main corpus of sociology, if that word be taken in a scientific rather than in a philosophic sense. But this body of specialized science suffers several grave defects. It is (a) unsystematized, and therefore, since lacking in real unity, is ill-adapted to the concerted activity on which assured progress depends; (b) uninformed by the master concepts on which the scientific foundations of sociology were originally laid; (c) inadequately related to biology and the other established sciences which, preliminary to sociology, compose an essential part of the equipment needed for the culminating study of society in evolution.

IV. THE CONTRIBUTION OF PATRICK GEDDES TO SOCIOLOGY
AND SOCIAL RECONSTRUCTION

We are now ready to go back to Geddes. His prime sociological contribution came, first, through his concrete and many-sided study of actual groups and communities. In this study, practice alternated with theoretical development. Second and not less important was his attempt to systematize and order these experiences by creating a framework which would not merely contain his own material but serve equally as a focus for studies, both generalized and specialized, that might be made by others. He attempted nothing less than the art of ideological cartography. Like the work of the pre-Columbian map-makers, it was to lead to new explorations and conquests in the actual world.

I cannot attempt in this short study to explain and comment upon all Geddes' diagrams, or even to present adequately the most significant ones. It is important, however, to outline the general method that he used, which others may revamp and develop.

Perhaps the largest part of Geddes' thinking was done on squared paper, which he folded rather than ruled; and the major categories on his intellectual maps were arranged in triads, in which a subject and an object were connected by a third category indicating action or function—therefore often a verb. Take the simplest of these triads:

from organism, functioning, and environment Geddes went on to the sociological equivalent of folk, working, and place. From this point of view it was important never to think of these categories as separate, except as a momentary convenience of thought. By using an intellectual map it was possible to keep them present simultaneously to the eye and to the mind—hence his occasional reference to this type of operation as "simultaneous thinking."

But these categories are neither separate nor inert. Hence if they are drawn on a diagonal in the middle of nine squares, the remaining boxes can be used to show their possible forms of interaction. Instead of picking activities and ideas at random, Geddes first evolves them from their fundamental logical categories as these categories are derived from experience. What is the outcome of this method? The outcome of using it is that one becomes aware of facts and relations that may not immediately be given in either observation or experience—just as, when the periodic table was first formulated, the unfilled spaces called attention to elements that were not yet discovered but whose general characteristics could be predicted from their position in the table.

If place, work, and folk are the fundamental categories of any society, then geography, economics, and anthropology, considered in their broadest sense, are the fundamental sciences of sociology. But the factor of time and the accumulation of the social heritage modify this simple scheme. The human group not merely is influenced by its environment but learns to dominate it; by improving its tools and weapons it creates a store of free energy that is available for art and thought and religion and play; and it criticizes its laws and customs and modifies its social heritage by deliberate selection. Hence human society comprehends polity, culture, and art, as well as work, folk, and place. If the concept of determinism applies usefully to life on the lower level, the concept of creative freedom applies to its upper levels. Holland made the Dutch; but the Dutch, with their dikes and their windmills and their land reclamation, also made Holland.

The fake dilemma of determinism versus free will Geddes rejects in sociology as he had rejected it previously in biology. Life, as he puts it, is not merely a matter of environment working on the passive organism but also a matter of the organism, in insurgent mood, working on the environment. In fact, even in its most passive state, it modifies the environment, as the animal does by inhaling air and giving out a larger amount of carbon dioxide. Both reactions are given in experience. In other words,

$$\text{Life} = \frac{OFE}{EFO} \ .$$

Approaching society from the level of choice and creative activity— that is, essentially from the level of the city—Geddes sees through Comte's eyes the division of all social groups into spiritual and temporal powers and into active and passive members. But, as a social philosopher, Geddes saw the weakness not merely of earlier social orders but of Comte's too rigid classification of their systems, particularly as expressed in the medieval polity. These functional elements—chiefs and people, intellectuals and emotionals—have a way of hardening into castes. The function becomes isolated and specialized; in the course of transmission it becomes stereotyped, and finally it fails to express its original content. The "chief" whose opinions are deservedly respected in the motor works becomes the arbiter of education as well, whereas, functionally, with respect to education he is merely one of the "people." So the man of the people may remain a day laborer all his life, through lack of opportunity, whereas functionally, like Burns, he may be a poet. In short, Geddes turned Comte's static divisions of society into dynamic ones, for, to him, each functioning social group had its appropriate regrouping of chiefs, people, emotionals, and intellectuals. He was always, however, dissatisfied with this terminology; perhaps the best substitute that he achieved was "leaders, workers, energizers, and initiators."

If Geddes' central diagram of thirty-six squares is an attempt to chart the field of social life, his bookcase diagram is a map of the biological and social sciences, by means of which this life is more clearly presented and integrated in thought.

This diagram is divided into an upper and a lower department: the upper deals with the group, the lower with the individual. With respect to time, four vertical compartments are divided into three sections: at the extreme left, the past; at the extreme right, the future or the possible; and the middle two, the present. These sections again are divided into the static and the dynamic. Giving these squares their proper values in biology, one has the following:

Paleontology	Taxonomy	Ecology	Phylogeny
Embryology	Anatomy	Physiology	Ontogeny

Is there the same sort of parallel between the essential sciences of biology and those of sociology as there is in society between organism, function, and environment and folk, work, and place? Geddes' answer to this is clear:

History and Archeology	Ethnography	Economics (and Politics)	Philosophy of History
Biography	Anthropography	Economics (detailed)	Biography (critical)

Only with great reluctance and with due caution may one substitute other categories from those which Geddes himself used. Nevertheless, the diagram will perhaps gain wider assent if one takes as the individual unit of sociology the group instead of the individual, and for the collective unit a whole society with its congeries of groups. Again, instead of the old terms "economics" and "politics," which are too limited, one might substitute social ecology, and for the individual aspect the functional study of component institutions.

It will be noted that this diagram gives a place to social philosophy, from Plato and Aristotle down to Karl Marx and John Dewey. But, instead of supposing that social philosophy or dialectic thinking can be a substitute for social science in the study of society, it limits philosophy to the possible. At the same time, by introducing the future and the possible as, so to speak, a legally bounded terrain in social thought, Geddes breaks with the nineteenth-century notion that valid thought must concern itself solely with the past and with those aspects of reality that do not imply either revaluation or action. Indeed, for Geddes, as for Dewey, thought was incomplete until it had passed back again into life and modified it. The weakness of the sociological precursors was that their "possible" rested on insufficient scientific data as to the past and the present. The weakness of the so-called "scientific" school today is that what it calls the future—when it chooses to consider that dimension of time—is in reality the past, since no allowance is made for chance, creative thoughts, and plans and for those emergent elements that are never clearly definable within the past social complex. Geddes' conception of man and society allowed not merely for outwardly conditioned responses but also for those that had an origin *within* the personality or the group; and, like Lloyd Morgan, whose work he valued, he knew the importance of "prospective reference" and anticipatory responses.

For the reader who wishes to go further with Geddes' social logic, I would refer to Amelia Defries' description of Geddes in *The Interpreter Geddes,* where he will find a complete layout of the "36," and to the series of diagrams Geddes included in two of the books he wrote with J. Arthur Thomson, *Biology* and *Life: Outlines of Biology.* It was Geddes' mission to restore, on a modern level, the essential structure of Greek thought as described by George Santayana—"physics" and "dialectics." He was one of the few non-Marxian scientists, outside the mathematical disciplines, who realized the importance of dialectic thinking and who, in the very act of acknowledging his debt to Comte, broke outside the narrow positivism of Victorian science.

This systematization of knowledge was, I must repeat, an important part of Geddes' life-work. His aim was to effect a passage from the dispersed, specialized, one-sided, narrowly pragmatic thinking that has dominated the last three hundred years to a synthetic, organic, and related mode of thinking—and thus of acting. It was not that he rejected, or failed to esteem, the separate results of highly specialized research. What he rejected was the notion that the separate compartments of thought or life could be kept separate. There was no guaranty that the accumulation of such separate particles of knowledge was bound—like the individualistic profit-seeking of the Victorian era—to produce a wealth of knowledge for the community. He saw that, on the contrary, knowledge became infertile and impoverished to the extent that it was, as he put it, "dis-specialized": becoming divorced from life, it failed to produce interesting hypotheses or to reflect vital dilemmas. For a specialism to be valid, it must be capable of reciprocal interaction with the entire body of thought that surrounds it. It needed, however, more than a metaphysical intuition to create this new wholeness. Hence, while Geddes appreciated the philosophic approach of both Jan Smuts and, still more, Whitehead, he believed that synthesis required a method as well as a formula: to live the life was a vital part of knowing the doctrine.

One turns finally to Patrick Geddes as a social philosopher. Beyond his ideological synthesis was the living example of the man himself. He was, above all, the philosopher of life. Though full of admiration for our technical triumphs, his life was dedicated to turning men away from the worship of things, from preoccupation with the impedimenta of existence, to the service of life itself. The paleotechnic period that began in the eighteenth century and devoted itself to mass production and power expansion and the general quantification of existence—was for Geddes a period of vital starvation: the peasant and the North Sea fisherman were for him higher biological types than the successful cockneys who looted a railroad system or cornered the grain market. In his work on city development, from the early report on Dunfermline to his final reports on Indore and Jerusalem University, he sought to reintroduce into Western civilization a balanced and life-maintaining environment. The nurture of children and the care of gardens, the mating of lovers and the building of homes, were for him the central tasks of civilization. The whole masculine world of machines, with its rigors and strenuous efforts and asceticisms, had meaning only to the extent that it furthered the elemental needs of life and afforded an opportunity for those higher growths of art and culture that spring out of a communal effort. Similarly, while Geddes acknowledged the many acute contributions of the urban mind, he looked forward to a new cycle of thought and activity when the more rustic types would come to the fore again; hence one of the acute problems in planning was to provide for the effective interaction of town and country on every level, from the growth of food to the propagation of thought.

Filled with awe and wonder and delight over the fact of life itself, Geddes rejected none of its manifestations; abstract thought was for him as real as an orgasm, and the hygiene of the digestive tract and the movement of the bowels were as important for clear thinking as the refinements of logic. So, too, he rejected those partial visions of life that sum themselves up in this or that philosophy or religion, or, rather, he accepted everything about them except their partiality. He could learn from the streetsweeper as well as from Bergson; the Hindu Brahmin had a glimpse of life not vouchsafed to the disciple of Marx; and, wherever Geddes encountered the living touch of experience and feeling, he seized it. This omnivorousness, this inclusiveness, this tremendous appetite for so many diverse parts of reality, which had been achieved on an emotional level by Walt Whitman, was attained on a more intellectual plane by Geddes. In weaker minds with less capacity to appropriate and assimilate, the process would be described as "eclecticism"; but in Geddes one feels that there is a beginning of that deeper world-wide understanding which is necessary for our intellectual health and our social salvation.

As a social philosopher Geddes was against the absolute state and *for* the functional organizations of cities and regions; against bureaucracy and militarism and *for* the voluntary action of groups; against mass regimentation and *for* the gradual leavening of action by education and example; against sessile aristocracies and ignorant democracies and *for* that aristodemocracy which he saw arising in the Scandinavian countries; against a verbalistic and pecuniary culture with the sham education of the three *R*'s in their crude form and their recent disguises and *for* a vital culture which combined the three *H*'s—head, heart, and hand. As for the positive movements that he started, one can only say that what is sound in regional planning, regionalism, and city development today either owes a direct debt to Geddes or was anticipated by his own earlier thought. Geddes the social philosopher rounds out the work of Geddes the systematic sociologist. And it may be that in the century to come Geddes will have an effect upon the ordering of our civilization even more powerful than that which Rousseau and Marx have successively exercised. If that turns out to be true, it will be partly, perhaps, because he was a better sociologist.

BIBLIOGRAPHY

BOOKS AND ARTICLES BY PATRICK GEDDES

The Classification of Statistics. Edinburgh, 1881.

An Analysis of the Principles of Economics. Edinburgh, 1885.

Civic Survey of Edinburgh. Edinburgh, 1911.

City Development: A Study of Parks, Gardens, and Culture Institutes. Edinburgh, 1904.

The Masque of Learning. Edinburgh, 1912.

Cities in Evolution. London, 1915.

Ideas at War. Lectures given with GILBERT SLATER, some of whose material was incorporated in the manuscript. London, 1917.

Report to the Durbar of Indore. 2 vols. London, 1920. The most exhaustive and the most important of Geddes' city-planning reports.

John Ruskin, Economist. "Round Table Series." Edinburgh, 1886.

Autobiographical papers: "Talks from My Outlook Tower," *Survey Graphic,* February–September, 1925.

Sociological papers in the series "Publications of the Sociological Society." London, 1905, 1906, 1907.

"Essentials of Sociology in Relation to Economics," *Indian Journal of Economics,* III, Part III (1922).

BOOKS BY PATRICK GEDDES AND J. ARTHUR THOMSON

The Evolution of Sex. 2 vols. London, 1888.
Evolution. New York, 1912.
Sex. New York, 1914.
Biology. New York, 1925.
Life: Outlines of Biology. New York, 1931.

BOOKS BY PATRICK GEDDES AND VICTOR BRANFORD

The Coming Polity. London, 1917.
Our Social Inheritance. London, 1918.
The Coal Crisis and the Future: A Symposium. Edited by VICTOR BRANFORD. London, 1926.
Coal—Ways to Reconstruction. Supplement to *The Coal Crisis.* London, 1926.

BOOKS BY VICTOR BRANFORD

St. Columba. Edinburgh, 1912.
Interpretations and Forecasts. New York, 1914.
Science and Sanctity. London, 1923.
Living Religions. London, 1925.
The following pamphlets in "Papers for the Present" series: *A Citizen Soldier, The Banker's Part in Reconstruction, The Modern Midas, The Drift to Revolution, A Rustic View of War and Peace.* London, 1917–20.
Articles on sociology in *Chambers' Encyclopaedia* (1928) and *Encyclopaedia Britannica* (14th ed.).

For a comprehensive study of the life and work of Geddes, see PHILIP BOARDMAN, *Patrick Geddes: Maker of the Future.* Chapel Hill, N.C., 1944.

CHAPTER XVII

WILLIAM GRAHAM SUMNER: SPENCERIANISM IN AMERICAN DRESS

HARRY ELMER BARNES

I. GENERAL CHARACTERISTICS OF SUMNER'S SOCIOLOGICAL THOUGHT

AMONG the sociologists of America there is little doubt that the late William Graham Sumner (1840–1910) of Yale University was the most vigorous and striking personality. Because Sumner was probably the most inspiring and popular teacher that either Yale University or American social science has ever produced, his direct contact with thousands of students was more important for the development of sociology in the United States than his own published works upon the subject. Consequently, in even a brief introduction to his contributions to sociology, an attempt to interpret his personality and methods, as revealed in his writings and in written and oral estimates of former students at Yale, is more essential than it would be in the case of most American sociologists.

Despite the fact that Sumner frequently emphasized the necessity for an objective point of view in social science and decried any attempt upon the part of a sociologist to moralize,[1] it is impossible for a reader to emerge from a protracted examination of Sumner's economic, political, and sociological writings without becoming convinced that Sumner was primarily a preacher, in the true sense of that term.

Trained originally for the ministry and serving for a short time as an ordained curate of the Episcopal church, Sumner tells his readers[2] that he left the ministry because he wanted to be able to turn his attention to political, economic, and social questions rather than to the preparation of sermons on theological subjects. It is hard to escape the conviction that he turned his professorial career in these more fertile fields into an intellectual ministry which has been unexcelled for its success, influence, and inspiration by that of any other American teacher.

Sumner was as subtle in his preaching as Jefferson was in his political epistolography, for he constantly disclaimed any attempt to do more than set forth concrete facts in a candid manner. Yet his *What Social Classes Owe to Each Other* is, above all, an exhortation to independent thought and action, self-reliance, and individual initiative; and the element of the preacher is not entirely absent even in *Folkways*. If one adds to this initial zeal the influence of a commanding personality; wide learning; a splendid, if not entirely accurate or consistent, dogmatism; and a mastery of incisive English, which makes his essays models of terse nineteenth-century critical prose, it is not difficult to understand Sumner's reputation as a teacher or his dominating influence at Yale.

Sumner's writings are intensely dogmatic, and he was an uncompromising foe of all the unscientific sentimentality which permeated so much of the quasi-sociological writings and movements of Sumner's generation. His basic message to his students and readers in this respect has been concisely epitomized by one of his leading students as "Don't be a damn fool!"

Sumner's dogmatism, however, was not entirely logical or consistent. For example, he stated that he did not believe in either metaphysics or psychology and that he had always tried to prevent sociology from being infected by either. Nevertheless, he frequently indulged in a rather elementary type of metaphysics of his own, and his *Folkways* is unquestionably the most important objective treatment of a very essential portion of social psychology that has ever been written.

As Professor Albion Woodbury Small remarked, Sumner's position in the development of sociology in the United States has not been definitely determined. While it is true that, as Professor A. G. Keller asserts, Sumner was always primarily a sociologist in method and point of view, there can be no doubt that he built up his academic and literary reputation chiefly in the fields of economics and political science as an exceedingly vigorous advocate of "hard money," free trade, and laissez faire. Again, while Sumner may claim a definite priority over any other American teacher in introducing a serious course in sociology into the university curriculum, he never published a systematic exposition of sociology, and his great monograph, *Folkways,* did not appear until three years before his death. These circumstances doubtless account for the fact that few persons who have not been Yale students or who have not been intimately acquainted with Sumner's academic work are aware that Sumner may accurately be classed as a sociologist. One need not be surprised that Professor Small was "shocked" in 1907 by the proposal of Sumner as president of the American Sociological Society. The extent of Sumner's interest and activity in sociology was not fully apparent until Professor Keller completed Sumner's projected work in four volumes, *The Science of Society* (1927–28). For the most part, however, this is an amplification of the methods and content of the earlier *Folkways*.[3] It has been ably digested and summarized in Professor Keller's *Man's Rough Road* (1932).

Sumner's own published works on sociology, aside from several brief essays, were almost entirely limited to his *Folkways*. Of this work it is not inaccurate to say that it is unsurpassed as a sociological achievement by any single volume in any language and that it has made the sociological treatment of usages, manners, customs, mores, and morals essentially a completed task.

So far as one can judge from his essays and lectures upon sociology, from his autobiographical sketches, and from Professor Keller's comments, Sumner's sociological views were colored by his economic and political predispositions and were inspired by the general attitudes and methods of Darwin, Spencer, and Julius Lippert. An evolutionary view of social life and development, a slight predilection for the use of biological concepts, and a firm conviction of the pre-eminent value of ethnography as the "data" and, to a large extent, the substance of sociology are the dominant features of Sumner's sociological thought. He seems to have been little influenced by, or acquainted with, the contemporary systematic sociological literature of America or Europe; and Professor Keller states that he even had little respect for such works. The doctrinal resemblance of Sumner's work to that of Spencer is to be seen in his political individualism, his reliance primarily on the ethnographic method, and his opposition to war and imperialism. The most extended expression of Sumner's views on the nature of the social sciences are to be found in Part VII of the third volume of his posthumous *Science of Society*.

It seems that Sumner's position in American sociology may be at least tentatively summarized as follows: He was the first teacher of sociology in the country from the standpoint of both time and ability; his *Folkways* is one of the finest treatments of a special field of sociology that has yet appeared; his sociological writings were primarily concrete and descriptive rather than abstract and theoretical; and his views regarding social initiative or "collective telesis," to adopt Ward's terminology, were exceedingly biased and archaic, being almost a *reductio ad absurdum* of the laissez faire individualistic position.

No extended analysis of Sumner's *Folkways* can be attempted within the scope of the present chapter, but it is essential that its fundamental conceptions be pointed out. As the subtitle of his work indicated, it is "a study of the sociological importance of usages, manners, customs, mores, and morals." The work is essentially an attempt to explain the origin, nature, value, and persistence of certain of the most important and characteristic group habits. Briefly, Sumner's theory of the folkways is that, guided in a general way by the instincts which he inherited from his animal ancestors and by the psychophysical capacity to distinguish pain from pleasure, man has gradually built up, by a process of trial and error, certain types of group conduct which have been found by experience to be conducive to the successful outcome of the struggle for existence. These group habits or folkways operate primarily on a subconscious or habitual level. They acquire greater power as time passes, through the force of tradition, habit, and religious sanction.

When the folkways reach the stage at which they are raised to the level of conscious reflection and are regarded as adapted to securing the continued welfare and prosperity of the group, they thereby become transformed into mores.[4] The mores, supported by group authority, are the chief agency through which societal selection operates. The mores determine what shall be regarded as right or wrong modes of conduct in any group, morality thus being not absolute and universal but relative and local. The question of the evolution of the mores and the ability of society consciously to change them was discussed by Sumner in many passages of his works, and he made it plain that he did not believe that members of any group are competent to discuss and criticize the validity of their own mores, much less to change them by predetermined action.[5] The following selected and rearranged quotations from the *Folkways* epitomize Sumner's theoretical position with respect to the mores:

Men in groups are under life conditions; they have needs which are similar under the state of the life conditions; the relations of the needs to the conditions are interests under the heads of hunger, love, vanity, and fear; efforts of numbers at the same time to satisfy interests produce mass phenomena which are folkways by virtue of uniformity, repetition, and wide concurrence. The folkways are attended by pleasure or pain according as they are well fitted for the purpose. Pain forces reflection and observation of some relation between acts and welfare.

At this point the prevailing world philosophy suggests explanations and inferences, which become entangled with judgments of expediency. However, the folkways take on a philosophy of right living and life policy for welfare. When the elements of truth and right are developed into doctrines of welfare, the folkways are raised to another plane. They then become capable of producing inferences, developing into new forms, and extending their constructive influence over men and society. Then we call them the mores.

The mores are the folkways, including the philosophical and ethical generalizations as to societal welfare which are suggested by them, and inherent in them, as they grow. They are the ways of doing things which are current in a society to satisfy human needs and desires, together with the faiths, notions, codes, and standards of well living which inhere in those ways, having a genetic connection with them. By virtue of the latter element the mores are traits in the specific character of a society or a period. They pervade and control the ways of thinking in all the exigencies of life, returning from the world of abstractions to the world of action, to give guidance and to win revivification.

At every turn we find new evidence that the mores can make anything right. What they do is that they cover a usage in dress, language, behavior, manners, etc., with the mantle of current custom, and give it regulation and limits within which it becomes unquestionable. The limit is generally a limit of toleration. The mores set the limits or define the disapproval.

The most important fact about the mores is their dominion over the individual. Arising he knows not whence or how, they meet his opening mind in earliest childhood, give him his outfit of ideas, faiths, and tastes, and lead him into prescribed mental processes. They bring to him codes of action, standards, and rules of ethics. They have a model of the man-as-he-should-be to which they mould him, in spite of himself and without his knowledge. If he submits and consents, he is taken up and may attain great social success. If he resists and dissents, he is thrown out and may be trodden underfoot.

The mores are therefore an engine of social selection. Their coercion of the individual is the mode in which they operate the selection. It is vain to imagine that a "scientific man" can divest himself of prejudice or previous opinion, and put himself in an attitude of neutral independence towards the mores. He might as well try to get out of gravity or the pressure of the atmosphere. The most learned scholar reveals all the philistinism and prejudice of the man-on-the-curbstone when the mores are in discussion. The most elaborate discussion only consists in revolving on one's own axis. When the statesmen and social philosophers stand ready to undertake any manipulation of institutions and mores, and proceed upon the assumption that they can obtain data upon which to proceed with confidence in that undertaking, as an architect or engineer would obtain data and apply his devices to a task in his art, a fallacy is included which is radical and mischievous beyond measure.[6]

In addition to his notion of the mores, the other fundamental conception in Sumner's sociological theory was the assumption that social, as well as organic, evolution is almost entirely an automatic, spontaneous process which cannot be extensively altered by social effort. In the light of Sumner's admitted obligation to Spencer, it seems reasonable to suppose that Sumner's view of social development either was directly derived from the latter or was strengthened by Spencer's vigorous exposition of this doctrine, particularly in his *Study of Sociology*. The following passage is the best summary of Sumner's views on the subject of the automatic evolution of society and the futility of social initiative:

If this poor old world is as bad as they say, one more reflection may check the zeal of the headlong reformer. It is at any rate a tough old world. It had taken its trend and curvature and all its twists and tangles from a long course of formation. All its wry and crooked gnarls and knobs are therefore stiff and stubborn. If we puny men by our arts can do anything at all to straighten them, it will be only by modifying the tendencies of some of the forces at work, so that, after a sufficient time, their action may be changed a little, and slowly the lines of movement may be modified. This effort, however, can at most be only slight, and it will take a long time. In the meantime, spontaneous forces will be at work, compared with which our efforts are like those of a man trying to deflect a river, and these forces will have changed the whole problem before our interferences have time to make themselves felt.

The great stream of time and earthly things will sweep on just the same in spite of us. It bears with it now all the errors and follies of the past, the wreckage of all the philosophies, the fragments of all the civilizations, the wisdom of all the abandoned ethical systems, the debris of all the institutions, and the penalties of all the mistakes. It is only in imagination that we stand by and look at and criticize it and plan to change it. Everyone of us is a child of his age and cannot get out of it. He is in the stream and is swept along with it. All his sciences and philosophy come to him out of it. Therefore the tide will not be changed by us. It will swallow up both us and our experiments. It will absorb the efforts at change and take them into itself as new but trivial components, and the great movement of tradition and work will go unchanged by our fads and schemes.

The things which will change it are the great discoveries and inventions, the new reactions inside the social organism, and the changes in the earth itself on account of changes in the cosmical forces. These causes will make of it just what, in fidelity to them, it ought to be. The men will be carried along with it and be made by it. The utmost they can do by their cleverness will be to note and record their course as they are carried along, which is what we do now, and is that which leads us to the vain fancy that we can make or guide the movement. That is why it is the greatest folly of which a man can be capable, to sit down with a slate and pencil to plan out a new social world.[7]

It would be interesting to know to what extent Sumner's rather vehement support of laissez faire was derived from his reading of Spencer and how far it was the outcome of his practical experience in American municipal politics, early in his career. At any rate, Sumner's dogmatic opposition to the doctrine that social reform can be effected through the agency of political machinery may be pardoned, as it would be a rare individual who could emerge with any other viewpoint from the simultaneous influence of Spencer's *Study of Sociology* and three years' experience in American city politics.[8]

II. SPECIFIC CONTRIBUTIONS TO SOCIAL AND POLITICAL THEORY

A. THE NATURE OF THE STATE

Though a professor of political science, Sumner never published any systematic treatment of political theory.[9] His reputation as a contributor to social and political theory rests upon a clear and vigorous elaboration of certain specific topics, chiefly the differentiation between democratic and republican government, a defense of laissez faire, and a condemnation of imperialism.

Sumner's conception of the state was extremely practical and matter of fact. He had little patience with the transcendental theories of writers like Hegel, who regarded the state as "perfected rationality" or an "ethical person." He says, in summarizing his analysis of the validity of the dogma that the state is an ethical person:

> It appears, therefore, that the assertion that we ought to conceive of the state as an ethical person does not rest upon any such solid analysis of the facts of life and the nature of the state as would make it a useful and fruitful proposition for further study of social phenomena, but that it is a product of the phrase-mill. It is one of those mischievous dicta which seem to say something profound; but, upon examination, prove to say nothing which will bear analysis.[10]

Sumner held that the state, as an abstraction, is nothing more than "all-of-us." In actual practice, "it is only a little group of men chosen in a very haphazard way by the majority of us to perform certain services for all of us."[11]

B. FORMS OF GOVERNMENT

Sumner was also opposed to the dogmatic statement that any type of government is absolutely the "best" under all circumstances. Like Montesquieu, he made a strong plea for the recognition of the principle of relativity in the excellence of political institutions. The "best" government for any particular people is simply that type which is best adapted to the general social, economic, and intellectual conditions which prevail: "We must abandon all hope of finding an absolutely 'best' system of government. If we study human nature and human history, we find that civil institutions are only 'better' and 'best' relatively to the people for whom they exist, and that they can be so called only as they are more closely adjusted to the circumstances of the nation in question."[12]

Though Sumner denied that there could be any absolutely or universally "best" government, there was, nevertheless, no doubt in his own mind as to what type of government was best adapted to the United States of his day. He was an uncompromising advocate of a conservative constitutional republic, based upon a sound system of representation. Such a government he defined, following Alexander Hamilton, as a "form of self-government in which the authority of the state is conferred for limited terms upon officers designated by election."[13] Sumner's political tenets were founded upon a curious, if interesting, combination of a Hamiltonian admiration of an aristocracy of talent; the ardent Jeffersonian defense of individualism, laissez faire, and free trade; and the conservative Republican advocacy of "hard money."

Sumner laid great stress upon the necessity of clearly differentiating between a "pure" democracy and a representative republic. Democracy is based upon the principle of equality and involves the direct participation of the people in every act of the government. The aim of a republic, on the other hand, is not equality but the securing and guaranteeing of civil liberty. Sumner held that democracy is an error in principle, in so far as it rests upon the assumption of the inherent equality of mankind. He said on this point that "the assertion that all men are equal is perhaps the purest falsehood in dogma which was ever put into human language; five minutes' observation of facts will show that men are unequal through a very wide range of variation."[14]

From this error of democracy in principle and as a result of its non-adaptability to the government of a large area, Sumner held that the attempt to preserve the ideals and practices of "pure" democracy in the federal and state governments of the United States was a dangerous anachronism and a menace to civil liberty and effective administration. With admirable clarity Sumner points out the fact that a "pure" democracy is fitted only for the administration of small local units, such as rural townships. The United States has completely outgrown the possibility of successfully employing this type of a democratic system in the federal or state governments. In adopting the necessary system of representation, we have carried over the extremely dangerous dogma of the older rural democratic local government that all men are equally fit to hold office and that officeholding is the legitimate privilege of every person. This general disregard of the necessity for expert guidance and for special talent in the holding of public office is the chief defect of our political system. Its other main imperfection is its impotence in the face of plutocratic and partisan interests.

If our political system is to be successful in the future, it must restore a proper estimation of the value of real statesmanship, purify the principle of representation, and improve the civil service in opposition to the antiquated dogmas and practices of pure democracy. None of these indispensable prerequisites of a successful republican system can be expected, however, without an intelligent and politically educated electorate.

C. THE PROBLEM OF SOCIAL REFORM THROUGH STATE ACTIVITY

There can be no doubt that Professor Sumner's reputation as a political theorist rests primarily upon his defense of laissez faire and his advocacy of a restriction of the functions of the state. He was easily the most able and tireless exponent in this country of the individualistic social philosophy which writers like Wilhelm von Humboldt and Spencer had upheld in Europe. Sumner's arguments in favor of laissez faire center around three main propositions: (1) that it is morally wrong to extend state activities, inasmuch as the burdens are not distributed in accordance with the benefits received; (2) that the state is proved by history to be incompetent as compared with private enterprise, and, moreover, when it extends its activities, it neglects its proper function of maintaining order and preserving liberty; and (3) that, since social evolution is primarily a product of nonvolitional forces, the interference of the state in an attempt to accelerate the process of evolution cannot fail to be mischievous and an impediment to progress.[15]

The fundamental purpose for which states exist, according to Sumner, is to secure and preserve civil liberty. Civil liberty he defines as "the careful adjustment by which the rights of individuals and the state are reconciled with one another to allow the greatest possible development of all and of each in harmony and peace."[16] In other words, the problem of state activity can be expressed in the abstract as follows: "Can we get from the state security for individuals to pursue happiness in and under it and yet not have the state itself become a burden and hindrance only a little better than the evil which it wards off?"[17] In practice this problem reduces itself to the simple question: "What ought Some-of-us do for Others-of-us?"[18]

It is in his answer to this practical question that Sumner makes his most original and distinctive defense of the principle of laissez faire, which he renders in his picturesque terminology as "mind your own business!"[19] Nearly all examples of an extension of state activity involve an agreement between A and B, who are "the ignorant social doctors," as to what C, who is the "Forgotten Man," shall do for D, who represents the class that has failed in the struggle for existence. The Forgotten Men make up that great self-respecting middle class in society. Being industrious, independent, and unobtrusive, this class attracts little attention, but, in reality, it is incomparably the most important of all social classes in its contribution to every phase of civilization.[20]

While this middle class never asks for any assistance from the government for itself, it invariably has to defray a disproportionate share of the expense of every extension of state activity: "It's the 'Forgotten Man' who is threatened by every extension of the paternal theory of government. It is he who must work and pay. When, therefore, the statesmen and social philosophers sit down to think what the State can or ought to do, they really mean to decide what the Forgotten Man shall do."[21]

The expense which is inherent in every extension of state activity always falls upon the middle class, but this class gets little or no benefit from these added burdens and tends to be crushed or diminished by them. Inasmuch as this class is, beyond all comparison, the most important element in the population, any extension of state action tends to menace the most valuable group in society for the benefit of those whose very need of assistance marks them off as inferior.[22]

It is important to note that Sumner does not defend laissez faire from a purely metaphysical individualistic standpoint but maintains that, from the strictly sociological point of view, a curtailment of state activity is indispensable. Sumner's answer to his famous question, "What do social classes owe to each other?" is that the sole duty of one class to another in society is to maintain an attitude of good will and mutual respect toward the other and to strive to bring about liberty and security, so that every class may improve its opportunities. Under no circumstances should one social class attempt to redistribute the achievements or products of the other classes.

In extending its activity into new and questionable fields, the state, Sumner holds, is losing its grip upon its primary function of providing "peace, order, and security." The extra-legal powers which have been usurped by party leaders and labor organizations have already vitiated the ability of the state to give security to the populace, and this practically means a revival of the "private war," so common in primitive society. Paternalistic legislation also provides a means for insidious and corrupt plutocratic interests to give themselves legal security in carrying on their exploitation of society.

History has never proved the state to be as competent as private enterprise, and the government of the United States has never shown a degree of intelligence and efficiency at all comparable to that exhibited by our private enterprise. As we have no reason to believe that the capacity of the state is likely to be improved, the only alternative is to restrict as much as possible the functions of the state and to leave the greatest possible opportunity for the development of the more competent private enterprise and personal initiative. The most urgent necessity in regard to the state is not to increase the sphere of its activity but to improve the performance of its legitimate functions.

Sumner's last argument in favor of laissez faire involves the question of the possibility and desirability of achieving the improvement of society by direct state action, in other words, the problem of the amenability of social evolution to artificial acceleration. Sumner's theory on this point is a combination of the ideas of Burke and the Romanticists on the historical development of institutions and the impossibility of making a sudden break with the past with Spencer's conception of the automatic and nonvolitional nature of social evolution. The attempt to reform social conditions by direct legislative action, he believed, is foredoomed to failure because of the spontaneous nature of social evolution and the impossibility of taking into account all the factors involved in any particular case: "Social improvement is not won by direct effort. It is secondary, and results from physical or economic improvements. That is why schemes of direct social amelioration always have an arbitrary, sentimental, and artificial character, while true social advance must be a product and a growth."[23]

The conviction that social improvement can be effected by direct action, then, is but one of those schemes for lifting one's self by one's bootstraps which have been discredited by natural science but have found a last intrenchment in social science.

In the place of Ward's term "attractive legislation," Sumner coins that of "speculative legislation" to designate all schemes to alter the existing social order by direct legislative action. After the manner of Burke, he declares that all "speculative legislation" is opposed to the fundamental principles of the Anglo-American legal and political systems, which are marked by "slow and careful growth, historic continuity, and aversion to all dogmatism and abstractionism."[24] The very complexity of social conditions prevents "speculative legislation" from achieving the desired results: "It is a characteristic of speculative legislation that it very generally produces the exact opposite of the result it was hoped to get from it. The reason is because the elements of any social problem which we do not know so far surpass in number and importance those which we do know that our solutions have far greater chance to be wrong than to be right."[25]

Another important reason for distrusting the efficacy of direct legislative action for social reform is to be found in the fact that, even if the plans for reform were perfectly scientific as theoretical abstractions, they would be likely to fail in their practical application. They would have to be put into operation, not by the learned reformers, but by the incompetent and avaricious machine politicians who constitute our body of public officials.[26]

In view of all these important objections to an extension of state activity, Sumner maintained that it was not only a matter of theoretical importance but also a patriotic and civic duty for all intelligent men to resist any increase of state interference. It is even futile to hope that politicians can make such changes in the social order as will retain the useful elements in the past and secure the benefits of innovations. It is a mere waste of time to reflect what the state might accomplish if politicians could attain real wisdom and integrity, for it is generally agreed that they never can do so. In short, Sumner advocated a greater efficiency in the exercise of the legitimate or "police" functions of the state and maintained that progress must come through the gradual and unconscious operation of social, economic, and intellectual forces.[27]

D. SOVEREIGNTY, LIBERTY, AND POLITICAL RIGHTS

Sumner's discussion of the problems of sovereignty, liberty, and rights is not particularly important or entirely consistent, though in certain points it is suggestive. He was not inclined to assign much importance to the concept of sovereignty. "Sovereignty is the most abstract and metaphysical term in political philosophy." It is undefinable and hence abused by all writers on political science. In another reference to the subject, however, he apparently regards sovereignty as identical with ultimate political power in a state and holds that the location of this power in a society is the criterion for classifying states.

In regard to liberty, Sumner is particularly insistent that there is no real liberty apart from law and political authority. Sumner distinguishes three different types or conceptions of liberty: anarchistic, personal, and civil. The anarchistic view of liberty, which was prominent in the earlier writings of Rousseau, maintains that man is free from all social responsibility. According to this fallacious view of liberty, no member of modern society can be said to possess liberty, unless it be the tramp. Personal liberty simply means a freedom from artificial impediments in the struggle for existence. Civil liberty is "a status created for the individual by laws and institutions, the effect of which is that each man is guaranteed the use of all his own powers exclusively for his own welfare."[28] As has already been pointed out, Sumner held that it is the chief purpose of the state to produce and preserve civil liberty.

Sumner was not entirely consistent in his discussion of political rights. In one reference to the subject he denied that the conception of natural rights possesses any validity whatever. In another analysis of the subject he held that the conception possessed a very considerable value and stated that "natural rights, as opposed to chartered rights, means that every man must, in the view of social order and obligation, be regarded as free and independent, until some necessity had been established for restraining him."[29] In his latest treatment of the subject Sumner reached what may be called a distinctly sociological conception of rights, namely, that they are "rules of the game of social competition which are current now and here." To be effective, they must be "recognized in laws and provided for by institutions."

E. IMPERIALISM AND EXPANSIONISM

Not only was Sumner an ardent advocate of laissez faire in domestic or internal policies, but he also vigorously criticized the imperialistic tendencies in the United States which took form about 1896 and culminated in the Spanish-American War and the conquest of several Spanish colonies. In both cases his fundamental argument was the same.

Imperialism, like paternalistic legislation, imposes upon the population burdens which quite outweigh the benefits which are forthcoming. The increased expenses of government are thrown upon the middle class, and imperialistic administration necessitates a curtailment of liberty and the adoption of militaristic measures which seriously threaten the existence of free republican government and industrial democracy.[30] Sumner's attack on imperialism was an effective answer to Benjamin Kidd and to Sumner's American contemporary, Franklin H. Giddings, who, in his *Democracy and Empire,* was ardently defending the new American imperialism.

Sumner made no attempt to dogmatize as to the exact size of the state whch is most desirable, but he laid down the general proposition that in every case there is a maximum size of the political unit which is most advantageous under the given circumstances. In each instance it is the task of the best statesmanship to determine the size which is most expedient. The tendency of the statesmanship of the nineteenth century to make nationality, in its ethnic sense, the test of the expedient size of the state has been proved fallacious. Sweden and Norway are homogeneous as regards nationality but have not been able to form a compact political unity, while Austria-Hungary, though extremely heterogeneous from the standpoint of nationality, was welded into a fairly coherent and stable political unit.

If territorial expansion proceeds beyond this expedient size, though it may enhance the prestige of the ruler or governing classes, it does not give added strength to the state. Under the present international system of unrestricted travel and enterprise, new territory acquired by a state means merely an increase in its burdens and liabilities and brings no adequate return. Not since the abolition of the old mercantilistic colonial system has additional territory proved an asset to a state.

More serious than the financial liabilities which are bound to be incurred by an imperialistic policy is the reaction of imperialistic ideas and practices upon the politics of the state. The whole imperialistic complex is fundamentally opposed to republicanism and industrialism. It invariably creates an attitude of political arrogance and chauvinism. When conquered territories are populated by peoples widely different in culture from the conquering state, they must either be admitted into the state to participate in government or be ruled as subjects. In the first case, corruption or disintegration is likely to take place, while the second alternative involves a sacrifice of republican principles. Imperialism invariably creates militarism, which is at all points opposed to industrial republicanism. It favors plutocracy by diverting the attention of the people from the sinister acts of corrupt interests at home. If persisted in, imperialism is bound to transform the United States into an empire and to render our republic merely a transitional form. Finally, only a person of defective intelligence would maintain that the accomplishments of the United States in war are better calculated to inspire patriotism than its achievements in peaceful pursuits.[31]

Sumner riddles some of the stock arguments which are usually adduced in favor of imperialism. He argues that no state is fitted to judge when another is adapted for self-government or to decide what constitutes a stable government in another state. On such grounds a conquest of the United States might be justified from the standpoint of certain other nations. Again, it is a very dangerous fallacy to claim that a nation must conquer adjoining territory to protect its present dominions. It was claimed that the United States must have Hawaii to protect California; according to this doctrine, the conquest of the Philippines would render necessary the acquisition of China, Japan, and the East Indies to protect the Philippines. "Of course this means that, on the doctrine, we must take the whole earth in order to be safe on any part of it, and the fallacy stands exposed."[32] Had Sumner lived to December 7, 1941, and Pearl Harbor, he would have seen the complete and tragic vindication of his prophecies as to the logical and final outcome of American imperialism. The following extracts admirably summarize the main arguments of Sumner against imperialism:

Any extension will not make us more secure where we are, but will force us to take new measures to secure our new acquisitions. The preservation of acquisitions will force us to reorganize our internal resources, so as to make it possible to prepare them in advance and to mobilize them with promptitude. This will lessen liberty and require discipline. It will increase taxation and all the pressure of government. It will divert the national energy from the provision of self-maintenance and comfort for the people, and will necessitate stronger and more elaborate governmental machinery. All this will be disastrous to republican institutions and democracy. Moreover, all extension puts a new strain on the internal cohesion of the pre-existing mass, threatening a new cleavage within. If we had never taken Texas and northern Mexico we should never have had secession.[33]

The issue [involved in imperialism] is nothing less than whether to go on and maintain our political system or to discard it for the European military and monarchial tradition. It must be a complete transformation of the former to try to carry on under it two groups of political societies, one on a higher, the other on a lower plane, unequal in rights and powers; the former ruling the latter perhaps by military force.[34]

It is well for Sumner's complacency and peace of mind that he did not survive into the days of the New Deal and the second World War. The extensive social legislation of the New Deal and our participation in a great imperialistic war would have outraged every fiber of Sumner's being.[35] Even more vehement would have been his reaction to President Truman's proposal in March, 1947, that the United States become a sort of twentieth-century Byzantine empire.

F. SUMMARY OF SUMNER'S CONTRIBUTIONS TO SOCIAL THOUGHT

In summary, one may reasonably observe (1) that Sumner took over both Darwinian and Spencerian evolutionism and embodied them in his social thinking; (2) that he followed Spencer in holding that social evolution is inherently an automatic process, with which social effort should not interfere; (3) that he applied more comprehensively than any other American sociologist the ethnographic and comparative methods of the European anthropologists and ethnographers; (4) that he produced the outstanding sociological analysis of the origin and nature of moral codes and social customs; (5) that he formulated the most forceful American statement of the evolutionary basis of individualism and laissez faire; (6) that his arguments are the most impressive American critique of the conception of social planning and governmental activity; and (7) that he was the outstanding American sociological opponent of militarism and imperialism, comparable in this way to L. T. Hobhouse in England.[36]

NOTES

1. Cf. his *What Social Classes Owe to Each Other* (New York, 1883), p. 155 (hereafter cited as *"Social Classes"*).

2. Cf. "A Sketch of William Graham Sumner," *Popular Science Monthly,* June, 1889, pp. 261–68; reprinted in *The Challenge of Facts and Other Essays* (New Haven, 1914). For the most satisfactory accounts of Sumner as a personality and the salient facts of his life and academic career see H. E. Starr, *William Graham Sumner* (New Haven, 1925); and A. G. Keller, *Reminiscences of William Graham Sumner* (New Haven, 1933).

3. Volume I deals with the nature and evolution of the mores, industrial evolution and economic institutions, and political institutions and ideas; Vol. II treats of religion and religious mores; Vol. III handles marriage, the family, and sex mores generally; Vol. IV is an extended and valuable case book, illustrating the ethnographic method as applied to sociology.

4. W. G. Sumner, *Folkways: A Study of the Sociological Importance of Usages, Manners, Customs, Mores, and Morals* (Boston, 1907), pp. 2–4, 28–29, 30, 33–34, 59, 521–22; see also *The Science of Society* (4 vols.; New Haven, 1927–28), Vol. I, Part I.

5. *Folkways*, pp. 97–98. Sumner's disciple and successor at Yale, Professor A. G. Keller, has extended his master's discussion of the mores with respect to automatic evolution and conscious alteration in *Societal Evolution* (New York, 1915; new ed., 1931), chaps. iv–vi.

6. Pp. 30, 33–34, 59, 97–98, 173–74, 521–22. By permission of Ginn & Co.

7. "The Absurd Attempt To Make the World Over," written in 1894 and reprinted in *War and Other Essays*, pp. 208–10. This statement, written a decade after the appearance of the *Social Classes*, and the opinion expressed more than ten years later in *Folkways*, which was quoted above, constitute a definite answer to Professor Small's query (*American Journal of Sociology*, May, 1916, p. 733) as to whether Sumner ever changed his views regarding the efficacy of social effort and initiative. By permission of the Yale University Press.

8. Sumner was an alderman in New Haven from 1873 to 1876. Sumner's works which form the basis of the analysis of his social and political theory are, in addition to *Folkways* and *The Science of Society*, his *What Social Classes Owe to Each Other*, and his collected essays. The latter are contained in the following volumes:

a) *Collected Essays in Political and Social Science* (New York, 1885). This contains the following essays which deal with political theory: "The Theory and Practice of Elections" (pp. 98–139); "Presidential Elections and Civil Service Reform" (pp. 140–59).

b) *War and Other Essays* (New Haven, 1913). The pertinent selections in this are: "Sociology" (pp. 167–92); "The Absurd Attempt To Make the World Over" (pp. 195–210); "State Interference" (pp. 213–26); "The Fallacy of Territorial Expansion" (pp. 285–93); "The Predominant Issue" (pp. 337–52).

c) *Earth Hunger and Other Essays* (New Haven, 1913). Particularly valuable are the following: "Rights" (pp. 79–83); "Equality" (pp. 87–89); "Liberty" (pp. 109–203); "Fantasies and Facts" (pp. 207–79); "Democracy" (pp. 283–333).

d) *The Challenge of Facts and Other Essays* (New Haven, 1914). Especially to be noted are "Legislation by Clamor" (pp. 185–90); "The Shifting of Responsibility" (pp. 193–98); "The State as an Ethical Person" (pp. 201–4); "The New Social Issue" (pp. 207–12); "Speculative Legislation" (pp. 215–19); "Republican Government" (pp. 223–40); "Democracy and Responsible Government" (pp. 243–86); "Advancing Political and Social Organization in the United States" (pp. 289–344); "Introductory Lecture to Courses in Political and Social Science" (pp. 391–403).

e) *The Forgotten Man and Other Essays* (New Haven, 1918), containing also a bibliography of Sumner's works and an index to the last four volumes of essays. A list of Sumner's published books and articles is also to be found in *War and Other Essays*, pp. 377–81.

f) *Selected Essays of William Graham Sumner* (New Haven, 1924). This is a judicious selection of essays taken from the preceding five volumes. It is the most representative brief anthology of Sumnerian thought.

g) The latest selection and anthology is *Essays of William Graham Sumner* (2 vols.; New Haven, 1934).

9. The nearest approach to a comprehensive statement of his political theory is to be found in *Collected Essays in Political and Social Science*, pp. 98 ff.; see also *The Science of Society*, Vol. I, chaps. xvi–xx. For his general social theory the best anthology is the *Selected Essays of William Graham Sumner*.

No sociologist save Comte has ever been blessed or cursed by such reverent discipleship as has Sumner. A Sumner Club has been maintained at Yale from 1914 to the present day. It published an interesting bulletin on Sumner's ways and thoughts. Recently, Professor M. R. Davie has edited a symposium on the relation of Sumner's thought to current problems, *Sumner Today* (New Haven, 1940).

10. *The Challenge of Facts*, p. 203.

11. *Social Classes*, p. 9; see also *The Science of Society*, Vol. I, chaps. xvi, xx. It is obvious that Sumner's view of the state as a practical institution is identical with the conception of government as held by the best political scientists.

12. *The Challenge of Facts*, p. 244.

13. *Ibid.*, p. 226.

14. *Earth Hunger*, p. 88. Were Sumner alive, his views on Bolshevism would not be likely to lack the characteristic Sumnerian vigor (see *Sumner Today*, p. 111).

15. *Social Classes, passim; War and Other Essays*, pp. 208–10, 224–25; *Earth Hunger*, p. 299. It is of fundamental importance to note that none of Sumner's arguments for non-interference is based upon the conventional individualistic tenets.

16. *The Challenge of Facts*, p. 239. In this rather vague and equivocal definition, Sumner barely escapes bringing forth a product of the "phrase mill," as he liked to call the source of all rhetorical or metaphysical definitions. For Sumner's most mature discussion of liberty see *The Science of Society*, I, 622 ff.

17. *War and Other Essays*, p. 128.

18. *Social Classes*, p. 12.

19. *Ibid.*, p. 120.

20. *Ibid.*, pp. 126, 148–49.

21. *Ibid.*, p. 150.

22. *Ibid.*, pp. 148–51. This vital point in Sumner's political theory is analyzed and criticized by Professor F. H. Giddings, *Democracy and Empire* (New York, 1900), pp. 110–21. Sumner's attitude is, of course, the argument that Guizot employed in defending the French middle class during the assault upon its financial power in the Restoration period. Showing how Rome had fallen, not because of immorality or paganism but on account of the extinction of the middle class by unjust taxation, Guizot tried to make it clear that France was inviting a similar fate by weakening the *bourgeoisie*.

23. *Social Classes*, pp. 160–61; cf. also *War and Other Essays*, pp. 208–10; and *Earth Hunger*, pp. 283 ff.

24. *The Challenge of Facts*, p. 215.

25. *Ibid.*, p. 219; cf. also Spencer, *The Study of Sociology*, pp. 270–71.

26. *Earth Hunger*, p. 287. These arguments against large-scale state activity, which have just been enumerated, embody Sumner's main theoretical contributions to the subject. For minor considerations and questions of detail see *Earth Hunger*, pp. 283–87, 300–301. It is, of course, well known that the specific curtailment of state action in which Sumner was most interested was an abolition of the system of protective tariffs in the United States.

27. *Social Classes*, pp. 162, 167; *Earth Hunger*, pp. 304–5; *War and Other Essays*, pp. 208–10. There is no evidence that Sumner ever changed his views regarding the futility of attempting to accelerate social evolution by legislative effort. His successor, Professor A. G. Keller, has discussed this problem further, and argues that any artificial acceleration of evolution in society must be achieved indirectly through an improvement of the "mores of self-maintenance" (*Societal Evolution*, esp. chap. v).

28. *Social Classes*, p. 34; see also *The Science of Society*, I, 622 ff.

29. *Earth Hunger*, pp. 223. For Sumner's most complete discussion of natural rights see *The Science of Society*, I, 600–606.

30. *War and Other Essays*, pp. 285 ff.

31. *Ibid.*, p. 334. Sumner's remarkable discussion of the part that war has played in social processes and social evolution, as well as his accurate prediction that European "defensive" preparedness for war would ultimately lead to a general European conflict, is contained in his *War and Other Essays*, chap. i.

32. *Ibid.*, p. 351.

33. *Ibid.*, p. 292.

34. *Ibid.*, p. 246; cf. also the nearly identical arguments advanced by L. T. Hobhouse, *Democracy and Reaction* (London, 1905), chaps. ii and viii. The arguments of Sumner are criticized by Giddings, *op. cit.*, pp. 269–90. While Giddings' criticism is by no means as effective as in the case of his analysis of Sumner's doctrines on state interference, chaps. i, xvii, and xx of Professor Giddings' work constitute the most vigorous defense of imperialism yet contributed by an American sociologist.

35. See the recent volume *Sumner Today, passim*.

36. For a fine summary of Sumner's social theory see L. L. Bernard, "The Social Science Theories of William Graham Sumner," *Social Forces*, XIX (1940), 153–75.

CHAPTER XVIII

ALBION WOODBURY SMALL: PROMOTER OF AMERICAN SOCIOLOGY AND EXPOSITOR OF SOCIAL INTERESTS

HARRY ELMER BARNES

I. INTRODUCTION

WE SHALL attempt in the following pages to present an estimate of the work of Albion Woodbury Small (1854–1926), considered in its relation to the history of modern sociology as a whole. An article by Annie Marion MacLean in the *American Journal of Sociology* (July, 1926), and a chapter by Edward Cary Hayes in Odum's *American Masters of Social Science* have described his personal life and academic career, and we shall bring that interesting story into the present chapter only in so far as it is directly related to the nature and influence of Small's sociological doctrines and objectives.

It is also obvious that we cannot in the space available for this article present a summary of all Dean Small's varied and voluminous writings in the field of sociology and social economics. We shall limit ourselves primarily to (1) an analysis of the origins of his sociological interests and doctrines; (2) the leading stages in the progress of his sociological thinking and writing; (3) his chief books, as related to his sociological thought; (4) his fundamental sociological conceptions; and (5) his academic and editorial activities that bear upon the growth of sociology.

II. THE BACKGROUND OF SMALL'S SOCIOLOGICAL INTERESTS AND EQUIPMENT

While Small was, from the standpoint of chronology, influence, and activities, one of the "founders" of sociology, his writings were a sort of transition from the "systematizers," like Comte, Spencer, Ward, Giddings, and Stuckenberg, who dealt with all, or nearly all, the various fields and problems of sociology, to the subsequent generation of specialists who have approached social analysis from the standpoint of methodology, anthropogeography, biology, psychology, cultural analysis, institutional history, social economics, or human betterment. Small soared magisterially at times with the systematizers; at other times he made extremely profound and cogent contributions to social economics; and he always believed himself to be notably furthering the cause of sociological methodology. While, in his later years, he looked upon himself as in large part a specialist, concentrating upon the problems of methodology, he lacked the training to function effectively as a rigorous methodologist. What he meant, for the most part, when speaking of "method" was, in reality, an attitude toward, or the results to be gained from, social analysis. He was, likewise, too much absorbed in his general sociological interests to break away long enough to produce any large amount of specialized writing in the fields in which he was particularly proficient, namely, history, social economics, and social politics.

In the comprehensive summary of the history, problems, and fields of sociology contained in his article on "Sociology" in the *Encyclopedia Americana,* Small points out that, until very recently, the majority of American sociologists were not trained as sociologists from the beginning of their academic careers but were recruited from the fields of theology, history, economics, or political science.

In his own case Small was "recruited" from all these fields. Though he did not serve long as a preacher, he was trained in theology at the Newton Theological Institution from 1876 to 1879. The years 1879–81 Small spent in Germany at the universities of Leipzig and Berlin, where he pursued his studies in the above-mentioned subjects. Particularly important were his courses under the great German social economists, Gustav Schmoller and Adolf Wagner. It was here that he delved deeply into the subject of the conflict of interests and classes in human society and was thoroughly indoctrinated with the constructive German views as to the propriety and effectiveness of state supervision of the social process. These two basic doctrines were the core of Small's thinking in social science and his ablest contributions to sociological thought in America.

After teaching at Colby College for some years, Small attended Johns Hopkins University during the year 1888–89, and here he continued his historical studies. The "Adams School" of historians based their work in part upon the dubious Teutonic and Aryan hypotheses, as

applied to the evolution of political institutions; but they were, nevertheless, primarily interested in that comparative and genetic approach
to historical problems which is of special value to the sociologist as
training in the problems of social genesis. While at Johns Hopkins, Small
produced an important and undeservedly ignored monograph on *The
Origins of American Nationality*. Though his experience at Johns Hopkins helped to impress upon Small the significance of the genetic approach to social institutions, he never forgave the historians for their
narrowness, their provincialism, their perversion of method from a
means into an end itself, and the limited and superficial scope of their
interests. In his discussion of Professor F. H. Giddings' paper on "A
Theory of Social Causation" at the New Orleans meeting in 1903 he
said, in part, of the historians:

> The quarrel of the sociologists with the historians is that the latter have learned
> so much about how to do it that they have forgotten what to do. They have become
> so skilled in finding facts that they have no use for the truths that would make
> the facts worth finding. They have exhausted their magnificent technique in dis-
> covering things that are not worth knowing when they get through with them.
> These discoveries may be taken up by somebody else and brought into their mean-
> ing relations, but history, as it is mostly written today, does not come within sight
> of these relations. The historians are locating cinders on the face of the glacier, but
> they overlook the mountain ranges that carry the glacier.
>
> When we once start to study human affairs, there is no stoppingplace, on any
> other ground than confession of mental incompetence, till we reach answers to
> these questions: What are the essentials in human relations? In what varieties do
> these essentials appear under different circumstances? How do we account for these
> universals and their accidents? What pointers does this knowledge give us about
> our own conduct?[1]

Economics, political science, and history, in the order named, were
Small's chief stock in trade in his sociological work. To these he added
a broad synthetic aim, with the end in view of diminishing the narrowness and suspicion prevalent among the various branches of social science and of pooling their mutual resources and results in one common
service, namely, that of a clearer and more profound understanding of
the social process as a whole. Small was, however, in no sense a master
of anthropogeography, biology, psychology, or anthropology, which
placed definite limitations upon his efforts to attain a comprehensive
approach to the analysis of the social process. He was also relatively innocent of statistical methods, which was a grave handicap to his ambitious efforts in the field of general sociological methodology.

III. THE GENESIS OF SMALL'S SOCIOLOGICAL THINKING

In his *General Sociology* Small states that the history of sociology may be described as "a gradual shifting of effort from analogical representation of social structures to real analysis of social processes." This characterization also admirably describes the progress of Small's own sociological achievements. Owing to his reading of Schäffle and the other "Organicists," his earliest sociological writings exhibit the influence of this group of writers, whose chief interest lay in the elaboration of the analogies between the individual organism and the social organism. This is particularly evident in Books III and IV of his *Introduction to the Study of Society*. Yet he was never guilty of any of the absurdities of many of these writers in going to grotesque extremes in elaborating such analogies. He used the analogical method in a very sensible and discriminating manner as an effective mode of illuminating his description of social processes and institutions.

His studies with the German economists, especially Schmoller's exposition of the conflict of classes, impressed upon Small the importance of material interests in the social process. His work on the history of economics in the nineteenth century convinced him, however, of the narrowness of the classical economists' view of interests, a conviction which was buttressed by his own theological and religious training and by the fundamentally ethical orientation of his thought from his student days to his death.

This led Small to the conviction that the cataloguing and classification of a broader and more inclusive schedule of human interests and the description of their emergence, conflict, and adjustment in human society constitute the key to any truly dynamic sociology. He worked along this line himself during the last decade of the nineteenth century, and, about 1900, he came upon the leading works of Gustav Ratzenhofer, who had simultaneously developed the same mode of approach to social analysis. Small's *General Sociology* is a synthesis of his own views, independently arrived at, with the contributions of Ratzenhofer. It was his study of the struggle and accommodation of social interests that brought Small to his larger conception of society as a "becoming" or "emerging" process, which constitutes the dynamics of his system.

The conception of the *group* as the core of organized interests and the unit of the social process led Small to what he called his "methodological" studies, namely, his discussions of sociology as primarily a study of man and society viewed in relation to the group basis of life. He never tired of emphasizing this point of view, and almost his last intellectual effort was a circular letter of September 11, 1924, on this subject, brought forth by Professor Malcolm M. Willey's review of his *Origins of Sociology*.

Though the ethical element was never absent from Small's writings and teachings, his interest in social betterment increased as years went on. Indeed, from the first, he held that sociology owed both its origins and its justification to its potential services as a guide to a valid program of social reform. To him ethics was not primarily a matter of sexual purity but an improvement of social institutions and intellectual life. Both the wrecking of a major railroad system, through the predatory manipulation of high finance, and the obstructive stupidities of a bigoted fundamentalism seemed to him worse sins than adultery. He was particularly interested in the mitigation of capitalism and in the substitution of service for profit as the basic motive of economic organization and activity. His general notions in this field were expressed in his *Between Eras: From Capitalism to Democracy*, and much more systematically in his famous university course on "The Conflict of Classes."

There is thus to be seen in the development of Small's sociological interests a logical sequence of doctrinal evolution. An intelligent appreciation of the organic analogy emphasized the primary significance of function as compared with structure. The analysis of function led to his conception of the importance of the manifestation and accommodation of interests in society. This, in turn, created the notion of society as a process of social conflict, ultimately transformed under state control into socialization and co-operative endeavor. The social process was, however, seen to be a group affair, and this made it evident that sociology is primarily an analysis of the group aspects of life. Finally, the understanding of the social process is a purely academic matter unless the information so gathered can be exploited in the service of social betterment, which fact makes it clear that the ultimate purpose of sociology is to initiate and encourage a broader approach to social ethics.

IV. SMALL'S CHIEF WRITINGS AND THEIR PLACE IN
SOCIOLOGICAL LITERATURE

With the possible exception of his *Between Eras*, Small's books all grew out of his classroom lectures and seminar discussions. This accounts in part for the colloquial nature of some of them and the lack of literary and textual finish which characterizes most of them. Tables of contents and extensive excerpts from books analyzed were freely embodied in the text of his books. Even many of his articles published in the *American Journal of Sociology* and subsequently embodied in his books were read in his classes or seminars.

His first publications in the field of sociology were three syllabi for a course in social science in Colby College, the first of these being the earliest printed foundation of a course in sociology in this country. Next came his *Intrcduction to the Study of Society,* in the preparation of which he had the collaboration of his student and colleague, George M. Vincent. This was published in 1894, two years after he went to the University of Chicago to become head of the new department of sociology there. It was a pioneer work in which he endeavored to chart the field of sociology and to present its main problems within the scope of a college manual. It dealt with the province and development of sociology, described the evolution of society from isolated agrarian entities to the modern metropolitan groups, analyzed social structures and functions on the basis of the organic analogy, and risked a highly rudimentary excursion into social psychology. If the work seems an archaic curiosity at the present time, this is only an indication of the progress in social science since 1894, when the book was literally an intellectual adventure.

By all odds the most substantial and enduring of Small's work was his *General Sociology,* published in 1905 and reprinted many times thereafter. The first part of the book is a sketch of representative stages in the history of sociology. Then comes a presentation of Ratzenhofer's conception of sociology as primarily a classification of human interests and an analysis of their significance in the social process. Next follows a detailed discussion of the social process, in which Ratzenhofer's conceptions are extensively supplemented by those of Small. The work concludes with a sociological consideration of ethical problems and methods. This section constitutes a profound and courageous effort to relate the ethical concepts and problems of society to the social process and to provide a positive basis for ethical judgments and social betterment. In many respects the book contains basic contributions to economic and politics that are quite as important as those to sociology itself.

Following the *General Sociology* came the *Adam Smith and Modern Sociology,* published in 1907. Here Small considered Smith a harbinger of modern sociology, on the basis of Smith's economic-ethical doctrines. Giddings had, a decade before, traced at least his own version of sociology to the psychological theory of sympathy in Smith's *Theory of Moral Sentiments*. As Small interpreted Smith, he was very really a forerunner of Small from the standpoint of his analysis of the social process. According to Small, *The Wealth of Nations* was, in reality, a treatise on sociology with a special emphasis on the economic processes of society. As Small says:

If one were to come upon *The Wealth of Nations* for the first time, with a knowledge of the general sociological way of looking at society, but with no knowledge of economic literature, there would be not the slightest difficulty nor hesitation about classifying the book as an inquiry in a special field of sociology..... Smith set a new standard of inquiry into the economic section of the conditions of life, while life presented itself to him as, on the whole, a moral affair, in which the economic process is logically a detail..... Modern sociology is virtually an attempt to take up the larger program of social analysis and interpretation which was implicit in Adam Smith's moral philosophy, but which was suppressed for a century by prevailing interest in the technique of the production of wealth.[2]

It would be difficult to state more precisely in the same number of words Small's own view of socioeconomic problems or the nature of his major contribution to the science of society. Small's book on Smith is, incidentally, an effective indictment of the tendency of the economists —or "pecuniary logicians"—of the last century to concentrate upon the wealth interest in society, to exaggerate its significance, and to consider it in relative isolation from the other social factors. Small expresses his view on this matter in the following paragraph:

Applying these generalities to the case in hand, the question which the sociologist is always implicitly asking of the economist is: To what extent are you making your analyses and passing your valuations of economic activities as though they were bounded by the wealth interest alone, and to what extent do your analyses and valuations take account of the whole process of moral evolution within which the wealth interest is an incident? Economic theory, in England and America, throughout the nineteenth century made the wealth interest unduly prominent in the process of moral evolution, and thereby introduced confusion into the whole scale of moral valuation. The present essay makes a beginning of showing this in detail. The principal methodological thesis which the exhibit is to support is that a sufficient interpretation of life to be a reliable basis for social programs must express economic relations at last in terms of the whole moral process. This is true of political economy in so far as it purports to be more than a technology of things. To the degree in which political economy proposes to establish norms for evaluating the activities of persons, it must answer to the whole moral process in which all the activities of persons derive their meaning.[3]

Small's most erudite volume, *The Cameralists,* was the fourth in the list of his publications. This was a thorough study of that type of German social, economic, and political doctrine which was, in a rough way, the analogue of British mercantilism. Small was interested in cameralism, both as a forerunner of the synthetic social science for which he was laboring and as an example of the exploitation of social science to guide public policy and social betterment. He thus explains the interest which led him through this painstaking but thankless compilation:

This system of ideas and of practice had been developing since 1555. It did not correspond in its subdivisions with later academic definitions of the social sciences. It started not as a general theory but as a formulation of administrative expediency. It set forth with the frank purpose of subordinating everything within the control of the state to the state's problem of existence. The central question to which cameralism elaborated answers was: The ruler being all-powerful over his territories and his subjects, what policies, and what details of practice in pursuance of the policies must he adopt, in order to make his rule most secure at home, and in order to provide most abundant means of asserting himself against other rulers? It would require but little reflection to prepare against surprise at what happened. Under the circumstances of the time, this question necessarily led to answers which amounted to prescribed programs covering the entire outward life of the subjects of German rulers. It soon became evident to the advisers of those rulers, and to the administrators of their states, that their problem involved not merely physical factors, but that it was a question of training the whole population for all the different sorts of useful work of which human beings are capable. From generation to generation the men who developed cameralistic theory and practice saw more and more clearly that if the rulers of German states were to command abundant resources, they must rule over resourceful people. This meant that the people must be trained physically, mentally, morally, and technically. In the end, therefore, cameralistic theory covered everything in the lives of the citizens, from farm work to religious worship. The machinery for administering this theory grew more and more complex. In detail its organization differed in one state from that in another. Its main purpose was everywhere the same, viz., to make the people as amenable as possible to all the discipline necessary to insure maximum performance of all the physical, mental, and moral processes tributary to the strength of the ruler.

It need not be pointed out that this program involved dealing from this special point of view, with every sort of activity which has since come under the attention of political science and political economy in their latest forms. In so far as cameralism dealt with economic questions in the later sense, it treated them as matters primarily of the state, not of individuals. German economic theory, therefore, was collectivistic in the highest degree. Only incidentally, and in a wholly subordinate degree, was it individualistic. It was a theory of, for and by the government.[4]

Small's fifth book, *The Meaning of Social Science,* was a telling attack upon the unfortunate tendency to departmentalize the social sciences in

the nineteenth century, with the resulting suspicion, jealousy, narrowness, and incomplete analyses of social situations. Small's healthy contempt for the departmental bigotry of the social scientists constitutes
a leading thread running through all his writings. It appears as early
as his first syllabus prepared in the eighties at Colby College, and in
one of his very latest published reviews he came back to the matter with
all his old time vigor:

Without essential perversion, the story of the social sciences in the United States
during the past generation might be told under the figure of a pack of mongrels
foraging for their keep and each snarling at each whenever one found a consum-
able bite. All the needed reduction of exaggeration in the analogy might be
effected by the substitute that until recently the typical American social scientist has
acted as though he feared that the supply of truth in the world is not enough to
go around, and that his share of its might run short if anybody else went in search
of it along any but his own beaten paths. The social scientists have manifested
a maximum of short-diametered clannishness each toward his own kind, and a
minimum of magnanimity toward everybody else. The result has been stunted
and shriveled social scientists and social science.[5]

The major theses defended in *The Meaning of Social Science* are:
(1) that knowledge of society must be unified, however much specialization may be needed in different types of investigation; (2) that there
can be no adequate social science which does not take into account all
phases of human experience and their interaction upon one another;
and (3) that the chief purpose of social science is to arrive at a valid
appraisal of human values, with the aim of promoting the creation of
a more adequate and just social order. Some of his more decisive statements upon these points follow:

Whatever else may be true or false about sociology, its reason for existence is
something which does not shut it off nor set it apart from other social sciences. On
the contrary, its essence is an assertion which must be the center of all sane social
science, namely, that knowledge of human experience cannot at last be many; in
the degree in which it approaches reality it must be one knowledge.....
Sociologists declare that the experience bounded by the reactions between men
and physical nature, on the one hand, and the reactions of men with one another,
on the other, is an interconnected experience, and that we shall have a science of
it only in the proportion of our insight into the way and degree in which each item
of this experience is affected by every other item of it.[6]

Much the most striking and original of Small's works was his *Between
Eras: From Capitalism to Democracy,* published in 1913. This is one
of the most outspoken and courageous books yet published in America,
but the peculiar nature of the presentation of the material in the form

of dialogues prevented any extensive circulation of the work, and it created little stir.

Between Eras is as relentless a criticism of our conventional unmitigated capitalism as can be found in Veblen's *Theory of the Leisure Class, The Theory of Business Enterprise,* and *Absentee Ownership;* in Tawney's *Acquisitive Society;* or in the Webbs' *Decay of Capitalist Civilization.* In arriving at his critical attitude toward capitalism and his unusually frank and capable analysis of capitalistic institutions, Small was greatly influenced by Schäffle, Schmoller, and Veblen, but, beyond all others, by Werner Sombart, whose *Moderne Kapitalismus* came into his hands about 1905.

Small adopted the quasi-socialistic thesis that nature and labor are the sole ultimate factors in productivity. He showed the ethical bankruptcy of the profit economy and thoroughly exposed the wastes, inefficiency, and injustices of capitalistic exploitation. He attacked the whole conception of the inheritance of immense fortunes, carrying with them extensive financial and industrial control. He made clear the fictitious nature of the divine-right theory of unlimited private property, which was the veritable cornerstone of our American *Politik* and economic system. In the place of the profit economy he would substitute the conception of production for human service under state supervision. Inheritance should be severely limited and labor given its just share in the control of industrial enterprise and social policy. As a startling and suggestive work, *Between Eras* can, without exaggeration, be compared with Plato's *Republic,* and its dialogues are much more cogent and relevant for contemporary readers than those contained in the work of the great Greek.

The same line of analysis, in a somewhat more conservative vein, was carried on by Small in one of his last utterances—an article on "The Sociology of Profits," published in the *American Journal of Sociology* for January, 1925. The fundamental principles and positions expounded in *Between Eras* were set forth in much more thorough and formal fashion in Small's famous course on the "Conflict of Classes," and it is a great misfortune that the material in this course was never published systematically in book form.

While it was printed in the *American Journal of Sociology* for May, 1916, Small's "Fifty Years of Sociology in the United States" (1865–1915) was in reality a book.[6a] It is an invaluable source for the history of

American social science, particularly in its academic aspects, and it contains much autobiographical material. It was based upon unique personal reminiscences and careful research. The monograph also contained much upon the development of sociological methods and objectives. It is admirably supplemented by his article on "The Future of Sociology," which appeared in the *Publications of the American Sociological Society* for 1920. He also left unpublished a work on the history of sociological method in the United States which we may hope will ultimately see light.

Small's last work was his *Origins of Sociology,* published in 1924. It is a comprehensive history of outstanding tendencies in German social science during the nineteenth century. Particular attention is given to those Germanic influences which helped to shape American social science between 1800 and 1900. As an authority on the subjects covered in this book, Small was without a rival in the United States.

In this work he selected the following topics to illustrate the development of social science in Germany during the nineteenth century: (1) the Savigny-Thibaut controversy as illustrative of the development of the concept of continuity in the historical and social process; (2) Eichhorn's emphasis on the complexity of social and historical situations; (3) Niebuhr's contributions to the scientific scrutiny and evaluation of historical sources; (4) Leopold von Ranke's insistence upon adequate documentation in historical narrative and generalizations; (5) the organization of source and archival material through the labors of Pertz, Waitz, and the editors of the *Monumenta;* (6) cameralism and the rise of objectivism in the social sciences; (7) the rise of systematic economics with Adam Smith and the classical school; (8) the development of systematic historical methodology by Bernheim; (9) the development of economics along the lines of comparative economic history by Wilhelm Roscher; (10) Karl Menger and presentation of the psychological point of view in economics; (11) Karl Knies and the entry of the ethical factor into economic science; (12) Schäffle, Schmoller, Wagner, and the professorial sociologists, who insisted upon the social and ameliorative point of view in economic and political activity; (13) the Treitschke-Schmoller controversy, which illustrated the clash of the individualistic and social points of view in *Politik;* (14) the contributions of Albert Schäffle in the way of introducing the sociological approach to economics; (15) the work of the Ahrens–Von Mohl group in developing the sociological orientation in German political science; and, finally, (16) the rise of the sociological movement in the United States.

In addition to these books, Small contributed many articles to the *American Journal of Sociology,* though most of them were later reprinted in book form. Whatever the verdict which historians of sociology may pass upon the value of his discussions of methodology and his positive sociological theory, there can be no doubt that Small's written work falls primarily under the heading of the history of social theory, especially Germanic social theory and its influence upon American social science. No other man did so much to make the fundamental contributions of modern German social science available to American readers.

While Small was a man of wide erudition and possessed of a very fertile and alert mind, he lacked almost every quality which goes to make an attractive writer. In part, this was due, as pointed out above, to the fact that his books were mainly the publication of classroom notes and lectures, sometimes admittedly without any alteration or revision. His style was extremely verbose and discursive. There were also endless repetitions of the same thought and phraseology. His major points and contentions were almost always sound and suggestive, but their phrasing was often tortuous and confused, a condition which was intensified by the involved nature of his verbal style.

It is true that Small exercised an influence upon American sociology greater and more salutary than any other individual except, perhaps, Giddings; but he did it chiefly through his intellectual courage and integrity, his great energy as a teacher, his real erudition, his capacity to charm and inspire students by his gracious and kindly manner, and his influence as the editor of the world's foremost sociological journal. We may well wonder what his national and international influence might have been if the cogency and penetration of his thinking had equaled that of Giddings or if his writing had possessed the verve and lucidity of Ross. In a letter of December 11, 1924, to the present writer, commenting on my review of the *Origins of Sociology,* Small, with characteristic candor, admitted these stylistic defects:

As to form, you are of course utterly right. My mother once asked me with a deep sigh, "Why is it that you never publish anything that contains either gospel or entertainment?" I could only admit the soft impeachment, and leave the subject with an unsatisfying answer. I do not remember that I have ever written anything, except things to be spoken, without feeling myself trailed by some coming man who could carry the job nearer to completion. All my life I have felt myself under mandate to get out stuff in the rough, which would be a challenge to somebody to work it over, or to get out more and better stuff of a more ultimate order. I have never been able to address myself to book *readers*, but only to potential book *makers*, and I have already felt that, with them, as makers not of literature but of technical treatises, not form, but substance, and pointers toward more substance. matters.[7]

In fairness to Small, however, it should be pointed out that his stylistic defects are to be found chiefly in his theoretical works. His critical reviews, and especially his treatment of concrete historical materials, as exemplified by his *Beginnings of American Nationality*, often exhibited clarity and directness.

V. DOMINANT POINTS IN SMALL'S SOCIOLOGICAL THEORY

We may now devote our attention to a brief summary of Small's central and dominant contributions to sociology. In the first place, he was thoroughly converted to Lester F. Ward's view that the only adequate guidance in adjusting man to the complex conditions of modern life and in effecting orderly social change must be sought in the social sciences. Small was, however, fully aware of the rudimentary and timid nature of the social sciences at the present time. In his circular letter of September 11, 1924, he frankly admitted this in the following words:

As to the so-called social sciences, on the average and as a rule, they have not passed far out of the homely wisdom stage of development. If we apply the acid test to the total output of what we now call the social sciences, from Herodotus down, and including the 1924 vintage, each social science has consisted of 95 parts *omnium gatherum* of all sorts of pertinent and impertinent selections from the scrap heaps of human experience, promoted in a few later generations by use of bibliographies and card-indexes, combined with five parts of critically authenticated first-hand discovery strictly pertinent to some accurately defined problem. On the whole, every social scientist, whether he preferred to call himself historian, economist, sociologist, or what not, has actually, in ninety-five hundredths of his activities been a rationalizer at large, and only in five percent of his activities has he concentrated upon close investigation of strictly defined problems, by use of an adequate method. I am prepared for correction as to my arithmetical terms. It is conceivable that the ratio may turn out to be 94% general discursiveness and 6% serious science, but that will not fatally affect the principle.[8]

Yet the social sciences are being rapidly improved in their objectivity and quantitative methodology. We shall probably be correct in expecting that they will have reached a status which will make them adequate for social guidance fully as soon as society is ready to accept advice from this quarter. Small devoted his professional life to the advancement of both these programs: the improvement of the social sciences and the increase of their public prestige.

Small's conception of the nature of sociology underwent important modifications along with the general progress of his sociological thinking. In his *Introduction to the Study of Society,* he presented the view that sociology is primarily a general synthetic science, embodying an organization of all the knowledge concerning man which has been accumulated or is being gathered by the special social sciences. Subsequently, he became preoccupied with Ratzenhofer's approach to sociology from the standpoint of the struggles of "interest-groups," and he approved Simmel's notion of sociology as a type of methodology concerned with the nature and forms of social groups. Small, accordingly, developed his later contention that sociology is "a collection of techniques for exposing group relations in human affairs" or, again, "sociology is that variety of study of the common subject-matter of social science which trains attention primarily upon the forms and process of groups." Perhaps the best of his later definitions of sociology is that contained in his *Americana* article:

> The sociological technique is that variant among the social science techniques which proceeds from the perception that, after allowing for their purely physical relations, all human phenomena are functions not only of persons, but of persons whose personality on the one hand expresses itself in part through the formation of groups, and on the other hand is in part produced through the influence of groups. In brief, sociology is that technique which approaches knowledge of human experience as a whole through investigation of group-aspects of the phenomena.[9]

Small himself recognized the transformation of his views on this subject and repudiated to some extent his earlier omnibus conception of sociology. In his article on the "Future of Sociology" he admitted:

> In proportion as sociology becomes responsibly objective it will leave behind its early ambition for a hegemony over social sciences, and it will realize its destiny of functioning within a federation of scientific activities. With widening and clarifying of social consciousness, it must become progressively evident that a single technique, no matter how penetrating, can at most lay bare only certain constituent aspects of the total social process.[10]

His view of sociology thus passed from a notion of a synthesis of the special social sciences to a notion much more like that of Giddings, namely, that of sociology as the elemental or basic social science. Yet Small never departed from his original healthy notion that the study of society must be a unified and co-operative process, in which sociology and the special sciences should carry on an intelligent and co-ordinated division of labor. Sociology may not legitimately aspire to be an over-science or a complete synthesis of all existing knowledge concerning society. But it must always operate in the closest rapport with the special social sciences and must appropriate the latest contributions from each of the latter which can aid in arriving at a more comprehensive and profound understanding of the group life of man as the core of the social process. To quote once more from Small's letter of September 11, 1924: "I have never been able to admire the ideal of a scientist as a man who should confine his personality within the bounds of his specialty. On the contrary, my conception of the ideal scientist is a consummate technician in his own specialty, or specialties, but over and above that a reliable liaison officer between his specialty and all other divisions of knowledge, including the arts of converting scientific knowledge into human advantage."[11]

The same spirit emerges from the following paragraph, taken from his article on the "Future of Sociology":

We may well congratulate ourselves upon the complete absence from our horizon of signs that the near future of sociology is to be sectarian. Differences of opinion there are among us in plenty. We differ about emphasis, about method, about vocabulary, about choices of immediate programs. All this makes for health. On the other hand, there is nothing among us remotely parallel with the quarrels in the eighteen-eighties between the economists of the "classical," the "historical," and the "Austrian" communions, not to speak of the minor sects. We are not a jangle of party proclamation—"I am of Paul, and I of Apollos, and I of Cephas." Various as our expressions are in outward appearance, we are bound together by common consciousness of a vocation to see that group aspects of human experience receive their dues in all attempts to interpret or to control human affairs.[12]

In his *Americana* article Small recognizes the present trend in sociology away from the older practice of attempting a systematic presentation of the whole field of sociology in one general treatise and toward specialization in what may be called "schools" or "provinces" of the subject. He distinguishes some six fields into which contemporary sociology has been differentiated: (1) methodology, (2) group psychology, (3) social analysis, (4) social survey, (5) social diagnosis and (6) drafting of specific programs for social betterment.

While Small himself wrote and discoursed incessantly during the last fifteen or twenty years of his life concerning "method" and "methodology" in the social sciences, it may be doubted if he used this term in a strictly accurate sense or recognized exactly what "methodology" means. Despite his rather complete divorcement from obscurantism, Small's early training and methods of thought were an almost insuperable handicap to his ambition as a specialist in sociological methodology. His early training was in philosophy and theology, and, despite his subsequent intellectual emancipation, he tended to think and write in a philosophical and metaphysical strain and to deal with imponderable abstractions. His mental patterns were of the prescientific and premethodological stage of social science.

Strictly speaking, sociological method is a combination of the broad, synthetic approach of sociology to human and social problems with the appropriate techniques of investigation and synthesis for the particular field which is to be studied and organized. Most sociologists agree that the methodology of sociology must be the *scientific* method of empirical inquiry; and some, such as Giddings, Ogburn, Lundberg, and others, insist that the scientific method in sociology means the quantitative or statistical method. Professor Ellwood, among others, has vigorously attacked this narrow conception of sociological method, in his book on *Methods in Sociology* (1933), and contends that there are important fields of sociological study for which the strictly statistical method is not suited. Such writers hold that, in social problems, there are necessarily value-judgments which are not comparable to the problems dealt with by the scientific method applicable to the physical sciences. Indeed, Howard Becker contends that sociological problems are primarily qualitative rather than quantitative and, hence, cannot be adequately handled by the statistical approach.

Small possessed almost no knowledge of modern statistics, which prevented him from dealing thoroughly with quantitative sociological methodology. Likewise, of the special fields of sociology, he had a competent command of technical knowledge only in matters of historical, economic, and political analysis, and here he did work of great distinction.

The fact is that what Small was pleased to call "sociological method" was, in reality, a sort of combination of the general sociological approach with what he regarded as the province and objectives of sociology. Methodology, then, was to Small chiefly definitions of sociology and its subdivisions; invention and elucidation of sociological categories; discussions of the province of sociology; and suggestions as to the ultimate ethical objectives of sociology. This is well illustrated by his summary definition of sociological method in his *Meaning of Social Science:* "This method is throughout objective investigation and evaluation of human experience, with the purpose of constructing valuations into more complete realizations."[13] Some may object that the present writer is too narrow or technical in his definition of sociological methodology; but, even if we concede that Small was correct in his conception of methodology, we must admit that, except in the politicoeconomic province, he wrote and talked primarily *about* sociological method instead of indicating just what it is.

The pivotal element in Small's own sociological system was the notion of human interests and their social control. The analysis of the origins, expression, adjustment, and more intelligent direction of human interests constituted the essence of both the analytical and the ethical aspects of his systematic writings.

The concept of interests and interest-groups as the clue to the dynamics of the social process has a long history, going as far back as Aristotle. It was basic in the thought of the "Fathers," from Madison to Calhoun. In modern sociology it took its origins from the ideas of the economists and from the fundamental work of Ludwig Gumplowicz in his elucidation of the essence of the *Rassenkampf.* His disciple, Gustav Ratzenhofer, still further elaborated this formula, and Small constructed his system on the basis of his own views and those of Ratzenhofer. The cardinal importance of this phase of his work Small pointed out as early as 1903 in his discussion of Giddings' paper on "A Theory of Social Causation" at the New Orleans meeting of the American Sociological Society, two years before the publication of the *General Sociology:*

We need to know, in the concrete, just how human interests have combined with each other in every variety of circumstance within human experience. There has never, to my knowledge, been a fairly successful attempt to schedule efficient human interests in general, till Ratzenhofer did it less than ten years ago in *Das Wesen und Zweck der Politik.* With this work sociology attained its majority. Henceforth, all study of human relations must be rated as provincial, which calculates problems of life with reference to a less comprehensive scheme of interests than his analysis exhibits.[14]

As early as 1893,[15] Small had formulated a schedule of human interests in six groups:[16] (I) the primary or "Health Interest," subdivided into three constituent elements: (1) the "Food Interest," (2) the "Sex Interest," and (3) the "Work Interest"; (II) the "Wealth Interest"; (III) the "Sociability Interest"; IV the "Knowledge Interest"; (V) the "Beauty Interest"; and (VI) the "Rightness Interest."

The emergence of these interests in society, their conflicts and adjustments in the form of group activity, carried on under the mitigating mediation of the state, and the progressive development of ever greater appreciation of the importance of the higher types of interests, constitute the social process, which is the vital subject matter of all dynamic sociology. Small summarizes his views on these critical matters in the following selections, which we have taken from the *General Sociology:*

In a word, then, the energies that have their basis of action in the human animal differentiate into impulses that cause the actions of that animal to radiate. The individual that comes into being through this differentiation is the resultant of the different interests that wrestle with each other in his personality. The career of that individual, and of all individuals combined, is persistent struggle, on the one hand, of the interests in the individual, by virtue of which he is what he is at any moment, and, on the other hand, of the combination of interests in one individual with the combination of interests in all the others.....

So far as I am able to account for the activities of men, they all run back to motives that have their roots in combinations of this health-interest with interests that arrange themselves in five other groups. Men have a distinct interest in controlling the resources of nature, in asserting their individuality among their fellows, in mastering all that can be known, in contemplating what seems to them beautiful, and in realizing what seems to them right. I have not been able to find any human act which requires, for explanation, any motive that cannot be accounted for by specialization and combination of these interests. Each of the groups has subdivisions, more or fewer than those of the first. All men, however, from the most savage to the most highly civilized, act as they do act, first, because of variations in the circumstances of their environment, both physical and social; second, because of variations and permutations of their six elementary interests.....

Without affirming that either conflict or conjunction of interests is the essence of the social process, we may say that, in form, the social process is incessant reaction of persons prompted by interests that in part conflict with the interests of their fellows, and in part comport with the interests of others. The ratio of the conflict and of the harmony is also infinitely variable. The kinds of conflict and harmony are likewise variable. In general, conflict is the obvious phase of association in earlier stages of the social process, while conjunction of interests grows more evident in later stages.....

We must at the outset disarm the prejudice that States are merely political organizations. That notion is parallel with the economic provincialism just noticed. The modern State is both a political organization and an economic system, but it is much more. The State is a microcosm of the whole human process. The State is the co-operation of the citizens for the furtherance of all the interests of which they are conscious.....

Whatever else the State may or may not do, this at least is its constant role, viz.: The State always brings to bear upon the individuals composing it a certain power of constraint to secure from them, in all their struggles with each other, the observance of minimum established limits of struggle. This is not a hypothetical statement of what the State might, could, would, or should do. It is a literal generalization of what every State actually does. It is an objective statement of a cardinal fact in the social process.....

Civic society organized as the State is composed of individual and group factors, each of which has in itself certain elements of political independence.....That is, each has interests seemingly distinct from the interests of the others. Each has some degree of impulse to assert these interests in spite of the others. Thus the State is a union of disunions, a conciliation of conflicts, a harmony of discords. The State is an arrangement of combinations by which mutually repellent forces are brought into some measure of concurrent action.....

At present we may use the terms "socialization" and "civilization" interchangeably. Each is a phase of the other. We have just seen how struggle—i.e., the specialization of interests—unwittingly pays tribute, and become vassal to, socialization. It turns the interests which are antagonists of each other into a common social stock, administered by a group composed of all the previously conflicting groups.....

Civilization, so far as it is bounded by national limits, consists in enlargement of the content of the common spiritual substance, until it approaches inclusion of all interests, so far as they depend upon concerted conduct; leaving scope for independence only in those activities in which free individual movement best realizes the common interests.....

Our whole life—from our eating and sleeping, to our thinking, and trading, and teaching, and playing, and praying, and dying—is a part of the social process. In us the process has its lodgement. In the process we live and move and have our being. Instead of not being concerned with it, nothing else is our concern, so far as we are citizens of the world. We do not know our personal concerns until we see through and through the social process.....

Human experience composes an associational process. The elements of that process are interests lodged in individuals. These interests may be reduced to least common denominators containing relatively simple essentials, but in the conditions of actual life, even at the most primitive stages, the interests express themselves in wants capable of infinite variation and combination. The individuals thus stimulated seek satisfaction of their wants, and efforts to this end bring them into contact with each other. At first these contacts are more evidently collisions; interest clashes with interest. The immediate result is formation of groups for offensive and defensive purposes. These groups in time vary more and more from the primitive animal type. As the variation increases, association becomes an accelerated process of differentiation or permutation of interests within the individuals, of contacts between individuals, of conflict and of co-operation among individuals and the groups into which they combine. Incidental to this pursuit of purposes, and to the process of adjustment between persons which results, individuals enter into certain more or less persistent structural relationships with each other, known in general as "institutions," and into certain more or less permanent directions of effort which we may call the social functions. These social structures and functions are, in the first instance, results of the previous associational process; but they no sooner pass out of the fluid state, into a relatively stable condition, than they become in turn causes of subsequent stages of the associational process, or at least conditions affecting details of the process. There comes a time when some of the individuals in association begin to reflect upon the association itself in a fragmentary way. They think of their family, their clan, their tribe, their nation, as having interests of its own, instead of confining themselves to impulsive action stimulated merely by their individual interests. These men coin and utter thoughts and feelings and purposes which become current in their group. There are thenceforward more or less distinct group-programs co-ordinating the instinctive endeavors of the individuals, and producing a certain mass-movement, in addition to the molecular motions, in the associational process. That is, the groups, as such, entertain purposes, and combine their efforts with some degree of reference to them. With this consummation the associational process is in full swing. All that follows is merely differentiated in detail. Interpretation of specific stages or areas of human experience is consequently a matter of qualitative and quantitative analysis of the experience in terms of these primary factors. History, or our own current experience, records its meaning in the degree in which it discloses the form, the quality, the force, and the proportions with which these various powers of the different elements and conditions of association participate in the given action.[17]

Small held that knowledge is worth while only in so far as it contributes to the betterment of society: "The primary and chief function of science is to act as all men's proxy in finding out all that can be known about what sort of a world this is, and what we can do in it to make life most worth living."[18]

The only valid guide to social change is the scientific knowledge available in the premises, presented by a co-operating group of scientists, representing the various fields of knowledge involved:

The most reliable criterion of human values which science can propose would be the consensus of councils of scientists representing the largest possible variety of human interests, and co-operating to reduce their special judgments to a scale which would render their due to each of the interests in the total calculation.

This declaration of principles, and the program which it implies would not be the abdication of science. It would be science stripped of cant. It would be science with its eyes open. It would be science with its decks cleared for action!

From this outlook there is nothing utopian whatsoever in anticipating the development of institutes of social science, composed not alone of academic men, by any means, but reinforced more and more by scientific men of action functioning as councils of elder statesmen, and focusing all the wisdom within human reach upon the conduct of men's affairs.[19]

Conforming to the above criteria and objectives of useful knowledge in general, sociology is of ultimate importance only in so far as it furnishes the basis for an intelligent and efficient control of the social process and a progressive improvement of human culture and social institutions:

If sociology is profitless, by all means let it alone. Wisdom is justified of her children, but she is always compromised when the unwise claim her maternity.....

Sociology has arrived at the outlook that human experience is the evolution of purposes in men, and of the action and reaction of men upon one another in pursuit of these changing purposes within conditions which are set by the reactions between men and physical nature.....

To do the right thing, except by accident, in any social situation, we must rightly think the situation. We must think it not merely in itself, but in all its connections. Sociology aims to become the lens through which such insight may be possible. There must be credible sociologists in order that there may be far-seeing economists and statesmen and moralists, and that each of us may be an intelligent specialist at his particular post.[20]

Small makes the following constructive and dynamic suggestion as to the social basis of fundamental ethical judgments: it is the function of the social process to increase the sum total of human satisfactions through an ever more perfect realization of vital human interests. The only valid criterion of "good" or "bad" is whether any act or policy speeds up or retards the social process:

If we are justified in drawing any general conclusions whatever from human experience thus far, it is safe to say that the social process tends to put an increasing proportion of individuals in possession of all the goods which have been discovered by the experience of humanity as a whole, and that all social programs should be thought out with a view to promotion of this tendency.....

All the systems of ethics, and all the codes of morals, have been men's gropings toward ability to express this basic judgment: That is good for me or for the world around me, which promotes the on-going of the social process. That is bad, for me or for the world around me, which retards the on-going of the social process.[21]

While Small rightly contended that all worth-while sociology must directly or indirectly contribute in differing degrees to the uplift of humanity, yet he conceded that not all uplift is sociology:

It will continue to be our misfortune if we persist in using the word sociology as an omnibus designation for all the different functions which are performed by the different types of people who in general make desire for human improvement the ostensible motive for their efforts. Instead of designating precision in the judgment of scientific men such indiscriminate use of a term confuses and compromises everything to which it is applied. When Lester F. Ward was spending certain hours of each day contributing to paleo-botany, and certain other hours of the same days wrote *The Psychic Factors of Civilization* he did not ask people to call paleo-botany social psychology nor vice versa. If he had he would simply have furnished an extreme illustration of the fallacy of the sociologists in trying to make terms for functions coincide with the persons functioning.[22]

In spite, however, of his courageous assertion of the ultimate validity of scientific knowledge as the basis for social judgments, Small was never quite able to escape from the religious background of his career and training. This is well brought out in an eloquent paragraph from *The Meaning of Social Science:*

No man has lived his life to the full who is not at last, in one preserve of his personality, a mystic. It is a grub's life not to feel out after the connections of what we can know with what we cannot know; after the fulfillment of what we have been or might have been in what we may be. From the first to last religions have been men's more or less conscious attempts to give finite life its infinite rating. Science can never be an enemy of religion. Stop the stress and strain, the rush and roar, the fuss and bluff of modern life long enough for the deeply human in us to have his chance, and the more science we have the more are we awed and lured by the mystery beyond our ken; the more do the unsatisfied longings in us yearn for larger interpretation.[23]

VI. GENERAL ESTIMATE OF SMALL'S PLACE IN AMERICAN SCIENCE

Briefly to summarize Small's contributions to sociology which are embodied in his books, we should give first place to his work as a historian of sociological thought. Here he was the most voluminous American contributor of his generation. He rendered a real service in interpreting the development of Germanic social science in such a fashion as to be of great utility to American readers. This was an achievement of the highest importance and, in all probability, was one which would not have been performed at all if Small had not executed it.

He was also a tireless worker in promoting the cause of sociology in all his writings. No other American writer devoted so much attention and energy to the program of justifying the existence of sociology as a subject of academic standing and professional importance. He was the leading propagandist of sociology in this country, employing the term "propagandist" in its best sense as a form of highly animated and enthusiastic education.

Small was likewise an indefatigable contributor to the indispensable, if somewhat thankless, field of delimiting and justifying the province of sociology and stating what he believed to be its objectives. If these last two contributions are interpreted, as Small himself interpreted them, to mean an elucidation of the problems of sociological methodology, then he was our most voluminous contributor to this department of sociological endeavor.

In conjunction with the supplementary work of Ratzenhofer, Small excelled any other sociologist writing in the English language in the thoroughness of his elaboration of the interest concept and the group idea as sociological clues. No other American sociologist has rivaled him in the development of the concept of the social process or in his emphasis upon the significance of its dynamic interpretation.

Finally, Small was exceeded only by Lester F. Ward in the persistence and ardor of his contention that sociology is to be justified, if at all, through its potential contributions to the triumph of scientifically guided social betterment. In other words, he always insisted that, in its fundamental goal, sociology is social ethics. He gave to this latter subject a broad foundation which distinguished it from its usual interpretation as the rationalized pseudo-scientific mental operations of the prohibitionist, vice-crusader, and smut-censor. He made it a dynamic and comprehensive agent for the general elevation of society, the deepening of the meaning of human life, and the improvement of social institutions. His writings were an appropriate and genuine outgrowth of his personality. This high ethical import of his writings was consistent with a personal character of real nobility and unusual generosity.

Significant as are the above contributions to sociology through the written word, the writer of this chapter is thoroughly convinced that Small's permanent influence upon sociology through his writings will ultimately prove slight and ephemeral as compared with the impress of his personality and personal activities upon the development of the sociological movement. In other words, Small was a much more significant figure in the campaign to establish sociology as a valid field of academic and professional endeavor than he was in sociological literature, magisterial though his position may be in this latter regard.

First and foremost, in determining Small's place in sociology, the writer would put his methods, ideals, and influence as a teacher. He possessed a singularly gracious personality, combined with an impressive dignity that was never forbidding. He at once secured the confidence of his students, and his many academic duties never led him into carelessness or neglect with respect to the legitimate needs of his classes. He carried a relatively heavy teaching schedule throughout his entire academic career, in spite of the fact that he was not only head of the department of sociology and editor-in-chief of the *American Journal of Sociology* but also dean of the Graduate School of Arts and Literature for nearly twenty years, having been appointed in 1905. He introduced thousands of students to the sociological idea, and he trained many of the professional teachers of sociology who are now expounding the subtle secrets of the science between the Alleghenies and the Pacific.

Particularly significant as an outgrowth of his teaching activities was his direction of the University of Chicago department of sociology for over thirty years. This was for a generation the only adequate and well-balanced faculty of sociology that had yet graced a graduate school in the United States. Small was a man of real tolerance of viewpoint and true catholicity of interests, and this led him to build up a sociology department that represented a great diversity of points of view and specialized interests, e.g., Henderson, Vincent, Thomas, Park, and their successors. This was of particular value to Chicago students, and it also served to disseminate throughout the country a broad conception of the nature of sociology and a wide array of the facts embodied in its subject matter. This was of immensely greater value than the inculcation of the essential elements of any single system of sociology, however impressive that system might be. The divers conceptions of the members of the Chicago department were reflected in the training and equipment of the many students who exposed themselves to the instruction of the Chicago staff and carried the knowledge thus acquired to teaching posts in all parts of the country.

Next to his teaching and departmental supervision, Small's most important work in promoting sociology lay in his founding and editing of the *American Journal of Sociology*. Established in 1895, this has been by all odds the most important sociological journal in the world during the last half-century. While now supplemented by the *Journal of Social Forces* and the *American Sociological Review*, it still carries more important monographic articles than either of the other two and must be reckoned the most significant of the three in respect to the discussion of theoretical issues in the sociological field. The *American Journal of Sociology* has served as a medium of expression for sociologists the world over.

Small's extensive acquaintance with European literature and personalities was of vital importance in securing contributions from the leading European sociologists. It also furnished a place where many ambitious young sociologists risked their first published ventures in the field. Small was never pontifical as an editor, and he encouraged young men to publish their materials in his journal if their contributions were articles of merit. It would be an interesting exercise to ascertain just how many important American sociologists of the present generation first broke ground in a literary way in the *American Journal of Sociology*. In recent years a combination of limitations of space and a great increase in the rate of publication of sociological books have tended to make the reviews in this journal very brief and sometimes casual. Yet for a generation this periodical was almost the only place in which American readers could acquaint themselves with the progress of sociological literature. There cannot be any doubt whatever that Small's service to the development of sociology through his editing of the *American Journal of Sociology* was in itself of greater consequence than all his own books combined.

In addition, Small was a leading figure in the development of modern sociology through his work in connection with the American Sociological Society and its meetings and activities. This society was founded in Baltimore in 1905 and has constituted the chief arena for sociological discussion and for the clarification of sociological opinion since that time. It has also furnished the nucleus for the organization of special committees of sociologists for the promotion of research and teaching. The papers read at the annual meetings have been published with unusual completeness in the so-called annual *Publications* of the society. They constitute an admirable source for the history of sociological opinion in this country, as well as containing much information on a great variety of technical and special problems. It will scarcely be denied by anybody that while he lived Small carried more of the burdens associated with the work of the Society than any other three men in the organization, and to him also fell, to a large extent, the task of editing for publication the papers read at the annual meetings. Small was always very active at these annual meetings, promoting discussion both in the formal sessions and in informal gatherings. He was much more in his element here than in the compilation of learned treatises. Moreover, his extensive travels and lecturing in this country and abroad served to promote the exchange of opinions between American and European social scientists. Likewise, he was the means of bringing to Chicago and elsewhere in this country a number of distinguished European social scientists, who left their impress upon this side of the Atlantic.

Further, the writer is going to risk what to many will seem a startling, if not absurd, contention, namely, that in his written work and even more in his teaching, Small's chief contributions were made to the fields of economics, and political science rather than sociology. His *Adam Smith*, his *Between Eras,* his *Cameralists,* and much of his *Origins of Sociology* constitute cardinal contributions to institutional economics. If he had seen fit to put into print the well-organized material from which he gave his famous course on the "Conflict of Classes," he would have produced a work which would have made him a rival of Veblen as an original and courageous economist. His course on Karl Marx and his doctrines and influence were likewise chiefly an exercise in economic dynamics and the history of economic thought.

In the field of political science Small's *General Sociology* may safely be called the most profound book published on the subject in this country between Calhoun's *Disquisition on Government* and A. F. Bentley's *Process of Government,* the latter of which was based upon the contributions of Small and Ratzenhofer.[24] Throughout most of his teaching career he gave a course under various titles which dealt with the sociological basis of the state and civic policy. There is little doubt that, a half-century hence, the historical student of Amerian political theory will find much more of permanent value in Small's writings than in those of a dozen contemporary political scientists of the conventional pattern. Small is likely to have a high place in the history of functional political science in the United States.

In other words, while it was a great gain for sociology that Small devoted his professional life primarily to this subject, it was a real misfortune to Small that he did not occupy himself more specifically with either economics or political science. His mind was better adapted for this type of analysis than for work in the more highly theoretical field of general sociology. Likewise, he would have been a far better stylist in these fields, for in these less theoretical and abstract subjects his thought and expression were much more clear, direct, and precise. In short, his work would have been more profound, articulate, and influential.

Finally, one cannot overlook Small's contributions to ethics. He was truly a pioneer in the foundation of the sociological attitude toward ethics. He powerfully promoted the movement to take the subject out of supernaturalism and metaphysics, as well as to remove it from the narrow conception of a rigid guide for an archaic view of sexual purity. He worked to identify it, instead, with the effort to promote a broader and more comprehensive view of social justice and human happiness.

As a final estimate of Small's place in American sociology the present writer would hold that among the first generation of our sociologists Small's status in advancing the subject matter of sociology was second only to that of Ward and Giddings, while in promoting the professional and academic position of sociology, he was without any close rival.

NOTES

1. *Publications of the American Economic Association, Third Series*, V, No. 2 (1904), 178–79.

2. *Adam Smith and Modern Sociology* (Chicago, 1907), pp. 1, 235, 237. For a bibliography of Small's books, articles, and reviews see *American Journal of Sociology*, July, 1926, pp. 49–58.

3. *Adam Smith and Modern Sociology*, pp. 23–24.

4. Article "Sociology," in *Encyclopedia Americana*, XXV (1920), 209–10.

5. *American Journal of Sociology*, July, 1925, p. 89.

6. *The Meaning of Social Science* (Chicago, 1910), pp. 9, 10, 61.

6a. This was republished in 1947 in the *American Journal of Sociology*.

7. Letter to author, December 11, 1924.

8. P. 3.

9. P. 208.

10. *Publications of the American Sociological Society*, XV (1920), 192.

11. P. 5.

12. P. 193.

13. P. 273.

14. *Publications of the American Economic Association, Third Series*, V, No. 2 (1904), 181.

15. The year in which *Wesen und Zweck der Politik* was published in Leipzig.

16. *General Sociology* (Chicago, 1905), chap. xiv.

17. *Ibid.*, pp. 197–98, 205, 226, 242, 252–53, 363, 472, 551, 619–20.

18. *The Meaning of Social Science*, p. 260.

19. *Ibid.*, pp. 242–43.

20. *General Sociology*, pp. 728–29; *The Meaning of Social Science*, p. 88.

21. *General Sociology*, pp. 522, 676.

22. Open letter to M. M. Willey, September 11, 1924, p. 6.

23. P. 275.

24. The author obviously refers here to Small's contribution to the analysis of the actual processes of government and not to his influence upon formal academic political science. Here he was far less influential than the professional political scientists like Woolsey, Burgess, Willoughby, and Lowell. The writer bases his judgment upon the assumption that it has already become evident that the analysis of political processes is of greater significance than the definition of political terms and concepts.

CHAPTER XIX

WILLIAM ISAAC THOMAS: THE FUSION OF PSYCHO-LOGICAL AND CULTURAL SOCIOLOGY

Harry Elmer Barnes

WILLIAM ISAAC THOMAS (1863–1947), one of the key members of the great department of sociology set up by Professor Small at the University of Chicago following 1893, is regarded by many students of sociological theory as the most erudite and creative of American social psychologists. In his later years Thomas extended his conceptions and methods to what might be called a "psycho-cultural" approach to social phenomena. Certainly, no other sociologist excels Thomas in his mastery of the subject or in a firm command of the auxiliary sciences essential to the successful exploitation of the field of ethnic and psychological sociology. Unfortunately, Thomas confined his systematic exposition of psychological sociology to his university lectures, which were never published. His published contributions to the subject are relatively few and fragmentary, woven into extensive documentary studies. But his general position and method can be reconstructed and summarized with relative confidence and accuracy.

Few leading sociologists have had a more curious and informal preparation for the cultivation of their subject. Thomas was reared in Tennessee, where he loved to roam in the woods with a gun. As he says: "My own childhood was of a strictly manual, perceptual-motor type, taking the direction of rifle shooting, which was the main sport of mountain people. My zeal for this was fanatical. I reckon that I passed not less than seven years of my youth in the woods alone with a rifle, without a dog, shooting at a mark, and regretting the disappearance of large game and the passing of the Indian and pioneer life."[1]

Ultimately, Thomas attended the University of Tennessee but paid no attention even to such rudiments of the social studies as were then taught. Rather, his main interests were in Greek culture and in biology. His Greek teacher interested him in German scholarship, and his biology professor in Darwinism and evolution, more than a generation before Tennessee discovered the dangers inherent in teaching evolution. For a time after his graduation Thomas taught Greek, Latin, French, German, and English at the University of Tennessee and then went to the University of Berlin to study. At Berlin and later at Göttingen, Thomas concentrated on philology; then he returned to teach English at Oberlin College for three years.

Thomas' first contact with sociology came from reading the reports of the American Bureau of Ethnology while at Tennessee and Spencer's *Principles of Sociology* while at Oberlin. In the spring of 1894 he learned of the establishment of the Department of Sociology at the University of Chicago under Professor Small and noted that attractive courses were offered in sociology and anthropology. Following the drive for new experience, he decided to enroll. But even when he arrived in Chicago to study sociology, most of his attention and interest were bestowed upon courses marginal to sociology, such as physiology with Jacques Loeb and brain anatomy with Adolf Meyer. While respecting them personally, he disclaims any important influence on his thinking by his formal teachers of sociology: "I do not feel that I have been greatly influenced by any of my teachers of sociology. My interests, as I have indicated, were in the marginal fields and not in sociology as it was organized and taught at that time, that is, the historical and methodological approach of Professor Small and the remedial and correctional interests of Professor Henderson." But, during his period of study and early teaching at Chicago, Thomas did arrive at the attitudes and methods which later dominated his professional activities in the field of sociology. He summarizes them as follows:

(1) I never became influenced by philosophy as offering an explanation of reality; (2) I kept notes of reading and classified and reclassified materials so that I eventually had at hand, with exact references, all that interested me in sociological and marginal literature; (3) I read widely and in marginal subjects—biology, psychology, ethnology—and acquired a habit of rapid reading; (4) I explored the city. This last was also largely a matter of curiosity. I remember that Professor Henderson, of sainted memory, once requested me to get him a bit of information from the saloons. He said that he had never himself entered a saloon or tasted beer.

About this same time, or a little later, Thomas developed the idea that more could be gleaned from *inspecting* both literature and social situations than from encyclopedic reading of formal sociological materials. He says that he was led to this conclusion by reading all the existing German theses on a certain sociological theme and deciding that they were so extremely banal and futile that they appeared to have no value or merit save that they were written in a foreign language.

Immediately after he received his Doctor's degree in 1896, Thomas again went to Europe. He traveled about, inspecting and observing, as far as the Volga. On this trip he was struck with the fruitful idea of a comparative study of the European nationalities, which was later to bear fruit in his great work on *The Polish Peasant in Europe and America* (1918–21), with Florian Znaniecki. It was in connection with his book on the Polish peasant that Thomas developed his conception of the importance of the life-history and personal-documentation approach to the study of sociological themes and issues. Thomas later gathered material for a work on immigrant Jews which he expects to publish. Thomas retired from the University of Chicago in 1918, and, except for some casual instruction at the New School for Social Research and at Harvard University, he devoted himself from that time onward to study, travel, and writing.

If Thomas was not greatly affected by his university teachers of sociology, there were several important personal influences on his sociological thinking. He was cordial to John Dewey's instrumentalist philosophy, and George H. Mead and Charles Horton Cooley had some influence upon his thinking with respect to personality, the social mind, and the social process. From Florian Znaniecki he may have gained the impulse to fuse the functional-psychological approach with a consideration of the cultural object or value element in the social situation. Thomas' contact with John B. Watson in the 1920's emphasized the concepts of behavioristic psychology. In his later years he was influenced by his wife, Dorothy Swaine Thomas, which is reflected in his increasing respect for the methods of quantitative investigation in social science. But the influence of others on Thomas has often been exaggerated. His was a singularly original and independent mind. Further, even in the case of most of those who had any real influence on him, Thomas' reciprocal influence upon such associates was fully as great.

As we have noted, Thomas never wrote a systematic work on sociology or social psychology, but he made many important contributions to these fields, though his writings, like his interests, were marginal rather than central to systematic sociology. His anthropological interests led to his monumental *Source-Book for Social Origins* (1909) and his later *Primitive Behavior* (1937). In the former the psychological approach was dominant, in the latter the cultural mode of comparison and analysis. His *Sex and Society* (1907) was a healthy release from the prudery of conventional academic sociologists. Unquestionably, his greatest published work was the five-volume masterpiece on the *Polish Peasant,* in which he developed and combined the life-history, personal-documentation, and culture-value approach and outlined the conception of the "four wishes." This book also put the study of immigrant maladjustment on a sound, scientific basis. Thomas made important contributions to the volume on *Old World Traits Transplanted,* by R. E. Park and H. A. Miller (1921). *The Child in America* (1928) combined his interest in psychology, education, and the social situation. At the time of its publication, no other book even approached it as a discerning and stimulating summary of all the cogent information concerning the psychological and cultural setting of child experience and development in this country.

II. THE DEVELOPMENT OF THOMAS' METHOD OF PSYCHOCULTURAL ANALYSIS OF THE SOCIAL SITUATION

As we have noted, Thomas' methodological principles and leading sociological generalizations have to be drawn from key passages scattered throughout his numerous works, the main body of which tends to be source material or other descriptive data. His views and methods grew gradually over the years and took definite form in the long methodological introduction to the *Polish Peasant.* Thomas' methodological conceptions and his interpretations of personality and society were further developed in his chapter in the symposium on *The Unconscious* (1927); in the *Proceedings of the Second Colloquium on Personality Investigation* (1930); in the Brookings Institution *Essays on Research in the Social Sciences* (1931); in the theoretical portions of *Primitive Behavior;* and in the *Critiques of Research in the Social Sciences* (1939).

In a notable paper read before the Congress of Arts and Sciences at St. Louis in 1904, Thomas presented his views on the province of social psychology, indicating its importance to the social scientist.[1a] He held that social psychology is "an extension of individual psychology to the phenomena of collective life," and he suggested some of the chief problems with which it should concern itself. Among these are: (1) crises and shocks in the experience of the social group, with their results upon culture and social organization; (2) the emergence and influence of great personalities; (3) the results of the contacts of social groups; (4) social organization; (5) the psychology of the temperament of races and social groups; (6) the relation of educational systems to social evolution; and (7) the problem of the parallelism between the mental development of individuals and that of the race.

In 1907, Professor Thomas published his *Sex and Society,* which was, probably, the most important American contribution to the sociology of sex at the time the book appeared. Especially significant are the chapters on "Sex and Primitive Social Control" and "Sex and Social Feeling." On the whole, the author, while indicating significant differences between the sexes, criticizes the tendency to regard woman as an inferior being, properly kept in a subordinate position.

Thomas' long period of study and reflection on primitive society and culture bore fruit in 1909 in his *Source-Book for Social Origins,* an admirable collection of material bearing upon the culture and social life of primitive man.[2] The Introduction to this work included a brief analysis of certain sociopsychic factors as keys to the interpretation of society and culture. Among these concepts he emphasized, in particular, control, attention, habit, and crises. In his idea of "crisis," Thomas anticipated by many years Arnold Toynbee's mechanism of "challenge and response."

Between 1918 and 1921, Thomas, as we have noted, published, in collaboration with Florian Znaniecki, a notable series of volumes on the problem of immigration and adjustment, entitled *The Polish Peasant in Europe and America.* At the beginning of the first volume the authors presented a long Methodological Note, which is regarded by some authorities as the most important American contribution to the methodology of sociological investigation.

Znaniecki participated in the *Polish Peasant* mainly in the role of a translator, but he did contribute the "values" concept, for which Thomas

has given him full credit. The greater portion of the Method(
Note was the work of Thomas. Thomas stressed the importance
history and personal documentation in research, and his basic i
the "point-by-point" approach—the idea that science moves ahead from
a first "guess" to a second "guess" and so on. This emphasized his fundamental assumption that any "theoretical" formulation must be regarded
as highly temporary and subject to many later modifications and developments. We may now turn to some of the theoretical points offered in
the Methodological Note.

Here is to be found a brief review of various attempts to state social
theory and social causation in "particularistic," i.e., "single-track," terms.
After indicating the inadequacy of these, Thomas goes on to formulate
his own social psychology as "precisely the science of attitudes" in reference to object-values.[3] These terms, "attitude" and "value," help us "to
understand and to control the process of *becoming*." The *attitude* is individual—the peculiar response organization, implicit or explicit, of the
personality. But attitudes cannot be understood by themselves alone.
We must take into account the other term in the equation, namely,
"value."[4] Value is the object of the activity of the individual. Any object
may become a value by the injection of meaning into it, and meaning
is socially determined.[5]

> By a social value we understand any datum having an empirical content accessible
> to the members of some social group and a meaning with regard to which it is or
> may be an object of activity. Thus, a foodstuff, an instrument, a coin, a piece of
> poetry, a university, a myth, a scientific theory, are social values.....
> By attitude we understand a process of individual consciousness which deter-
> mines real or possible activity of the individual in the social world.....The atti-
> tude is thus the individual counterpart of the social value; activity, in whatever
> form, is the bond between them.[6]

The following passages develop thoroughly the distinction between
the scope and the province of social psychology and sociology:

> Thus, the field of social psychology practically comprises first of all the attitudes
> which are more or less generally found among the members of a social group,
> have a real importance in the life-organization of the individuals who have devel-
> oped them, and manifest themselves in social activities of these individuals. This
> field can be indefinitely enlarged in two directions if the concrete problems of
> social psychology demand it. It may include attitudes which are particular to cer-
> tain members of the social group or appear in the group only on rare occasions,
> as soon as they acquire for some reason a social importance; thus, some personal
> sexual idiosyncrasy will interest social psychology only if it becomes an object of
> imitation or of indignation to other members of the group or if it helps to an

understanding of more general sexual attitudes. On the other hand, the field of social psychology may be extended to such attitudes as manifest themselves with regard, not to the social, but to the physical, environment of the individual, as soon as they show themselves affected by social culture; for example, the perception of colors would become a socio-psychological problem if it proved to have evolved during the cultural evolution under the influence of decorative arts.

Social psychology has thus to perform the part of a general science of the subjective side of social culture which we have heretofore usually ascribed to individual psychology or to "psychology in general." It may claim to be *the* science of consciousness as manifested in culture, and its function is to render service, as a general auxiliary science, to all the special sciences dealing with various spheres of social values. This does not mean that social psychology can ever supplant individual psychology; the methods and standpoints of these two sciences are too different to permit either of them to fulfil the function of the other, and, if it were not for the traditional use of the term "psychology" for both types of research, it would be even advisable to emphasize this difference by a distinct terminology.

We have seen that social psychology has a central field of interest including the most general and fundamental cultural attitudes found within concrete societies. In the same manner there is a certain domain which constitutes the methodological center of the sociological interest. It includes those rules of behavior which concern more especially the active relations between individual members of the group and between each member and the group as a whole. It is these rules, indeed, manifested as mores, laws, and group ideals and systematized in such institutions as the family, the tribe, the community, the free association, the state, etc., which constitute the central part of social organization and provide through this organization the essential conditions of the existence of a group as a distinct cultural entity and not a mere agglomeration of individuals; and hence all other rules which a given group may develop and treat as obligatory have a secondary sociological importance as compared with these. But this does not mean that sociology should not extend its field of investigation beyond this methodological center of interest. Every social group, particularly on lower stages of cultural evolution, is inclined to control all individual activities, not alone those which attain directly its fundamental institutions. Thus we find social regulations of economic, religious, scientific, artistic activities, even of technique and speech, and the break of these regulations is often treated as affecting the very existence of the group. And we must concede that, though the effect of these regulations on cultural productivity is often more than doubtful, they do contribute as long as they last to the unity of the group, while, on the other hand, the close association which has been formed between these rules and the fundamental social institutions without which the group cannot exist has often the consequence that cultural evolution which destroys the influence of these secondary regulations may actually disorganize the group. Precisely as far as these social rules concerning special cultural activities are in the above-determined way connected with the rules which bear on social relations they acquire an interest for sociology. Of course, it can be determined only *a posteriori* how far the field of sociology should be extended beyond the investigation of fundamental social institutions, and the situation varies from group to group and from period to period. In all civilized societies some part of every cultural activity—religious, economic, scientific, artistic, etc.,—is left outside of social regulation, and another, perhaps even larger, part, though still subjected to social rules, is no longer supposed to affect directly the existence or coherence of society and actually does not affect it.

It is, therefore, a grave methodological error to attempt to include generally in the field of sociology such cultural domains as religion or economics on the ground that in certain social groups religious or economic norms are considered—and in some measure even really are—a part of social organization, for even there the respective values have a content which cannot be completely reduced to social rules of behavior, and their importance for social organization may be very small or even none in other societies or at other periods of evolution.[7]

The fundamental methodological principle, therefore, of both sociology and social psychology—"the principle without which they can never reach scientific explanation"—is this: "The cause of a social or individual phenomenon is never another social or individual phenomenon alone, but always a combination of a social and an individual phenomenon." Or, in more exact terms: "The cause of a value or of an attitude is never an attitude or a value alone, but always a combination of an attitude and a value."[8]

Further, it may be maintained that:

. . . . a nomothetic social science is possible only if all social becoming is viewed as a product of a continual interaction of individual consciousness and objective social reality. In this connection the human personality is both a continually producing factor and a continually produced result of social evolution, and this double relation expresses itself in every elementary social fact; there can be for social science no change of social reality which is not the common effect of pre-existing social values and individual attitudes acting upon them.[9]

Contrary to the usual practice, Thomas regarded social psychology as a broader social science than sociology.[10] He held that sociology is a "special science of culture," concerned with the "theory of social organization," while social psychology is "the general science of the subjective side of culture." Social psychology studies "the attitudes of the individual towards *all* cultural values of the group." Sociology studies "only one type of these values—social rules—in their relation to individual attitudes."[11]

Quite independent of Freud, Thomas, out of his own investigations, developed a set of fundamental wishes, four in number, which express the principal attitudes that one finds in individuals. The impulses behind these wishes are: (1) the desire for new experience or fresh stimulations; (2) the desire for recognition; (3) the desire for mastery, or the "will to power"; (4) the desire for security.[12]

On the side of the objective reality, there exist "definitions of situations," delimited ways of reacting, which modify and control the four wishes. Moreover, these "definitions" become organized into schemes or rules of action and in this way serve to determine the "run of attention" of the group toward certain values of the group (family, clan, religious body, guild, state, etc.) and the consequent ignoring of others. Conflict arises when the definitions of the situation change too rapidly for the individual, as well as when there exists a hiatus between the fundamental wishes and these definitions in more static societies. These points are illustrated in the study of the Polish peasant both in Europe and in the chaotic industrialism of America.[13]

Thomas elaborated his idea of the four wishes and their sociological implications in his work on *The Unadjusted Girl* (1923). After the publication of this latter book, Thomas abandoned his use of the "wishes" formulation in this phraseology. He was both surprised and somewhat shocked at its popularity. The "wishes" seemed to him to become in too many quarters mere intellectual fetishes which stultified, rather than stimulated, research. The change in his phraseology was evident in his chapter on "The Configurations of Personality," in the symposium on *The Unconscious* (1927), where the wishes appear as "fields" or "classes" of values: (1) new experience; (2) desire for response; (3) desire for recognition; and (4) security.

In addition to the life-history and fundamental-wishes approach to the psychology of the individual personality and the culture-value concept, the third vital element in Thomas' sociological interpretation of individual and social behavior is the notion of the social situation. This he summarizes in the following manner in his *Child in America:*

> The behavioristic or situational approach .... ignores or minimizes instincts and original nature and studies behavior reactions and habit formation in a great variety of situations comparatively. It assumes that whatever can be learned about original nature will be revealed in its reactions to these various situations. We regard this approach as the only one capable of giving a rational basis for the control of behavior.[14]

In his later work on *Primitive Behavior,* Thomas used the social-situation concept as a basic technique for the interpretation of culture and behavior:

> Employing the term "culture" to represent the material and social values of any group of people, whether savage or civilized (their institutions, customs, attitudes, behavior reactions), the structuralization of cultures, their diversification and the direction of their development, the total configuration of the patterns they contain, and the reaction of the personalities to the cultural situation can best be approached in terms of *the definition of the situation.* An adjustive effort of any kind is preceded by a decision to act or not act along a given line, and the decision is itself preceded by a *definition of the situation,* that is to say, an *interpretation* or *point of view,* and eventually a policy and a behavior pattern.[15]

This approach to sociology through a functional-dynamic psychology of the individual personality, on the one hand, coupled with the importance of the culture-object or -value, on the other, constitutes, to the mind of the writer, an extremely important advance over the older theories. Its attempt to integrate the individual with the cultural factors in social causation and the creation of the social situation is outstanding. For instance, Thomas, speaking of the causes of social progress, stresses the following factors: (1) individual initiative, creative ability, and the accompanying outstanding individual attitudes; (2) the level of culture of the group; (3) the "run of attention" in the group, especially of those individuals of capacity, in terms of the "values" which the group culture holds to be valid.[16] This view might, without difficulty, be utilized to harmonize the alleged opposing views of the culture theorists, such as Boas and his school, and those who follow the Galtonian tradition in emphasizing the place of individual initiative and innate capacity for social development and cultural change.[17]

An authoritative epitome of Thomas' comprehensive approach to the study of personality and culture is his own summary, embodied in a notice to the American Sociological Society, of which he was then president, justifying his selection of "The Relation of the Individual to the Group" as the general topic to be discussed at the coming meeting of the society. This brings out well the breadth of his approach to the subject, both as to the divers methods of studying the evolution of the human personality and as to the multiplicity of techniques and sciences essential to a full understanding of personality:

Our conception of the relation of "experience" to the development of the "person" has been undergoing a rapid modification. "Environment" is no longer regarded as a scene of action for the person, but as material out of which the personality itself is built. "Integration" and "conditioning," as first elaborated by Sherrington and Pavlov, have been further developed by the physiologists, neurologists, and psychologists, and have an important position in sociological method. The "Gestalt" psychology has contributed to the concept of integration as a totality of elements, and of meaning as appearing always in a context and upon a background. The sociologists are now producing important studies on "social distance" and "social position." The social psychologists are working out comparisons between the social classes, and between urban and rural populations, from the same standpoint. The anthropologists are taking the same attitude toward the questions of cultural areas and migrations of peoples, and the question of inferiority and superiority of races. The psychiatrists connected with the child-guidance clinics, even those who formerly gave a preponderating importance to the factors of heredity, are being forced by their own case-studies to seek the sources of the behavior difficulties of the child in his relation to the family and the groups with which he comes into contact at his various age-levels.[18]

The conclusions to which his studies had brought him, on the matter of personality, attitudes and values, a decade after the publication of the Methodological Note in the *Polish Peasant,* are well presented in the above-mentioned symposium on *The Unconscious:*

I am assuming, at least for the initial standpoint for the study of the formation of personality, that there are certain satisfactions, objects of desire, which men always and everywhere want and seek to secure, and we may speak of these satisfactions as values. These values will also be found to fall into classes or fields, corresponding partly with instinctive or unlearned action tendencies and partly with learned or conditioned tendencies. We may speak of the action tendencies as attitudes and of the values as stimuli.

From this standpoint a personality would be regarded as the organization of attitudes, and personalities would be distinguished among themselves by their greater or less tendency to seek their satisfactions, play their rôles, in this or that field of the values. . . . .

Viewed as a configuration, a personality would be a background of attitudes and values common to everybody, upon which certain attitudes and values, or constellations of attitudes and values, assume a prominent or perhaps a dominant position.[19]

In December, 1938, Thomas' *Polish Peasant* was subjected to a critical analysis by leading American social scientists under the auspices of the Social Science Research Council. A long analysis and critique of the book had been prepared in advance by Professor Herbert Blumer, of the University of Chicago, and this critique and the book were then discussed at length at a Round Table presided over by Professor Warren S. Thompson, of Miami University. Thomas and Znaniecki were present to comment. Thomas laid special stress upon the development of his conceptions and methodological principles in the twenty years since the book had been published. In general, he agreed with Blumer's appraisal and critique. A letter from Thomas to Professor Robert E. Park was introduced into the discussion. In this Thomas had outlined his famous "point-by-point" procedure, which he regards as his most important contribution to the methodology and techniques of social science:

It is my experience that formal methodological studies are relatively unprofitable. They have tended to represent the standpoint developed in philosophy and the history of philosophy. It is my impression that progress in method is made from point to point by setting up objectives, employing certain techniques, then resetting the problems with the introduction of still other objectives and the modification of techniques. . . . .

In all this, there is no formal attention to method but the use of some imagination or mind from point to point. The operator raises the question, at appropriate points, "What if," and prepares a set-up to test this query. . . . .

We move from point to point without necessarily any formidable attempt to rationalize and generalize the process. It is only, in fact, so far as sociology is concerned, since we abandoned the search for standardized methods based largely on the work of dead men, that we have made the beginnings [in truly empirical social science] which I have indicated.[20]

At the close of the Round Table conference, Professor Read Bain, of Miami University, well stated not only the significance of the *Polish Peasant* for methodology in social science but also the contribution which Thomas has made to empirical social science:

The Polish Peasant is a monumental instance of the revolt against "armchair" sociology which began about 1900 and has progressed to such an extent that sociologists increasingly regard themselves as natural scientists. Few present day sociologists fail to give lip-service, at least, to this conception of sociology and they also profess to base their theories upon actual or possible empirical research.[21]

NOTES

1. The biographical material on Dr. Thomas is derived mainly from a personal memorandum prepared by him and supplied to the author of this chapter.

1a. *American Journal of Sociology*, January, 1905, pp. 445–55.

2. Chicago, 1909.

3. *The Polish Peasant in Europe and America* (5 vols.; Chicago, 1918–21), I, 27. Republished in 2 vols. (New York, 1927). See Herbert Blumer's admirable summary of the methodological contributions of *The Polish Peasant* to sociology and social psychology, in *Critiques of Research in the Social Sciences*, I (New York, 1939), 81–82.

4. *The Polish Peasant*, I, 21–26, 45, 48.

5. Thomas would agree in the main with the theory of meaning and social consciousness developed by George H. Mead at Chicago (see his "Social Consciousness and the Consciousness of Meaning," *Psychological Bulletin*, VII [1910], 397 ff.).

6. *The Polish Peasant*, I, 21–22.

7. *Ibid.*, pp. 30–31, 34–35.

8. *Ibid.*, p. 44.

9. *Ibid.*, III, 5.

10. *Ibid.*, I, 33–37.

11. *Ibid.*, p. 33.

12. *Ibid.*, I, 73.

13. Cf. W. Trotter, *Instinct of the Herd* (London, 1918); G. Wallas, *The Great Society* (New York, 1914); and, above all, W. F. Ogburn, *Social Change* (New York, 1922).

14. *Op. cit.*, p. 561.

15. *Op. cit.* (New York, 1937), p. 8. By permission of the McGraw-Hill Book Co.

16. *Source-Book for Social Origins* (Chicago, 1909), Introd., pp. 18–22.

17. Cf. Kimball Young, *Mental Differences in Certain Immigrant Groups* ("University of Oregon Publications," Vol. I, No. 11 [1922]), chap. v, for an attempt to harmonize these opposing views.

The writer desires to express his gratitude to Professor Young, a former student of Professor Thomas, and to Professor Read Bain, for indispensable aid in drawing up this brief formulation of Thomas' contributions.

18. *American Journal of Sociology*, March, 1927, p. 814.

19. *Op. cit.* (New York, 1927), pp. 143–44.

20. *Critiques of Research in the Social Sciences*, I, 166–67.

21. *Ibid.*, p. 192.

CHAPTER XX

THE SOCIOLOGICAL THEORIES OF
EDWARD ALSWORTH ROSS

William L. Kolb

I. THE NATURE OF ROSS'S SOCIOLOGICAL WRITINGS

FEW writers in the field of sociology have been able to put the results of their speculation and research before the reading public in as interesting and vivid a fashion as has the sociologist who is the object of our attention in this chapter. There is little doubt that the reputation which Edward Alsworth Ross (1866-1951) enjoys in sociological circles today is due in large measure to his ability to present his ideas in a manner which attracts the lay reader as well as the professional sociologist. Although his tendency to popularize has at times led Ross into the pitfalls of overeasy generalization, it must be recognized that sociology owes a great deal to Ross for arousing public interest concerning certain of its problems and methods.

This emphasis on getting ideas across to the general reader seems to be the result of a fusion of a genuine scientific interest in societal phenomena with a strong desire to aid in solving the problems which the peoples of the world have been called upon to face. It is possible to trace the presence of this combination of interests in Ross from his graduate student days at Johns Hopkins through his periods of teaching at Indiana, Cornell, Stanford, Nebraska, and, finally, Wisconsin. As his autobiography reveals, Ross's zeal for social reform has more than once involved him in difficulties with various groups and has been equaled only by his insatiable curiosity concerning the regularities to be found in social life.[1]

No other American sociologist has had so interesting and colorful a life as has Ross. While a voluminous writer on sociological subjects and a conscientious and brilliant university teacher for nearly fifty years, Ross was as much a publicist and social reformer as he was a professional sociologist. A graduate of Coe College, he studied at Berlin and Johns

Hopkins universities and received his doctorate at the latter in 1891. His graduate training was more strictly in the field of economics and finance than in sociology.

Ross accepted a professorship in economics at the University of Indiana in 1891 but remained there only a year, moving to a chair in economics and finance in Cornell in 1892. This was a short stay, also, for he assumed a professorship in sociology at Leland Stanford in 1893. Here he developed a great reputation as a teacher but was dismissed in 1900 for too great frankness in describing the coolie labor used by Leland Stanford in building the Central Pacific Railroad, as well as for other evidences of liberal thought. He then accepted a professorship in sociology at the University of Nebraska in 1901 and remained there until 1906, when he moved to Wisconsin, where he held the chair in sociology until his retirement in 1937. It is pretty generally conceded that Ross was the most dramatic and effective classroom teacher in the history of American sociology. While not a meticulous scholar, he was a man of vast learning and was unrivaled among sociologists in his command of the raw materials of public affairs and world events.

Ross maintained a deep interest in social reform from his youth onward, and he wrote and lectured extensively against the evils of plutocratic society and partisan politics. His *Sin and Society* attracted the attention and received the approval of Theodore Roosevelt. He was an inveterate globe-trotter and studied social change and reform movements at first hand from Mexico to Russia and from India to Sweden. He was, at one and the same time, the incarnation of the sociologist who believed that social sciences should promote social reform and the despair of the cloistered devotees of statistical research and professorial timidity.

The duality of approach—scientific and reformist—shows itself in even more marked form in Ross's writings than it does in other aspects of his life; and, while the fusion of these two attitudes in his personality has prevented his producing any book which subordinates one point of view completely to the other, his writings can be conveniently classified according to the predominance of one or the other standpoint.

Among the more important of his works which were written primarily from the scientific point of view are *Social Control, The Foundations of Sociology, Social Psychology,* and *Principles of Sociology.*[2] The first of these is perhaps the most important and enduring of all Ross's writings. In the author's own words it consists of "a survey of the foundations of order," in which Ross, after dismissing the possibility that a complex society can exist on the basis of what he terms "a natural order," attempts to establish the thesis that social order exists because of the conscious control of the individual on the part of society.[3] The study of social control, according to Ross, is part of the domain of social psychology, which, in turn, is part of the larger field of sociology.[4] In spite of the fact that Ross is handicapped in his analysis by the individual-society contrast and that his division of social psychology into individual and social ascendancy, with social ascendancy, in turn, divided into social influence and social control, serves no particularly useful purpose, this book still stands as one of the best analyses available of the problems involved in social control.

The Foundations of Sociology contains Ross's conception of the field of sociology and its relations to some of the other social sciences. The work consists primarily of a series of constructive criticisms of the writings of other men about such topics as "The Scope and Task of Sociology," "The Sociological Frontier of Economics," "The Unit of Investigation of Sociology," etc. The most striking aspect of the book is that, despite Ross's defining sociology in such a way as to include the other social sciences, the map of the sociological field which he presents in the chapter on "The Unit of Investigation in Sociology" indicates a field for specialized research which does not encroach on the domains of the other social sciences.[5]

In his *Social Psychology* Ross turns his attention to the planes and currents of "feeling, belief, or volition—and hence in action—which are due to the interaction of human beings....."[6] These planes and currents are analyzed in terms of Tarde's concepts of conventionality and custom based on imitation, united with the biological conception of human nature which was prevalent at the time and with some of Le Bon's ideas concerning crowd psychology.

The study of the main body of the phenomena which constitute the subject matter of sociology, i.e., social processes, is to be found in the *Principles of Sociology*. In this work the basic concept of social interaction is broken down. The various processes in which individuals engage and which result in the formation of subjective products, such as the planes and currents mentioned above, and objective products or actual human groupings and social structures are presented and analyzed.

Turning for the moment from Ross's writings, which we have designated as essentially written from the scientific viewpoint, we find that a still greater number of his books have been written as appeals for reform or as popular presentations of specific cultures. One of the earliest of these was his *Sin and Society,* a work written in the spirit of the muck-rackers of the turn of the century, castigating those individuals who are free from personal vice but engage in antisocial conduct which harms others, which Ross designates as sin.[7] Pointing out how the morality of the early twentieth century tended to control vice rather than sin, he pleaded for a reorientation and extension of morality so that sin may be controlled.

Nowhere is Ross's interest in social reform more clearly revealed than in his *Changing America.*[8] The purpose of the book is to bring the citizen's conception of social problems into closer alignment with the actual problems of the day, and in it Ross deals with such matters as women in industry, contemporary commercialism, and capitalist influence over the press. The last few chapters are devoted to a description of social conditions in the Middle West and to the promise which this region holds for American society. While *Changing America* consists of a discussion of several social problems, *The Old World in the New* deals with the specific problem of immigration into the United States.[9] Approaching the problem from a sociological point of view, Ross attempts to point out that unrestricted immigration will result in the fall of the standard of living and the degeneration of some important social institutions.

Almost a decade later Ross brought his discussion of social problems in the United States up to date in his *Social Trend,* and in this popular book is to be found the germ of *Standing Room Only,* which followed in a few years.[10] Although he has been forced to modify the thesis of overpopulation which is presented in this work, owing to the decline of population growth in the western European world since 1920, Ross still feels that the thesis is true of other parts of the world.[11]

Ross showed his customary intellectual alertness by being the first American sociologist to interest himself actively in the Russian revolution of 1917, which he investigated on the spot. His *Russia in Upheaval* (1918), *The Russian Bolshevik Revolution* (1921), and *The Russian Soviet Republic* (1923) were among the best of the early interpretations of that great social transformation. He also studied the social changes in Mexico and in 1923 wrote a book on *The Social Revolution in Mexico.*

He further investigated the social changes taking place in contemporary China and India.

Although the volumes mentioned above are far from completing the list of the books that Ross has written, they are representative of the type of writing which he has done in the spirit of reform. Most of Ross's later works are either of this sort or are popularized treatments of social phenomena in other countries and are written in a much less scientific vein than such books as his *Social Control* or *Principles of Sociology*. While there is little doubt that his popularized works have attracted many people to sociology who would not have been interested otherwise, and with all due regard for the contribution which Ross has made to the cause of sociology in such a manner, the purpose of this chapter directs our attention away from the popularizing function that his writings have performed and turns it toward the contribution he has made to the development of general sociology.

II. THE ESSENTIALS OF ROSS'S SOCIOLOGICAL SYSTEM

Any discussion of the system of sociology that is present in Ross's work must deal with the four books which were mentioned as being written primarily from the scientific point of view: *Social Control, The Foundations of Sociology, Social Psychology,* and *Principles of Sociology*. Although chronology would indicate that the works be taken up in the order listed, a clearer conception of his system can be developed if we start with *The Foundations of Sociology*. The chapter on "The Unit of Investigation in Sociology" presents a comprehensive map of the field of study for the sociologist as Ross conceived it.[12] The basic unit of sociological investigation, although not the sole unit, is the social process:

> The five units so far favorably considered—groups, relations, institutions, imperatives, uniformities—are products. They precede the individual and survive him. To the onlooker they appear as gods or fates, moulding the lives and disposing upon the destinies of ordinary men. Nevertheless, they have all risen at some time out of the actions and interactions of men. To understand their genesis we must ascend to that primordial fact known as the social process.[13]

According to Ross, if we choose any of the other five units as the basis for the investigation of social phenomena, we soon arrive at an impasse that does not permit further exploration, since it is the process that lies behind every other form of sociological data that is of fundamental importance. If, on the other hand, we begin with the social process, we can trace out the development of the phenomena which go to make up the other classes of data. Ross divides the processes involving human interests into three different classes for purposes of analysis: preliminary, social, and reconstructive. The first of these classes is made up of processes which are not strictly social, since they do not involve "the action of man on man," but which render man amenable to the social processes.[14] One illustration of such a process would be the influence of a common occupation in molding people to such an extent that they would be receptive to being drawn into the same society. Once processes of the preliminary variety have operated over a long enough period of time, the actual social processes may come into play, and it is out of the workings of these that groups, institutions, etc., are produced. The processes which disturb these social products, which have grown and solidified over a period of time and prevent them from becoming completely static, are the reconstructive processes.

These processes, of course, do not comprise the whole of the system, since some provision must be made for the analysis of the products of the social processes. The products Ross considers to be either subjective or objective: institutions, uniformities, and imperatives are classified as subjective, while groups and social relations are thought of as objective. The latter are objective in the sense that they "evince themselves in behavior" and can be observed without communicating with the participants. Institutions are subjective, since they are a sanctioned grouping or relation, though the actual grouping may or may not conform to the sanctioned grouping, while imperatives are subjective, because they are sanctioned actions or beliefs. The uniformities are subjective, since they are beliefs and feelings, but they are not binding.[15] Despite the fact that the old dichotomy of objective and subjective is no longer held to be valid, Ross has succeeded in marking off the division which is still widely used to separate social psychology and sociology, and he has, moreover, dealt with the contents of both categories as being the product of social interaction.

The outline presented above is the scaffolding of Ross's system of sociology as it is described in *The Foundations of Sociology,* and for our purposes the rest of his scientific writing must be regarded as an attempt to fill out this framework. Before proceeding to an analysis of his system, it is necessary to discover the foundations upon which Ross builds, i.e., under what conditions does he believe that social processes, the basic units of sociological investigation, occur?

While the phenomena which compose the rest of the system are the products of social interaction, we must look elsewhere for the source of social interaction itself, and Ross finds this source in the "social forces." These social forces are nothing more than the desires which motivate human beings and are blended into the complex patterns of interests "which shape society and make history." Some of these desires have always been present in the form of biological needs and are later modified by the cultural environment, e.g., the appetitive desires such as hunger, thirst, and sex, while others have developed only after man has become a cultural being, e.g., religious, ethical, and intellectual desires.[16]

The difficulty with this theory of the social forces is the same that plagues other theories of the same sort and is one of the centers of controversy in sociology at the present time: the tendency to reify certain classifications of social phenomena and then use the reified classifications as causal factors in the analysis of the rise of the phenomena. If this use of desires and interests on Ross's part is regarded as a convenient classification of the conditions under which social interaction arises, criticism of it must wait for an analysis of the results which Ross has secured with it. This, of course, leads us to consider the manner in which Ross has dealt with the social processes and how he has actually related his concept of social forces to social interaction.

When we turn to Ross's discussion of the social processes, however, we find that the gap between the social forces and social interaction is not bridged in any generalized formulation but only in examples of how specific traits of human nature determine specific social responses. Thus combat reactions are used to infer that man inherits a struggling response, and the struggling response is, in turn, used as a means of explaining combat reaction. Moreover, with a few exceptions, the examples which are used are not carried over into the discussion of the social processes. It must be concluded that the social forces have little to do with the working-out of the system, since the classificatory device which they offer is not used as such.[17]

In his discussion of the social processes in the *Principles of Sociology,* Ross modifies his system to a certain extent. The preliminary processes are broken up into two sections: one an analysis of the environment, in which it is pointed out that environment serves essentially as a limiting factor in the development of society; and the other a discussion of the relationship of occupation to social function. On the other hand, the reconstructive processes are discussed mainly under the heading of "The Social Population," where the effects of population change, urbanization, and the sex ratio are indicated.

The social processes proper are considered under the several different categories. Association, communication, domination, and exploitation are regarded as being the processes which are most intimately tied up with the genesis of society.[18] How association can be regarded as a process in its own right rather than as a symbol denoting the other social processes is not clear in Ross's writing, and the fact that it is not clear indicates that there is little ground for the assumption that he makes. A similar difficulty is encountered in dealing with the process of communication, in that all other processes are carried out largely through the medium of communication, so that it must be considered to be a phenomenon of a different order. Ross's discussion of the forms of domination and exploitation, as being persistent and recurrent processes, is doubtless correct; but why they and not other processes should be regarded as being the most important in the genesis of society is difficult to perceive. This is particularly true, if we regard society as consisting of the network of social relations that are set up by the social processes.

Ross's attempt to deal with the processes of opposition, conflict, competition, and adaptation is hampered severely by his interest in what he considers to be the good and bad effects of these forms of interaction, and the discussion is limited largely to such topics as wholesome opposition, services of economic competition, and antagonistic effort.[19] If, however, it is realized that this interpretation of good and bad can be translated to mean the strengthening or weakening of a particular group, whether that group be good or bad, the description of these processes becomes much more satisfactory. Moreover, the grouping of opposition, competition, and conflict into a single unit reveals an awareness on Ross's part that there is some common element which renders them akin to one another. The nature of this common element is never revealed, with the result that it is left to the reader's own discretion to decide whether or not these processes do belong together. The uniting of the discussion of the processes of co-operation and organization into a single section also bears witness to this tendency to order the processes around a never revealed common element.[20] It should be obvious by this time, however, that the former are grouped together because they are essentially dissociative processes, while the latter are considered in the same section because they are associative.

A different factor serves as the combining element in the classification of the processes of stratification, the rise of gross inequalities, gradation, and segregation under the heading of class and caste.[21] This factor seems to be that, although dissociative, the primary function which these processes serve is that of differentiation. They are the processes by which division of labor and of benefits develops, and they prevent society from showing a dead level of uniformity. If it is thought that this factor does not explain his placing of equalization and social circulation under the same heading as the above, it must be remembered that, just as adaptation is considered as the process which offsets conflict and competition, so the processes of equalization and social circulation are included under the heading of class and caste because they tend to offset the complete dominance of gradation, stratification, etc.

The processes of socialization, estrangement, and liberation are considered in the same class by Ross because he feels that their greatest importance lies in the relationship which they establish between the individual and society, while ossification, decadence, transformation, etc., are considered under the heading of social regress and progress. The heterogeneity of the classification is still further emphasized by the fact that anticipation, simulation, individualization, deterioration, and balance are not considered as social processes at all but are regarded as sociological principles.[22]

Only one conclusion can be reached from the above description of Ross's treatment of the social processes: systematization of the social processes, as such, exists only in incipient form, and then according to diverse, implicit principles. Some of the processes are systematized according to whether or not they are associative or dissociative, and others are classified as contributing to the growing complexity of society; still others are grouped according to their influence on the relationship between the individual and society. Such systematization amounts essentially to no systematization at all, since no relationship is established between the processes which are classified according to one principle and those grouped around a different standard of judgment.

This does not mean that Ross's discussion of each individual process is invalid, but only that no method is set up by means of which we can relate one process to all the other processes in terms of a certain common element, which all represent to a certain degree. Certain predictions can be made concerning the occurrence and the results of the occurrence of each process, but these generalizations cannot be constructed into a systematized body of knowledge. Had any one of the principles by which Ross classified the processes been carried through consistently, the analysis could have been regarded as systematic, and the validity of the system would have depended upon the increased understanding of social phenomena which it made possible. As it is, the material concerning the processes contains some valid analysis of particular processes and some suggestive principles for future classification but cannot itself be regarded as a systematic description of the social processes. The effects of this carry over into the other aspects of Ross's map of the sociological field. They make rather difficult the demonstration of how the phenomena which go to make up the other divisions are produced by social interaction. The latter, of course, is one of the primary duties that Ross laid upon himself when he outlined his system of analysis, and it is the object toward which most of the remainder of our investigation will be directed.

Ross restricts his analysis of the objective products of social interaction to a brief discussion of groups in the *Principles of Sociology,* and even this discussion is limited essentially to those groups which are regarded as being the product of other than the social processes. Moreover, social processes are "group-makers" to the extent that they, like other phenomena, mark ".... off certain persons from others, or establish a community of interest....."[23] This limited presentation of the role of the social processes in the formation of groups does not, of course, offer a satisfactory explanation of how social interaction is responsible for the formation of groups.

Social Psychology and *Social Control* deal primarily with the subjective products of social processes, and in these works Ross points out in detail the fashion in which certain phases of individual mentality and action are determined by the society in which the individual lives. Much has been made of the fact that, in the latter work, Ross has attempted to show that a natural order can develop out of the instinctive behavior of man; but it must be remembered that he casts aside this natural order as not being sufficient to support a complex society and then proceeds to point out how order is brought about on a social basis.[24] Although Ross deals to some extent with the agencies of control which are external to the individual controlled, i.e., law and public opinion, he places primary emphasis on those controls which are social in origin but are internalized in the individual and are an essential part of his personality and are subjective products of social interaction in the meaning of Ross's use of the term. Whether or not the control which is exerted is consciously directed toward certain ends or not seems to be a relatively minor matter. Indeed, except for his mentioning it in the Introduction, Ross pays little or no attention to the restriction that he has theoretically placed on himself. It is for these reasons that *Social Control* is still unsurpassed as a listing of the various means of social control and of the types of behavior which these agencies control. The weakness of the work lies where we might expect it: in the explanation of how these subjective products become part of the personality of the individuals who are controlled by them.

It is in Ross's description of the influence of custom that we see this weakness most clearly illustrated. The individual may obey custom because he is afraid of the consequences which are to follow, but Ross points out that custom is largely self-enforcing, meaning that the fear of external factors need not enter the situation. Thus we get a picture which, in almost every way, corresponds to the most sophisticated theories of social control; but Ross then attributes this self-enforcing quality of custom to the power of suggestion and habit:

The secret of this power must be sought, in the last analysis, in suggestion and habit. The child receives the ideas, precepts, and likings which are to become the organizing factors of its life, because it has no habits, because it is not yet obsessed by other ideas and feelings, because it wants something that may help it to bring order out of the chaotic contents of its mind, and because the hunger of a growing creature makes it greedy for mental aliment. On the other hand, the adult who has passed the suggestible age and emerged from the family chrysalis, allows the early organization of his life to dominate him because habit is strong and the wrench of mental adjustment is painful.[25]

The point must be re-emphasized that Ross sees that a connection exists between social interaction and attitudes, mind, and other so-called "subjective" phenomena but hides the essential element of the problem behind the symbols—suggestion and habit. So again he fails to bridge the gap between one segment of his system and another. This applies not only to his treatment of the factors involved in social control over a long period of time but also to his treatment of the material concerning all psychic planes and currents which are due to social interaction. A good part of the *Social Psychology* is taken up with the phenomenon of suggestibility and the part it plays in transferring to another group the ideas, habits, and attitudes of one group of individuals. It is true that Ross is interested primarily in the broad uniformities of attitudes, ideas, and habits that people possess within a given society rather than in the development of the unique personality in social interaction. But the problem, in so far as it is connected with the process by which these attitudes are internalized, is essentially the same, whether they be the attitudes of a small group or attitudes which are present throughout a whole society. He fails to answer the question as to the conditions under which the social mind develops.[26]

We must conclude, therefore, that that section of Ross's system which deals with the subjective products of social interaction cannot be regarded as being actually systematic. His discussions concerning specific factors in social control and other particular problems, such as crowd behavior and mob mind, are brilliant and useful, but each of them forms a separate and distinct piece of work. There is little relationship demonstrated between the phenomena, since their basic relationship must grow out of the fact that they are products of social interaction, and Ross is unable to show how they are so produced.

III. A CRITICAL APPRAISAL OF ROSS'S SOCIOLOGICAL DOCTRINES

Ross's system as a whole must then be regarded as a map of the sociological field, and a map in which the connection between the various areas is not clearly demonstrated. The map, however, does contain the basic dividing line along which sociology has continued to grow, in that social interaction is the core of systematic sociology, while groups, attitudes, mind, etc., are regarded as products of the social processes. As a system, however, it is definitely unsatisfactory. The two basic requirements of a system of scientific theory are that the relations between the major divisions be demonstrated and that within each major division the various phenomena dealt with be clearly related. Ross's system meets neither of these requirements: the social processes are not successfully related to one another, nor are the products of interaction related to one another. Ross fails to establish his hypothesis that what he calls "social products" are actually produced by social interaction. As has been pointed out before, this does not invalidate the results which Ross has secured in dealing with the problems presented by various individual phenomena; it indicates only that Ross has not successfully erected his findings into a system.

How much influence on systematic sociology Ross's map of the sociological field has had is difficult to determine. Blackmar and Gillin adopted Ross's outline of the social processes, with some modification, and Von Wiese and Becker have utilized Ross's material to some extent.[27] In the latter case, however, it is primarily a use of the specific description of certain processes, since the authors have systematized the processes according to one consistent standard throughout.

The influence which Ross's writing will have in the future will also probably stem from his description of specific problems and processes. Systems superior to Ross's system in consistency and explanatory power have already been developed, and their existence minimizes the possibility that his system as such will ever have a great deal of importance for formal social theory. Future interest in his system must be essentially of a historical nature.

NOTES

1. *Seventy Years of It* (New York, 1936).

2. *Social Control* (New York, 1901); *The Foundations of Sociology* (New York, 1905); *Social Psychology* (New York, 1908); *Principles of Sociology* (2d ed.; New York, 1930).

3. *Social Control,* title-page.

4. *Ibid.,* pp. vii–viii.

5. *Foundations of Sociology,* p. 98.

6. *Social Psychology,* p. 1. It is realized that what has been said here about these books has been said countless times before, and it is included only to set the stage for the more lengthy analysis which is to follow.

7. *Sin and Society* (Boston, 1907). For a survey of Ross's contributions to public problems see the article on Ross by Harry Elmer Barnes, in the English *Sociological Review,* April, 1923.

8. New York, 1914.

9. *The Old World in the New* (New York, 1914).

10. *The Social Trend* (New York, 1922). The first two chapters deal with the problem of population increase and migration; see also *Standing Room Only* (New York, 1927).

11. *Seventy Years of It,* pp. 226–29.

12. *The Foundations of Sociology,* pp. 71–99.

13. *Ibid.,* pp. 90–91.

14. *Ibid.,* pp. 88–90.

15. *Ibid.*

16. *Ibid.,* pp. 149–81.

17. One of the exceptions is his discussion of opposition. Ross points out that interference of interests leads to the processes of opposition, competition, and conflict (*Principles of Sociology*, p. 149).

18. *Ibid.*, pp. 93–146.

19. *Ibid.*, pp. 149–262.

20. *Ibid.*, pp. 265–310.

21. *Ibid.*, pp. 313–71.

22. *Ibid.*, pp. 375–498, 531–85.

23. *Ibid.*, p. 515.

24. *Social Control*, pp. 41–61.

25. *Ibid.*, pp. 184–85. Ross's use of suggestion is similar to his use of the social forces. Suggestion is inferred from the behavior of individuals and then used to explain that behavior. This use of the term prevents a detailed discussion of the conditions under which attitudes, ideas, and habits of others are taken over into the personality in question.

26. Compare this point of view with that of Kimball Young, "Social Psychology," in H. E. Barnes (ed.), *The History and Prospects of the Social Sciences* (New York, 1925), pp. 156–209, and particularly pp. 161–62.

27. F. W. Blackmar and J. L. Gillin, *Outlines of Sociology* (New York, 1915), pp. 296–307; see also G. Lundberg, *Foundations of Sociology* (New York, 1939), p. 248; L. von Wiese and Howard Becker, *Systematic Sociology* (New York, 1932). Consult Index in the latter work for references to Ross.

CHAPTER XXI

THE SOCIOLOGICAL IDEAS OF PITIRIM ALEXANDROVITCH SOROKIN: "INTEGRALIST" SOCIOLOGY

HANS SPEIER

I. THE CULTURAL BACKGROUND AND PERSONAL EQUATION IN SOROKIN'S WRITINGS

PITIRIM A. SOROKIN is one of the most prolific writers in contemporary sociology. Because of his broad historical interests, his systematic grasp of factual detail, and his aptitude for facile theoretical reasoning, he occupies a place of distinction among the sociologists of our time. This place would have been his due, even if he had never written the four volumes of *Social and Cultural Dynamics* which are his most spectacular, but not his most important, contribution to sociology.

Sorokin is of Russian origin. His parents were peasants. He was born in Touria in 1889 and studied at the Psycho-neurological Institute and at the University of St. Petersburg, where he received his Doctor's degree in sociology in 1922. From 1914 to 1916 he taught at the Psycho-neurological Institute and from 1917 to 1922 at the University of St. Petersburg and at the Agricultural Academy. In 1917, Sorokin was editor-in-chief of the *Volia Naroda,* a moderately progressive paper. He was also a member of the Executive Committee of the All-Russian Peasant Soviet, of the Council of the Russian Republic, and secretary to Alexander Kerensky, the Russian prime minister in 1917. In 1918 he became a member of the Russian Constitutional Assembly.

Sorokin's experiences during the Russian revolution exerted a profound influence on his political attitudes and on his social theories. His hatred of communism, many of his antiprogressive and reactionary political opinions, and his rejection of the ideals of modern, Western civilization as a whole may be traced to this period of his life.

Sorokin claims that he believed in egalitarian principles at the beginning of the Russian revolution but that his observations of life in Russia during the revolutionary period led him to realize that this belief was untenable.[1] His *Leaves from a Russian Diary 1917-1922*[2] contains many gripping details of the Russian revolution. Apart from being a valuable source for the student of the revolution, this diary offers many clues for understanding the personal background of Sorokin's later works. During the revolution Sorokin completed his *System of Sociology* (2 vols., 1920; in Russian). His Marxian critics found many faults in this work. They criticized, in particular, the author's insistence on the importance of racial homogeneity for sociopolitical unity, on the unchangeable character of the Jewish race, and on the physiological basis of social inequality.[3]

Sorokin was sentenced to death by the Bolshevik authorities in 1922. Former students intervened in his behalf, and the death penalty was converted into banishment from the country. In 1923, Sorokin came to the United States. From 1924 to 1930 he was professor of sociology at the University of Minnesota, and in 1930 he was called to Harvard University.

Sorokin's first sociological book in English, *The Sociology of Revolution*,[4] is not one of his major works. It contains theoretical propositions which he later discarded, such as the theory of social equilibrium.[5] It is not primarily a study of the social conditions and social causes of revolutions but a treatise on the pathology of human behavior. Both the causes and the characteristics of revolutions are interpreted in terms of various conflicting psychologies which are not reconcilable with one another, except for the fact that they all minimize the importance of man's rational conduct. Sorokin's main line of reasoning in this book is derived from psychological doctrines in which the instinctive, "irrational" nature of man is stressed. Under the influence of Pareto, whom Sorokin read when the Russian revolution was in its initial phase, and also under the influence of Freud and Pavlov, Sorokin emphasized the limited power of human reason. Unfortunately, the weakness of reason is implemented by the evil nature of human instincts, which renders man a rather weird being. A revolution occurs when the balance of reason and instinct is suddenly disturbed on a mass scale. Then, man, as a social being, is reduced to an uninhibited, instinctive animal that shakes off the fetters of custom, morals, and law. Revolution is, thus, essentially anarchy and destruction, as instinct is essentially destructive.

Revolution is evil, since man is evil unless he is restrained by fear, force, or faith. Revolution is crime on a mass scale.

While the book contains many interesting facts on mass behavior in the Russian and earlier revolutions, it does not display an understanding of the historical conditions of revolutionary change. In particular, it fails to deal with the ideas that go into the making of revolutions. Because of Sorokin's emotional bias, which pervades both the general structure and the particular statements of the book, *The Sociology of Revolution* does not rank among the outstanding contributions in this field of sociological research; but, for the same reason, the book offers the best revelation of the personal equation in the author's outlook on man and society.

In the third volume of his more recent work, *Social and Cultural Dynamics*,[6] Sorokin returned once more to the analysis of revolutions. There he studied the fluctuations of internal disturbances through time, analyzing 1,622 revolutions and other internal conflicts in the history of Greece, Rome, and Europe as to the social area, the duration, the intensity of the disturbance, and the masses participating in it. This investigation is based on a much broader historical survey than the earlier study of revolution. While Sorokin repeats that the main difference between crime and revolution is one of magnitude only,[7] he does not reiterate his earlier misanthropic psychological doctrines. Instead, he advances a general interpretation of the social conditions of revolutions, viz., that "the main and the indispensable condition for an eruption of internal disturbances is that the social system or the cultural system or both shall be unsettled." One will hardly be inclined to regard this statement as especially illuminating. Sorokin tries, however, to increase the significance of his findings by attacking a number of popular theories to which he takes exception. Thus his curves on the frequency of revolutions show that the twentieth century has been one of the most turbulent periods of history, and he exclaims: "This conclusion will certainly startle all the manufacturers and consumers of the 'sweet applesauce' theories that civilization is progressive through a process of orderly change toward universal peace."[8] Here, as in many other of his polemics, Sorokin neglects to consider that the readers whom he deserves are not quite so naïve as the views which he attacks.

In yet another volume Sorokin discussed revolutions, treating them together with famine, pestilence, and war as one of the four most terrible disasters that befall mankind. *Man and Society in Calamity*[9] is devoted to a study of the effects of these disasters on the human mind, human behavior, the vital processes, social mobility, social organization, and "cultural" activities. There is again a wealth of quotations from historical sources and monographs in this book, but the analytical findings are disappointing by comparison. Sorokin's main thesis is the "law of diversification and polarization of the effects of calamity." It does not seem unfair to regard this law as the elaboration of a commonplace when its meaning is explained as follows: "The effects of a given calamity are not identical—indeed are often opposite—for different individuals and groups of the society concerned."

Sorokin's first major contribution to sociology in English was his *Social Mobility,* published in 1927.[10] In this work, Sorokin analyzed the phenomena of vertical and horizontal mobility, their nature, causes, and consequences. The wealth of quantitative data and the rich historical documentation of the volume have made it an indispensable textbook for anyone interested in social stratification. Sorokin discusses not only social mobility but also certain differential characteristics of social classes which have been studied by earlier sociologists, such as longevity, health and bodily features, intelligence, and character traits. Furthermore, the book contains a brief theoretical discussion of the nature and causes of social stratification. In *Social Mobility* Sorokin's political opinions determine the course of his investigation to a lesser extent than in his *Sociology of Revolution.* They are not entirely suppressed, however, in favor of scientific detachment. In his study of social mobility and stratification he found many of Pareto's ideas suggestive.[11] Specifically, with Pareto and a number of other modern critics of democracy, Sorokin considers it "a matter of necessity" that the leaders of politics and business must be immoral; they are either "lions" or "foxes."[12] At the same time, the "scepticism and destructive criticism" of modern intellectuals is presented as resulting from a deplorable lack of "any firm and sacred convictions," which Sorokin attributes in this work to the mobility of modern society, or, to put it in his own inimitable way: "Intellectuals of our epoch are a mixture of Protagoras, Gorgias, Socrates and Montaigne."[13] He concluded *Social Mobility* with a declaration of personal preference for the mobile type of society, which at that time he liked "too much to prophesy its funeral."[14]

Contemporary Sociological Theories, his next publication,[15] is one of the best introductory texts in the field. It most satisfactorily demonstrates his impressive erudition. By its invariable simplification of the theories presented for review and criticism, by its pedagogically skilful presentation, and by its successful attempt to consider theories in the light of factual findings, the book excels most similar writings on the history of social theory. Its bibliographical usefulness is considerable, since the book contains ample reference to works in five or six different languages.

Sorokin's contributions to rural sociology are embodied in a monumental *Source Book in Rural Sociology,* in three volumes,[16] prepared jointly with Carle C. Zimmerman and Charles J. Galpin under the auspices of the United States Department of Agriculture and the University of Minnesota, and a manual, *Principles of Rural-urban Sociology,* written jointly with Carle C. Zimmerman,[17] which is a concise summary of the *Source Book.* The outstanding value of the *Source Book* consists in the systematic presentation of selected passages from classic investigations of rural life in many different cultures. Data from numerous societies provide the rural sociologist with a wealth of factual material for comparative studies of contemporary rural life in America with that of other civilizations, past and present. Some of the conclusions which Sorokin suggests at the end of his *Principles of Rural-Urban Sociology* are of the same ethos that pervades his main work on social and cultural change. Thus he advocates a "deep spiritual revolution .... towards reinforcement and regeneration of the Stoic attitudes towards life instead of the Epicurean."[18] Among other things, this revolution would retard the "progressive extinction of the offspring" of the upper classes and counteract the "progressive impoverishment of the racial fund."[19]

Before turning to Sorokin's main work, mention should be made of another study which he undertook with Clarence Q. Berger on *Time Budgets of Human Behavior.*[20] This work is based on a collection of records which approximately one hundred individuals kept from day to day during a period of four weeks. These individuals were asked to record accurately the kinds of activities in which they engaged during the twenty-four hours of the day and precisely how much time was consumed by each activity. A part of the book is devoted to a factual discussion of human motives on the basis of "motivation schedules." For a period of two weeks the individuals whose time budgets were investigated recorded also the motive or motives for their varied activities. Finally, the authors deal with the problem of the predictability of human behavior and of social processes. One hundred and six individuals were asked to predict their own behavior accurately a day, several days, a week, or a month in advance, "listing exactly all the activities which would occupy them on the stated days from the moment of rising to that of retiring. Any activity with a duration of five minutes had to be listed separately....." As was to be expected, the authors found that the errors in prediction were considerable and increased as the prediction extended further into the future. To this result there are added others of equal importance; for example, *"The more stable and routine the social life in which an individual lives and acts, the more clock-like its functioning from day to day, the higher the accuracy of prediction."*[21]

The volume closes with an eloquent chapter devoted to warnings against "reckless" "scientific" forecasting and large-scale social planning. "Perhaps," we are told, "the percentage of right *guesses* compared with wrong ones was rather higher in institutions like the Pythia of Delphi or the famous oracle of Apollo than in the contemporary predictions supposedly based firmly upon science."[22]

Still another book, *Russia and the United States*,[23] was written during the war when American sentiment ran high in praise of the Red Army and the Russian people. Today the volume is interesting mainly for the light it throws upon the conflict between anti-Bolshevik and pro-Russian feelings in the author's heart. The conflict was resolved in favor of the pro-Russian feeling. Sorokin attacked American apprehensions of "Russian communism, atheism, 'imperialism' and 'barbarism,' " regarding them as altogether unfounded. He tried to prove the essentially democratic nature of Russian life before and after the destructive phase of the revolution and found that the United States and Russia exhibited a most extraordinary similarity in moral standards, social institutions, cultural creativeness, etc. The "mutual, cultural and social congeniality of the two nations" held the promise of even closer co-operation between them in the future. "It is refreshing to sense, within the otherwise dark and chaotic maze of events, so beneficent a destiny."[24]

When the merit of this book is assessed in the light of subsequent events, it should not be forgotten that the "vital interests" of the two nations fall, strictly speaking, under the heading of international relations. Sorokin did not really examine these interests anywhere in his book but approached his subject more freely from a "sociocultural" point of view. Instead of talking about Manchuria, China, Korea, or about the Balkans, Germany, Austria, Italy, the Middle East, etc., he pleaded at the time, as an American citizen, for good will toward America's ally.

We have tried to indicate how all Sorokin's major writings are the expressions of a personality with firm convictions, convictions of a kind which are not too popular in modern democracy. Much as Sorokin the scholar tries to control his valuations which have inspired him in all his endeavors, his books are distinguished from many other monographs and textbooks in the social sciences by the evidence of a struggle in the author's soul between political passion and "scientific objectivity," objectivity being an ideal too often proclaimed by those who fail to be inspired by anything. One may justly doubt whether, in Sorokin's publications, this struggle is always resolved in favor of objectivity. Those who disagree with his valuations and preferences will, indeed, be inclined to deny most vigorously that it is so resolved. Some critics have contended that Sorokin's sociological writings are a long and elaborate —almost classic—demonstration of the validity of Max Weber's contention that the interjection of "value-judgments" vitiates sociology as an objective social science.

A more dispassionate answer can be given only after Sorokin's valuations are understood more clearly. Precisely what are his preferences? Are they dogmatic or critical? Do they differ in any way from the reactionary opinions of men who do not devote much time and energy to social philosophy? In short, are they prejudices or ideas? In order to answer these questions, we must turn to Sorokin's main work, which contains the most explicit exposition of his social philosophy.

II. "SOCIAL AND CULTURAL DYNAMICS": ITS THEME AND METHODOLOGY

Social and Cultural Dynamics[25] is a very ambitious study. It covers the history of civilization for the last twenty-five hundred years and contains numerous excursions into the history of many civilizations in order to ascertain the forms and kinds of sociocultural change.

Fundamentally, the work is a gigantic re-examination of the theory of progress which, in popular form, has dominated the philosophical views of many social scientists in the nineteenth century and has exerted a deep influence upon the mores of modern Western society. The theory contained not only the prospect of an ever increasing efficiency of man's control over nature—making for greater safety and comfort—but also of an ever increasing liberation of man from prejudice, ignorance, and destructive passions.

Even in its heydey this doctrine was not uncontested. There have been numerous scientists who tried to prove that the history of cultures resembles organic birth-growth-decline-death cycles, to be compared with recurring cyclical movements rather than a progressively ascending line. Leaving aside various refinements and modifications of these two basic doctrines of historical change, there has also been a much more radical criticism of the theory of progress: it has been denied that certain fundamental tenets of the theory of progress are sound. Briefly, the theory of progress endows different stages of history with significantly varying degrees of moral worth; and implies that the present may shine in the complacency of superiority as long as it lasts. This characteristically "modern" attitude was created by the advance of modern natural science, its marvelously effective application to man's control over nature, and the overwhelming prestige which quantitative methods acquired.[26]

The modern theory of progress is also an outgrowth of the increased *philosophical interest in history,* and it has been shown that this interest, which begins, roughly speaking, with Francis Bacon, emerged with the systematic doubt of the efficacy of rational moral precepts. A radical criticism of the theory of progress and of the ethical notions which it embodies would have to re-examine the relevance of historical investigations for moral considerations, on the one hand, and the adequacy of quantitative methods for dealing with this philosophical problem, on the other hand. Sorokin falls short of this kind of radical criticism. He discusses the philosophical problems which he raises, to a large extent, with the help of quantitative methods, but without ever disentangling the ethical problem of what is good from the essentially meaningless one, namely, how good was man in different periods of history. In other words, Sorokin's study of history is imbued with the spirit of the doctrine that he desires to refute. For this reason the work is an "expression"—or "derivative," to use Pareto's term—of our civilization rather than a critique of our civilization.

Sorokin comes to the conclusion that, viewed in historical perspective, there has not been any progress, nor has there been any cyclical movement. What he finds is *fluctuation:* fluctuation of the basic types of culture, fluctuation of the types of social relationships, fluctuation in the concentration of power, in economic conditions, in the occurrence of conflict—fluctuations everywhere.

The data from which this generalization is derived are taken from an area as varied as civilization itself. The first volume of *Social and Cultural Dynamics* deals with forms of art; the second with systems of truth, ethics, and law; the third with numerous social relationships, groups, and institutions, from the family to the state and from the church to economic conditions. It also contains a monumental study of about one thousand wars and sixteen hundred revolutions, and an inquiry into the relation between culture, personality, and conduct. Thus the research which went into the making of *Social and Cultural Dynamics* is truly enormous. It was undertaken with the help of numerous specialists. Even so, the encyclopedic enterprise would have been impossible had it not been for the fact that the research was confined to investigations which are, strictly speaking, unhistorical. The historical phenomena were not studied in order to understand their specific historical character but rather in order to "grade" them! Works of historians and occasionally also—for example, in the section on law—original documents were used with the single question in view: If all cultural phenomena are divided into a small number of classes, into which of these classes do the phenomena under investigation fall? Are they good, satisfactory, or bad?

The terms designating these classes are, of course, not quite so simple. They vary, in fact, from one cultural domain to another. For example, the opposing categories for classifying the "topics" of painting, sculpture, architecture, music, and literature are *religious* (good) and *secular* (bad); for their styles, *symbolic* (good) and *visual* (bad). The corresponding terms for social relationships are *familistic* (good) and *contractual-compulsory* (bad). Again, all pairs of categories are co-ordinated, since they are derived from a pair of basic values. The names of these basic values are *ideational* and *sensate*.

Once the historical phenomena are thus reduced to a basic index, i.e., subsumed under one of the classes, it becomes possible to compare the frequencies through time of the indices within any given series of phenomena. By doing the same for other series, frequencies in various series can be compared. No matter how heterogeneous the various departments of culture are; no matter how surprising it may appear to compare families with symphonies or states with systems of philosophy, once a common denominator of values—"externalized" in family, symphony, state, or philosophy—is established, the circle is squared.

In many respects Sorokin's sociological approach to history reminds one of the methodology of the old unilateral evolutionists in ethnological theory, who started out with an assumed and prearranged scheme of universal evolution and then searched for materials to round out the skeleton outline and vindicate the evolutionary scheme, having little regard for the cultural context from which they wrenched their data.

This, in brief, is the procedure which Sorokin follows in his attempt to arrive at generalizations about social and cultural change, namely, regarding almost everything in the history of mankind as an index of a strictly limited number of values.

The historian will consider this treatment of historical data, in which the most divergent phenomena are torn from their historical context and put in the same "class," as very strange indeed. He may well wonder what the significance of this cumbersome undertaking can possibly be when, on the highest level of generalization, the period of absolutism in the sixteenth and seventeenth centuries is made to appear *identical* with the period between the two world wars. Nor will he be convinced that the statistical method has been used with proper caution, when, even in its application to economic facts, it leads to such startling results as the following one, in which the understanding of historical circumstances is entirely neglected in favor of drawing a time curve, cutting across the most heterogeneous systems of economic organization: the general economic situation in France was "satisfactory" (rather than "bad" or "excellent," etc.) in the twelve following years, 1115, 1350, 1480, 1585, 1610, 1650, 1685, 1740, 1785, 1800, 1920, and 1925.[27]

Much as the historian may be at a loss to recognize the merit of such procedures and results, the moralist may reserve his judgment until he understands precisely what Sorokin's scale of values is. Unfortunately, Sorokin knows more definitely what is bad than what is good. Everything *sensate* is definitely bad. Contemporary society is bad, because the values externalized in contemporary society are hedonistic, utilitarian, and relativistic. Sorokin likes to dwell on the syndrome of the contemporary crisis of Western civilization in both America and Europe, in order to persuade his readers that they have made a mess of everything noble, decent, and good. His eloquence is that of a professorial Abraham, a Santa Clara.

It should be noticed that in his grandiose historical perspective there is not much difference between America and Europe,[28] nor is there any essential difference between democratically organized societies and non-democratic societies. It is characteristic of sensate "culture mentality" that people take seriously the "slogan," "Give me liberty or give me death," whereas the much superior ideational mentality "is little interested in political and civil rights and declarations, in various political devices to guarantee the liberty of speech, press, convictions, meetings, and overt actions; in the constitution, in free government, and the like."[29] On the other hand, the rise of totalitarianism is also indicative of sensatism; only, it is not "sensate liberation" but "sensate curbing" of the individual.

In any case, we must find our way back to the values of ideationalism, the culture of faith, or to the idealistic types of culture, which is the culture of reason. Unlike Spengler, Sorokin is not a straightforward prophet of doom. To be sure, sensatism will perish; but, after a catharsis, new values, i.e., the old values of idealism or ideationalism, will be once more externalized in society. In the end, then, everything will be well, until the new culture will again reach its "limit" and, by the operation of "immanent change," presumably make room for a new sensatism. In short, there is no final doomsday, there is only condition: a fluctuating prophecy of recurring doomsdays alternating with recurring days of a more fortunate lot of man.

In the fourteenth book of Augustine's *Civitas Dei* we read: "Epicurean philosophers lived after the flesh because they placed man's highest good in *bodily pleasure;* and .... those others do so who have been of opinion that in some form or other bodily good is man's supreme good." According to Augustine, the next higher level of life is represented by the Stoics, "who place the supreme good of man in the soul." Since "both the soul and the flesh, the component parts of man, can be used to signify the whole man," both Epicureans and Stoics (and Platonists) live "according to man." Or one may say that they live according to *reason,* if reason can be divorced from faith. Only the Christian, in his *faith,* lives according to God.

Sorokin's basic distinction between "sensate," "idealistic," and "ideational" bears more than a faint resemblance to the ideas expressed in this quotation from Augustine. Sorokin's basic philosophy may be regarded as a modern vulgarization of early Christian thinking. The distinction between senses, reason, and faith is retained as a universal principle of division of the types of men, cultures, and "systems" within each culture. The hierarchization of these values, however, is blurred. The idea of a supreme good is given up in favor of a relativistic point of view, tempered by eclectic professions of absolute standards. Throughout his work some kind of hierarchy of the three values is implied, as is particularly evident from the expressions of contempt, disgust, and revulsion in which Sorokin indulges whenever he describes the "sensate sewers" of our time. However, it is not the truth of faith which ranks highest, as one might expect from familiarity with the tradition which Sorokin follows in distinguishing the three values. Rather, he "prefers" idealism to ideationalism. Again, ideationalism is constructed as a compromise between sensatism and idealism, which blurs the distinctions further. Finally, the methods used in *Social and Cultural Dynamics* are those of "sensate science," which has induced a malicious critic to remark that the work may be a satire on modern social science.

The three kinds of truth are first distinguished and utilized in classifying philosophical systems, as well as cultural epochs. They are irreducible, and, consequently, Sorokin, the antirelativist, presents an elaborate system of historical relativism. In the fourth volume of his work, however, this relativism is suddenly revoked. In the first three volumes, Sorokin speaks of the three basic "systems of truth," leaving the reader at a loss as to what the author means by "truth," or, rather, plainly admitting a pluralism of three different kinds of truth. In the fourth volume, two new kinds of truth are introduced under the name of *integral truth,* which "embraces" "all three forms of truth,"[30] and *absolute truth,* which is reserved for God. The integral truth is called "three-dimensional" by Sorokin, because its sources are intuition, reason, and the senses. Sorokin claims that his "integralist sociology" has accomplished "a profound revolution" in the social sciences, because "instead of dispensing with anything valuable in the cognitive sense, in any of the systems of truth," the integralist method contains them all and is hence fuller and more adequate than any of them taken separately.[31]

Integral truth resembles the type of "synthetic" thinking which Karl Mannheim invented, in order to rid his "sociology of knowledge" of the epistemological difficulties arising from the "perspectivism" of "situationally determined" types of thinking. Both Sorokin and Mannheim speak of the relative and "partial" truth of the philosophies they reject, and then they emerge from the welter of relativism with a pretentious claim of a "supertruth." Mannheim proposes that his "sociology of knowledge" may serve as a foundation of all social science; Sorokin claims that his integral truth is closer to the absolute truth than any one-sided truth. This claim, characteristic of all those who try to reconcile historicism with philosophy, hardly merits serious refutation. But, as an intellectual curiosity, it may be noted that Sorokin does not hesitate to elevate his own thinking above the one-sidedness of all philosophers of the past whom he regards as representatives of idealitionalism, idealism, or sensatism, respectively: "Hence the greater adequacy of the integral system of truth—compared with partial or one-sided truth .... over each of these systems."[32]

Within the confines of this chapter it is impossible to do justice to the great number of discussions contained in the four volumes of Sorokin's work. Two of them may be singled out for brief analysis, however, since they are especially important for understanding the structure of the work, viz., the problem of cultural integration and the general theory of social change.

Sorokin distinguishes between various meanings of cultural "integration." Cultural elements may be (1) merely adjacent in time or space but independent or contradictory in meaning; (2) associated with one another, because of adaptation to an "external" factor; (3) functionally or causally interdependent; and (4) "internally" or "logico-meaningfully" united.

For two reasons the choice of the term "logico-meaningful" for the highest form of integration is not fortunate. Both functional and external forms of integration are meaningful and not all cases of logico-meaningful integration are logical. For example, the relationship between the motor and the battery in an automobile is functional, that between refrigerators and sun suits and other light clothing is external; yet the fact that the automobile is supposed to move and that both refrigerators and sun suits are related to the prevalence of a warm climate indicate that the integrations are not strictly meaningless in either case. Again, logical integration is claimed not only for certain interrelationships of cultural elements that we encounter in the form of verbal propositions, such as statements in written documents, but also for nonverbal cultural elements, such as monuments and music, and for relationships between different classes of cultural elements, such as a specific family organization, a style of culture, a specific type of personality, and a particular kind of legal code. Sorokin himself admits that many units which he calls logico-meaningful are not logical units in the formal sense of the word "logic."

It appears, therefore, that what is meant by "logico-meaningful integration" is a type of integration which exists with reference to an arbitrarily selected norm, while "causal-functional integration" refers to the structure of the whole whose parts are functionally interdependent. Association due to an external factor is, of course, functional, too; but in this case integration exists only in view of the fact that social data are dependent upon nonsocial facts (climate, natural resources, etc.). By stressing the importance of logico-meaningful integration and by proclaiming it to be the highest form of integration, Sorokin is in a position to reject as insufficient or faulty those theories of culture which take cognizance only of that form of integration which depends on an external factor. Also, by differentiating spatial adjacency and integration in a narrower sense of the term, Sorokin makes allowance for the existence of unintegrated elements in a culture. Such elements are called "congeries." Sorokin repeatedly points out that any empirically given culture contains logico-meaningful systems and, in addition, congeries, although in the historical parts of his work he does not indicate which elements of the culture under investigation fail to be integrated. Sorokin takes exception to all theories of culture which insist on the functional interdependence of *all* cultural elements without admitting the possibility of unintegrated elements. Similarly, he rejects the "atomistic" theories which deny the existence of *any* integration, and in doing so he falsely regards any denial of a philosophy of history as a process with an integral meaning as a denial of the interdependence of various cultural elements in a given period of time.

Sorokin's analysis of culture centers around the logico-meaningful integration, i.e., around integration of culture with reference to norms. External phenomena of culture, such as objects, events, processes, are regarded as "incarnations" or "realizations" of the internal aspect of culture. In its organized form this internal aspect of culture consists of systems of thought which are "woven out of the inner experience" of a culture. Another term frequently used to designate this internal aspect is "culture mentality." External aspects of a culture are taken into account "only as manifestations of its internal aspects. Beyond this, they cease to be a part of an integrated system of culture."[33] This quotation confirms the statement that what is meant by "logico-meaningful integration" is integration with reference to norms. In addition, it indicates the antimaterialistic orientation of Sorokin's sociology. Sorokin's system may indeed be regarded as intellectualistic.

For purposes of analysis the external aspects of culture—say, the state organization or the prevailing family system—can be identified as integrated parts of a culture only if these social institutions can be translated by the analyst into normative terms and if, in addition, these norms are found to be identical, or at least compatible, with the basic values, sensate, idealistic, ideational, and their modifications. Sorokin, however, does not proceed according to this cumbersome method. He takes a short cut which is methodologically ingenious. Instead of investigating the philosophy, the art, the social institutions, the codes, the techniques, and the resources of a given society in order to understand the historical nature of these phenomena before proceeding to an analysis of integration, he takes as a starting-point a series of classifications of the various departments of culture in *all* periods, as has been indicated above. All these classifications are, from the beginning and by definition, compatible with the fundamental types of culture mentality. It is this procedure which renders his historical investigations unhistorical in the strict sense of the term.

In his general theory of social change Sorokin rejects the "externalistic" doctrines, according to which the changes that a cultural "system" undergoes are caused by external, environmental factors, for example, changes in the family structure by industrialization. The logical objection to all these theories is, according to Sorokin, that they postpone rather than solve the problem of change. By explaining a change of (*a*), say the family, by a change of (*b*), say industrialism; and the change of (*b*) by a change of (*c*), say the population structure; and the change of (*c*) by a change of (*d*), say the climate, an unlimited regression is introduced. This regression often involves the further difficulty of explaining transformation in one sphere, where much change occurs, in terms of causes located in another sphere, where less change occurs, as is especially evident in the explanation of social change in terms of climate.

In this case, as rather frequently in his writings, Sorokin does not fairly present the theory that he rejects in its most reasonable form, which is more difficult to criticize than its popular, simplified version.

Thus Sorokin attributes to the "externalistic" theories of social change the presupposition that change rather than "unchangeableness" of a sociocultural system needs explanation, whereas Sorokin himself stresses quite rightly that life is always changing and that unchangeableness rather than change needs explanation.

The occurrence of social change is, indeed, a universal fact, but the inquiry into the reason for this fact is part of the metaphysical problem of what life is. The various "externalistic" theories offer hypotheses regarding the causes of *specific* changes, not of the principle of change itself. Thus it is perfectly sensible to investigate the dependence of social life on climate or geography without investigating the metaphysical problem of change and stagnation, or of life and death. The scientific criticism, as distinguished from the metaphysical one, of such externalistic theories would have to determine whether the proposed causal dependence can be reversed, as, for example: Are climate and geography dependent upon social life? It would have to inquire to what *extent* and *degree* the hypothesis is correct; to what *extent* and *degree* other causal factors have to be introduced into the explanation of specific changes, etc. In short, the externalistic theories are not necessarily incompatible with the principle of *immanent change,* to which Sorokin adheres and to which he devotes a very stimulating discussion.

While it is generally true that "change needs much less explanation than any case of unchangeableness," it also remains true that any specific case of change needs as much explanation as any specific case of unchangeableness. Now Sorokin does recognize "externalistic" causes of social change, in addition to the principle of immanent change, but he attributes only a *subsidiary* significance to the externalistic principles and claims immanent change to be the primary principle. No protagonist of the externalistic doctrines will, however, go so far as to suggest that a state can by any effort of external factors be changed into a night club;[34] all protagonists of the externalistic doctrines will give implicitly more credit to the principle of immanence than Sorokin is inclined to give to intelligence, in the case of his opponents. On the other hand, Sorokin's emphasis on the principle of immanent change leads very easily to an attitude of resignation regarding the scientific explanation of specific changes. If everything changes anyhow and primarily according to the principle of immanent change, why bother much about *explaining* specific social changes? It will be noticed that this logical outcome of Sorokin's doctrine closely corresponds to his skepticism regarding forecasting and social planning. If everything changes anyhow and primarily according to the principle of immanent change, why bother much about *effecting* a specific change in society?

In conclusion, it may be said that Sorokin's main work revives the tradition of the encyclopedic endeavors of the early sociologists like Comte and Spencer. The greatest compliment that can be paid to it is that it invites comparisons with other contemporary attempts to arrive at an integrated philosophical view of human history, such as Spengler's or Toynbee's, or with other contemporary studies of the crisis of our time, such as Huizinga's. In such comparisons, however, Sorokin does not fare too well. Even Spengler excels him in historical judgment, imagination, and taste. H. Leisegang's older study, *Denkformen* (1928), offers a more penetrating analysis of the basic differences between various "types" of thinking than does Sorokin's integralist sociology. With all due respect for the gigantic labor that went into *Social and Cultural Dynamics,* for many stimulating discussions in this work, and especially for Sorokin's courageous attacks on many cherished errors in contemporary social science, one cannot help concluding that the work, as a whole, suffers from the persistent interjection of personal prejudices and that it combines the faults of European and American social science: unclear metaphysics and the application of quantitative techniques to philosophical problems which evade figures and curves.

NOTES

1. Hans Kasspohl in the *Introduction* to the German edition of Pitirim Sorokin's *Sociology of Revolution* (1925): *Die Soziologie der Revolution* (Munich, 1928), p. 18.

2. New York, 1924.

3. Kasspohl, *op. cit.*, p. 16.

4. Philadelphia, 1925.

5. See his criticism of this theory in "Le Concept d'équilibre est-il necessaire aux sciences sociales?" *Revue internationale de sociologie,* September–October, 1936. An abbreviated version of this article is contained in Sorokin's *Social and Cultural Dynamics,* IV (New York, 1941), 677–93.

6. (New York, 1937), pp. 383–508.

7. *Ibid.,* III, 501.

8. *Ibid.,* III, 478.

9. New York, 1943.

10. New York, 1927.

11. *Contemporary Sociological Theories* (New York, 1928), p. 60, n. 83.

12. For the context in which Sorokin uses these terms of Pareto cf. *Social Mobility,* p. 310.

13. *Ibid.*, p. 520.
14. *Ibid.*, p. 544.
15. New York, 1928.
16. Minneapolis, 1930–31.
17. New York, 1929.
18. *Principles of Rural-urban Sociology*, p. 635.
19. *Ibid.*, p. 632.
20. Cambridge, Mass., 1939.
21. *Time Budgets of Human Behavior*, p. 170 (italics Sorokin's and Berger's).
22. *Ibid.*, p. 179.
23. New York, 1944.
24. *Russia and the United States*, p. 209.
25. Vols. I–III (New York, 1937); Vol. IV (1941). A popularization of these four volumes appeared later under the title *The Crisis of Our Age* (New York, 1941). The methodology employed in his main work is discussed and summarized in *Sociocultural Causality, Space, Time* (Durham, N.C., 1943).
26. For two of the most penetrating discussions of this subject, cf. Edmund Husserl, "Die Krisis der europäischen Wissenschaften und die transcendentale Phaenomenologie," *Philosophia*, I (1936), 77–176; and Jacob Klein, "Die griechische Logistik und die Entstehung der Algebra," *Quellen und Studien zur Geschichte der Mathematik*, Abteilung B: *Studien*, II (Berlin, 1934), 18–105, and III (Berlin, 1936), 122–235.
27. *Social and Cultural Dynamics*, III, 236, Fig. 4.
28. See "Socio-cultural Trends in Euro-American Culture during the Last Hundred Years," *A Century of Social Thought* (Durham, N.C., 1939), pp. 96–125. In this essay Sorokin tries to prove that "any contention that American and European cultures are different is wrong." They are "identical .... in all essential traits!"
29. *Social and Cultural Dynamics*, III, 167.
30. *Ibid.*, IV, 763.
31. *Sociocultural Causality, Space, Time*, p. 230.
32. *Social and Cultural Dynamics*, IV, 764.
33. *Ibid.*, I, 55.
34. The example is Sorokin's (cf. *ibid.*, IV, 604).

INDEX OF NAMES

Vesalius, Andreas, 69

Vico, Giovanni Battista, 24, 25, 40, 46, 56–57, 73, 75

Vincent, George M., 76, 414

Virchow, Rudolf, 70

Vitruvius, 13–14

Voltaire, F. M. Arouet de, 21, 24, 46, 47, 58, 69

Wagner, Adolf, 410

Wagner, Alfred, 144, 145, 160

Wallas, Graham, 349

Walras, Leon, 181

Walton, Henri, 232

Ward, Lester Frank, 6, 56, 75, 100, 102, 126–42, 172, 332, 361, 394, 402, 421, 429, 431

Watson, John B., 438

Waxweiler, Émile, 295

Webb, Beatrice and Sidney, 418

Weber, Max, 56, 148, 150, 244–45, 286, 303, 308, 309, 310, 311, 312, 320, 324, 327, 468

Westermarck, Edward Alexander, 71, 166–79

Wheeler, G. C., 344

Wiese, Leopold von, 159, 287, 294–306

Willcox, O. W., 51

Willey, Malcolm M., 413

Worms, René, 82

Wundt, Wilhelm, 82, 127, 144–45

Young, Kimball, 447

Zeller, Eduard, 60

Zeno, 9

Zimmerman, Carle C., 466

Znaniecki, Florian, 295, 438

PHOENIX BOOKS

in Sociology